PREACHING
IN AMERICAN
HISTORY

PREACHING
IN AMERICAN
HISTORY

SELECTED ISSUES IN THE AMERICAN PULPIT,
_____ 1630–1967

*prepared under the auspices of the Speech
Association of America*_____

DEWITTE HOLLAND, EDITOR _____
JESS YODER AND HUBERT VANCE TAYLOR,
_____ **ASSOCIATE EDITORS**

ABINGDON PRESS • NASHVILLE ⊕ NEW YORK

PREACHING IN AMERICAN HISTORY

Copyright © 1969 by Abingdon Press

Standard Book Number: 687-33816-6
Library of Congress Catalog Card Number: 69-18453

Quotations from *The Pulpit Speaks on Race* by
Alfred T. Davies, ed., are used by permission of
Abingdon Press.

Quotations from *Who Speaks for the Church?*
by Paul Ramsey are used by permission of Abingdon
Press.

Quotations from editorial comment in *Christianity
Today,* XII, November 24, 1967, are used by permission.

Quotations from Rolland W. Schloerb, "An Uneasy
Conscience About Killing," copyright © 1943, *Christian Century Foundation,* are reprinted by permission from the September 1943 issue of *The Pulpit.*

Quotations from Reinhold Niebuhr, "Moralistic
Preaching," copyright © 1936, *Christian Century
Foundation,* are reprinted by permission from the
July 15, 1936 issue of *The Christian Century.*

Quotations from Edward Scribner Ames, "What Is
Religion For?" copyright © 1930, *Christian Century Foundation,* are reprinted by permission from
the February 1930 issue of *The Pulpit.*

SET UP, PRINTED, AND BOUND BY THE
PARTHENON PRESS, AT NASHVILLE,
TENNESSEE, UNITED STATES OF AMERICA

This volume is dedicated to Ernest J. Wrage, 1911–1965, president of the Speech Association of America in 1963. His untimely death took from us a brilliant teacher and respected scholar. These studies in American preaching grow out of his issue-centered concern for speech as a vital force both shaping free society and being shaped by it. Several of the authors of these essays were inspired by his dramatic and provocative lectures at Northwestern University. His landmark article, "Public Address: A Study in Social and Intellectual History," together with American Forum *and* Contemporary Forum, *volumes which he co-authored with Barnet Baskerville, influenced others to appreciate his method of analysis.*

May these essays enable many to share his vision and encourage others to continue studies of his well-beloved American forum.

CONTENTS

INTRODUCTION

The Puritan fathers of our nation arrived in New England with a strong heritage in preaching. Daily, on the six-week voyage from England, they heard two hour-long sermons. Since that time there have been shifts in emphasis and method, but the strong pulpit heritage continues, and weekly thousands of sermons are delivered from Protestant, Roman Catholic, and Jewish pulpits in America. Judged quantitively, preaching then occupies a very large place in the culture of America. No other kind of public speaking holds nearly as large a place.

Countless books have been written on the phenomenon of preaching. The vast majority of them are homiletical or inspirational in intent. Few works, however, have sought to describe and interpret the basic issues presented through preaching in the American pulpit. The classic work in the field of the history of preaching is that done by E. C. Dargan in the early 1900's. He presented a nonprovincial chronical covering the entire period of Christian preaching, but focused on great pulpit personalities and the techniques of their sermonizing. Others have written what are, essentially, single denominational histories of preaching, usually centering on homiletical techniques or biography. Ernest Thrice Thompson hinted at evaluating the ideas of preaching in his *Changing Emphases in American Preaching*, although he directed his study to a very limited period.

American preaching, then, from a substantive point of view, has never been adequately described and interpreted, nor has such an analysis ever been attempted except from restricted sectarian points of view. Recognition of this fact, coupled with the unusual status of research in preaching done in the speech profession, and the interests of the writers of this volume have guided the formulation of the purposes of our study. This volume is a collection of essays seeking to describe and interpret some of the major topics of the American pulpit from 1630 through 1967. The chapters use a common system of analysis in attempting to describe what American churches said through their pulpits.

Preaching as a specialized form of public address has been studied in the speech field for a number of years, and a large body of research findings has accumulated. With rare exceptions this material lies quite hidden away in university libraries. Most of our essayists are generally familiar with the methods and findings of this research and often draw upon them as a framework for the study peculiar to this volume.

Twenty men of varying occupations and theological persuasions, working through the Speech for Religious Workers Interest Group of the Speech Association of America prepared this book. Two are full-time pastors, four are seminary teachers, and the others are college and university teachers, with the exception of one who is an advanced theological student. Each man has a theological degree or an advanced academic degree in speech, and several have both. This diversity of training helps to make for a narrowing of the gap between the scholarship efforts of the theological seminaries and the universities. The purposes, then, of this study are

1. to aid students (rhetorical or theological) and preachers to become aware of large amounts of research in preaching that may be found in university libraries;
2. to help bridge the gap between the work of the university rhetorician and the seminary homiletician;
3. to expose the interrelationship between the course of American history and the events of the American pulpit;
4. to reveal the place of the American pulpit in the dynamic interaction of opposing forces that shaped the American churches and in part helped to shape American society.

It is important to note that popularity of a topic or its inclusion on a list of topics in systematic theology were not criteria for inclusion in the subjects analyzed. The direction of the essays was chosen by knowledgeable men during several hours of dialogue on the basic question, "What major topics has the American pulpit controverted?" A period of testing by preliminary research suggested alterations in the list of original topics, and subsequent limitations of time and materials further shaped the final subjects.

Great preaching personalities, biography, inspiration to preach, sermonic techniques, or theories of preaching are not focal points of this work; rather, the task is to present an analysis of the ideas in conflict on major topics of the American pulpit. Admittedly, the researchers have been influenced by the work of the intellectual historians who with their overview of ideas tie together the events of history. This work borrows some of the topics of the intellectual historian but seeks to develop its own tools and system of analysis. We are necessarily concerned for American church and secular history and general theological developments as they impinge upon our research and provide a background for understanding of our analysis. We necessarily deal with actual sermons by anyone who may have spoken on our topics.

Famous men are treated in this analysis, but the attention is not meant to be on, for instance, John Cotton, Jonathan Edwards, or Martin Luther King, Jr. Rather, the focus is on the debates surrounding them, on issues with which they dealt in the pulpit. Some of these issues were simultaneously discussed, although we have sought here to outline them in rough chronological order. Our system of presentation is not meant to suggest that there are clear points in time when an issue is debated. Indeed, a truly significant issue never seems to be fully resolved, but periods of climax in emphasis do appear. It is on a series of such climaxes that this volume centers.

Insofar as it appeared relevant to the study, the report describes preaching by Roman Catholic, Jewish, and Protestant clergymen. In some instances, men who were not regularly ordained spoke relevantly to the issues at hand, and their contributions are noted. Not ministerial fame but availability of records was a principal criterion for consideration. In many cases we talk about lesser known men, even unknown men, because they too engaged our issues, and we have a record of their struggles.

The writer of each essay obliged himself to address certain basic topics in his report:

1. Definition and vivification of the issue being treated;
2. Description of the factors giving rise to the issue;
3. Analysis of the conflict of ideas on the issue as presented in sermons;
4. Tracing and interpretation of developments from the interaction on the issue.

Each writer was free to make additional relevant comments and was encouraged to develop the most appropriate organization of his material. With some very minor exceptions, the reports are faithful to the required topics. Breadth, time expanse, and significance of the issue, together with availability of materials worked to produce widely differing approaches in the reports. Even so, a unique perspective on the substance of the ideas of the American pulpit is presented, a perspective not known to be found in other current works on American preaching.

While this collection is unique, it does not purport to cover all the important issues of the American pulpit. Chapters on "Church Unity Through Restoration" and "The Nature of the Church Reflected in Sect Polemics" were dropped. Both of these are especially relevant to the unique experience of the church in America. Both are probably as important as some of those included, but time and space factors forced them out.

The reader will certainly note different depths of research, varying styles of reporting, and probably some simple unevenness of general quality. Hopefully, the extensive nature of the research will help to excuse these shortcomings.

This work was intended to describe, analyze, and interpret without presenting bias or advocacy. However, depending on the reader's point of view

13

he may find either bias or advocacy. Our writers are scholars and researchers, yet they are human beings, and each inherently has his own vantage point from which he finds and interprets materials. Indeed, the unique vantage point of each researcher surely has affected the sort of materials which he found. This limitation may have some bearing on the limited amount of non-Protestant preaching reported. However, in defense of this point, there appears to be a relatively limited amount of Jewish and Roman Catholic preaching records from which to work when compared with the massive amount of materials on Protestant preaching. What we have produced, then, is largely, though not completely by any means, a work on Protestant preaching in American history. We feel that it is a movement in the right direction and prepares the way for a genuinely comprehensive work on religious speaking in America.

The essays cover a period of some three and a half centuries, but almost half of the issues described fall within the twentieth century. Whether there have actually been that many real pulpit issues in our time cannot finally be said now. The proximity of the problems and the abundance of available materials on these more recent debates certainly enlarge our view of them. History's long view will tell us of the wisdom of our choice.

Works most important in the development of the essays are listed in the Bibliography. A number of minor sources used in the study and quoted directly in the text are not reported there. Original footnote documentations in a given essay present complete bibliographic descriptions. Our researchers used extensively well over one hundred libraries in their preparation. Unfortunately but understandably, a few bits of bibliographical information were lost.

The reader may wish to study this collection in a topical pattern in preference to the basic chronological sequence of the essays. This can be done by considering

1. the four basic topics under one of which each essay falls:
    a. divine authority,
    b. political institutions,
    c. the nature of the church and/or the Kingdom of God,
    d. human rights;
2. man's growing perception of the dignity and responsibility of man;
3. man's changing perception of the nature of God;
4. topics with inherent commonality such as:
    a. "Preaching on Slavery," and "The Thrust of the Radical Right,"
    b. "The Social Gospel," "Popular vs. Experimental Religion," and "The Challenge of the Secular,"
    c. "Civil War Preaching," and "Preaching on Issues of War and Peace,"
    d. "The Rise of Unitarianism," "The Voice of God: Natural or Supernatural," and "The Fundamentalist-Modernist Controversy."

14

The serious student will certainly find other helpful ways to approach the essays.

A companion volume of sermons representing the polarity of the issues of this volume is complete and will be available soon. It contains sermons, biographical sketches of the men who preached them, and brief analytical essays on the issues.

DEWITTE HOLLAND
TEMPLE UNIVERSITY

1

THE ROLE OF PREACHING IN AMERICAN HISTORY

_____Harold A. Bosley_____

Any appraisal of the phenomenon of preaching in the history of American churches must begin by relating it to the role of preaching in the Christian tradition. Preaching, in the American experience, while exhibiting a freedom, flexibility, and effectiveness unsurpassed by any other country or continent in Christendom, is not peculiar to our experience. It is, in fact, one of the oldest forms of witnessing in the history of the Hebrew-Christian tradition, and throughout the ages preachers have adjusted their messages to contemporary needs and problems. Therefore an adequate introduction to the special interest of this volume must deal with the nature and meaning of preaching in Christian history.

The first and really all-important fact to be kept in mind by one who would understand the church and the office of preaching is *the divine dimension* in both. Let the historian miss this, and he will miss the truly distinctive thing about the church and preaching. Both insist that their *raison d'être* is to be found in the revelation of the will of God for man which came in Jesus the Christ. Neither the church nor any of her activities makes sense apart from this firmly held and time-tested conviction.

A second consideration is the fact that, from the beginning, preaching has been one among many functions or activities of a Christian community or a Christian church; for the Christian community is by its nature a community concerned with mission. Actually the church cannot be considered apart from mission; to be a church is to be a mission—a community entrusted by God with witnessing to the gospel. The most effective witness of the church has been simply to be the church, the community which centers its life, work, and very being in God's claim on it and its response to that claim.

Preaching was one of the first ways in which the church responded to the trust placed in her by God through the Christ event in history. Teaching was another—and in the early church the offices of teaching and exhortation went hand in hand. The development of the sacraments became still another

17

medium of witnessing to the steady claim of the church to be the people of God—for the sacraments were regarded as those moments and acts whereby God's grace came to man with genuine though mysterious efficacy. Nor can we ignore the simple routines of group life as we list the forms of witnessing used in the church. That badly misused and sadly overused word "fellowship" continues to be essential to any understanding of the relevance and power of Christian churches among all peoples over their historic career.

A third general consideration is that the forms of the church, including preaching, are shaped by the total social context even as they seek to shape that context and direct it into new forms. To adopt a contemporary word: the vital church is and has always been in unbroken dialogue with the world. While the office of preaching is one of the primordial and continuing activities of the church, the ways in which men have preached—content, manner, form—have varied from age to age and culture to culture. No one form bears the seal of ultimate or divine efficacy and validity even though the office of preaching itself does.

The Role of Preaching in the New Testament [1]

Preaching is one of the basic functions of every church group described in the New Testament. This was true of the community gathered around Jesus of Nazareth, who "came preaching." His public ministry was devoted completely to the proclamation of the gospel of the imminence of the kingdom of God. The records tell of his preaching, teaching, and healing ministry in behalf of that Kingdom. While many questions about his public ministry remain to be investigated, the four Gospels bear unflawed witness to the centrality of his preaching endeavors. The writer of the Gospel of Matthew organizes the material of his Gospel around several great preaching-teaching discourses of Jesus.

One of the tests Jesus gave the disciples, according to Matthew, was to send them in pairs to preach the gospel (Matt. 10:5 ff; also Luke 9:1 ff). Luke tells of the sending of seventy-two in pairs to announce the advent of the Kingdom (Luke 10:1 ff). And at the end of his public ministry Jesus charged the disciples with what has come to be known as the great commission: "Go forth to every part of the world, and proclaim the Good News to the whole creation" (Mark 16:15 NEB).

Jerusalem and Antioch seem to have been the earliest centers of the primitive church—though others certainly developed rapidly in Rome, Ephesus, and Corinth. In each case, the records we have reveal a community bent on intense missionary activity, one phase of which was to send preachers with

---

[1] Some of the material in the remainder of this chapter has been taken from some of my previous writing and adapted to the theme at hand. The opening chapters of *The Church Militant* and *Preaching on Controversial Issues* have supplied most of the aid.

the good news of the gospel to those who had not heard it and to bring into existence another Christian community to carry on the work. The apostles (the twelve who had been set apart by Jesus) had two great tasks: (1) to be open through prayer to the promptings of the Holy Spirit; (2) to preach the gospel (Acts 6:1-6). Peter and Paul were appointed by God to take the gospel to the Gentiles—and were so accepted by other apostles, known as "the pillars," who seem to have remained in Jerusalem despite occasional severe persecution.

It is an interesting tribute to the role of preaching in the primitive church that the book of *The Acts of the Apostles* revolves in large measure around eleven sermons: five by Peter, one by Stephen, and five by Paul. Each of these is a magnificent statement of faith couched in terms of judgment and a call to "repent and believe the good news." The remainder of this book tells of the journeys taken by the apostles, principally Peter and Paul, as they fulfilled the great commission. While it is difficult and finally impossible to separate fact from hallowed tradition in many details, the indisputable historical fact is that the twelve apostles were associated with the founding of most of the major churches in the eastern half of the Mediterranean world.

Such spiritual ancestors were a sturdy lot, to say the least. They call to mind Pearl Buck's description of her missionary father—Fighting Angel. They are the soul, the living, eternal soul, of the church militant. Though we are inclined to put them on tall pedestals, the simple fact is that, in real life, they were uncomfortably like us. They were ordinary people made extraordinary by their devotion to the will of God as they found it in Jesus the Christ. Their lives and efforts were a crisscross of good and evil, strength and weakness, lucid insight and incredible blindness. That, better than anything else, explains why the tradition which they molded and perpetuated and which we have inherited must be dealt with always in a spirit of critical appreciation.

Since the phrase "the church militant" may be unfamiliar to some, a word of explanation may be in order as we apply it to the church engaged in preaching the gospel. Traditionally, the history of the life and the work of the church has been regarded as falling into two stages: the church militant and the church triumphant.

The church militant is the church at work in the redemption of the world. The church triumphant is the church whose work is done. The church militant knows that she lives in a world that is dying of sin, of alienation from God, and believes it to be her divine commission to confront that world with the gospel claim that in Jesus the Christ we have "the way, the truth, and the life" which alone, when accepted and followed, can lead us into an experience of the grace of God that will transform life and grant us a new day in the human enterprise. The church triumphant, by contrast, will be the ideal state of the church when she has accomplished her mission, when, like the Good Shepherd, she has brought her entire flock into the safety of the one fold.

Here in this world as it is, where all have sinned and come short of the glory of God, where our sins always find us out, and where the entire human enterprise is shot through and through with the consequences of the sins of men, the church is and must forever be the church militant, the church at work in the redemption of the world; the church that will not, because she cannot, rest until in the providence of God that end is won.

When this is spelled out in concrete tasks in our world today, there is an enormous temptation to write it off as a quixotic adventure, as a futile and foolish charge of a brigade of light-headed idealists. The only adequate antidote to that feeling of defeatism—and it is a sure cure—is to renew acquaintance with this tradition of the "fighting angels" which has meant so much as a formative force and factor in the life of the church. Once we see the church militant in courageous, aggressive, purposive action in eras that seemed as dark for those who lived in them as ours does to us today, we will begin to hear the mighty roll of the drums of God above and beyond yet always within the tumult of our own times.

As we might expect, the church has been on the march almost steadily since her inception. Time after time she has struck her tents and moved out to new fields with her gospel. Starting out as an unwanted stepchild of Judaism, she early discovered that she had to make a choice between ekeing out a precarious existence as a Jewish sect or breaking her racial and cultural ties with Judaism and appealing to all men in a spirit of catholicity that was to etch itself into the theology and the organizations of the church. The struggle between those who preferred to stay bound and those who wanted to go free, while brief, was intense enough to appear in a marked way in the New Testament. Yet the issue seems never to have been in doubt. The divine commission to go to the ends of the earth was ringing in the ears of all who heard the call of Jesus the Christ, and finally drowning out the fears of the fainthearted and providing a sense of divine power for those who were willing to be guided and governed by loyal obedience to it.

The men of this message were not content to try to stand alone, much less keep the gospel to themselves. They created groups of believers wherever they went. And in these groups the foundations of social revolution were laid; masters and slaves were equal and equally free in the sight of God and each other; the rich shared with the poor; the well cared for the sick, the widows, and the orphans. The faith of all was fanned to a new intensity. Every member of the group became a missionary to friends, neighbors, and whomever he met.

Outstanding leaders, like Paul, Peter, Apollos, were sent from one great city to another to present the message with tongues of fire. These men with a message became a group with a mission, the mission of bringing all men,

20

regardless of race, nationality, or status in life, into a fellowship with Christ and with those who believed in him. They threw bridges over gaps between and among men and cultures that hitherto had seemed unbridgeable: between Jew and Gentile; between barbarian and Greek; between slave and Roman. They could do this because the message that made them march was for all men. It arose from the heart of one of Israel's fondest hopes, and it spoke to the needy heart of men everywhere.

Groups of Christians sprang up with such amazing rapidity all over the Roman Empire that in three brief centuries the Emperor Constantine not only revoked the imperial policy of persecuting them but actually adopted Christianity as the state religion. Charles Norris Cochrane, after studying the relationships of that period, says quite simply in his *Christianity and Classical Culture,* "The theme of this work is the revolution in thought and action which took place during the first four centuries of the Christian Era."

Or as Will Durant has put it in the conclusion to his tremendous book, *Caesar and Christ:*

There is no greater drama in human record than the sight of a few Christians, scorned and oppressed by a succession of emperors, bearing all trials with a fierce tenacity, multiplying quietly, building order while their enemies generated chaos, fighting the sword with the word, brutality with hope, and at last defeating the strongest state that history has known. Caesar and Christ had met in the arena, and Christ had won.[2]

But the church militant was not through when she took the Roman Empire into receivership. Her missionaries fanned out north, east, and west among the peoples who had come only partially, if at all, under the civilizing rule of Rome. They followed the Roman roads as far as the roads went, then they took to the rivers and forest trails. Wherever men were they went. And when the ships of Spain, Portugal, France, and England struck westward in search of new worlds, these intrepid evangelists, Catholic and Protestant alike, were aboard. When, in due time, the ships came home with their fur traders and explorers, the evangelists were not with them; they were teaching and preaching the gospel, sometimes writing a famous chapter of history, sometimes simply disappearing into the wilderness never to be heard from again. We need not approve of the fanaticism and bigotry which characterized many of them and which have left their exploits under so dark a shadow, in order to thank God for them all and for a faith that makes man march!

The Role of Preaching in the Reform Movements in Christendom

As the church moved into the medieval period it not only became more powerful but also lost the prophetic zeal that had spread the gospel across

[2] Will Durant, *Caesar and Christ* (New York: Simon and Schuster, 1944), p. 652.

Europe. It was so intent on seizing and maintaining the control of economic and political power that it appeared to forget the spiritual hungers of ordinary people.

Prophetic voices like that of Savonarola were lifted briefly against the state of the church. His scalding condemnation of the church set all Italy astir and finally earned him the conjoined wrath of pope, prince, and people. But his vigorous proclamation of the gospel as judgment on the church and princes of the Italian states stirred the ashes of prophecy, and some embers began to burn again.

The rapid growth and spread of the monastic and conventual movements bore witness to many faithful churchmen's awareness of the church's need to recover its apostolic piety and work. Saint Dominicus and Saint Francis, to cite only the better known ones, founded orders for service, sending preaching friars all over Europe, establishing houses of their orders and using them as centers for an intensive cultivation of surrounding areas with the preaching of the gospel and caring for men at the point of need. In both movements the expressed desire of the founders and followers was to emulate the simple life of Jesus the Christ and to save men by bringing them into the church. While the church hierarchy was suspicious, initially at last, of these efforts, fearing that they might lead to schism, their founders declared their loyal obedience to the church. Even though the early ardor of the movements cooled somewhat with the passing of time, they continued to be vital centers for teaching and preaching the gospel and continue to be so today.

Not all brotherhood movements fared so well. For three hundred years before Luther, small groups sprang up all over Europe among common people who hungered for faith and fellowship. With few exceptions, the church was pitiless in her attitude toward them and brutal in her dealings with them.

One of the greatest orders of the Roman Catholic tradition, the Society of Jesus, came into existence as an answer to the Reformation. Ignatius Loyola, its founder, was determined to equip the faltering church with new energy and power. His order did just that. Its record of missionary activities in all quarters of the world is unsurpassed by that of any other church. Under its guidance the evangelistic fervor of the church was rekindled, and its missionary priests spread to every continent.

The Reformation came on the wings of the preaching of the reformers who surged to the fore in France, Switzerland, Germany, Bohemia, and Scotland. While the writings of these men set forth the doctrines of dissent, their preaching not only called groups of dissenters into being but nourished them into full-blown churches. It was Luther's sermons, even more than his powerful tracts, that kept the fires of dissent stoked to white heat throughout his lifetime. Dissenters like Erasmus might write their criticisms in lucid prose

22

and remain within the church, but Luther thundered his dissent from the pulpit and stirred men to radical thought, vigorous action, and eventual schisms. While many of Luther's writings gave solid channeling to the energies of dissent, it was his preaching that kept the waters tumbling through those channels.

Nor did he stand alone as the preaching reformer. Who would separate the Reformation in England and Scotland from the preaching of John Knox? Harried from place to place by royal decree, he stuck to his task until he had made his point. George Fox was a dynamic aggressive street-corner preacher when he was not in prison. It was his powerful word that shook William Penn and, indeed, the ecclesiastical establishment of all England.

It is fortunate that Luther, Zwingli, Calvin, Knox, and Penn were "fighting angels." Had they been anything less, the movements of dissent nourished by them would have died at an early age. They felt compelled of God to march against the enormous power of the Roman Catholic Church at those points where they believed it to be in error, and against the Holy Roman Empire which was supporting the church. Right or wrong, it took courage to lift the Bible and say: "The Word of God is to be found in this book rather than in the words of the pope." It took courage to survey the sacramental system of the church, untouched for ages, and say, "We will keep only those sacraments that have a foundation in Scripture." It took a tremendous faith in God and man to challenge the power of the priesthood by proclaiming "the priesthood of all believers." It took scholarly insight as well as courage to translate the Bible from Latin into the language of the people and make it available for wide-scale reading and study. Tyndale was burned for doing it, and Luther would have suffered the same fate if his enemies had been able to lay their hands on him at the right time.

Nor was the Roman Catholic Church the only form of religious establishment to hear the preachers of dissent. In fact, the great churches of the Reformation, without exception, found themselves facing the challenge of dissent within their own ranks before many years had passed. While this was true in the churches of northern Europe, the American tradition is particularly indebted to the forces of dissent that were articulated in England against the established church there.

The great state churches, Roman Catholic and Protestant alike, tried to control such movements of dissent by threat and persecution and, upon occasion, by all-out crusades. But nonconformists continued to erupt and challenge the state churches even as they laid plans to emigrate to new lands in order to enjoy freedom of worship.

One such eruption occurred in a rural area of England in the seventeenth century. A small group of sincere people refused to conform to the religious laws of the country. They insisted upon setting up their own liturgy and life

23

without reference to the state church and state laws governing religious assembly and procedures. In fact, they were very critical of the established church. Discriminatory laws, mob violence, and actual persecution finally convinced them that they would have to give up either their homeland or their desire to worship God as they saw fit. Consequently, they made ready to move to Holland, and did move. After a long period of almost heart-breaking difficulty they discovered that this was not the answer to their need, and they began to investigate the possibility of coming to the new lands to the West and building a home where they might realize their desire for an unfettered worship of God. After another period of great anxiety and even greater difficulty, the actual transfer of the small colony to America was accomplished. They found themselves clinging precariously to the eastern edge of an unexplored and literally unknown world.

Soon other religious groups from Europe followed suit. The Puritans, the Quakers, the Roman Catholics from England; the Huguenots from France; the Moravians from the Rhine Valley; the Presbyterians from Scotland and Ireland, to name but a few, headed westward. In every case we discover the activity of learned and eloquent men whose interpretation of the gospel fortified the determination of such groups to sacrifice every creature comfort they might enjoy in the old countries as they searched for the most precious jewel of all—the right to worship God according to the dictates of their own conscience.

In 1730, one of great preaching traditions in Christendom began to take form and define itself in terms of the tasks at hand. A group of sincerely religious students at Oxford University, among whom were John and Charles Wesley, felt called of God to challenge the evils of their day. First, they sought to purify their own lives in order that they might become acceptable interpreters of the word of God. Then, with relentless consistency, they sought to purify all else. They brought the established church under judgment for tolerating evils in her own life as well as in public life. They tackled the sins of society with great gusto. To a clergy, many of whom loved and knew the joys of an easy and favored life, they recommended fasting and abstinence. To a church that enjoyed the support and esteem of the upper classes, they recommended a new and profound concern for those in need: debtors, prisoners, widows, and orphans. Upon a ruling class that loved and exploited its prerogatives to the full, they sternly urged the duty of providing a godly example for the people. Bible in hand, they and their recruits went the length and breadth of their homeland with a zeal that, to this day, seems unbelievable. Many of them broke under the rigors of their efforts, but not before they had brought all England to a stage of active ferment. Angry, frightened churchmen closed their churches to these "fanatics," but the open fields lay close by, and the meetings were held there.

The age of this development is pictured by one authority with this terse judgment: "It was an age of bleak tragedy for ordinary people." Historians of the established church of England have given equally sharp judgments on prevailing conditions. One writer has gone so far as to say that the church was "never less deserving of the name of 'Church' than then." Still another writer says, "The darkest period in the religious annals of England was that prior to the preaching of Whitefield and the two Wesleys."

It is an interesting thing to study the form the preaching of the gospel took in this situation. Bishop Francis J. McConnell expressed it in a single sentence: "What Wesley taught was the worth of man in the eyes of God."

This simple, searching message opened the eyes of ordinary people to God's love for them as revealed in Scripture, particularly the New Testament; it called them to love God utterly and to live in humble obedience to him; it led them to study his Word and share their experiences of his love and power; it gave point and purpose to their lives both here and hereafter. Here, again, we have a restatement in terms of the eighteenth century of the message that the preachers of the gospel had taken from one end of the Mediterranean world to the other in the first and second centuries: "For God so loved the world, that he gave his only begotten Son, that whosoever believeth in him should not perish, but have everlasting life." Wesley and his preachers were men with this message, and they went everywhere.

Before Wesley died, over seventy thousand adults professed membership in the Methodist societies of England. What is more, a reform movement was well under way within the established church. Social reforms had a new and powerful spiritual ally in the life of England. An eminent scholar has given it as his opinion that the Methodist movement was a powerful factor in averting in England a parallel to the French Revolution. Be that as it may, we know that ordinary people found a new lease on the spiritual energies for life through it. Coal miners, factory workers, sailors, and farmers walked with new dignity. And this is what counts.

Nor was the ferment that originated in the soul of the Wesleys confined to England. John Wesley sent his preachers wherever they could get transportation to go. The spirit in which he sent them is well revealed in a brief note to one of his preachers named George Shadford: "Dear George: The time has arrived for you to embark for America. . . . I let you loose, George, on the great Continent of America. Publish your message in the open face of the sun, and do all the good you can. Yours affectionately, J. Wesley."

The Role of Preaching in the Planting and Growth of the American Churches

William Warren Sweet, the most industrious and tireless fact-finding historian of churches in early America, wrote many books himself and inspired his students to write many more. Toward the end of his life he chose the Beckly Lectureship in England as the occasion for a summing up of a lifetime of research and reflection in *The American Churches*.[3] This little volume, a gem of conciseness and clarity, begins with the observation that Protestantism in Europe at the time of the great emigrations to the New World in the seventeenth century had developed into "right- and left-wing churches." The right-wing churches were those recognized and established by law as state churches; the left-wing churches "repudiated the right of the civil arm to interfere in any way with matters of religion and conscience."[4] An equally significant difference is seen in the emphasis the left-wing churches placed in the "inner, personal character of religion, [in the fact that they] played down its institutional character, and put much less stress upon creeds and sacraments."[5] Sweet makes the point that, while both types of churches crossed the Atlantic, the left-wing "radical" type made the greatest contribution to the thought and life of the New World. "All the great concepts for which American democracy stands today, individual rights, freedom of conscience, freedom of speech, self-government, and complete religious liberty, are concepts coming out of the left-wing phase of the Reformation."[6]

The right-wing type of Protestantism dominated the American scene for nearly sixty years, but near the turn of the eighteenth century the sects, or left-wing types, flooded the colonies and pressed westward. Under the grinding experience of the frontier the two types lost their sharp opposition and tended toward each other in the life of the evolving churches in the New World.

Some historians have been inclined to debate the importance of a religious motive in the founding of the colonies in this country. Yet the records of the colonies as planted and in operation leave no doubt as to the reality and power of such a motive. That preaching was one of the most powerful factors in this experience of emigration and settlement is an uncontested historical fact. The sermons preached in these small groups of people, striving desperately to hold and deepen a beachhead in a new, unknown, and frequently hostile world, brought comfort and courage from biblical example and admonition. Like Abram, the colonists, they said, have been called of God to leave behind all security save God and follow his leading into an unknown country; they, like the Israelites at the end of their sojourn in the wilderness, have been brought of God to the edge of the Promised Land; they, like the early Christians, have been called of God to build a new

---

[3] William Warren Sweet, *The American Churches* (Nashville: Abingdon-Cokesbury, 1948).
[4] *Ibid.*, p. 14.
[5] *Ibid.*
[6] *Ibid.*, p. 15.

Jerusalem on the virgin soil of the new land; they, like Paul, have responded to a divine call to go to a far country that the gospel might be preached to all men.

The Bible lay at the center not alone of their rude pulpits but of their rugged life as well. It was the divine calling of the minister (for the Puritans, an ordained man) under the guidance of the Holy Spirit *to open the word of God* to them in such fashion as to explain God's way and will with and for them. By means of analogies (frequently far-fetched) the preacher would find a reassuring word for them in hours of crisis: during famine, under Indian attack, when threatened by civil strife; when facing an election. The Election Day Sermon was, second only to Easter, the occasion for solemn and helpful scripturally based admonitions as to the kind of men needed to govern the new Israel. Upon these occasions the minister, usually by indirection and through allegory, would bring to bear upon the squirming candidates for public office the high and holy standards of conduct expected of Solomon (as a ruler) or some other biblical governor or king.

Each time a new group of colonists decided to move deeper into the wilderness, to Hartford or Sturbridge or even western New York (a dangerous move into a country claimed by the French and the homeland of the fierce Mohawk Indians), they, through their pastor, would explain their decisions to themselves and to their neighbors in biblical terms. One thing is clear in all this: the colonial communities had a vivid awareness of their dependence upon God and his word in holy Scriptures; they regarded the pastor as the man of God appointed by divine decree to guide them in the way everlasting as that way is found in the Bible.

Not that all the religious ministrations of these early communities were left to the minister! The elders were elected, ordained, and given the tasks assigned elders in Holy Writ. But they did not preach—that was one of the special tasks of the office of the minister. He, like the early apostles, was supposed to be in his spiritual watchtower at all times seeking a vision of God's word and will for his people. He was charged with the task of opening the Word to them for grace and for judgment.

No survey of the churches in colonial America would be complete without mention of the "Great Awakenings" which swept the colonies like a mighty tempest.[7] This round of revivals did more to break the chain of European custom and rite in the New World than any other single event. It occurred about a hundred years after the founding of the first colonies and lasted for the better part of fifty years. If found the churches already settled in a comfortable routine and addressing themselves to the privileged few. Beginning in the middle colonies in the 1720's, it spread rapidly to New England and to

[7] William Warren Sweet, *Religion in Colonial America* (New York: Charles Scribner's Sons, 1942), chap. 9.

the southern colonies. In each area it was centered in the vigorous preaching of men like George Whitefield, Theodore Frelinghuysen, William and Gilbert Tennent, Jonathan Edwards, William Robinson, Samuel Davies, Devereux Jarrett. Far from being simple emotionalism, the Great Awakenings not only stimulated left-wing Protestantism in its personal salvation and experience-centered religion, but they also produced profound educational, social, and humanitarian effects.[8]

Since the pressing daily needs of colonial communities were radically different from those of Europe, ministers who had been trained in the Old World and had spent the early part of their lives there, sought and found new ways of illustrating the Word once they came to the colonies. The frontier made an early and indelible mark on them for the simple reason that they could not ignore it. For example, hunger, even famine, was a frequent visitor and a constant threat; epidemics swept through the settlements; good men and true needed to be found for public office, and the sermons preached upon those occasions spoke to such needs.

The pulpit of American churches was not really emancipated from the influence of the Old World until the Great Awakenings strained the ties with the Old World, and schools in the New World began to train men for the ministry. When Harvard and Yale began to send men into the ministry of the various churches the ties that bound those churches to the Old Country were weakened and finally broken. Presbyterian, Unitarian, Congregationalist, and Episcopal churches came increasingly under the leadership of men who had been born and educated in the New World with few if any ties to the Old World.

This process of severance went on dramatically in the Methodist Church, to illustrate from the experience of one. While Wesley was alive the American wing of the Wesleyan movement began to live outside the Church of England. After the Revolutionary War all binding ties between British and American Methodism were severed, and this without losing the guiding thought of Wesley as found and treasured in his sermons, *Journal*, and many letters on churchmanship. But when the Methodist circuit riders began to penetrate to the frontier villages and followed the inevitable trail westward, they became thoroughly American in outlook and endeavor. While they continued to revere Wesley, they had no thought of being bound to or by either the mother church in England or the Protestant Episcopal Church in this country. Almost none of even the fully ordained men had any training outside this country. The idiom in which they spoke as well as customs and institutions and problems were identifiably American.

We sense the inevitability of both the dialogue between inherited faith and the New World and their profound effect on each other in the volumi-

[8] *Ibid., passim*, esp. pp. 311 ff.

nous documentation now available on the origins and growth of the churches in the eighteenth century. Wallace Guy Smeltzer's study of *Methodism on the Headwaters of the Ohio*[9] shows the preacher as the cutting edge of a growing church. Here we read of "Eli Shickle, a young man of deep piety, and an exhorter or local preacher in our church," who conducted religious services along the Ohio frontier in 1772. Five years later a Robert Wooster "came West at the suggestion of Bishop Asbury to look after the flock in the wilderness." Under his preaching "souls were awakened and converted to God." [10] We get some notion of the isolated kind of life led by these preachers from the fact that the Berkeley Circuit in Pennsylvania in the 1780's was composed of "twenty-four preaching places" that were covered by schedule every four weeks. An eloquent entry in the journal of Robert Ayres will sum up the actual role of the preacher on the frontier.

Friday, May 18, 1787: Rode nine miles and preached to a small congregation and rode the same evening four miles to Friend Hawkins and tarried. Saturday, 19th: Preached to a congregation in the Chapel. Met the large Society and had a difficulty to settle. Rode the same evening four miles to Mr. Brynton's and tarried. Sunday, 20th: Rode six miles to Roberts Chapel and preached with liberty. Met the Society.[11]

Similar items can be found in the journals of preachers in every sect or church operating in America at that time. What was written of the early Quakers was true of the frontier preachers: The gospel was as a hammer and an anvil in them. It drove them forth into every nook and corner of the needy land, and they considered the vast continent as their parish." [12]

Some Dominant Themes for Sermons in the American Churches

Sermon themes in the American churches fall roughly into several general categories with the emphasis shifting from church to church, period to period, and preacher to preacher.

First and always a primary concern was the Word of God as found in the Bible. This emphasis crossed all denominational and sectarian lines in the New World. It was the duty of the preachers to "open the Book" on Election Day in staid New England or to a rain-swept handful of settlers in the upper Ohio region. The Book was their pillar of cloud by day and of fire by night. It was God's Word to them. It told of God's purpose in the creation, maintenance, and redemption of their world and their lives in that world. Through

[9] Wallace Guy Smeltzer, *Methodism on the Headwaters of the Ohio* (Nashville: The Parthenon Press, 1951).
[10] *Ibid.*, pp. 40-41.
[11] *Ibid.*, p. 46.
[12] Sweet, *The American Churches*, p. 45.

the preacher it spoke to them of their sin, their lostness, their need for God; it opened the way to forgiveness, reconciliation, and the salvation of their souls through all eternity.

Secondly, the preachers were concerned with a vital personal experience of salvation. Whether cast in the semi-superstitious phrases of a backwoods preacher or the elegant periods of a well-trained Boston divine—the determination to make faith real, relevant, and all-important to the listener can be felt in every sermon we have.

Thirdly, the preachers were concerned with correct doctrine, and here heresies, schisms, and sectarianism ran rife. Every church tradition is peppered with such sequels, especially the right-wing churches which stressed tradition and order even more than their brethren of the left. The new wine kept bursting old wineskins. The proliferation of sects in America began early and continues to this day, with some preachers or groups of preachers insisting on what they believe to be either a "new gift of the spirit" or a return to an older idea or position that is being forsaken by modern trends.

Fourthly, the acid debate between Protestants and Roman Catholics lost none of its bite on the long ocean voyage from Europe. The New England sermons ring with assaults on the Roman Catholic Church: its doctrines, sacraments, authority, and practices. Simple civility, let alone genuine tolerance, is a rare virtue in vigorous religion, and the sermons preached in the churches of early America are more often exhibits of rank intolerance and misrepresentation of differing religious positions than calls to compassion and understanding. Regrettably human though this is, it provided the preacher with a concrete if largely fictitious enemy in the neighborhood.

Fifthly, the preachers were always concerned with personal morality and public order. Sometimes by analogy, sometimes by direct reference, the moral standards of the community were laid on the altar for the cleansing fire of the Holy Spirit. Not always wisely nor with humble spirit, the preacher set himself to this task whenever he proclaimed the gospel. Novels like *The Scarlet Letter* and *Saints and Strangers*, taken together with the thousands of records of trials in churches in which members are made to answer for unjust weights in their store, lying about service rendered, loose living, etc., spell out the concrete ways in which the gospel was focused on life.

Finally, the preachers invariably found themselves involved in issues of general controversy in their day.

The history of each church in our country furnishes not one but many instructive examples of the way in which the preachers spoke up on highly controversial matters. The first ministers to come to this country set the pattern or, rather, fashioned here in our tradition the ancient pattern of the church, for getting involved in controversial issues is as old as the prophets of ancient Israel.

A quick perusal of Mary Baldwin's study of *The New England Clergy and the American Revolution*[13] or Ola Elizabeth Winslow's book *Meetinghouse Hill: 1630-1783* [14] furnishes ample evidence of the breadth and depth of the concern of our first preachers as they studied the problems that were troubling their people. We sense the justice of the conclusion that the clergymen of the colonies were as responsible as the statesmen for kindling and fanning the flames of revolution that swept on through a tragic course to freedom.

Miss Winslow comments on the way in which the preachers concerned themselves with the moral considerations that underlay the concrete controversies over the Stamp Act and various other specific matters, and those considerations were freedom, liberty, equality, responsibility, and justice. One worthy divine, Jason Haven, preaching the election sermon in Massachusetts said:

People indeed generally apprehend some of their most important civil rights and privileges to be in great danger. How far these apprehensions are just, is not my province to determine. The Ministers of religion will unite their endeavors, to investigate and declare, the moral cause of our troubles.[15]

It is not hard to see why Miss Winslow gives the title "Pulpit Drums" to the chapter in her book which chronicles facts like these:

Under stress of perilous events town and parish were again one as in the earliest days. The meetinghouse once more became the center of community life to a degree more nearly complete than any of the voting generation (in the 1770's) would well remember. Once again it was the town arsenal, with "Powder and Balls" under lock and key in the "Garrett" or, more conveniently still, just under the pulpit. The Rev. John Adams of Durham, New Hampshire, preached Sunday after Sunday with the town's supply of powder directly under his feet. So did other "warm Patriots" among the clergy, and doubtless found their eloquence and the effects of it greatly improved thereby. The meetinghouse was also the recruiting center, the place of rendezvous for troops, the point of departure when it came time to go. Later, as messengers brought back news from the front, it became the broadcasting station, whenever the bell or beat of the drum called the inhabitants together for announcement.[16]

While these men lived and spoke at the time when the pulpit of the Christian church was more widely heard and heeded than at any subsequent period in our history, it would be a mistake to infer that there was complete agreement among the clergymen who spoke up with such effectiveness on

[13] Mary Baldwin, *The New England Clergy and the American Revolution* (Durham, N.C.: Duke University Press, 1928).

[14] Ola Elizabeth Winslow, *Meetinghouse Hill: 1630-1783* (New York: The Macmillan Company, 1952).

[15] *Ibid.*, p. 269.

[16] *Ibid.*, pp. 273-74.

31

the great issues of that troubled period in our nation's life. The record, unfortunately, reads otherwise. Ministers loyal to the king and ancestral ways were insulted and frequently asked to leave their churches and usually the town. The fissure in their fellowship was so deep that the Protestant Episcopal Church, to cite the one hardest hit by it, had to sever her legal ties with the mother church in England when independence had been won.[17]

But deeper than even these serious differences of opinion on what ought to be done about the problems at hand were two areas of complete agreement among the clergy: they agreed both in the absoluteness of their concern for the moral principles involved and in their uncompromising conviction that it was their sacred duty to speak out on them. Even as they disagreed violently on the meaning of the facts involved in the issues, they agreed that facts of far-reaching importance were involved and deserved their public attention and consideration.

If we look into the matter, we shall find that this tragic agreement-disagreement pattern underlies the creation and perpetuation of the divisions which have cropped up with appalling profusion in the church life of our country. The pre-Civil War period was easily the most trying one for all major religious bodies then in existence on a wide scale in this country. All were riven by deep splits on the issues involved in the brewing storm; only a few were able to avoid outright schisms in their polity. Preachers, north and south alike, approached the knotty problems of slavery, freedom, states' rights, etc. in a spirit of profound dedication as well as division. It is easy enough for us today to laugh (or weep) over their *non sequiturs* and special pleadings born of blind, emotional partisanship, but we would do well to endeavor, by an act of healthy imagination, to set ourselves down in their day. It may be doubted whether we would have done much better than they or nearly so well as some of them did. Struggling to get their hands on decisive facts that would clarify the issues before them, they plunged into scripture, history, biology, and social and political thought. That they emerged with some bizarre interpretations in all these areas should surprise no one who has lived through the last two world wars and hears all about him today the roar of the third one. The most rabid defender of slavery sounds exactly like the rabid defenders of war in our time.

[17] Catholic and Jewish preaching drew little public attention in colonial America. These groups were, in fact, small in number and influence until well into the early national period of the United States. The growth of industry coupled with mass migrations of Catholic workers to America brought large numbers of European trained priests to our soil. Growth of business and need for skilled craftsmen brought Jews to the growing nation. Rabbis naturally came along. Catholic and Jewish ministries, like the Protestants before them, were busied initially with house-building and housekeeping tasks and thus were even later in preaching on public issues. Currently, however, the hewing of wood and the carrying of water behind, Catholic priests and Jewish rabbis are among the most incisive of the outspoken.

Yet it is easy to miss the obvious point that, short of guaranteeing infallibility to preachers, this is precisely what we should expect when the sense of concern and commitment of the preacher focuses upon the tangled issues of our day. No one knows better than he how difficult they are; no one need tell him how inadequate he is to deal with them. But deal with them he must and will, and as wisely as he knows how but without the claim, much less the guarantee, of infallibility. Silence may be golden, as the proverb has it, for most men most of the time, but not so for the preacher confronted by the unfolded issues of the life of his time. Nor will he hesitate long about speaking his mind as carefully and as forcefully as he can lest he prove to be in error in either or both insight and judgment. The one thing he cannot do is keep silent in their presence. If he belongs to the great tradition of preaching, he will know that it is better to be wrong than be silent in the face of the problems that are tormenting the thought and lives of his people. It is easy to explain mistakes, for all honest men will understand and sympathize; it is impossible to explain silence, for none will listen.

Little sympathy need be wasted on the so-called "swing away from the social gospel" which some say is characteristic of the last thirty years. If there is such a trend, and there is real evidence of it in certain quarters, then, in fair interpretation, it is a swing away from a forthright facing in religious terms of the vital concerns of our life and time and, strictly speaking, must be regarded as an unwitting and unintentional demonstration of the irrelevance of religion. A religious faith that will not concern itself with the vital issues in the life of a person or a people is a mean and doomed thing. It is more a delusion than an opiate and deserves the scorn which ethically sensitive people are not slow to heap upon it.

Every important person in the social gospel movement from Walter Rauschenbusch to Shailer Mathews and Arthur Holt knew full well the necessity of driving the roots of Christian social action deep in Christian faith. In fact, their greatest writings are concerned with this point. Something of this profound concern and commitment radiates the great social gospel documents written by churchmen. The two most influential are the encyclical *Rerum novarum* by Pope Leo XIII and Rauschenbusch's masterpiece *Christianity and the Social Crisis*. Neither of these outstandingly influential documents is blessed with infallibility of judgment, but both exhibit *the absoluteness of concern* which is one of the distinguishing marks of the Christian love that seeks expression through the witness of the pulpit. Both Catholic and Protestant churches have nurtured and brought to maturity this concern in many concrete ways. Out of it has grown the strong effort of both to understand and minister to the problems of labor and agriculture, for example. In these movements and others like them individual churchmen let their aroused and informed Christian consciences come to bear on concrete vital problems and spoke their minds with real persuasiveness. No amount of criticism and opposition (encountered in tidal waves) could soften their indictment of evil, much less silence it.

Preaching in the Contemporary World

When stray voices are lifted saying that preaching is no longer an effective means of proclaiming the gospel, two things must be said in reply: (1) the forms and modes of preaching are extremely flexible; (2) if the gospel is the central gift of the church, then the proclamation of it is as important as ever.

On the matter of flexibility, the preacher must now be able to use radio, television, share in panel discussion, participate in talk-back sessions, as well as preach the formal sermon at the service of worship. The length of the sermon, the kind of service of worship, when, by whom, and to whom the sacraments are administered—these are variables.

But the fact of preaching and the administration of the sacraments is constant and will last as long as the church does, and that is as long as the gospel is to be preached. Peter Taylor Forsyth insists that, "With preaching Christianity stands or falls because it is the declaration of a Gospel. . . . It is the Gospel prolonging and declaring itself." [18] Rudolf Bultmann would agree.[19]

Yet proclaiming the gospel in the contemporary church will lay as heavy a burden of preparation on the preacher as practicing medicine does upon the doctor.

Where despair is transformed by hope; where ideologies which stress the meaninglessness of life are confronted with the gospel of ultimate and relevant meaning—there the preacher meets his parishioners and needy non-parishioners these days. The hard battle for a reasonable, experience-centered faith is where the preacher finds his young people now, and he must be ready for the demanding encounter with them. The ecumenical movements abroad in the world are battering down the lines of division between traditions, and an effective preacher must be able to preach across denominational and sectarian lines. The social and political upheavals of our day demand knowledge and attention, and the preacher who is to apply the gospel to the problems people face will have to deal with these as well as with the Bible. The "revolution of rising expectations" will outlast several generations, yet it will be one of the most important centers of attention for the effective preacher.

---

[18] Peter Taylor Forsyth, *Positive Preaching and the Modern Mind* (London: The Independent Press, 1949), p. 5.

[19] Rudolf Bultmann, *Theology of the New Testament*, I (New York: Charles Scribner's Sons, 1951), 301-2.

34

The search for a peaceful means of settling international conflicts is now top priority for the preacher as well as for the diplomat.

To ask who is sufficient for these demands is to invoke the ancient answer: no one by and of himself; but one called of God and obedient to him may face them with assurance.

2

PURITAN PREACHING AND
THE AUTHORITY OF GOD

_____Eugene E. White_____

The founding saints who attempted to establish in New England a "city upon a hill" were collateral descendants of John Calvin, and their commonwealth was an oblique reflection of Geneva. Both John Cotton and John Calvin rejected images, restricted the role of music, considered the Lord's Supper a spiritual rather than a physical communion, and conceived of the church as a body of convinced believers. Neither anticipated the imminent coming of the Lord. As a consequent, both endorsed the role of the elect and of the parallelism of church and state as constituting the divinely appointed means of establishing a holy commonwealth on earth. Both advocated pervasive and rigorous civil controls to promote the purity of man's spiritual and secular life. Both proclaimed the transcendence and purity of God, the impotence and depravity of man, original sin, predestination, and justification by faith.

Despite these and other substantive agreements concerning the nature of man and the universe, Puritanism was probably not a direct derivative of Geneva Calvinism imported into England by home-coming Marian exiles. More likely, if it was not a theology indigenous to England, as suggested by Leonard J. Trinterud, it drew primarily from the covenantal theories of the Rhineland reformers, with the Geneva influences being substantial but not genesic.[1] Before Puritanism crossed the ocean, English systematizers had thrust a protective theology of multiple covenants between man and the blinding glare of a completely transcendent God. Painstakingly evolved through the interaction of numerous minds, the system was sufficiently ambiguous to accommodate the appearance and substance of God to the needs of man: in its "conditional" aspects covenant theology filtered the unbearable harshness of absolutism, mitigating God's terrifying unpredictability, partially penetrating his awesome mystery, and rendering less than perfect his authority; in its "absolute" aspects, however, covenant theology ultimately exposed naked man to an all-powerful God. (Inasmuch as the

---

[1] See Everett H. Emerson, "Calvin and Covenant Theology," _Church History_, XXV (June, 1956), 136-44; Leonard J. Trinterud, "The Origins of Puritanism," _Church History_, XX (March, 1951), 37-57; Jens J. Möller, "The Beginnings of Puritan Covenant Theology," _The Journal of Ecclesiastical History_, XIV (April, 1963), 46-47.

conditional and absolutist aspects of Puritan covenant theology will be considered throughout this essay, it is perhaps sufficient here to explain that in the federal, or covenant, theology God offers salvation to all men who fulfill his condition: to believe him and to obey him. Only God, however, can supply the means of satisfying his condition. Saving faith cannot be achieved by man. It is a divine free gift from a sovereign God who has arbitrarily predestined those who will receive it.[2]) In his American sermons, John Cotton stressed the absolutism of the covenants more consistently than did William Perkins, perhaps the most important formulator of the Puritan covenant theology, or John Preston, the greatest propagandist of the system. Nevertheless, Cotton and the generality of first-generation colonial ministers —who, though not as extreme in their absolutism as Cotton, were probably more severe than their English colleagues—were the beneficiaries, as well as the prisoners, of both the conditional and absolutist aspects of the covenant theology.

Ennobled and sustained by their belief in the covenant of grace, the church covenant, and the social covenant,[3] John Winthrop's people subdued the wilderness and built a vigorous, aggressive order, devoted to the service of God and the extirpation of sin. With the peculiar vitality so characteristic of Calvinistic peoples, they turned to the tasks of creating a civilization: building roads, catching fish, selling cloth, expanding commerce, pacifying the frontier, codifying the laws, quarreling with English authorities, plowing, harvesting, establishing schools, applying the principles of representative government, developing a judicial system, warring with the French, and so on.

In the process of causing New England to blossom, however, the people themselves changed—imperceptibly, yet ineluctably. From the beginning it had been possible for them to feel some protection from the awesomeness of an absolute God: if God had voluntarily entered into compacts with the elect, then God had bound himself and, therefore, was not unlimited in the application of his power. During the passage of years the will-to-believe had induced many minds to leap progressively from the wish to the hope and, ultimately, to the active acceptance of this crucial extension: if, as the covenantal theories taught, it were possible not only for the elected person to enter into covenant with God but also for the imperfect individual church and the imperfect society to do so, perhaps man was not totally impotent— without hope or merit; perhaps he possessed within himself substantial means to further his own salvation.

The encouragement of hope contained in the covenants had helped the original colonists to endure the frequent preachments of carnal man's abject

---

[2] For example, see John Von Rohr, "Covenant and Assurance in Early English Puritanism," *Church History*, XXXIV (June, 1965), 195-203.

[3] For definitions and discussions of these covenants, consult the topic headings of subsequent sections of this essay.

depravity and impotency. Then, as civilization moved up the rivers and spread over the land and as liberating currents of enlightenment, of tolerance, and of recognition of the innate dignity and worth of man eventually reached New England and penetrated the thinking of the people, the hope for personal salvation very likely grew stronger and the fears of an incomprehensible, capricious God diminished. Although during the first century of the New England experiment the Puritan doctrine remained essentially the same, and although the pulpit imprecations of man's sinful nature perhaps increased in volume and intensity, much of the substance gradually disappeared from the timeworn expressions.

By the 1730's, societal attitudes and practices had so magnified man and thereby diminished the majesty and authority of an unknowable God that New Englanders were unprepared for the absolutist preaching of Jonathan Edwards. Brushing aside the protectiveness of the conditional aspects of federal theology, Edwards taught that under the covenant totally depraved man could achieve salvation only through the mercy of a totally sovereign God.[4] Responding to his preaching with the flash fire of the Great Awakening, New England soon flinched from the awful consciousness of an absolute God, and in 1750 the people of Northampton drove Edwards from his pulpit.

Puritan theology had partially humanized the Reformation God, and societal practices had carried the transformation even further; by rejecting Edwards' attempt to return to the intense purity of John Cotton's Reformation ideal, New England had irrevocably committed itself to the uncharted reaches of the modern age.

Covenant Theology, Protestant Thought, and the Needs of Man

God's covenant is his contract with man, concerning the obtaining of life eternal, upon a certain condition. This covenant consists of two parts: God's promise to man, man's promise to God. God's promise to man is that whereby He bindeth Himself to man to be his God, if he perform the condition. Man's promise to God is that whereby he voweth his allegeance unto his Lord and to perform the condition between them.[5]

The covenant theology of the Puritans, and hence the conception of divine authority which was manifested in their preaching, was conditioned by the psychological and societal needs of man and by three basic assumptions of

[4] See Robert C. Whittemore, "Jonathan Edwards and the Theology of the Sixth Way," *Church History*, XXXV (March, 1966), 60-75; Conrad Cherry, *The Theology of Jonathan Edwards* (Garden City, N.Y.: Doubleday & Company, 1966).

[5] William Perkins, A *Golden Chaine: Or, the Description of Theologie*, p. 32, in *Workes* (London, 1612), I. The italics are mine. In this excerpt, as in all others drawn from coetaneous works, when archaic spelling and punctuation might distract or obfuscate, they have been modernized.

Protestant thought: individualism, the antithetic natures of God and man, and election.

COVENANT THEOLOGY AND PROTESTANT THOUGHT. In the century before the Reformation some scholastics had attacked the metaphysical concept of "universals" which had undergirded the Catholic Church and had provided the prevailing concept of reality. According to the earlier teachings of the Catholic systematizer Thomas Aquinas, reality consisted of "great universals": thus, the Church and Holy Roman Empire were superunities, earthly extensions of ultimate being. If meaning lay not in universals but in unrelated particulars, as some dissenting scholastics claimed, the conclusion necessarily followed: both Church and Empire were compacts, consisting of individuals who had entered into contractual agreements. In 1521 before the Diet of Worms, Martin Luther carried this emphasis upon particulars to the ultimate degree of individualism and established its central position in Protestant thought: "The pope," Luther told his inquisitors, "is no judge of matters pertaining to God's word and faith. But the Christian man must examine and judge for himself." The voluntary assent of the believer became a seminal principle in the development of Puritan covenant theology.[6]

In reforming Catholic theology and worship in order to place greater responsibility upon the individual, Luther did not go as far as Calvin. The Puritans continued Calvin's emphasis, developing their religious experiences around individual participation: in distinction to the Catholic reliance upon ceremony, the Puritans centered their services upon the preaching of the Word; in contrast to the alleged Catholic practice of discouraging personal knowledge of, and personal interpretation of, the Bible, Puritans employed "plaine" and "painful" preaching to teach "even the meanest sort"; in opposition to the Catholic "dumb listening" to Latin ritual, Puritans encouraged the taking of sermon notes and the discussing of sermons in family circles and prayer groups; in emphasis of the pulpit at the expense of the altar, Puritans redesigned church interiors; in substitution for the passivity of the mass and choir singing, Puritans instituted the personal involvement of spiritual communion and of congregational singing of Psalms.

Not only did Luther, Calvin, and other Protestant reformers emphasize individualism, but they also centered much of their theology around the nature of the individual, his relationship to God, and his desperate need for

---

[6] For representative differing emphases on Puritan individualism, see Christopher Hill, *Society and Puritanism in Pre-Revolutionary England* (New York: Schocken Books, 1964), chap. 14, "Individuals and Communities," pp. 482-500; Charles H. and Katherine George, *The Protestant Mind of the English Reformation 1570-1640* (Princeton, N.J.: Princeton University Press, 1961), pp. 85-87, 192-201; M. M. Knappen, *Tudor Puritanism* (Chicago: The University of Chicago Press, 1939), pp. 346-48; Clinton Rossiter, *The First American Revolution* (New York: Harcourt, Brace & World, 1956), pp. 71-72, 92-93; Max Lerner, *America as a Civilization* (New York: Simon and Schuster, 1957), I, 298.

reformation. As the Reformation spun out its violent course, from the quartering and burning of the body of Ulrich Zwingli, to the fires of Smithfield, and to the Massacre of St. Bartholomew, the Protestant thought emerged with reasonable clarity. A polar antithesis existed between God and man. God was absolute: all-powerful; incomprehensible; perfect. In terms of his justification for salvation, man was totally debased and must be remade. To be reshaped in the image of God, man must be foreordained from eternity to receive the saving gift of faith. Because of his fall from grace, natural man no longer possessed the spiritual insights which were necessary to understand God and the reflection of divine goodness which was necessary for salvation. Devoid of all redeeming qualities, man could no nothing to influence his spiritual state. Natural man was incapable of good works. Salvation was completely a gift. It could not be earned, and God would not heed the unelected persons' cries for help. Man was absolutely—terrifyingly—helpless.

COVENANT THEOLOGY AND THE NEEDS OF MAN. Neither Luther nor Calvin was primarily disturbed, however, by the plight of man. Unlike essentially negative thinkers, such as Ernest Hemingway in his basic theme "Man can't win—but he can be brave," the great reformers taught a positive, revivalistic faith. "Man can either win all or lose all. In either case, however, his fate has already been determined, and it is bootless for him to be overly concerned about his personal salvation." According to Luther, man should forget himself in the love of God and in the exemplification of Christ. According to Calvin, he should lose himself in honoring, admiring, and serving the sovereignty of God. Both reformers were men of great faith and burning zeal. Both were men of action, and they preached a theology of revivalism. With the help of other reformers they moved a mountain, and the gigantic revival they agitated changed the course of history.

After the immediacy of the Reformation had passed and searching questions had replaced burning faggots as the means of determining doctrine, Catholics, Lutherans, Anglicans, Calvinists, and others—all turned to a meticulous re-examination of theological matters. It soon appeared to many persons that although the *Institutes*[7] may have provided an intellectually defensible basis for the Reformation, it was inadequate to withstand the emerging challenges of the post-Reformation period.

If Calvin had not gone far enough in spelling out the details of his theology, perhaps he—and especially the Reformed scholastic theology which from Calvin's period on was significantly more severe than the Frenchman's teachings—had gone too far in predicating the Pauline polarity of debased, impotent man and total God: inscrutably mysterious in his secret will;

---

[7] Published originally in Basel, 1536, the *Institutes* has been reissued many times. An excellent recent edition is *Calvin: Institutes of the Christian Religion*, ed. John T. McNeill and trans. Ford Lewis Battles (Philadelphia: The Westminster Press, 1960), 2 vols.

implacably righteous; completely unforgiving of the direct and derived sins of the unelected; absolutely just; completely unpredictable; ineffably loving; and perfectly rational. In at least two ways the absolutism of Calvinism and Reformed Orthodoxy created severe theological problems. First, the Reformed deity was too conflicting in his allness, too savage, too distant, too strange, and too different to be easily lovable or servable. Second, since Calvin had written out of the white heat of his own devotion, lesser men with a less intense acceptance of the will of God could not help bursting through the self abasement required by the *Institutes* to cry, "What can I do to be saved?" After this question came the inevitable query, fraught with peril to the established order: "If election is completely out of my hands and if nothing I do will help or hinder my salvation, why should I bother about morality?"

To some extent the Puritan theology of the covenants developed as an attempt to resolve these theological problems. The initial concepts of the religious covenant-contract, with its conditional promise by God and its matching requirement of faith and obedience by man, were taught in England during the reign of Henry VIII by innovators who probably derived their orientation from Rhineland reformers. During the last years of the sixteenth century and the first decades of the seventeenth, the Puritans brought the covenantal theories to a mature fruition. It seems probable that in evolving the complicated dialectics of Puritan theology the English divines were responding to the felt—if not expressed—need of making God seem less remote and more believable and servable, yet not be a refraction of the Anglican God. Accepting as ultimate truths the individual responsibility of man, the antithetic natures of God and man, and election, the theologians developed a system of interlocking covenants, including the social covenant, the church covenant, and the covenant of grace. No sharp break with the *Institutes* or with Reformed Orthodoxy, the "new" theology endorsed the absolutes of total God and totally depraved man, and the never-dying echoes of such preachments from the pulpit helped to shape New England society throughout the colonial period and beyond.[8]

Covenant theology provided an unobtrusively rationalized basis for the relationship between God and man; it identified sin as the enemy; it prescribed continuous, conscious striving for regeneration by the individual as a means of securing the fulfillment of the covenants; it endorsed the preaching of the Word as the chief ordinary means of communication from God to man, of eradication of sin, and of attainment of salvation.

---

[8] For an example of the use of threatening materials by a framer of the covenant, see William Perkins, *A Powerful Exhortation to Repentance*, pp. 411-27, in *Workes* (Cambridge, Eng., 1613), III; for examples by New England ministers, see Thomas Hooker, *The Saints Guide* (London, 1645), esp. pp. 24-26, Solomon Stoddard, *The Falseness of the Hopes of Many Professors* (Boston, 1708).

Puritan covenant theology also contained new emphases and obfuscations, however, which so contributed to the undoing of the saints in the New World that even Jonathan Edwards, armed with new insights from Locke and Newton, could not salvage what then remained of the holy common-wealth. Although the federal theology was based upon thoroughly orthodox absolutist principles, its conditional promises encouraged a posture which tended to magnify man's efforts and to minimize the doctrine of election. In the writings of English Puritans, such as William Perkins, John Preston, William Ames, Paul Baynes, and Richard Sibbes, there runs a recurrent emphasis upon the conditional aspects of the covenants, frequently at the expense of the absolutist values. This focus upon the mercy of God, the willingness of God to bind himself in contracts with man, and the efficacy of the covenants, perhaps, can be epitomized by these representative extracts from the sermons of John Preston:

God made the world . . . for His glories sake, to make manifest that now . . . was to communicate His mercy and His goodness to the creature. . . . His mercy then must needs be His Glory. . . . Doubt not then, but that when you come to ask at His hand any request that is meet for you, He will be ready to grant it, for it is His glory to shew mercy. . . . Doubt not then . . . of obtaining what you desire at His hands. . . .[9] So then if you will desire salvation, and happiness, and the strength of the *Inward man*, you shall have it. . . .[10] Saith the *Lord* . . . I am willing to enter into covenant with thee, that is, I will bind myself, I will engage myself, I will enter into bond, as it were, I will not be at liberty any more. . . . There shall be a mutual engagement between us, and it shall continue forever, both to thyself and to thy posterity. . . .[11] If one plead the *covenant* hard with God and tell him it is a part of His *covenant* and He must be just, He cannot be a *covenant-breaker*, . . . He cannot deny thee, He will put away thy sins.[12]

Thus, the backdrop of this essay is provided by the English covenantal theories, which perhaps were borrowed from the Rhineland reformers during the reign of Henry VIII and which later matured into full fruition as the Puritan federal theology. When transplanted to New England, this heritage shaped the form and substance of Puritan preaching, as well as the Puritan concept of the authority of God.

The Social Covenant

Neither is it only a consolation to know the great things which God hath by covenant promised unto us, but it is a foundation to all godliness and holy

[9] John Preston, *Riches of Mercy to Men in Misery* (London, 1658), pp. 29, 30.
[10] *Ibid.*, p. 68.
[11] John Preston, *The New Covenant* (London, 1629), p. 70.
[12] *Ibid.*, p. 225.

walking before God . . . as beseems those whom he hath taken into covenant with Him, to be a peculiar people to himself.[13]

WINTHROP AND "A MODEL OF CHRISTIAN CHARITY." To the colonists on board the *Arbella* their task of establishing a Zion had been ordained by God, and the success of their venture depended upon their fulfilling the terms of their social covenant with God. During the passage, they listened to an exceedingly important lay sermon, entitled "A Model of Christian Charity," by their appointed governor, John Winthrop. Although Winthrop was not a theologian, his sermon was an unusually clear explanation of the nature of the social contract and of its importance to the Puritan experiment. A close examination of the implications contained in his message helps to explain how the incessant stress upon this doctrine during the first generations of New England's dynamic development ineluctably produced alterations in Puritan preaching and the concept of divine authority.

Before the saints had embarked from Southampton, John Cotton, who had come down from Lincolnshire, had reassured them that, as the vanguard of a Great Migration, they were responding to the will of God. Cotton's text had been II Samuel 7:10: "Moreover I will appoint a place for my people Israel, and will plant them, that they may dwell in a place of their own, and move no more." Weeks later, in mid-Atlantic, the challenges of sea and wilderness may have seemed less menacing as Winthrop promised his hearers, "We shall be as a City upon a Hill, the eyes of all people . . . upon us," [14] and as he reviewed the familiar outlines of the analogy which gave meaning to their pursuit. By their forsaking the security of England to set up a holy commonwealth in the new world, they had become a chosen people, sharing with each other in a special covenant with God. "We are a company professing ourselves fellow members of Christ," Winthrop said, "for the work we have in hand, it is by mutual consent, through a special overruling providence and a more than an ordinary approbation of the churches of Christ, to seek out a place of cohabitation and consortship, under a due form of government both civil and ecclesiastical."

Here was both promise and threat: church and state would be separate and distinct, but they would work in closest cooperation to establish and maintain a universal saintly deportment. Like other Englishmen, the passengers knew that through natural law and social contract God had ordained the governments under which men lived and, therefore, that persons should accord obedience to the authority of the state. In their thinking and in the

[13] Peter Bulkeley, *The Gospel Covenant . . . Preached in Concord in New England* (London, 1651), (2nd ed.), "The Epistle Dedicatory," n. p.

[14] "A Model of Christian Charity," in *Winthrop Papers* (Boston, The Massachusetts Historical Society, 1931), II, 282-95, and in *The American Puritans*, ed. Perry Miller (Garden City, N.Y.: Doubleday & Company, 1956), pp. 79-84.

thinking of other Englishmen, the authority of the rulers—both civil and ecclesiastical—was clearly established in Old Testament passages, such as II Kings 11:17: "And Jehoiada made a covenant between the Lord and the king and the people, that they should be the Lord's people; between the king also and the people." So long as the rulers did not transgress their divinely commissioned authority, as revealed in scriptural warrants, the people were duly bound to obey.[15] Such obligatory obedience, incumbent upon all peoples sharing ordinary contractual relations with the deity, applied with extraordinary intensity to the passengers upon the *Arbella:* because God had entered into a special covenant with them, they bore correspondingly greater obligations to submit to his agents.

Also familiar and acceptable to the listeners was Winthrop's explanation of the purpose of their experiment. "The end," he said, "is to improve our lives to do more service to the Lord, the comfort and increase of the body of Christ whereof we are members, that ourselves and posterity may be the better preserved from the common corruptions of this evil world, to serve the Lord and work out our salvation under the power and purity of His holy ordinances." Then, in brisk cadence he stated the pith of his thought: "Thus stands the cause between God and us: we are entered into covenant with Him for this work; we have taken out a commission, the Lord hath given us leave to draw our own articles. We have processed to enterprise these actions upon these and those ends; we have hereupon besought Him of favor and blessing."

Even the legalism of Winthrop's language struck sympathetic cords of memory as he explained how the passengers were to tell whether God had accepted them into social covenant. "Now, if the Lord shall please to hear us and bring us in peace to the place we desire, then hath He ratified this covenant and sealed our Commission." Such a sealing of the contract would mean, of course, "that the Lord our God may bless us in the land whither we go to possess it." So obvious was the reliability of God's honoring his obligations in the agreement that Winthrop did not dwell on this point, saying principally: "We shall find that the God of Israel is among us . . . when He shall make us a praise and glory, that men shall say of succeeding plantations: 'The Lord make it like that of New England.' " This allusion to Israel—as in the previous instance of the text of Cotton's Southampton farewell sermon—linked the listeners with the Old Testament covenant.

God's loyalty to the social covenant was unquestioned. Man was the unpredictable element. After warning that God "will expect a strict perfor-

---

[15] See William Ames, *Conscience with the Power and Cases Thereof,* Book V, 162-63, 164-69, in *Workes* (London, 1643). The pagination in this volume, as well as in others cited hereafter, is somewhat irregular. In each case, however, sufficient guidance is provided to enable the reader to find the passage without difficulty.

mance of the articles contained in" the covenant, Winthrop made clear the nature of this performance: "Now the only way to avoid this shipwreck" of noncompliance with the terms of the agreement "and to provide for our posterity is to follow the counsel of Micah: to do justly, to love mercy, to walk humbly with our God. For this end, we must be knit together in this work as one man." The climax of Winthrop's application followed swiftly. "If we shall neglect the observation of these articles which are the ends we have propounded . . . the Lord will surely break out in wrath against us, be revenged of such a perjured people, and make us know the price of the breach of such a covenant. . . . We shall surely perish out of the good land whither we pass over this vast sea to possess it."

As the listeners all understood, unlike the covenant of grace which pertained to personal salvation, the social covenant, as an outward or external covenant, bound all men together as one community under God.[16] In fulfilling their obligations of good deportment under the social covenant, they knew that they would not be, thereby, enhancing their individual chances for salvation. Their individual adherence to the terms of the social contract was essential, however, to the Puritan community. If God had especially designated them, as he had earlier selected the people of Israel, to establish the land of promise and serve as a model for all others, he would judge them collectively as a people. Any unpunished individual breech of the covenant would be considered by God as a sin by the whole community, and the entire society would be punished. If the volume and character of the sins committed by individuals should warrant, God would withdraw from the covenant, leaving the society to flounder helplessly in a natural state.

SUCCESS AND FAILURE. As soon as the settlers stepped ashore from the *Arbella* and her sister ships, they began to establish the conformist society necessary to carry out their half of the social covenant. The incoming tides of settlers, some twenty thousand in the next ten years of the Great Migration, were directed into societal patterns designed to encourage them to "do justly, to love mercy, to walk humbly with our God." For society to "be knit together in this work as one man," the founders coalesced three separate elements—the civil government, the ecclesiastical foundation, and the people—into the closest approach to a monolithic state then existing in the Western World. Paradoxically, and critically important to the eventual unraveling of the social covenant, the ministers possessed less direct authority than in any country in Europe. In the first decades, however, they possessed exceptional

---

[16] In a true holy commonwealth, of course, the "circle" of persons admitted to the covenant of grace would conform exactly with those engaged in the social covenant. As Winthrop and his followers knew, however, a perfect equation between the two covenants would not exist in New England.

prestige and influence. For a brief time, especially due to their efforts, the covenanted society indeed seemed to be a "city set upon a hill." [17]

Throughout the century the ministers undergirded the New England Way with the syllogisms of divine authority. Even after the covenant concept had lost most of its potency, the clergy continued to defend the coercive cast of church and state. In an election sermon of 1703,[18] the Rev. Solomon Stoddard warned the Massachusetts governor and the General Court: "The abuses that are offered unto a people by their rulers and the abuses that are offered unto the rulers by the people are deeply resented by God." Only "while rulers and ruled do attend their relative duties," he said, will God "continue His relation to them." In the first place, so Stoddard pointed out, "God hath appointed divers orders of men." "Some should be rulers, and others ruled," because otherwise "all things would run into confusion." In both the commonwealth and the church, the "principal foundation of . . . power is divine ordination." Although men may appoint persons to civil and religious positions of authority, "the offices themselves are appointed by God, and men may neither augment nor diminish their power." In the second place, both the people and the rulers must conduct themselves according to God's will. For their part, the people must not provoke God's wrath by failing to render "that reverence and obedience that they owe to their rulers." Furthermore, to support the rulers they must maintain a spotless behavior, govern their families well, and keep a close surveillance of others, reporting all observed "wickedness, swearing, drunkenness, and sin." For their part, the civil rulers must be "nursing fathers to the church." Inasmuch as "reformation is the condition of the public covenant between God and the land," Stoddard entoned, "it is your duty to lead in it . . . to bring the country to an outward conformity." Not only must rulers themselves "be good examples to the people" in order to "stir up others to imitation" but they must also labor "to reform the prophaneness, the pride, and sensuality of the land": they must exert close supervision over education; appoint only godly men to "places of power"; "use all proper means for the suppression of heresy, prophaneness, and superstition, and other corruptions in worship"; be "men of zeal and men of courage for the suppressing of sin." Despite their best efforts at repression, Stoddard warned, "many times there will be a breaking out of sin." Therefore, rulers must constantly be alert to detect and punish

---

[17] According to Darrett B. Rutman, the Puritan community became "fragmented from almost the very beginning," and the Winthropian ideals experienced a rapid and steady decline. *Winthrop's Boston: Portrait of a Puritan Town, 1630-1649* (Chapel Hill: The University of North Carolina Press, 1965), esp. pp. vii-ix, 274-79.

[18] Solomon Stoddard, *The Way for a People to Live Long in the Land That God Hath Given Them* (Boston, 1703). The excerpts in this paragraph have been drawn from pp. 4, 5, 8, 10, 11, 14, 15, 16, 17, and 21. Also, see Stoddard's *An Examination of the Power of the Fraternity*, appended to *The Presence of Christ with the Ministers of the Gospel* (Boston, 1718).

"flagitious crimes." Unless the "people do their duty to inform rulers, and rulers theirs in bearing due testimony against them," the sins of particular individuals would become "public guilt" and God would "charge these sins upon the country." [19]

A key concept in both Stoddard's election sermon and Winthrop's lay sermon on the *Arbella* was the suppression of sin.[20] Although the smallest happenings were prescribed by providence (as William Ames[21] pointed out, "God did so dispose all things . . . a man killing another by chance . . . the lot cast into the lap . . . little sparrows falling to the ground . . . all the hairs of a man's head . . . the lilies, flowers, and grass of the earth"), man was considered to be responsible and, hence, punishable for his actions. To both Stoddard and Winthrop, sin meant any nonconformity in thought or action. Thus, in the earliest days the catalogue of sin included any attempt to rise above one's betters, any persistent complaint against established wages or prices, any substantive divergent religious expression, any schismatic political thinking. If unpunished, such sins would provoke God to retribution. In a specially covenanted land, the transgressions of individuals would displease God, who would thereupon punish the entire society; when the people repented, as could be demonstrated by official days of humiliation and fasting, God would relent and withdraw the affliction.[22] Any unusual hardship upon the people was not a chance occurrence: it indicated that God was displeased with man's failures, and repentance was in order.

With the success of the social covenant dependent upon the suppression of sin, it is understandable that Puritan preaching would concentrate upon the prevention of aberrant behavior. Alterations in the thinking and behavior of the people inevitably occurred, however, as the population increased in numbers and diversity, as commercialism burgeoned and a new merchant class rose to challenge the Puritan hegemony, and as problems over the charter arose with the English authorities.[23] The ministers were disturbed by the changes in society and, failing to understand their causation, consid-

---

[19] Inasmuch as appeals to the General Court to enforce arbitrary civil controls do not appear in other writings of Stoddard, it is probable that in this election sermon he was responding to the circumstances of the speaking occasion and that he recognized that the temper of the Court and of the people would not permit a return to the authoritarianism of the past.

[20] Of course, sin also received much attention in the treatises of the English framers of the covenant. See William Perkins, *The Cases of Conscience*, Book I, in *Workes* (London, 1613), II.

[21] William Ames, *The Marrow of Sacred Divinity*, p. 29, in *Workes*.

[22] For contemporary accounts concerning days of humiliation, consult the indexes of *Records of the Governor and Company of the Massachusetts Bay in New England*, ed. Nathaniel Shurtleff (Boston, 1853-54), 5 vols.

[23] See Bernard Bailyn, *The New England Merchants in the Seventeenth Century* (Cambridge, Mass.: Harvard University Press, 1955); James A. Henretta, "Economic Development and Social Structure in Colonial Boston," *The William and Mary Quarterly*, XXII (January, 1965), 75-92.

ered them sinful vitiations of the social covenant. So concerted was their focus upon sin that by the late 1660's a stereotyped sermonic lamentation for the sinfulness of the land had been developed. In 1679, a Reforming Synod, fearing for the safety of the social covenant, catalogued the prevailing sins under a dozen heads and called for emergency efforts toward reformation.[24] During the remainder of the century and well into the next, a dominant sermon form was to elaborate upon one or more of the social ills catalogued by the Synod and then to call for purgation. The problem was sin; the solution was reformation.

As Winthrop had pointed out, however, in order to control sin and to compel a reformation of manners, society must be "knit as one man." Unfortunately for the Puritan cause, such integration over the long term was virtually precluded by their Congregational system, which called for an official separation of church and state. An impossibly high standard of inter-cooperation was demanded of the people, the church, and the state: the people must remain pious and patiently subservient to their civil and ecclesiastical rulers; the clergy must stay united and retain exceptional influence; the magistrates must continue to be acutely responsive to the counsel of the clergy, zealously active in promoting the cause of religion, and in complete and arbitrary control of the population. Furthermore, for society to be "knit as one man," the power of a police state must exist in some fiat of command, as in the Massachusetts Bay Charter.

Long before Jonathan Edwards took over the Northampton pulpit from his grandfather, Solomon Stoddard, all these requisites for the repression of sin had been lost, and New England could not seriously claim to be in special covenant with God. A steady stream of convulsions had shaken New England, eventually fragmenting the once monolithic society. A partial list of these catastrophes, picked almost at random, is sufficiently indicative: Anne Hutchinson and the Antinomian controversy; Roger Williams and the festering sore of Rhode Island; Dr. Robert Child and his Presbyterian conspirators; the escalating of Parliamentary intervention; problems of currency; revulsion following the witch hangings; the loss of the Charter; the forced acceptance of the new charter with mandatory provisions for tolerance; continuous serious Indian uprisings on the frontier; the on-again and off-again wars with the French; the splitting of the polity into Liberal and Tory factions; the magistrates' growing indifference to the advice of the clergy; the diminishing influence of the clergy and the increasingly serious divisions

---

[24] The list included the following: decay of the spirit of Godliness; pride—disrespect for superiors, ostentatious dress, and controversy in the churches; heresy; swearing and sleeping during services; Sabbath-breaking; decline in family discipline; contentious spirits; sexual immorality and excessive drinking; lying; worldliness; refusal to reform; decline of public responsibility. See *The Necessity of Reformation. . . . What Are the Evils That Have Provoked the Lord to Bring His Judgments on New England? . . . What Is to Be Done . . . ?* (Boston, 1679).

among them. Despite the numerous days of humiliation on which both civil and ministerial leaders had expiated upon the sins of the land and called for reformation and divine forgiveness, the series of "afflictions" had continued unabated. Well before Edwards urged a great revival, reasonable men could only conclude that New England was no longer in special covenant with God.

RHETORICAL CAUSES AND EFFECTS. For the purpose of this essay, the essential point is not that the social covenant failed but that this failure is related to Puritan preaching and the concept of divine authority. The pervasive emphasis upon the social covenant served to enlarge the sphere of human striving and, thereby, to constrict the sovereignty of God. Several factors contributed to this effect.

First, in preaching the social covenant, the ministers of necessity concentrated upon sin. The basic means of determining whether the colonists were fulfilling their social contract with God was to assay their outward manifestations of piety. For, as Winthrop had stated on the *Arbella*, "We are commanded this day to love the Lord our God, and to love one another, to walk in His ways and to keep His commandments and His ordinance and His laws and the articles of our covenant with Him." Nonfulfillment of these conditions would void the contract, he had warned: "If our hearts shall turn away so that we will not obey, but shall . . . worship . . . other gods, our pleasures and profits . . . we shall surely perish." Inasmuch as the continued prosperity under the social contract depended upon the extirpation of sin, the ministers redundantly denounced wickedness and called for reformation and, during the early years at least, the magistrates zealously reinforced the clergy. Instead of buttressing the social covenant, however, this emphasis of the Puritan establishment upon sin-reformation-forgiveness-prosperity eventually contributed to its undoing and to the diminishment of the absolute values of covenantal theology.

Second, the ambiguities inherent in the social covenant theology were reflected in the preaching of the doctrine. In numerous sermons, New England ministers hailed divine power as being unlimited, but qualified this absolutism by advancing the doctrine of the social covenant as a means of conditioning God's judgments. Such implications of man's capability to affect his destiny obscured the central principle of the social covenant: "He 'indents and covenants' with every people that, if they repent, He will repent. He does not, of course, repent the way a man repents, but though He never changes His will, He does sometimes will a change, and when nations repent, He turns His judgments into mercies. 'But the change is in the nation, not in God.' " [25] As the generations passed and as the social covenant gradually lost its validity, the ministers grew less careful to recognize that "the change is in the nation, not in God."

[25] William Haller, *Liberty and Reformation in the Puritan Revolution* (New York: Columbia University Press, 1955), p. 29.

49

Third, the incessant emphasis upon sin-reformation-forgiveness-prosperity distracted the colonists from serving God to enhance his glory, with no thought of gain for self or society. The probable end effect of such preaching was to encourage them to believe that pious behavior would influence what had already been pre-ordained and that, if their actions did not contain spiritual merit in themselves, at least they possessed *quid pro quo* values: if man behaved well, God would honor his covenant agreements and cause the land to prosper. Thus, God would seem to accommodate his sovereignty to the behavior of man. God must wait upon man's pleasure, instead of the reverse. Thus, it became easy for man to overlook that God "never changes His will" and to consider that God was bound—harnessed—by the social covenant. According to this reasoning, God was perfect; he could not renege on his guarantee and still remain perfect; therefore, he could no longer be completely sovereign in the application of his power.[26]

Fourth, as Perry Miller suggests, the constant denunciations of sin may have produced the reverse psychological effect of facilitating the ongoing process of societal change: "There is something of a ritualistic incantation about them; . . . they are purgations of soul; they do not discourage but actually encourage the community to persist in its heinous conduct. The exhortation to a reformation which never materializes serves as a token payment upon the obligation, and so liberates the debtors." [27] Inasmuch as societal changes proved inevitable and irresistible, unrequited calls for reform probably served to purge feelings of guilt; in their long-range effect, they also probably contributed to the decline in the status of the clergy, to the stereotyping of the sermons, to the deterioration of the church covenant, and to significant changes in the preaching of the covenant of grace.[28]

Fifth, the endless thematic repetition of sin-reformation-forgiveness-prosperity may have weakened the absolute values of the covenant of grace. Puritan theologians had always agreed that man's deportment was an inexact index of his spiritual state and that, although justification and sanctification were inseparable, sanctification *followed* justification.[29] Nevertheless, it was generally agreed that man's behavior provided the best available test of his condition of grace; the English covenant theologian William Ames argued

[26] For examples of sermons containing emphasis upon sin-reformation-forgiveness-prosperity, see the following: Increase Mather, *Ichabod . . . A Discourse Shewing . . . That The Glory of the Lord Is Departing from New England* (Boston, 1702); Cotton Mather, *A Midnight Cry* (Boston, 1692); Solomon Stoddard, *The Danger of Speedy Degeneracy* (Boston, 1705); Thomas Shepard, *Eye-Salve* (Cambridge, Mass., 1673); Urian Oakes, *New England Pleaded With* (Cambridge, Mass., 1673).

[27] Perry Miller, *Errand Into the Wilderness* (Cambridge, Mass.: Harvard University Press, 1964), pp. 8-9.

[28] For a discussion concerning the preaching of the church covenant and of the covenant of grace, see pp. 51 and 59 of this essay.

[29] For example, see John Preston, *The Saints Qualification* (London, 1637), p. 285.

that there were identifiable "signs of true sanctification";[30] and the colonial minister, Peter Bulkeley, went to the extreme of saying that sanctified behavior was a "safe" indicator of justification.[31] With sin and pious behavior receiving such prime emphases in the pulpit, it became increasingly difficult for the people to remember that true piety was the result of saving faith, rather than its cause. Furthermore, if man's behavior might possibly influence God within the external social covenant, might not his good works influence God within the internal covenant? If man through his own efforts might seem to earn prosperity for the commonwealth, could he possibly earn the greatest blessing of all, salvation?

The preaching of the social covenant helped produce the self-confident vitality that enabled New England to survive and to develop into a dynamic society. It also probably elevated the stature of man, reduced the absolutism and inscrutability of God, and helped prepare the way for quasi-Arminianism.

The Church Covenant

Those have a nearer and deeper engagement, and beside the bond of Christianity, have the bond of church-confederacy, which in a peculiar manner engageth the one to the other more than any other Christians in the world . . . so they have special power one over another, and that by virtue of the covenant.[32]

APPLICATION OF THE CHURCH COVENANT. Fundamental to Winthrop's conception of the holy commonwealth was the second external covenant, the autonomous church in covenant with God. Augustine had taught, and the great continental reformers had reiterated, that there were two churches: the invisible one which included all those whom God selected from eternity to receive the purity of saving grace, and the visible one which embraced living persons who professed faith. In their attempts to reform Christianity, neither Luther nor Calvin went beyond the admonition of Augustine to strive toward purity in the visible church by excluding the unrepentant and open sinners. Both assumed that inasmuch as only an indeterminate few had been elected by God, and inasmuch as a majority of those professing faith had been denied saving grace and had been excluded from the invisible church, the earthly church could not be spotlessly pure. Although over the centuries various reform groups, such as the Donatists, had attempted to purify the visible church by excluding all but the elect, Luther and Calvin rejected such perfectionism, believing that it was impossible to identify with

[30] These signs were "a reformation of all the powers and faculties of the whole man . . . a respect to all the Commandments of God . . . a constant care to avoid all sin . . . a walking before God . . . a combat betwixt the flesh and the spirit." Ames, *Conscience with the Power and Cases Thereof*, Book II, p. 27, in *Workes*.

[31] Bulkeley, *The Gospel Covenant*, p. 252.

[32] Thomas Hooker, *A Survey of the Summe of Church Discipline* (London, 1648), Part III, 2.

51

certainty those who possess saving grace. Calvin was content to offer three general tests for church membership: Does one profess faith? Does one lead a righteous life? Does one participate in the sacraments? Such criteria basically involved external manifestations, rather than the extensive probing of one's inward spiritual state. Even the profession of faith was primarily the public recognition by the individual of his belief in God and his acceptance of the creed.[33]

In his *Visible Saints*, Edmund S. Morgan demonstrates that the restriction of church membership to visible saints was not practiced by the English Puritans or Separatists, nor by the Pilgrims or Puritans in New England during the very earliest years of settlement.[34] Instead, this exclusionary policy began in the Massachusetts Bay colony in the mid-1630's and spread from there to Plymouth and to Old England. The passengers on the *Arbella* did not take with them a fully developed concept of the church covenant because, prior to the calling of the Long Parliament in 1641, the English Puritans had no practical opportunity to reform the churches and, therefore, had not worked out all the important elements of the covenant.[35] During the first half-dozen years of settlement, Winthrop's company apparently accepted into full church membership all supplicants who professed faith and led exemplary lives. By 1636, however, the church covenant was interpreted to apply only to those who could relate a convincing experience with saving grace. This critically important change of interpretation came about partly because of changing theological concepts within the colony—for instance, John Cotton arrived in 1633 and soon endorsed restrictive church membership—and partly because of political necessity: following the extension in 1631 of citizenship to all church members,[36] the great number of immigrants, many of them obviously less than saints, threatened to overwhelm the original company.

Thus, in two critically important ways, the New England Puritans went beyond the practice of Augustine, Luther, Calvin, and the framers of the covenant theology. On the one hand, for admittance to church membership they demanded more than man could achieve through his own efforts: man could achieve "historical faith" by listening to the preaching of the Word

[33] *Calvin: Institutes of the Christian Religion*, II, 1022-23.

[34] Edmund S. Morgan, *Visible Saints* (New York: New York University Press, 1963), pp. 64-152.

[35] According to Geoffrey Nuttall, the divergence of English Puritans into Presbyterians and Congregationalists did not occur until after 1640. *Visible Saints: The Congregational Way, 1640-1660* (Oxford: Basil Blackwell and Mott, 1957), pp. 8-14. Also, see Hill, *Society and Puritanism in Pre-Revolutionary England*, pp. 28-29, 252-56.

[36] Unlike New Haven and Massachusetts Bay, Connecticut did not limit citizenship to church members. *Records of the Governor and Company of the Massachusetts Bay in New England*, ed. N. B. Shurtleff (Boston, 1853), I, 87; (1854), IV, Part I, 420. Stephen Foster, "The Massachusetts Franchise in the Seventeenth Century," *The William and Mary Quarterly*, XXIV (October, 1967), 613-23.

and by accepting biblical truths, but only God could provide grace. On the other hand, they elevated man to an unprecedented status: the visible saints were thought capable of sufficiently penetrating God's will to identify those whom he had probably elected to save.

In their own view, by assigning themselves the ability to judge the inward spiritual state of others, the New England Puritans were committing no monstrous expansion of the capacity of man. In the first place, they considered that by virtue of their own assumed election they had been freed from much of the stain of sin and, therefore, could freely will to execute spiritually meritorious acts. They made no claim to infallibility of judgment and did not attempt to equate the visible church with the covenant of grace. Their purpose was to make the earthly church as pure as possible by limiting membership to those who seemed clearly to possess the signs of election.[37] In the second place, they were merely carrying the rational thrust of Puritan thought to a logical conclusion. Puritans believed that orderliness was godliness.[38] The universe was system and pattern. Each of the arts and sciences, every idea, every action had its assigned place and relationship in the divine scheme.[39] Because original sin had occluded the vision of natural man, he could not always perceive that the seeming dissonance of man's actions, which sprawled chaotically upon the time-space dimensions of the universe, actually manifested God's harmonious and beautiful plan. During the first decades of the seventeenth century, various English divines, hoping that they possessed the improved insights afforded by saving grace, attempted to discover the pattern by which God drew elected persons closer to him and eventually revealed to them that they possessed grace. They concluded, and broadcast widely in sermons and tracts, that the elected indeed seemed to follow a predictable sequence: from knowledge, through conviction and despair, to faith and assurance.[40] Inasmuch as Puritans generally agreed that a morphology of conversion existed, it was a natural extrapolation for Increase Mather and other colonial ministers to conclude that saving grace "is a discernible thing" and can be judged with reasonable accuracy.[41]

[37] See A Conference Mr. John Cotton Held at Boston with the Elders of New England; Cotton, A Coppy of a Letter of Mr. Cotton of Boston (London, 1641); Cotton, A Sermon Preached . . . at Salem, 1636 (Boston, 1713); Thomas Hooker, A Survey of the Summe of Church Discipline (London, 1648), esp. Part I, 60-67, and Part III, 4-8; Thomas Lechford, Plain Dealing or News from New England, Introduction and Notes by J. Hammond Trumbull (Boston, 1867), esp. pp. 18-36.

[38] It is indicative that John Cotton defended the New England Way in his The Keys of the Kingdom of Heaven (London, 1644) by the analogy of two keys: the key of knowledge and the key of power, which is either a key of order or a key of jurisdiction. See esp. chap. 2.

[39] Ames, The Marrow of Sacred Divinity, pp. 23-32, in Workes.

[40] See Perkins' Cases of Conscience, p. 13, in Workes, II, his A Golden Chaine, pp. 79-80, in Workes, I, and his Two Treatises, p. 457, in Workes, I. Also, see Ames's Conscience with the Power and Cases Thereof, pp. 8-12, in Workes.

[41] Increase Mather, The Order of the Gospel (Boston, 1700), pp. 17-21, 23-38.

So rigorously did the saints scrutinize the spiritual state of candidates that by the early 1640's their exclusive church policy was being attacked by the emerging Presbyterians in England.[42] In their defense, the colonists protested that, although they probably had been too severe in their judging, they had not aimed for perfectionism and, furthermore, had not achieved it—New England, they said, was beset with sin.

Two of the imperfections of society, which by the latter 1640's had become increasingly serious problems, were correlatives: the decrease in church membership and the status of the baptized but unconverted children of church members. Although the founders recognized that Abraham's covenant did not guarantee the universal transmission of saving grace to the seed of the saints, they, nevertheless, practiced infant baptism.[43] It was anticipated that when the children grew toward maturity they would claim a saving experience and would be admitted into full membership. To the consternation of the Fathers, increasing numbers of baptized children grew up without being able—or willing, as the case might be—to testify publicly to their possession of grace. Even more troublesome under the church covenant, these unregenerate persons were begetting children of their own. To resolve this crisis, the synod of 1662 proposed a "half-way covenant" by which the baptized but unregenerate children of the founders would continue to be considered partial church members and their own offspring would be eligible for baptism and partial membership. Neither they nor their children would be admitted to the Lord's Supper or given voting privileges, however, until they could demonstrate signs of election.[44]

An immediate effect of the halfway covenant was to rend the uniformity of New England thought. Many ministers and magistrates, as well as large numbers of the laity, believed that the policy was unscriptural and would impair the purity of the church.

Nevertheless, despite the initial opposition to the baptizing of partial church members, and despite the fact that the halfway covenant did not prevent the continued decrease in the relative number of full church members, the ministers gradually began to intensify their efforts to reach the unchurched, by extending halfway membership to persons without a family history of church membership. Although the founders had considered that the sacrament of baptism was a covenantal seal which could be dispensed

[42] According to Larzer Ziff, by the end of 1645 "only 1,708 of the close to 20,000 residents of Massachusetts Bay had been admitted to citizenship." *The Career of John Cotton: Puritanism and the American Experience* (Princeton, N.J.: Princeton University Press, 1962), p. 210.

[43] See Hooker, *A Survey of the Summe of Church Discipline*, Part III, 8-32, esp. 15.

[44] For the text of the *Platform* of the synod of 1648 which stated that the church consisted of "proved saints" and "the children of such who are holy," see *A Platform of Church Discipline . . . at Cambridge* (Cambridge, 1649). The majority report of the synod of 1662 was published as *Propositions Concerning the Subject of Baptism and Consociation of Churches* (Cambridge, Mass., 1662).

only to visible saints and their children, it seemed reasonable that, if baptism could be administered to the saints' grandchildren who possessed only historic faith, it could also be administered to persons outside the church who claimed "federal" holiness. Within twenty-five years or so, it became general practice to open partial church membership, with the privilege of baptism for oneself and one's offspring, to any person who was knowledgeable concerning doctrines and the Scriptures, who led an upright life, and who professed faith.[45] Throughout the remainder of our period the composition of most churches probably continued to consist of an inner core of full communicants, a larger congregation of half-way members, and a periphery of the unchurched—members of society who were not affiliated with the church but who were forced to attend services and to help pay for the maintenance of the church.[46]

CHANGES IN THE RHETORIC OF THE CHURCH COVENANT. After the adoption of the half-way covenant, as the disparity between the external church covenant and the covenant of grace widened, various changes occurred in the rhetoric of the pulpit. First, the failure of the baptized children to seek full church membership was widely accepted as a repudiation of the original church covenant, a falling away from the religious zeal of the Fathers. As Morgan has pointed out, however, "the half-way covenant had nothing to do with the population at large." "Since the second generation of New Englanders was . . . actually the first generation in which every church member did have to pass the new test, a comparison of membership statistics in the first decades, if they were available, would not" accurately measure comparative religious devotion. Even though the half-way covenant was "neither a sign of decline in piety nor a betrayal of the standards of the founding fathers," [47] the alleged declension soon became a whip, used repeatedly to flagellate the congregations.

Second, in addition to preserving the remnant church covenant as a significant social force—by sweeping a greater segment of the populace under its canopy, and in addition to preserving the purity and safety of the inner church—by restricting to visible saints the Lord's Supper and the privilege of voting on church matters, the half-way covenant made both possible and necessary a change in the direction of the Puritan sermon.

[45] Morgan, Visible Saints, pp. 139-52; Perry Miller, The New England Mind: From Colony to Province (Cambridge, Mass.: Harvard University Press, 1953), p. 113.

[46] As early as 1635, the General Court provided for fining those who failed to attend church meetings. Records of the Governor and Company of the Massachusetts Bay in New England, I, 140. For additional references to compulsory church maintenance and attendance in the Bay Colony, consult the indexes of this work. For reference to compulsory church attendance in the Connecticut codification of laws in 1650, see The Public Records of the Colony of Connecticut, ed. J. Hammond Trumbull (Hartford, 1850), p. 524.

[47] Morgan, Visible Saints, pp. 136-37.

In overview perspective (we shall return to this point in *The Covenant of Grace*), the preaching during the first generation had been sober, albeit intense, explanations of the meaning, justification, and application of scriptural doctrines. The cast of the sermons was basically disputative and expositive, rather than violently or furiously hortative. The composition of the church auditory, the universal acceptance of faculty psychology, Puritan theology, and the morphology of conversion—all conjoined to produce a "plaine" and "painful" style of preaching.[48] The exultation and challenge of establishing a Zion in the wilderness helped the founders maintain much of the original zeal which had impelled them to cross the Atlantic. The visible saints did not need to be convinced and scourged to action. They either believed—with the nagging doubts which characterized the truly blessed—that they possessed saving grace, or they ardently hoped that they did. They were the consequential persons in the church and commonwealth, and it was primarily to them that the sermons were directed.[49]

To the founders, true faith was based upon knowledge; it must be preceded by the understanding of, and the rational assent to, the Christian doctrines extracted from biblical truths. Understanding and acceptance of religious principles came before the personal experience of faith[50] and must adhere to the primacy of the faculty of judgment and to the sequence of the faculties which God had ordained. The founders would have agreed thoroughly with the Rev. du Moulin's assessment:

Now seeing there are many faculties of the soul, that is of greatest dignity, which is called the mind or Understanding; for it gives light unto the Will, and sitting at the helm doth steer and guide the Affections, from whence it is called . . . the regent or the empress. The principal ornament and perfection of this Understanding is the knowledge of the truth, which is so affected to the mind as light unto the eye.[51]

God's intent was so literally apparent in the Scriptures that, if a text were clearly explained and the laws of logic followed in extrapolating the meanings, all hearers would be convinced and impressed—that is, all auditors except perverse sinners whose faculties of the Understanding and the Will were corrupted by original sin. Warmth of the spirit was, of course, an essential characteristic of true faith—and of a successful sermon—but Affections should be evoked only after the faculty of the Understanding had accepted

---

[48] For example, see Perkins' *Epistle to the Galatians*, p. 222, in *Workes*, II, and his *Of the Calling of the Ministerie*, p. 430, in *Workes* (Cambridge, 1613), III.

[49] In *The Puritan Family* (Boston: Boston Public Library, 1956), pp. 90-104, Edmund S. Morgan develops the thesis that the New England Puritans sought to preserve their faith rather than to extend it and, as a result, turned the church "into an exclusive society for the saints and their children." Also, see Rutman, *Winthrop's Boston: Portrait of a Puritan Town 1630-1649*, pp. 135-63.

[50] See Perkins, *A Golden Chaine*, p. 80, in *Workes*, I.

[51] Pierre du Moulin, *A Treatise of the Knowledge of God* (London, 1634), p. 1. The Rev. du Moulin was minister of the Reformed Church at Paris.

the intellectual and moral truth of the matter and the Will had embraced it. Furthermore, the release of the Affections should remain under the supervision of the Understanding and the Will.[52]

According to the rhetorical theory of the founding fathers, the sermon form should follow the sequence of the faculties. The thrust of the sermon may be epitomized by several key sentences from the notes which were recorded by Henry Dunster as a student at Cambridge University and which are probably indicative of his lectures on rhetoric, delivered as president of Harvard College:

After explication proves the Doctrine, which you may do by any arguments in logic . . . after you have proved . . . that it is, then show . . . why it is so. Such Reasons may be taken from the cause, effects, or end. . . . In handling the Doctrine be as plain as may be, only look what concerns the understanding of the Doctrine. Look especially at the logic, the rhetorical passages are only profitable in the Uses when you come to the Affections. After proof of the Doctrine & Reasons [is] given, then take away Objections, & answer these, that false logic may not seem to oppose the truth. . . . From the Doctrine come to Application to the soul wherein consists the life of preaching. You shall first apply it to the Understanding. 2ly [Secondly] to the Will & Affections for therin consists the labor; & as to teach & inform the Understanding, so to stir up the people's heart to the thing taught.[53]

As will be made clearer in the later discussion, the composition of the sermon reflected both the sequence of the faculties and the morphology of conversion, in which knowledge and conviction preceded humiliation and the raptures of spiritual union.

An important new dimension was added to the calculus of the sermon, however, when baptized but unconverted persons were admitted to the churches in such increasing amounts that they eventually greatly outnumbered the full communicants. Possessing only federal holiness, halfway members were assumed to be damned. Nevertheless, they differed significantly from the nonmembers who were compelled to attend services. By virtue of their having been baptized, their faculties had been freed from the total paralysis of original sin. Instead of being utterly impotent, they possessed some slight ability to improve their spiritual condition. Therefore, a more active striving for grace and saintly deportment could logically be demanded of them, and a greater intensity of eternal punishment could be predicted for them.[54] Before long, however, some ministers were addressing them as though they possessed ability to perform or not, as they willed. It gradually

[52] For an interpretation of the relationship between faculty psychology and Puritan theology, see Eugene E. White, "Master Holdsworth and 'A Knowledge Very Useful and Necessary,'" *The Quarterly Journal of Speech*, LII (February, 1967), 1-16.

[53] Henry Dunster MS., Massachusetts Historical Society. For a similar statement, see Ames, *The Marrow of Sacred Divinity*, pp. 154-62, in *Workes*.

[54] See John Cotton, *The Grounds and Ends of the Baptisme of the Children of the Faithful* (London, 1647); Thomas Shepard, *The Church-Membership of Children* (Cam-

became customary to exhort them to strive to attain grace, as well as to lead exemplary lives, and to chastise them for their failures. As the sermons became more hortatory, less effort was exerted to restrict emotive materials to the section on "Application" or "Uses," and such appeals tended to intrude within the "Doctrine" and "Reasons" segments, previously theoretically devoted to logical explanation and analysis.[55] Furthermore, near the end of the century, preachers began to direct a greater amount and intensity of attention to the eternity and torments of hell.[56]

One of the important evidences of the changing rhetoric under the church covenant was the preaching which took place at covenant renewals. In addition to requiring the baptized but unregenerate parents to repeat their covenant vows at the baptism of their children, the practice developed, during the last quarter of the century, of setting aside a special day for all halfway members publicly to own the covenant. On the appointed day of humiliation, the minister would deliver a jeremiad which lamented the sins of the land and the lassitude of the congregation, and then the partial members would in unison renew their vows to God and the church. Ministers began to use these ceremonies as a means of increasing the pressure upon the unregenerates to strive for election. As a fulcrum to pry such persons from spiritual inertia, they came to place greater reliance upon exhortation and threats of hellfire and brimstone. Thus, the mass renewals of the covenant tended to focus greater emphasis upon the self-actuation of persons who might be, or might not be, destined for salvation.[57]

In response to changes within the church, the preaching of the church covenant had swung far from the absolutism of Calvinism and Reformed Orthodoxy: man should honor and adore God without undue concern about his own salvation, because, after all, the selection of saints had been determined from eternity. The preaching under the church covenant, much like that under the social covenant, had come to assume a *quid pro quo* complexion: the striving for faith, as well as the reformation of manners and behavior, would possibly result in personal and societal blessings.

---

bridge, Mass., 1663); Hooker, *A Survey of the Summe of Church Discipline*, Part III, 8-32, esp. 17; Bulkeley, *The Gospel Covenant*, Part II, 151-66; Increase Mather, *The First Principles of New England, Concerning the Subject of Baptisme and Communion of Churches* (Cambridge, Mass., 1675).

[55] This does not mean, of course, that the Statement of the Text, Doctrine, and Reasons were compartments hermetically sealed against all emotive matter or expression.

[56] See, for example, Samuel Willard, *The Barren Fig Trees Doom* (Boston, 1691); Increase Mather, *The Greatest Sinners Exhorted* (Boston, 1686) and his *Impenitent Sinners* (Boston, 1698); Cotton Mather, *A Midnight Cry*; Solomon Stoddard, *The Tryal of Assurance* (Boston, 1698), *The Safety of Appearing at the Day of Judgment* (Boston, 1687), *The Efficiency of the Fear of Hell to Restrain Men from Sin* (Boston, 1713), and his *The Falseness of the Hopes of Many Professors*.

[57] See Cotton Mather, *A Midnight Cry*; Samuel Willard, *Covenant-Keeping* (Boston, 1682).

DECLINE OF THE CHURCH COVENANT. A majority of New Englanders probably continued to accept the church covenant to the end of the first century of the Puritan experiment. Well before that time, however, the covenant had become only an abortive remnant of the conception of John Winthrop in 1636: the independent covenanted church based upon biblical warrant and gathered of visible saints, united as one man. In the Connecticut Valley the Reverend Solomon Stoddard rejected the church covenant as unscriptural, and he struck at the Congregational principle of the autonomous church by banding the neighboring churches into a Presbyterian-like consociation. In 1708 the Saybrook synod, called into being by the Connecticut General Court, incorporated Stoddard's theories into its *Platform*.[58]

Even the greatest pillars of the church covenant, Increase and Cotton Mather, recognized the need for greater control over individual churches and, thereby, over the individual person. The ineffectual, quasi-Presbyterian *Proposals* of five eastern ministerial associations which the Mathers endorsed in 1705 further undermined the church covenant.[59] The founders of the liberal Brattle Street Church, established in 1700, denied scriptural warrant for a church covenant limited to visible saints.[60] Even the stalwart defender of the church covenant, John Wise, weakened its claim to validity, by admitting that its existence depended upon social compact rather than upon the Bible.[61] The most serious attack upon the church covenant was Stoddard's widely publicized return to the anti-intellectual concept of a truly inscrutable God. A church based upon visible saints was an absurdity, Stoddard proclaimed, because visible signs of election were thoroughly unreliable indices of true grace. Except for recalcitrant sinners, Stoddard swept everyone in his community into full church membership, and over the years he coerced them into five revivals. Outside the Valley, probably most of the ministers clung to what was left of the church covenant. Their preaching under the covenant, echoing much of the earlier rhetoric, tended to continue the drift from absolutism toward Arminianism.

The Covenant of Grace

Therefore he that offends herein, in denying God the glory of His great, tender unspeakable mercy, whereby He would glorify Himself most in the covenant of

---

[58] *A Confession of Faith . . . at Saybrook* (New London, 1710).

[59] See Williston Walker, *Creeds and Platforms of Congregationalism* (New York, 1893), pp. 463-96. (Paperback ed.; Philadelphia: The United Church Press, 1960.)

[60] *A Manifesto or Declaration, Set Forth by the Undertakers of the New Church Now Erected in Boston* (Boston, 1699); Increase Mather, *The Order of the Gospel*; Benjamin Colman, *Gospel Order Revived* (New York, 1700); Cotton Mather, *A Collection of Some of the Many Offensive Matters, Contained in a Pamphlet, Entitled the Order of the Gospel Revived* (Boston, 1701).

[61] John Wise, *A Vindication of the Government of New England Churches* (Boston, 1717), esp. p. 30.

grace, he offends God most. Therefore, let us at such times as God awakens conscience, be so far from thinking that God is unwilling to cure and help us, as to think that hereby we shall honor God more by believing, than we dishonored Him by our sin.[62]

As the previous discussion has suggested, the preaching of the social covenant and of the church covenant may have gradually moved the New England society in the direction of Arminianism and reduced the antithesis between God and man. The focus of this section concerns the nature and the results of the preaching of the covenant of grace, the covenant upon which the other covenants depended for their validity and their effectiveness.

THE TRANSPLANTED CONFORMATION OF THE COVENANT OF GRACE. In Puritan thinking, the problem of man was that, because Adam had been the representative of the entire human race, all succeeding generations had been fatally stained by the original sin. Before the fall, God had arranged with Adam a covenant of good works which provided for his salvation. Because Adam's sin voided the saving qualities of the covenant, both he and all his descendants warranted damnation. Thereafter, only through divinely dispensed grace could man's claim to salvation be justified. Although all men deserved to be damned, God predestined a minority of them to receive election, as a manifestation of his mercy and generosity. Some Puritan theologians attempted to "humanize" this seeming cruelty, by claiming that God damned the majority of living and yet-to-be-born persons because he knew in advance that they would be sinful. The main stream of thought followed William Perkins, however, in justifying God's assignment of most men to hell simply on the basis that it pleased him to do so. Inasmuch as everyone deserved hell, it was gracious for God to save even a few.[63]

Because of original sin, the operation of man's faculties was severely impaired, but not completely paralyzed.[64] God employed these faculties to guide man to the discovery and application of the arts and sciences, the principles of health and government, cooperative social and civic behavior, family love, and so on. Such knowledge and deportment were necessary to the earthly survival of the race; but any good works which man might render thereby in improving himself or society possessed no saving merit in the sight of God.

In regard to spiritual matters, it should be emphasized, original sin had caused a total paralysis of natural man's faculties. Of the various faculties,

---

[62] Richard Sibbes, *The Returning Backslider* (London, 1639), p. 150.

[63] See Perkins, "Preface" of *A Golden Chaine*, p. 24, in *Workes*, I; Preston, "Four Sermons," p. 48, in *The New Covenant*.

[64] For representative references, see Perkins, *A Graine of Mustardseede*, p. 637, in *Workes*, I; John Preston, *The Saints Qualification* (London, 1637), pp. 31-79. Preston here discusses the consequences of original sin and the corruption of the Understanding, of the Will, of Memory, of Conscience, of Sensitive Appetites, and of Affections.

the one which received the greatest opprobrium from the Puritan theologians was the Will. Located in the heart, the Will was the "faculty of *assenting*," that is, of "embracing or eschewing" the conceptual messages which were sent to it from the Understanding, located in the head. The function of the Understanding was to determine the *"truth* and *falsehood"* and the "goodness or badness" of a matter and to pass the ideational judgment down to the Will for acceptance or rejection. If a man's Will were spiritually paralyzed, he could not "will or nill" according to divine righteousness. He was not only dead in sin but he was also unable to recognize the enormity of his guilt or to do anything about it. His Will could neither choose morally nor could it pass along suitable commands to the Affections and to the effector mechanism of the body.[65] The paralysis of his Will and other faculties could be lifted only by his rebirth: by his becoming aware that he possessed saving grace, as a free, unearned gift from God. The condition, cause, and remedy of man's predicament was clear, therefore. He was helpless because he had inherited from Adam a sinful nature which merited damnation, and he could be saved only through the predetermined, unmerited intervention by God.

By the end of the sixteenth century, many Englishmen were unwilling to follow Luther and Calvin's admonition not to fret about salvation but to concentrate upon the task of glorifying, honoring, and adoring God. Perhaps drawing the nub of their conception from Book III of the *Institutes,*[66] English divines worked out a rationale for salvation by which sensitive man could live in a darkly mysterious universe under the lowering terrors of a capricious, cruel, and vengeful God. In a series of concatenated doctrines they shaped the faceless deity into an image, possessing recognizable and reliable human values. Through the covenant of redemption, God accepted the sacrifices of Christ as redeeming mankind, and through the corollary covenant of grace he extended salvation to Christ and to his followers. Saving grace was persevering and, under the covenant, could not be withdrawn from anyone to whom it had once been given.

The most difficult task of the covenanters was to evolve rational procedures by which man could attain the experience of grace, without violating the conception of election or of the spiritual passivity of man. Out of the melange

---

[65] I am following here the thinking of William Perkins and William Ames. See, esp., Perkins' A *Discourse of Conscience,* p. 517, in *Workes,* I and Ames' *Conscience with the Power and Cases Thereof,* Book I, 2-4, 15-22, in *Workes.* On pp. 2 and 3, Ames compares his interpretation of the Understanding and the Will with that of Perkins. In *The New Covenant,* pp. 151 and 168, John Preston offers the different view that the function of the Understanding is to determine the truth or falseness of a matter and that the function of the Will is to decide its moral quality and then to accept or reject it. Also, see Sir Miles Sandys, *Prudence the First of the Foure Cardinall Virtues* (n., 1635), pp. 85-89.

[66] Book III, "The Way in Which We Receive the Grace of Christ: What Benefits Come to Us From It, and What Effects Follow," in *Calvin: Institutes of the Christian Religion,* pp. 537-1008.

of writings on this matter emerges a configuration, integrating faculty psychology and the morphology of conversion.

Inasmuch as the major faculty involved in man's spiritual helplessness was the Will,[67] the simplest solution would have been for the covenanters to find some way to "reactivate" this faculty and, thereby, to enable man to "will" himself to salvation. Despite occasional strong assertions to the contrary,[68] at times Perkins and Preston very nearly seemed to advocate this very thing.[69] Also, in their emphasis on sin, the covenanters sometimes appeared almost to consider pious deportment to be *de jure* evidence of a divinely blessed Will, a throwback to the pre-Reformation covenant of good works.[70] As we have already seen in the discussion of the church and social covenants, the lid to this Pandora's box of the Will was to be opened so frequently and so incautiously during the New England experience that it finally became unhinged.

In the formulation of the basic morphology of conversion, it appeared clear to the framers of the covenant that regeneration could not be particularized in the Will but, instead, involved the entire nature of man.[71] Although the receiving of grace was a deeply felt emotional experience which necessitated the commitment of the Will, it also contained an intrinsic ideational component which required preparatory guidance by the Understanding. Faith was idea, as well as tone and feeling. Man must first understand Christian doctrines and believe them to be true; secondly, he must accept and be humbled by the righteousness of the doctrines, including his own damnation; then—providing, of course, that God had already so willed it—he might experience the flooding of his being with saving grace. Inasmuch as God invariably adhered to the laws of nature, which in the case of man always operated through the faculties, and inasmuch as God created man as an *ens rationis* and always treated him as such, the Understanding was still the king of the faculties, and the entire faculty sequence was involved in the process of reformation.

[67] For instance, William Ames writes that "The first cause therefore of the goodness or sinfulness of any act of man is in the Will. Secondly, liberty also of election is formally in the Will: that therefore anyone doth yield obedience to God, or refuseth to do so, proceeds from the Will." *Conscience with the Power and Cases Thereof,* Book III, 91, in *Workes.* Elsewhere he writes, "The Will is the most proper and prime subject of this grace, because the conversion of the Will is an effectual principle of the conversion of the whole man." *The Marrow of Sacred Divinity,* p. 112, in *Workes.*

[68] See Perkins, *A Treatise of Gods Free Grace and Mans Free Will,* pp. 733-34, in *Workes,* I; Preston, *The New Covenant,* Sermon II, pp. 37-66.

[69] For example, see Perkins, *A Treatise Tending unto a Declaration, Whether a Man Be in the Estate of Damnation, or in the Estate of Grace,* p. 372, in *Workes,* I, and Preston, *Riches of Mercy to Men in Misery,* p. 68.

[70] Preston, *The New Covenant,* "Four Sermons," p. 56. Also, in *The New Covenant,* see p. 93. The reader is reminded that in many of these works the pagination is irregular. In this particular treatise, the "Four Sermons" segment is numbered separately.

[71] Ames, *Conscience with the Power and Cases Thereof,* Book II, 27, and *The Marrow of Sacred Divinity,* p. 5, in *Workes.*

The covenanters were agreed that nothing in Christianity or in the pursuit of salvation was contrary to sense and reason. Therefore, the Understanding should ordinarily be disciplined before the sequence of the succeeding faculties, i.e., the Will, the Imagination, and the Affections, could be summoned to divine pursuits. If the Understanding—the center of the conscience—were corrected, the rest of the faculties would probably conform suitably to the "truth," passed along by the Understanding.[72] Because of the exceptional importance which God had attached to man's rational nature, the Puritans placed great stress upon knowledge and logic. In terms of consistency within the absolute values of the covenant, the constant and ambiguous stress of the covenanters upon reason amounted both to overemphasis and obfuscation. "All the grace that a man hath," John Preston preached, "passeth through the understanding; and therefore if a man would be strong in grace, let him labour to get much light, to get much truth, much knowledge in his mind: for certainly all the difference between . . . men in Christianity" and those who are not, is "that one is more enlightened, he hath more knowledge, he hath more truth revealed to him, which truth carries grace with it." [73] "If you be rich in knowledge, it will make you rich in grace likewise," [74] Preston argued, thereby almost seeming to equate right thinking with salvation: "If the mind be right the Will will follow; and if the Will will follow, be sure the affections will follow." [75] Thus, it very nearly seemed that conviction or acceptance of Christian doctrines could effect more than "historic faith." The power to "think" one's self into salvation appeared to be nearly within the reach of man. As in the case of the Will, the emphasis of the covenanters upon the Understanding, when transferred to the New World, eventually contributed to the undoing of the holy commonwealth.

Despite the basic premise of man's spiritual impotency, the powerful thrust of the covenant of grace came from its capacity to energize man to strive for grace. God had designed the means for salvation to consist of attending to the preaching of the Word, studying the Scriptures, praying, partaking of the covenants, and constantly striving to emulate Christ's example.[76] In the course of such exertion, those who were elected would experience the presence of saving faith. Those who were not elected, naturally, would never receive the experience. Nevertheless, because this was the appointed route to everlasting life, all who hoped to be saved had to make the effort. In their attempts to encourage man to initiate and to maintain spiritual

[72] Ames, *Conscience with the Power and Cases Thereof*, Book I, 2-4, in *Workes*; Perkins, *A Discourse of Conscience*, pp. 517, 549-52, and *A Declaration of the True Manner of Knowing Christ Crucified*, p. 627, in *Workes*, I.

[73] Preston, *The New Covenant*, pp. 207-8; Sibbes, *The Excellencie of the Gospel Above the Law* (London, 1739), p. 141.

[74] Preston, *The New Covenant*, p. 211.

[75] Preston, *ibid.*, pp. 132, 204, and *Breastplate of Faith and Love* (London, 1634), 5th ed., p. 204.

[76] Ames, *Conscience with the Power and Cases Thereof*, Book IV, 1-98, in *Workes*.

striving, some of the framers of the covenant at times skirted close to pronouncing a universal calling. Although William Perkins, Richard Sibbes, and other covenanters repeatedly stressed the absolute values of the covenant, they also preached that a touch of grace was sufficient to salvation and that if a man felt a faint stirring in his heart, he could anticipate that he was saved.[77] Faith has saving qualities, Perkins observed, not "because it is a perfect virtue, but because it apprehends a perfect object." Therefore, "If our faith err not in his object, but be rightly fixed on the true causes of our salvation, though it be but a weak faith, and do no more but cause us to will, desire, & endeavor to apprehend Christ, it is true faith, and justifieth; the weakness of it shall not hinder our salvation." [78] Such beginnings of faith, they advised, could be encouraged and strengthened by steadfast pursuance of the appointed means.

An earnest seeker needed more than exhortations, however. He needed a route that was distinctly marked, one on which his progress could be charted. By studying the progress of man from the state of sin to the status of visible saints and by applying the principles of faculty psychology, Perkins, Ames, and others plotted with considerable general agreement a morphology of conversion. Knowledge and understanding of scriptural truths constituted the first stage. Then in succession came conviction, "legal fear" and humiliation, awareness of the possible presence of faith, unsettling struggle between feeling assured and doubting the possession of grace, and, eventually, assurance of personal salvation.[79]

The covenant of grace, as delineated above, constituted the most significant theological heritage brought to New England by Winthrop's company on the *Arbella*. Although societal pressures in the New World molded the covenant into somewhat different contours, its conformation remained basically consistent with the principles of the original framers of the covenant of grace, and its vitality provided the *vis vitae* for Puritan preaching throughout our period.

THE VIS VITAE OF THE COVENANT OF GRACE. During the first generation of the New England experience, the ministers in general, and those in particular who followed John Cotton, perhaps tended to reflect more closely the absolute values of the covenant of grace than did the English framers themselves. In contrast to Paul Baynes, Richard Sibbes, and John Preston,

---

[77] Perkins, *A Graine of Mustardseede*, pp. 636-44, and *A Golden Chaine*, p. 80, in *Workes*, I; Perkins, *Cases of Conscience*, pp. 19, 27, in *Workes*, II; Sibbes, *The Bruised Reede, and Smoaking Flax* (London, 1630).

[78] Perkins, *Epistle to the Galatians*, p. 283, in *Workes*, II.

[79] For example, see Perkins, *Cases of Conscience*, p. 13, in *Workes*, II, *A Golden Chaine*, pp. 79-80, in *Workes*, I, and *Two Treatises*, p. 457, in *Workes*, I. Also, see Ames, *Conscience with the Power and Cases Thereof*, pp. 8-12, in *Workes*.

who sometimes seemed to reach out toward a doctrine of universal calling, and in contrast even to William Perkins who redundantly stressed reprobation but who also seemed to bring salvation almost within the grasp of the eager seeker, the colonial ministers probably emphasized more strongly the helplessness and the sinfulness of man and the awful glory and majesty of God. The tone of their sermons seemed to be somewhat more censorious and threatening[80] and to be basically less optimistic concerning man's chances for salvation.[81] Although they did not go to the absolutist extremes of John Cotton, very likely most ministers emulated Cotton in stressing that man must be elected for union in Christ before he can work effectually toward salvation,[82] that no gracious conditions or qualifications exist in the soul before grace,[83] that God's mercy is manifested in his justice, and that he plans damnation for all those he has not elected to save.[84]

Some ministers, however, responded differently from the generality of the clergy to the theological pressures of establishing a Zion in the wilderness. For instance, to Thomas Hooker, who left the Bay Colony at the time the more stringent church requirements were initiated, incipient stirrings within the breast might well be evidences of grace.[85] If the symptoms of grace occurred early in one's seeking, as they customarily did, man could optimistically continue the task of spiritual improvement.[86] Nevertheless, even Hooker stressed the impossibility of carnal man's assisting himself toward salvation.[87] Even Hooker failed to heed the admonition of Perkins, "The minister of the word in preaching is in the judgment of charity to presume that all his hearers be elect, leaving all secret judgment to God," [88] and

---

[80] This should not be interpreted to mean that Puritan ministers at this time deliberately sought to evoke convulsionary conversions.

[81] The partial result of such preaching may be seen in the Reverend Michael Wigglesworth's records of several testimonies given in his church by candidates seeking membership. See Edmund S. Morgan's edited version of Wigglesworth's "Diary" in the *Transactions* of the Colonial Society of Massachusetts, XXXV (Boston, 1951), 426-44. The entire "Diary" affords a fascinating insight into the Puritan character. *Ibid.*, pp. 311-419.

[82] Cotton, *A Treatise of the Covenant of Grace, as It Is Dispensed to the Elect Seed* (London, 1671), 3rd ed. See, for example, pp. 125-35, 218-19. Esp. useful in these regards is Cotton's *A Sermon Preached . . . at Salem, 1636.*

[83] *A Conference Mr. Cotton Held at Boston with the Elders of New England . . . Written by Francis Cornwell* (London, 1646), pp. 1-6.

[84] Cotton, *The Saints Support and Comfort* (London, 1656), Sermon III.

[85] In his *Visible Saints*, pp. 96-97, Morgan reports new documentary evidence which indicates that substantive differences existed between Hooker and Cotton.

[86] In addition to being a powerful preacher, Hooker wrote searching tracts on the psychology of conversion. See his *The Application of Redemption* (London, 1656), *The Faithful Covenanter* (London, 1644), *The Covenant of Grace Opened* (London, 1649), *The Soules Preparation* (London, 1632), *The Soules Exaltation* (London, 1638), *The Soules Humiliation* (London, 1637), *The Soules Ingrafting into Christ* (London, 1637), *The Unbelievers Preparing for Christ* (London, 1638).

[87] Hooker, *The Saints Guide* (London, 1645), esp. pp. 87-140.

[88] Perkins, *A Warning Against the Idolatrie of the Last Times, and an Instruction Touching Religious or Divine Worship*, p. 709, in *Workes*, I.

he violated Perkins' injunction, "Always, in the very hatred of sin, let the love of the person appear in the speeches, and let the minister include himself (if he may) in his reprehension, that it may be more mild and gentle." [89] Even Hooker did not conform to the style of preaching which Perkins defended against those "that mislike the preaching used in these days [i.e., by the English Puritan ministers] because we use not severity, and personal reproofs." [90]

In important respects it was Peter Bulkeley who prepared the way for future changes of emphasis. Bulkeley emphasized God's mercy, saying in a sermon, "In the covenant of works, God's highest end is the glorifying of His justice . . . rewarding good, and punishing evil, condemning sin; but in the covenant of grace, he shows himself a God gracious and merciful, forgiving iniquity." [91] Also, in a manner reminiscent of the English covenanters, he brought salvation almost within reach of the sincere seeker:

Seeing God's end in the covenant of grace is to glorify His grace in us, we may by this in some measure discern what part we have in the grace of this covenant. . . . It may serve for direction unto all such, as desire to enjoy the blessings of this grace which God offers in His covenant, let them seek it with the same mind that God offers it, with a purpose and desire to have grace exalted and magnified. . . . In this way we cannot miss of obtaining that thing we seek for at God's Hand.[92]

In addition, Bulkeley connected morality so closely with grace that pious behavior seemed indicative of justification. "It is a warrantable and safe way," he preached, "for a man by and from his sanctification to take an evidence of his justification, and of his estate in grace before God." [93]

Over the years, as has been discussed earlier in this essay, New England came under attack from English Presbyterians for its exclusionary church policies, church membership dropped off, ministers turned a greater amount of their attention to the unchurched and to the baptized but allegedly unregenerate members of their congregations, and a host of other political, social, economic, and religious problems disturbed the commonwealth. Under these impingements, the preaching of the covenant of grace underwent significant incremental changes. The main stream of Puritan expression tended to stress gradually more and more the conditional aspects of the covenant, to magnify man's role in the process of securing conversion, and, albeit giving voluminous lip service to the concept, to de-emphasize the

---

[89] Perkins, *The Arte of Prophecying*, p. 669, in *Workes*, II.

[90] Perkins, *Epistle to the Galatians*, p. 317, in *Workes*, II. This does not mean, of course, that Perkins and other English Puritan ministers did not upon occasion preach imprecatory sermons. For a sermon containing threatening materials, see Perkins' *A Powerful Exhortation to Repentance*, esp. pp. 423-27, in *Workes*, III.

[91] Bulkeley, *The Gospel Covenant*, pp. 82, 83, 84.

[92] *Ibid.*, pp. 85, 86, 87.

[93] *Ibid.*, p. 252. Contrast with *A Conference Mr. Cotton Held at Boston with the Elders of New England*, pp. 6-37.

implacability, the capriciousness, the inscrutability, the inhumanness, the absoluteness, the allness of God. Thus, the pendulum, which during the first generation had swung toward greater severity and greater emphasis upon absolute values, returned to the more moderate position of the English framers of the covenant and then, in the teachings of Cotton Mather and others, continued its excursion toward a more "liberal" philosophy. With the oversimplification necessitated by limitations of space, the movement toward rational piety may be illustrated by its extreme prophet, Cotton Mather.

Toward the close of his frenetic career, the New England commonwealth which Cotton Mather sought to influence was only faintly reminiscent of Winthrop's city upon the hill. Although religion was still central, the minister-magistrate absolutism which had been endorsed by the generation of his grandfathers, John Cotton and Richard Mather, had long since faded into the unrenewable past. For several decades, as perhaps the most perceptive observer of the declivity of the holy commonwealth, Mather had attempted to evolve a new theological accommodation to the times. Almost desperately he clung to the remnant church and social covenants and to the veneration of the ideals of the founders. At the same time, however, he knew that the cosmology of the past was doomed and that a quasi-Arminian preaching of the covenant of grace could not contain the emergent spirit of the new age. Although during his earlier career he was sometimes ambiguous and indecisive, in his autumn years Mather was both daring and creative in his efforts to harness the forces of society to the cause of religion. Instead of attempting to stop the course of history or to bend it backward into the medieval caverns from which it had come, he attempted to capture the stream itself, to turn its vast energies into religious effort. By means of a pervasive pietism, Mather sought to transform secular, fragmented New England into a religiously unified and conformist society.

Of his various works advocating the Matherian system of pietism, perhaps the most noteworthy is the last of his major writings, the *Manuductio ad Ministerium*, by which Mather encouraged a new type of ministerial leadership.[94] In the first section of this tightly structured little book, Mather guided the ministerial candidate through the several stages of his development in pietism. By meditating deeply and frequently upon death, the candidate should come to a pervasive awareness that the "true END *of life*" is "the SERVICE OF THE GLORIOUS GOD." To achieve the "fixing" of "this *veneration*," the candidate was counseled to spiritualize all his daily activities, by applying to himself the questions and answers provided in a lengthy catechism. "But you will not come to *this*" discipline, Mather warned, "until the glorious GOD . . . give you a *new heart*, and cause a *regenerating*

[94] Cotton Mather, *Manuductio ad Ministerium. Directions for a Candidate of the Ministry* (Boston, 1726). See Eugene E. White, "Cotton Mather's *Manuductio ad Ministerium*," *The Quarterly Journal of Speech* XLIX (October, 1963), 308-19.

work of His grace to pass upon you." Strikingly different from John Cotton, Mather approached the morphology of conversion with great optimism, all but denying the implacability and inscrutability of God: *"Plead* it, that you may be *justified.* Plead it, with a *comfortable persuasion* of your finding a *kind reception* with your SAVIOUR. Don't think, that you *honor,* but that you *reproach* your SAVIOUR, if you doubt your *kind reception* with Him." Only by means of a perfunctory sentence did Mather maintain the semblance of identification with the absolutism of John Cotton: "If GOD be with you in this action, your *conversion* to GOD is now accomplished." Any doubts which might have been aroused by this qualification were probably dissipated by the optimism of the immediately following sentence: "Every thing in *heaven* and *earth* and *hell* now looks with a most *joyful aspect* upon you." In the orthodox sequence of conversion, sanctification automatically followed justification; in the Matherian scheme, piety was the consequent: "Being thus brought into an *happy state* of *reconciliatin* [sic] to GOD, you are *prepared,* yea, you cannot but be *disposed* . . . that ESSAYS TO DO GOOD, may fill your life, and be the very *spirit* and *business* of it, and the principal *delight."* [95]

Although the spirit and methodology of pietism should infuse all pastoral duties, it was especially important that preaching be pietistic. By applying *"motions* of PIETY" in conjunction with certain principles which Mather recommended concerning sermon preparation and delivery, the minister would "become the mirror, or conduit, or conveyor of GOD's truth to others." One of the *"affections"* which Mather prescribed was a greater emphasis upon the person of Christ than was typical of the time: "Your *sermon* must . . . have the *blood* of your SAVIOUR sprinkled on it, and His *good* SPIRIT breathing in it." [96] Another motion of piety was to "show the people of GOD, how to take the comfort of their *eternal election,* and *special redemption,* and *ensured perseverance;* and at the same time fetch mighty incentives to *holiness,* from those *hopes,* which will forever cause those that have them to *purify themselves."* [97]

In addition to his substitution of spontaneous natural reason for the labored intellection of formal logic, Mather urged that the sermon should not be directed first to the cognitive faculties and then to the emotive ones, but that by means of the *"motions* of PIETY" it should be directed to man as an integrated creature with mind and emotion conjoined. Instead of recommending that appeals to the emotions be limited to the "Application"

[95] Mather, *Manuductio ad Ministerium,* pp. 4, 15, 16, 17, 18, 20. Mather's emphasis upon "doing good" is reminiscent of Richard Baxter's *How to Do Good to Many* (London, 1682) and of Preston's *The Deformed Formes of a Formall Profession* (London, 1641). Also, see Cotton Mather's *Bonifacius: An Essay Upon the Good, that Is to Be Devised and Designed* (Boston, 1710).

[96] Mather, *Manuductio ad Ministerium,* pp. 78, 91, 94, 95, 96.

[97] *Ibid.,* p. 97.

68

segment of the sermon, he exhorted the ministerial candidate to become a *"fire kindler"*: "I would have you usually try, as much as with *good judgment* you can, to set the *truths on fire,* before you part with any *head* that you are upon; and let them come *flaming* out of your hand with excitations to some *devotion* and *affection* of Godliness into the *hearts* of those whom they are addressed unto." "Exhibit the *terms of salvation,* and the proposals of the Gospel," and "the *desires of* PIETY, in such a manner, that they must have their *hearts burn within* them." [98]

In his final years, Mather attempted to substitute tolerance, quasi-Arminian self-enablement, daily spiritualizing, and a program of doing good deeds for the outmoded focus of John Cotton upon systematic theology, traditional creeds, and state religion. In the *Manuductio,* he ignored the church and social covenants, and he converted the covenant of grace into a relatively painless seeking of, and a radiantly assured finding of, salvation. The rational emotionalism of Cotton Mather's pietism represented a heightened optimism that helped push man out of the cave of Reformed Orthodoxy into the modern era.

If Cotton Mather represented the extreme extension of Puritan preaching toward rational pietism, a contrasting extreme may be epitomized by Solomon Stoddard,[99] the pope of the Connecticut Valley. Previously noted in this essay for his ecclesiastic and liturgic reforms, Stoddard was also extremely significant for his applying the rhetoric of revivalism to the covenant of grace. In some ways, his preaching resembled that of both Mather and the English framers: he accepted the covenant of grace as a contractual agreement irrevocably binding upon both God and man;[100] he stretched preparation at least as widely;[101] he considered a single act of faith "sufficient unto salvation";[102] at times he seemed to open the gates of salvation to all earnest seekers; he characterized faith as "a rational understanding action" and man as a "reasoning being." Not infrequently he demonstrated a seemingly orthodox adherence to faculty psychology[103] and to the primacy of reason, by observing that, inasmuch as God has given man "an understanding and free will," he does not deal with men "as sticks and stones by mere force," but

---

[98] *Ibid.,* pp. 104, 105.

[99] Among the elements which are neglected in the simplified schema presented here of Mather vs. Stoddard, is the rationalism found in the preaching of "liberals" like Charles Chauncy and the distinctive blend of reason, emotion, and sophistication found in the preaching of Benjamin Colman of the Brattle Street Church.

[100] For example, see Stoddard's *The Way to Know Sincerity and Hypocrisy Cleared Up* (Boston, 1719), pp. 137-38.

[101] See Stoddard's *A Guide to Christ* (Boston, 1714), Preface, and his *The Safety of Appearing at the Day of Judgment* (2nd ed.; Boston, 1729), pp. 174-85.

[102] Stoddard, *A Treatise Concerning Conversion* (Boston, 1719, p. 4, and *The Safety of Appearing at the Day of Judgment,* p. 86. Stoddard preached and published a sermon concerning this point: *The Sufficiency of One Good Sign* (Boston, 1703). No copies of this treatise are known to exist, however.

[103] In contrast to his occasional acceptance of orthodox faculty psychology, Stoddard

he "prevails upon their hearts in a way suitable to their nature." [104] This meant that God employed the sequence of the faculties: "The Will always follows the last dictates of the Understanding. The Understanding is the guide of the Will." When God implanted "spiritual illumination" in the Understanding, the Will automatically embraced it. "Men would offer violence to their nature, if they should do otherwise." [105]

In critically important ways his preaching of the covenant of grace differed from Mather's.[106] Except possibly for the treatises of Thomas Hooker, Stoddard's extensive writings represented the most profound and penetrating probings of the psychology of conversion, prior to Jonathan Edward's *Religious Affections*.[107] His conversionary preaching produced five "harvests" during his long tenure in Northampton and conditioned the people in the Valley to respond somewhat later to the revivalistic preaching of Edwards. Despite the ambiguities and contradictions which pervaded his rhetoric, a main thrust of Stoddard's preaching was clearly his emphasis upon absolutism—an absolutism which in stridency of expression probably exceeded anything heard in America up to this time, and in tonus and fiber was closer to the teaching of John Cotton than to that of the English framers of the covenant of grace. In contrast to the dignity which rational piety accorded to men, Stoddard referred to them as "vermin," "dead fish," and "polluted creatures." In contrast to his own endorsement of the importance of the Understanding and the rationality of religion, he dwelt on the corruption of natural reason and proclaimed that men's Wills are "spiritually blind and cannot see the evil of hell," and, hence, their "feet go down to death, their steps take hold on hell." [108]

In Mather's preaching the freedom of choice which God offered to man seemed an approachment to real choice. Almost in the same words that Edwards was later to employ, the Northampton parson agreed with Mather that the ultimate recognition by God of the rational nature of man was his awarding to him of "great freedom of choice": *the DECREES of GOD does not at all infringe the liberty of man*." [109] At this point, however,

---

also at times denied the separation of, and the sequential nature of, the Understanding and the Will. For example, see his *The Safety of Appearing at the Day of Judgment*, p. 6.

[104] Stoddard, *Three Sermons Lately Preach'd at Boston* (Boston, 1717), p. 67.

[105] *Ibid.*, p. 78; *A Treatise Concerning Conversion*, p. 35.

[106] For a dramatic contrast, compare Stoddard's *A Guide to Christ* with Cotton Mather's *Manuductio ad Ministerium*, his *Reasonable Religion* (Boston, 1700), and his *A Man of Reason* (Boston, 1718), and with Increase Mather's *A Discourse Proving That the Christian Religion Is the Only True Religion* (Boston, 1702).

[107] For Perry Miller's assessment of Stoddard's writings, see *The New England Mind: From Colony to Province*, pp. 232-33, 282.

[108] Stoddard, *Those Taught by God the Father* (Boston, 1712), p. 5, and *The Safety of Appearing at the Day of Judgment*, p. 3.

[109] Stoddard, *A Guide to Christ*, pp. 62-63, and *A Treatise Concerning Conversion*, p. 14.

Stoddard, as his grandson was to do later, moved toward the polar extreme from Mather: man's self-love, he argued, compels him always to misuse "his great freedom of choice," and, inclined as he is by the baseness of his nature, man must invariably *"chuse the ways of sin."* [110] Before one could receive assurance, he had to pass from the *"outward call"* of conviction through a terrifyingly traumatic passage of humiliation in which his Will was broken, and he no longer questioned his "fitness to be damned" or objected to God's sending him to hell for "His own glory." [111]

In contrast to the basically rational, benevolent, and predictable God of the *Manuductio*, Stoddard's God was starkly impersonal, jealous, arbitrary, vindictive, and absolute; a God who derived pleasure from sending the unregenerate to hell. Convinced that "fear and dread of hell" are the propulsions that "make men do what they do in religion," he exceeded all other ministers in stressing the nearness, the inevitability, and the painful torments of hell. Repeatedly he took his listeners on hypothetical descents into the pit: "How will you cry out when tumbling into the lake that burns with fire and brimstone? . . . You will wring your hands, and tear your hair, and gnash your teeth, and curse your day, and fill hell with outcries and lamentations." [112] Paradoxically, in apparent contradiction of his concentration upon the impotent and debased nature of man and the inscrutable and absolute power of God, Stoddard upon occasion would comfort the distraught sinner: Do not "scare your self causelessly," God "will reject no man that will come. . . . It is an universal offer without an exception." [113] In language very similar to that of Mather's, Stoddard would assert: "There is an absolute connection between faith & salvation: if you believe in Christ that will be a sure sign of election." [114]

At times Stoddard appeared to arrive at the same ultimate universalism that Mather seemed to endorse. Also, both he and Mather substantially accepted the process to conversion taught by the English framers of the covenant of grace. Nevertheless, the Stoddardian route to faith was vastly different from the comfortable, assured path described in the *Manuductio*. Stoddard's exhortations focused upon the stage of humiliation, converting it into a terrifying and agonizing experience which sometimes resulted in cataclysmic conversion.[115] It was out of this divergent approach that Solomon Stoddard initiated the rhetoric of revivalism in America.

---

[110] Stoddard, *Three Sermons Lately Preach'd at Boston*, pp. 34-64, and *The Necessity of Acknowledgment of Offenses* (Boston, 1701), pp. 28-29.

[111] This strain ran through all his preaching. For an example, see his *The Defects of Preachers Reproved* (New London, 1724), pp. 11-13.

[112] For instance, see Stoddard's *The Efficiency of the Fear of Hell*, pp. 23-27, 37, *The Falseness of the Hopes of Many Professors*, pp. 19-21, *The Presence of Christ* (Boston, 1718), pp. 27-28, and *The Safety of Appearing at the Day of Judgment*, pp. 158, 231.

[113] Stoddard, *The Safety of Appearing at the Day of Judgment*, pp. 84, 258.

[114] Stoddard, *Three Sermons Lately Preach'd at Boston*, p. 30.

[115] According to Stoddard, the work of preparation ordinarily takes "a great deal of

71

The Divine Platform: Imitable by the Creatures

In every artificer . . . there is a platform aforehand in the mind which when he is about to work he looks into, that he may fit his work to it; so also in God, seeing He worketh . . . with greatest perfection of reason, such a platform is to be conceived to preexist before in His mind, as the exemplary cause of all things to be done. . . . The platform of all things is the Divine Essence, as it is understood of God himself as imitable by the Creatures, or so as in some sort the image of that perfection or some footstep thereof may be expressed in the creatures. . . . A platform in the mind of man . . . is collected of things themselves: and so things are first in themselves, then they come unto the senses of men, and then to the Understandingw, [sic] here they can make some idea to direct the following operation. But . . . all things are first in His mind before they are in themselves.[116]

If there is a key to the understanding of "Puritan preaching and the authority of God," perhaps it may be found in the above-cited quotation from William Ames' *The Marrow of Sacred Divinity*. The theology of the covenants represented a rational attempt to understand the universe and man's role in it. God had planned the world according to the "platform" in his mind. It was incumbent upon man to discover to the fullest possible extent the details of the divine plan and to organize his life accordingly. The external church and social covenants prescribed the interrelationships which should exist between God and man in the areas of church and state. The covenant of grace, with its morphology of human striving, represented the pattern by which God had structured man's course to justification and sanctification. To discover and understand the manifestations of God's design, as well as to interpret correctly his Word in the Scriptures, required the keenest type of intellection, reinforced by mental discipline acquired through the study of formal logic. Religion was intensely personal and emotional; but it was first reasonable and reasoning!

When the covenantal patterns and the sermonic patterns were applied to the conditions in the New World, at first they worked exceedingly well. Then, as circumstances changed, they worked less well. The nature of society altered to such an extent that the social covenant disintegrated and virtually disappeared; the church covenant was forced into configurations which would have seemed strange and alien to John Cotton; the stress of Cotton and his followers upon the absolute values of the covenant of grace gradually gave way to a greater emphasis upon the conditional values, the efficacy of man's striving for faith, and the automatic, causal relationship between faith and salvation; the neat compartmentalization of the mind into the faculties and of the sermon into parts devoted to understanding, reasoning, and feeling

---

time," but conversion "is wrought in the twinkling of an eye." A *Treatise Concerning Conversion*, p. 2.

[116] Ames, *The Marrow of Sacred Divinity*, pp. 24-25, in *Workes*.

gradually yielded to an awareness of man as a unified being with his reason and emotion conjoined.

Undoubtedly the events of the first century of the New England experience shook the faith of the Puritans in their ability to perceive the divine "platform." Nevertheless, instead of their being thrown back upon blind submission to the unknowable and the unchangeable, the major thrust of the changes which occurred in their thinking, their theology, and their preaching, was to elevate the status of man and to diminish the inscrutability, the implacability, and the uncontrollable exercise of God's power. Although appeals to the emotions may have become more open, more strenuous, and more pervasive, the dominant stream of Puritanism continued to accept the reasonableness, the rationality, of religion. Even in Cotton Mather's preaching of emotional piety, there was no abdication of the intellect, no abandonment of the intellectual reaches of man's struggles with his environment, spiritual as well as physical.

To this dominant force in the New England society, a counterforce was developing in the anti-rational, anti-intellectual teachings of Solomon Stoddard. The five revivals which he agitated in Northampton were minor electrical disturbances in comparison to the hurricane of the Great Awakening which soon swept the land. In the pulpit of his deceased grandfather, Stoddard, in the most revivalistic community of the New World, the young and intense Jonathan Edwards unleashed the thunderbolts of a new rhetoric based upon insights drawn from Locke and Newton and of a terrifying absolutism: total divinity of God and absolute depravity and helplessness of man. For a decade the storm rocked New England, dividing its people and its churches. When it subsided, Edwards was renounced by his own congregation and driven from his pulpit.

Although many persons would continue to hold Edwards' views of absolutism and of the basically emotional character of the religious experience, the land had entered into covenant with the modern era. Incrementally and undesignedly, the Puritan preaching of the covenants had helped prepare the New England community for the emerging man-dominated world, one in which self-confident humans increasingly rely upon human means in their ongoing struggles to conquer the earth, the universe, matter and energy, the origination of life, and death itself.

3

MAN AND HIS GOVERNMENT: ROGER WILLIAMS VS. THE MASSACHUSETTS OLIGARCHY

Leon Ray Camp

During the period of his Massachusetts ministry (1631-35), Roger Williams allegedly first formulated his principal ideas on political and religious freedom, and it was also during this time that he was one of the principal challengers of the Massachusetts Bay governing group in Boston. It is to our interest to trace the growth of his ideas over the half-decade, though we should be aware that his sermons are not extant.

Pulpit Qualifications

As a minister, Williams was eminently qualified to assume a preaching position in New England. His credentials included a Cambridge University degree and additional graduate work.[1] He could read several languages including Dutch and Hebrew.[2] While at Cambridge he participated in numerous disputations before the student body, heard lectures on rhetoric, and took part in student declamations. As a matter of requirement, he read Aristotle, Plato, Livy, Cicero (including *De Oratore*) as well as Demosthenes, Causinus' *De Eloquentia*, and Quintilian's *De Institutione Oratoria*.[3] Cambridge students were expected not only to absorb the concepts of rhetoric but to practice them as well. As one tutor of Williams' time at Cambridge remarked, "Without these [concepts] you will be baffled in your disputes, disgraced and vilified in public examinations, laughed at in speeches and declamations." [4]

---

[1] He was admitted to the university on June 29, 1623. *Rhode Island Historical Society Collections*, XVI (Providence: Knowles and Vose, 1838), 80.

[2] Roger Williams to John Winthrop, July 12, 1654. Nearly all of Williams' letters were collected and published in 1874. Roger Williams, *Letters of Roger Williams*, ed. John R. Bartlett (Providence: Narragansett Club Publications, Providence Press, 1874), VI, 356. Cited hereafter as Williams, *Letters*.

[3] William Costello, *The Curriculum at Seventeenth Century Cambridge* (Cambridge, Massachusetts: Harvard Press, 1958), p. 42. Cited hereafter as Costello, *Curriculum*.

[4] Emmanuel College Library, MS. 48, cited in Costello, *Curriculum*, p. 42.

74

The early seventeenth-century Cambridge scholastic curriculum with its accompanying texts produced a hardy breed of scholar. Skilled in imitation, he was not urged to become an original thinker. Students were expected to listen attentively to all lectures, take part in public disputations (in Latin or Greek), and present speeches to classmates which presumably stressed knowledge of the classics.[5] The scholastic system relied heavily upon dispute and contention as a principal means of conveying information.[6] Lecture titles, for example, were subdivided into topics which could be phrased into questions for disputation. The disputation was a universally accepted and integral part of student life. Such disputations were conducted by a moderator who supervised the students' oral command of Latin, as well as their knowledge of Aristotles' rhetoric or dialectic (whichever was the subject of the classroom disputation).[7] The students also participated in more formal and public disputations before the student body. In these cases, the topic selected was of a much broader nature, usually involving some question of theological importance.[8]

During Williams' stay at Cambridge (ca. 1623-28), students were constantly encouraged by both rule and example to argue and discuss their knowledge with their friends. Williams' speeches as a student are not extant. Nevertheless, since academic regulations required all to participate in the exercises mentioned, we may properly assume that Williams must have taken part in them.[9] The effects of the scholastic system are evident throughout his speeches and writings. As a Cambridge graduate and minister in the New World, he used his disputation skills again and again.[10]

[5] University regulations required four public lectures a week in theology, civil law, medicine, and mathematics, and five in language, philosophy, dialectic, and rhetoric. *Statuta Academiae Cantabrigiensis* (Cambridge, England: Cambridge University Press, 1785), pp. 145-47.

[6] See David Masson, *The Life of John Milton* (London: McMillan, 1877), I, 77; and Tudor Jenks, *In the Days of Milton* (New York: A. S. Barnes, 1905), p. 70, for additional information about early seventeenth-century education.

[7] All students were expected as a matter of routine rule to have a command of correct colloquial Latin. James B. Mullinger, *University of Cambridge* (Cambridge England: Cambridge University Press, 1911), III, 136.

[8] For some dissident reflections upon the scholastic system by seventeenth-century scholars as reprinted, see Charles H. Cooper, *Annals of Cambridge* (Cambridge: Warwick and Company, 1908), III, 616. Some critics felt that the undergraduates were being taught by unprepared instructors who also neglected the students' "learning and manners."

[9] Costello, *Curriculum*, pp. 17, 30.

[10] Williams' letters also reflect his argumentative spirit. He frequently referred to, or made use of, such words as arguments, debate, contention, and propositions. See, for example, Williams, *Letters*, Williams to Robert Williams, February 22, 1651, and Williams to Winthrop, October 27, 1660 (VI, 206-9 and 314-15). For an example of his written argument, see his letter to the General Court of Massachusetts, May 12, 1656 (VI, 299-304). His letters are generally organized in a topical pattern that seems excessively rigid to the modern reader because Williams often divided and then repeatedly subdivided each topic of discussion.

Williams' First Pulpit

Before his departure for Massachusetts Williams accepted his first pulpit call in Essex County, High Laver at Otes Manor, in the house of Sir William Masham. Although we do not know the exact circumstances of the call, the Masham household probably suited Williams' thinking rather well. As a student, he had been exposed to the anti-high church and anti-royalist spirit which prevailed at Cambridge. Sir William, it appears, was of the same mind. He had been imprisoned by the government for resistance to the monetary policies of James I and was released in January, 1628. Between that date and his departure for the New World in late 1630, Williams was able to meet many important people who were religious non-conformists if not also anti-royalist. Various records indicate that Williams knew Sir Thomas Barrington, John ("Ship Money") Hampden, John Pym, John Eliot, Oliver Cromwell, and the noted English lawyer Sir Edward Coke.[11] Before his departure he also met and occasionally argued with Hugh Peter, John Cotton, and Thomas Hooker.[12]

It is, of course, difficult to read English and American seventeenth-century religious and political history without encountering the names above.[13]

Influences on Williams

There were at least two major environmental influences upon Williams. At Cambridge, an institution regarded by some high government officials as a center of anti-royalism, Williams received his education. As an educated churchman, he doubtless knew of the verbal battles being fought over control of the English pulpit. Anglican ministers, charged the nonconformists, were guilty of moral excesses, lacked education, and failed to deal with the needs of the common man. These abuses were compounded when Anglican ministers read their sermons in Latin (which many commoners could not understand) and from manuscripts which were frequently copied from books or other sources not familiar to the listening audience. Eventually, some ministers recognized these as harmful and attempted to persuade their congregations in a more extemporaneous fashion. But the ministers who changed their sermons to meet their audiences' needs frequently found themselves in

[11] Precisely how well he knew the above individuals is a matter of conjecture. The Mashams and Barringtons were close friends and related by marriage. On at least one occasion, Williams served as a messenger and family informant on parliamentary difficulties to the Barringtons in London.

[12] Roger Williams, *The Bloudy Tenent Yet More Bloudy* (London, 1652), as reprinted entire and in facsimile, ed. S. L. Caldwell (Providence: Narragansett Club Publications, Providence Press, 1870), IV, 65.

[13] In regard to a study partly dealing with Williams' Cambridge friends, see George A. Stead, "Roger Williams and the Massachusetts-Bay," *New England Quarterly*, VII (1934), 238.

trouble with the government. Under the repressive policies of the government, Archbishop William Laud had been ordered to enforce the use of manuscript sermons which endorsed absolute monarchism. The extemporaneously prepared sermon presumably was not "safe" enough in the hands of ministers who might deviate from the theme of monarchism.

A second major influence upon Williams' life was his friends and acquaintances. As a boy, he had been a reporter and shorthand scribe for Sir Edward Coke, the noted champion of English common law. Coke, a principal antagonist of royal authority, had been imprisoned in the Tower in 1621 by King James. In addition to the other political antagonists mentioned earlier, Williams also knew the principal leaders of the English colonization movement. Indeed, it was either en route to or following a meeting of colonization leaders that he met Thomas Hooker and John Cotton and, while still on horseback, argued with them about common prayer.

Going to the New World

We do not know exactly when Williams made the decision to leave England. Apparently, he, Hooker, Cotton, and many other prominent Puritans were contemplating a departure for New England in 1629. Essex County, where Williams preached, has been described as a hotbed of Puritan sentiment as well as a center of opposition to royal rule.[14] Archbishop William Laud, whose jurisdiction included Essex County, diligently pursued his policy of stamping out religious dissent. Because of Laud, Hooker fled to Holland, while others stayed and were imprisoned.[15]

We do know that many of Williams' friends were planning to go or had already arrived in the New World by 1630. With this knowledge of colonization plans and leaders, it is not surprising that Williams decided to go to Massachusetts. No doubt he had decided sincerely to go anyway, since his "conscience was persuaded against the national church and ceremonies, and bishops." According to Williams' own admission, however, Bishop Laud had "pursued me out of this land." [16]

Because of his associations in England, Williams knew the general character and type of settlement in Massachusetts. Indeed, the colony was well known as a "remote plantation" as well as a "world of dangers." One writer, attempting to dissuade the eminent John Winthrop from leaving England, asserted that New England was a "barbarous place where is no learnynge and

[14] Charles M. Andrews, *The Colonial Period of American History: The Settlements* (New Haven: Yale University Press, 1964), I, 384. A balanced study of the persecution dealt out to the independent and dissident minded by the royalists is well told in this Pulitzer Prize winning volume.

[15] *Ibid.*, I, 375-85.

[16] Williams, *Letters*, Williams to Anne Sadleir, daughter of Sir Edward Coke, VI, 239.

lesse cyvillytie." [17] If New England was a place of "lesse cyvillytie" it was also a place of religious and political dissidence. As early as 1624 the Pilgrims had expelled the Rev. John Lyford for *suspected* adherence to the Anglican Church ritual and ceremonies. In Salem, an especially independent location, two brothers were deported to England for espousing the official liturgy of the Church of England. In another case, a Thomas Morton had been expelled from the Massachusetts Bay area because of his moral laxity with the nearby Indians. Before Williams' arrival in Boston on February 5, 1631, there were enough cases of expulsion and reports of rebelliousness to cause many loyal Englishmen to have second thoughts about the loyalty of New England.[18]

The Boston Church Rebuffed

The Rev. Williams arrived at a propitious time in New England.[19] The good ship Lyon brought food to a starving group of colonists "much afflicted with scurvy." Some had been forced to live in tents during the winter, and this caused many deaths. Before Williams' arrival, however, the revered church teacher John Wilson had decided to return temporarily to England.[20] It was his vacant post which Williams allegedly was offered. Apparently, the Boston church had not heard anything derogatory of the new arrival. But after appropriate and considered "examination and conference" with Winthrop and the church leaders, he "conscientiously refused" the position. In his own words, "I durst not officiate to an unseparate people, as . . . I found them to be." In addition, Williams also refused to join the congregation and told the Boston church that local area magistrates did not have the legal power to punish people for infractions of the first four commandments.[21]

Although other critics have bypassed this incident, the confrontation merits study because it constitutes Williams' first challenge of the Bay oligarchy. His refusal to accept the office of church teacher was enough in itself to generate anger—presuming the post was in fact offered. Most

[17] *Winthrop Papers*, ed. The Massachusetts Historical Society (Boston: Plimpton Press, 1931), II, 105. (Letters to Winthrop from Robert Ryece, August 12, 1629.) Cited hereafter as Winthrop, *Papers*.

[18] See Henry M. Dexter, *As to Roger Williams and His Banishment from the Massachusetts Plantation* (Boston: Congregational Publishing Society, 1876). Dexter alleges there were nineteen cases of banishment or expulsion from the Bay prior to Williams' case in 1635.

[19] John Winthrop, *History of New England* (Boston: Phelps and Farnham, 1825), I, 41. Because students may not have easy access to the edition noted, I have also used John Winthrop, *History of New England*, ed. James Kendall Hosmer (New York: Charles Scribner's Sons, 1908), I, 57-58. The Hosmer edition, like the 1825 copy, is a reprint of Winthrop's *Journal* entire. Cited hereafter as Winthrop, *Journal*.

[20] Winthrop, *Journal*, I, 61.

[21] Williams, *Letters*, Williams to John Cotton, March 25, 1671, VI, 351-57.

sources of the time fail to record the offer, but there is evidence that Williams did argue the extent and legality of magisterial power.[22] It was apparently during the "examination and conference" that Williams refused to join the congregation either as a member or elder, and also attacked the right of the magistrates to punish for violations such as breaking the Sabbath and swearing.

What is the meaning of this first challenge to the oligarchy? It is important to remember that the first settlers in Boston had left England as *members* of the Church of England. While in England, they had wished reforms within the church. When the reforms were not enacted, many moved to New England. The persecution by Archbishop Laud harried some out of England, but even then the desire of the Puritans, as they were eventually called, was to remain within the established church of the mother country. Thus, Winthrop had helped build the colony upon the premise that even though the Puritans were *geographically* separated from the mother church—and detested her rituals and ceremonies—the colonists were still members and a part of the Anglican Church. Archbishop Laud was not one to tolerate the vagaries of this hairsplitting argument, and Roger Williams in Boston refused to accept the hypocrisy of the arrangement.[23]

There are no verbatim records of the "conference," but we can be sure Williams asked some questions which the oligarchy did not want debated in public. In all probability, he asked: How can you people call yourselves members of the Anglican Church? You deliberately discard her prescribed sermons. You detest her ritual and ceremony. You expel or banish those who espouse Anglican worship practices. You cut yourself off from contact with those officials in England who endorse Anglicanism. Wouldn't it be much simpler just to declare yourselves *entirely* separate from the Anglican Church and be honest? [24]

Williams knew the answers to his own questions. The rub of the matter was that even though the colonists *could* declare themselves separate and

[22] Winthrop, *Journal*, I, 62.

[23] Clinton Rossiter, in his Pulitzer Prize winning *Seedtime of the Republic* (New York: Harcourt, Brace & World, 1953), points out, "In the very act of crossing the Atlantic, these non-separatist Puritans became separatist Congregationalists" (p. 162). In essence, the Puritans were avoiding church policy by asserting the "competency of each body of believers to form its own church-estate and to choose and ordain its own officers" (p. 162).

[24] The Puritans apparently attempted to "cleanse" their own church practices and meetings of all Anglican "excesses." As one doctrinaire Puritan wrote: "Let the matter and forme of your Churches be such as were in the Primitive Times (before Antichrists Kingdome prevailed) plainly poynted out by Christ and his Apostles, in most of their Epistles, to be neither Nationall nor Provinciall, but gathered together in Covenant of such a number as might ordinarily meete together in one place, and built of such living stones as outwardly appeare Saints by calling." Captain [Edward?] Johnson, *A History of New England* (London, 1654), as reprinted entire and ed. J. F. Jameson (New York: Charles Scribner's Sons, 1910), pp. 25-26.

79

not a part of the Anglican Church in England, the repercussions would have been disastrous. Such a declaration and separation from the mother church would confirm what Laud probably already suspected, i.e., that the colonists were guilty of treason. Technically, a formal separation would have freed the oligarchy from the question of hypocrisy which they steadfastly refused to deliberate. Politically, Williams was raising a hornets' nest. To have acceded to his arguments would have at least forced the oligarchy out of power, or worse, since Williams was urging an act tantamount to religious secession.

The Reverend Williams of Salem

On this occasion of public argument, the Boston leaders decided to "forbore proceeding with him," and Williams withdrew. Upon arriving in Salem, he assumed the post of church teacher which had been left vacant by the death of one of the Salem elders, the Rev. Francis Higginson.[25] Salem must have seemed as likely as any place in Massachusetts to go for an independent spirit like Williams. Earlier, on May 11, 1629, one of the town leaders had reassured Governor William Bradford at Plymouth that those at Salem would "as Christian brethern be united by a heavenly and unfeigned love," and that they would work for "sweet harmony" within the local church.[26] Apparently, since both the Rev. Ralph Skelton and Higginson had been officially silenced in England for nonconformity, Governor Bradford wanted some indication that matters religious were properly ordered in Salem. He had good reason to need reassurance. The Rev. John Bright had attempted to preach in Salem but could not agree with the nonconformists there and voluntarily left for England. Two brothers had earlier been deported from Salem because of conformity to the Anglican pattern.[27]

When the oligarchy heard that the Salem church had called Williams to be their official teacher, a letter of warning was sent to them. The Boston group told the Plymouth Deputy Governor John Endicott that they "marvelled" that the church "would choose him [Williams] without advising with the council" and asked Salem to "forbear to proceed till they had con-

[25] William Hubbard, *A General History of New England, from the Discovery to 1680* (Cambridge: Hillard and Metcalf) as reprinted entire (Boston: Charles C. Little and James Brown, 1848), p. 203. The first published edition of this work was in 1815. The copy referred to herein is the second edition of that work reprinted entire from the earlier copy and collated with the original manuscript (1680).

[26] Nathaniel Morton, *New England's Memoriall: or A brief Relation of the most memorable and Remarkable Passages of the Providence of God, manifested to the Planters of New England in America With special Reference to the first Colony thereof, called New-Plimouth* (Cambridge: Printed by S. G. and M. F., 1669), p. 73.

[27] *Ibid.*, pp. 74-77. See also James Davis Knowles, *Memoir of Roger Williams, The Founder of the State of Rhode Island* (Boston: Lincoln, Edmands and Company, 1834), p. 41.

ferred about it." [28] Even though Plymouth was technically out of the jurisdiction of Boston, the oligarchy wasted little time in asserting its power.
Herbert L. Osgood, in his excellent *The American Colonies in the Seventeenth-Century*, comments, "If this was an official act of the board of assistants, it was not justified by an existing law of which we have knowledge,
and it is to be regarded as one of the earliest assertions of the authority of
the civil power to warn and restrain the individual churches in the interest
of uniformity." [29] Williams was now a marked man because of his encounter
with the Bay leaders. Apparently, they were quite able to recognize a troublemaker when they saw one, and equally able to assert their power in a
formidable manner, for Williams left Salem.

Teacher Williams, Plymouth

In August, 1631, Williams was called to Plymouth as church teacher. At
first, he found favor with Bradford and others there. Nathaniel Morton, a
contemporary, wrote that he was "well accepted" as an assistant minister
and church teacher.[30] Bradford described him as "godly and zealous, having
many precious parts, but very unsettled in judgmente." When he came to
Plymouth, he was "freely entertained, according to their [the church's]
poore abilitie." Williams "exercised his gifts amongst" the congregation
and was "admitted a member of the church." His teaching was "well approved, for the benefite whereof I still blese God, and am thankfull to him,
even for his sharpest admonitions & reproufs, so farr as they agreed with
truth." [31]

In September of 1632, Governor Winthrop and a delegation from the
Boston church traveled to Plymouth where they met Governor Bradford
and the local church group there. At the time, the Plymouth congregation
was upset over the theological meanings of titles awarded to people generally
and to "unregenerate," i.e., unconverted, individuals specifically. Williams
made use of his disputation talents learned at Cambridge by "propounding"
the topic into a debate question—which has not been preserved—and the
Rev. Ralph Smith, the local minister, spoke on the topic. Williams preached
next, with Governor Bradford following. The revered Elder William Brewster of the Plymouth congregation also spoke on the topic, as did several

[28] Winthrop, *Journal*, I, 62. The Salem church admitted Williams to office the same
day the letter was sent (April 12, 1631).
[29] Herbert L. Osgood, *The American Colonies in the Seventeenth Century* (New York:
Columbia University Press, 1930), I, 226.
[30] Morton, *New England's Memoriall*, p. 78, Hubbard's account seems identical word
for word in comparison to Morton's on Williams early Massachusetts ministry (see p. 203).
[31] William Bradford, *History of Plimoth Plantation*, Commonwealth edition (Boston:
Wright and Potter Printing Company, 1901), p. 370.

others.[32] Governor Winthrop was then asked his opinion. Although the speeches given are not extant, we do have something of the main arguments as presented by Winthrop. The Boston leader told the group not to worry about titles and names as they might or might not apply to "unregenerate" men. His principal argument was that titles were neither theological nor moral but arose from English civil custom and were used principally in courts, if at all. Therefore, the common Plymouth practice of calling a neighbor "good man," for example, was entirely within the province of sharing friendship with someone you liked, regardless of his spiritual condition. The meeting ended when deacon Samuel Fuller reminded the congregation of the financial necessities of the church and all "put into the box" and left.[33]

Contrary to some accounts, Williams did hold church office formally and preached regularly.[34] Later, in a letter to John Cotton, Jr., he recalled his Plymouth pastorate when he commented: "I spake on the Lord's days and

[32] Winthrop, *Journal*, I, 92-94, and Cotton Mather, *Magnalia Christi Americana, or, The Ecclesiastical History of New England, From Its First Planting In the Year 1620, Unto the Year of Our Lord, 1693*, first American edition, from the London edition of 1702 (Hartford: Roberts and Burr, Printers, 1820), I, 117. See Knowles, *Memoir of Roger Williams*, p. 51. Elder William Brewster—not an ordained minister—was a highly respected "pillar of the colony," according to Hosmer (p. 93, n. 3).

[33] Winthrop, *Journal*, I, 92-94.

[34] Perry Miller has stated that Williams was not ordained and only "occasionally" preached while in Plymouth (*Roger Williams, His Contribution to the American Tradition* [New York: Atheneum Press, 1966], p. 19). Miller provides no source identification for either allegation. Since the ordination records in Williams' area were burned during the English civil war, it is difficult to establish whether Williams was officially admitted to orders (see James Ernst, *Roger Williams, New England Firebrand* [New York: The Macmillan Company, 1932], p. 58). I am inclined to believe Williams was ordained, for several reasons:

(1) Williams' associations in England were as much religious as political. He knew rather well, it seems, such people as John Cotton, Thomas Hooker, and John Winthrop before he left England.

(2) Winthrop himself named Williams a "godly minister." Winthrop was not one to bandy complimentary titles around. His *Journal* gives the unmistakable impression that Williams was greeted as a minister the day he arrived in Boston.

(3) Nathaniel Morton, a contemporary historian of that time (and a source not very friendly to Williams), plainly states that Williams held office in Plymouth as an Assistant Minister (*New England's Memoriall*, p. 78).

(4) Williams was familiar with the importance of ordination and its relationship to the ministry. In his *Bloudy Tenent Yet More Bloudy* (pp. 63-65), he states that a "Minister cannot administer before ordination (no more than a husband enjoy his spouse before marriage) which is the putting of him into, and the investing of him with, his Authority, as we see both in the priests of the law, and the Ministers of the Gospel."

The evidence presented herein is admittedly circumstantial, but it is of value in assessing the validity of Miller's allegation. His second assertion that Williams "occasionally" preached at Plymouth is equally difficult to assess because Miller failed to define the term "occasionally." The influence which Morton as a contemporary source attributes to Williams seems to imply that the minister preached quite regularly (pp. 78-81). Williams himself provides evidence to the contrary of Miller's assertion (see n. 35 for reference).

week days, and wrought hard at the hoe for my bread (and so afterward at Salem), until I found them both professing to be a separated people in New England (not admitting the most godly to communion without a covenant), and yet communicating with the parishes in Old [England?] by their members repairing on frequent occasions thither." [35]

The letter above provides a clue to the development of Williams' views. He had earlier told the Boston leadership that he could not "officiate" with them because they had refused to separate from the Anglican Church of England. While there is no evidence that the Plymouth church issued a formal manifesto of their religious principles, Williams indicated that he felt he had persuaded the congregation to become separated from the Anglican Church, if not also from the Boston group as well. Apparently, however, Williams overstated his case or was definitely optimistic about his effectiveness. Governor Bradford in his *History of Plymouth Plantation* wrote that in 1633 Williams "begane to fall into some strange opinions, and from opinion to practise; which caused some controversie between ye church & him." [36] Bradford implied that Williams was having a sufficiently persuasive success with the congregation that the church was in danger of splitting. Whether Williams was "discontented" with this possibility as a result of his preaching is not certain. At any rate, he requested a dismissal from the church in order to return to Salem. The Plymouth church granted it and several people followed him to his new pastorate.[37]

It is important to note here that Williams' dismission does not constitute a dismissal in the sense of being expelled. Church membership was exceedingly important not only for its spiritual or religious benefits, but for its political value. One of the principal qualifications to be a "freeman" was church membership—in this case, in a Boston-approved church. Whether or not Williams ever took the freeman's oath is disputed.[38] He was, however, a member of an approved church by virtue of his election to office. His dismission, therefore, was a notice of intent that he was still in good standing but simply wished to move his church membership.

Of his Plymouth ministry we have little in the way of detail. Available records amply indicate that he pursued his ministry with the Indians and

[35] Williams, *Letters*, Williams to John Cotton, March 25, 1671, VI, 356.
[36] Bradford, *History of Plimoth Plantation*, p. 370.
[37] Morton, *New England's Memoriall*, p. 78.
[38] See Knowles, *Memoir of Roger Williams*, pp. 43-44, who alleges that Williams did take the freeman's oath in 1631. The minister did not take the oath if the primary sources of that time are accurate (and they may be deliberately silent on this point). I am inclined to believe Williams did not take the oath for the simple reason that the oath required swearing allegiance to the governor, deputy governor, and assistants as well as the "commonalty" of Massachusetts. Charles Andrews has pointed out that when the Bay company officials made up the oath while in England (1629), allegiance to the king was required. In 1631, however, this part of the oath was deleted (Andrews, *The Colonial Period of American History*, I, 435, notes 1, 2, 3).

learned something of their dialects.[39] Eventually his friendships with them helped the Massachusetts Bay colony avoid entanglement in a war with the Narragansetts. Although we do not know exactly what Williams preached, various sources testify that he was regarded as a warm friend of the Indians and that they reciprocated the friendship. Williams' letters to his friends indicate that he did not particularly enjoy living in their "smoky holes," however. Years later, in 1670, when on diplomatic business with the Pequod Indians as an agent of the Massachusetts Bay, he confessed that he was afraid of the natives. As he stated it:

My business forced me to lodge and mix with the bloody Pequod ambassadors, whose hands and arms, methought, wreaked with the blood of my countrymen, murdered and massacred by them on Connecticut river, and from whom I could not but nightly look for their bloody knives at my own throat also.[40]

Williams' Plymouth ministry was formative in several ways. His cultivation of friendships with the neighboring Indians eventually led him to translate the Narragansett dialects into transcriptions and publish these in book form. His knowledge of Indian problems may have helped lead him to champion their rights later at his banishment trial in 1635. But in 1633 as afterwards, Williams "worked on the hoe" like the other colonists. He was by no means a cloistered scholar in Plymouth. This would probably have been impossible. He preached both to whites and Indians, apparently acquired some linguistic skills, and worked as a manual laborer. It can, of course, be argued that this pattern is not much different from that of other area ministers from 1630 to 1635. What is different about Williams' ministry, however, is that he attempted to practice what other ministers had only discussed, i.e., preaching to the Indians. The English colonization leaders had always talked of "heathen conversion." Precisely what they had done about it by 1635 is not clear. Williams, however, saw this phase of his ministry as necessary.[41]

Back to Salem

In the early fall of 1633, Williams and his family moved to Salem. Some of his followers in Plymouth moved along with him. The deliberateness of

[39] Williams, *Letters*, Williams to John Winthrop, n.d., 1632, VI, 1-3.

[40] Williams, *Letters*, Williams to Major Mason, June 22, 1670, VI, 333-51. Williams also indicates that friendship with the Indians was difficult for him at times because of the "great cost and travail." *Letters*, Williams to John Whipple, Jr., July 8, 1669, VI, 329.

[41] In 1652, Williams wrote that there existed a "twofold Ministry of Christ Jesus." The first was with the "already Christian and Converted," the second was "to convert and beget to Christ." Roger Williams, *The Fourth Paper, Presented by Major Butler, To the Honourable Committee of Parliament, for the Propagating of the Gospel of Christ Jesus* (London: Giles Calvert, West-End of Paul's, 1652), as reprinted entire and in facsimile, ca. 1898, p. 11.

the move on the part of Williams and his adherents suggests that they felt Salem would be a good place to live and practice their faith. Superficially, at least, such was the case. Ralph Skelton, a nonconformist, was the minister there, and the congregation was known to dislike high-church practices. Because of their independence, it is probable that the Boston group did not look favorably upon the Salem church. Plymouth Governor Bradford had at one time been doubtful of their stability, but this had been repaired when John Endicott had promised "sweet harmony."

While in Salem, Williams spoke out against ministerial association meetings because he feared they "might grow in time to a presbytery or superintendency, to the prejudice of the churches' liberties." [42] John Winthrop belittled Williams' prophecy of the possibility of uniform church control, not realizing that the possibility was later to turn into fact. The Rev. Skelton also objected to the meetings, but Winthrop concluded in his *Journal* that the ministers "were all clear" that "no church or person can have power over another church; neither did they in their meetings exercise any such jurisdiction." Apparently Winthrop had forgotten the earlier interference by the Boston church with Williams' 1631 Salem church position. Williams and Skelton had not.

The Flag Problem

Williams' views and statements about "popishness" or Roman Catholicism have been adequately recorded both by himself and others.[43] When he preached against "badges of superstition" and particularly against the inclusion of the cross in the king's flag as a relic of "antichristian superstition," one of the Salem General Court assistants, John Endicott, ripped the cross out of one of the royal flags in Salem with the apparent endorsement of the townspeople.[44] The results of this defacement of the English flag were momentous. Some denounced it as treasonous; others upheld the act as desirable because the cross was too "popish." The Massachusetts militia was split down the middle as to their position. Some soldiers refused to march with the defaced flag; others declared that "they'd sooner turn Heathens and yield to ye Enemy than follow or fight under a Popeish Idol." The legality of the act was debated throughout the colony or, as one anonymous document states, "ye whole Collony seemed to be in an uproar." On November 7, 1634, one of the elders of the Watertown church brought the "Mighty

[42] Winthrop, *Journal*, I, 113.

[43] For some esp. vitriolic comments about Roman Catholics, see his *George Fox Digg'd Out of His Burrows* (London, 1672), as reprinted entire and in facsimile, ed. J. Lewis Diman (Providence: Narragansett Club Publications, Providence Press, 1874), V, 70, 133, *et passim*.

[44] The story of the defacement is told by Hubbard, *A General History of New England*, pp. 164, 165, and 205.

Matter" up in Boston General Court.[45] Richard Davenport, the Salem ensign-bearer in charge of the now defiled flag at Salem was required to appear at the next session of the court to answer charges of defacing the king's colors.[46] John Winthrop's *Journal* indicates, "Much matter was made of this, as fearing it would be taken as an act of rebellion." On November 27, 1634, the court of assistants met and decided to write to Winthrop's brother-in-law, Emmanuel Downing, in England to ask him for his advice.[47] Their purpose was to "disclose the truth of the matter" to Downing. Also, the court decided to "punish the offenders," although available records do not indicate that any sentences of punishment were levied against either Davenport or Endicott.[48] In effect, the court postponed its decision until later.

On January 19, 1635, the *ministers* of the Bay were called into meeting to debate the problem. They came away divided on the subject. They, too, "deferred it to another meeting." [49] The next court meeting of March 4 produced similar results. Winthrop stated in his *Journal*, "the court could not agree about the thing." [50] Although the decision of how to deal with defacing was postponed, the militia was told that "all the ensigns should be laid aside." [51] Secondly, a committee must have been chosen to study the problem because at the next session of the court on May 6, 1635, Winthrop wrote that "the Commissioners chosen to consider of the act of Mr. Endicott concerning the colrs att Salem did reporte to the Court." The court's decision was to censure Endicott and deprive him of the privilege to hold office for one year.[52] Even this relatively mild sentence was enacted with some trouble. As one source describes it, "after many teadious Debates, It [the sentence] was Carryed by three Votes that tho' their Brother had down well and acted like a Good tender Conscion'd Christian,

that yet nevertheless he had not done prudently, and tho that he did not deserve any punishment for ye Act it self; yet that he ought to be discharged his place in ye Government for ye same for going so bunglingly about it, and for fear that their Charters and Priviledges should be a Seizure from ye King make an attonement for ye same.[53]

[45] Winthrop, *Journal*, I, 137-38.

[46] *Records of the Governor and Company of the Massachusetts Bay in New England* (Boston: William White, 1853), I, 133. This volume is a reprinted collection in facsimile of the earliest of the official Bay records. Cited hereafter as *Records*.

[47] Winthrop, *Journal*, I, 141.

[48] *Ibid.*

[49] *Ibid.*, I, 145.

[50] *Ibid.*, I, 147. At the same session, one Israel Stoughton was denied the right to continue to hold office because he questioned the oligarchy's use and extent of civil powers.

[51] *Ibid.*

[52] *Ibid.*, 149.

[53] Sir Henry Vane [?] in Harleian Manuscript No. 4880, folio 86, as reprinted in Howard Millar Chapin, *Roger Williams and The Kings Colors, The Documentary Evidence* (Providence: E. L. Freeman Company, 1928), p. 19. I am indebted to the pamphlet noted above for the locations of some of the research materials dealing with the flag crisis. I have, of course, independently consulted the various sources whenever available.

Although Winthrop was concerned about the defacement because it would give "occasion to the state of England to think ill of us," [54] he apparently was not worried about English repercussions. His solution was to have each of the officials deal with his neighbors, "to still their minds, who stood so stiff for the cross, until we should fully agree about it, which was expected, because the ministers had promised to take pains about it, and to write into England, to have the judgments of the most wise and godly there." [55]

The Anti-Royalist Tract

In January, 1636, the General Court had apparently received the "wise and godly" advice from Downing in England, for the group decided to allow each militia company its own choice as to "what colrs they shall have." [56] By 1636, however, Williams had been expelled from Massachusetts. In order to evaluate some of his additional encounters with the oligarchy leading to his banishment, it will be necessary to return to the late fall of 1633, when Williams wrote an anti-royalist treatise which he sent to the governor of Plymouth colony, William Bradford. Although the tract was an attack upon the royal patent system (and only incidentally concerned with religious freedom), it evoked no response from Bradford. Governor John Winthrop, however, reacted differently when he forced Williams to send him a copy.

The Boston group called a meeting of the governor and the assistants and "took into consideration" the political broadside written by the stubborn minister.[57] They decided Williams should be officially informed of their displeasure by John Endicott, Assistant to the General Court from Salem. For some reason Endicott had been absent from the "consideration" session just mentioned. Winthrop was asked by the assistants to write a letter to the absent official explaining Williams' latest attack and detailing the court's feelings. Endicott was urged to "confute the said errors" with the minister and then show evidence that Williams had retracted his statements.[58]

Although his treatise is not now extant, we have something of the major heads of Williams' arguments from Winthrop's letter to Endicott. The governor cited the following four:

1. that he charge the Kinge James with a solemn pub[lic]k lye.
2. that he chargethe both Kinges and others with blasphemy for calling Europe Christendom, or the Ch[ristia]n world etc.

[54] Winthrop, *Journal*, I, 149.

[55] *Ibid.*, I, 151.

[56] Chapin indicates this decision to have been made on March 3, 1636. Winthrop's *Journal* does not indicate this to be true. The *Journal* states under date of February 1, 1636, that the decision was made "at the last general court" (174). This would place the date of decision in January of 1636.

[57] Winthrop, *Journal*, I, 116.

[58] *Ibid.*, I, 117.

3. for personall application of 3 places in Rev[elations]: to our present Kinge Charles.
4. for concluding us all heere to lye under a sinne of uniust [unjust?] usurpation upon others possessions: and all these to be maintayned and published by a private person etc:[59]

The Winthrop letter containing Williams' alleged principal arguments also includes the governor's analysis of the treatise. Of his opposition to Williams' document there is no doubt, for he comments: "If it be not treason, yet I dare saye, it is strange boldnesse, and beyond the Limitts of his callinge." Winthrop seems to have believed that this new challenge to authority was more than a minor trouble for New England, for he told Endicott that if Williams "loued the peace of these Churches as Paul did those, he would not (for smale or no occasion) have provoked our Kinge against us." [60]

Winthrop dismissed Williams' first argument with two broad rhetorical questions which seem to defend King James as one of the "Lord's anointed." Presumably, kings could not lie once they had achieved divine status. Of the second argument, Winthrop alleged that the "Israelites . . . were called the Circum[ci]sion and the people of God" and intimated that Europe was similar to Israel. Although he admitted that Europe contained "pagans," this did not deter him from labeling Europe as Christian. In his words, "I am perswaded it is no Blasphemy (when I would distinguish a nation, that professeth the Faith of Jesus Christ—be it in trueth or not—from other nations which professe him not) to saye they are Ch[ristia]ns."

Williams' third alleged argument which denigrated King James's morals was in turn challenged by Winthrop. The Bostonian did not deny the accusations of immorality; rather, he questioned Williams' judgment in making the allegations. As he expressed it: "I would gladly knowe, to what good ende, and for what Use of Edification, he should publish these things in this lande." If Winthrop knew anything intimate of His Majesty's moral practices, he did not reveal it. Through correspondence he may have heard some malicious rumors about the king, of course, but it is doubtful that the Puritan divine would have debated the topic with Williams anyway—particularly in the Endicott letter since it represented the official thinking of the Bay assistants. We do not know what Williams' treatise revealed about the king either, although the minister's friends in England included the stiffest of anti-royalists.

The fourth argument which asserted that New Englanders had unjustly usurped the land from the Indians by virtue of a corrupt royal patent system received lengthy treatment from Winthrop. He defended the system partly by explaining the legal processes involved in obtaining land in New

[59] Winthrop, *Papers*, III, 146-49 (Winthrop to Endicott, January 3, 1634).
[60] *Ibid.*, III, 148.

England, partly by asking questions which Endicott presumably was to have Williams answer and by implying that, since Williams had not seen the original patent, he was not qualified to question it. Concluding his review of the Williams treatise in rebuttal, Winthrop commented, "If we had no right to this lande, yet our God hathe right to it, and if he be pleased to give it us (takinge it from a people who had so longe usurped him, and abused his Creatures) who shall controll him or his termes?" [61] It is clear Winthrop felt that the Boston group had the right to "controll" land used only by Indians. Presumably, "controll" meant ownership, or at least the right to purchase.

It was at least inexpedient of Williams to challenge the oligarchy—he was under the eye of the Boston group anyway. But when he denied the legality of the royal patent system, he was denying the authority of the crown. Winthrop was correct in assessing Williams' treatise as treason. Of course, when the minister asserted that His Majesty was also a liar, an adulterer, and an equal to Satan, Winthrop's reaction seems modest.

John Endicott, the court assistant at Salem who had been charged by Winthrop to "confute" Williams' "errors" in thinking, was apparently successful. Williams mailed a "very modest and discreet answer" about the treatise and before the next court session he "appeared penitently, and gave satisfaction of his intention and loyalty." [62]

Williams also told Winthrop that if the court desired, he would offer his book or any part of it to be burned.[63] Although the available evidence does not indicate the disposition of the text, it is not now extant. It is possible that the court impounded it, for the book is not one of Williams' published works. At any rate, because of his submissive attitude, Williams was not punished at all. He was, however, required to give promise that he would not continue to preach his "divers dangerous opinions."

What implications can be drawn from this episode about Williams as an initiator of religious and political freedom? If the records of his contemporaries are correct, individual freedoms and rights were never mentioned as a central issue. If Williams believed the area of individual rights in an aristocratic system to be important at this time, he did not mention it. It is, of course, dangerous to assume anything about his ideational position on religious and political freedom from the reading of evidence provided by his enemies. Winthrop's *Journal*, as well as the official court letter to Endicott which urged Williams to submit, established the Salem pastor as an anti-royalist. Secondly, the evidence indicates that Williams believed the royal land grant "patent" system to be unjust if not corrupt.

Even though the court agreed that Williams' "strange boldness" was near

[61] *Ibid.*, III, 149.
[62] Winthrop, *Journal*, I, 117.
[63] *Ibid.*

treason, they freed him upon his promise to keep quiet. Why? Since the court letter to Endicott was more severe than Winthrop's private reactions as disclosed in his *Journal*, it is probable that Winthrop, as leader of the oligarchy and a personal friend of Williams, persuaded the group of assistants to deal rather kindly with the opinionated minister. It is equally probable that Endicott, both as a friend and a representative of the court, discussed the treatise with his Salem companion to bring him around to the recognition of his "errors." Whatever did take place between Williams, Winthrop, and Endicott has not been recorded. At any rate, there were grounds for Williams' banishment by December, 1633. His submission and "intention of loyalty" were apparently enough for the court to forego punishment of the offender. Indeed, by January 24, 1634, when the court officially passed sentence on Williams, it had been decided that "the aforesaid offensive passages in his book" were not "so evil as at first they seemed." As part of his "intention of loyalty," however, Williams was required to take the oath of allegiance to the king or retract his statements.[64]

English Developments

After this encounter with the Boston group, Williams returned to his pastorate in Salem, although the church had been warned by the Boston oligarchy not to accept him.[65] In August of 1634, Ralph Skelton, the minister in charge, died, and Williams assumed Skelton's position. Before this date, however, several things happened in England which directly influenced the Bay Colony and indirectly affected Williams. Earlier, on February 12, 1634, the English government had decreed that all persons going to New England would henceforth be required to take an oath of allegiance to the king before departure, and secondly, that immigrants enroute to New England by ship would be required to hold services according to the established church practice. On April 28, 1634, the existence of a new supergoverning body (the Commission for Regulating Plantations) was decreed. Rather ominously, Archbishop Laud was declared its head.[66] On July 1, 1634, John Humphrey and his wife arrived in Boston from England bearing the ill tidings. Humphrey was a man of wealth and influence who providentially arrived with both gunpowder and muskets. Additionally, he told Winthrop that the English government would soon call in the Bay Colony royal patent.[67] For the settlers, this signified that English officials would soon cross the ocean to close down the "promised land." Appropriately, the

---

[64] *Ibid.*, I, 119. James Ernst in his biography errs on the date of Williams' submission at court. The court met on January 24, 1634 rather than March 4, 1634, to dispose of the Williams case.

[65] *Ibid.*, I, 62. Knowles, *Memoir of Roger Williams*, p. 49.

[66] Andrews, *The Colonial Period of American History*, I, 410-14.

[67] Winthrop, *Journal*, I, 127.

colonists began defense preparations. On September 18, 1634, official copies of the decrees arrived by ship.[68]

Sometime between September and November Williams preached his sermon against the use of "popish" symbols and rites in worship ceremonies which caused the magistrate John Endicott to cut the cross from the royal flag in Salem. Perhaps taking advantage of the anti-royalist spirit, Williams again preached against the patent system and also used his pulpit to declare that the church of England was so corrupt it had become "anti-christian." When the Boston oligarchy heard that Williams had broken his promise to keep quiet, they ordered him to appear before the court. On April 30, 1635, Williams and Endicott both appeared before the court and were "clearly confuted." No sentence was passed on either of them, but there was a lengthy debate about Williams' conduct before "all the ministers" of the Bay who controlled the government. Less than a week later, Endicott was required to return to court to explain his role in the flag defacement case. As stated above, the court declared him ineligible for office in the Bay for one year. The oligarchy also decided that the defacement had laid a "blemish" upon the "magistrates as if they would suffer idolatry," "giving occasion to the state of England to think ill of us." [69] Although further deliberation about the defacement was deferred until later, it is clear that both Endicott and Williams had challenged the aristocracy to the point of no return.

At the same session, the ruling magistrates elected John Haynes as governor. They also refused to hear popular grievances against the court and, after deferring further policy decisions on the flag defacement case, there was concern expressed that some of the magistrates had, in the absence of specific laws, "in many cases" proceeded to handle cases "according to their discretions." The court agreed that a committee should be appointed to "frame a body of grounds of laws," after which the ministers of the Bay would examine the accused, and then the court would take action.[70]

Salem Denied Land

Sometime in 1634, before the court session just mentioned, several of the Salem townspeople forwarded a petition to the Boston officials requesting the purchase of more land. The petition was received, debated, and refused.[71] The reasons: the Salemites had dared summon Williams as their teacher against the will of the oligarchy and secondly, Williams himself was under

[68] *Ibid.*, I, 134-35. *Records*, I, 146-47.
[69] Winthrop, *Journal*, I, 150.
[70] *Ibid.*, I, 149-51.
[71] *Ibid.*, I, 154. The petition was apparently in the hands of the court at least by May 3, 1635, although this is not clear in Winthrop's *Journal*. Court sessions were not often held during the winter months because of travel difficulties. At any rate, the petition was denied on July 12, 1635.

the contempt of court for breaking his promise to avoid preaching "dangerous opinions." Indeed, the minister was present for the court session to answer charges against himself.[72] According to the list of charges in Winthrop's *Journal*, Williams was guilty of preaching that the magistrates did not have the legal power to punish for breaches of the first four commandments except in such cases "as did disturb the civil peace," that the magistrates did not have the legal power to administer oaths to "unregenerate" men, that "a man ought not to pray" with unregenerate men, and lastly, "that a man ought not to give thanks after the sacrament nor after meat." Tacked on to this list is the comment, "and that the other churches were about to write to the church of Salem to admonish him of these errors." [73]

Ideas in Controversy

Even though Williams' ally, John Endicott, had been removed from the group, there was still "much debate . . . about these things." Williams "obstinately" maintained his opinions (which were "erroneous, and very dangerous"). Winthrop's *Journal* and John Cotton's recollections as well as those of Cotton Mather are sparing of Williams' comments during the session.[74] Apparently, Williams also denounced the patent system in a "violent and tumultous" manner. Denying that the land was unused when the colonists arrived, Williams asserted that the Indians had hunted "all the Country over." Like the "Kings and Noblemen" of England who claimed "great forests" in order to hunt, the Indians pursued the same practice and used the land in the same manner. The English nobility claimed the land they hunted on as their own, and the Indians claimed the same. The court officials declared Williams' analogy concerning the English nobility and the Indians invalid, since the nobles "did greater service to Church and Commonwealth." And, they alleged the Bay area was unoccupied in the early days of settlement since the Indians had been "swept away" by divine Providence who had visited "contagious diseases" upon the red man. These arguments "did not satisfy Mr. Williams." Apparently, either Williams' compassion for the Indian or his regard for better logic prevented him from blaming God for pestilential calamities.

The officials also declared that they "did not disturb the huntings of the Natives," but in fact kept "their [the Indians'] Game fitter for their taking; for they take their Deer by Traps, not by Hounds." Furthermore, unlike the

---

[72] *Ibid.*

[73] *Ibid.* The last charge is appended to the *Journal* as if it was hastily thrown in perhaps to add weight to the charges against Williams. Nowhere is there evidence, however, that the stubborn minister knew he was to be "admonished" of his errors by the "other churches." Was it criminal that Williams did not know he was "about" to be "admonished"?

[74] *Ibid.* Cotton's reflections were written ten years later (1644). See John Cotton, *A Reply to Mr. Williams His Examination* (London, 1644), reprinted entire and ed. R. A. Guild (Providence: Narragansett Club Publications, Providence Press, 1867), II, 46-50.

Indians who were alleged occasionally to burn forest in order to flush game for food, the colonists used the forests "for the nourishment of tame beasts," "habitation of sundry Tenants" and, lastly, for timber. There is no record of Williams' answers to the above arguments. Since he knew and preached to the Indians around Salem and Plymouth, it is probable that he was well aware of Indian hunting habits. Precisely how Williams might have questioned the assumption that hunting deer by hound made the Indians' "Game fitter for their taking" would be interesting to read. Were the Indians such poor hunters that they could not hunt game except by burning the forests? One also wonders if the Indians did not use the forests for the same purposes as the white man. The Indians did, of course, use timber for canoes and firewood. But the Bay officials were absolutely right in arguing that they used timber for "habitation." Apparently the white man could have a preeminent right to the forests if he used them as a supply source for housing.

Neither Cotton's nor Winthrop's commentary reveals the order in which the specific charges against Williams were debated. The eminent Puritan preacher John Cotton, however, indicated that the allegations concerning the uses and extent of magisterial power were the second major cause for Williams' banishment.[75] Williams generally denied that the magistrates had the power to punish infractions of the first four commandments and, additionally, asserted that civil magistrates had jurisdiction only in civil law. As Williams is alleged to have stated it, the civil authorities' power extended only "to the bodies, and goods, and outward state of men." It is plain that the stubborn reformer wished a split between church and state. Williams himself pinpointed the issue involved in his expulsion: "Why was I not yet permitted to live in the commonwealth, except for this reason, that the commonwealth and church is yet but one, and he that is banished from the one, must necessarily be banished from the other also." [76]

The Boston court decided, however, to defer the decision on Williams until the next court session. As Winthrop stated it: "time was given to him and the church of Salem to consider of these things till the next general court, and then either to give satisfaction to the court, or else to expect the sentence." The court also decided that the Bay churches themselves should express their opinion on the case and that their opinions would help the court decide what to do.[77]

The Salem church took advantage of this allowance and instantly wrote letters to the other churches reacting indignantly to the land petition denial and Williams' treatment. Williams himself wrote letters to his friends around the Bay or at least helped others in Salem to write letters denouncing the

[75] Cotton, A Reply to Mr. Williams, II, 47-48.

[76] Roger Williams, Mr. Cottons Letter Lately Printed, Examined and Answered (London, 1644, reprinted entire and ed. R. A. Guild (Providence: Narragansett Club Publications, Providence Press, 1867), I, 327.

[77] Winthrop, Journal, I, 154.

treatment given him.[78] He also wrote the Salem church stating that unless they formally separated themselves from the Boston group and their control, he would have to leave. Winthrop reported that the "whole church was grieved herewith." [79] The zealous minister continued to force the issue by sending letters containing the same information to other churches in the Bay.

Banished

At the September 1 court session, Endicott was present and was allowed to deliver a protest speech justifying the letter barrage in defense of the Salem church's actions. This offended the officials who had decided that the letters were "against the magistrates and deputies," and so Endicott was "committed," i.e., jailed. For some reason, however, the Salem official recanted and, after he had "acknowledged his fault," was released without further punishment. During this time, Williams was ill in Salem and unable to speak in his own behalf in the pulpit.[80]

In October, the distinguished Puritan preacher Hugh Peter arrived in Boston and brought news of additional persecution from England. The son of Governor Winthrop also arrived and brought with him men, money, and ammunition for the defense of the colony. When the October court session met, they heard Williams defend his letters to the other churches by complaining of injustice and oppression as well as his decision to renounce communion with the Salem church if they did not separate from the Boston oligarchy. After the letters were denounced as "antichristian pollution," Thomas Hooker "disputed" with Williams but "could not reduce him from any of his errors." The stubborn troublemaker was then ordered banished.[81] When he returned home, he again told the Salem group to separate. They refused because they had already written a letter to the court "acknowledging their fault in joining with Mr. Williams in that letter to the churches against them." What really happened was that the Boston officials had told the Salem church they could have the land they wanted if they would get rid of Williams. The church opted for the land. Williams, now a man without a legal home and a pastor rejected by his own church, left Massachusetts.

---

[78] *Ibid.*, I, 155. The oligarchy was very displeased with Williams' upstaging of the court by initiating a letter-writing campaign of defense. Because of this campaign, the legally elected Salem representatives were excluded from court sessions until they gave "satisfaction" to the court.

[79] *Ibid.*, I, 157.

[80] *Ibid.* Endicott may have realized that submitting was better than standing up to the court. His friends had already been locked out of the court sessions, so he could not expect help from them.

[81] *Ibid.*, I, 162-63.

Summary and Interpretation

We have attempted to trace the Massachusetts ministry of Roger Williams and his challenges to the oligarchy to determine the development of his ideas on religious and political freedom. Before Williams left England he had adopted a position antithetical to that of the established church of England. When he arrived in Boston, he found what to him seemed to be a hypocritical arrangement of a church which allegedly was Anglican but in fact was not. That the Boston church had decided to delete Anglican worship ceremonies from their own services, however, did not bother Williams. Both he and the Winthrop group were in agreement that ceremonies and rituals during services were excesses. Such excesses made the church "impure," and Williams is alleged to have often preached for church reform while in New England. On the *need* for reform, both Williams and the tightly knit group of aristocratic-minded Boston leaders were in accord.

Because the source of these excesses was the parent English church and because the established church there was also the official religious institution of the realm, any denunciation of the church was also a denunciation of the state. This made life difficult for the religious nonconformists in England, because at heart few of them were extremely anti-royalist. But when the king helped the bishops persecute those who dissented, several thousands of Englishmen and their families fled to the Massachusetts Bay colony. Williams and the colonists were, in the main, rather fiercely protective of their independence in the New World. Many of the Bay citizens had been forced out of England because of their religious dissidence, and they doubtless detested any form of royal persecution.

The Boston group differed with Williams, however, in that they were not unhappy with the duplicity of retaining the Anglican name (and thus avoiding legal problems) without utilizing Anglican worship forms and practices. Williams disliked this arrangement and angered the Boston officials when he accused them of dishonesty. When Williams first met the officials he also told them that the civil authorities in the Bay did not have the power to punish for infractions of the first four commandments, except when such infractions "disturbed the peace." Because of this position, Williams has often been unfairly criticized as being something close to an anarchist. The charge evades Williams' assertion that a person should not be required *by law* to say grace at mealtime or to avoid drinking if as a matter of conscience the individual felt he wanted to. Matters such as drinking or praying were individual acts, not punishable by the state and particularly not by a state ruled by ministers. If a person declined to say grace before meals, this was his right and no one could tell him to do otherwise. Williams retained this position on the extent and legality of civil power throughout his Massachusetts ministry.

If the Winthrop letter to Endicott is accurate, Williams was anti-royalist in attitude by 1633. It may be that he was of that persuasion before he left England. Certainly he had ample opportunity to become anti-royalist at Otes Manor in view of his acquaintances and friends there. Because Williams was seemingly against so many things as a Massachusetts minister, some critics have alleged he was principally a negativist. This allegation obscures the fact that the oligarchy often denied the means of effecting social change. During Williams' ministry the Boston group refused to allow freemen to examine the charter and other documents of incorporation, excluded from office those with whom it disagreed (including the forced locking out of legally elected officials), and engaged in duplicity and bribery to gain its goals.[82] Although the oligarchy did not, of course, rule this way all the time, they did treat Williams and the Salem church in a shady and illegal manner prior to the 1635 banishment case.

Williams himself failed to provide enough information about his Massachusetts preaching to determine an accurate tracing of the development of his ideas on political liberty and religious freedom. The materials available on this period (most are from sources unfriendly to Williams) seem to confirm that his anti-Laudian and anti-royalist feelings were strong. Eventually, before his banishment case came to trial in 1635, we know he was also against the idea of a combination church-state. His only practical answer on this idea while in the commonwealth, however, was to urge the Salem church to disaffiliate from the Boston group. He must have made his principles rather attractive from the pulpit, since the church nearly did exactly what he asked.

Williams' crime against the Bay was not necessarily in holding opinions which some people in the colony already accepted, but in using the highest office in the colony to promulgate his opinions. The Massachusetts pulpit of 1630 to 1635 was the center of power, and Williams abused it when he continued verbally to assault the governmental arrangement which bowed to the wishes of ministers in order to keep the colonists in line. Williams compounded his crime by pursuing other options open to him. He was friendly with the Indians (and dared to argue that they were equal to the white man) and apparently sought to convert them. He wrote letters to his friends urging them to resist the Boston officials. Even the King of England received Williams' views—although His Majesty's reply, if any, has not been recorded. The bumptious troublemaker left no persuasive stone unturned in order to achieve his separatist goals.

When Williams' preaching and ideas proved effective enough to attract adherents, the oligarchy had no other feasible choice but to expel the obstinate minister. Not to have done so could have brought about the downfall

---

[82] *Records*, I, 165. See Rossiter, *Seedtime of the Republic*, p. 183.

of the ruling aristocracy. The rulers recognized Williams for what he was—an argumentatively powerful minister who used his religious office as a tool to urge the substitution of a popular government for an autocratic arrangement. For Williams

the Soveraigne, originall, and foundation of civill power lies in the people. . . . A People may erect and establish what forme of Government seemes to be the most meete for their civill condition: It is evident that such Governments as are by them erected and established, have no more power, nor for no longer time, then the civill power or people consenting and agreeing shall betrust them with. This is cleere not only in Reason, but in the experience of all commonweales, where the people are not deprived of their naturall freedome by the power of Tyrants.[83]

As to the powers of the civil officials and religion,

All Civill States with their Officers of justice in their respective constitutions and administrations are . . . essentially Civill, and therefore not Judges, Governours or Defendours of the Spirituall or Christian State and Worship. It is the will and command of God that . . . a permission of the most Paganish, Jewish, Turkish, or Antichristian consciences and worships, bee granted to all men in all Nations and Countries. . . . God requireth not an uniformity of Religion to be inacted and inforced in any civill state; which inforced uniformity (sooner or later) is the greatest occasion of civill Warre.[84]

But the citations above are from Williams' pen of 1644, not 1635. While in Massachusetts, he never systematically detailed his philosophy of freedom, although later in Rhode Island his followers were rather successful in developing a popular government. Williams was not a great thinker or a distinguished theologian. He does deserve a high place in the American heritage, however, for as a political activist he was the initiator of the now traditional American idea of the separation of church and state.

[83] Roger Williams, *The Bloudy Tenent of Persecution* (London, 1644), as reprinted entire and in facsimile, ed. S. L. Caldwell (Providence: Narragansett Club Publications. Providence Press, 1867), III, 249-50.
[84] *Ibid.*, III, 3-4.

4

THE RHETORIC OF SENSATION CHALLENGES THE RHETORIC OF THE INTELLECT: AN EIGHTEENTH-CENTURY CONTROVERSY

Edward M. Collins, Jr.

The eighteenth century was a time in which the established religious order came under question. In England John and Charles Wesley began an evangelical revival in reaction to the inertia of the Church of England. In Germany Spener and Francke challenged the established order under the name of Pietism. In America religious enthusiasm swept over the colonies from Georgia to New England.

These movements had an underlying unity.[1] All were concerned with a reformation of personal religion rather than revision of doctrine. They sought to awaken the people to a deeper religious life than they had hitherto experienced. Pietism emphasized the priesthood of all believers by stressing the emotional and aesthetic qualities over the ritualistic and intellectual.[2] John Wesley stressed the doctrine of "free grace" whereby all men could have a personal experience with God. In America emphasis was shifting from the rational self-discipline of the Enlightenment to a religion of experience.[3]

The religious movement in the American colonies, known as the "Great Awakening," was far more extensive than the famed revival begun under Jonathan Edwards.[4] The Great Awakening should more properly be called "Great Awakenings," as the turmoil ranged in space over the entire eastern seaboard, and in time from 1734-35 to the decade of 1740-50. Professor H. Richard Niebuhr wrote concerning these religious movements that America "cannot eradicate, if it would, the marks left upon its social memory,

---

[1] Vernon L. Stanfield, "The Preaching of the Great Awakening and Its Contribution to Political Liberty" (unpublished Th.D. thesis, Southern Baptist Theological Seminary, Louisville, Kentucky, 1947). Stanfield's position is that the Great Awakening in the colonies was a separate movement and was not related, for example, to the Wesleyan movement in Great Britain.

[2] William Gerald McLoughlin, _Modern Revivalism: Charles Grandison Finney to Billy Graham_ (New York: The Ronald Press, 1959), p. 8.

[3] H. Shelton Smith, Robert T. Handy, and Lefferts A. Loetscher, _American Christianity: An Historical Interpretation with Representative Documents_ (2 vols.; New York: Charles Scribner's Sons, 1960), I, 310. See also James H. Nichols, _History of Christianity, 1650-1950_ (New York: The Ronald Press, 1956).

[4] F. M. Davenport, _Primitive Traits in Religious Revivals: A Study in Mental and Social Evolution_ (New York: The Macmillan Company, 1917), p. 94.

upon its institutions and habits, by an awakening to God that was simultaneous with its awakening to national self-consciousness." [5] Both the religious and political awakenings suffered birth pangs. Conflict arose; sides were taken. Jonathan Edwards of Northampton, Massachusetts, emerged as the chief apologist for the revival; Charles Chauncy of Boston became the prime antagonist; and James Davenport became the example of extremism in the prosecution of the movement. Examination of the writings and preaching of these men shows the various forces and counterforces that created the intellectual polarity of revivalism and orthodoxy in the eighteenth century.

New England Background

Although the spiritual stirrings of the eighteenth century were international in character, certain forces peculiar to colonial life contributed to the Great Awakening in New England. The literature of the period, for example, is filled with descriptions of the sad state of morals and religion. Jonathan Edwards, writing of the conditions prevalent in his own parish about 1730, complained that it was a time of licentiousness, night walking, frequenting taverns, lewd practices, and mirth and jollity in conventions of both sexes.[6] A number of causes for the spiritual apostasy which Edwards described may be identified.

The ideal in early Massachusetts was the founding of a Puritan theocracy, a state composed entirely of Puritan Christians. Such a system can survive, however, only if it can perpetuate itself and keep foreign elements at a minimum. The original theocracy met these criteria in that it had been composed of people who were born or reared in England, had been baptized, and, upon experiencing conversion, been received into the church. The system then was transplanted to New England where in the second generation there were many good people who, although baptized, had never experienced conversion. Because of this they were not permitted full membership nor were their children offered baptism.[7]

The exclusion of some persons from full religious participation seemed to augur a decline in piety.[8] To avert this trend the "halfway covenant" was devised.[9] It provided that children whose parents were church members could

[5] H. Richard Niebuhr, *The Kingdom of God in America* (Chicago: Willett, Clark, and Company, 1937), p. 126.

[6] Jonathan Edwards, *The Works of President Edwards in Four Volumes* (New York: Robert Carter and Brothers, 1881), III, 232.

[7] Charles Edwards Parks, *The Beginnings of the Great Awakening* (Lancaster, Massachusetts: Society of the Descendants of the Colonial Clergy, 1943), p. 21.

[8] See Williston Walker, A *History of the Congregational Churches in the United States* (New York: The Christian Literature Company, 1894). See also Perry Miller, *The New England Mind* (New York: The Macmillan Company, 1939 [Cambridge, Mass: Harvard University Press, 1953]).

[9] Provisions of the halfway covenant can be found in "The Answer of the Elders and Other Messengers of the Churches, Assembled at Boston in the Year 1662," *The Results of Three Synods* (Boston, 1725).

be baptized and with the exception of admittance to the Lord's Table enjoy most of the privileges of church membership. Two avenues thus were open to church membership, birth or experience, with full privileges of membership available only by the latter. A thorny problem arose, however, over what to do when these quasi-members did not have a conversion experience. Furthermore, should *their* children be admitted to baptism? The General Court of the Bay Colony in 1662 allowed that a person's child could be baptized if he was a church member, understood and professed publicly the doctrine of Faith, and was not scandalous in life.[10]

The modifications effected by the halfway covenant struck directly at the heart of Calvinistic doctrine. Originally New England divines had agreed that "Visible Saints are the only true and meet matter, whereof a visible Church should be gathered." [11] The "visible saints" were the regenerates under the covenant of grace while the unregenerates occupied a status of second-class citizenship.[12] The halfway covenant changed the requisite of admission to the covenant from regeneration to "not scandalous in life." [13]

The final breach in the Calvinistic doctrine occurred in 1707 when "the venerable Stoddard," influential minister at Northampton and grandfather of Jonathan Edwards, published a sermon in which he maintained that the Lord's Supper was a converting ordinance and that sanctification was not a necessary qualification for the partaking of it. Also, he contended that conversion was not necessary to full church membership or even to the filling of the ministerial office.[14] Thus, instead of emphasis on man's depravity and the need for God's grace, there arose a belief in Arminian self-sufficiency. Sainthood was equaled with respectability; morality became the chief end in life.[15] Regeneration assumed an inexplicable character while "good works" became the chief duty. Such a belief caused religion to become a matter of the institution rather than a matter of the heart.[16] As a result, piety waned,

[10] Williston Walker, *Creeds and Platforms of Congregationalism* (New York: Charles Scribner's Sons, 1893), p. 328. Two Synods had met previously to attempt to settle this question of who was eligible for baptism. The Cambridge Synod (1646-48) postponed action. The Synod in Boston in 1657 reached the conclusion that children of halfway covenanters should be admitted to baptism.

[11] Thomas Hooker, *A Survey of the Summe of Church Discipline* (London, 1648). Preface.

[12] The preface to the *Cambridge Platform*, published in 1648, is concerned primarily with vindicating the practice of admitting to the communion only the regenerate. This system of administering the ordinances laid the foundation for what has been called "The New England Style of Preaching."

[13] Thomas Clap, *A Brief History and Vindication of the Doctrine Received and Established in the Churches of New England* (New Haven, 1755), p. 5.

[14] F. L. Chapell, *The Great Awakening of 1740* (Philadelphia: American Baptist Publication Society, 1903), p. 14.

[15] Gaius Glenn Atkins and F. L. Fagley, *History of American Congregationalism* (Chicago: The Pilgrim Press, 1942), pp. 99 ff.

[16] The decline in piety had not abated by the end of the seventeenth century which led to several ministerial conferences hopefully to bring firmer control of ecclesiastical

godliness declined,[17] and the covenant became a covenant of equals with God, who owed man deliverance because of his merit. Arianism and even Socinianism were attracting followers.[18]

Edwards Preaching in 1734

Such were the conditions, when in the spring of 1734 Jonathan Edwards preached a series of sermons on justification by faith, the justice of God in the damnation of sinners, the excellency of Christ, and the duty of pressing into the kingdom of God.[19]

These sermons struck directly at the heart of the halfway covenant and the prevailing Arminian influences. They stressed the doctrine of God's sovereignty. Edwards agreed with Locke's epistemology, for his own observation had led him to an acceptance of God in nature, and his own spiritual experience convinced him that God could be known by man. Although experienceable, God is under no obligation to save anyone. Adam's fall caused man to lose favor and any claim of mercy with God. By birth man is depraved, and he must acknowledge his helplessness before God and his absolute dependence on him for salvation. Not only is man unnecessary to God, but he is loathsome in his sight.[20] Ordained grace is given to those who have been chosen for salvation, but satisfaction must be made for those who are foreordained to eternal life. Redemption was accomplished by the vicarious sacrifice of Jesus Christ who on the cross erased the debt for the elect. Such in brief were the points in Edwards' sermons and in essence the elements of his theology.

These sermons produced a general quickening of the religious spirit and the beginning of the Great Awakening in New England.[21] Describing the religious change in Northampton, Edwards wrote: "The Work of God, as it was carried on, and the number of true saints multiplied, soon made a glorious

---

affairs. Chief among the conferences were the "Reforming Synod" held in Boston in 1679 and the Saybrook Conference in 1705 which resulted in the Saybrook Platform.

[17] John White, New England's Lamentaitons [sic], Under These Three Heads, The Decay of the Power of Godliness; The Danger of Arminian Principles: The Declining State of our Church-Order, Government and Discipline, With the Means of These Declensions, and the Methods of our Recovery (Boston, 1734).

[18] John M. Mecklin, The Story of American Dissent (New York: Harcourt, Brace & Company, 1934), pp. 45-46.

[19] In 1738 Edwards published Discourses on Various Important Subjects, Nearly Concerning the great Affair of the Soul's Eternal Salvation, a collection of sermons that he preached during the 1734-35 revival. The sermons lack emotional appeal, being directed primarily to the intellect. The apparent reason for this approach is that Edwards regarded doctrinal confusion as the chief reason for decline in piety.

[20] See Jonathan Edwards, "A Careful and Strict Enquiry into the modern prevailing Notions of That Freedom of Will, which is supposed to be essential to Moral Agency, Virtue and Vice, Reward and Punishment, Praise and Blame" (Boston, 1762).

[21] Other revivals had broken out earlier under the preaching of a number of evangelical pastors in various parts of the colonies.

101

alteration in the town; so that in the spring and summer following, anno 1735, the town seemed to be full of the presence of God." [22] Remarkable conversions were recorded under the spell of his preaching.[23]

Such dramatic response to Edwards' preaching cannot be ascribed to his possession of any of the common qualities of the evangelistic orator. Here was the settled pastor evangelizing, rather than the itinerant Whitefield, Tennent, or Davenport. Here then is the mystery: how was it that the Calvinistic theologian preached like and gained the same effect as an evangelist?

In the delivery of his sermons he was unsensational. His voice, neither loud nor strong, had little inflectional variety.[24] An obituary in the New York Mercury, April 10, 1758, stated "that . . . in middle life he appeared emaciated by intense study and hard labour; hence his voice was a little low for a large assembly, but much helped by proper emphasis . . . and great distinctness in pronounciation." He did not use gestures,[25] and a heavy dependence on his manuscript prevented any direct rapport with his congregation.[26]

Edwards' success as an exhorter and evangelist lay in the structure, content, and style of the message rather than in the delivery. In structure, he was methodical and consistent. His sermons normally contained a statement of the text, an exposition of the doctrine under the proposition, a development of the doctrine under preannounced divisions, and an application of the doctrine. However finely divided, the sermon always gave an impression of unity and coherence.[27]

The style of Edwards was the plain style. Yet, at the same time it was full, varied, and interesting. According to Gardiner, "there are many passages in them of wonderful charm as well as many of great sublimity and rhetorical power." [28] His words were often picturesque, making use of metaphor, an-

---

[22] Edwards, Works in Four Volumes, IV, 323.

[23] Statistics vary as to the number of persons converted. J. E. McCullock, "The Place of Revivals in American History," Methodist Review, XXI (1902), 681-97, places the figure at 300. Solomon Clark, Historical Catalogue of the Northampton First Church (Northampton, 1891), pp. 40-67, prints 550 names as converts in the 1734-35, 1740-42 revivals.

[24] Samuel Hopkins, The Life and Character of the Late Reverend, Learned, and Pious Mr. Jonathan Edwards, president of the College of New Jersey (Boston, 1765), p. 48.

[25] See James McGraw, Great Evangelical Preachers of Yesterday (Nashville: Abingdon Press, 1961), p. 52. See also W. P. Trent, John Erskine, S. P. Sherman, Carl Van Doren, The Cambridge History of American Literature I (New York: The Macmillan Company, 1956), which states that Edwards' practice was "to hold the manuscript volume in his left hand, the elbow resting on the cushion on the Bible, his right hand rarely raised but to turn the leaves, and his person almost motionless" (pp. 60-61).

[26] Ralph G. Turnbull, Jonathan Edwards: The Preacher (Grand Rpaids: Baker Book House, 1958), p. 99. Turnbull offers the thesis that because most of Edwards' manuscripts are in notes and outlines it is impossible to state that he adhered to one method of delivery.

[27] Jonathan Edwards, Selected Sermons of Jonathan Edwards, ed. H. Norman Gardiner (New York: The Macmillan Company, 1904), pp. xxi, xxiii.

[28] Ibid., p. xxiii.

tithesis, and iteration,[29] easy, familiar, and at times even colloquial, but never sensational or vulgar in the manner of some of the itinerants. His style reflected variety, beauty, and novel collocations,[30] while revivalism added the factor of immediacy. He realized that if an impression were to be made it needed to occur simultaneously with the communicative act. An immediate impact and confrontation were called for. In this regard Edwards anticipated Kierkegaard by realizing that the heart is the first recipient of an idea. Perry Miller summarizes Edwards' style when he writes: "Edwards' sermons are immense and concentrated efforts to get across, in the simplest language, the meaning of the religious life, of the life of consciousness, after physics has reduced nature to a series of irreversible equations, after analysis of the mind has reduced intelligence to sensory conditioning." [31]

Edwards the evangelist motivated men by appeal to fear. In terrible and imprecatory language he proclaimed the wrath and anger of God.[32] By prodigious intellectual strength, by setting forth premises that were terribly real, by marshaling overwhelming evidence, he shocked and terrorized his hearers. And it is precisely at this point that the Calvinistic theologian gained the effect of the evangelist. Neither the Puritan manner of preaching[33] nor the formality of New England would shock people into an awareness of the primordial oneness of word and idea. The oratory of the time scratched the intellect but did not touch the heart. As Tracy pointed out: "After all that can be said of the power of love and of kindness, and the winning accents of mercy and the like, it remains an awful truth, that men will not give an efficient attention to these things, till they have been first brought to see their need of them." [34] Edwards convinced them of their need. He carried his hearers to the very pit of hell itself by preaching so that his words would immediately demand a confrontation with the senses. He combined reason and the data of experience with a supernatural sense of God's grace.

Such preaching thrust Edwards into the role of chief apologist for the revival. In Boston, Charles Chauncy, of the established ministers who op-

[29] For a thorough discussion of Edwards' use of tropes and figures of speech, see Jonathan Edwards, *Images or Shadows of Divine Things*, ed. Perry Miller (New Haven: Yale University Press, 1948).

[30] Edwards, *Selected Sermons*, p. xxiv.

[31] Perry Miller, *Jonathan Edwards* (New York: W. Sloane, Associates, 1949), p. 148.

[32] Edwards' most famous sermon was preached at Enfield on July 8, 1741, "Sinners in the hands of an angry God." God's wrath as a theme for a sermon abounds elsewhere, for instance in a discourse of May, 1735, "Wrath upon the wicked to the uttermost," or of April, 1739, "The eternity of hell torments," or April, 1741, demonstrating the future punishment of the wicked to be unavoidable and intolerable. Other subjects are: "The Justice of God in the damnation of sinners," "The torments of the wicked in hell no occasion of grief to the saints in heaven," and "Wicked men useful in their destruction only."

[33] For a thorough discussion of the New England style of preaching, see Betty May Levy, *Preaching in the First Half Century of New England History* (Hartford: The American Society of Church History, 1945).

[34] Joseph Tracy, *The Great Awakening* (Boston: Charles Tappan, 1845).

posed the revival, was most active in opposition. In the writings and preaching of these two men the intellectual polarity of revivalism and orthodoxy can be most clearly seen.

Edwards Defends Revivalism

Edwards wrote four treatises defending revivalism. The first, a revised letter to Benjamin Colman, described the revival of 1734-35 in Edwards' church at Northampton.[35] It was highly subjective in reporting the various happenings and, by offering very little criticism of the revival itself, branded him as its friend.

By 1741, when George Whitefield and Gilbert Tennent had kindled the fires of revivalism in New England again, Edwards was called upon to defend the movement a second time. In September, 1741, he delivered a sermon at the Yale commencement on "The Distinguishing Marks of a Work of the Spirit of God, Applied to that Uncommon Operation that has Lately Appeared on the Minds of Many of the People in New England. . . ."[36] In this treatise he championed the cause of revivalism more objectively than he had done previously. He first discussed the negative side of conversion, describing as irrelevant to a spiritual work such things as extreme intensity, physical effects, noisiness, effects upon the imagination, examples, and errors that could result from such activity. He then stated the criteria by which the distinguishing marks of the Spirit of God can be determined: (1) to increase esteem of Jesus, (2) to lessen esteem of the pleasures of this world, (3) to have a high regard for Scripture, (4) to become an apostle for truth, (5) to become an apostle of love to God and man.[37] He exhorted his audience "by no means to oppose or do anything in the least to clog or hinder the work: but on the contrary, do our utmost to promote it."[38] In strong and unequivocal language he had stated his opinion on revivalism; he was not invited to speak at Yale again.

Edwards' third defense came in 1743 when he published a five-part work, entitled *Some Thoughts Concerning the Present Revival of Religion in New England*.[39] This work not only amplified the Yale sermon; it also changed

---

[35] Jonathan Edwards, A *Faithful Narrative of the Surprising Work of God in the Conversion of Many Hundred Souls in Northampton, Massachusetts, A.D. 1735* (London: Printed for John Oswald, 1735). Edwards described the various ways that conversion could be brought about and gave in detail a description of the conversion experience of Abigail Hutchinson and Phebe Bartlet.

[36] Jonathan Edwards, *The Distinguishing Marks of a Work of the Spirit of God, Applied to That Uncommon Operation That Has Lately Appeared on the Minds of Many of the People in New England* (New York, 1832).

[37] *Ibid.*, pp. 578-88.

[38] *Ibid.*, p. 596.

[39] Jonathan Edwards, *Thoughts on the Revival of Religion in New England, and the Way in Which It Ought to Be Acknowledged and Promoted* (New York: Dunning and Spalding, 1832).

the emphasis of his defense of the revival as it had progressed to that point. Before, his strategy had been to persuade people to join in the work. Now he felt it necessary to direct the first portion of the treatise to a defense of the revival as a true work of God. According to Edwards the truthfulness of the revival should be judged *a posteriori* not *a priori*, by the effect not the cause.[40] He then inserted the argument that probably constitutes the nucleus of his defense:

All will allow that true virtue or holiness has its seat chiefly in the heart, rather than in the head: it therefore follows from what has been said already, that it consists chiefly in holy affections. The things of religion take place in men's hearts, no further than they are affected with them. The informing of the understanding is all vain, any farther than it affects the heart; or which is the same thing, has influence on the affections.[41]

Edwards chastised those ministers and officials who rejected the revival on the grounds of rationalism or indifference. "At such a time as this," he wrote, ". . . he [God] expects that his visible people, without exception, should openly appear to acknowledge him in such a work, and bow before him, and join with him." [42] Anticipating the objections from the antagonists of the revival and the rationalizations of those who supported it, Edwards clearly showed that there were portions of the revival that needed to be corrected.[43] The treatise concluded with a discussion of the ways in which the revival should be promoted.

In 1746 Edwards published his final apology for revivalism, *A Treatise Concerning Religious Affections*. Frank Hugh Foster says that "It may be said to have given the determining principle to the whole school of thinking which was to bear the name Edwardean." [44] Perry Miller agrees by calling it "the most profound exploration of the religious psychology in all American literature." [45] This work was Edwards' severest attempt to deal with the fundamental question of revivalism, namely, the defining of the soul's relation to God. Before, in his writings and sermons, he had defended, interpreted, and even criticized revivalism, but this work directed itself to the fundamental question of "What are the distinguishing qualifications of those that are in favour with God, and entitled to his eternal rewards?" [46] Edwards took the position that the inclination involves the will and the mind. This relationship is essential in that Edwards was trying to make clear the absolute

[40] *Ibid.*, p. 118.
[41] *Ibid.*, p. 123.
[42] *Ibid.*, p. 211.
[43] *Ibid.*, p. 369.
[44] Frank Hugh Foster, A *Genetic History of the New England Theology* (Chicago: The University of Chicago Press, 1907), p. 91.
[45] Miller, *Jonathan Edwards*, p. 177.
[46] Jonathan Edwards, *The Works of President Edwards, in Ten Volumes* (New York: S. Converse, 1829), V, 1.

identity of the will and emotions. The will is not distinct from the affections. As a matter of fact, his principal contention was that "true religion, in great part, consists in the Affections." [47] Religious experience is part of an organic whole and cannot be compartmentalized into understanding, judgment, or will. This centrality of religious feeling in Edwards' thinking was foreshadowed in his work *A Divine and Supernatural* (1734), and was further developed in *The Nature of True Virtue*, published posthumously in 1765. The whole point boiled down to the fact that "there is no true religion where there are no religious affections." [48] If religion is understood correctly, it will affect the heart.

Chauncy Attacks Revivalism

While Edwards preached and wrote in defense of the Great Awakening, Charles Chauncy emerged as its chief antagonist. Both men supported the revival in its early stages; indeed, in 1741 Chauncy imitated the rhetoric and language of Edwards' famous Enfield sermon by preaching ". . . you hang, as it were, over the bottomless pit, by the slender thread of life, and the moment that snaps asunder, you sink down into perdition." [49] By 1742-43, however, the battle lines were clearly drawn. While the attacks and defenses that followed were not in the form of direct confrontations,[50] it clearly was understood that each occupied the place of leadership in his respective camp.

Chauncy's attack on the revival centers around two writings. Prior to 1743 he attacked mostly through a camouflaged position. For example, in 1742 his oblique attack consisted of an anonymous letter and quite possibly the infamous "A Faithful Account of the French Prophets . . . ," [51] a work which attempted to associate by implication the enthusiasm of the French Prophets with the revivalists. He first attacked the revival directly in a sermon preached the Sunday after the Harvard commencement of 1742.[52] The printed version contains an open letter to James Davenport in which he

[47] Edwards, *Works in Ten Volumes*, V, 12. Edwards was rejecting Locke's premise that the will is perfectly distinguishable from affections. See also Jonathan Edwards, *Freedom of the Will*, ed. Paul Ramsey (New Haven: Yale University Press, 1957), pp. 137 ff.

[48] Edwards, *Works in Ten Volumes*, V, 31.

[49] Charles Chauncy, *The New Creature Describ'd and Consider'd as the Sure Characteristick of a Man's being in Christ: Together with some Seasonable Advice to those who are New Creatures* (Boston, 1741), p. 20.

[50] Miller, *Jonathan Edwards*, p. 177. Miller points out that one of the peculiarities of the Chauncy-Edwards debate is that throughout Edwards refused to call Chauncy by name.

[51] *A Faithful Account of the French Prophets, Their Agitations, Extasies, and Inspirations: To which are added, Several other remarkable instances of Persons under the Influences of the like Spirit, in various Parts of the World, particularly in New England . . .* (Boston, 1742).

[52] Charles Chauncy, *Enthusiasm described and Caution'd Against. A sermon Preach'd at the Old Brick Meeting House in Boston, the Lord's Day After the Commencement, 1742* (Boston, 1742).

expressed the hope that the sermon would deter Davenport from any further wild displays of the imagination in preaching. The sermon itself threw enthusiasm into the pot with everything that was considered a violation of the orthodoxy of the time. As he pointed out: "It [enthusiasm] has made men fancy themselves to be prophets and apostles; yea, some have taken themselves to be Christ Jesus; yea, the blessed God himself. It has, in one word, been a pest to the church in all ages, as great an enemy to real and solid religion as perhaps the greatest infidelity." [53] In March, 1743, a work entitled *The Late Religious Commotions in New England Considered. An Answer to the Reverend Mr. Jonathan Edwards' Sermon, Entitled The Distinguishing Marks of a Work of the Spirit of God . . .*[54] was published in Boston and erroneously attributed to Chauncy. In addition to a point by point refutation of Edwards' *The Distinguishing Marks*, the work also directed itself to an examination of William Cooper's Preface to Edwards' sermon. The anonymous work is a rather feeble attempt to meet Edwards' arguments and constitutes only a prelude to the major work of the antagonists, which was to follow.

Late March, 1743, issues of the *Boston Weekly News Letter* carried simultaneously an announcement of the publication of Edwards' treatise *Some Thoughts Concerning the Present Revival,* and the forthcoming publication of what was to be Chauncy's major effort of the conflict, *Seasonable Thoughts on the State of Religion in New England, A Treatise in Five Parts.*[55] Hardly coincidental, this juxtaposition brought the writings of the two men into direct clash. Point by point Edwards' position is stated and dealt with. Enthusiasm and antinomianism are the destructive forces. Amassing voluminous evidence, Chauncy indicted the revival for errors of doctrine, emotions, censoriousness, claims of immediate inspiration, and itinerant preaching. Three hundred and thirty-two out of the four hundred and twenty-four pages were devoted to these "dangerous tendencies," while the remainder of the book constituted almost an incidental addendum of refutation to the remaining four parts of Edwards' treatise. Important to this discussion is the fact that with this work Chauncy attacked publicly the revival as a whole and Edwards in particular.

Edwards and Chauncy Contrasted

Both Edwards and Chauncy were astute observers of the revivals. The differences of opinion resulted not from the observations themselves, rather

[53] *Ibid.,* p. 15.

[54] *The Late Religious Commotions in New England Considered. An Answer to the Reverend Mr. Jonathan Edwards' Sermon, Entitled, The Distinguishing Marks . . . By a Lover of Truth and Peace* (Boston, 1743).

[55] Charles Chauncy, *Seasonable Thoughts on the State of Religion In New England, A Treatise in Five Parts* (Boston: Green, Bushell and Allen for T Fleet, 1743).

from the conclusions to be drawn.[56] Edwards argued that you could not condemn the effects of good works because of isolated violations of accepted conduct. Chauncy countered that because so many errors and disorders occurred you could not classify them as isolated but as a natural part of revivalism. He could not allow Edwards the point that true religion necessitated holy affections. The "things of a bad and dangerous tendency" were real and needed immediate refutation.

Chauncy believed that the affections were different from and independent of the will. In *Seasonable Thoughts*, he argued that instead of "raised affections" the enlightened mind should be the basic criterion of religious experience. As a rationalist Chauncy assumed that Edwards' defense of affections meant that he was defending religious emotionalism at the expense of the intellect.[57] While admitting that emotions in and of themselves were not bad, he accused Edwards of overstimulating them so that men were not reasonable under their powers.[58]

Edwards' basic premise was that the emotions and will are not separate entities.[59] All acts of one are in a sense acts of the other.[60] Beyond the mere amalgamation of the two phenomena, however, the emotions are necessary in the moving of men to the great things of religion. Religion, by its very nature, involves emotion. His quarrel with Chauncy and all like rationalists was that they reduced all religious experience to a merely intellectual enterprise.[61] To Edwards, this was impossible; as he said, "there never was any considerable change wrought in the mind or conversation of any person, by any thing of a religious nature, that ever he read, heard or saw, that had not his affections moved." [62] The activity of the affections, therefore, serves as the foundation for Edwards' theory of preaching. The direct and primary responsibility of preaching is to impress divine things on the emotions of men. While the preacher may be able to inform, teach, or delight, he cannot expect to move or to persuade unless he can touch the affections.

The divisive forces of the Awakening thus were the inability of Chauncy and the other Boston ministers to grasp the significance of revivalism, and, secondly, the inadequacy of the same group of ministers to understand and judge Edwards' interpretation of a religion of the heart. Chauncy's criticisms of Edwards in particular and revivalism in general indicate that he did not fully comprehend the subtle ramifications of Edwards' concept of affections in the interpretation of revivalism. Always, whether in sermons or in other

---

[56] *Ibid.*, pp. 307 ff.
[57] Perry Miller, "Jonathan Edwards' Sociology of the Great Awakening," *The New England Quarterly*, XXI (March, 1948), 51.
[58] Douglas J. Elwood, *The Philosophical Theology of Jonathan Edwards* (New York: Columbia University Press, 1960), p. 140.
[59] Edwards, *Thoughts on the Revival*, pp. 117 ff.
[60] *Ibid.*, pp. 231 ff.
[61] *Ibid.*, p. 141.
[62] Edwards, *Works in Ten Volumes*, III, 2, 5, 7.

writings, Chauncy created a dichotomy between "emotion" or "imagination" on the one hand and "judgment" or "reason" on the other. Such a sharp contrast distorts the meaning behind Edwards' concept of a more sensitive relationship of idea and affection.

The intimate relation of the concept of affections to the conversion process was the major factor that created the polarity between Edwards and Chauncy. This same concept formed the foundation of a second polarity in the Great Awakening that was far more extreme and violent in its activity—the conflict between itineracy and extreme emotionalism in revivalism, represented by James Davenport, and orthodoxy, again represented by Chauncy.

Davenport on Revivalism

To Chauncy, Davenport represented everything that was evil in the revival. Whitefield, Tennent, and other itinerants also came under Chauncy's condemnation, but not so severely as Davenport. While granting that Whitefield and Tennent showed respect for reason, revelation, and propriety, he criticized them for allowing excessive emotionalism as a reaction to their preaching. Davenport, on the other hand, he accused of throwing aside everything that stood for good taste and propriety, of intentionally fostering extreme emotionalism and hysteria,[63] and even of deserving a prominent place among Quakers, French Revivalists, Familists, and Antinomians.

Davenport cannot be placed in the same categories as Whitefield, Tennent, Antinomians, Quakers, or any of the other classifications given him by Chauncy. Among those who participated in the revival, he stands by himself. He, above all, was responsible for discrediting the revival and quickening the spread of Presbyterianism on the one hand and Unitarianism and Universalism on the other.[64]

Davenport's fundamental thesis of religion consisted of the complete surrender of a person to God's will. It was precisely at the point of how one could determine divine will that Davenport was both at such extreme variance with Chauncy and the progenitor of a religious tradition called Strict Congregationalism. According to the Strict Congregationalists, God shows man in mystical ways which ones are saved and which are not.[65] Davenport influenced the Strict Congregationalists to accept lay preaching and spontaneous emotional utterances as being divinely inspired, and to reject formal worship and the educated ministry. He further maintained that ultimate authority lay in the emotions, that a person could not sin after conversion, and that the

[63] Chauncy, *Seasonable Thoughts*, pp. 5-6.
[64] Tracy, *The Great Awakening*, p. 137.
[65] Solomon Paine, *A Short View of the Differences Between the Church of Christ and the Established Churches in Connecticut* (Newport, 1752), pp. 1-5.

revival was preliminary to imminent judgment.[66] The Strict Congregationalists adhered to most of Davenport's beliefs, but in their confession of faith they revealed the continuing influence of Calvinism by disagreeing with him on the matter of the ultimate authority of Scripture, the progressive authority of sanctification, and the disavowal of imminent judgment.[67] The points of agreement outweighed the points of disagreement, however, and an alliance was formed between Davenport and the Strict Congregationalists that in turn created a conflict not only with Chauncy but also with other revivalists like Whitefield, Tennent, and Edwards. None of these men approved of separatism or lay preaching, and none accepted the idea that the converted could know one another.[68]

Davenport's view of religion was based on divine revelation through the emotions. The central concept was the afflatus. Any intense thought or emotion was interpreted as divine revelation.[69] The medium through which the afflatus was transmitted could be anything such as scripture reading, an idle remark, preaching, or an intense dream. Whatever the method, the feeling had to be interpreted as divine, and any person, revivalist or not, who failed to heed the impulse was interfering with the will of God.[70] No other person of importance in the revival held this view.

This strange man, born in 1716 at Stamford, Connecticut, was the son of a clergyman and the great grandson of John Davenport of New Haven. Graduated from Yale in 1732, and licensed to preach in 1735, he became pastor of a congregation at Southold, Long Island, in 1738.[71] In 1740 he met and was strongly influenced by George Whitefield who also indicated a mutual attraction to him by writing that he had "never known anyone to keep so close a walk with God." [72] Imitating Whitefield's itineracy, he traveled to Stonington, Connecticut, in 1741,[73] and approximately a year later arrived in Boston,[74] accompanied by his "armour bearer" [75] and sing-

---

[66] *Boston News Letter*, June 24, 1742.

[67] *Confession of Faith and Form of Government of the Strict Congregationalist Churches* (Brooklyn, 1823), pp. 37-38.

[68] See George Whitefield, *Some Remarks on the Late Charge of Enthusiasm*, p. 21; Gilbert Tennent, *The Necessity of Holding Fast the Truth*; pp. 48-49; Jonathan Edwards, *Thoughts on the Revival*, p. 145.

[69] Chauncy, *Seasonable Thoughts*, p. 152.

[70] *Ibid.*

[71] See William Chalmers, *Historical Sketch of Associated Congregationalism in Suffolk County* (MS, 1891), p. 26.

[72] George Whitefield, *Continuation of His Journal* (London, 1741), p. 10.

[73] *Boston Postboy*, August 10, 1741.

[74] *Boston Evening Post*, July 5, 1742.

[75] *Boston Evening Post*, July 5, 1742. "He has got a Creature with him as a Companion, whome some call an Armour-Bearer, who assists him in praying and Exhortations at private houses. He always stands with him upon the same Eminence when he is Preaching. For my part, when I see them together, I cannot for my life help thinking of Don Quixote and Sancho-Pancha."

ing as he marched through the streets.[76] By this time the revival had created sharply divided camps and the clergy feared that it was losing any semblance of control.[77] Their fears were well founded, for the appearance of Davenport in Boston soon created an unbridgeable chasm.

As early as 1740, Davenport's emphasis on total surrender to the Holy Spirit had caused his preaching to lose any semblance of order. As he relied more and more on spontaneous utterances, his sermons became more and more chaotic.[78] He once preached to a group of people in a parish house for twenty-four consecutive hours, after which he suffered a high fever for several days.[79] Trumbull describes Davenport's tone and manner of speaking.

With his unnatural and violent agitations of the body, he had a strange singing tone, which mightily tended to raise the feelings of weak and undiscerning people, and consequently to heighten the confusion among the passionate of his hearers. This odd, disagreeable tuning of the voice in exercises of devotion, was caught by the zealous exhorters, and became a characteristic of the Separate teachers. The whole sect was distinguished by this sanctimonious tone.[80]

A contemporary account in Boston adds to Trumbull's description:

He has preached every day since upon the Commons to pretty large Assemblies but the greatest part very far from admiring him, or being willing to give him Countenance—when he first descends the Rostrum, he appears with a remarkably settled composed Countenance, but soon gets into the most extravagant Gesture and Behaviour both in prayer and preaching. . . .He does not seem to be a Man of Any Parts, Sprightliness or Wit. His Sermons are dull and heavy, abounding with little low Similitudes. He has no knack at raising the Passions, but by a violent straining of his lungs, and the most extravagant wreathing of his Body, which at the same time that it creates laughter and indignation in the most, occasions great meltings, screaming, crying, swooning and Fits in some others.

[76] "Complaints Against James Davenport for Extravagant Services" (MS, May 28, 1742). A fellow itinerant, Gilbert Tennent, after first condoning the revivalistic activities of Davenport, later criticized him for his street singing and denunciation of the clergy. See *Boston News Letter*, July 15, 1742, and *Boston Evening Post*, September 27, 1742.

[77] Joshua Gee, *A Letter to the Reverend Mr. Nathaniel Eells* (Boston, 1743), p. 9.

[78] "Declaration of a Council on Long Island Concerning the Reverend James Davenport," William Buell Sprague, *Annals of the American Pulpit*, III (New York: R. Carter and Brothers, 1857), p. 846. Davenport relied entirely on the Holy Spirit to direct his thoughts. He rarely knew what he was going to say before he entered the pulpit. Furthermore, he condemned ministers for standing in the way of divine inspiration by preparing their sermons.

[79] Many scholars believe that this illness was the chief factor in Davenport's mental breakdown that resulted in two trials that pronounced him judicially insane; once by the Colonial Assembly at Hartford, and once by the jury that acquitted him at Boston. See Benjamin Colman, *Declaration of a Number of the Associated Pastors of Boston and Charlestown Relating to the Rev. Mr. Davenport and his Conduct* (Boston, 1742), pp. 4-5.

[80] Benjamin Trumbull, *A Complete History of Connecticut*, II (New Haven, 1818), 160, 161. See also, *Boston Postboy*, September 25, 1741. Some ministers of the established churches as well as the Separatist ministers imitated Davenport's "sing-song" method of delivery.

People in fits, tho' often almost suffocated for want of air, are not suffered to be removed into more open air, lest the Spirit should be disturbed in its Operations. He boldly asserts, that Man cannot be convinced and doubt about it, any more than have the Air blow upon him and not feel it. . . . Some think he is crazy, others that he is not, but that he is a rank Enthusiast, which last Opinion I am most inclined to.[81]

In addition to this firsthand account of Davenport's preaching, we have twenty-six verses by a contemporary anonymous bard describing his oratorical activities. Two verses will suffice:

> One hand he waves and sets two stays
> from hymn, not David's metre
> For doubtless he takes him to be
> an unconverted creature.
>
> With mind perplexed he looks a text
> and seems most dreadful glad,
> And on he'll run as sure as gun
> and talk like any mad.[82]

And mad he probably was. With screams of agony and facial contortions he imitated Christ on the cross.[83] He fostered and encouraged hysterical laughter, groans, shouting men and shrieking women.[84] The "services" concluded with Davenport walking home accompanied by his frenzied converts, almost a mob,[85] and his trusted "armour-bearer."

It is little wonder that Davenport came to represent everything that stood for extremism in the Great Awakening. His critics in general and Chauncy in particular cut a sharp dichotomy between apostleship and Davenport's brand of fanaticism. According to Hooper, for example, the enthusiasts (as fanatics were called) were persons who "persuade themselves that they are the particular Favorites of Heaven and that every vain notion that settles strongly in their Fancies is the Effect of divine Inspiration." [86]

Chauncy and Davenport Contrasted

Chauncy could not tolerate the theology or the rhetoric of Davenport. The preface to Chauncy's sermon "Enthusiasm Described and Caution'd Against . . ." includes a letter to Davenport in which he is chided for his activities in New England:

[81] *Boston, Evening Post*, July 5, 1742.
[82] "A Curious New Sonnet Dedicated to the Street Musicians," (Boston, 1742).
[83] *Boston, News Letter*, June 24, 1742.
[84] *Boston, News Letter*, July 15, 1742.
[85] *Boston, Postboy*, September 23, 1741. See also *Diary of Joshua Hempstead*, June 6, 1741.
[86] William Hooper, *The Apostles Neither Enthusiasts Nor Impostors* (Boston: Rogers and Fowle, 1742), p. 21.

What good you may have been the means of elsewhere, I know not: But I am well assured, instead of good, you will be the occasion of much hurt, to the interest of religion in these churches. Your manner in speaking, as well as what you say, seems rather calculated, at least some times, to disturb the imagination, than inform the judgment: And I am fully persuaded, you too often mistake the mechanical operations of violent voice and action, for impressions of another kind.[87]

To Chauncy salvation was accomplished by a slow, patient process rather than by emotion. Accordingly, the work of the spirit "does not lie in giving men private revelations but in opening their minds to understand the publick ones contained in Scripture." [88] Nor does the spirit "lie in sudden impulses and impressions, in immediate calls and extraordinary missions." [89] He did not disallow the conversion experience; he simply equated it with moral behavior. Chauncy's salvation was salvation by character where man acclimated his will to divine will. It was a process whereby all the faculties that had been given to man were used to create the highest possible moral life. He was, in short, a rationalist who opposed undue emotionalism.

Chauncy and Davenport approached revivalism from diametrically opposite vantage points.[90] Davenport believed in revelation through emotion; Chauncy believed in reason. These two extremes in the Great Awakening could not hope to agree.

Edwards Synthesizes the Polarity

The contrasting views of Chauncy and Davenport were brought into clearer focus by Edwards, for it was he who attempted to synthesize the positions of the extreme revivalists and those who clung tenaciously to orthodoxy and institutionalism. As John E. Smith points out:

We may say that JE's [Jonathan Edwards] ideas involve a greater sensibility than Chauncy's rationalism could grasp and that his sensibility involves more of idea than the emotionalism of John Davenport could allow. The intimate relation between the two poles brought about by the concept of affections is the real meaning of JE's "middle ground" in the revival disputes. Part of the tragedy is that neither extreme understood the genius of this transcending third position.[91]

[87] Chauncy, "A Letter to Mr. James Davenport," *Enthusiasm Described and Caution'd Against*, p. ii.

[88] *Ibid.*, p. 17.

[89] *Ibid.*

[90] For a further discussion of the antagonism between the institutional and evangelical types of piety, see Blake, *The Separates or Strict Congregationalists of New England*, 1902; Trumbull, *History of Connecticut*, I, chap. 8; Tracy, *The Great Awakening*, 1842, chap. 17; M. L. Greene, *The Development of Religious Liberty in Connecticut*, 1905, chap. 10; Isaac Backus, *History of New England with particular reference to the denomination called Baptist*, 1777-96, II, chaps. 16, 17.

[91] Jonathan Edwards, *A Treatise Concerning Religious Affections*, ed. John E. Smith (New Haven: Yale University Press, 1959), p. 3.

The genius of Edwards' position was the recognition that revivalism and orthodoxy need not constitute an either-or relationship but a combination-of and a dependency-upon relationship.

Edwards first takes the side of the revivalists by clearly affirming that true religion is centered in the inner nature of man. Like Wesley, Edwards saw that the great truths of religion are not truths of the head followed by truths of the heart. First they are truths of experience, and later they become truths of the intellect.[92] Moral rules and good works are desirable and acceptable to the Christian life, but they must be built upon the fundamental inclination of the heart.

The existentialist of today would find rapport with Edwards' position that the individual needs to discover anew a sense of his own presence. Kierkegaard and all the existentialists who have followed have rebelled with Edwards against a theoretical concept of salvation. The individual needs to taste, to feel, to hear, to see religion. "Hence it follows," according to Edwards, "that wherever true religion is, there are vigorous exercises of the inclination and will towards divine objects: but by what was said before, the vigorous, lively, and sensible exercises of the will, are no other than the affections of the soul." [93] Religion cannot be a notion that in turn results in morality, good sentiment, and institutionalism. Again Edwards takes the position that "true religion is evermore a powerful thing; and the power of it appears, in the first place, in its exercises of the heart, its principal and original seat. Hence true religion is called the power of godliness, in distinction from external appearances, which are the form of it. . . ." [94] Edwards realized that true religion has to be firsthand experience, otherwise it is doomed to abstraction and rationalism.

The renewed emphasis on the first-person experience was what the revival was all about in the first place. Not only did it leave theological [95] and institutional [96] divisions in its wake, but it changed the whole concept of preaching as well.

Before the revival the clerics had followed the general tradition of Puritan preaching. This tradition had dictated that the minister should pay attention to the techniques of pulpit oratory. The sermons were to be prepared carefully after much meditation and prayer, written down and presented from memory or closely read from the manuscript, and contain close reasoning

---

[92] Edwards, *Works in Ten Volumes*, V, 95 ff.

[93] *Ibid.*, V, 13.

[94] *Ibid.*

[95] Edwin S. Gaustad, *The Great Awakening in New England* (New York: Harper & Brothers, 1957). Gaustad lists four distinguishable theological divisions as a result of the Great Awakening: The Extremists, Traditional Orthodoxy, Liberals, New Divinity. See also Edwin S. Gaustad, "The Theological Effects of the Great Awakening in New England, "*Mississippi Valley Historical Review*, XL (March, 1954), 681-706.

[96] Gaustad, *The Great Awakening in New England*, chap. 7.

within a logical development.[97] The sermon was scholarly without being ostentatious. The Bible was the root of all authority. Whatever doctrine was developed for the day had its origin and justification in the Bible.[98] Clerics worked for the plain style. While simple, concrete illustrations were sought, allegorical exempla were scorned because they were too elaborate and smacked of popery.[99] The organizational patterns were an outgrowth of the influences of the rhetorics of both Ramus and John Flavel. Ramus' emphasis on dichotomies encouraged Puritan preaching to adopt an either-or pattern as well as an inductive pattern based upon the argumentative generalization.[100] John Flavel in his work *Husbandry Spiritualized* influenced the organizational pattern of Puritan preaching by insisting that the starting point be an actual experience, treated in the form of allegory or metaphor, followed by the extraction of a religious moral.[101] Whatever the method or influence, Puritan preaching prior to the Great Awakening was the age of pulpit oratory. With critical acumen the members of the congregation judged the homiletical effectiveness of the sermon by its technique and spiritual truth. Puritan preaching was, according to Davenport, "centres of intellectual, moral and spiritual virility." [102]

Revivalism Affects Preaching

The Great Awakening completely disrupted the Puritan style of preaching. From the time of the revival it was no longer possible for a minister to be successful in the pulpits solely by his homiletical prowess. As a result of the revival the people demanded that the minister be spiritually alive himself. Whether a sermon was homiletically a work of art was no longer the criterion. A sermon now was judged by its effect. Style was secondary to conversion; organization gave way to immediacy. No longer did a sermon direct itself in close reasoning through the inductive process to a theoretical theological issue; rather, the sermon called for the sinner to admit his dependence on God and repent. The minister was judged by whether or not he could bring about this experience. If a minister appealed to logic or used notes or prepared his sermon, he was only standing in the way of a direct confrontation with God. The rhetorical rebellion against the Puritan style was epitomized in its extreme form by Davenport. Nonetheless, it also appeared in the

[97] George V. Bohman, "The Colonial Period," *A History and Criticism of American Public Address*, ed. William Norwood Brigance (New York: McGraw-Hill, 1943), pp. 23-24.

[98] Levy, *Preaching in the First Half Century of New England History*, p. 13.

[99] See G. R. Owst, *Literature and Pulpit in Medieval England* (Cambridge: The University Press, 1933), chaps. 4-7.

[100] For a full discussion of the influences of Ramus on New England thought and preaching, see Miller, *The New England Mind*, pp. 116-53.

[101] Edwards, *Images or Shadows of Divine Things*, pp. 13-14.

[102] Davenport, *Primitive Traits in Religious Revivals*, p. 95.

preaching of Tennent and Whitefield and, at times, even Edwards. The method of preaching sprang logically from their concept of the doctrine of regeneration.[103]

Conclusion

Edwards had come to realize that preaching a theoretical understanding and justification of Christianity as had been done by Chauncy and all like institutionalists as well as himself at one time was inadequate. It left the hearer on the outside of any type of experience or personal engagement. On the other hand, Edwards insisted that any personal experience needed to be tied to the understanding. Understanding is the integral force between the heart and the will. And it is precisely at this point that Edwards synthesized the positions of revivalism and orthodoxy. He saw along with Tennent and Whitefield and even Davenport in his more moderate moments that genuine religion begins with the heart. It cannot be proved; it must be experienced. Despite this avowal of the religion of the heart he sided with Chauncy by differing with the revivalists at two crucial points. First, unlike Whitefield, Tennent, and Davenport, he would deny that extraordinary powers and ecstatic behavior constituted conversion. He was critical of placing undue emphasis on impulses and impressions:

Some that follow impulses and impressions go away with a notion that they do not other than follow the guidance of God's word, and make the scriptures their rule, because the impression is made with a text of scripture that comes to their mind, though they take that text as it is impressed on their minds and improve it as a new revelation, to all intents and purposes, or as a new revelation of a particular thing.[104]

Edwards felt that in the case of rancorous and harsh-tongued persons, the process of conversion was not only incomplete but interfered with. It was no guarantee of religious experience that a person shouted, had convulsions, or cried. The truly converted person was calm.[105]

The second disagreement with the revivalists was his unwillingness to put the intellect in contrast to religious experience. He was a scholar, and he refused to follow the persistent error of the revivalists that "book learning" was detrimental to a full and complete religious experience and that ignorance was synonymous with incorruption and innocence.[106]

On the side of the revivalists, Edwards affirmed the validity of religious experience; on the side of orthodoxy, he affirmed that any religious experience

[103] Mecklin, *The Story of American Dissent*, pp. 219-20.
[104] Edwards, *Thoughts on the Revival*, p. 295.
[105] *Ibid.*, pp. 150-51.
[106] *Ibid.*, p. 296.

must be subjected to critical judgments. Affections cannot validate themselves, they must be put to a test beyond their own control. The manifestation of the affections must be judged against the life of the converted as pictured in the New Testament.

The double-edged form of Edwards' premise, direct experience coupled with the intellect, brought revivalism and orthodoxy into proper focus and made the contrast less sharp. He made it possible to understand a Davenport or Whitefield or Tennent as they attempted to tear asunder the conventions and staid assumptions of the highly rationalistic society in which they were preaching and at the same time appreciate Chauncy's conviction that religious experience without some control is just as heretical. Davenport and the other revivalists said, feel your religion; Chauncy and the other established ministers said, follow your intellect. Edwards said, combine them. The crucial issue for both revivalism and orthodoxy was the doctrine of regeneration, how a man might be born anew into the Kingdom of God. The power of Edwards' doctrine is that uncompromisingly he demanded that both the approach of revivalism and the approach of orthodoxy be preserved.

5

THE RISE OF UNITARIANISM IN AMERICA

Thomas Olbricht

Now that a century and a half have passed, it is obvious that the rise of Unitarianism shook Puritan theology at its very foundations. The controversy which ensued was crucial not only for the ongoing stream of American religion, but also to American life and culture. From the standpoint of the history of preaching, the controversy was crucial for it was primarily oral, even though many of the speeches eventually appeared in print. The books of sermons are legion, with every important New England minister of the period publishing at least one volume. The crucial documents of the controversy were sermons or lectures. As Conrad Wright states, "Channing's Baltimore Sermon, Emerson's Divinity School Address, and Parker's South Boston Sermon have long been accepted as the three great classic utterances of American Unitarianism." [1]

The repercussions of the controversy were felt largely in the genteel society of eastern Massachusetts. But the fire smoldered in upper New England and New York among Baptist groups who were heirs of the evangelical awakenings. The result was the formation of two religious bodies, the Universalists and the Christian Connexion.[2] These groups attracted primarily the uneducated, but their theology in many facets paralleled that of the Harvard elite. For Unitarians proper, however, a great deal of truth is contained in the jibe that Unitarians believe in the fatherhood of God, the brotherhood of man, and the vicinity of Boston. Because of the limitations of space this essay will concern only the controversy on the seaboard.

The Beginnings

When a crack first began to show in New England theology, it appeared not at the doctrine of the Trinity, but at the doctrine of man. Rumblings of

[1] Conrad Wright, _Three Prophets of Religious Liberalism: Channing, Emerson, and Parker_ (Boston: Beacon Press, 1961), p. 3.

[2] For the Universalists, see Ernest Cassara, _Hosea Ballou_ (Boston: Beacon Press, 1961). For the Christian Connexion, see Thomas H. Olbricht, "Christian Connexion and Unitarian Relations 1800-1844," _Restoration Quarterly_, 9:3, 1966.

Arminianism, which affirmed human ability, go back to Charles Chauncy in the age of Jonathan Edwards. Chauncy opposed Awakening theology with the rationalism and tolerance of the Age of Reason.[3] Orthodox New England Calvinism emphasized original sin, predestination both to heaven and hell, and the belief that salvation is the result of unmerited grace apprehended in conversion by an act of the Holy Spirit. In the orthodox view, human history was the stage on which God produced great drama; in which he was playwright, set designer and director, with no deviation from his script permitted.

Those who affirmed the emerging theology to which they themselves attached the name "liberal" believed, in contrast, that man had potential for both good and evil and that he could respond piously as well as sinfully. Life was the stage of trial and discipline in which man with the assistance of God, freely given to all, could overcome sinfulness. In this revision history was still divine drama, but God the director permitted the actors to cast themselves in the roles which they wished to play. The first affirmations of human freedom later gave way to the more pronounced transcendentalist view which argued for the essential dignity of human nature. God's role thus was even further reduced, for he turns the keys to the playhouse over to man who now writes the script, designs the set, and himself directs the drama.

The label Unitarian is thus a misnomer if by it is suggested that the *raison d'être* was anti-Trinitarianism.[4] The doctrine at stake was not the doctrine of God's nature, but God's sovereignty and man's freedom. But Unitarians did reject Trinitarianism on the ground that it was mystical and not to be found in Scriptures. The early Unitarians were Arian in outlook, affirming that Jesus was a preexistent deity, but created by God, hence subordinate to him. The earliest church in America to openly affirm Unitarianism was King's Chapel in Boston, an Episcopal congregation. King's Chapel accepted the Unitarian label in 1785. It was not until about thirty-five years later, in 1819, that the liberals in the church of the New England establishment accepted the title in self-identity.

The Early Controversy

As the eighteenth century hastened toward the nineteenth, the controversy among those of Puritan heritage grew increasingly open, and relationships more strained. Regardless, exchange of pulpits continued even among those who felt themselves at odds theologically.[5] The liberals argued that God gave

---

[3] See Conrad Wright, *The Beginnings of Unitarianism in America* (Boston: Beacon Press, 1966).

[4] Wright, *Three Prophets*, pp. 6, 7.

[5] For example Joseph Buckminster, the father of Joseph S. Buckminster, spoke at his son's ordination despite theological differences. Eliza Buckminster Lee, *Memoirs of Rev. Joseph Buckminster D.D. and of His Son, Rev. Joseph Stevens Buckminster* (Boston: William Crosby and H. P. Nichols, 1849), pp. 141 ff.

man reason and the freedom to employ it so that man could attain a semblance of righteousness on his own. Those most controversial in their preaching were not the ones who later were best known. Men such as Buckminster and Channing were irenic in spirit and less inclined to polemical preaching, and they were situated in Boston in contrast to the controversialists who could be found in the outlying towns.

Aaron Bancroft was obviously such a willing combatant.[6] The manner in which he identified the lines of difference is instructive:

Professors with us, at the present day, may be classed in two great divisions, Calvinists and Liberal or Unitarian Christians. Perhaps the most distinguishing point of difference between them respects the office of reason in the sacred concerns of religion. The Calvinists style themselves the orthodox, evangelical professors; and they require that the mysteries of revelation, as they dominate them, should be received, though these cannot be explained, in humble submission to Divine Wisdom.[7]

The primacy of reason was held by many of these combatants as the main ground for dispute. William Emerson, the father of Ralph Waldo, charged in an 1803 ordination sermon that "sound reasoning and an appeal to historical facts are their [the ministers'] only means of establishing the truth and importance of Christian principles." [8] The importance which these men attached to reason is seen in numerous sermons on the reasonableness of Christianity which reflect an indebtedness to John Locke and the European tradition of rational Christianity. A sermon by Joseph S. Buckminster titled "The Reasonableness of Faith" reflects this interest: "Faith is in fact, the most reasonable thing in the world. . . . Faith is reasonable, because it is the involuntary homage which the mind pays to the predominence of evidence. Faith that is not founded on testimony is no longer faith." [9]

The gift of reason did not, however, obviate the need for scriptures. It was precisely in interpreting the scriptures that reason found its province. The minister, according to Thaddeus Harris, must be mighty in the scriptures and a man of "extensive erudition" in order to fulfill his duty in respect to nat-

---

[6] Aaron Bancroft (1755-1839) was minister of the Second Church, Worcester, 1786-1839. Sermon materials are found in Aaron Bancroft, *Sermons on those Doctrines of the Gospel and on Those Constituent Principles of the Church which Christian Professors have made subject of Controversy* (Worcester: William Manning and Son, 1822).

[7] *Ibid.*, p. 26.

[8] William Emerson, "A Sermon Delivered March 2, 1803, at the Ordination of the Rev. Thomas Beede to the care of the Church of Christ in Wilton" (Amherst, New Hampshire: Joseph Cushing, 1803), p. 12. Emerson (1769-1811) was minister, First Church, Boston, 1799-1811. For an analysis of the earliest interest in reason, see Wright, *The Beginnings of Unitarianism in America*, chap. 6, "Rationalism 1755-1780," pp. 135-60.

[9] Joseph S. Buckminster, "The Reasonableness of Faith," Sermon XV in *Sermons by the Late J. S. Buckminster with a Memoir of His Life and Character* (Boston, 1814), p. 144. Joseph S. Buckminster (1784-1812) toured Europe and brought back three thousand books on biblical criticism. He was preparing to teach a course on that subject at Harvard Divinity School at the time of his death. See George Ticknor, "Memoirs of the Buckminsters," *Christian Examiner*, XLVII, 1849, p. 186.

ural and revealed religion. Furthermore, he will employ reason to defend the faith against the skeptics since reason will enable him to "illustrate the evidence of miracles, to defend truth against the subtle objections, cavils, and sophisms of philosophical unbelievers [and] to exhibit Christianity in all its certainty and excellence." [10]

Despite implications to the contrary, the orthodox accepted reason as a tool for theological construction, as had their Puritan forefathers. The Awakening with its emphasis on religious experience had in some measure eroded the ground of reason, but not completely.[11] So Bancroft charged, "Indeed, we perceive that Calvinists never reject the authority of reason, when it can be brought to support their positions." [12] But those who espoused the New Divinity more openly embraced reason in their theologizing than Bancroft was willing to admit. Nathanael Emmons made his position clear by contrasting opposing extremes:

In treating on revealed religion men have often run into two extremes. Some have been fond of finding mysteries everywhere in the Bible; while others have been equally fond of exploding all mysteries from divine revelation. Here the truth seems to lie in the medium.[13]

Emmons was particularly chagrined by the liberal charge that the doctrine of the Trinity was irrational. He responded that the Trinity was not repugnant to the dictates of sound reason and affirmed the need for the law of non-contradiction: "Any doctrine, which necessarily involves a contradiction, is repugnant to reason, and demonstrably false. For it is out of the power of the human mind to conceive, that a real contradiction be true." [14] For Emmons, as for the Liberals, reason was necessary as a theological tool. The question rather centered around the limits of reason.

The liberals affirmed the supremacy of reason, for it was a gift bestowed by God which in turn set man at liberty to order his moral life on his own. As Bancroft stated it, "God has imparted to man the attributes of reason and liberty. These constitute him the subject of a moral government and make him capable of virtuous action." [15] In Calvinistic theology man could only

[10] Thaddeus Mason Harris, "A Sermon Preached at the Ordination of the Rev. Samuel Osgood in Springfield, January 25, 1809" (Springfield: Thomas Dickman, 1809), pp. 6, 7. Harris (1768-1842) was minister at Dorchester 1793-1836.

[11] The theology which resulted from the Awakening was the "New Divinity" or "Edwardean Theology" because of Jonathan Edwards. Important early leaders were Joseph Bellamy and Samuel Hopkins. Later leaders were Nathanael Emmons and Timothy Dwight. See Clifton E. Olmstead, *History of Religion in the United States* (Englewood Cliffs, New Jersey: Prentice-Hall, 1960), pp. 186-87.

[12] Bancroft, *Sermons*, p. 26.

[13] Nathanael Emmons, *Sermons on Some of the First Principles and Doctrines of True Religion* (Wrentham: Nathaniel and Benjamin Heaton, 1800), p. 85. Emmons (1745-1840) was a graduate of Yale and by marriage related to a number of Hopkinsian ministers. He settled at Franklin as minister in 1769 and remained there until his death.

[14] Emmons, *Sermons*, pp. 95-96.

[15] Bancroft, *Sermons*, p. 18.

respond morally by a special act of God. His faculties were disintegrated to such an extent that virtue was impossible if man was left to his own resources.

Human freedom was seen by the liberals as the crux of their disagreement with the orthodox. Bancroft presented a series of sermons on the five distinct propositions in the "Calvinistick system of theology." [16] They concerned election, salvation, total depravity, effectual calling, and evangelical obedience. In each case he found these doctrines to be a denial of human freedom. The doctrine of election was especially odious in this regard:

God has chosen a certain number in Christ, unto everlasting glory, before the foundation of the world, according to his immutable purpose, and of his free grace and love, without the least foresight of faith and good works, or any conditions performed by the creature; and that the rest of mankind he was pleased to pass by, and ordain them to dishonour and wrath for their sins, to the praise of his vindictive justice.[17]

After presenting this Calvinistic view he set out to refute it. "I shall make the attempt to prove that neither reason nor revelation supports the doctrine of election, in the meaning of the above proposition." [18] James Freeman in a manner less polemical, also affirmed freedom as opposed to determinism in a sermon titled, "Necessity." [19] It seems likely that the specific doctrine of necessity he had in mind was that of Edwards. He argued that neither scripture nor reason support the view that human action is determined. "The doctrine of necessity, whether true or not, is not taught in the Sacred Scriptures." [20] Reason shows it invalid because it is ludicrous when carried to its proper conclusion:

. . . if the doctrine is true, it must extend to everything; not only to actions, but to motives; not only to consequences, but to causes; every link of the chain must be indissoluble. There can be but one agent in the universe: God must be the author of everything which exists of evil, as well as good, of sin, as well as holiness.[21]

In the sermon Freeman did not cite scriptures. He depended mostly on deductive arguments for the force of his persuasion.

The case for freedom was argued primarily by opposing original sin, a cardinal Calvinistic doctrine. The gist of the Calvinistic view was that Adam sinned and in turn set the future of the human race. The support of Emmons for the doctrine was on the grounds that Adam in his choice determined man's position before God.

[16] *Ibid.*, pp. 209 ff. He preached five consecutive sermons on these subjects from his Worcester pulpit.

[17] *Ibid.*

[18] *Ibid.*, p. 210. For earlier controversy, see Wright's "The Freedom of the Will, 1754-1773," pp. 91-114, in *The Beginnings.*

[19] James Freeman, *Sermons and Charges,* new ed. (Boston: Carter, Hendee and Company, 1832).

[20] *Ibid.*, p. 308.

[21] *Ibid.*

God placed Adam as the public Head of his posterity, and determined to treat *them* according to *his* conduct. If he persevered in holiness and obedience, God determined to bring his posterity into existence holy and upright. But if he sinned and fell, God determined to bring his posterity into existence morally corrupt or depraved. Adam disobeyed the law of his Maker; and according to the constitution under which he was placed, his first and single act of disobedience made all his posterity sinners.[22]

Because of man's inability to overcome original sin, God acted on his behalf in Jesus Christ. In this manner, though man could not overcome the taint of Adam in his own freedom, God enabled him to win the victory through Jesus Christ.

It was because of an affirmation concerning the doctrine of the Trinity that the Unitarians were finally willing to accept the title by which they became known. One of the reasons they reluctantly accepted the name was that European Unitarians had long been involved in doctrinal struggles and had gone farther in humanizing Jesus Christ than the New Englanders were prepared to follow. They had enough trouble on their hands with their own doctrinal beliefs without adding those of European Unitarianism.[23] Even as late as 1812, Francis Parkman insisted that Freeman was the only "Unitarian" minister in Boston.[24] But the reappraisal of man's nature as sinner brought a reexamination of the atonement, and hence the person of Jesus Christ. The American Unitarians were Arians in a true sense, because they claimed divinity for Jesus Christ even though he was a lesser deity than God and subordinate to him.

The Unitarian affirmation concerning Jesus Christ is indicated in Bancroft's second sermon, titled, "Jesus Christ does not possess the attributes of Supreme Divinity." The grounds for rejecting the doctrine were biblical:

We reject the doctrine of the trinity because, by its admission, we must receive it as a doctrine of revelation, and as a term of Christian fellowship, a number of words which either have no meaning, or amount to a plain contradiction; and because, in our apprehension the doctrine is opposed to the particular and the general language of Scripture respecting the character of God.[25]

Rather than the traditional formulation of one God in three persons, all three divine from eternity, Bancroft affirmed that Jesus Christ is a being of derived existence and without the attributes of supreme deity.[26] Furthermore, he is a being distinct from God and, as Arius argued, subordinate to him.[27] In

---

[22] Emmons, Sermon XIII, "On Original Sin," *Sermons*, p. 308.

[23] See Wright, *Beginnings*, pp. 200 ff. For the European background, see Earl Morse Wilbur, *A History of Unitarianism in Transylvania, England, and America* (Cambridge: Harvard University Press, 1952).

[24] Francis Parkman, "Letter to the Rev. Mr. Grundy, of Manchester," *Monthly Repository*, VII, 1812, 201.

[25] Bancroft, *Sermons*, p. 30.

[26] *Ibid.*, p. 33.

[27] *Ibid.*

another sermon, Bancroft argued from a number of scriptures, especially the Gospel of John, to prove his point. He charged that the Trinitarians object to the "common meaning of the term person; in their reasonings they adopt it in its usual sense." [28] He admitted, however, that not all Unitarians affirmed the same about Jesus Christ, making a distinction between the American and the European Unitarians:

Unitarian Christians of the present day may be divided into two classes. One of these believe that our Savior existed prior to his appearance on earth, the other maintain that he was merely a man, chosen by God to be his distinguished Prophet to his brethren of the human family; to whom the Spirit of inspiration was given without measure; and who was invested with power. [29]

The reply of the orthodox was that even though the Trinity concept defied full rational explanation, it had to be accepted because it was a revealed doctrine. So Emmons says:

Of all religious mysteries, the distinction of person in the Divine Nature, must be allowed to be the greatest. Accordingly upon this subject, there has been the greatest absurdity as well as ingenuity displayed in attempting to explain a real mystery. But though a mystery cannot be comprehended, nor consequently explained; yet it may be stated and distinguished from real absurdity. [30]

The reason the mystery of the Trinity cannot be explained is because "it is not fimiliar [sic] to any other distinction in the minds of mortal beings." [31] Nevertheless, if one can conceive three human persons, he can likewise conceive three divine persons even though the being of God is obviously different from the being of man.[32] On these grounds the doctrine is both reasonable and scriptural:

Though perhaps, the bare unassisted power of reason would have never discovered, that God exists in three Persons; yet since the Scripture has revealed this great mystery in the divine existence, reason has nothing to object against it. Reason can see and acknowledge a mystery, though it cannot comprehend it. [33]

From these sermons the arguments of the Unitarians and their opponents emerge. These predispositions of the ministers also affected the means whereby they communicated their message. Since they saw reason underlying all theological construction, one would expect an influence on structure and style. Likewise, since the scripture was declared to be the final court of appeal for all matters of faith, one would expect the scriptures to play a crucial role in argumentative proof.

The earlier sermons of the period follow a rigid structural pattern which

[28] *Ibid.*
[29] *Ibid.*, p. 45.
[30] Emmons, *Sermons*, p. 85.
[31] *Ibid.*, p. 87.
[32] *Ibid.*, p. 97.
[33] *Ibid.*, pp. 98, 99.

is typical of the time. In this pattern the arguments are first announced, followed by exegesis of the scripture cited, and the sermon ends with an application to the hearers if warranted. This type development is found in Bancroft's sermon, "On the Doctrine of Election." [34] William Emerson even followed this pattern in speaking to a military group in 1799.[35] Within this general pattern the main divisions stand out in a skeletal manner. The latter is the case with the sermons of James Freeman even though he departs from the more traditional threefold development. Nathanael Emmons structured his sermons in much the same way even though not so rigidly as did Bancroft. Thaddeus Harris set forth the skeletal structure as he began an ordination sermon:

In discoursing on the passage of Scripture selected as a text, I shall attempt, 1st, to show what is implied in a Minister's taking heed to himself; 2ndly, what is intended of continuing in them; and then point out the encouragement he has to order his private behaviour and public ministrations in this wise and becoming manner.[36]

The rationalistic predilection hence is reflected in the sermon structure, the divisions being obvious and rationally conceived.

The style of these sermons also reflects the penchant for reason. Very few metaphors or literary allusions are employed. Some of the sermons may be described as eloquent, but in a manner which is compatible with the overall rationalistic approach. Style of this sort may be found especially in the sermons of Bancroft and Emerson. Buckminster has a clear cogent style, but only occasionally is the language elegant. His argument is cogent and moves clearly, but it is not built in the schematic fashion of sermons at the end of the century. His structure thus harbingers the freer sermon organization which becomes commonplace a decade later. In style, however, he reflects the clear-cut, nonmetaphorical use of language which grows out of a rationalistic frame of mind.

The argument in these sermons, in keeping with the emphasis on reason, is largely deductive. Scripture is sometimes cited as a proof text and hence employed inductively. But more often a scripture is presented, explained, then applied to a specific doctrine or action. This deductive use of scripture is obvious in William Emerson's "On the Peculiar Business of a Christian

---

[34] Bancroft, *Sermons,* pp. 210 ff.

[35] William Emerson, "Piety and Arms," A Sermon preached at the request of the ancient and honourable Artillery Company in Boston, June 3, 1799, The Anniversary of the Election of Officers (Boston: Manning & Loring, 1799). At the beginning of the ordination sermon for Beede, Emerson stated, "In going forward with this subject, it may be proper for me, in the first place, to give a particular exposition of the text. Secondly, I will mention some of the leading articles of the Christian doctrine. And, thirdly, I shall say, that the preaching of these doctrines is the proper business of a Christian minister" (p. 7).

[36] Harris, "Ordination of Rev. Samuel Osgood," p. 4.

Minister." [37] In a number of these sermons divisions of the text served as the main points in the sermon. Toward the end of this early period of the controversy, the use of the citation of scripture declined as is obvious in Buckminster's sermons. He may refer to an incident in the Bible, but he seldom quotes it. He also points in a new direction by referring with some frequency to extra-biblical materials such as the Talmud, Philo, and Josephus.[38]

The Middle Period

The middle period, so designated here, extends from William Ellery Channing's sermon, "Unitarian Christianity," delivered in 1819, to Ralph Waldo Emerson's, "The Divinity School Address" of 1838. Channing's sermon marks the realization of the Unitarians that they were forced to a separate existence, while Emerson's sermon prefaces the new theology of the transcendentalists. In this period the motifs of early Unitarianism are preserved, but new directions in preaching may be found.

In reading Channing's sermon on "Unitarian Christianity," one is struck by the manner in which the ideas presented reiterate what we have noted in earlier sermons. This approach on Channing's part was intentional since his purpose was to defend those views which Unitarians already held in common. The function of the sermon was not the presentation of views before unannounced, but to formulate a statement which Unitarians could recognize as a rallying point in their dispute with the orthodox. The speech was given in Baltimore at the ordination of the Rev. Jared Sparks, May 5, 1819, with many Boston ministers present. Their lengthy travel suggested strong support of Unitarian views. The result was so encouraging that many Unitarians saw in it the dawn of a new day.[39]

Channing was aware that the Unitarians had been criticized for their stand on reason. "We are particularly accused of making an unwarrantable use of reason in the interpretation of Scripture. We are said to exalt reason above revelation, to prefer our own wisdom to God's." [40] The gist of his argument was that since the Bible is written for men in human language, human reason is necessary in order to interpret it. As to interpretation, Channing offered the program of continental biblical criticism as opposed to older New England approaches. In this he was moving beyond the earlier Unitarian

---

[37] Emerson, Beede ordination sermon.

[38] Buckminster, *Sermons*, "Never Man Spake Like This Man," p. 24.

[39] For events leading to the sermon, see Wright's *Three Prophets*, pp. 5-19.

[40] The pages cited here are those in Wright, *Three Prophets*, p. 49. Compare Channing's sermon "Evidences of Christianity" in *Discourses by William Ellery Channing* (Boston: Charles Bowen, 1832), Vol. II, p. 4. "I begin with the position, that there is nothing in the general idea of Revelation at which reason ought to take offense, nothing inconsistent with any established truth, or with our best views of God and nature." Also the sermon, "Christianity is a Rational Religion," Vol. II, pp. 114 ff.

methods, but his colleagues were already aware of the method through the teaching of Buckminster, Andrews Norton, and Channing himself.[41] For these men, revelation or the scriptures are addressed to rational creatures, and reason must be employed if they are to be interpreted aright:

Say what we may, God has given us a rational nature, and will call us to account for it. We may let it sleep, but we do so at our peril. Revelation is addressed to us as rational beings. We may wish, in our sloth, that God had given us a system, demanding no labor or comparing, limiting, and inferring.[42]

The imperative to use reasoning in biblical interpretation is here clearly seen. Early in the sermon Channing made it clear that Unitarian thought was solidly biblical, and that reason is the vehicle through which the message is appropriated. Later generations of Unitarians may have looked elsewhere, but not those of Channing's age. Channing contended that "whatever doctrines seem to us to be clearly taught in the Scriptures, we receive without reserve or exception." [43]

From statements about reason and biblical interpretation Channing turned to specific doctrines, namely, the oneness of God as opposed to the Trinity, the unity of Jesus Christ, the moral perfection of God, the atonement, and human piety. His arguments in this section vary little from those of earlier Unitarian sermons. He charged that the orthodox view of God was tri-theism, thus the doctrine is "irrational and unscriptural." [44] He asked biblical support from those who advanced the doctrine of the Trinity: "From the many passages which treat of God, we ask for one, one only, in which we are told, that he is a threefold being, or that he is three persons, or that he is Father, Son, and Holy Ghost." [45] In spite of his request for scripture, Channing advanced only one reference himself. His arguments were drawn from the desirability of unity, the silence of the apostolic fathers, and the oneness of worship. He approached his arguments on the other doctrines with similar supporting materials. He argued the unity of Christ on the ground that Christ does not mention that he has two minds. He did indicate the names by which Jesus is called in the New Testament, but without citing specific passages. The manner in which he argued is consonant with his comments on preaching in a sermon at the ordination of E. S. Gannett; "Christianity now needs dispensers, who will make history, nature, and the improvements of society tributary to its elucidation and support; who will show its adaptation to man as an ever progressive being." [46]

[41] Andrews Norton (1786-1852) was appointed Dexter Lecturer on Biblical Criticism at Harvard in 1813. He taught there until 1830.

[42] Wright, *Three Prophets*, p. 55, sermon by Channing.

[43] *Ibid.*, p. 48.

[44] *Ibid.*, p. 58.

[45] *Ibid.*, p. 59.

[46] Channing, "The Demands of the Age," *Discourses*, III, 140.

Henry Ware, Jr. held compatible views and argued in much the same manner. In a sermon "Jesus the Mediator" he argued that contrary to what the orthodox profess, the biblical view" intimates no mysterious union of natures by which the Mediator is God as well as man . . . but simply declares the plain, intelligible fact that 'there is one God, and one Mediator between God and men, the man Jesus Christ.' " [47] He thus affirmed that God is one being and Jesus another. Jesus Christ as Savior does not save from the "Curse of man's original condition," since this represents a false concept.[48] Man is free to choose either good or evil. "The Christian dispensation is a provision of means for the regeneration of free, intelligent, voluntary agents, existing in a state of probation." [49] Jesus rather is one who assists man in his own efforts at overcoming sin:

He redeemed them, not by literally paying any ransom to their masters, nor by providing substitutes in their stead, nor by offering in any way an equivalent for their service; but by opening for them a way of escape, through which they might pass to freedom and independence, and guiding them in it by his presence and power.[50]

Ware thus aligned himself with a view of the atonement which is identified with that of Abelard.

Lyman Beecher is representative of those who opposed the Unitarians during the middle years.[51] In a sermon delivered at Worcester, Massachusetts, October 15, 1823, at the ordination of the Rev. Loammi Ives Hoadly, Beecher set forth what he called the "Evangelical System" as opposed to the "Liberal System." [52] The Evangelical System, as he saw it, espoused free human agency, atonement for sin by Jesus Christ, the act of the Holy Spirit in conversion, the providential government of God, and the existence of God in three persons.

In the manner in which he affirms human freedom, Beecher has moved away from a strict Calvinism. In this he was by no means alone among the orthodox. As Channing observed, "Unconditional Election is seldom heard among us. The Imputation of Adam's sin to his posterity, is hastening to join the exploded doctrine of Transubstantiation." [53] It is this position which Ware explicitly denied in his sermon. The influence of the Holy Spirit in conversion was objected to by the Unitarians on Lockean grounds, con-

[47] Henry Ware, Jr., "Jesus the Mediator," *The Works of Henry Ware, Jr.* (Boston: James Munroe and Company, 1847), p. 44. Ware, whose father was also a Harvard professor, was ill in early life. Born in 1794, he died in 1843.

[48] *Ibid.*, p. 62. Sermon V, "Jesus the Saviour."

[49] *Ibid.*, p. 66.

[50] *Ibid.*, p. 68.

[51] Lyman Beecher, a Yale graduate, was born in 1775, and held pulpits in New York, Connecticut, and Hanover Street, Boston. The sermon cited here is in Ernest J. Wrage and Barnet Baskerville, *American Forum* (New York: Harper & Row, 1960).

[52] *Ibid.*, p. 101.

[53] Channing, "The Demands of the Age," *Discourses*, III, 154.

tending that conversion comes by hearing the Word of God, not via a mystical spiritual experience. The Unitarians did not object to providential government but gave greater power to human efforts than the orthodox. Beecher stands firm for the doctrine of the Trinity, presenting typical arguments. Thus it would appear that in some respects the evangelicals provided a watertight dyke against the flood of Unitarian arguments at certain locations, while at others the waters seeped through. The tendency was for the orthodox to move in the direction of the Unitarians, but there was no move in the converse direction.

In an interesting statement about his sermon method, Beecher observes that it has been customary to support doctrines by citing proof texts and affirming the reasonableness of the liberal position. Beecher, in contrast, proposed to avail himself "of collateral evidence only." [54] His evidence, in the manner of Channing, is taken from the history and life of the church. On the doctrines of the Trinity and the nature of Jesus Christ, he argues from the fourth-century decisions as to who were the heretics.[55] As to the piety in the church he argues that Evangelical churches were as pious as the Unitarians.[56] In his method of argument in this sermon, Beecher duplicates the method of Channing in the "Unitarian Christianity" address.

Of great homiletical interest in this period is the fact that the sermons move away from older forms. No longer does one find a precise presentation of the arguments, the texts exegeted, or application made. No longer do the main points occur in skeletal fashion. The style continues to reflect logical cogency, but movement toward impressing rather than arguing appears. Scripture, though still appearing in the sermons, is now employed in a different way. Among the Unitarians one finds fewer and fewer sermons which are developed exegetically, nor is scripture often cited for inductive proof. References to the scriptures are general; for example, in the New Testament Jesus calls himself or is called Son of God but never God. The result is a sermon which flows more freely, arriving more directly at the point to be made. One reason may be that the controversial context demands greater freedom and more direct handling of sermon materials.[57] Channing noticed the change in preaching and declared that "preaching is incomparably more practical than formerly." [58]

[54] Wrage and Baskerville, *American Forum*, p. 101.
[55] *Ibid.*, pp. 111-13.
[56] *Ibid.*, p. 109.
[57] Channing's sermons were not typically polemical. He says in the Sparks ordination sermon, "I have spoken doctrines which you will probably preach; but I do not mean, that you are to give yourself to controversy. You will remember, that good practice is the end of preaching, and will labor to make your people holy livers, rather than skillful disputants" (p. 87).
[58] Channing, "The Demands of the Age," *Discourses*, III, 154.

The Rise of Transcendentalism

Finally, we are interested in those controversies involved in the rise of Transcendentalism. This new polemic differs from the old in that the dispute is now with those within Unitarianism rather than those without. An early indication of new developments in Unitarianism was Emerson's "The Divinity School Address" delivered before the Senior Class at Harvard Divinity School, Cambridge, on July 15, 1838. Those who extended the invitation were not aware of the volatile nature of the views which Emerson intended to express. It is clear that Emerson is faithful to his Unitarian background at certain points, but the disturbance was created by his undercutting both the commonly accepted Lockean epistemology, and the affirmation that the miracles attest to the validity of Christianity. In respect to his doctrine of man, Emerson carried a step further the affirmation of man's ability.[59]

The Divinity School Address has two main points: inadequacy in Unitarian theology, and inadequacy in church ministry. As to theology, Emerson contended that truth, rather than being derived from experience, is apprehended by intuition. "The intuition of the moral sentiment is an insight of the perfection of the laws of the soul." [60] To Emerson the intermediate step of the association of sensations was bypassed for direct intuition. In particular this undermined the Unitarian method of biblical interpretation, but Emerson did not bother to notice that. His second charge was that Jesus Christ, as other prophets, announced truths transcending human contingencies. Since these truths stand on their own, no miracles are needed to validate them. In his famous phrase he charged that "the word Miracle, as pronounced by Christian churches, gives a false impression; it is Monster." [61] In his denunciation of the ministry, Emerson charged that ministers are not open to the intuitions of the soul in the manner that religious giants of the past have been. His complaints about how the church and ministry have become outmoded sound almost like the 1960's though his given reason for the problem was a failure to respond to the soul. Callousness to social injustices is cited now as the main evidence of the irrelevance of the church. In addition, his proposal was not to throw off existing forms but to revitalize them: "Rather let the breath of new life be breathed by you through the forms already existing. For if once you are alive, you shall find they shall

---

[59] For an analysis and background for the speech, see Wright, *Three Prophets*, pp. 19-32. See also the essay by Herbert A. Wichelns, "Ralph Waldo Emerson," in *A History and Criticism of American Public Address*, ed. William Norwood Brigance (New York: McGraw-Hill, 1943) II, 501-25. Other materials include *The American Transcendentalists*, ed. Perry Miller (Garden City, N. Y.: Doubleday & Company, 1957) and Octavius Brooks Frothingham, *Transcendentalism in New England* (New York: Harper & Row, 1959).

[60] Wright, *Three Prophets*, p. 92.

[61] *Ibid.*, p. 97.

become plastic and new. The remedy to their deformity is, first, soul, and second, soul, and evermore, soul." [62]

Apparently Emerson did not intend to stir up excitement with his address, as his failure to pursue the argument which followed indicates. The address hit a responsive cord since the young ministers had for some time felt uneasy about the traditional emphasis on reason and Lockean epistemology. The Seminary faculty, however, were chagrined for they feared the public occasion on which the speech was given would stamp the address as official Unitarian sentiment.

Andrews Norton of the Harvard Divinity School replied to the Emerson speech in "A Discourse on the Latest Form of Infidelity, Delivered at the Request of the 'Association of the Alumni of the Cambridge Theological School' on the 19th of July, 1839." [63] In his speech Norton worked at length to establish the importance of the Christian miracles. It was here that Emerson touched a nerve, for Unitarians had long differentiated themselves from the deists on the ground that the faith depended on the actual occurrence of the miracles. Norton finds the source of the "new infidelity" to be in Europe, especially Germany. The language used in German theology, he charges, is Christian as to doctrines, but "devoid of their essential meaning." [64] This is the case because "it strikes directly at the root of faith in Christianity, and indirectly of all religion by denying the miracles attesting the divine mission of Christ." [65] If the miracles are denied, then "Nothing is left that can be called Christianity. . . . Its essence is gone; its evidence is annihilated." [66]

Later in the address Norton attacked Emerson's search for absolutes. "To the demand of certainty, let it come from whom it may, I answer, that I know of no absolute certainty." [67] He also rejects Emerson's penchant for intuition. "There can be no intuition, no direct perception, of the truth of Christianity, no metaphysical certainty." [68] In closing he takes a jab at intuition, identifying it as emotion. "Gentlemen, I have addressed your understandings not your feelings." But this is not to deny feelings a role in religion, since "Christianity cannot be rightly apprehended without the strongest feeling." [69] Norton was well aware of the points at which Emerson attacked traditional Unitarianism; but whereas Emerson appeared to consider his chief objection to be rationalistic epistemology, Norton felt compelled to answer foremost his attack on miracles.

[62] *Ibid.*, p. 111.
[63] Andrews Norton, A *Discourse on the Latest Form of Infidelity* (Cambridge: John Owen, 1839).
[64] *Ibid.*, p. 10.
[65] *Ibid.*, p. 11.
[66] *Ibid.*, p. 22.
[67] *Ibid.*, p. 30.
[68] *Ibid.*, p. 32.
[69] *Ibid.*, p. 36.

Norton's address did not go unanswered. George Ripley, who had already called into question the traditional view of miracles in the *Christian Examiner* in 1836, responded with "The latest form of Infidelity Examined: A Letter to Mr. Andrews Norton." [70] Ripley went at considerable length to argue for freedom of thought pointing out that such freedom was sought by the early Unitarians. Interestingly, this is a typical rhetorical ploy for new moments since they feel constrained by traditional views. At this point in its existence a new moment calls for freedom in order to get a foot in the door. Ripley saw a need for a new theology, since "the religion of the day seemed too cold, too lifeless, too mechanical for many . . . and that a new direction must be given to their ideas, or they would be lost to Christainity." [71] Those who saw the need for new directions "become convinced of the superiority of the testimony of the soul to the evidence of the external senses." [72] He also affirmed that the truths which early Christianity discovered through intuition were more impressive than the mighty works or miracles.[73] He further chided Norton for citing authorities who no longer carried any persuasive force. His chief arguments therefore revolved about the manner in which traditional Unitarian theology, now some thirty years old, was becoming antiquated.

Theodore Parker's sermon at the ordination of the Rev. Charles C. Shackford in the Hawes Place Church, Boston, on May 19, 1841, added further fuel to the flames of controversy.[74] Parker titled the sermon "The Transient and Permanent in Christianity." Because the occasion was an ordination service, this address, too, like Emerson's "Divinity School Address" took on added significance. As was typical for New England ordination services, a number of ministers were present and participated. Among Unitarian fears was the anticipation that orthodox ministers would charge that Parker's speech was official Unitarian doctrine, and their fears were not unfounded.[75] Parker, unlike Emerson, was not about to abandon the ministry. He continued to defend his point of view after the speech, and failed to respond favorably to the suggestion of his colleagues that he withdraw from the Unitarian ministry.

In his address Parker built along lines already laid down by Emerson. He charged that years of controversy among Christians indicated that a distinction needed to be made between the permanent and the transient in Christianity. The transient, for Parker, is to be located in forms and doctrines,

[70] George Ripley, *The Latest Form of Infidelity Examined: a Letter to Mr. Andrews Norton* (Boston: James Munroe and Company, 1839). Ripley (1802-80) trained for the ministry and later went into journalism.

[71] *Ibid.*, p. 11.

[72] *Ibid.*, p. 12.

[73] *Ibid.*

[74] Wright, *Three Prophets*, pp. 113-49.

[75] See Wright's material on the background for the speech, pp. 32-43. Also, Roy C. McCall, "Theodore S. Parker," in Brigance, *History and Criticism*, pp. 238-64.

while the permanent has to do with the "divine life of the soul, love of God, and love to man." [76] Such love is found uniquely in Jesus Christ. "So the Christianity of Jesus is permanent, though what passes for Christianity with Popes and catechisms, with sects and churches, in the first century or in the nineteenth century, prove transient also." [77] He charges that the development of doctrine in the history of the church has distorted Christianity.

One of the chief areas in which he goes beyond both traditional Unitarianism and Emerson is in affirming the current German biblical criticism of the 1840's. He charged that false claims have been made for the Bible; that it does not claim that Christianity rises or falls on its accuracy or completeness. Rather, Christianity depends on faith in Jesus Christ, and in order to recover the original faith it is he who must be sought and mutant doctrines bypassed:

> To turn away from the disputes of the Catholics and the Protestants, of the Unitarian and the Trinitarian, of Old School and New School, and come to the plain words of Jesus of Nazareth, Christianity is a simple thing; very simple. It is absolute, pure Morality; absolute, pure Religion; the love of man; the love of God acting without let or hindrance. [78]

Parker longed for the time when sectarian theologies and institutions would pass away and permanent Christianity emerge. The problem with the sermon was that it criticized orthodox and Unitarian alike and thus entertained controversy. If it was Parker's intent to stir up dispute, then he was not disappointed.

The stylistic changes between these transcendentalist sermons and those of the early Unitarians are obvious. While structure is not absent in either of these major addresses of Emerson and Parker, it is by no means skeletal in the manner of the sermons at the turn of the century. Rationalism, denounced by both these speakers, no longer serves as the ground for the communication vehicles employed. [79] In the sermons of Emerson and Parker may be found flights of eloquence with reference to nature and history. One finds only some of this in the earlier sermons. In an intuitionist philosophy, an impressionistic unfolding of material is valid. But if reason is queen, as in Unitarian earlier days, then such a rhetorical approach is inappropriate. The Transcendentalists felt no need to interpret a biblical text though Parker employs one for his sermon. Viewpoints in the scriptures come in for oc-

---

[76] *Ibid.*, p. 118.
[77] *Ibid.*, p. 121.
[78] *Ibid.*, p. 140.
[79] The movement away from reason is seen in later Unitarians. See Henry Bellows, *Re-Statement of Christian Doctrine in Twenty-five* (New York: D. Appleton and Company, 1860), esp. Sermon III, "Paradox—Its Place in Religious Statement and Experience," pp. 42 ff. Bellows (1814-82) was ordained in 1838 as minister of the First Unitarian Church in New York. Also James Walker (1794-1874), President, Harvard, 1853-60, who talks about mystery in a sermon "The Mediator," in *Reason, Faith and Duty*, Sermons preached chiefly in the Chapel (Boston: Roberts Brothers, 1877), pp. 3 ff.

casional attention, but proof texts are neither cited nor propositions found in scripture, except for a case or two in Parker's speech. If truth can be apprehended directly via intuition, then the scriptures are not the only or even the most important source of truth. It is apparent, then, that a shift in one's view of truth and the manner in which it is derived has a concomitant effect on the manner in which those truths are communicated.

Conclusion

Unitarianism is an interesting epoch in the history of American preaching. It reflects the breaking away from older patterns of thought which afflicted much of America in the first half of the nineteenth century. It is also a harbinger of the theological revolt toward the end of that century. While the later revolt was not an exact duplication of the earlier, many points in contention were the same. Thus we are carried into the twentieth century, and to appreciate the contemporary pulpit fully, a knowledge of the Unitarian epoch is important. This is the case despite the fact that in some quarters Unitarianism is no longer considered to be mainstream American Christianity. But whether the same ideas are argued or not—and a number continue to be—one recognizes in these sermons rhetorical strategies which are easy to uncover in the contemporary pulpit over much of America. Some Unitarian ideas, if not the label, have managed to escape the boundaries of Boston.

6

BUILDING MEN FOR CITIZENSHIP

—Raymond Bailey—

Nineteenth-century political theorists busily engaged themselves debating the ability of man to govern himself. The preachers of the period were no less polemical, and the major question which occupied them was closely akin to the chief political issue. Simply stated, it was, "Is man a free moral agent, responsible for his conduct, endowed with choice, or is he under an unalterable decree of an omnipotent God?" (This issue was a continuation of the clash described in the essays on the Authority of God, and the Rise of Unitarianism. In this chapter the debate moves to the frontier.) How these questions were answered had a profound effect on the development of American institutions.

The Political and Intellectual Climate of the United States

The Revolution ended the isolation of America and brought it into touch with European philosophy and literature. It was a period of great intellectual ferment. The ideas of the enlightenment with a ringing declaration of the worth and dignity of the individual influenced American thought and action. Thomas Paine was widely read, and the ideas of Jefferson and Franklin were published throughout the nation.

The war for independence was a prelude to the ideological war of the political parties. The federalists were devoted to the existing order and the concept of a strong central government to preserve it. The democrats, led by Jefferson and influenced by the French revolution, stressed individualism.

While the nation's leaders debated theories and philosophies, the people were concerned with pragmatic devotion to economic and social independence. Religion did not escape the turmoil which permeated the country. The religion of a people does not develop in a vacuum but is the product of constant interaction with the political and economic facets of society. The American pulpit was to be a sounding board for the discussion of the individual's role in society. Religion was to provide a catalyst for deep emotional commitment to the democratic ideal.

The Status of Religion at the Close of the War

The end of the Revolution found organized religion in America in a state of disruption and decline. It was estimated that in 1790, ninety percent of America was unchurched; moreover, many Americans were not just indifferent to religion, they were blatantly hostile to it.[1] The reasons for this situation were many and varied, ranging from general irreligion to a popular revolt against orthodoxy and authority in any form. Deism and transcendentalism, although not new to America, had been given impetus by French rationalism and the revolt against authoritative religion and were suddenly thrust into popularity. The popularity of deism was enhanced by some of its patriotic proponents, particularly Thomas Jefferson, Benjamin Franklin, and Thomas Paine. Paine's *Age of Reason* was one of the most widely read works of the nineteenth century, and its caustic style was well received by the skeptic masses.

Deist sentiment was not new in America, but hitherto it had been confined to an aristocratic elite who frowned upon any widespread dissemination of their views because they believed that the "superstitions" of religion did little harm and actually had the beneficial effect of promoting morality among the common people and thus helped to preserve good order in society. In the first flush of enthusiasm evoked by the French Revolution, however, Deism was transformed into a popular movement, and pamphleteers began to attack the churches as the great enemies of progress.[2]

Unitarianism and its offspring transcendentalism, with their practical emphasis on man working together with nature to achieve a utopian state, had great appeal to Americans on the fringe of an unconquered continent.

The exaltation of man, of all men; the doctrine that all power, all wisdom, comes from nature, with which man must establish an original and firsthand relationship; the relegation of books to a secondary place in the hierarchy of values; the insistence that instinct is good and must be obeyed . . . all these ideas were closely related to the democratic impulse.[3]

Unitarianism found an able spokesman in the person of William Ellery Channing. As pastor of the Federal Street Church, Boston, he enunciated the doctrines of Unitarianism and avowed man's responsibility to man. The

[1] Albert Barnes, quoted in H. Richard Niebuhr and Daniel D. Williams, eds., *The Ministry in Historical Perspective* (New York: Harper & Row, 1956), p. 247.
[2] Winthrop S. Hudson, *Religion in America* (New York: Charles Scribner's Sons, 1965), p. 131.
[3] Merle Curti, *The Growth of American Thought* (New York: Harper & Row, 1943), p. 304.

real controversy came not between orthodoxy and non-Christian groups but within the Christian community. Lyman Beecher, a leading popular preacher theologian of the day, took it upon himself to do battle with the Unitarians hoping to destroy their *heresy*.

The Challenger Becomes the Challenged

In 1823, Beecher used the occasion of an ordination to deliver a sermon which he entitled, "The Faith Once Delivered to the Saints." His purpose was to demonstrate how the "liberal system could not possibly be the faith once delivered to the saints." [4] However, the sermon antagonized the hyper-Calvinists, and he himself became a target for their attacks. In the sermon he declared:

Men are free agents, in the possession of such faculties, and placed in such circumstances as render it practicable for them to do whatever God requires. . . . Such ability is here intended as lays a perfect foundation for government by law, and for rewards and punishments according to deeds.[5]

Thus Beecher declared that God held men responsible for their actions and that man's obligation to God included "certain duties" to his fellowman. The sermon met with severe criticism from conservative quarters, and the dispute ultimately led to Beecher's trial as a heretic and a hypocrite in 1835.

The effect of adopting this open view of redemption and the hope it promised man is evident in the scope of Beecher's preaching. In many ways he was an early prototype of the reform preacher as he boldly spoke out against the evils of his day. Beecher declared that the American republic was of "heavenly origin" and that the laws of the nation should be based on the laws of God. Following the death of Alexander Hamilton by a bullet fired from the gun of Aaron Burr, he denounced dueling as a "great national sin. The duelist is a murderer; and, were there no sentence of exclusion from civil power contained in the word of God, the abhorrence of murder should exclude from confidence these men of blood." [6]

A short time later he established himself as a temperance leader by declaring intemperance to be "the sin of our land and a threat to the hopes of the world, which hang upon our experiment of civil liberty." [7] Thus he laid the foundation for the direct involvement of the pulpit in directing the

[4] Barbara Cross, ed., *The Autobiography of Lyman Beecher*, Vol. I (Cambridge: The Belknap Press of Harvard University, 1961), 412.
[5] *Ibid.*
[6] Henry C. Fish, *Pulpit Eloquence of the Nineteenth Century* (New York: Dodd, Mead & Company, 1871), p. 412.
[7] Lyman Beecher, *Beecher's Works*, Vol. I (Cleveland: John P. Jewett and Company, 1851], 349.

citizenry toward civil responsibility. However, this was only an early shot; the most intense battle was to be fought by other warriors on another front.

The Influence of the West

America was growing rapidly, and it soon became apparent that the emerging West was to be a major factor in determining what kind of adult this fast-growing infant nation would become. The presidential election of 1800 marked the development of the West as a significant factor in politics.

"The existence of an area of free land, its continuous recession, and the advance of American settlement westward, explains American development." [8] Thus historian Frederick Jackson Turner explained the development of American culture and American institutions. Turner attributed the uniqueness of American institutions to the demands of an expanding people adapting to the challenges of conquering a continent. Whether or not Turner overestimated the importance of the frontier is a matter of speculation for the historians; however, no one can refute the fact that the opportunities of the new country, its vast store of natural resources, and the simplicity of primitive society profoundly affected the molding of American character. The development of American religious character has been affected no less than its social and political character by the influence of the frontier. The constantly changing society of the ever westward moving American frontier provided a hothouse climate for the germination and growth of a vital and practical American religion.

The Mind of the Frontier

Status in frontier society was determined, not by what a man inherited, but by what he could produce, by what the combination of head, hand, and heart could win from the wilderness. Frontier life developed its own mentality; unique intellectual traits that were conducive to the creation of a nation.

Coarseness and strength combined with acuteness and inquisitiveness; that practical, inventive turn of mind, quick to find expedients; that masterful grasp of material things, lacking in the artistic, but powerful to effect great ends; that restless, nervous energy; that dominant individualism, working for good and for evil and withal that bouyancy and exuberance which comes with freedom—these are traits of the frontier. [9]

In the West, freedom and equality were not theoretical abstractions, but realities. The ruggedness of the wilderness and the unpredictableness of

[8] Frederick Jackson Turner, *The Frontier in American History* (New York: Henry Holt & Company, 1921), p. 1.
[9] *Ibid.*, p. 15.

138

nature combined to create a new breed of adventurer. The people were individualistic because they had to be; they were reliant upon self and nature; dependence on other people rarely extended beyond the immediate family. Optimism resulting from a confidence in land and their ability to use it kept them always moving and always working. They were proud and aggressive, qualities which many times led to keen competition in frontier games. Contests were very often finally decided by vicious fights. Each man wanted to outproduce, outbuild, outdrink, and outfight everyone else. They were drunk with the democratic spirit, and the only laws by which they were bound were the laws of nature. Their distrust of authority was evidenced by disgust for any government or government activity which sought to restrict them. For the most part the people of the frontier were materialistic and anti-intellectual with no time for books and no interest in in any cultural activity that was not utilitarian. They were hard, crude people who worked hard when they worked and played hard when they played. "The drinking of whiskey, the fighting, and the swearing were accompanied by repellant conditions of living. . . . Social relations were loose and undisciplined." [10] The fervency with which they approached their work and their play was not to be diminished when applied to religious conviction and expression.

New Ideas Demand New Expression

The grace of sophisticated liturgical religion would not have survived on the American frontier and indeed never got started there. To meet the needs and demands of Americans reveling in the new freedom, there had to be a new concept of Christian experience and worship. Albert Barnes, dynamic, new-school Presbyterian, defined the new evangelical concept:

This is an age of freedom, and man *will* be free. The religion of forms is the stereotyped wisdom or folly of the past, and does not adapt itself to the free movements, the enlarged views, the varying plans of this age. The spirit of this age demands that there shall be freedom in religion; that it shall not be fettered or suppressed; that it shall go forth to the conquest of the world.[11]

It was this same Barnes who was later charged and tried for heresy in Philadelphia for teaching that man is free and that God loves every man.

The frontiersman was not long in developing an appropriate mode of religious expression. It was natural, in keeping with the rest of his life, that his religious expression be flamboyant and free. Such was the phenomenon commonly called the campmeeting. The exact origin of it is a matter of dispute, but many scholars attribute it to the ministry of James McGready, a Presbyterian preacher. Logan County, Kentucky, was the site for a series of

[10] Albert J. Beveridge, *Abraham Lincoln: 1809-1858*, I (Boston: Houghton Mifflin Company, 1928), 53.

[11] Niebuhr and Williams, *The Ministry in Historical Perspective*, p. 223.

prolonged outdoor revival meetings conducted by McGready during the period from 1797-1799.

These camp meetings had the atmosphere of a medieval fair, as the people gathered from far and wide to socialize and to find God. The meetings were crude and loud; the preachers whipped themselves into an emotional frenzy, and as the intensity increased the congregation would give themselves physically and vocally to the overt expression of their feelings. Charles Johnson in his book *The Frontier Camp Meeting* records McGready's own description of the climax of one of these services:

No person seemed to wish to go home—hunger and sleep seemed to affect nobody—eternal things were the vast concern. Here awakening and converting work was to be found in every part of the multitude. . . . Sober professors, who had been communicants for many years, now lying prostrate on the ground, crying out in such language as this: "I have been a sober professor: I have been a communicant; . . . O! I see that religion is a sensible thing . . . I feel the pains of hell in my soul and body! O! how I would have despised any person a few days ago, who would have acted as I am doing now!—But O! I cannot help it!" . . . Little children, young men and women, and old grey-headed people, persons of every description, white and black, were to be found in every part of the multitude . . . crying out for mercy in the most extreme distress.[12]

These camp meetings met with unusual success as they adapted religion to the needs of the people and the realities of the frontier situation. "The frontiersman was different. He lived, worked, and died hard. It was natural that he should convert hard." [13] The unrestrained spirit of the wide-open spaces and the feeling of personal liberation had now carried over to religion. Religion joined government and social structure in the Americanization process.

The folk religion of the exuberent, optimistic, and undisciplined frontier represented a bizarre, but none the less genuine expression to the spirit of romanticism. The religion had power. It helped to subdue the grosser evils of the frontier. It made an impression on American Society that persisted far into the 20th Century.[14]

The revivalism of the camp meetings had a profound and lasting effect on American life, and these effects were not limited to the illiterate and poor. A European visitor made this observation:

These revivals are looked up to and supported as the strong arm of religion. It is not only the ignorant or the foolish, but the enlightened and the educated also, who support and encourage them, either from a consideration of their

[12] Charles Johnson, *The Frontier Camp Meeting* (Dallas, Texas: Southern Methodist University Press, 1955), p. 37.

[13] Bernard A. Weisberger, *They Gathered at the River* (Boston: Little, Brown & Company, 1958), p. 29.

[14] Ralph Henry Gabriel, "Evangelical Religion and Popular Romanticism in Early Nineteenth Century America," *Church History*, XIX (March, 1950), 39.

utility or from that fear, so universal in the United States, of expressing an opinion contrary to the majority.[15]

The popularity of the camp meetings and the widespread acceptance of the revival techniques were symptoms of new attitudes and new values which were becoming deeply ingrained in the American character. There was on the one hand a fear of anarchy which would destroy civilization and on the other hand a determination to assert individual freedom.

The Americanization of God

The new freedom brought with it a multiplicity of problems. If every man was equal, who was to determine a code of conduct for him? Obedience was not in the vocabulary of the individualist. Some reasoned that the only one qualified to establish a code of conduct was the one responsible for this land of milk and honey, God. Therefore, to many, religion became the means of social control. Many came to see the gospel as social as well as individual, that is, they saw the reconstruction of society as a result of the reconstruction of the individual life. Albert Barnes saw God as the only power sufficient to meet the evil of the day. "The only power in the universe which can meet and overcome such combined evil is the power of the spirit of God. There are evils of alliance and confederation in every city which can never be met except by a general revival of religion." [16]

Edward Beecher, one of the preacher sons of Lyman, wrote in "The American National Preacher" in 1835, that the task of the church in America was "to reorganize human society in accordance with the law of God." [17] The laws of God were to become the laws of America. America was the promised land; some even went so far as to equate it with the kingdom of God. Robert J. Breckinridge, a leader of the old-school Presbyterians and son of Senator John Breckinridge, speaking at General Assembly in Nashville in 1856, declared, "At present it is enough to say, that as for us and our Presbyterian Church in this great country, we have come to the Kingdom of God." [18]

In a sermon entitled "The Bible a Code of Laws," Lyman Beecher declared man's responsibility for his conduct. "Man, the subject of these laws, possesses indisputably, all the properties of an accountable agent, understanding, conscience, and the faculty of choice; and in the scripture is

[15] Captain Frederick Marryat, A Diary in America, ed. S. W. Jackman (New York: Alfred A. Knopf, 1962), p. 295. This account relates Captain Marryat's response to a tour of America made in 1837-38. The narrative was originally published in three volumes in London in 1839.

[16] Albert Barnes, quoted in Timothy L. Smith, Revivalism and Social Reform (Nashville: Abingdon Press, 1957), p. 152.

[17] Edward Beecher, "The Nature, Importance, and Means of Eminent Holiness Throughout the Church," The American National Preacher, X (June-July, 1835), 193.

[18] Fish, Pulpit Eloquence, p. 278.

recognized as accountable." [19] If men were to be held accountable for their conduct, then they had to be made aware of their responsibility. The success of democracy was seen by many to be dependent upon man's ability to discipline himself. Andrew Jackson enunciated this principle in his inaugural address of 1829.

I believe man can be elevated: man can become more and more endowed with divinity; and as he does, he becomes more God-like in his character and capable of governing himself. Let us go on elevating our people, perfecting our institutions, until democracy shall reach a point of perfection that we can acclaim with truth that the voice of the people is the voice of God.

The New Theology

This new concept of religion with its emphasis on man's restraint being self-imposed, and its emphasis on what Lyman Beecher had called "certain overt duties," led away from Calvinistic doctrine that declared that men had no control over their destiny. The revivalist movement was evolving a new doctrine of conversion which placed stress on human responsibility. It was the democratic strain of the freedom of will which appealed so strongly to the frontiersmen. "The theology of the revival reflected the new spirit of democracy. It stood for the sovereignty of God, but departed from Calvinism in its emphasis on the work of man." [20] A people free from tyrannical government and controlled economy refused to be bound to an inflexible religious system. The practical theology of the West placed the emphasis on man's freedom and his ability to improve his own lot. William Warren Sweet, the prolific writer of American religious history, points out that "the churches which were most successful on the frontier were those which in their organization and practice most embodied the democratic ideas of the young nation." [21] Revival preaching offered grace to all who would repent, be regenerated by the Spirit and walk therein. Men believed that they were free and that this freedom should extend to the spiritual as well as the temporal.

Charles G. Finney:
Apostle of Liberty and Responsibility

The boldest and most articulate exponent of the new doctrine of man was Charles Grandison Finney, generally conceded to have been the forerunner of modern revivalism. Finney was studying law when in 1821, nearing his

[19] Lyman Beecher, *Sermons Delivered on Various Occasions* (Boston: Saxton and Miles, 1845), p. 142.

[20] Clifton E. Olmstead, *History of Religion in the United States* (Englewood Cliffs, New Jersey: Prentice Hall, 1960), p. 257.

[21] William Warren Sweet, *Religion in the Development of American Culture 1765-1840* (New York: Charles Scribner's Sons, 1952), p. 442.

thirtieth birthday, he was converted to the Christian faith. In his *Memoirs*, he vividly recounts the ecstasy of the experience. He had a vision of the Lord and felt a "mighty baptism of the Holy Spirit." [22] Immediately following this experience he turned from the study of law to theology. From the very beginning of his career in the ministry, Finney asserted his independence from tradition and orthodoxy. He declined to attend college but chose instead to work out his theology through a personal study of the scriptures. He was ordained in July, 1824, and immediately launched a lifelong career as an evangelist, dedicating his later years to theological education and the sharing of his evangelistic techniques. Although his seminary lectures and later sermons are extant, his early sermons were unwritten and, according to him, often unprepared: "I had not taken a thought with regard to what I should preach; indeed this was common with me at the time. The Holy Spirit was upon me, and I felt confident that when the time came for action I should know what to preach." [23]

It is no wonder that Finney met with great popularity with the common people, for he spoke their language and his illustrations were drawn from everyday experiences. His revival messages were uncluttered by theological jargon that was usually dominant in the more orthodox preaching of the day. Finney delighted in the live options contained in preaching unfettered by specific preparation and notes. "We can never know the full meaning of the gospel," he said, "till we throw away our notes." [24] Much of his effectiveness resulted from his ability to combine "reason and emotion, faith in the Bible and faith in human intelligence." [25]

The absence of theological jargon from his sermons in no way concealed his position in regard to Calvinism and predestination. Finney boldly declared an unlimited atonement which he translated to unlimited potential for man. It is man who chooses, and if he makes the wrong decision he cannot blame God.

"God so loved the world," meaning the whole race of men. By the "world" in this connection cannot be meant any particular part only, but the whole race. Not only the Bible, but the nature of the case shows that the atonement must have been made for the whole world.[26]

God made possible man's emancipation from sin, but finally it is man himself who determines his spiritual and social destiny. The evangelist pro-

[22] Charles G. Finney, *Memoirs of Rev. Charles G. Finney Written by Himself* (New York: Fleming H. Revell Company, 1876), p. 20.

[23] *Ibid.*, p. 62.

[24] Robert T. Oliver, *History of Public Speaking in America* (Boston: Allyn & Bacon, 1965), p. 385.

[25] William Gerald McLoughlin, *Modern Revivalism* (New York: The Ronald Press, 1959), p. 67.

[26] Theodore W. Engstrom, *Master Preachers of All Ages* (Grand Rapids, Michigan: Zondervan, 1951), p. 95.

claimed that man was free but that he was freed for a purpose. He proclaimed that any man who would turn from his sinful ways and appropriate through Christ the love of God, could become a contributing member of society. His philosophy as expressed in his preaching was that men made right with God would make society right. He taught that when men exercised their freedom to chose God, the social order would be reconstructed and that this could be accomplished in no other way. Finney preached a religion of service and good works.

"Look at the utility of benevolence," said Finney in the second part of his 'New Heart' sermon. "It is a matter of human consciousness that the mind is so constituted that benevolent affections are the source of happiness; and malevolent ones the source of misery." Because "benevolence is good will, or willing good to the object of it" it follows that "if we desire the happiness of others, their happiness will increase our own, according to the strength of our desire." In other words, the more vigorously a man pursued do-goodism, the more he tasted "the cup of every man's happiness."
And inasmuch as "God's happiness consists in his benevolence," therefore do-goodism, by advancing the happiness of the universe in general, advanced the will of God. On this basis it was natural for Finney to say of young converts. "They should set out with a determination to aim at being useful in the highest degree" and "if they can see an opportunity where they can do more good, they must embrace it whatever may be the sacrifice to themselves." In the light of these statements it is not surprising that many of Finney's converts engaged in the manifold reform movements of the day with the dedicated, and often self-righteous, zeal of persons assured that they were serving the Lord.[27]

Finney quickly became the primary target for the attacks of the orthodox Calvinists. He deftly defended the doctrine of election while at the same time clinging to man's freedom of choice. In the conclusion to a sermon entitled "Doctrine of Election" the following points were expounded:

Foreknowledge and election are not inconsistent with free agency, but are founded upon it. The elect were chosen to eternal life, because God foresaw that in the perfect exercise of their freedom, they could be induced to repent and embrace the Gospel. . . . I have said that the question is as much open for your decision, that you are left as perfectly to the exercise of your freedom, as if God neither knew or designed any thing in regard to your salvation.[28]

Finney insisted that God's election and the work of the Holy Spirit were not inconsistent with individual responsibility.

It has been common for those who believe that sinners are unable to change their own heart, when sinners have inquired what they should do to be saved, to substitute another requirement for that contained in the text, and instead of commanding them to make a new heart, have told them to pray that God would change their heart. . . . Sinner! instead of waiting and praying for God to change

[27] McLoughlin, *Modern Revivalism*, pp. 102-3.
[28] Charles G. Finney, *Sermons on Important Subjects* (New York: John S. Taylor, 1836), pp. 217-18.

144

your heart, you should at once summon up your powers, put forth the effort, and change the governing preference of your mind.[29]

He declared that men had two alternatives, either to serve Satan and their own selfish interests, or to serve God and seek the benefit of others. According to his formula, dedication to the public good was the inevitable sequel to an experience with God.

Self-gratification becomes the law to which he conforms his conduct. It is that minding on the flesh, which is enmity against God. A change of heart, therefore, is to prefer a different end. To prefer supremely the glory of God and the public good, to promotion of his own interest; and whenever this preference is changed, we see of course a corresponding change of conduct.[30]

Charles Finney vigorously proclaimed the freedom and perfectibility of man. Man was free to choose God and free through God to construct his society. To Finney, liberty and responsibility were coterminous and incorporated in the gospel of Christ.

The Defenders of the Faith

The orthodox preacher steeped in the Puritan Calvinism of the eighteenth century viewed the preaching of Finney and his colaborers as anathema. Sweet in *Religion in the Development of American Culture* related a conservative minister's evaluation of the *heretical* concept of the equality of men:

One New York preacher for example roundly condemned the men who broached "the pompous doctrine that 'all men are born both free and equal' in the teeth of all the providence of God, in whose unsearchable wisdom, one is born in manger and another on a throne. The axiom of 'equal rights,' " this gentlemen continues, "is infidel, not christian, and strikes at all that is beautiful in civil, or sacred in divine institutions." [31]

The Calvinists, deeply disturbed by the spread of what they considered a heinous distortion of the Word of God, were quick and incisive in their attack. Jedidiah Morse was representative of those who sought to defend the faith. Morse, who served the First Congregational Church in Charleston, Massachusetts, from 1789 to 1829, discussed the responsibility and objective of the Christian ministry before the convention of Congregational ministers in Boston in 1812. According to him, man's part in the plan of salvation "is to aid in the accomplishment of the revealed plan of God for recovering lost sinners." [32] Another minister expressed man's relationship to God's plan

[29] *Ibid.*, pp. 36-37.
[30] *Ibid.*, p. 15.
[31] William Warren Sweet, *Religion in the Development of American Culture* (New York: Charles Scribner's Sons, 1952), p. 442.
[32] Jedidiah Morse, *Sermon Before the Congregational Convention* (Boston: Samuel T. Armstrong, 1812).

with this statement, "One must be willing, nay ever anxious, to spend his eternity in hell, if it should chance to please God to send him there." [33] The battle was not fought along denominational lines for, with the exception of the Methodists, most were divided on the issue. For instance one Baptist preacher is quoted as saying: "Sinners, I have no Gospel for you, I am only sent to preach to God's people, to feed his sheep and lambs, God will save his elect in spite of men and devils—means or no means—no difference, God will save them." [34] Another of the same faith declares: "Jesus Christ is God's elect; and when sinners believe in the Savior, they are elected, and not before; this is all the election I read of in the Holy Scripture." [35]

Robert Breckinridge summed up the attitude of the Calvinists toward the new breed when he stated:

The universal doctrine of error is that man can do and must do something more or less, which, as merit, condition, or occasion, shall secure his salvation. . . . There is a great defection from the bosom of Protestantism, in which its erring children have let slip the fundamental point of God's method of saving sinners and while they profess to abhor the man of sin, are in reality unwitting instruments of his will. [36]

George Junkin, Chief Prosecutor

One of the most vigorous opponents of the freedom school was George Junkin. After serving eleven years as pastor at the Milton, Pennsylvania, church, he entered upon a long career of educational administration. As the schism between the Old School Presbyterians with their Calvinistic orientation and the New School party with their emphasis on the human element widened, Junkin became the primary prosecutor of the heretics. It was he who instigated the heresy trial of Albert Barnes and later authored a publication entitled *The Vindication, Containing a History of the Trial of the Rev. Albert Barnes*. Junkin articulated his position before the General Assembly on May 15, 1845, in a sermon entitled "Truth and Freedom." [37] He characterized free-will as "the strongest link in the chain of human bondage," and went on to describe the condition of the sinner and his "utter incapacity . . . to break off his chains and restore himself to true moral freedom." [38] He reinforced the complete sovereignty of God in the matter of the restoration of fallen men. "The word of God everywhere represents

[33] Peter W. Elsbree, *The Rise of the Missionary Spirit in America; 1790-1815* (Williamsport, Pennsylvania: n. p., 1928), pp. 147-48.

[34] Hosea Holcomb, *A History of the Rise and Progress of the Baptists in Alabama* (Philadelphia: King and Baird, 1840), p. 96.

[35] *Ibid.*, p. 53.

[36] Fish, *Pulpit Eloquence of the Nineteenth Century*, pp. 278-79.

[37] Published by R. P. Donogh and Company, Cincinnati, 1845. There is a copy in the Columbia Theological Seminary library, Decatur, Georgia.

[38] *Ibid.*

regeneration, faith, repentance as graces of God's Holy Spirit, wrought in his people, by His Almighty energies and leading them in the way, by the truth to the enjoyment of life everlasting." [39]

The Rev. Junkin admitted that this position had direct implications in terms of man's relationship to his fellowman and to the state. He developed the concept in terms of those preordained to damnation being represented by Adam, and those predestined to redemption being represented by Christ. This principle of representation was purported to be the model for the government of the United States.

But the principal point of special adaptation is the free-grace scheme . . . the precursor to a free system of government . . . found in its federative or representative principle. We have only to transfer this prominent feature of our theology, into government, ecclesiastical and civil, and religious and political liberty are both secured. [40]

Here the federalist strain becomes apparent. Men are not spiritually free to plot their lives; their representative, Adam, has staked out the path they must follow, and it is the will of God that it be so. The logical application of this principle to political endeavor requires that society's destiny be left to the decision of duly elected representatives.

The Effects of the Controversy

It is difficult to ascertain cause and effect in the scope of historical event and subsequent action. Did the new theology expounded by Finney and those he represented bring about new direction to American life, or were Beecher, Finney, and others only expressing the functional beliefs of a majority of the people? At least, even the most conservative evaluation of the effects of the evolution of a democratic theology in America must recognize that the movement (chaotic and unorganized as it was, it *was* a movement) gave form and verbal expression to the feelings of democratic Americans. The people of the United States came out of the revolution with the firm conviction that an earthly utopia was a real possibility and that men could free themselves from the tyranny of the old order. They fought desperately against those who wanted to substitute an aristocratic oligarchy for the European monarchies. These people, tempered by oppression and war, were motivated by "belief in equality so profound in that the American almost confounded equality of opportunity with equality of ability, together with an intense, militant individualism that resented all restrictions and was restless, buoyant, self-assertive and optimistic." [41] Believing that they

[39] *Ibid.*
[40] *Ibid.*
[41] Alice Felt Tyler, *Freedom's Ferment* (Minneapolis: The University of Minnesota Press, 1944), p. 18.

147

were economically and politically free, they demanded spiritual freedom as well. And yet, they were not willing to reject their religious heritage; the rigorous life and the disappointments and frustrations, which were for many a daily occurrence, required an undergirding faith in an ultimate strength beyond even the elements of nature. The inability of law and the civilizing forces of an established community to keep pace with the moving frontier made the restraints of religion an indispensable commodity. One observer of the period noted the ameliorating influence of religion:

In a free community the follies of the frontier are harmless. The points on which he [the man in the fluid frontier society] differs from those around him are rarely of a nature to produce injurious effects on his conduct as a citizen. But the man without religion acknowledges no restraint but human laws; and the dungeon and the gibbet are necessary to secure the rights and interests of his fellow-citizens from violation. There can be no doubt, therefore, that in a newly settled country the strong effect produced by camp meetings and revivals is on the whole beneficial. The restraints of public opinion and penal legislation are little felt in the wilderness; and in such circumstances, the higher principle of action communicated by religion, is a new and additional security to society.[42]

These forces combined to drive men to discover a doctrine of the relationship of God and man more consistent with their life and practice. Although not intellectually concerned with theological principles, they found in the sweep of revivalism a religious expression which served their needs and expressed their feelings. The contributions of the religious movements of the early nineteenth century were significant. The people found a faith that, while making demands in terms of their personal conduct, was not degrading to their concept of the basic worth and dignity of the individual; furthermore, it provided for them a sustaining confidence and hope. The humanitarian movements of the latter part of the nineteenth century grew out of the rich soil of the evangelistic religion of the early part of that century. Timothy L. Smith in his interpretation of revivalism arrives at the thesis that "whatever may have been the role of other factors, the quest for perfection joined with compassion for poor and needy sinners and a rebirth of millennial expectation to make popular Protestantism a mighty social force long before the slavery conflict erupted into war." [43]

By and large, Americans came to accept the idea that the blessings of God to be realized in the building of his Kingdom on earth depended on their willingness to roll up their sleeves and to build it. Thus any serious study of a given society must include a study of its religion. Religion tends to give form to the practicing philosophy expressed in economy and government. The preaching of the evangelical movement of the first half of the

---

[42] Attributed to Thomas Hamilton, a European visitor to America in the early nineteenth century, in Alice Felt Tyler, *Freedom's Ferment*, p. 41.

[43] Smith, *Revivalism and Social Reform*, p. 149.

nineteenth century reinforced the democratic ideal. Divine unction was a final seal to the hope for a free society of promise. The identification of American goals with the goals of God added more fuel to the fires of hope and determination, kindled by what had originally been an instinctive desire for security. These fires were not to be extinguished. The religious part of the westward movement in which the personality of the pulpiteers was dominant had a profound influence on the development of American culture.

7

ON ENTERING THE KINGDOM: NEW BIRTH OR NURTURE

_____D. Ray Heisey_____

When Congregationalist Dr. Edward D. Griffin raised the question in one of his "Sabbath Evening" lectures in the famed Park Street Church, Boston, in 1813, "whether regeneration is progressive or instantaneous," he was anticipating an issue whose discussion later would shake New England theology to its foundations.[1] It was not a new issue but its importance for the implications regarding religion in America reached an unprecedented height during the first half of the nineteenth century. Thus during the decades when Calhoun and Webster were debating the essential nature of the Constitution, the pulpit in America was debating the nature of the process of entering the kingdom of God. In order to become a Christian, the question was asked, is it necessary for everyone to experience an individual, instantaneous conversion, or can it be accomplished for some by the process of proper nurturing?

The New Birth Point of View

In answering the above question with the reply that "it must be instantaneous," the Boston minister was echoing the prevailing New England theology of his time. It was called the experience of the "new birth," from the biblical injunction of Jesus to Nicodemus that he "must be born again."

Three elements were identified with conversion by the new birth: a recognition of one's moral depravity, a radical and sudden change in the affections, and a repentance of sin under the influence of the Holy Spirit.[2] The new

---

[1] Edward D. Griffin, A Series of Lectures, Delivered in Park Street Church, Boston (3rd ed.; Boston: Crocker and Brewster, 1829), p. 91; Theodore T. Munger, Horace Bushnell: Preacher and Theologian (Boston: Houghton Mifflin Company, 1899), p. 67.

[2] Charles G. Finney, Sermons on Important Subjects (3rd ed.; New York: John S. Taylor, 1836), p. 62; Charles Wadsworth, "A Sermon preached in the Arch Street Presbyterian Church," April 11, 1858 (Philadelphia, 1858), pp. 23-24. Wadsworth's sermon apparently was privately published. It is found in a bound collection of individual sermon pamphlets in the Oberlin College Library, Oberlin, Ohio.

150

birth was an inward, supernatural renovation of heart which expressed itself in outward life. At such time, and only at such time, as this new birth occurred, the person was a new creature in the Kingdom, capable of subsequent growth as a Christian.

The Christian Nurture Point of View

In contrast to the new birth approach was the position which claimed that spiritual life could result from growth in an appropriate organic environment. It precluded the necessity of a moment in time in which the person experienced a radical conversion from his sinful state. It assumed that the spiritual life of Christian parents was infused into the life of the child, who grew "up into Christ by the preventing or anticipating grace of their nurture in the Lord." In the words of Horace Bushnell's now famous proposition, "the child is to grow up a Christian, and never know himself as being otherwise." [3]

It should be made clear that the Christian nurture position did not exclude conversion and a radical change for those who needed such a supernatural transaction. The main point was that the radical change was not required "of such as are already subjects of the change, and many are so even from their earliest years." [4]

This view rested squarely on the traditional concept of human depravity but differed from the "new birth" approach in emphasizing the fact that the regenerating power of the Spirit of God can be transmitted by "the organic unity of the family" just as well as, or better than, the individualism of "the way of earnest repentance."

Origins of the Controversy

New England theology in the early part of the nineteenth century was in a state of transition, causing inevitable conflict. On the one hand, the Calvinist theologian exalted God as "the sole author" of regeneration, and, on the other, the pastor's practical interest wanted "to clear away obstacles and stimulate activity on the part of sinners and so eventually to elicit the act of conversion." [5] Frank Hugh Foster claims that by 1819 New England theology had modified the old Calvinistic doctrines considerably, substituting for "the arbitrary will of God" his character, love; "for a sinful nature, a

[3] Horace Bushnell, *Christian Nurture* (New Haven: Yale University Press, 1947), p. 4.

[4] Horace Bushnell, *Sermons for the New Life* (5th ed.; New York: Charles Scribner's Sons, 1859), pp. 108-9.

[5] Frank Hugh Foster, *A Genetic History of the New England Theology* (Chicago: The University of Chicago Press, 1907), p. 527.

nature occasioning sin; for imputation, a strict personal responsibility; for a limited, a general atonement; for a bound, a free will." [6]

Further evidence of the transition is seen in the attempt of the eminent Princeton theologian Charles Hodge, to interpret the older Calvinists in a newer light. Samuel H. Cox of the Laight Street Presbyterian Church, in a sermon preached at the opening of the synod of New York on October 20, 1830, had claimed that the "old Calvinists" were guilty of "false and ruinous" dogmas. These included the beliefs that God is the sole agent of regeneration, that it is wrong to require a sinner to repent immediately and believe the gospel, and that the offer of salvation is not made to every hearer. Hodge replied to this sermon in a published essay in which he tried to show that the old Calvinist authors expressly disclaimed the opinions that Cox had imputed to them, and that these opinions were not really deducible from any of the principles which they held.[7]

Though theology at the time was in the process of being modified, the strength of its major tenets should not be underestimated. Natural depravity, with varying definitions, was accepted by most religious groups. Lyman Beecher, illustrative of the traditional New England mind, defined it to mean "that there is nothing in [man], of which religion is the natural effect or consequence, without a special divine interposition." [8]

Another major doctrine in New England theology as related to the revivalists was freedom of the will. Some evangelists taught that though man was depraved, he had the ability to respond to "special divine interposition" with a change of mind. This meant, of course, that children, unable to comprehend the theoretical doctrines of depravity, divine grace, and regeneration, were excluded from the system. They were not excluded from the indictment of the human race, but there was no provision for their salvation until they became old enough to understand.[9] Children of Christian parents were expected to grow up like children of those outside the church, "out of covenant with God" and in need of the same measures as others to bring them to God.[10]

The concepts of innate sin and the freedom of man to respond to God's grace led, understandably, to a doctrine of conscious conversion. When full freedom of the will was "made the chief factor in the first experiences of the Christian life," [11] the deliberate act of exercising the will in a moment of decision took on great importance in a system of salvation. Thus an emphasis

----

[6] *Ibid.*, p. 282.

[7] Charles Hodge, *Essays and Reviews* (New York: Robert Carter and Brothers, 1857), pp. 3-4.

[8] Lyman Beecher, "The Native Character of Man," *The National Preacher*, II, No. 1 (June, 1827), 1.

[9] Daniel D. Addison, *The Clergy in American Life and Letters* (London: The Macmillan Company, 1900), p. 295.

[10] Hodge, *Essays and Reviews*, p. 316.

[11] Munger, *Horace Bushnell*, pp. 72-73.

was placed on decision-making, including a repentance of sin and a turning to God.

Propagating the Church Through Revivalism

The emphasis on conversion and freedom of the will led to revivalism as the primary means of implementing these theories and of extending the domain of the church. Foster says:

The overemphasis of covenant relations and the importance of baptism in the period before Edwards had led him and his followers . . . to correct certain disastrous results by a corresponding overemphasis on conversion as an epoch in the conscious experience of the believer. And the development of the theory of the will at New Haven had led to a great revival epoch.[12]

The early decades of the nineteenth century were called "the age of revivals." Particularly in New England the revival fires burned where Lyman Beecher, Charles G. Finney, Asahel Nettleton, and others were the chief promoters.

The "protracted meetings," as revivals were sometimes called, often continued for days or even weeks. The preaching of certain evangelists was often "an exciting kind" in order to get people to respond. New measures were introduced into the services by Finney in the late 1820's, such as "the anxious-seat" to which sinners could come for receiving salvation. The "anxious-seat" was used originally to save the pastor the work of calling upon the many in the audience who "were exercised." Certain men became "evangelists" in order to assist the pastors, "who were borne down with the multiplicity of their arduous labours."[13]

Revivals were looked upon as an extensive means of reforming the nation by awakening the "larger portions of the community" and attacking the empire of "the enemy."[14] They found an atmosphere conducive for growth, not only among the established churches in New England, but also in the individualism of frontier religion.[15]

Excesses of Revivalism

The practice of revivalism, itself a useful means of gaining converts for the church, was susceptible to numerous evils. The Protestant pulpit did not hesitate to enumerate these evils.

To begin with, critics claimed that revivals fostered an unnatural attitude toward promoting religion. Princetonian Charles Hodge pointed out that it

[12] Foster, Genetic History, pp. 413-14.

[13] Cornelius C. Cuyler, The Signs of the Times (Philadelphia: William S. Martien, 1839), pp. 120-22.

[14] Lyman Beecher, "Resources of the Adversary, and Means of Their Destruction," The National Preacher, II, No. 5 (October, 1827), 69.

[15] Alice Felt Tyler, Freedom's Ferment: Phases of American Social History to 1860 (Minneapolis: The University of Minnesota Press, 1944), p. 35.

was an error to think that extraordinary seasons of revival were the only, the greatest, and the best means of promoting the Christian faith.[16]

A second evil, obvious to the critical pulpit, was the fact that many conversions proved impermanent. Cornelius Cuyler of the Second Presbyterian Church, Philadelphia, cited a case in point where two hundred and ten persons were admitted to communion during the last ten days of a five-week meeting. Within four months the pastor was dismissed, and within eighteen months the church disbanded.[17] Such incidents must have provoked James A. Thome, professor of rhetoric at Oberlin College, to point out that often as few as twenty or even five remained steadfast out of "one or two hundred hopeful conversions."[18] And Congregationalist Roswell D. Hitchcock, preaching in 1858, said that "the real genius of a true discipleship" is not "excitement of feeling" but "a resolute and manly service." And, he added, if revivals now were to produce more lasting results than they did in 1740 or 1828, a greater appreciation of this real genius would be necessary.[19]

Third, the censurers argued that revivals resulted in defective Christian character. Even where the conversion may have been real, said Cuyler, Christians who are hastily admitted to the church are frequently unwilling to submit to authority, are ignorant of the doctrines of the gospel, and are lacking in those graces "which adorn the Christian when the confirmation of the new man is fully developed."[20]

Fourth, revivals encouraged the neglect of the ordinary means of grace. The ordinances became "insipid or distasteful" to people accustomed to great waves of religious excitement. The churchgoers, after having experienced a popular protracted meeting, would be little influenced by "the ordinary ministrations of the sanctuary."[21]

Fifth, revivals caused neglect of "the divinely appointed means of careful Christian nurture,"[22] particularly among children where, it was claimed, character is mainly determined.[23] Without adequate evidence evangelists assumed all were in need of conversion.

Christian Nurture: A Reaction

It was out of the background of overemphasis on revivals that the Christian nurture position developed. Horace Bushnell was its strongest advocate

---

[16] Hodge, *Essays and Reviews*, p. 320.

[17] Cuyler, *Signs of the Times*, p. 133.

[18] James A. Thome, "Evangelism and Evangelists," *The Oberlin Quarterly Review*, I, No. 2 (November, 1845), 204.

[19] Roswell D. Hitchcock, "True Religion, A Service," *The New York Pulpit in the Revival of 1858* (New York: Sheldon, Blakeman, and Company, 1858), p. 358.

[20] Cuyler, *Signs of the Times*, p. 135.

[21] *Ibid.*, p. 127; Hodge, *Essays and Reviews*, pp. 321-22.

[22] Hodge, *Essays and Reviews*, pp. 321-22.

[23] Munger, *Horace Bushnell*, p. 70.

and during the middle years of the nineteenth century he published several works stating his arguments. His 1838 essay, "Spiritual Economy of Revivals of Religion," was followed in 1842 by another entitled "Growth, not Conquest, the True Method of Christian Progress." The Massachusetts Sabbath School Society later published two of his lectures called "Discourses on Christian Nurture" but had to withdraw them from sale because of opposition. In 1847 Bushnell republished the two discourses along with a defense of them, the two earlier essays and two additional sermons on related themes.

Bushnell's theory of Christian nurture was born out of intense personal reaction to the revivalism, the rationalism, and the individualism of New England theology. He rejected the revivalism of his era, not because it was in itself wrong, but because revivals, with the attendant evils and excesses, hindered him in his work as a pastor. He felt that the life of the church should be propagated not by unnatural means, such as "the artificial firework, the extraordinary, combined jump and stir" of revivals, but by the natural means of the influence of an organic environment consisting of the family and the church.

Bushnell revolted against the rationalism of New England theology by rejecting the idea that the Christian faith consisted of a neat set of theological propositions to be accepted and acted upon.[24] He could not follow in the school of Jonathan Edwards and had little sympathy for "a theology defended, modified, taught, preached and applied by formal logic." Where others, such as N. W. Taylor, first professor of theology at Yale Divinity School, stood confidently on their logic, Bushnell rested on the trustworthiness of his insight, intuition, and his experience as a pastor and a father.[25]

He reacted to the extreme individualism of revivalistic theology in New England by calling for the church to return to its historic position on the organic relation between parents and children. He reminded the church that the doctrine of free will is carried too much to an extreme when little or nothing is made of organic laws.[26] He explained his organic concept, as opposed to individualism:

And the intention is that the Christian life and spirit of the parents, which are in and by the Spirit of God, shall flow into the mind of the child, to blend with his incipient and half-formed exercises; that they shall thus beget their own good within him—their thoughts, opinions, faith, and love, which are to become a little more, and yet a little more, his own separate exercise, but still the same in character. The contrary assumption, that virtue must be the product of separate and absolutely independent choice, is pure assumption.[27]

[24] William A. Johnson, *Nature and the Supernatural in the Theology of Horace Bushnell* (Lund: CWK Gleerup, 1963), p. 60.

[25] Munger, *Horace Bushnell*, pp. 41-42.

[26] Bushnell, *Christian Nurture*, pp. 20-21.

[27] *Ibid.*

For rationalism, Bushnell wanted to substitute intuition; for revivalism, Christian nurture; for individualism, organic relationships.

New Birth Preaching

The foremost proponent of the new birth concept was, undoubtedly, the evangelist Charles G. Finney (1792-1875). Finney, a trained lawyer, experienced a radical conversion in his adult life and became a highly successful evangelist in western New York and throughout the northeastern United States. He preached for conversions, always with the unrelenting purpose and direct manner of a courtroom lawyer seeking a favorable verdict for his client. Finney brought to his preaching the concise method of a brief. A typical example of his logical thinking is seen in the following excerpt:

The first point to be established, under the fourth head of this discourse, is, that impenitent sinners *hate* God. I shall pursue the same method, appeal to the same sources for proof, and go into the same field and gather facts to establish the truth of this position that I did in proof of the position that men do not love God. My appeal is to the well known laws of mind, as they are seen to develop themselves in the transactions of every day.[28]

Lyman Beecher (1775-1863), Presbyterian minister and advocate of free will, was another great revivalist of the period. He tried to keep the spirit of revivalism alive in his own pastorates and participated himself as an evangelist in other churches. He tended to oppose, however, the excitation and "new measures" of Finney's group. This New England clergyman was a stout defender of the orthodox faith against the encroaching Unitarianism of his day. In his Worcester sermon of October 15, 1823, "The Faith Once Delivered to the Saints," Beecher stated as one of the arguments for the orthodox faith that its preaching "was attended with sudden anxieties, and deep convictions of sin, and sudden joy in believing; followed by reformation and a holy life." [29] In short, the faith delivered to the saints produced revivals of religion.

Another evangelist, but of the old-fashioned form of Calvinism, was Asahel Nettleton (1783-1844). Nettleton believed in and conducted revivals, but also opposed the radical measures employed by Finney. His own meetings he kept regular, orderly, and solemn. In his pulpit manner he was not particularly captivating or exciting. One of his contemporaries says that there was "nothing to make you admire the man, or his writings, or his speaking; or in any way to divert your attention from the truths which he uttered." [30]

Edward D. Griffin (1770-1837), Congregationalist minister, professor of

[28] Finney, *Sermons on Important Subjects*, p. 119.

[29] Lyman Beecher, "The Faith Once Delivered to the Saints," *Sermons Delivered on Various Occasions, 1806-1827* (Boston: T. R. Marvin, 1828), p. 235.

[30] Bennet Tyler, *Memoir of the Life and Character of Rev. Asahel Nettleton* (Hartford, Connecticut: Robins and Smith, 1845), p. 357.

sacred rhetoric at Andover and president of Williams College, was also a great promoter of revivals. Like Nettleton, Griffin was of the Old School, believing that conversions and revivals were appointed by God and not the result of natural means. The historian Henry C. Fish wrote of Griffin in 1857 that "it would be difficult to find the individual in our country, since the days of Whitefield, who has been the instrument of an equal number of conversions." He possessed "surprising powers of pulpit oratory" and was known for his emotional but dignified voice, his clarity of thought, his command of audiences, and his carefully prepared sermon manuscripts.[31] His approach in the development of a sermon was to clarify the thesis, develop each argument with full explanation and an abundant quoting of scripture, and conclude with "Inferences," or an application of the subject.

The primary argument for the necessity of the new birth was that *man is "totally depraved,"* a condition which renders him incapable of loving God and reforming himself. In a striking sermon Finney defined "total depravity" as the state of supreme selfishness, or "a controlling and abiding preference of self-gratification, above the commandments, authority, and glory of God." [32] Lyman Beecher, in a sermon published in *The National Preacher* in 1827, developed at great length his thesis of the meaning of the natural character of man's heart. "The entireness of human depravity," he concluded, "consists in the constant voluntary refusal of man to love the Lord his God, with supreme complacency and good will." [33]

The supporting evidence for the depravity argument generally came from two sources. The first source was the Bible, in the words of Jesus to Nicodemus, "Except a man be born again, he cannot see the kingdom of God." This verse became the fountainhead of all argument claiming the necessity of the new birth. The second source cited was universal experience. In a sermon entitled, "God Cannot Please Sinners," Finney argued that the heathen, by offering sacrifices to appease their offended gods, were acknowledging "in the most public manner" the fact that they have violated their consciences.[34] Even such action, he said, indicates the self-evident nature of the necessity of the new birth.

Regarding the nature of the new birth, the proponents claimed that *the change from a condition of moral depravity to one of holiness must, by its very nature, be instantaneous.* In one of his Park Street lectures entitled "Regeneration Not Progressive," Dr. Griffin argued that, if being born again means that one now loves God more than himself, "nothing can be plainer than that the change is as sudden as the entrance of the first drop that falls

[31] Henry C. Fish, *History and Repository of Pulpit Eloquence*, II (New York: M. W. Dodd, 1857), 470.

[32] Finney, *Sermons on Important Subjects*, pp. 116-17.

[33] Beecher, *The National Preacher*, II, No. 1 (June, 1827), 14.

[34] Finney, *Sermons on Important Subjects*, pp. 182-83.

into a vessel." [35] One cannot, he said, be "destitute" of holiness and not undergo an instantaneous change in order to begin loving God. For a sinner, who has loved the world supremely, said Beecher, to set his affections "on things above" requires a "real, and great, and instantaneous" change.[36]

In addition to the fact that the new birth was claimed to be instantaneous, *it was also noted to be a conscious turning away from sin in an individual act of repentance.* Revivalists repeatedly emphasized repentance as the essence of being born again. It involved, on the one hand, a sorrow for and abandonment of sin, and, on the other, an acceptance by faith of Christ. In a sermon preached in the Arch Street Presbyterian Church, Philadelphia, on April 11, 1858, Presbyterian clergyman Charles Wadsworth said, "To come to Christ is to turn from your sins in penitence, and cast yourselves in faith on the merits of your Redeemer." [37] A Baptist minister, William Hague, of New York City, pointed out that true repentance means: (1) a change of mind, (2) spontaneous sorrow on account of the nature and evil of sinful dispositions, and (3) an inward moral force which produces a real transformation of life and conduct.[38] Finney told his listeners that they must confess their sins and believe the record God gave of his Son.[39]

A final aspect of the nature of the new birth concerned the element of ability and freedom of the will. The Old School theology declared that the *new birth depends entirely on the intervention of God's sovereign will.* This traditional Calvinistic position is represented in the sermon "Regeneration Supernatural" by Edward Griffin of Boston's Park Street Church. He denied that the sinner cooperates in any way with the supernatural force of God's will. Not by mechanical means, or by the influence of motives, or even by the laws of nature was the change in conversion effected. Griffin said,

that love should start up out of enmity in a moment, uncaused but by itself, is altogether incredible, and never was and never will be believed by any rational mind. The moment regeneration is proved to be an instantaneous change, from unabated enmity to supreme love, the argument for the self-determining power is forever ruined.[40]

That the new birth is a sovereign act of God was undeniable to Asahel Nettleton. He never engaged in any of the measures employed by Finney and others to facilitate the decision to become a Christian. He always maintained that a revival, and likewise a conversion, was dependent entirely

[35] Griffin, *A Series of Lectures*, p. 101.
[36] Beecher, *The National Preacher*, II, No. 1 (June, 1827), 14.
[37] Wadsworth, "Sermon Preached in the Arch Street Presbyterian Church," p. 23.
[38] William Hague, "True Repentance," *The New York Pulpit in the Revival of 1858*, p. 144.
[39] Charles G. Finney, *Sermons on Gospel Themes* (Oberlin, Ohio: E. J. Goodrich, 1876), pp. 161 ff. See also J. A. Clark, *Awake Thou Sleeper* (2nd ed.; New York: Robert Carter, 1845), "There is only one way in which any human being can enter Heaven; and that is by being born again and made a new creature in Jesus Christ." p. 31.
[40] Griffin, *A Series of Lectures*, p. 111.

upon God. He emphasized the doctrine of eternal and particular election as the foundation of all hope with respect to man's salvation.[41]

In contrast to the position that the new birth is caused entirely by the sovereign act of God was the New School doctrine that *the sinner can, by an act of the will, change his mind, thus bringing about his own conversion.* In a sermon entitled, "It Is the Duty of Sinners to Make Them a New Heart," Congregationalist Nathanael Emmons claimed that "the united evidence of reason, scripture, and experience," shows that a new heart consists in nothing but "new, holy, voluntary exercises of the mind." Since this was true, and true also that sinners were free "to exercise benevolence instead of selfishness," it was quite clear to Emmons that sinners were not passive but active in regeneration.[42]

The foremost advocate of human participation in the act of conversion was Charles Finney. In what may be considered one of his most noted sermons, "Sinners Bound to Change Their Own Hearts," [43] Finney went back to the Old Testament to the command of Ezekiel, "Make you a new heart and a new spirit," and bound the command upon every sinner in his audience. Explaining that a change of heart was really the voluntary change in "the governing preference of the mind," Finney claimed that every sinner was obligated to choose, of his own free will, a new disposition which prefers holiness to sin, and the glory of God to self-gratification.

The arguments of new birth preaching followed lines of appeal that were quite clearly volitional and rationalistic. In a sermon on "How to Change Your Heart," Finney emphasized the importance of reasoning with the sinner, as opposed to appealing to fear or hope. Appeals, he said, which produce "much feeling and many tears" but which fail to provide "that discriminating instruction which the sinner needs in regard to his duty and the claims of his Maker, will seldom result in a sound conversion." [44] Although, according to critics, Finney engaged in emotional appeals, he is known primarily for the courtroom manner of giving great attention to the logical development of his argument. His devotion to reason is seen in the question, "If the intelligence cannot be safely appealed to, how are we to know what the Bible means? for it is the only faculty by which we get at the truth of the oracles of God." [45]

[41] Tyler, *Memoir of . . . Asahel Nettleton*, pp. 204, 213, 231. See also Lyman Beecher's *Views of Theology* (Boston: John P. Jewett and Company, 1853) where he says that the love of God is never a quality of a man's heart as a consequence of his natural birth. It is, in all cases, the result of a "special divine interposition." p. 53.

[42] Nathanael Emmons, *Sermons on Various Important Subjects of Christian Doctrine and Practice* (Boston: Samuel T. Armstrong, 1812), pp. 174, 178, 180. Another example of this emphasis may be seen in S. Edwards Dwight, *Select Discourses* (Boston: Crocker and Brewster, 1851) which includes a sermon entitled, "Make You a New Heart." p. 203.

[43] Finney, *Sermons on Important Subjects*, pp. 1-42.

[44] *Ibid.*, p. 65.

[45] Quoted in Hodge, *Essays and Reviews*, pp. 247-48.

Lyman Beecher also typified the rationalism of the new birth position in the closing appeal of his sermon, "The Native Character of Man." He attempted a logic-tight argument, an either-or position which demanded a decision in his favor. "You have now before you the evidence," he charged, "that men are not religious by nature; and that this destitution implies the universal and entire depravity of man, and the necessity of a great and sudden change in the affections, by the special influence of the Holy Spirit." He concluded, "And will you, dare you, in the presence of such evidence, reject it in favour of the dictates of mere inclination? . . . This fearful truth will still remain, The sinner must be born again, Or drink the wrath of God." [46]

Impact of New Birth Preaching

Part of the impact of revivalistic preaching has already been noted in terms of certain excesses which often resulted from revivals.

A second effect was that revivalistic preaching stimulated the great emphasis on individualism already prominent in American life at that time.[47] The new birth appeal was by its very nature an appeal to the individual. Evangelistic preaching was very productive among frontier minds which have been characterized as having "an intense, militant individualism that resented all restrictions and was restless, buoyant, self-assertive, and optimistic." [48] Conversion, it was claimed, brought a new and free life to burdened and depraved men.

A third impact of revivalistic preaching was the enhancement of religion and holiness in the life of its converts. The widespread influence of revivals was claimed by Finney in his *Memoirs* when he said that the converts of his revivals "are still living, and laboring for Christ and for souls, in almost, or quite, every state in this Union." [49] It was claimed that Asahel Nettleton's revivals built up the local churches, strengthened the hands of the pastors, elevated the standard of orthodoxy, checked the prevalence of vice, and improved the standard of morals.[50] His biographer noted, for instance, he would not admit converts into the church who did not entirely abandon the habit of drinking.[51] The church historian H. Shelton Smith has said that the great influence which religion exerted over the lives of Americans in the nineteenth century was, to a considerable extent, a contribution of revivalism.[52]

[46] Beecher, *The National Preacher*, II, No. 1 (June, 1827), 16.
[47] H. Shelton Smith, Robert T. Handy, and Lefferts A. Loetscher, *American Christianity: An Historical Interpretation with Representative Documents* (New York: Charles Scribner's Sons, 1963), II, 17.
[48] Alice Felt Tyler, *Freedom's Ferment*, p. 18.
[49] Charles G. Finney, *Memoirs* (New York: A. S. Barnes, 1876), pp. 221-22.
[50] Bennet Tyler, *Memoir of . . . Asahel Nettleton*, p. 235.
[51] *Ibid.*, pp. 216-17.
[52] Smith, *et al.*, *American Christianity*, p. 19.

Revivals may have encouraged social reform. The career of Finney himself aptly illustrates how the preaching of the new birth could change a man and channel his energies into the cause of humanitarian reform.

Christian Nurture Preaching

We have record of only one outstanding man during this period who may be considered the proponent of Christian nurture. Horace Bushnell (1802-76) was reared in a strong Christian home which fit him well for his creative thinking about matters religious. He wrote of his mother that "she was concerned above all things to make her children Christian, she undertook little in the way of an immediate divine experience, but let herself down, for the most part, upon the level of habit" [53] Bushnell's younger brother said that they were "born in a household where religion was no occasional and nominal thing, no irksome restraint nor unwelcome visitor, but a constant atmosphere, a commanding but genial presence." [54]

Bushnell graduated from Yale in 1827, tutored there while he pursued law studies, and finally entered the Theological School in New Haven. He was ordained pastor of North Church in Hartford, Connecticut, in 1833, and spent his adult life as a pastor-preacher. He tried his hand at revivals and even cooperated with Finney at the time of his evangelistic meetings in Hartford, but was never very successful.[55]

Though he always had a hearing among a select audience, Bushnell was not a "popular preacher." He thought too deeply and too independently to accommodate the generation. Theodore Munger, one of his foremost biographers, says: "His brilliance and fervor flashed and burned at too great a distance to be discerned by the multitude. . . . Sermons and delivery fitted each other like die and image. The sincerity of the word was matched by the quiet confidence of his bearing." [56]

Bushnell's sermons were always written out fully and carefully and read from manuscript until duties and ill health in later life forced him to extemporize.

With the facts of moral depravity, the subsequent necessity of regeneration, and the supernatural elements in regeneration, Bushnell had no quarrel. He accepted without question these fundamental premises of the revivalists.[57] His conflict was not with the *fact* of regeneration but with the current manipulations of it in the life of the church.

[53] Munger, *Horace Bushnell*, p. 10.
[54] *Ibid.*, p. 7.
[55] See the bibliography for suggested biographies of Bushnell.
[56] Munger, *Horace Bushnell*, pp. 278-79.
[57] In a sermon on "Regeneration," Bushnell made very clear, and without equivocation, that Christianity brings a supernatural transaction; regeneration is not mere human development or self-culture of what is already in man. If it were, then it were only "a fungus growing out of the world." *Sermons for the New Life*, p. 109.

161

In contrast to the three propositions put forth by the revivalists—that the new birth is instantaneous, consists of repentance of sin, and is produced either by a sovereign act of God or by an act of the individual will—Bushnell put forth only one proposition: the child should grow up a Christian and never know himself otherwise. This proposition is developed at length in his book *Christian Nurture*, first published in 1861.[58] The original two discourses mentioned earlier comprise the first two chapters of this book.

The first discourse consists of what Bushnell called the *argument from human evidence*. The proposition had at least four supporting arguments:

(1) That children should grow up Christian is *reasonable*, given the contrary supposition. There could be no worse implication given to children, he said, than that they are to reject God until a mature age. Where is the authority to make children feel that they are "old enough to resist all good, but too young to receive any good whatever?" Christian education, based on the premise that children are to be brought up for future conversion, is no different from unchristian education and thus does actual harm.

(2) That children should grow up Christian is *wise*, given the corruption of human nature. Assuming moral depravity, he asked, when should we think it wisest to undertake or expect a remedy? "When evil is young and pliant to good, or when it is confirmed by years of sinful habit?" Children are never too young, he claimed, for good to be communicated to them. There is nothing to forbid children from being led, in their first moral act, to cleave unto that which is good and right.

(3) That children should grow up Christian is *possible*, given the desire of the parents and the experience of other Christians. Bushnell asserted that it is generally accepted that children of deeply pious parents are more likely to have children who display early the same piety. Granted this, he argued, what forbids the hope that if parents "were riper still in their piety, living a more single and Christ-like life, and more cultivated in their views of family nurture, they might see their children grow up always in piety towards God?" This proposition was also argued from the experience of other Christians, such as the well-known seventeenth-century English preacher Richard Baxter who "could recollect no time when there was a gracious change in his character." Further he cited the church in Germany and the Moravian Brethren, deeply pious people, whose power rested on their system of Christian education.

(4) Finally, that children should grow up Christian is *natural*, given the organic relation between parent and child. This was Bushnell's strongest and most fully developed point. He affirmed the sovereignty of society—the church, the state, the school, the family—over the individual. A separate man, living wholly within and from himself, is a mere fiction. The child, after

[58] The present discussion is based on the edition reprinted by Yale University Press in 1947. All quotations in this section are from the first two chapters of this volume unless otherwise noted.

birth, must still be considered within the matrix of parental life for many years, "And the parental life will be flowing into him all that time, just as naturally, and by a law as truly organic, as when the sap of the trunk flows into a limb." In a sermon on "Unconscious Influence," he said, "We overrun the boundaries of our personality—we flow together. . . . And thus our life and conduct are ever propagating themselves, by a law of social contagion, throughout the circles and times in which we live." [59]

This, then, is *the argument from human evidence*—Christian nurture is reasonable, wise, possible, and natural.

Bushnell's second major argument, *the argument from divine revelation,* was developed in the second of his two discourses. Again, he presented several supporting arguments to his theory that children should grow up Christian:

(1) It is in accordance with the character and will of God. God desires and has promised that spiritual grace will be given as necessary to parents both for them and their children.

(2) It is in accordance with the expectations of the Old and New Testaments. Bushnell quoted the Old Testament, "Train up a child in the way he should go, and when he is old he will not depart from it." This training, he asserted, is not for "future conversion." The New Testament phraseology is "Bring them up in the nurture and admonition of the Lord," implying the existence of a divine nurture.

(3) It is in accordance with the prophesied universality of the Kingdom. Bushnell foresaw a time, generally accepted by the churches, he said, when all shall know God. He devoted an entire chapter in his book to this doctrine, arguing that God will finally propagate the world by an increase from within the church. If we believe, he continued, that Christianity has the intention, the instruments, and powers "to claim all souls for its dominion," why not begin now?

(4) It is in accordance with the scriptural recognition of organic connection between parent and child. The character of children, in the Scriptures, is often regarded as derivative from their parents. "The Scriptures have a perpetual habit of associating children with the character and destiny of their parents."

(5) It is in accordance with infant baptism which rests on the recognition of organic connection between parent and child. Bushnell drew this argument from the symbolism of the rite. Baptism, he said, supposes "a seal of faith in the parent, applied over to the child on the ground of a presumption that his faith is wrapped up in the parent's faith; so that he is accounted a believer from the beginning." He argued that he who accepts the rite of infant baptism must also accept the doctrine of Christian nurture.

The appeal of Bushnell's arguments was grounded not on the rationalism

[59] Bushnell, *Sermons for the New Life,* p. 186.

of the new birth approach, but on the naturalness of human experience and the superiority of divine revelation. Whereas Finney and other revivalists emphasized the priority of reason and the individual decision of a mature person, Bushnell stressed the priority of experience and the influence of environment in an organic relationship between parent and child. Both positions called upon scripture for support; both were interested ultimately in the same end—making men Christian; both insisted on using right means, but differed as to what the best means were. Finney looked to dogma and reason, Bushnell to experience and intuition.

Impact of Christian Nurture Preaching

Bushnell's point of view added strong fuel to the fire of the Unitarian controversy of the period. The most vocal enemy was Bennet Tyler, president of the Hartford Seminary. He was responsible for getting the Sunday School Association to withdraw its publication of Bushnell's discourses, and, by persistent writing and ecclesiastical action, he attempted to shatter Bushnell's position.[60] "Educated by angels, amid the glories of heaven," Tyler insisted, a child would remain a sinner.[61] Tyler's main objection, in which he was joined by J. W. Nevin of the German Reformed Church and Charles Hodge of Princeton, was that the discourses smacked of naturalism. The Unitarians, of course, favored his work; this evoked much noise from his enemies who were sure that, if the Unitarians were in favor of it, it must be wrong.

By stressing the natural connection between the faith of parents and that of the child, Christian nurture preaching tended to bring back to New England theology a balance in methods of conversion.[62] Bushnell reinstated the Christian family as the primary means by which grace could be communicated. He returned to the corporate theory of church growth by nurture, thereby offering an alternative to the individualism of revivalism. Hodge, in his review, anticipated much good from Bushnell's work, since, he said "there is perhaps no one doctrine to which it is more important in our day to call the attention of the people of God" than that "children of believers will become truly the children of God." [63]

In thus returning to the covenant theory implicit in salvation through the family, Bushnell's theory turned the attention of the church to children. Here again was a method of providing for children in a system of grace. Long neglected, the children of Christian parents could now experience regeneration *in childhood*.

---

[60] A. J. W. Myers, *Horace Bushnell and Religious Education* (Boston: Manthorne and Burack, 1937), p. 19.

[61] Quoted in Barbara Cross, *Horace Bushnell: Minister to a Changing America* (Chicago: The University of Chicago Press, 1958), p. 71.

[62] Foster, *Genetic History*, pp. 414-15.

[63] Hodge, *Essays and Reviews*, pp. 305, 310.

Christian nurture preaching also greatly influenced later theology. Bushnell's biographer, T. T. Munger, claims that *Christian Nurture* achieved in New England theology an influence second only to that of Edwards.[64] Charles C. Cole, American intellectual historian, agrees with this estimate in suggesting that in terms of influence Bushnell did for nineteenth-century theology what Edwards had done for the eighteenth.[65] Bushnell liberated theology from the stranglehold of rigid, rationalistic Calvinism. He transcended individualistic psychology and arrived at a view of social dependence and social responsibility consonant with the views of later social psychologists and social reformers.[66]

A final impact to be mentioned was Bushnell's influence on preaching. The style of preaching in his day was as rigid as its theology. Whatever the subject, everything was viewed through several dominant doctrines which determined in advance what was to be said.[67] Most sermons were argumentative discourses, beginning with a thesis, a statement of what was to be "proved," and often an outline consisting of what the subject does not mean, what it does mean, and why it is true. Bushnell pushed through this superimposed structure to the openness and freshness that came by seeing straight into the nature of things. Christianity to him was not dogma, but life. This emphasis is seen even in the titles of his published sermons, *Sermons for the New Life* (1858) and *Sermons on Living Subjects* (1872).

Theologian George Adam Smith is said to have called Bushnell the preacher's preacher because of his great influence upon preaching in America. William Warren Sweet says, "It is not an exaggeration to say that the best preaching in America during the last half of the nineteenth century largely stemmed from Horace Bushnell, who was a prophet rather than a theologian." The great contribution of Bushnell, Sweet continues, was "to restore the Christ of the Gospels, and to lift Him up as a living, pulsing, appealing personality." [68]

Conclusion

In 1907, J. Franklin Jameson said before the American Historical Association that "of all the means of estimating American character . . . the pursuit

[64] Munger, *Horace Bushnell*, p. 95.
[65] Charles C. Cole, *The Social Ideas of the Northern Evangelists 1826-1860* (New York: Columbia University Press, 1954), p. 54.
[66] Quoted in Johnson, *Nature and the Supernatural*, pp. 30-31. Johnson summarizes Bushnell's impact on later theologians in terms of these emphases: (1) the immanence of God, (2) the idea of evolutionary growth, (3) the inherent goodness of man, and (4) the historical Jesus. These, Johnson suggests, characterize what has been called the "Social Gospel" movement, p. 237.
[67] Munger, *Horace Bushnell*, p. 285.
[68] William Warren Sweet, *Religion in the Development of American Culture 1765-1840* (New York: Charles Scribner's Sons, 1952), pp. 202-3.

of religious history is the most complete." [69] The examination of the early nineteenth-century controversy over the nature of entering the Kingdom is a good case in point. Finney and Bushnell, as representatives of the opposing revivalistic and Christian nurture approaches, are seen to be men not just preaching sermons, but men making history. They reveal remarkably well the developing character of young America. The first half of the nineteenth century was the formative period in the history of the American people. As Sweet contends in his *Religion in the Development of American Culture 1765-1840*, "We are dealing with people in motion, vast streams of them, each and all of them moving away from the old home, the old community, the old school, the old church, and the restraints and influences which all of these things imply." [70] Not only were the economic and political institutions taking shape, but the religious attitude of mind was in ferment. The orthodox and the conformists went to battle to defend the faith. The prevailing pioneering spirit and the nonconformist attitude which wanted to break loose from the old ways of thinking existed in religion. What Sweet says of the people regarding the westward movement may be said of both Finney and Bushnell regarding their relation to established religion and theology. Finney was moving away from New England Calvinism in proposing that sinners could change their own hearts and in employing new measures to induce them to change. Bushnell, an outstanding example of a nonconforming individualist, was moving from the contemporary New England mind in proposing that a crisis experience in religion give place to the more natural process of Christian growth.

Revivalism continued to appeal to the rugged individualism of the frontier. And though Bushnell's teaching had a great impact in the theological world, it did not lessen the force of revivalism. The revivalistic pattern carried far and cut deep into American religious life. The basic patterns of the early nineteenth-century revivals continued strongly, says H. Shelton Smith, "to shape Protestant thought and practice into the post- [Civil] War period." [71]

On the other hand, Bushnell's Christian nurture found its way gradually into the organized patterns of religion. It appealed to the developing sense of social responsibility that was to emerge full-grown later in American life. As far as the Protestant church at large was concerned, the accepted means of entering the Kingdom came to rest on Bushnell's side. The progressive leaders in religion and in education accepted the fundamental premises which shaped Bushnell's proposition.[72] Revivalism, as a thing in itself, was not supplanted, but it was replaced as the primary means of growth among churches.

[69] Quoted in Sweet, *ibid.*, p. vii.
[70] *Ibid.*, p. 312.
[71] Smith, *et al., American Christianity*, p. 17.
[72] See Myers, *Horace Bushnell and Religious Education*, chap. VI, for a full discussion of this point.

Thus there were elements in American religious life to which both revivalism and Christian nurture appealed. The struggle on this issue may be considered symbolic of the development of the American mind and character. Revivalism was calling for the faith of Americans to be ruled by dogma and individualism. Christian nurture was pleading for the faith of the young nation to be guided by its intuition and the organic force of social relationships. Both ideas jostled for public acceptance. Clergymen of both sides were making a vital contribution in providing "the substance and framework of an American forum" on the important religious issue of the nature of entering the Kingdom.

8

PREACHING ON SLAVERY
1831-1861

_____*Hubert Vance Taylor*_____

A twofold revolution was in progress in the United States between 1831 and 1861 as this nation confronted the issue of slavery. Demand for national opposition to slavery, first heard insistently in 1831, led to the election of Lincoln; demand for the preservation and extension of slavery, increasingly clamant after 1831, led to formation of the Confederate States of America. Both demands shaped significant changes in public opinion. The thirty-year ferment increasingly split our nation into discreet sections with antagonistic political philosophies rooted in antithetical attitudes toward both the Declaration of Independence and the Constitution. Documents that less than a century earlier had united the states now divided them. In 1861 the sections thus divided mustered men in Blue and Grey as they turned from forum to field.

On the battlefield combatants defended causes that for some became righteous crusades before the first shell burst. Three decades of heated forum conflict had forged links between both pro- and antislavery arguments and God's Truth. During the first decade abolitionists sought doctrinal and disciplinary official church actions declaring slaveholding sinful and denying communion to unrepentant slaveholders. With the Bible in one hand, the South denied the doctrine's validity and the discipline's propriety while, with the Constitution in the other, she declared Congress powerless to act upon the abolitionist petitions that flooded Washington. When problems of territorial expansion pressed slavery questions upon Congress during the second decade, political and moral concerns were increasingly intertwined. Some preachers asked adherence to religious conscience and application of moral principle in politics; some statesmen pleaded for Christian fidelity to contracts or support for sacred national goals. Although the majority, desiring peace rather than decisive and divisive choice, entered the third decade with the Compromise of 1850, yet when a territory sought statehood, the slavery question could not be avoided. Armed conflict in Kansas soon heated forum furnaces that forged support for conflicting righteous crusades. The Blue and

168

the Grey both shouldered arms with the conviction that God's truth marched on their side.

The Church and Slavery

The pulpit was a party to the revolutionary activity forging such support. Boston's Wendell Phillips protested, "Calling a slave-holding nation a Christian nation—that is the fatal error: encouraged by the pulpit, which forms the mind on which your statesmen are to act." [1] John S. Preston, South Carolina's spokesman before the 1861 Virginia state convention, warned, "Its representative [of religion] the Church, has bared her arm for the conflict—her sword is already flashing in the glare of the torch of fanaticism. . . . With demonic rage they [the brethren at the North] have set the Lamb of God between their seed and our seed." [2] Thus pulpit justification of slaveholding was condemned by northern abolitionists while the South deplored the abolitionist effort to mount a Christian antislavery crusade. Meanwhile moderate pulpit voices proposed mediating measures or urged Christians to maintain peace by avoiding entangling secular affairs. Roman Catholics and Lutherans, with few exceptions, avoided pulpit involvement; Baptist, Methodist, and Presbyterian denominations all eventually divided along a sectional axis after prolonged ecclesiastical controversy. [3]

A comparison of some early and late ecclesiastical actions indicate the change of opinion that culminated in schism. In 1784 the Methodist General Conference directed that communion be denied to members who would not free their slaves, but in 1845 southern members erected a separate denomination after the Conference refused to condone slaveholding by electing a slaveholder to the bishopric. [4] In 1787 and again in 1818, the Presbyterian General Assembly directed its members to seek as a duty the complete abolition of slavery. By 1861 Southern Presbyterians were defending the erection of a separate denomination with the argument that slaveholding was not an evil relationship because the early church of the prophets and reformers—the pre-1787 Christians—had approved slavery throughout the

---

[1] *National Anti-Slavery Standard*, May 18, 1843, in Willard H. Yeager, "Wendell Phillips," *History and Criticism of American Public Address*, ed. William N. Brigance (New York: Russell and Russell, 1960), I, 341.

[2] See Dwight Lowell Dumond, *Antislavery Origins of the Civil War in the United States* (Ann Arbor, Michigan: The University of Michigan Press, 1939), p. 40.

[3] Madeline Hook Rice, *American Catholic Opinion in the Slavery Controversy* (New York: Columbia University Press, 1949), pp. 69, 151; Robert Fortenbaugh, "American Lutheran Synods and Slavery, 1830-1860," *Journal of Religion*, XIII (1933), 75-77, 83-84; William W. Barnes, *The Southern Baptist Convention, 1845-1953* (Nashville: Broadman Press, 1954), p. 25; Donald G. Mathews, *Slavery and Methodism: A Chapter in American Morality, 1780-1845* (Princeton: Princeton University Press, 1965), pp. 242-64; Hubert V. Taylor, "Slavery and the Deliberations of the Presbyterian General Assembly, 1833-1838" (unpublished Ph.D. dissertation, Northwestern University, 1964), pp. 160-62.

[4] Mathews, *Slavery and Methodism*, pp. 16, 193, 264.

ages.[5] Such shifts in opinion followed upon extensive pulpit activity. The three-decade period, 1831-61, defines a time of marked pulpit involvement with the slavery issue. In the pages to follow this period will be studied in ten-year periods indicating the larger context of slavery and reporting representative sermons.

Preaching and Slavery

An analysis of some one hundred sermons, admittedly only a small sample of the whole body of such speech during the decades preceding the Civil War, reveals to some degree pulpit approaches to the slavery issue. The sermons, all based upon a biblical text and delivered in a church, represent a geographical spectrum of the nation.[6] Many were occasional sermons. Some were heard on special days such as Thanksgiving, the Fourth of July, Fast Day, or in connection with meetings of church courts or societies. Others were Sunday sermons influenced by events such as the 1837 murder of Elijah Lovejoy, the 1838 burning of Pennsylvania Hall, the Compromise of 1850, the 1854 Kansas-Nebraska Act, the 1859 attack upon Harper's Ferry, or the election of Lincoln in 1860.[7]

The immediate audience for such discourse was frequently large. In Boston, Theodore Parker drew thousands.[8] In Brooklyn, some two thousand or more regularly heard Henry Ward Beecher between 1850 and 1861.[9] In New Orleans, B. M. Palmer's famous 1860 sermon was heard by a Thanksgiving audience of about two thousand (four times the size of the congregation).[10] The immediate audience for the preachers in the abolitionist revivals can scarcely be estimated, but considered collectively it must have been large because of the extensive activity of the revivalists and the intense excitement they generated.

The position of the church in society during the period suggests that influential men heard the preachers' appeals. "A large assembly of intelligent and respectable citizens of Charleston" heard J. H. Thornwell, Presbyterian

[5] H. Shelton Smith, Robert T. Handy, and Lefferts A. Loetscher, *American Christianity: An Historical Interpretation with Representative Documents* (New York: Charles Scribners' Sons, 1963), pp. 180, 208, 209.

[6] Sermons from Boston, Buffalo, Cleveland, Cincinnati, Philadelphia, New York, Richmond, Charleston, New Orleans, and other cities have been studied.

[7] Almost every northern pulpit protested the Kansas-Nebraska Act. See Charles C. Cole, Jr., *The Social Ideals of the Northern Evangelists, 1826-1860* (New York: Columbia University Press, 1954), p. 215.

[8] Earl Morse Wilbur, *A History of Unitarianism in Transylvania, England, and America* (Cambridge: Harvard University Press, 1952), p. 461.

[9] William C. Beecher and Samuel Scovillle, *A Biography of Rev. Henry Ward Beecher* (London: S. Low, Marston, Searle and Rivingtons, 1888), p. 224.

[10] Wayne C. Eubank, "Benjamin Morgan Palmer's Thanksgiving Sermon, 1860," *Antislavery and Disunion, 1858-1861*, ed. J. Jeffery Auer (New York: Harper & Row, 1963), p. 297.

of South Carolina, defend the rights of masters in 1850.[11] Palmer's 1860 audience was largely upper class and white collar.[12] Statements made in church courts and conferences were heard by denominational leaders—both clerical and lay—who were shaping public opinion.

The larger audience received printed sermons distributed by churches, church courts or societies, or read entire sermons or abstracts in the press. Palmer's 1860 sermon received wide press coverage, and some eighty to ninety thousand copies were printed in New Orleans alone.[13] Thornwell's 1850 sermon in Charleston received a thirty-page review in New Haven's *New Englander*.[14] Beecher's sermons appeared regularly in the *Independent* from 1859-61 and Parker's were regularly and widely noted in the press.[15]

Some signs of the effect of these sermons are apparent, and some opinions have been voiced. The abolitionist revival and crusade of the first decade is judged decisive, for it determined that the slavery philosophy would not dominate the entire nation.[16] Many preachers were stirred into action by the crusade that made reformation of the church one of its first objectives. By the end of the second decade the denominational tide in the East and the West was decidedly proabolitionist.[17]

In the South, meanwhile, sermons proclaiming the duties of slaves and the rights of masters became plentiful and popular.[18] Churchmen there were early convinced that the Bible justified slavery, and both Baptists and Methodists divided on a North-South axis in 1845 when northern brethren refused to share this conviction.[19] When Thornwell in 1860 decried northern infidelity to the Constitution as sin, he countered abolitionist repudiation of slaveholding as sinful. Radicals in both sections had some theological justification for their positions. Preachers had planted germinal ideas and developed these into actions that helped lead the nation toward the crisis of 1861.

1830–1840

A radical attack upon slavery was launched in the North during the decade of the 1830's. Since 1817 the Colonization Society had provided a gradual

---

[11] James H. Thornwell, *The Rights and Duties of Masters* (Charleston: Walker and James, 1850), p. iii.

[12] Eubank, "Benjamin Morgan Palmer's Thanksgiving Sermon," pp. 296, 297.

[13] *Ibid.*, p. 309.

[14] *New Englander*, XII (February, 1854), 93-124.

[15] Beecher and Scoville, *A Biography of Rev. Henry Ward Beecher*, pp. 32, 321; Henry Steele Commager, *Theodore Parker: Yankee Crusader* (Boston: Little, Brown and Company, 1936), p. 145.

[16] Dumond, *Antislavery Origins of the Civil War*, p. 5.

[17] Smith, Handy, and Loetscher, *American Christianity*, pp. 175, 176.

[18] William Sumner Jenkins, *Pro-Slavery Thought in the Old South* (Chapel Hill: The University of North Carolina Press, 1935), pp. 213, 214; George D. Armstrong, *The Christian Doctrine of Slavery* (New York: Charles Scribner, 1857), pp. 88, 89.

[19] Mathews, *Slavery and Methodism*, p. 264; Barnes, *The Southern Baptist Convention*, p. 25.

approach to emancipation, but with the establishment of the American Antislavery Society in 1833, a new demand for immediate action was institutionalized. William Lloyd Garrison signaled the attack in the first issue of *The Liberator,* January 1, 1831. Militant devotees enlisted rapidly to implement a program of moral suasion first designed to convince masters to free slaves voluntarily and later extended to seek church and governmental action against slaveholders. Circulars flooded the mails to the South while petitions went to church courts and Congress. State and local antislavery societies proliferated, antislavery presses proclaimed immediatist principles and programs, abolitionist preachers generated fervent revivals.

Based upon a moral philosophy that declared both slaveholding and prejudice against color sinful, this program sought immediate repentance for sin and action to remove sin. Action was sought not only from individuals but also from the body politic; a nation that had the power to abolish slavery in the District of Columbia should act, and churches that had authority to deny communion to unrepentant slaveholders should exercise their disciplinary power.

Reaction in the North to these radical demands was frequently violent. Mobs stormed abolitionist meetings, destroyed their presses, attacked their speakers and editors. In such reaction the abolitionists discovered the issues of free speech, free press, and free assembly.

In the South efforts to protect the slavery system increased. From request for sectional balance of power in 1830, John C. Calhoun turned in 1837 to demand federal protection for state institutions. The decade opened with a slave insurrection in Virginia that forced lengthy debate of the slavery question in a special state convention. When in 1832 that state decided to legislate a more stringent Slave Code rather than abolish slavery, the reactionary course of the South was set. Now only justification of slavery as a positive good was tolerated. Silence of emancipation talk was sought through attempts to close the mails to abolitionist propaganda and to mute discussion of slavery in both church and civil forums.

But the effort to enforce silence was indicative of the scope of abolitionist activity in the North. The antislavery crusade was a widespread and powerful religious revival.[20] The majority of the preachers serving under the American Home Missionary Society through the northwest were active abolitionists in 1838.[21] Apparently these preachers had met some success in their efforts to make slavery a moral question, for Calhoun complained in Congress that

---

[20] Dumond, *Antislavery Origins of the Civil War,* p. 35; Matthews, *Slavery and Methodism,* p. 166.
[21] Frederick Irving Kuhns, *The American Home Missionary Society in Relation to the Antislavery Controversy in the Old Northwest* (Billings, Montana: Privately printed, 1959), pp. 1, 8.

172

public men were forced by the preaching of the sinfulness of slaveholding to stand for or against slavery as a matter of conscience.[22]

Undergirding the preaching were new thought forms. An intuitional ethic challenged the established utilitarian ethic.[23] Concern for immediate application of right principles replaced sober reasoning about the consequences of an action. These fixed, unchanging principles were laws of God written into the original nature of man and recognized by man intuitively.

> The framework of nature, formed on the model of the divine law, cannot fail, when enlightened by celestial truth, to employ its original susceptibilities and powers, in direct, determined, ceaseless opposition to iniquity. In his efforts to reform mankind, the philanthropist may bring all these powers and susceptibilities into full and active subserviency to his design. He has only to adjust his exertions to an accurate discrimination between right and wrong, and human nature, from the most retired recesses of the soul, will rush forth to his assistance.[24]

So fixed in man were these principles that when he determined to do the right thing the entire force of his original nature—that nature "formed on the model of the divine law"—rushed to aid in the accomplishment of his intent. Fixed also was God's determination to reward reformers who employed their powers in opposition to evils, and to punish the unrepentant who stubbornly resisted his law.[25]

From such views of God's law and man's nature abolitionists derived their doctrine of the sinfulness of slaveholding. Since God had created all men as moral agents who could only realize their moral potential by choosing obedience to his law—that law to which their understanding and conscience were tuned—denying any man such freedom of choice by making him subservient to a master's will was sinful.[26] Slavery, they insisted, was a moral question and not merely a political question as the Colonization movement had viewed it.[27] It was a sinful system of the kind of oppression repeatedly condemned in the Bible.[28] Guilt for the sin was shared by the entire nation that permitted perpetuation of slavery, and non-slaveholding Christians were duty bound to warn slaveholders of God's certain judgment and punishment.[29] The South's plea for noninterference with her unique institution

[22] *Debates in Congress*, XII, ii, 2184-88.

[23] Wilson Smith, *Professors and Public Ethics* (Ithaca, New York: Cornell University Press, 1956), pp. 186, 188, 208.

[24] Beriah Green, *Four Sermons Preached in the Chapel of Western Reserve College* (Cleveland: Office of the Herald, 1833), p. 14.

[25] *Ibid.*, p. 7.

[26] Gilbert H. Barnes and Dwight L. Dumond, eds., *The Letters of Theodore Dwight Weld and Angelina Grimke Weld and Sarah Grimke, 1822-1844* (New York: Appleton-Century, 1934), I, 120.

[27] Green, *Four Sermons*, p. 24.

[28] James Taylor Dickinson, *A Sermon* (Norwich: Anti-Slavery Society, 1834), pp. 6-14. In this Fourth-of-July sermon, published by the Anti-Slavery Society, Dickinson supported the abolitionist position with numerous references to scripture.

[29] *Ibid.*, pp. 4, 5.

could no longer delay action mandatory if the Union was to escape God's punishment. Local laws protecting slavery should be nullified by men obedient to the higher law of God.[30]

Not all northern preachers accepted this doctrine with its radical demand for immediate action. The Colonization Society had many friends. Some denied that slaveholding was categorically sinful and warned against impolitic immediate action. Let southern men have time to correct abuses in the slavery system through gradual legislative changes, they asked.[31] Even the Quakers, who had prodded the national conscience on the slavery question since colonial days, now for the most part rejected the radical approach with its attendant violence.[32] Moderate spokesmen, recalling French radicalism, feared the tyranny of an anarchic majority and turned attention toward southern pleas for obedience to existing laws and for united action against destructive revolutionary forces in society.[33] Actions in church courts during the decade suggest that most northern churchmen were eager to maintain peace and were not convinced by radical immediatist rhetoric. Methodist leaders in 1836 sought silence on the whole question of slavery; Congregationalists in New England began to deny abolitonist use of their pulpits in the second half of the decade; Roman Catholic clergymen condemned Garrisonian thought as contrary to Christian morality.[34] Mob violence was not always blamed upon the abolitionists, however, for when antislavery speakers were attacked and their places of meeting burned, some preachers defended freedom of speech and assembly.[35] These asked responsible legal action against proslavery mobs. One mediating position recognized that Christians could not interfere with civil institutions legally established, but they could labor to change laws by the will of the people expressed constitutionally.[36]

Southern sermons voiced interpretations of both God's law and natural law that clashed with abolitionist views. Equating the terms "servant" and "slave" in the scriptures, Presbyterian James Smylie of Mississippi thus found

[30] *Ibid.*, p. 18.

[31] Horace Bushnell, A *Discourse on the Slavery Question* (Hartford: Case Library, 1839), pp. 5, 16; George Duffield, A *Sermon on American Slavery: Its Nature and the Duty of Christians* (Detroit: J. S. and S. A. Bagg, 1840), pp. 21, 22; Joshua L. Wilson, *Relation and Duties of Servants and Masters* (Cincinnati: Hefley, 1839), p. 32.

[32] Thomas E. Drake, *Quakers and Slavery in America* (New Haven: Yale University Press, 1950), pp. 141-49, 157-62.

[33] Edwin Hall, "Submission to Civil Authority," *American National Preacher,* XIII (March, 1839), 3-40; see Richard Hofstadter, *The American Political Tradition and the Men Who Made It* (New York: Vintage Books, 1958), pp. 81-84, for the role of this fear in American politics.

[34] Mathews, *Slavery and Methodism*, pp. 141-44.

[35] William Henry Furness, A *Sermon Occasioned by the Destruction of Pennsylvania Hall* (Philadelphia: J. C. Clark, 1838), p. 127; Beriah Green, *The Martyr: A Discourse in Commemoration of the Martyrdom of the Rev. Elijah P. Lovejoy* (New York: n. p., 1838), pp. 5, 6.

[36] Wilson, *Relations and Duties of Servants and Masters*, p. 30.

abundant testimony to the existence of slavery in biblical times. Searching for specific condemnation of slavery and finding none in the scriptures, he concluded that God's law did not condemn slaveholding as sinful, and therefore Christians had no duty to seek either immediate or gradual abolition.[37] His proslavery position soon became "violently and exclusively dominant" in most of the lower South.[38] Samuel Dunwoody, in a sermon published in 1837 by the South Carolina Methodist Conference, further claimed that God made express biblical provision for perpetual slavery and condemned the Negro race to continued existence in slavery.[39]

Samuel Crothers, an Ohio delegate to the 1833 American Antislavery Society meeting, attempted refutation of Smylie by drawing a distinction between Hebrew and pagan slavery. Hebrew slavery was voluntary servitude of a debtor, and provision was made for his emancipation. He was not kept in perpetual bondage. Thus God's law did not endorse the slavery system of the South.[40]

While the abolitionist declared civil law subordinate to natural law, the South identified natural law and God's law with the positive law of the particular states.[41] Dunwoody cited the New Testament injunction that Christians be obedient to the civil authorities, for such authorities were ordained of God. He then inferred that a slaveholder who acted under civil laws ordained of God could not be condemned as a sinner.[42] The pulpit, therefore, should be silent about slavery.[43] Already Thomas Dew, the political theorist, had credited God with the design of a society composed of superior and inferior men in which slavery was a good institution, and later on James Thornwell, the preacher, justified slavery as an ordinance of God.[44] In time, natural became identified with historical or habitual in southern thought, and slavery that had been a part of most societies in the past was justified as a part of the natural order of life.

[37] Walter B. Posey, *The Presbyterian Church in the Southwest, 1778-1838* (Richmond: John Knox Press, 1952), pp. 79, 80. Smylie's argument was later detailed in his *Review of a Letter from Chillicothe Presbytery* (Woodville: W. A. Morris, 1836).

[38] Leonard W. Bacon, *A History of American Christianity* (New York: Charles Scribner's Sons, 1901), p. 278.

[39] Samuel Dunwoody, *A Sermon Upon the Subject of Slavery* (Columbia: S. Weir, 1837), pp. 6, 10, 11.

[40] Samuel Crothers, *The Gospel of the Typical Servitude* (Hamilton, Ohio: Gradner and Gibbon, 1835), pp. 3, 5. For a detailed study of the forced constructions of scripture used in the slavery debate, see Caroline L. Shanks, "The Biblical Anti-Slavery Argument of the Decade 1830-1840," *Journal of Negro History* XVI, No. 2 (April, 1931), 132-57.

[41] Carl L. Becker, *The Declaration of Independence: A Study in the History of Political Ideas* (New York: Random House, 1942), p. 254.

[42] Dunwoody, *A Sermon Upon the Subject of Slavery*, pp. 12, 13.

[43] *Ibid.*, p. 24.

[44] Becker, *The Declaration of Independence*, p. 247; Thornwell, *Thoughts Suited to the Present Crisis* (Columbia: A. S. Johnston, 1850), p. 30.

1840–1850

Slavery's expansion into or exclusion from the territories was at issue in the decade of the 1840's. While some opposed any discussion of slavery in Congress, others pressed pro- or antislavery demands. Tempers were especially hot during the 1846-47 debates over the Wilmot Proviso where proponents asked exclusion of slavery from any territories acquired by the Mexican War while opponents denounced exclusion as northern aggression. The controversy moved toward crisis in 1849 when California, requesting entrance as a free state, threatened the Union's delicate balance of fifteen free and fifteen slave states.

Within the church, abolitionism continued to be both commended and condemned.[45] While some preachers declared slaveholding a civil matter over which the church lacked any authority and about which she should not speak, others proclaimed the doctrine and policies of the antislavery societies urging Christians to vote against the extension of slavery and to refuse to obey proslavery laws.

The demand from some northern pulpits for Christian political activity rested upon the supremacy of God's law and his opposition to slavery. Not only should unjust—and therefore ungodly—state laws be changed or nullified, but even the American Constitution should be changed, ended, or broken if it contradicted God's law.[46] Aimed at southern demands for fidelity to the sacred compact, the Constitution, and for acceptance of civil law as natural law, this demand was rooted in natural law and natural rights concepts once prevalent in Puritan England and Revolutionary America.[47] Conscience and moral sensitivity should determine national policy; the pulpit should enlighten conscience and shape moral judgment; persistent agitation and conscientious voting should establish new directions and legislate new laws.[48]

To preachers who impatiently watched the slavocracy gain power in Washington, the Mexican War was especially repugnant. Seeing it as a conspiracy to extend and perpetuate slavery, they called for popular protest or rebellion.[49]

---

[45] By 1851, Thornwell was echoing Calhoun's earlier complaint that the conviction that slavery was a sin was determining national policy, *Collected Writings* (Richmond: Presbyterian Committee of Publication, 1873), IV, 381-82.

[46] Theodore Parker, "A Sermon on Slavery," *The Collected Works of Theodore Parker*, ed. Frances Power Cobbe (London: Trubner and Company, 1863), V, 13.

[47] These concepts are exposed in Clinton Rossiter, *The Political Thought of the American Revolution* (New York: Harcourt, Brace & World, 1963), pp. 91, 92.

[48] Horace Bushnell, *Politics Under the Law of God* (Hartford: Case Library, 1844), pp. 12, 14, 15; S. S. Schmucker, *The Christian Pulpit, the Rightful Guardian of Morals, in Political no Less Than in Private Life* (Gettysburg: H. C. Neinstedt, 1846), pp. 22, 27; Horace James, *Our Duties to the Slave* (Boston: Richardson and Filmer, 1847), pp. 16-19; Lemuel Foster, *Inquisition for Blood* (Alton: Telegraph Office, 1847), p. 15.

[49] Parker, June 7, 1848, *Speeches, Addresses and Occasional Sermons* (Boston: Crosby and Nichols, 1857), I, 72, 73, 130-32; Schmucker, *The Christian Pulpit*, pp. 31, 32.

Denominational activity evidenced ferment. Slavery was a factor in the Presbyterian schism of 1838, and the continuing tensions between divisions of that church were indicated in rival Ohio church courts. The Synod of Cincinnati (New School) heard extended biblical support for the classical abolitionist doctrine in 1841, and two years later the Synod of Cincinnati (Old School) heard an eight-hour attack upon the abolitionist's scriptural argument and political philosophy.[50] Although establishment of the Wesleyan Methodist Connection of America in 1843 siphoned off the most radical element in Methodism, yet sectional division followed after the 1844 General Conference refused to repudiate the Methodist antislavery heritage.[51] Baptists rejected demands that slaveholders be appointed as missionaries in 1845, and southern dissidents withdrew to form a sectional church. Thus the North refused to approve slavery; meanwhile the abolitionist doctrine was refuted in the South, where antislavery radicals were labeled sinners who should be denied communion.[52]

Such rifts in church life were indicative of the increasing strains upon the weakening fabric of the Union. Alarmed pastors requested respect for an obedience to the Constitution as a solemn compact binding all Americans.[53] Let men obey laws. Let them reject insurrectionary efforts and appeals for insubordination, that were more evil than the slavery the proposed actions opposed.[54] The prevailing Quaker abhorrence of radical action was expressed in an 1843 Philadelphia sermon by George F. White.[55] Old School Presbyterians, scorning abolitionism, resolved that slaveholders should not be denied communion, for the scriptures did not term their institution sinful. They thus postponed sectional division until 1861.[56]

But voices of compromise and peace were doomed to be overpowered by four comparatively young voices that would be decisive during the final years of the debate. Theodore Parker was only thirty-one when he embraced the abolitionist doctrine in an 1841 sermon. By 1850, Unitarians had closed their church doors against this radical prophet, but crowds heard him every Sunday in Boston's Melodeon Theatre. Henry Ward Beecher, only thirty-four when he preached three antislavery sermons in Indianapolis, soon moved to Brooklyn's Plymouth Church where in 1847, on his first Sunday, he vowed

[50] Jonathan Blanchard, *Sermon on Slaveholding* (Cincinnati: n. p., 1842); George Junkin, *The Integrity of Our National Union* (Cincinnati: R. P. Donogh, 1843).

[51] Mathews, *Slavery and Methodism*, pp. 231, 265-80.

[52] W. T. Hamilton, *Duties of Masters and Slaves Respectively; or, Domestic Slavery as Sanctioned by the Bible* (Mobile: F. H. Brooks, 1844), p. 18.

[53] Gardner Spring, *The Danger and Hope of the American People* (New York: John F. Trow, 1843), p. 16; Henry A. Rowland, *The Frame-Work of Liberty* (New York: William S. Dorr, 1840), p. 24; Junkin, *The Integrity of Our National Union*, iv.

[54] Spring, *The Danger and Hope of the American People*, p. 18; Charles S. Porter, *Our Country's Danger and Security* (Utica: R. W. Roberts, 1844), p. 10.

[55] Drake, *Quakers and Slavery in America*, p. 161.

[56] *Biblical Repertory*, XVIII, No. 4 (July, 1854), 440.

to denounce slavery.[57] James H. Thornwell, only thirty-five when he moderated the 1847 Presbyterian Assembly that rejected abolitionism, would preach definitive proslavery sermons in the next decade and prepare the 1861 proslavery "Address to the Churches." With Thornwell in South Carolina was Benjamin Morgan Palmer who at twenty-five became pastor of Columbia's First Presbyterian Church in 1843. We can assume that Palmer shared Thornwell's 1847 conviction,

As to the other opinion [that the church should seek abolition], it mistakes entirely the true vocation of the Church. It is a spiritual body, and has no right to interfere directly with the civil relations of society. . . . As it is clear from the Bible that Slavery is not a sin, the Church, *as such*, has no more right to seek its extinction than to seek a change in the political structure of a nation.[58]

Such was the justification for silence in the pulpit on the slavery question, but this silence would eventually be broken, and Thornwell and Palmer would speak effectively for the radical South, while Parker and Beecher spoke for the radical North.

1850-1860

Sectional tensions were generally reduced by the Compromise of 1850, but its Fugitive Slave Act angered abolitionists, and its action against slavery in the District of Columbia aroused southern radicals. Four years later, concern for the Kansas-Nebraska Act's apparent repeal of the Missouri Compromise and its establishment of a doctrine of Congressional noninterference with slavery in the territories produced political realignments and the Republican Party. Fremont, the 1856 Republican candidate, advocated congressional control of territorial slavery to a nation made wary by bleeding Kansas of the impolitic popular sovereignty doctrine. Then the 1857 Dred Scott decision intensified opposition to the slavocracy. During the next year, Lincoln declared extension of slavery a moral issue and warned that national decision was mandatory. Antithetical sectional decisions were expressed defensively when, after federal force was employed at Harper's Ferry, Free Soil advocates declared Washington captured by the slavocracy, and after the election of Lincoln, the South charged Republicans would turn federal force against slavery. Tensions reduced by compromise in 1850 were tempered for conflict in 1861.

The South's scriptural justification for slavery and refutation of philosophical attacks are seen best in Thornwell. Upon the premise that society was an ordinance of God, not an invention of man, he considered slaves responsible agents voluntarily fulfilling the duties of the permanent station in which

---

[57] Parker, "Sermon on Slavery," *Works*, V, 1-14; Beecher and Scoville, *A Biography of Rev. Henry Ward Beecher*, pp. 196, 218.

[58] Thornwell, *Collected Writings*, IV, 501.

God placed them.[59] God assigned the duties of each station and an encroachment upon the rights of a person was anything that obstructed performance of the station's duties.[60] A Christian slave, one who had found true freedom in Christ, willingly gave his service to his master as unto Christ. The master's right to command and the slave's duty to obey were ordained by God.[61] Forty-one of his fifty-one pages supported the master's right to the slave's obedient service. Magnifying the struggle between opposing social systems, he said:

The parties in the conflict are . . . atheists, socialists, communists, red republicans, jacobins, on the one side, and the friends of order and of regulated freedom on the other. In one word, the world is the battle ground—Christianity and Atheism are combatants: and the progress of humanity the stake.[62]

Moderate Thanksgiving day sermons in the North that year frequently called for obedience to law and patience until courts could decide the legality of the compromise. Radicalism of all kinds was decried.[63] Slavery was condemned, but, since the union was their primary concern, obedience to the Fugitive Slave Act was mandatory.[64]

In Boston, Theodore Parker demanded disobedience to the Act that involved citizens of free states in the capture and return of fugitive slaves. The absolute, universal moral law required men to resist the pursuing marshal and rescue the slave in defiance of civil statutes. The fugitive had the natural right to kill the marshal in his self-defense. The marshal's duty to moral law was higher than his duty to his oath of office, and thus he should not enforce the Fugitive Slave Act. Every man's first duty—even the marshal's— was to his own integrity before God.[65] In Brooklyn, Samuel Spear asked use of lawful measures to correct unjust law, if possible, but stated that man

[59] Thornwell, *The Rights and Duties of Masters*, pp. 24, 25. The text for this sermon preached on May 26, 1850, was Colossians 4:5.

[60] *Ibid.*, p. 40. Becker, *The Declaration of Independence*, p. 253, notes that by 1850 Calhoun had rejected as fallacies derived from a false conception of nature the self-evident truths proclaimed in the 1776 Declaration. Thornwell shared this rejection.

[61] *Ibid.*, pp. 24, 25, 29, 30.

[62] *Ibid.*, p. 14. On Fast Day, December 6, 1850, the South Carolina General Assembly heard similar doctrine preached by Whitefoord Smith in his "God, the Refuge of His People" (Columbia: A. S. Johnston, 1850).

[63] John C. Lord, *"The Higher Law" in its Application to the Fugitive Slave Bill* (Buffalo: Geo. H. Derby, 1851); Henry Green, *Our National Union* (n. p., n. d.); N. S. S. Beman, *Characteristics of the Age* (Troy: Young and Hartt, 1851); William P. Breed, *Discourse Mainly Upon the Importance of the American Union* (Steubenville: Messenger & Job Office, 1850).

[64] Becker, *The Declaration of Independence*, pp. 241-44, indicates that northern business interests cried, "Liberty and Union, one and inseparable." But, more concerned for the Union than for principles of the Declaration, they began to call the self-evident truths of that document "glittering generalities" and abstractions.

[65] Parker, "The Function and Place of Conscience, in Relation to the Laws of Men: A Sermon for the Times," *Works*, V, 148, 150, 157, 160.

179

was bound to obey God's supreme law even if it led him to action for which he suffered civil penalty.[66]

When Congress debated the Kansas-Nebraska Act in 1854, charges of broken faith and establishment of a new policy were flung from northern pulpits. Violating compacts made in both the Missouri Compromise and the Northwest Ordinance, the Act would admit slavery to territory heretofore legally closed to it. Principles of the 1776 Declaration were at stake: Were all men born free, or was a slave's child born a slave as civil law decreed? Was this civil dictum "intrinsically right" so that it could be applied in a new territory? If right to be applied in one new territory it could be applied to every territory, every race.[67] Bushnell pleaded for maintenance of God-supported principle.[68]

But the Bill passed and almost every northern pulpit protested.[69] Everyman's freedom was now in jeopardy. The advance of slavery must be stopped.[70] The revolution against liberty was begun, for law and order now enforced tyranny.[71] Would men choose moral progress or moral regression, democracy or despotism? Let men recall New England monuments and holidays commemorating heroes who, in the name of justice defied creeds and kings.[72]

The cry against new policy was louder, the charge of slavocracy conspiracy more insistent, during the 1856 controversy over "bleeding Kansas." Let the pulpits declare the truth about slavery and persuade men to vote against its expansion.[73] Let Christians send arms into Kansas.[74] the physical attack upon Sumner in Congress had unmasked the brutal character of the slavocracy that designed to control the nation.[75] When federal force was used against John Brown at Harper's Ferry in 1859, the proslavery stance of Washington was fully revealed.[76]

[66] Samuel Spear, *The Law-Abiding Conscience, and the Higher Law Conscience; with Remarks on the Fugitive Slave Question* (New York: Lambert and Lane 1850), pp. 23-26.

[67] Charles Beecher, *A Sermon on the Nebraska Bill* (New York: Oliver and Brothers, 1854), pp. 5, 9, 10, 13.

[68] Horace Bushnell, *The Northern Iron* (Hartford: L. E. Hunt, 1854), pp. 14-22.

[69] Cole, *The Social Ideals*, p. 215.

[70] Theodore Parker, "The Dangers Which Threaten the Rights of Man in America," *Old South Leaflets* (Boston: n. d.), No. 80, pp. 8, 9.

[71] Thomas Wentworth Higginson, *Massachusetts in Mourning* (Boston: James Monroe and Company, 1854), p. 12.

[72] Parker, "The Law of God and the Statutes of Men," *Works*, V, 230, 231, 243; "The Dangers Which Threaten . . . ," V. 2, 4.

[73] Octavius B. Frotheringham, *The Last Signs* (New York: John A. Gray, 1856), p. 19; George Thacher, *No Fellowship with Slavery* (Meridan: L. R. Webb, 1846), p. 10; Noah Porter, *Civil Liberty* (New York: Pudney and Russell, 1856), p. 21.

[74] J. E. Roy, *Kansas: Her Struggle and Her Defense* (n. p.: Wright, Medill Day and Company, 1856), pp. 30-32.

[75] Frotheringham, *The Last Signs*, pp. 10, 16.

[76] Daniel Rice, *Harper's Ferry—Its Lessons* (Lafayette: Luse, 1860), pp. 7, 15-17; Beecher and Scoville, *A Biography of Rev. Henry Ward Beecher*, pp. 301-2.

The South, already alerted by Republican campaign appeals and the Harper's Ferry incident, reacted quickly to Lincoln's election. South Carolina called a secession convention to meet December 17. On November 21, a Day of Fasting and Prayer, Thornwell made secession a matter of Christian duty. By breaking solemn contracts, Carolina's opponents had committed the sin of perfidy: Congress had transcended powers granted her by the states; states had refused to restore fugitives and to grant slavery access to new territory. If the North desired release from obligations under the Constitution, then the South should be permitted release from hers. His peroration promised:

Thermopylae was lost, but the moral power of Thermopylae will continue as long as valour and freedom have a friend, and reverence for law be one of the noblest sentiments of the human soul. Let it be our great concern to know God's will. Let *right* and *duty* be our watchword, liberty, regulated by law, our goal; and leaning upon the arms of everlasting strength, we shall achieve a name, whether we succeed or fail, that posterity will not willingly let die.[77]

Duty to the South, the slave, the civilized world, and God demand the perpetuation and extension of slavery, said Benjamin Palmer on Thanksgiving, November 29, in New Orleans.[78] R. K. Porter reaffirmed the appeals to duty and to defense against an aggressively and lustfully crusading North that had departed from the truth of God.[79]

In the North reaction to secession was mixed. Some pulpits sought a middle way while others either advocated a permissive attitude toward secession or supported the southern rebellion. Rejecting all radical positions, the mediators asked respect for civil authority, toleration of slavery within the slave states, and patient waiting for circumstances to change.[80] Support for the South in New York City by a Presbyterian pastor and a Jewish rabbi rested upon biblical interpretation.[81] On the border some doubted that secession could be prevented or that border states should permit the North to attempt prevention.[82] In Boston, Wendell Phillips rejoiced that disunion finally arrayed the sides decisively after thirty years of debate. Let the South

[77] Thornwell, "Sermons on National Sins," *Collected Writings*, IV, 512, 522, 528, 530, 533, 547, 548. The Presbyterian Synod of South Carolina resolved that South Carolina represented God's truth in the crisis and gave her revolting citizens its blessing. *Southern Presbyterian*, December 8, 1860.

[78] Eubank, "Benjamin Morgan Palmer's Thanksgiving Sermon," p. 298.

[79] R. K. Porter, *Christian Duty in the Present Crisis* (Savannah: John M. Cooper, 1860), pp. 6, 11, 13, 15.

[80] George D. Boardman, *Loyalty to Law, the Duty of the Christian Patriot* (New York: French and Wheat, 1860); Horace Bushnell, *The Census and Slavery* (Hartford: L. E. Hunt, 1860); C. M. Butler, *Republican Loyalty* (Washington: Polkinhorn, 1860).

[81] Henry J. Van Dyke, "The Character and Influence of Abolitionism"; M. J. Raphall, "Bible View of Slavery," *Fast Day Sermons; or, The Pulpit on the State of the Country* (New York: Rudd and Carleton, 1861), pp. 127-76, 227-46.

[82] *Southern Presbyterian*, December 22, 1860, January 19, 1861. Among preachers cited were Thomas A. Hoyt, Louisville, and S. R. Wilson, Cincinnati.

go, he cried.[83] Henry Ward Beecher repudiated any pro Union compromise to appease the South and demanded strong federal action against secession.[84] He, too, rejoiced in decisive action. Now liberty, like Lazarus, was about to be given new life.[85]

The shots at Fort Sumter were for Phillips the "yell of pirates against the Declaration of Independence" as he shifted from desire for peaceful recognition of secession to advocacy of militant self-defense against the Confederacy.[86] Beecher charged the nation to draw opposing lines according to deep convictions. A peace that required two-thirds of the Union to accept slavery and surrender freedom of speech would only enervate the American eagle. Let men have faith in America as the refuge of liberty for all the earth. Let America go forward! [87]

Conclusions

Both aggressor and defender preachers stepped into American pulpits soon after 1830 to discuss slavery on the basis of scripture. Their sermons voiced moral and political concepts that had sprung from different sources and would develop pervasive sectional convictions. The primary issue was the sinfulness of slaveholding. Proclaiming biblical justification of slavery, and therefore denying the abolitionists' doctrine of slavery's sinfulness, the South moved on to claim divine ordination of the civil laws regulating slavery. Aggressor preachers appealed to Higher Law in their rejection of the sanctity of civil law. Such rejection sometimes called for civil disobedience and condemnation of the Constitution that compromised with slavery.

Church schisms during the second decade of the ferment signified growing sectional allegiance to conflicting doctrines. Aroused by the Mexican War, some northern preachers demanded increased pulpit efforts to shape a righteous national policy. Efforts of the slavocracy to extend and perpetuate slavery in new western territories should be blocked by voters who expressed their conscience, reaffirmed right principle, and rejected compromise. The development of the conscience of the voter was the task of the pulpit. Thus the South's demand for pulpit silence about slavery was countered by northern insistence that national decisions about evils were matters of religious conviction and therefore the concern of the preacher.

The Compromise of 1850 stimulated new justification of slavery in the

---

[83] Wendell Phillips, "Disunion," *Speeches, Lectures, and Letters* (Boston: Lee and Shephard, 1902), pp. 343, 345, 355.

[84] Sermons on November 29, 1860 and January 4, 1861; Beecher and Scoville, *A Biography of Rev. Henry Ward Beecher*, pp. 306, 307.

[85] Henry Ward Beecher, "Peace, Be Still," *Fast Day Sermons*, p. 291.

[86] Phillips, "Under the Flag," *Speeches, Lectures, and Letters*, pp. 400, 414.

[87] Sermon on April 14, 1861; Beecher and Scoville, *A Biography of Rev. Henry Ward Beecher*, pp. 310, 311.

South, intensified appeals to Higher Law in the North, and evoked appeals for compromise in both sections. Tensions were accentuated as new territories were acquired and decisions were made about their slave or free status. While northern preachers warned that the nation could not much longer exist half slave and half free, southern preachers invented arguments supporting disunion. The shots at Fort Sumter rang in the ears of men prepared by preachers to defend antagonistic sectional positions as God's truth.

Critics of these sermons must array the premises of the preachers and evaluate them in terms of enduring truth and contemporary life. Both sides could not be right, yet both sides claimed to be right. War did not decide the issue of truth, for war did not vanquish thought forms and convictions. Studies are needed to search out the basic thought patterns and to expose their relationship to the lives of the people who were moved to action by these preachers.

9

CIVIL WAR PREACHING

Charles Stewart

When the United States began to splinter following Abraham Lincoln's election in 1860, perhaps no group had been longer and more deeply involved in the sectional disputes than the clergy. Slavery became inextricably enmeshed in morals and religion soon after the completion of the American Constitution, and the pulpit found itself in a growing entanglement from which it could not escape.[1] During the decades from 1790 to 1840, clergymen migrated to sections of the country most compatible with their views on slavery.[2] This migration made sections even more one-sided and tended to leave both ardent abolitionists and slavery proponents without an effective opposition. Indeed, the abolition movement gained much of its impetus from ex-southern clergymen who moved to northern states determined to bring an end to the institution of slavery.[3]

Charles Darwin's theories, apparently undermining the fundamental religious premise that God controlled the universe and every action in it, did not invade the United States until after the Civil War. Thus the clergy in America, an avenue to the ear of God, was a significant molder of public opinion.[4] The immanence of God as a real force in human affairs was still an important factor in the thinking of Americans.[5] Abolitionists and defenders of slavery naturally turned to the Bible for proof that God did or did not approve of slavery, and the clergy, as authorities on biblical teachings, became spokesmen for both sides of the controversy.

However separate clerics were geographically, it became increasingly difficult for them to avoid the sectional issues, for their annual denominational

[1] Chester Forrester Dunham, "The Attitude of the Northern Clergy Toward the South, 1860-1865" (unpublished Ph.D. dissertation, Department of History, The University of Chicago, 1939), chap. 2.

[2] Dwight Lowell Dumond, *Antislavery Origins of the Civil War in the United States* (Ann Arbor, Michigan: The University of Michigan Press, 1959), pp. 6-8.

[3] *Ibid.*

[4] Dunham, "The Attitude of the Northern Clergy Toward the South," pp. 1-5; and Ralph Henry Gabriel, *The Course of American Democratic Thought* (New York: The Ronald Press, 1956), p. 28.

[5] Gabriel, *The Course of American Democratic Thought*, pp. 16-18.

184

assemblies brought representatives together from all geographical regions. The inevitable conflicts occurred. In 1845, long before the nation experienced actual political division, the Baptist and Methodist churches split into totally separate northern and southern churches.[6] Presbyterians, Episcopalians, and Lutherans maintained shaky unities until the nation itself divided; then, one by one, they too separated into northern and southern churches. Only relatively small religious groups, notably the Roman Catholics, Jews, and Cumberland Presbyterians, remained intact.[7]

When southern states began to secede in the months after Lincoln's election, clerical reaction seems to have been as mixed as public reaction. Some preachers felt that secession would not last, while others seemed to believe that a division would have its advantages. Some argued that peace could be maintained if the anti- and proslavery radicals would moderate their views, while others warned that a division of states so closely related for decades could only result in a bloody military conflict.[8] Some clergy pleaded for compromise, and others demanded a stern maintenance of "principle" at any cost.

The Civil War Begins

In the early morning of April 12, 1861, public and clerical speculations became purely academic, for the bombardment of Fort Sumter in Charleston harbor had begun. The nation was at war with itself. All serious attempts at compromise ended, and the majority of clergymen became ardent supporters of either the Union or the Confederacy.[9] Preachers soon discovered that they could avoid partisan politics in their sermons, but silence on supporting their respective governments would lead to severe criticism from their congregations.[10] Clergy preached sectional unity and loyalty before mass meet-

[6] Oliver Saxon Heckman, "Northern Church Penetration of the South, 1860-1880" (unpublished Ph.D. dissertation, Department of History, Duke University, 1939), pp. 11-13.

[7] *Ibid.*, p. 34. Groups like the Congregationalists, Unitarians, and Universalists were essentially northern denominations and thus did not split over sectional issues.

[8] The following sermons illustrate northern and southern preaching in the weeks prior to Fort Sumter: Henry A. Boardman, *What Christianity Demands of Us at the Present Crisis* (Philadelphia: J. B. Lippincott, 1860); Zachary Eddy, *Secession—Shall It Be Peace or War?* (Northampton, Massachusetts: Trumbull and Gere, 1861); C. C. Pinckney, *Nebuchadnezzar's Fault and Fall* (Charleston, South Carolina: A. J. Burke, 1861); and E. T. Winkler, *Duties of the Citizen Soldier* (Charleston, South Carolina: A. J. Burke, 1861).

[9] Stuart W. Chapman, "The Protestant Campaign for the Union" (unpublished Ph.D. dissertation, Department of History, Yale University, 1939), p. 16.

[10] Writers like Dunham, "The Attitude of the Northern Clergy," pp. 140-47, and Chapman, "The Protestant Campaign," pp. 248-73, note that some clergymen in both North and South were critical of the war and its administration, some even outright disloyal to the sections in which they resided. Writers also agree, however, that clerical disloyalty is difficult to assess and that the number of such clergymen was not large. Not a single note of disloyalty or even severe criticism of home section was found in the sermons analyzed for this study.

185

ings of citizens, state legislatures and assemblies, and church congregations. Sundays, days of fast, and days of thanksgiving offered them an abundance of speaking opportunities.[11]

During the four long and bloody years of the Civil War, Union and Confederate preachers never ceased to sermonize on the conflict; this much the records clearly show. But what specific issues and arguments did clergymen develop? In their opinions, what were the causes for which they were fighting? How did preachers adapt to their sectional audiences? How did their sermons change during periods of victory and defeat, or as the war dragged on for four years? To answer these questions, fifteen northern and fifteen southern sermons have been analyzed for each of three arbitrary periods of the war: (1) the early period, April 12, 1861, to January 1, 1862; (2) the middle period, January 1, 1862, to July 1, 1863; and (3) the late period, July 1, 1863, to April, 1865.[12] The total of ninety sermons includes manuscripts from Baptist, Episcopalian, Congregational, Universalist, Unitarian, Lutheran, Methodist, and Jewish clergymen.

The Early Period

By the time the guns were silenced at Fort Sumter, the martial spirit had captured the northern and southern states.[13] Enthusiastic pledges of support for either the Union or the Confederacy were exceeded only by confidence in a short and victorious conflict. Unionists were certain that the southern gentry would flee in terror at the sight of northern might, and Confederates were just as confident that, even if the northerners were brave enough to fight, they would plead for peace after their first defeat. Lincoln exhibited northern confidence when, on April 15, 1861, he issued a call for 75,000 volunteers to serve for only *three months.*

During the early months after Sumter, both sides prepared for the "decisive" battle that would either end succession or win southern independence. There were minor victories and minor defeats for each side, and strange names like Philippi Races and Big Bethel appeared in newspapers with the first casualty lists. All was ready by mid-July for the "showdown." A Union force of 30,000 men moved out of Washington and into Northern Viriginia,

[11] Chapman, "The Protestant Campaign," chap. 15.

[12] These periods appear to the author to have decisive starting and closing events and to include military, economic, and political incidents that clearly separate them one from another. The historical backgrounds presented for each period will aid in explaining the author's selection and delineation of the early, middle, and late periods.

[13] Discussions of the historical backgrounds of the three periods of the Civil War are based on the following sources: J. G. Randall, *The Civil War and Reconstruction* (New York: D. C. Heath and Company, 1953); Bruce Catton, *This Hallowed Ground* (Garden City, New York: Doubleday, 1956); Ralph Newman and E. B. Long, *The Picture Chronicle*, Vol. II: *The Civil War* (New York: Grosset and Dunlap, 1956); and Otto Eisenschiml and Ralph Newman, *The American Iliad*, Vol. I: *The Civil War* (New York: Grosset and Dunlap, 1956).

and from the south a Confederate force of 32,000 moved to confront it at Manassas Junction. A bitter and confused battle raged throughout the day (July 21, 1861) with the greater part of the fighting taking place along the little stream called Bull Run. For a time it appeared that the Union army would by victorious, but fresh Confederate reinforcements began a slow turn of the battle that became a frantic, disastrous rout of the Union forces. Washington, only a few miles away, was in grave danger. However, the Confederate army, badly bloodied, was in a state of disorder nearly as serious as that of the Unionists. The remainder of 1861 saw no major battles, but northern armies suffered losses at Springfield and Lexington, Missouri, and at Ball's Bluff near Leesburg, Virginia.

Thus, the early period ended with each side determined to win and a little less optimistic about a short, easy conflict. Southern states exuded confidence and pride in their victories. Northern states, with little to brag about, spent the winter months preparing for the decisive battles they felt would take place in the spring.

Early Period Preaching

Throughout the early period, government calls for days of fast or thanksgiving and military events prompted clergymen to preach on the war, its causes, its effects, and its probable outcome. The basic premise of these sermons was almost universally that God, as creator and ruler of the universe, controlled all earthly events and powers. The Rev. Thomas Smyth, pastor of the First Presbyterian Church in Charleston, South Carolina, declared, "The government of this world of ours . . . is upon His shoulder, and all power, over all flesh, is put into His hands. He supports all, permits all, restrains all, and limits all." [14] Northern clergymen were equally certain of God's power. "We should habitually recognize God as the determiner of events," the Rev. Seth Sweetser stated in the Central Church of Worcester, Massachusetts.[15]

Inevitably clerics concluded that if God determined all earthly events, then he must have caused war. Speaking before the Georgia Legislature on November 15, 1861, the Rev. Henry H. Tucker exclaimed that "it is all important for *us* to remember,—that GOD is in the war. *He* brought it upon us." [16] Scriptural texts like the following were selected to prove God's involvement in and approval of the war: "The Lord is a man of war: the Lord

[14] Thomas Smyth, *The Battle of Fort Sumter: Its Mystery and Miracle: God's Mastery and Mercy* (Columbia, South Carolina: Southern Guardian Press, 1861), p. 8. Delivered on June 13, 1861.

[15] Seth Sweetser, *The Strength of the Battle* (Worcester, Massachusetts: Transcript Office, 1861), p. 6. Delivered on September 26, 1861.

[16] Henry H. Tucker, *God in the War* (Milledgeville, Georgia: Boughton, Nisbet and Barnes, 1861), p. 7. Tucker was a professor at Mercer University.

is his name." [17] The reasoning supported by such texts not only helped to explain the occurrence of the Civil War, but it aided in removing latent opposition to the war; Christians could hardly oppose a war caused by God himself.

With God's part in the war firmly established, clerics could begin to turn the war into a glorious religious crusade. God would not have caused the war without some reason, and both northern and southern preachers were certain they knew his intentions. God, they concluded, was punishing the nation for its sins: Sabbath breaking, profanity, intemperance, vanity, business and political corruption. Sectionalism was not forgotten. A number of northern clergymen cited slavery as a sin and, thus, a cause of the war. Speaking in the State Street Church of Portland, Maine, the Rev. George Leon Walker declared that "the great sin of human oppression is at length disclosed as the sin of sins cleaving to the national soul." [18] "What will you do, O American empire, about this sin on thy soul?" Walker asked. "Will you submit to it? Will you be ruined by it? Or will you repent of it and put it away?" [19] Abolition still lacked support of both the northern populace and the Lincoln administration. By citing slavery as a sin, however, clergymen could attack the institution of slavery and the South on religious grounds and be less open to the charges of political preaching and abolitionism. Southern clergymen cited materialism, especially that of the North, as a sin and the leading cause for God's wrath. The Rev. Thomas V. Moore of Richmond, Virginia, said that "a long course of peace and prosperity, acting on our depraved nature, tends to emasculate and corrupt a people." [20] Ministers like Moore reasoned that the unprecedented prosperity of the United States had corrupted it to the point where God was forced to act. They made it clear, of course, that the agricultural South had been much less guilty of materialism and corruption than had the highly industrialized North.

Two vital questions remained once the cause of the war was established: when would the war end and who would be victorious. Clergymen answered the first question in line with their basic premise; the war would end, they declared, when God willed it. "Until they [sins] are repented of and forsaken, God will continue to smite us," the Rev. Thomas Moore warned in Richmond.[21] Unlike the public optimism rampant in both the Union and the Confederacy, a number of clerics predicted a long and brutal military strug-

---

[17] George D. Armstrong, *The Good Hand of Our God Upon Us* (Norfolk, Virginia: J. D. Ghiselin, 1861), p. 3. Presbyterian Church, Norfolk, Virginia, July 21, 1861; text from Exodus 15:3.

[18] George Leon Walker, *The Offered National Regeneration* (Portland, Maine: Advertiser Office, 1861), p. 10. Delivered on September 26, 1861.

[19] *Ibid.*, p. 11.

[20] Thomas V. Moore, *God Our Refuge and Strength in This War* (Richmond, Virginia: W. Hargrave White, 1861), p. 7. Delivered to the congregations of the First and Second Presbyterian Churches on November 15, 1861.

[21] *Ibid.*, p. 15.

gle. In the Beneficent Congregational Church of Providence, Rhode Island, the Rev. A. Huntington Clapp referred to previous "Divine chastisements" like insurrections, wars, depressions, and deaths of presidents, and concluded, "Other judgments . . . have made a temporary impression. It will not be so with this [Civil War]." [22]

And which side would win? The side favored by God, clergymen responded. "If God be for us who can be against us?" a New York minister asked.[23] Scriptural support of this assertion was abundant in northern and southern sermons. One text read, "And if ye go to war in your land against the enemy that oppresseth you, then ye shall blow an alarm with the trumpets; and ye shall be remembered before the Lord your God, and ye shall be saved from your enemies." [24] Preachers devoted sizable portions of their sermons prescribing ways to gain God's favor and, thus, to win the war. Obviously the sins for which God had caused the war needed to be repented. But above all, clergymen warned, victory would come only to the side which turned humbly to God and asked his help. Preaching in Savannah, Georgia, one week after the Confederate victory at Manassas Junction, Bishop Stephen Elliott said:

If we continue humble and give glory to God, we shall go on from victory to victory, until our independence shall be acknowledged and our homes be left to us in peace. But if we suffer ourselves to be elated and to ascribe our success to ourselves—if our heart be lifted up and we forget the Lord our God . . . then shall our peril be imminent, for the Lord hateth the proud and smiteth those who would rob Him of His glory.[25]

As with most wars, church attendance had fallen off during the exciting early months of the Civil War, and threats like Elliott's were probably aimed partly at drawing the people back to church services.[26]

Most clergymen agreed that a turning to God would gain his favor only if the penitent had a just cause for which he was seeking God's help. Interestingly enough, neither belligerent presented slavery as its cause.[27] Confederate preachers claimed that the South was merely fighting in self-defense,

[22] A. Huntington Clapp, *God's Purpose in the War* (Providence, Rhode Island: Knowles, Anthony and Company, 1861), p. 5. Delivered on May 12, 1861.

[23] Robert R. Booth, *The Nation's Crisis and the Christian's Duty* (New York: Anson D. F. Randolph, 1861), p. 21. Mercer Street Presbyterian Church, New York, May 12, 1861.

[24] Stephen Elliott, *The Silver Trumpets of the Sanctuary* (Savannah, Georgia: John M. Cooper, 1861), p. 3. Christ Church (Episcopal), Savannah, spring, 1861; text from Numbers 10:9.

[25] Stephen Elliott, *God's Presence with Our Army at Manassas!* (Savannah, Georgia: W. Thorne Williams, 1861), pp. 19-20. Christ Church (Episcopal), Savannah, July 28, 1861.

[26] Chapman, "The Protestant Campaign," pp. 385-97.

[27] Only one northern preacher of those studied claimed abolition of slavery to be the North's cause. Southern sermons that mentioned slavery usually referred to it as a reason for God's approval of the Confederacy.

189

to preserve its independence. For instance, the Rev. H. N. Pierce told his congregation in St. John's Church of Mobile, Alabama, that the Confederate
States wanted only peace and were being forced to fight. "Under these circumstances," Pierce concluded, "we may confidently ask for God's blessing
on our cause and look for His protection." [28] The Rev. George Armstrong of
Norfolk, Virginia, referred to the conflict as the "second 'war of independence.' " [29]

Union clerics were also concerned with who started the war—who was to
blame. They argued that southerners had been appeased for decades while,
at the same time, creating constant crises. What better proof than the firing
on Fort Sumter was needed to show that the South had caused the war,
northern clergymen asked? Attempts by clergy of each section to blame the
other for starting the war were curious because both had recognized God's
control over all things and had cited reasons why *he* had caused the war.
Perhaps they were adapting to two audiences: one that believed in an interfering and all powerful God and one that believed man caused worldly
events with a minimum of heavenly control.

The northern cause was stated emphatically by the Rev. A. L. Stone in
the Park Street Church of Boston on the Sunday following the fall of Fort
Sumter. "It is not an anti-slavery war we wage; not a sectional war; not a war
of conquest and subjugation," Stone declared, "it is simply and solely a war
for the maintenance of the Government and the Constitution." [30] This
cause, to preserve the government, was one God would support, clergymen
contended, because government was a divine institution. "It is true *now*
that government, as such, is ordained of God," the Rev. E. E. Adams stated
in Philadelphia, "All power is of God; He ordains law. He originates the idea
of civil compact." [31] Thus, northern preachers reasoned, rebellion is never
justified. Biblical passages like the following proved their case:

An evil man seeketh only rebellion: therefore a cruel messenger shall be sent
against him.

Whosoever therefore resisteth the power, resisteth the ordinance of God: and
they that resist shall receive to themselves damnation.

Render therefore unto Caesar the things that are Caesar's; and unto God the
things that are God's.[32]

[28] H. N. Pierce, "God Our Only Trust," *Sermons* (Mobile, Alabama: Farrow and
Dennett, 1861), p. 6. Delivered on June 13, 1861.
[29] Armstrong, *The Good Hand of Our God Upon Us*, p. 4.
[30] A. L. Stone, *The War and the Patriot's Duty* (Boston: Henry Hoyt, 1861), p. 18.
Delivered on April 21, 1861.
[31] E. E. Adams, *Government and Rebellion* (Philadelphia: Henry B. Ashmead, 1861),
p. 5. North Broad Street Presbyterian Church, April 28, 1861.
[32] Proverbs 17:11; Romans 13:2; Matthew 22:21.

The Rev. Lavalette Perrin of the Center Church in New Britain, Connecticut, read this last passage for his text and related how cruel the Roman government had been during Christ's time and that Christ had opposed rebellion against it. "How much more is this true, then, when rulers are upright, and the government just," Perrin argued. "Surely such a government is of divine authority, and rebellion against it is the highest crime against God and society possible to man." [33] What about the American Revolution of 1776? That case was an exception, clergymen reasoned, because the colonialists revolted not against the British government but for lack of it in the colonies. Preachers assured their congregations that no revolution would have taken place if the colonies had had a real part in the British government.

Was there evidence of God's favor during the early period of the war? Confederate preachers like Bishop Elliott of Savannah, Georgia, thought so, and pointed to southern victories. On the Sunday after the battle at Manassas (Bull Run), Elliott said that "God was evidently there, strengthening the hearts of our struggling soldiers and bringing the haughty down to the dust." [34] "And this victory has been given to us by God just at the moment when it was most important to us," he added.[35] Meanwhile, the Rev. C. S. Vedder, pastor of the Summerville Presbyterian Church in South Carolina, simply concluded, "It is God alone who has fought our battles." [36]

Unionists were hard pressed for evidence of God's approval. Some blamed the northern losses on inept military officers, while others rationalized that God chastened only those he loved, that God was cleansing the North of its sins and that losses were bringing increased European monetary investments into the North. The majority of Union preachers, however, turned to the history of the United States as proof of God's interest in the union of all the states. For instance, the Rev. John F. Bigelow, pastor of the Baptist church in Reeseville, New York, discussed God's role in American history during the colonial period and through the revolutionary and constitutional periods.[37] The characteristics and peculiarities of American society and geography were all parts of God's plan for a special nation in the Western hemisphere. "Surely," Bigelow concluded, "He will make their [Confederates] own wicked rage and demented foolhardiness, if they persevere in the attempts to sunder the Republic, the *means* of their chastisement, if not their destruction." [38] A few weeks after the defeat at Manassas, the Rev.

[33] Lavalette Perrin, *The Claims of Caesar* (Hartford, Connecticut: Case, Lockwood, and Company, 1861), p. 7. Delivered on August 18, 1861.

[34] Elliott, *God's Presence with Our Army at Manassas!* p. 13.

[35] *Ibid.*, p .14.

[36] C. S. Vedder, *Offer unto God Thanksgiving* (Charleston, South Carolina: Evans and Cogswell, 1861), p. 13. Delivered on July 28, 1861.

[37] John F. Bigelow, *The Hand of God in American History* (Burlington, Vermont: W. H. and C. A. Hoyt, 1861), pp. 4-29. Delivered on July 7, 1861.

[38] *Ibid.*, p. 36.

Daniel C. Eddy told his congregation in the Harvard Street Baptist Church of Boston, "We cannot have two or more republics on this soil. God and nature have forbidden it." [39]

Northern clergymen tended in the early period to stress the Christian nature of the war and fighting for one's country. War was not just a necessity to protect homes, they contended, but a God-ordained and approved duty. Thus, the Rev. A. L. Stone of Boston declared, "If war is a duty, it is a Christian duty, as sacred as prayer,—as solemn as sacraments." [40] There appear to be three possible explanations for northern and not southern clerical interest in the Christian nature of war. First, preachers may have felt a need to justify northern invasions of southern states. Second, recruits were needed by the thousands and Union victories were scarce. And third, this appeal negated the charge that the war was being fought to abolish slavery; it became God's war to preserve *his* government.

During the early period of the war, then, northern and southern clergymen based their "cases" on the premise that God controlled the world and all human actions. This premise led speakers to conclude that God caused the war and that he did so to punish the nation for its sins. Only by turning humbly to God with a just cause could either side be victorious. Clergymen of both sections shunned slavery as their reason for fighting—southerners pointed to independence while northerners offered preservation of divinely established government. Union clerics stressed the holy nature of war; it became a Christian duty. Confederate clergymen seemed content with their victories and to infer that God was undoubtedly on their side.

The Middle Period

The middle period—January 1, 1862, to July 1, 1863—began with an unrelenting series of Union attacks and victories. Fort Henry, Fort Donaldson, Nashville, and New Orleans fell in the west, while Roanoke Island, New Bern, North Carolina, Fort Pulaski in Georgia, and Fort Macon in North Carolina capitulated to Union assaults in the east. The Army of the Potomac under General McClellan landed on the Peninsula in May, and began its methodical march toward the Confederate capital of Richmond. Only the bloody Battle of Shiloh blemished the northern record of the first five months of 1862, but casualties were nearly equal, and the Confederates retreated.

Just when the southern cause seemed on the verge of collapse, the invincible team of Robert E. Lee and Thomas Jonathan "Stonewall" Jackson executed a series of attacks that sent the gallant Army of the Potomac, nearly 100,000 strong, reeling back down the peninsula. Mechanicsville, Gaines'

[39] Daniel C. Eddy, *Liberty and Union* (Boston: John M. Hewes, 1861), p. 19. Delivered on August 11, 1861.
[40] Stone, *The War and the Patriot's Duty*, pp. 21-22.

192

Mill, Savage Station, White Oak Swamp, and Malvern Hill became all too familiar names to northern readers as casualties soared into the thousands. The seven-day series of battles from June 25 to July 2 cost the Union army nearly sixteen thousand men. Richmond had been saved, and northern morale suffered severely.

During the next twelve months, the tide of battle turned ever against the Union forces. Confederate forces in the west moved through Tennessee into Kentucky and did not stop until mid-September when they faced Cincinnati from across the Ohio River. Meanwhile, in the east Union forces regrouped, received new commanders, and ran headlong into the second Battle of Manassas, from which they retreated with sixteen thousand fewer soldiers. Lee then decided to take the war to the north and crossed the Potomac into Maryland on September 5. Ten days later Lee's Army of Northern Virginia met the Union army in one of the bloodiest of all Civil War battles, Antietam. Lee and his battered army retreated into Virginia without interference from an equally battered northern army.

The fall and winter months witnessed a trading of blows, with Unionists scoring several victories in the west and Confederates scoring a lopsided defensive victory at Fredericksburg, Virginia: Union losses totalled 1,284 killed, 9,600 wounded, and 1,769 missing while Confederate losses totalled only 595 killed, 4,061 wounded, and 653 missing.

During the spring of 1863, General U. S. Grant tried his best to take Vicksburg, Mississippi, the last Confederate bastion on the Mississippi River, but by mid-May had settled for a siege of the city. In the east the Army of the Potomac tried once again to defeat the Army of Northern Virginia, this time in the Battle of Chancellorsville. The result was another of the bloody, indecisive battles that characterized action in the east until the end of the war. Union forces retreated toward Washington and, on June 15, Lee invaded the North for the second time. As the "middle period" came to a close, Grant's army was stalled in a siege of Vicksburg, and Lee's army was nearing the little college town of Gettysburg, Pennsylvania.

On the home fronts during the middle period, morale was plunging downward in the North and reaching new heights in the South. Lincoln faced increasing difficulties in recruiting vitally needed troops. The slavery issue came to a head on September 23, with a preliminary announcement of emancipation and then, on January 1, 1863, with the Emancipation Proclamation. Abolition of slavery was now a part of the Union cause. Southern sympathizers and those disgusted with the military situation were demanding peace and a change in the administration at Washington. The South was not without its problems, however, for European nations had failed to recognize the Confederacy, and the southern economy was suffering from the ever tightening Union naval blockade. Food and consumer goods were in short supply with little hope of relief. Heavy military casualties had forced the

Confederate Congress to pass an unpopular conscription law and equally unpopular tax laws to supply the southern armies.

Middle Period Preaching

The pulpits of North and South continued to be vocal in defending and
supporting their sections and, especially in the South, were more certain than
ever that an all-powerful God had caused the conflict raging in America.
Texts like the following appeared in Confederate sermons:

I form the light, and create darkness: I make peace, and create evil: I the Lord do
all these things.

That he might make thee know that man doth not live by bread only, but by every
word that proceedeth out of the mouth of the Lord doth man live.

The Lord hath prepared his throne in the heavens; and his kingdom ruleth over
all.[41]

A characteristic method for the development of such texts is illustrated in
these passages from a sermon delivered by the Rev. J. W. Tucker, a Presbyterian minister in Fayetteville, North Carolina:

Our Chief Magistrate in making this call to prayer, and this congregation in cheer-
fully responding to it, alike recognize the hand of God in the origin and progress
of this conflict. . . .
    There can be then no such thing as fortune or accidents—everything is of
providence and under the control of God. Every power in nature and man works
for God. . . .
    He [God] has a providence in all national revolutions. He directs, controls,
governs and regulates them. They are made to subserve His purposes, to advance
His glory, and to promote His cause.[42]

Statements like the above undoubtedly flowed more easily from mouths of
preachers who were on the "winning" side.

Clergymen were still concerned with God's reasons for having caused the
war, but there appeared to be two differences from the points of view expressed in the first period. First, there appeared to be less concern for justifying the war; it was a fact and, whether some people liked it or not, they had
to accept its existence. The second difference was in the listing of God's
alleged reasons for having caused the war. Sin was still cited as a major
reason, particularly in the North, but additional reasons were becoming
prevalent, and lists of common sins were less frequent. Two factors seemed
to determine the sins offered as highly distasteful to God: Lincoln's emancipation of the slaves and the worsening economic conditions in the South.
The Rev. John Weiss showed northern concern over the sin of slavery in a

[41] Isaiah 45:7; Deuteronomy 8:3; and Psalm 103:19.
[42] J. W. Tucker, *God's Providence in War* (Fayetteville, North Carolina: Presbyterian
Office, 1862), pp. 3-4. Delivered on May 16, 1862.

194

sermon delivered in Watertown, Massachusetts, on April 30, 1863, a Day of National Fast. "The sin of fifty years [slavery] rose wrathfully, and held its poisoned cup to the trembling lips of the country," Weiss declared.[43] He spent a sizable part of his sermon attempting to show that God was punishing the United States for the sins of slavery and hatred of Negroes.[44] Meanwhile, in the South, there was a growing concern over the sins of extortion and profiteering. On September 7, 1862, the Rev. J. W. Tucker delivered a sermon entitled "The Guilt and Punishment of Extortion," a message devoted entirely to the hoarding of consumer goods and profiteering in the South. "This sin is punished by the gradual destruction of all the higher elements and ennobling principles of man's nature under its blighting influence," Tucker warned.[45] On March 27, 1863, in the midst of continued Confederate victories, the Rev. William Norwood of St. John's Church in Richmond devoted a large part of his message to condemnation of speculators and profiteers. He claimed that widows, orphans, and crippled veterans were being denied food, clothing, and shelter because many southern businessmen were interested in gaining wealth from the war. [46] The pulpit was clearly reflecting the worsening conditions in the South and the growing condemnation of slavery in the North.

Sin was, however, only one of the causes cited during the middle period. Union preachers openly declared that slavery itself, apart from being a sin, caused God to plunge the nation into civil war. The Rev. James Freeman Clarke told his congregation in the Indiana Place Chapel of Boston, "We had seventy years given us by God, in any part of which we might have prevented this war by removing its cause [slavery]. But three generations have refused to do it." [47] Southern clerics, flushed by a long string of victories and certain that God was favoring their side, retorted that God had caused the war to punish a corrupt nation, a people even tampering with the godly institution of slavery. "I affirm that this revolution was as much a moral as a political necessity," Bishop Stephen Elliott stated in Christ Church, Savannah, "that corruption had become deep-seated in philosophy, in letters, in ethics, in religion as well as in politics. . . ." [48] "There is no instance upon record of such a rapid moral deterioration of a nation as has taken place in

[43] John Weiss, *Northern Strength and Weakness* (Boston: Walker, Wise and Company, 1863), p. 5.

[44] *Ibid.*, pp. 13-17.

[45] J. W. Tucker, *The Guilt and Punishment of Extortion* (Fayetteville, North Carolina: Presbyterian Office, 1862), p. 10.

[46] William Norwood, *God and Our Country* (Richmond, Virginia: Smith, Bailey and Company, 1863), pp. 13-15.

[47] James Freeman Clarke, *Discourse on the Aspects of the War* (Boston: Walker, Wise and Company, 1863), pp. 14-15. Delivered on April 2, 1863.

[48] Stephen Elliott, *New Wine Not to Be Put into Old Bottles* (Savannah, Georgia: John M. Cooper, 1862), p. 8. Delivered on February 28, 1862.

ours in the last forty years," Elliott concluded.[49] Other Confederate clergymen contended that God had caused the war to assure southern independence. The Rev. H. A. Tupper of Washington, Georgia, reasoned that the North would never have allowed the southern states to exist independently, "Hence, the Lord, who would deliver us from the snare, led [us] providentially and imperceptibly into the war." [50] Both northern and southern clerics agreed that God had also become angered because the populace had begun to ignore him.

When would the God-ordained war end? Union preachers were more outspoken on this question than Confederates, possibly because of their seemingly endless, bloody defeats, but both agreed that the war would end only when God willed it. Northern clergymen predicted a long and terrible war before sin would be adequately punished. We must "resign ourselves to whatever agonies Heaven, as terms of pardon, appoints," the Rev. Cyrus A. Bartol exclaimed in Boston's West Church, for "only after a long and painful purification, are we to be released." [51] The depth of northern pessimism was illustrated in a sermon delivered on April 30, 1863, late in the most foreboding part of the middle period. The Rev. Byron Sunderland of the First Presbyterian Church in Washington, D. C., declared, "The day of peace is gone from us; God only knows when, or if ever, it may return to this generation." [52] Although southern preachers generally agreed that the war would be a long one, a few cautiously predicted that total victory might be near. For example, Bishop Alexander Gregg told his audience in St. David's Church of Austin, Texas, that the end was not too distant, and he referred to the Confederacy as "a people wonderfully delivered." [53]

As could be expected, the status of the conflict in terms of victories and defeats was a major part of most sermons during the middle period. However, surprisingly few speakers mentioned specific battles and still fewer described any of the battles in detail. Southern clergymen unanimously claimed that God himself had given the Confederacy its victories after the southern people had turned to him in prayer and humility. The Rev. M. J. Michelbacher, preaching in the German Hebrew Synagogue of Richmond on March 27, 1863, exclaimed:

May we not reverently conceive, that the Almighty, in listening to our prayers, has in the High Courts of Heaven, graciously ratified our choice? the wonderful

---

[49] *Ibid.*, p. 9.

[50] H. A. Tupper, *A Thanksgiving Discourse* (Macon, Georgia: Burke, Boykin and Company, 1862), pp. 6-7. Delivered on September 18, 1862.

[51] Cyrus A. Bartol, *The Remission by Blood* (Boston: Walker, Wise, and Company, 1862), p. 9. Specific date unknown.

[52] Byron Sunderland, *The Crisis of the Times* (Washington, D.C.: National Banner Press, 1863), p. 35.

[53] Alexander Gregg, *A Sermon* (Austin, Texas: Texas Almanac Office, 1862), p. 9. Delivered on July 20, 1862.

victories of our arms in answer to our petitions, impress us in our faith therein with this belief—and, if this be so, *let him beware, who is slow to perform the first duty of the citizen [patriotism]!* [54]

That religious skeptics had been vocal during the early years of the war was revealed in a sermon preached by Bishop George F. Pierce before the General Assembly of Georgia on March 27, 1863. "The coincidence of these interventions with the prayer of the people have left no room for doubt," Pierce declared, "and have wrung from profane, even skeptical lips, the confession, God reigneth, and God is for us and with us." [55]

In two-thirds of the southern sermons examined in this study, clergymen agreed that the dual cause of independence and self-defense was the one favored by God and, if it remained the cause, then "we [will] retain the blessing of the Great Creator by our humility and righteousness before Him." [56] Only two clerics claimed slavery to be the Confederate "cause." [57] Thus, during the middle period, southerners became even less concerned about slavery while northern preachers, as we will continue to see, became ever more obsessed with the slavery issue. Perhaps Confederates were so sure of eventual victory that they felt the peculiar institution was safe, and, therefore, saw no need in defending it, a move that might alienate the non-slaveholding majority of southerners.

Union preachers, with no victories upon which to dwell, had to discuss northern disasters and, hence, why God was smiting the North. The main cause of failure offered from pulpits was couched in this passage of scripture chosen by the Rev. A. C. Thompson of Roxbury, Massachusetts: "If ye forsake him, he will forsake you." [58] Clergymen warned that the North had turned from God, was guilty of "profane self-conceit," [59] and that "our disasters may be God's method of delay, to bring us more into felt dependence on Him, and so more in harmony with His plans." [60] An equally important cause of God's apparent dissatisfaction, according to many clerics, was northern reluctance to emancipate the slaves. God, they contended, had withheld victories until Lincoln was forced to issue the Emancipation Proclamation. "The cause of the war is clearly slavery; and we tried for a long time

[54] M. J. Michelbacher, *A Sermon* (Richmond, Virginia: Macfarlane and Fergusson, 1863), pp. 8-9.
[55] George F. Pierce, *Sermon* (Milledgeville, Georgia: Broughton, Nisbet, and Barnes, 1863), p. 3. Episcopal bishop of Georgia.
[56] Michelbacher, *A Sermon*, p. 7.
[57] Perhaps southern preachers were keenly aware that slaveholders were a small minority in the southern population and thus cited a cause that *all* southerners might be likely to support.
[58] A. C. Thompson, *Military Success from God* (Boston: T. R. Marvin and Son, 1862), p. 8. Eliot Church, April 3, 1862; text from II Chronicles 15:2.
[59] Alexander H. Vinton, *Man's Rule and Christ's Reign* (New York: John A. Gray, 1862), p. 19. St. Mark's Church, New York, November 27, 1862.
[60] *Ibid.*, p. 25.

. . . to fight the war, and save the sin; and God would not suffer it," the Rev. Israel Dwinell exclaimed in the South Church of Salem, Massachusetts.[61] "Now we are openly and directly on the side of God; and now we may hope to have His favor," he concluded.

On a more optimistic note, northern preachers reasoned that, although God had severely chastened the Union, he would not allow it to perish. The Rev. Cyrus A. Bartol of Boston commented, "The country bleeds for its sins: it must bleed abundantly; though we trust it will not, like a sacrificial victim on a Hebrew altar, bleed to death." [62] Clergymen like Bartol predicted that more and greater defeats were probably in store for the North, but also that the war would eventually end and the Union would be saved.

Why would eventual victory belong to the North? The "cause" for which it was fighting was the answer, but, whereas restoration of divinely ordained government was the primary cause given during the early period, slavery was the cause cited during the middle period. "It is *this spirit of despotism* [slavery] that we are called to combat," the Rev. William A. Gaylord declared in Fitzwilliam, New Hampshire.[63] Restoration of divine government was still mentioned as a cause, but it was clearly subordinate to the abolition of slavery.

One final question remained. How could God's favor be maintained or attained for the duration of the conflict? Clergymen of both sections agreed that a humble turning to God and a reliance on him rather than on science, armies, industry, or human leadership were the only ways to obtain God's help. Several Union clerics added that slavery had to end once and for all.

Missing from Union and Confederate sermons were appeals to duty and patriotism that might have motivated men to enlist for military service. This was strange indeed because both sides were in grave need of additional men. The North had resorted to bounty and draft systems and the South to highly unpopular conscription laws. Clergymen would seem to have been in excellent positions to recruit, but, in the sermons studied at least, few attempts were made.

Middle Period Differences

Thus, preaching during the middle period reflected the status of the military conflict. Pessimism or optimism went with the side obtaining the best military results. God had caused the war, clerics agreed, but northerners saw God demanding an end to slavery and southerners saw him punishing a sinful, corrupt North. There was little optimism in either South or North that

[61] Israel E. Dwinell, *Hope for Our Country* (Salem, Massachusetts: Charles W. Swasey, 1862), p. 16. Delivered on October 19, 1862.

[62] Bartol, *The Remission by Blood*, p. 8.

[63] William A. Gaylord, *The Soldier God's Minister* (Fitchburg, New Hampshire: Rollstone Printing Office, 1862), p. 13. Congregational Church, October 5, 1862.

the end of the war was near. Confederate preachers generally ignored the issue of slavery, while Union preachers, hesitant to mention slavery in the early period, seemed obsessed with the issue during the middle period. Slavery was a cause of the war, a cause of Union defeats, a cause for which to fight, and a means of gaining God's favor, if it was abolished. Gone from sermons of this period were efforts to justify or condemn revolutions, attempts to place the blame for the starting of the war, and efforts to show that soldiering in defense of one's country was a holy, Christian duty. The war was stark reality, and some of these points undoubtedly seemed academic.

The Late Period

The late period of the Civil War (July 1, 1863, to April 1865) began with Confederate hopes for victory based on a long series of military successes and with Lee's Army of Northern Virginia approaching Gettysburg. Lee's invasion, if successful, would surely force Lincoln to sue for peace. But the war was simply entering a new phase, its bloodiest and its last. Increasingly sharp clashes occurred around Gettysburg on July 1 and 2, and, then, on July 3, Pickett's famous charge withered under intense fire from entrenched Union forces. The Battle of Gettysburg was over and Lee had lost more than 28,000 irreplaceable men. The Army of Northern Virginia would not invade the North again. News of the victory at Gettysburg barely reached northern cities before Grant telegraphed on July 4 that Vicksburg had surrendered with its 27,000 Confederate soldiers.

Confederate victories came to an abrupt end, and, during the next twenty months, the South would have little to cheer about. Union victories at Fort Smith, Arkansas, Knoxville and Chattanooga, Tennessee, and Brownsville and Corpus Christi, Texas, marked the remainder of 1863. In the lone southern "victory," Chickamauga, the South suffered almost 5,600 more casualties than did the North. The war of attrition that would grow in intensity during 1864 had begun. The Confederacy would lose more and more men it could not replace, and bits and pieces of its territory would fall one after the other into Union hands.

During the first half of 1864, Sherman began his march through the heart of the South, and Grant, now commander of all northern armies, began his move against Robert E. Lee—119,000 Unionists against 64,000 Confederates. The Battle of the Wilderness was followed by the Battles of the Bloody Angle and Cold Harbor, and, in less than thirty days, fifty-five thousand federals fell, nearly the number of Lee's entire army. Grant continued south, on to Petersburg, Virginia, where he would face Lee's army until the spring of 1865. The booming, industrialized North quickly replaced its losses of men and material, whereas the southern losses could not be replaced.

Except for a few days in early July, 1864, when Confederate General

Early's army charged past Union forces in the Shenandoah Valley, crossed the Potomac, and reached the Washington suburbs before meeting hastily organized Union defenders, Confederate military hopes were dismal. Southerners hoped, however, that northern discontent over the horrendous loss of lives and failure to win a "decisive" victory would lead toward peace and southern independence. Winter and spring of 1864-65 saw a continuous whittling away of southern armies and territory until early April when Lee surrendered his half-starved Army of Northern Virginia at Appomattox Court House. Although some Confederate forces remained in the field, the war was over.

During the final period of the war, graft, corruption, and profiteering were rampant on both sides of the Mason-Dixon Line. In the Confederacy, food, clothing, and shelter were scarce. The grand society was being reduced to rubble while the Davis government, much to southern dismay, was incapable of halting northern advances. Meanwhile, in the North, Lincoln's critics could not understand either why the war was being continued or why Union armies could not easily defeat the undermanned and ill-equipped Confederate armies. Lincoln was exceedingly pessimistic about his chances for reelection in 1864 (both radical Republicans and Democrats met in conventions, condemned him, and selected candidates), but the surrender of Atlanta and sufficient popular faith in an eventual Union victory gave him a second term, one that was to last only a few weeks.

Late Period Preaching

Members of the clergy tried gallantly during the late period of the war to bolster the morale of their sections, to rally support for their governments, and to convince their congregations that victory alone, and not surrender or compromise, was acceptable. The pastor of the Fourth Avenue Presbyterian Church in New York, the Rev. Howard Crosby, warned his congregation on September 11, 1864, "If we compromise with this rebellion we shall bring down [from God] woes most fearful on our country's future." [64] In the Centenary Church of Lynchburg, Virginia, the Rev. Leroy M. Lee declared, "Until they [northerners] choose to stop, we are compelled to fight. . . . Compromise would be treason against truth, country and God." [65] As the military scene progressively worsened for the Confederacy and public pressure for peace talks increased, southern clerics began to portray the horrors of a northern victory. For instance, the Rev. D. S. Doggett exclaimed in Richmond that, if the Confederacy should fall, northern heresies would "surge over the heritage of God," close southern churches, imprison ministers, and

[64] Howard Crosby, *God's View of Rebellion* (New York: E. French, 1864), p. 14. Delivered on September 11, 1864.

[65] Leroy M. Lee, *Our Country—Our Dangers—Our Duty* (Richmond, Virginia: Charles H. Wynne, 1863), p. 7. Delivered on August 21, 1863.

scatter church members.[66] "At one fell stroke," Doggett concluded, "religious liberty would be extinguished, and a ruthless tyranny would dictate terms of communion with the polluted crusaders of their altars." [67] At the same time, northern preachers spent more time than ever in justifying the war, a war, they argued, that God had approved to end illegal and sinful rebellion. Apparently the pulpits of North and South were intent on victory regardless of cost or duration of the conflict and were not numbered among those demanding peace.

As in the early and middle periods, clergymen claimed that God was all-powerful, that he had caused the war. Unlike the earlier periods, however, few northern or southern clerics devoted much time to establishing these claims or in speculating *why* God had caused the conflict. Perhaps speakers felt that these points had been adequately discussed during the first years of the war. The only exception was the issue of slavery. Several northerners argued as vehemently as ever that the "great national sin" of slavery had prompted God to cause the war.[68]

The main concern of sermons in the late period was the status of the conflict in terms of victories and defeats and its eventual outcome. Northern clergymen happily found themselves on the "winning" side, and they reacted much as southern clerics had during the middle period. The victories, they concluded, were from God. "*Our hopes?* They are unfailing because sustained by the marked interpositions of an Almighty God," the Rev. Charles Little stated in Cheshire, Connecticut.[69] Also like the southern sermons of the middle period, Union preachers reasoned that God had given victories in response to northern prayer. Referring to a recent day of fast, the Rev. Elisha Cleaveland of New Haven, Connecticut, exclaimed, "And how soon and signally have those prayers been answered!" [70] The righteous northern cause had also induced God to favor the Union armies, clerics added. Surprisingly, after their obsession with slavery during 1862 and early 1863, northern preachers presented the ending of rebellion against divinely ordained government, and not slavery, as the cause for which the North was fighting.[71] Perhaps northern clergymen, like the organized abolitionists, believed that the Emancipation Proclamation plus disruption of the institution by in-

---

[66] D. S. Doggett, *The War and Its Close* (Richmond, Virginia: Macfarlane and Fergusson, 1864), p. 13. Centenary Church, April 8, 1864.

[67] *Ibid.*, p. 13.

[68] Marvin R. Vincent, *The Lord of War and of Righteousness* (Troy, New York: A. W. Scribner, 1864), pp. 7-8. First Presbyterian Church, Troy, New York, November 24, 1864.

[69] Charles Little, *Relation of the Citizen to the Government* (New Haven, Connecticut: William H. Stanley, 1864), p. 14. Congregational Church, November 24, 1864.

[70] Elisha Cleaveland, *The Patriot's Song of Victory* (New Haven, Connecticut: Thomas H. Pease, 1864), p. 8. Third Congregational Church, September 11, 1864.

[71] Slavery remained an issue during the final period, but as a sin and a reason for God's having caused the war, not as the goal or "cause" for which the North was fighting.

vading Union armies had ended slavery forever. The turn of events from constant defeats to continuous victories was often explained in this manner: "A bad cause may be successful at the start. . . . The good cause is stunned and staggered by the first onset; but by and by it rallies, warming as it works, and striking harder and harder till the field is won." [72]

Confederates were naturally preoccupied with the deteriorating military scene. Some said that God was punishing southerners for their own good, and that "the ways of His providence are generally dark to mortal vision." [73] Others said the reasons for God's chastisement were clear and simple. Southerners had turned from God, clergymen contended, and were relying too much on man. In a sermon delivered before the General Assembly of Alabama, the Rev. I. T. Tichenor accused the South of relying too heavily on cotton to bring foreign recognition and too heavily on its armies and valor to win battles. "The day is past," Tichenor said, "when God will permit the nations of the earth to ignore Him." [74] Later he quoted the scriptural passage, "Put not your trust in princes," and claimed that southerners had failed to turn to God after the disasters at Vicksburg and Gettysburg, so God allowed them to suffer further reverses. [75]

The Rev. D. M. Gilbert, preaching in the Evangelical Lutheran Church of Savannah while Sherman's army was poised in Atlanta readying its march on Savannah, stated the reason why most southern clerics felt God had deserted the South. "It is because of our sins that the Almighty is so sorely chastening us," Gilbert said. [76] The "sins" expounded upon revealed the worsening conditions in the Confederate states. Profiteering, extortion, and speculation headed the list of sins, while desertion, treason, discontent, factionalism, and religious skepticism appeared frequently. The Rev. Charles Minnigerode of St. Paul's Church in Richmond referred to "coward, faithless selfish hearts," to "croakers" and to "want of faith," "the root of all that murmuring against God's providence." [77] Ministers severely criticized southerners who were trying to maintain a "business as usual" attitude in the face of defeats and mounting casualties. [78] Preaching in Christ Church of Savannah on September 15, 1864, Bishop Stephen Elliott accused south-

[72] R. D. Hitchcock, *Thanksgiving for Victories* (New York, 1864), p. 5. Plymouth Church, Brooklyn, September 11, 1864.

[73] John Paris, *A Sermon* (Greensborough, North Carolina: A. W. Ingold, 1864), p. 12. Kingston, North Carolina, February 28, 1864.

[74] I. T. Tichenor, *Fast Day Sermon* (Montgomery, Alabama: Advertiser Office, 1863), p. 10. Pastor of the First Baptist Church of Montgomery, August 21, 1863.

[75] *Ibid.*, p. 11. Text from Psalm 146:3.

[76] D. M. Gilbert, *A Discourse* (Savannah, Georgia: George N. Nichols, 1864), p. 11. Delivered on September 15, 1864.

[77] Charles Minnigerode, *He That Believeth Shall Not Make Haste* (Richmond, Virginia: Charles H. Wynne, 1865), pp. 7-8 and 4. Delivered on January 1, 1865.

[78] J. C. Stiles, *National Rectitude* (Petersburg, Virginia: 1863), pp. 16-17. Specific date unknown.

emers of attempting to maintain wealth and a life of ease in the midst of terrible suffering. He spoke of widespread refusal either to join the Confederate army or to support it materially.[79]

There was only one way to gain and to preserve God's favor until final victory, Union and Confederate clergymen contended, and that was to turn humbly to God and to place all trust in him. "We are learning . . . that our national salvation depends neither upon political sagacity, nor military strength," the Rev. Charles Wadsworth declared in San Francisco, "but solely on the protection of that great Arm that ruleth in Zion." [80] Southern preachers continued to argue, no matter how hopeless their chances seemed, that faith in God was enough for victory. On January 1, 1865, the Rev. Charles Minnigerode stated in Richmond, "let us do our duty as in His sight and to His glory, in His faith and His strength, and in obedience to His will, *and we cannot, we shall never fail!*" [81] As conditions in the South deteriorated steadily, audiences must have found it increasingly difficult to accept this reasoning.

During the final period, very few clergymen commented on the remaining length of the conflict, perhaps because the war seemed endless, but nearly all appeared convinced that their side would win. Unionists contended that God was opposed to rebellion against his earthly governments, and so he would ultimately give victory to the North. "We are one people, under one Government, and armed resistance to that Government is rebellion, and rebellion is accursed of God," the Rev. Howard Crosby said in New York.[82] He added that "the Bible speaks all one way; it denounces rebellion even against a Nero." [83] Northern clerics frequently referred to their early losses followed by great victories as proof of God's intention to defeat the Confederacy. The Rev. Henry Darling of Albany, New York, compared the southern rebellion to that of Absalom against David, and recalled that although God had allowed Absalom "a *momentary* triumph, yet, in the *end*, David was certain that it would be destroyed." [84] Condemnation of rebellion against divine government had been strong during the early period, had all but disappeared during the middle period when northern preaching seemed obsessed with the slavery issue, and then reappeared stronger than ever during the last years of the war.

Meanwhile, in the South, clerics were trying desperately to raise the

[79] Stephen Elliott, *Vain Is the Help of Man* (Macon, Georgia: Burke, Boykin and Company, 1864), pp. 6-8.

[80] Charles Wadsworth, *War a Discipline* (San Francisco: H. H. Bancroft and Company, 1864), p. 14. Calvary Church, November 24, 1864.

[81] Minnigerode, *He That Believeth*, p. 13.

[82] Crosby, *God's View of Rebellion*, p. 10.

[83] *Ibid*.

[84] Henry Darling, *Chastened, but Not Killed* (Albany, New York: Van Benthuysen's Printing House, 1864), p. 14. Fourth Presbyterian Church, August 4, 1864.

morale of the populace and to convince their listeners that ultimate triumph would belong to the Confederacy. Numerous rationalizations were presented with no single one dominating; most were reasons why God would favor the South. Clergymen reasoned, for example, that God wanted to protect slavery and, to do so, had to protect the South; that he approved the "purposes" of the Confederacy (slavery, self-defense, independence); that he knew the North was intent on destroying his heritage on earth; that he would not abandon the South after giving it so many victories in 1861, 1862, and 1863; that he always made evil forces lose after initial successes (the fact was ignored that the South itself was losing after "initial" successes); that he always chose new nations after a time of affliction; and that he was using the South as the defender of true republicanism, not "crass democracy." [85] Other reasons for future victory seemed naïve, even desperate. For instance, a few clerics argued that the Confederacy was united and better supplied than ever while northern resources were nearly exhausted. One clergyman said Lincoln's reelection would greatly aid the Confederacy because it would never surrender with Lincoln in power.[86]

During the final period, then, the preachers of both sides tried to convince their audiences that victory alone, and not surrender or compromise, was acceptable, regardless of cost in lives and wealth. Sermons were still based on the premises that God was all powerful and that he had caused the war, but less space was given to establishing these premises. Victories were the result of prayer, preachers argued, while defeats resulted from unrepented sins and a turning from God. The northern cause, for which God was giving it many victories, was the restoration of divine government to all the nation. Unlike the middle period, slavery was rarely mentioned as the northern cause. Southern sermons reflected the worsening plight of the Confederacy. Such "sins" as profiteering, extortion, speculation, desertion, treason, discontent, factionalism, and religious skepticism were cited by a large number of ministers. Northern clerics said God condemned all revolutions, so he would give final victory to the Union forces. Southern clerics presented a variety of rationalizations why the Confederacy could not lose.

Summary

Thus, Civil War preaching, northern and southern, was based on the fundamental religious premise generally accepted in pre-Darwinian America that God controlled the universe and every thing and action in it. This belief led clerics to conclude that God caused the war for his own purposes (to punish the nation for its sins, to end or to protect slavery, to end rebel-

[85] B. M. Palmer, A Discourse (Columbia, South Carolina: Charles P. Pelham, 1864), pp. 10-12. Before the General Assembly of South Carolina on December 10, 1863.
[86] Elliott, Vain is the Help of Man, p. 12.

lion or to assure southern independence), and that neither section could be victorious without turning humbly to God. When their side was winning, clergymen saw the victories as a direct result of prayer; when they were losing, they charged the populace with skepticism, sin, and turning from God.

The southern "cause" remained the same throughout the war: to assure and to preserve its independence. The northern cause changed according to events during the war periods. Hence, during the early period when abolitionism was still unpopular, Union preachers said restoration of divine government was the "cause." Then, during the middle period when the emancipation of slaves became a policy of the Lincoln administration, the ending of slavery was cited as the northern cause. Finally, when slavery seemed abolished, members of the clergy once again claimed restoration of government to be the North's cause.

Civil War sermons also reflected the ever-changing military, political, and economic conditions of the belligerents. Preachers were never as optimistic as the political and civilian populations regarding a quick, easy victory, but each argued to the end that his side would be the ultimate victor. Compromise and surrender were against God's will, they declared; victory alone was acceptable, regardless of the sacrifice. Few clergymen used appeals that might have aided their sections in recruiting desperately needed soldiers. On the other hand, they argued that God, and not science, armies, human leaders, or industry, could grant final victory.

In conclusion, then, Civil War sermons were based on the fundamental religious tradition of America, did change to reflect the varying "fortunes of war," and exhibited what could be regarded as a blind loyalty to the "native lands" of the speakers. In fact, if one salient attribute of all these sermons stands out, it is the universal conviction of the individual preacher that he and his congregation were "on the right side." Geography and/or vested interests of parishioners seem to have made a marked impression on the sermonic minds of the ministers.

10

THE VOICE OF GOD: NATURAL OR SUPERNATURAL

Harold Miller

In the years prior to the publication of Darwin's *Origin of Species*, the church in America had come to expect that new discoveries in science would establish, rather than contradict, revelation. Stowe Persons, writing in *Evolutionary Thought in America*, says regarding this tendency:

In the early years of the nineteenth century, Orthodox Protestant Christian thinkers, both in England and in America, absorbed the Deist argument in its rationalistic aspects by harmonizing natural religion with revelation. The one was found to strengthen and confirm the other.[1]

Thus, the harmony of revelation and natural religion actually provided a most powerful weapon for the orthodox apologist. Persons says that the emerging bulwark for the belief of the faithful was the doctrine of design. It was brought into being out of a fusion of natural and revealed religion.[2] As the prestige of science increased, the church found it increasingly expedient to use its findings to further her causes; she eagerly pointed to new discoveries as proof of the design of God in the laws of nature. In one of the most famous analogies in science and religion, the teleological argument is advanced by reference to Paley's watch and watchmaker, in which the complicated mechanism of the watch makes a chance arrangement of the parts seem absurd. The very complication of parts of the watch, and the universe for that matter, and the intricacy of their respective movements preclude a universe without a universe-maker. And so, all was at peace between science and religion up until 1859 and the publication of *Origin of Species*.

Darwin's *Origin* landed like a bombshell in the midst of the advocates of the doctrine of God's design in nature. Up until this time, there was no either-or between natural and supernatural; they agreed. But, with an emphasis on natural selection, in which the struggle for existence is carried on

---

[1] Stowe Persons, ed., "Evolution and Theology in America," *Evolutionary Thought in America* (New Haven: Yale University Press, 1950), pp. 422-23.

[2] *Ibid.*, p. 423.

by organisms which have minute differences, the idea of evolving species invaded the scientific world. Historian Bert J. Loewenberg, writing in the *American Historical Review*, discussed the early reactions of several leading American naturalists to the ideas of Darwin as published in *Origin of Species*.[3] He showed that while some of the leading scientists of America were receptive to Darwin's ideas of natural selection, few were willing to conclude that natural selection with design was valid. Loewenberg identified Agassiz of Harvard as the chief American naturalist to oppose the theory of natural selection. Agassiz prepared his final repudiation of the Darwinian theory, and it was published posthumously in the January, 1874, issue of the *Atlantic Monthly*. In that article Agassiz said:

The most advanced Darwinians seem reluctant to acknowledge the intervention of an intellectual power in the diversity which obtains in nature, under the plea that such an admission implies distinct creative acts for every species. What of it, if it were true? . . . The world has arisen in some way or other. How it originated is the great question, and Darwin's theory, like all other attempts to explain the origin of life, is thus far merely conjectural. I believe he has not even made the best conjecture possible in the present state of our knowledge.[4]

Even Asa Gray, another Harvard botanist and a leading American exponent of Darwinian evolution, felt it necessary to distinguish between evolution and evolution without design. As Gray said, "Agreeing that plants and animals were produced by omnipotent fiat does not exclude the idea of natural order and what we call secondary causes." [5]

But while the Darwinian theory was received with mixed reaction among scientists, it was odious to orthodox churchmen. The new view of origin conflicted directly with the traditional view of design: that God created by a special act of making different species out of that which was not already living. Stowe Persons, in discussing the major conflict between evolutionary science and Christian doctrine said:

In theology, as in many other fields of thought, the first major conflict over evolutionary ideas came in the wake of the Darwinian theory of natural selection. This was because Darwin proposed an explanation of the method of evolutionary change that was diametrically opposed to the Christian doctrine of design. Both theories were equally mechanical in character, and one or the other must give way. . . . If evolution occurred by means of natural selection from among random and universal variations, how could the process be identified with the belief in design? [6]

[3] Bert J. Loewenberg, "The Reaction of American Scientists to Darwinism," *American Historical Review*, XXXVIII (July, 1933), 687-701.
[4] Louis Agassiz, "Evolution and Permanence of Type," *Atlantic Monthly*, XXXIII, No. 95 (January, 1874), 101.
[5] Asa Gray, "Darwin and His Reviewers," *Atlantic Monthly*, VI, No. 36 (October, 1860), 406.
[6] Persons, "Evolution and Theology in America," pp. 425-26.

The power of Darwinism struck with fantastic force. As Robert E. D. Clark puts it:

Till Darwin's day the argument from design had reigned supreme. "Then," as Romanes put it, "with a suddenness only less surprising than its completeness the end came; the fountains of this great deep were broken up by the power of one man and never in the history of thought has a change been effected of a comparable order of magnitude." [7]

Thus, in a short time, Darwin had threatened thought and theology which was in building for decades and had significantly undercut a foundation stone of orthodoxy.

But the church and the other advocates of the doctrine of design did not give up without a fight. In fact, they did not give up at all.

The next few years were years of significant change and adjustment in the church. No longer did the scientists support the theologians. For Christian apologists some peace had to be made.

A study of American preaching during the last third of the nineteenth century indicates that the efforts to relieve the tension between science and religion went through several stages. It might be more accurate to say that there were several concurrent reactions which eventually culminated in the accommodation and endorsement of some variation of the evolutionary theory by most of the church; we may well refer to them as the reaction of ridicule, the reaction of confrontation, the reaction of accommodation, and the reaction of endorsement.

Ridicule, the Initial Reaction

It should not be assumed that Darwin's *Origin of Species* was the first attempt of its kind. Robert Chambers published his *Vestiges of the Natural History of Creation* in 1844. It received a generally favorable reaction but fell into disrepute with the sharp attacks of scientists as well as theologians. It is likely that Darwin hesitated to publish his *Origin* because of the sharp attack which *Vestiges* had received. When finally, in 1859, he published the *Origin of Species*, the reactions were mixed. The reviews in the *London Times, Saturday Review,* and the *Guardian* were generally complimentary, while those in the *Athenaeum* and the *Daily News* were negatively critical. It was the June, 1860, meeting of the British Association at Oxford which first propelled Darwin into the limelight of controversy.

There was a brief flurry of excitement at the first mention of his name in the Thursday, June 28, meeting of the British Association. But it was not until the following Saturday that the first public clash on the subject of

[7] Robert E. D. Clark, *Darwin: Before and After* (London: The Paternoster Press, 1858), p. 87.

evolution took place between advocates of the church and advocates of the scientific world. On that Saturday the Rev. Samuel Wilberforce, bishop of Oxford, delivered the first public attack on Darwin's theories. Clark describes the event:

The audience that turned up was so large that it was necessary to move from the usual lecture room to the library, which in turn was filled to standing. . . . Prof. Draper was . . . called upon to read his long and dull paper "The Intellectual Development of Europe Considered with References to the Views of Mr. Darwin and Others." For an hour or more he droned on and on while the audience listened, or pretended to listen, impatiently. The meeting was then opened for discussion. [Then Bishop Wilberforce] who had entered the meeting late and had pushed his way through the crowd fairly bristling with importance, jumped up and proceeded at once to deliver an oration against the new evolutionary hypothesis.[8]

Wilberforce's speech was not recorded in that meeting, but the *Quarterly Review*, published the next month, carried his manuscript on the topic. The degree of accuracy of the *Quarterly Review* article to the text of the speech is difficult to determine. Clark says that the article is said to have followed closely the lines of his attack in the speech.[9]

Bishop Wilberforce started the speech with high praises of Darwin and his past works; his first references to the *Origin of Species* were kind and complimentary. However, the bishop soon dropped the compliments and got to the analysis of the arguments of Darwinism. Developing his objections, the bishop turned first to the conclusion of the work, "that all the various forms of vegetable and animal life . . . have come down to us by natural succession of descent from father to son." [10]

If Mr. Darwin can, with the same correctness of reasoning [that Newton used to discover the law of gravity] demonstrate to us our fungular descent, we shall dismiss our pride, and avow with the characteristic humility of philosophy, our unsuspected cousinship with the mushrooms.[11]

In an effort to analyze the argument of *Origin of Species*, Wilberforce summarized the major arguments which are developed in the book: (1) that observed and admitted variations spring up in the course of descents from a common progenitor, (2) that many of these variations tend to an improvement upon the parent stock, (3) that by a continued selection of these improved specimens are the progenitors of a future stock being unlimitedly increased, and (4) that there is, in nature, a power continually and universally working out this selection, and so fixing and augmenting these im-

[8] *Ibid.*, p. 67.
[9] *Ibid.*, p. 68.
[10] Samuel Wilberforce, "The Origin of Species," *Quarterly Review*, CVIII (July, 1860), 231.
[11] *Ibid.*, p. 235 and p. 238.

provements.[12] In attacking the idea that there is a natural power which works out the details of natural selection, Bishop Wilberforce said:

We affirm positively that there is no single *fact* tending even in that direction [proving that variations are species in the act of formation]. . . . On what, then, is the new theory based? We say it with unfeigned regret, dealing with such a man as Mr. Darwin, on the merest hypothesis, supported by the most unbounded assumptions.[13]

The bishop became more brutal in referring to Darwin's wide use of time to help explain the process of evolution: "The other solvent which Mr. Darwin most freely employs to get rid of difficulties, is his use of time. This he shortens or prolongs at will by the mere wave of his magician's rod,"[14] and he eventually came to the eloquent conclusion:

Indeed, not only do all laws for the study of nature vanish when the great principle of order prevading and regulating all her processes is given up, but all that imparts the deepest interest in the investigation of her wonders will have departed too. . . . The whole world of nature is laid for such a man under a fantastic law of glamour, and he becomes capable of believing anything: To him it is just as probable that Dr. Livingstone will find the next tribe of negroes with their heads growing under their arms as fixed on the summit of the cervical vertebrae; and he is able, with a continually growing neglect of all the facts around him, with equal confidence and equal delusion, to look back to any past and to look on to any future.[15]

Perhaps the most famous section of the speech was deleted from publication in the *Quarterly Review*. It was reported from the meeting and confirmed by Thomas Henry Huxley's letters that Wilberforce actually concluded his speech by demanding whether Huxley received his monkey ancestry from his grandmother's or his grandfather's side of the family. Huxley, it was reported, said that he would rather be descended from an ape than from one who, "not content with equivocal success in his own sphere of activity, plunges into scientific questions with which he has no real acquaintance only to obscure them by an aimless rhetoric."[16] It was this statement which led some to say that Huxley would rather be descended from an ape than from a bishop.

Ridicule as a strategy to fight the ideas of evolution was widely applied in both England and America in those early years following the publication of the *Origin of Species*. The strategy which had been successful in the suppression of *Vestiges* should have worked, thought the religious leaders, in the defeat of this new writing.

Darwin's work and everything connected with it aroused virulent hostility throughout the 1860's and 1870's. Not a few of the clerical arguments were on the intel-

[12] *Ibid.*, p. 231.
[13] *Ibid.*, pp. 235 and 238.
[14] *Ibid.*, p. 250.
[15] *Ibid.*, p. 264.
[16] Clark, *Darwin: Before and After*, p. 69.

lectual plane of the minister who asserted that Darwinism would be established only when scientists could take a monkey from the zoo and by natural selection make him into a man.[17]

It was likely that the religious leaders of Darwin's day generally felt that the idea of evolution of the species was not a really serious threat in America and England and that ridicule was all that was necessary to defeat it. Bert J. Loewenberg, writing in the *New England Quarterly* regarding the controversy over evolution in New England indicated that wholesale denunciation of the kind used by Wilberforce was "the distinguishing note" of the period from 1859 to the death of American naturalist Louis Agassiz in 1873. Loewenberg attributed this strategy to "the newness of the evolutionary idea and the doubtful attitude of the scientists." [18]

The penchant for scorn did not end in the nineteenth century. A perusal of the speeches delivered by the "Fundamentalists" in the anti-evolution fights of the 1920's shows that, with some ministers and laymen, the strategy of ridicule remained a very popular one. For example, in a speech published in the *New York Times* of February 26, 1922, William Jennings Bryan criticized the evolutionists for compelling their believers to resort to absurd explanations:

Evolutionists, not being willing to accept the theory of creation, have to explain everything, and their courage in this respect is as great as their efforts are laughable. The eye, for instance, according to evolutionists, was brought out by "the light beating upon the skin," the ears came out of response to "air waves"; the leg is the development of a wart that chanced to appear on the belly of an animal; and so the tommyrot runs on *ad infinitum* and sensible people are asked to swallow it. Recently a college professor told an audience in Philadelphia that a baby wiggles its big toe without wiggling its other toes because its ancestors climbed trees; also that we dream of falling because our forefathers fell out of trees 50,000 years ago, adding that we are not hurt in our dreams of falling because we descended from those that were *not killed.*[19]

Here, as in other times and places in the speaking and preaching of the men who chose to fight evolution by ridicule, the strategy of the straw man argument is used; oversimplifying the opponents' arguments and then ridiculing that oversimplification.

It was not just the Protestant evangelicals who scorned the new theory. The Catholics had their Orestes A. Brownson who "urged a policy of no compromise with evolutionary biology." [20] The November, 1869, issue of the *Catholic World* reported that "The greater light thrown upon it [*Origin*

[17] Richard Hofstadter, "The Coming of Darwinism," *Evolution and Religion*, ed. Gail Kennedy (Boston: D. C. Heath, 1957), p. 11.

[18] Bert J. Loewenberg, "The Controversy over Evolution in New England," *New England Quarterly*, VIII, No 2 (June, 1935), 234.

[19] William Jennings Bryan, "God and Evolution," *Evolution and Religion*, ed. Gail Kennedy, p. 25.

[20] Hofstadter, "The Coming of Darwinism," p. 11.

of Species], the more glaringly palpable will become its absurdity. Scientists accept the hypothesis because their atheistic views are the chief inducement urging them to accept the theory." [21] And so, the first reaction of the church when it faced the crisis of 1859 was to scoff.

The Reaction of Confrontation

But not all the opponents of the theory were satisfied to scorn the new science. It was already proving itself attractive for the scientists and intellectuals of America. By 1873, when Louis Agassiz died, so many scientists had gone over to the side of the theory of natural selection as an explanation for the origin of species that Agassiz stood nearly alone against evolution. Even many of his students defected to the camp of the enemy, while many of the more devout scientists were finding no problem with accepting both a God of design and the theory of natural selection. The writings of Herbert Spencer had linked progress to natural selection, thus making it all seem less an effect of pure chance. "It was Spencer who used the phrase 'survival of the fittest' [which meant that progress was related to natural selection]. Thus the sting is drawn from Darwin's conception of the evolutionary process as an effect of blind chance." [22]

One of the scientists who held to his religious beliefs and at the same time endorsed evolution was Asa Gray, an eminent American naturalist. Gray, who had followed Darwin's progress, wrote in March, 1860, even before the British Association meeting:

Mr. Darwin holds the orthodox view of the descent of all the individuals of a species . . . from a single ancestor or pair. . . . The ordinary view—rendering unto Caesar the things that are Caesar's—looks to natural agencies for the actual distribution and perpetuation of species, to a supernatural for their origin.[23]

It was evident, too, that the spirit of many of the early critics had changed since the publication of *Origin of Species*. Thomas Huxley, in an 1871 speech, said: "As time has slipped by, a happy change has come over Mr. Darwin's critics. The mixture of ignorance and insolence which, at first, characterized a large proportion of the attacks with which he was assailed, is no longer the sad distinction of anti-Darwinian criticism." [24]

However, many leading American churchmen were not content to give up their conception of a doctrine of design so easily, or to adjust it to such a new idea.

Dr. Charles Hodge of Princeton Theological Seminary gave leadership to

---

[21] *Catholic World*, November, 1869, pp. 252-53.

[22] Gail Kennedy, ed., *Evolution and Religion*, p. vii.

[23] Asa Gray, "The Origin of Species by Means of Natural Selection," *Major Crises in American History*, ed. Merrill D. Peterson and Leonard W. Levy (New York: Harcourt, Brace & World, 1962), p. 78.

[24] T. H. Huxley, *Darwiniana* (New York: D. Appleton and Company, 1898), p. 120.

the idea that Darwinism and theology were incompatible. To accept one was to reject the other.

Hodge's most noted work in the study of evolution was his short book: *What Is Darwinism?* Though it was not in itself a sermon, the fact that it was written by a leading faculty member at Princeton Theological Seminary gave it significant credibility as a reference source for orthodox preachers who spoke against the doctrine of natural selection.

In *What Is Darwinism?* after a discussion of the importance of the problem of the origin of the universe, which Darwin proposed to answer, Hodge viewed the various "solutions" to the problems of the universe and its beginnings. First came the scriptural solution: "The truth of this theory of the immense [that God created the universe and all that is therein] rests . . . on the infallible authority of the Word of God." [25]

Pantheistic, Epicurean, Spencerian agnosticism, the hylozoic theory (the universe is eternal) and unscriptural forms of theism were dealt with and dismissed. Then, Hodge turned his attention to Darwin's theory, especially to the process of natural selection. He was careful to be quite complete in his arguments, restating, more or less fairly, the chief tenets of Darwinism.

But Hodge's reason for writing *What Is Darwinism?* was not only to show Darwin's error, but also to show that, for Christians, it was impossible to accept evolution. To demonstrate that Darwinism and orthodoxy are incompatible he differentiated between the terms "natural" and "supernatural"; "Natural," being antithetical to "supernatural" and implying that no plan exists.[26]

In the major section of his argument, Hodge set out to prove that Darwinism excludes teleology. He referred to Darwin's own writings, to the statements of the advocates of evolution, and to the arguments of its opponents. He quoted Darwin:

Have we any right to assume that the Creator works by intellectual powers like those of man? . . . In living bodies, variations will cause the slight alterations, generation will multiply them almost infinitely, and natural selection will pick out with unerring skill each improvement. Let this process go on for millions of years and we shall at last have a perfect eye.[27]

And in reaction to the passage, Hodge argued that "he constantly shuts us up to the alternative of believing that the eye is a work of design or the product of the intended action of physical causes." [28]

Turning to the testimony of the advocates of the theory, Hodge referred to some eminent Darwin supporters and their anti-theological statements:

[25] Charles Hodge, *What Is Darwinism?* (New York: Scribner, Armstrong and Company, 1874), p. 5.
[26] *Ibid.*, p. 41.
[27] *Ibid.*, pp. 59-60.
[28] *Ibid.*, p. 60.

Mr. Alfred Russel Wallace (naturalist), "I believe that the Universe is so constituted as to be self-regulating"; Professor T. A. Huxley, "When he first read Mr. Darwin's book, that which struck him most forcefully was the conviction that teleology, as commonly understood, had received its death-blow at Mr. Darwin's hands";[29] Dr. Ernst Haeckel, leading German scientist, "To the scientist matter is eternal. If anyone chooses to assume that it was created by an extramundane power, Haeckel says he will not object. But that is a matter of faith; and 'where faith begins, science ends.' Haeckel says that Darwin's theory of evolution leads inevitably to atheism and materialism." [30]

Finally, referring to the opponents of Darwinism, Hodge again supported the contradiction between Darwinism and orthodoxy. Agassiz and other notables were cited to prove the two positions incompatible.

In his final pages, Hodge laid out his major arguments against Darwinism as a reasonable belief. He identified four major reasons why he objected to the theory of evolution: its *prima facie* incredibility, the fact that its supporters made no pretense that the theory could be proved, the earlier rejection of evolution in V*estiges*, and the evidence for the fixedness of the species. The latter constituted his major argument. In it, he first identified the problem involved in definition of the term "species," then tried to show that evidence uncovered shows only improvement within species, that hybrids are sterile, that geology disproves it and that man is a reasoning being. Hodge then argued for life as originated by God:

Mr. Darwin . . . admits that life owes its origin to the act of the Creator. This, however, the most prominent of the advocates of Darwinism say, is giving up the whole controversy. If you admit the intervention of creative power at one point, you may as well admit it in any other. . . . If the stupendous miracle of Creation be admitted, there is no show of reason for denying supernatural intervention in the operations of nature.[31]

But perhaps Hodge was at his best when he argued for the contradiction between evolution and design:

The grand and fatal objection to Darwinism is this exclusion of design in the origin of species, or the production of living organisms. . . . That design . . . implies intelligence is involved in its very nature. No man can perceive this adaptation of means to the accomplishment of a preconceived end, without experiencing an irresistible conviction that it is the work of mind. No man does doubt it, and no man can doubt it. Darwin does not deny it. Haeckel does not deny it. No Darwinian denies it. What they do is to deny that there is any design in nature.[32]

He then summarized:

[29] *Ibid.*, p. 78.
[30] *Ibid.*, p. 90.
[31] *Ibid.*, p. 164.
[32] *Ibid.*, pp. 168-69.

The conclusion of the whole matter is, that the denial of design in nature is virtually the denial of God. Mr. Darwin's theory does deny all design in nature, therefore, his theory is virtually atheistical.[33]

To hear the respected Dr. Hodge so eloquently and reasonably say that the principles of Darwinism were exactly at odds with those of orthodoxy was enough for many. Whenever the orthodox set out to argue against compromise with evolution, Hodge's arguments pertained. During the twentieth century, the fundamentalists used his arguments to establish enmity between Darwinism and the biblical view of creation. References to the speeches of William Jennings Bryan, of William Bell Riley, and others show the frequent use of Hodge's arguments. His book and his speaking constituted American orthodoxy's major and most comprehensive statement against evolution.

The Reaction of Accommodation

But not all the American church people saw so much black and white as did Dr. Hodge. Many religious leaders were uneasy with his unequivocating position. If, as Hodge said, the acceptance of the theory of natural selection meant the certain rejection of Christianity and the acceptance of atheism, the growth of the popularity of the theory with scientists and intellectuals posed no uncertain threat to the timeliness and validity of the orthodox Christian position. According to Hodge, as more and more scientists accepted the idea of natural selection, more and more scientists and intellectuals would be lost to Christianity. There was no place in his thinking for an Asa Gray, a Christian who believed in evolution.

Happily, the movement to accommodate the popular belief of evolution to Christianity had its champions, too. The consigning of all believers in evolution to a position inimical to the church might be suitable if no one accepted evolution. But with the widespread espousal of the theory by scientists and intellectuals, the church was in danger of being cut off from a great many of these men. This was too great a price to pay for a church whose leaders had enjoyed corroborating their beliefs with those of naturalists. Some of them had to bridge the widening gap.

Perhaps the most prestigious American spokesman for accommodation was James I. McCosh, president of Princeton. Dr. McCosh had come to Princeton from Scotland in 1868. To step into that presidency recognizing that his position on evolution differed from the position of Charles Hodge took some deliberation. McCosh discussed this:

When I was called from the old world to the office which I now hold as president of an important college, I had to consider—I remember seriously pondering the

[33] *Ibid.*, p. 173.

question in the vessel which brought me to this country—whether I should at once avow my convictions or keep them in abeyance. . . . I decided to pursue the open and honest course. . . . I was not a week in Princeton till I let it be known to the upper classes of the college that I was in favor of evolution properly limited and explained.[34]

Although Dr. McCosh had criticised Darwinism and published objections to the theory of natural selection, he made an effort to accommodate some interpretation of the theory of evolution to the orthodox Christian view of religion. In 1888, he published his Bedell Lectures on the subject. In the preface to that series, Dr. McCosh reflected his concern that a rejection of evolution by the church might have problematic effects on students:

I have all along had a sensitive apprehension that the undiscriminating denunciation of evolution from so many pulpits, periodicals and seminaries might drive some of our thoughtful young men to infidelity, as they clearly saw development everywhere in nature, and were at the same time told by their advisers that they could not believe in evolution and yet be Christians. I am gratified . . . to find that I am thanked by my pupils, some of whom have reached the highest positions as naturalists, because in showing them evolution in the works of God, I showed them that this was not inconsistent with religion, and thus enabled them to follow science and yet retain their faith in the Bible.[35]

There were six Bedell lectures on Evolution. McCosh dealt with "The State of the Question," "The Organic History," "Powers Modifying Evolution," "Beneficence in the Method of Evolution," "Geology and Scripture" and "The Age of Man." The first, "The State of the Question," was the speech which summarized his point of view on the question. In it he defined evolution as "the drawing of one thing out of another." [36] He traced the chain of causes back to God as the first Cause, an assumption which he never questioned. Neither did he question the possibility of an immediate and instanteous creation:

The All-Mighty God, in all his works, might have acted immediately—that is, without any creature instrumentality, He might have produced crops and cattle, heaved up mountains and lowered plains, determined birth and death without the use of means of any kind.[37]

But, while admitting the possibility that God could have created without intermediate steps, he denied that this was the case; "God has been pleased to arrange instead that every physical event has a physical cause." [38]

In explaining the nature of causation, McCosh referred to "organized

[34] James I. McCosh, *The Religious Aspect of Evolution* (New York: Charles Scribner's Sons, 1890), pp. viii, ix.

[35] *Ibid.*, pp. ix, x.

[36] *Ibid.*, p. 1.

[37] *Ibid.*, pp. 1, 119.

[38] *Ibid.*, p. 2.

causes." His effort to relate evolution to Christian concepts led him to liken organic development to the maturing of children:

Of mature age, I know that I am developed from the boy of six as I remember him going to school. . . . We do not complain of these evolutions; we do not denounce them as atheistic. We are grateful for some of them; as, for example, that we have been nursed by a mother's love and watched over by a father's care. The new evolutions of plants and animal races which we are now called to consider, may only be a farther evolution of the old ones.[39]

Dr. McCosh not only tried to see the doctrine of evolution in as positive a light as is possible, he addressed himself to the controversy which had grown up between evolutionists and religious anti-evolutionists. He faced squarely the problem that Hodge created in his "all or nothing" analysis of the inherent atheistic qualities of evolution. He spoke of the young naturalist who feels that he must choose between religion and science:

The great body of naturalists, all younger than forty, certainly all younger than thirty, are sure that they see evolution in nature; but they are assured by their teachers or the religious press that, if evolution does everything, there is nothing left for God to do, and they see no proof of His existence.[40]

Here McCosh rejected Darwin's particular position on evolution:

Mr. Darwin . . . is constantly drawing the distinction in this form; between "natural selection" and "supernatural design," between "natural law" and "special creation" . . . [but] "the supernatural power" is to be recognized in the natural law.[41]

So, while accepting evolution, McCosh saw and pointed out the beneficent hand of God guiding the selection of the variation: a kind of supernatural selection. "God has provided the horse with its hard hoof for man, who to make it harder adds a shoe. I hold that there are as clear proofs of design in the hoof as in the shoe upon it." [42] And:

The principle of the survival of the fittest is a beneficent provision, as it preserves the strong and the useful, while the weak is allowed to die out and leave room for something else to take its place in the exuberance of God's works.[43]

In concluding his speech, McCosh left room for change of species:

I have never been able to see that religion, and in particular that Scripture in which our religion is embodied, is concerned with the question of the absolute immutability of species. Final Cause, which is a doctrine of natural religion, should

[39] *Ibid.*, p. 4.
[40] *Ibid.*, p. 6.
[41] *Ibid.*, p. 7.
[42] *Ibid.*, p. 15.
[43] *Ibid.*, p. 16.

217

be satisfied with species being so fixed as to secure the stability of nature. . . . Nature is kept steadfast and theism is satisfied, even though in rare circumstances a new species should be produced to diversify nature and make it equal to the duty of peopling the earth, which is certainly one of the purposes of God by which he widens the sphere of happiness."[44]

So, by admitting the possibility of God's benevolent intervention in the affairs of nature in the selection process, McCosh made it possible for budding young scientists to make peace between their scientific and religious views. Princeton had changed dramatically in the time between the death of Hodge in 1878 and the publication of McCosh's speeches in the 1880's. McCosh had articulated what was to be the beginning of the acceptance of some form of evolution by the American Protestant ministry. That the position was popular is evident from his testimony: "I have been gratified to find that none of the church has assailed me, and this has convinced me that their doubts about evolution have proceeded mainly from the bad use to which the doctrine had been turned." [45]

The Reaction of Endorsement

What McCosh had begun, many imaginative preachers eagerly continued. While most of the conservative literalists held to the hopeful lampooning of Wilberforce, or to Hodge's arguments which insisted that evolution was necessarily atheistic, many of the more liberal pulpits were used to endorse a form of theistic evolution. Such an endorsement came from Henry Ward Beecher.

Beecher, the pulpit orator of Plymouth Church in Brooklyn, was an enthusiastic supporter of evolutionary theology. He admitted his great indebtedness to Herbert Spencer's writings in the area of evolution theory, and he endorsed the view that survival of the fittest implied a God of grand design. His enthusiasm for the view was evident in the introduction to his volume of sermons on evolution:

For myself, while finding no need of changing my idea of the Divine personality because of new light upon his mode of working, I have trailed the evolutionary philosophy with joy. . . . The underlying truth, as a Law of Nature [that is, a regular method of the divine action] I accept and use, and thank God for it."[46]

Beecher preached his famous evolution sermons to his Plymouth Church congregation between May 18, 1885, and July 5, 1885. They were reported and revised by Beecher himself before publication. He approached the

---

[44] Ibid., p. 27.

[45] Ibid., p. ix.

[46] Henry Ward Beecher, Evolution and Religion (New York: Fords, Howard Shilbert, 1885), p. 3.

problem from many angles: "The Signs of the Times" rebuked men of religion for not discerning the work of God that was going on in their own times; "Evolution in Human Consciousness of the Idea of God" presented a discussion of the evolution of Christian thought about God; "The Two Revelations" considered man and matter as revelations of God's creative energy; "The Inspiration of the Bible" saw evolution as freeing the Scriptures from the bondage of literalism; "The Sinfulness of Man" tied the spiritual growth of man toward perfection (a sort of supernatural selection) to the evolutionary theory of natural selection; "The New Birth" demonstrated that regeneration is a culminating stage in the evolution of the species; "Divine Providence and Design" provided an identification of God as the designer of the universe; and "Evolution and the Church" considered the likely effects of evolution on the organized church. It was in the seventh sermon of the collection, "Divine Providence and Design," that he fully developed his arguments for a revised approach to design.

For "Divine Providence and Design," he took his text from Isaiah 46:5, "To whom will ye liken me, and make me equal, and compare me, that we may be like?" By way of introduction he developed an argument for the inscrutability of God and suggested that "Any formulation of the divine nature, which becomes definite, crystalline, philosophic, is a perpetual affront to the method of God's revelation, whether in Scripture or in science." [47] He then pictured science as an iconoclastic tool useful to destroy the false "idealizations of the Greek philosophy and of the hard and organic materialism of the Roman mind;" [48] to destroy also the "ignorant analysis and quibbling refinements of the schoolmen of Medieval ages," and, conversely, a tool to help man realize once again that God is inscrutable. [49]

Beecher then announced two divisions of his discussion:

It will be my design this morning, therefore, to discuss at least two of these matters—the question of design in creation and the question of a general and special Providence, as they stand related, not to the Scriptural testimony alone, but to what we now know of the course of natural law in this world. [50]

In advancing the argument for design in creation, he attacked atheism as taxing "credulity a great deal more than even the most superstitious notions do." [51] Having denied that matter originated in itself and began to progress from the origin, he stated his position "that evolution, if it allows for an original creation of matter and God as the original cause, is an acceptable explanation of nature. Time and matter being given and certain forces es-

[47] *Ibid.*, p. 110.
[48] *Ibid.*, p. 111.
[49] *Ibid.*
[50] *Ibid.*
[51] *Ibid.*

tablished, then the world, to be sure, could be unfolded as it is taught by Evolution." [52]

In addition to admitting evolution as a possible explanation for the development of species, Beecher argued for the contribution of evolution to a bigger and better concept of design:

It [design] is being restored in a larger and grander way, which only places the fact upon a wider space, and makes the outcome more wonderful. Special creation, and the adaptation in consequence of it, of structure to uses in animals, and in the vegetable kingdom of their surroundings, has always been an element of God's work regarded as most remarkable.[53]

He contrasted the "old view" of design with the "new view":

The old theory conceived God as creating things for special uses. . . . Thus God adapted all his creation . . . the climate and the soil and the circumstances. . . . Then comes evolution and teaches that God created through the mediation of natural laws; that creation . . . was a process of slow growth. . . . The adaptation then of plants to their condition did not arise from the direct command of the Great Gardener; but from the fact that from these infinite gradations of plants, only those survived and propagated themselves which were able to bear the climate and soil in which they found themselves.[54]

Driving home his idea of design of selection, Beecher asserted:

If single acts would evince design, how much more a vast universe, that by inherent laws gradually builded itself, and then created its own plants and animals, a universe so adjusted that it left by the way the poorest things, and steadily wrought toward more complex, ingenious, and beautiful results. Who designed this mighty machine, created matter, gave to it its laws, and impressed upon it that tendency which has brought forth the almost infinite results on the globe, and wrought them into a perfect system? Design by wholesale is grander than design by retail.[55]

Then taking the famous Paley watch-and-design argument, he brought it up-to-date and incorporated in it his concept of design by evolution:

If it be an argument of design that a man could make one watch, is it not a sublimer argument of design that there is a man existing who could create a manufactory turning out millions of watches, and by machinery too, so that the human hand has little to do but to adjust the parts already created by machines. . . . Is not the creator of the system a more sublime designer than the creator of any single act? [56]

Realizing that his first point could lead to a transcendent but not immanent God, a kind of God Emeritus, he shifted to the second major area of

[52] Ibid.
[53] Ibid., p. 112.
[54] Ibid., p. 113.
[55] Ibid., p. 115.
[56] Ibid., p. 116.

his sermon. Here he discussed the effects of a universal law of evolution on the doctrine of special providence over man and events. He showed that a belief in a God who is not personal and concerned for his people is a belief which is at best depressing.

He attacked on two grounds the notion that God would not intervene in natural laws. First, that it is not necessary to accept the fact that if he sets up laws he could not intervene and, secondly, that laws are not so unchangeable and irresistible as might be imagined. Here he said,

Of all things within the conception of the imagination, there is nothing gentler, nothing more pliable, nothing more applicable, nothing more controlable, than natural physical laws. They are more like the silk thread than they are like the needle that carries it.[57]

Thus, by putting one law against another, man can make laws do, by the fusion of human reason and human will, that which they would never do of themselves. A great many analogies were drawn here urging that God controls laws as man does with electricity, steamboats, and factories. "If, then, God cannot create a providence by using, not violating, natural laws, he cannot do what the meanest creatures on earth can do in some degree and measure." [58]

Beecher's conclusion referred to evolution as providing man with a better view of God—a God of design, but one who uses the laws he has designed to bring good things to his children. He concluded:

So, brethren, be not in haste to cast away, on the instruction or the misinterpretation of science, yet crude in many of its parts, that faith of childhood, that faith of your fathers, that faith which is the joy and should be the courage of every rightminded man, the faith that God's eye is on you, and that He cares, He guides, He defends, and will bring you safely from earth to eternal life.[59]

And so, with Beecher, the popular pulpit had begun to learn how to make its peace with evolution. This acceptance, though not universally applied throughout Christendom, showed that harmony was possible between the scientist and the one who believed in a God of design.

Conclusion

When theologians were faced with a theory of existence which ran directly counter to what had been popularly believed, they had to react. The reactions were not neat and orderly and did not proceed in a step-by-step adjustment of beliefs. Some men insisted on the literal biblical view of creation. These men persist until today. It is their strategy to deny the

[57] *Ibid.*, p. 120.
[58] *Ibid.*, p. 123.
[59] *Ibid.*, p. 124.

"fact" of evolution and to say that acceptance of any form of that belief is a denial of the inspiration of the Bible and will lead ultimately to atheism. To these men, the ridicule of Wilberforce and the logic of Hodge are still pertinent and useful.

But the mainstream of Christendom has bowed to the growing popularity of the evolutionary theory. A re-explanation of design in nature which gives an interpretation of science which allows for "in the beginning God created," and for an interpretation of scripture which allows for some form of modification and selection of characteristics, has been the goal of much of Christian theology since Darwin. That was the goal of McCosh and Beecher. While the enthusiasm of Beecher for evolution has not generally been the position of the American church, the prevailing attitude has been of cautious acceptance of the theory and an accommodation to it. The tension which was precipitated by the publication of *Origin of Species* in 1859 was relieved by the acceptance of the possibility of changing species, so long as that change was not accompanied by an insistence in the eternality of matter and a denial of design.

11

THE SOCIAL GOSPEL: PREACHING REFORM 1875-1915

William Bos

Clyde Faries

The latter part of the nineteenth century in the United States was a crucial period in economic and social development. It was an era of war-stimulated, rapid industrial growth, marked also by a fast-growing population and a fundamental sociological change from a rural to a predominantly urban way of life.

Socio-Economic Conditions

The period was, in general, one of rapid increase in national wealth, highlighted by the amassing of great fortunes by the Harrimans, the Rockefellers, the Mellons, and others. Post-reconstruction America witnessed a sharpened competition for wealth and a narrowed distribution of property. The new industrialism lifted burdens from the shoulders of those who managed the nation's wealth, only to lower them upon those who produced that wealth. A new middle class of prosperous merchants, minor business and industry executives, and professional people partially filled the widening gulf between the wealthy and the poor.

Farmers, laborers, and small businessmen watched profits and prestige of big business and industry soar while their own material wealth and social status began to decay. For example, the farmer's income dropped continuously from the 1870's until the turn of the century. Wheat went from $1.06 a bushel in 1873, to $0.75 in 1887, to $0.63 in 1896. Corn, following a similar pattern, fell from $0.43 to $0.30 in the same period, and cotton sank from $0.15 to $0.06 per pound.[1] Kansas grain farmers even burned corn when it became cheaper than fuel, and southern farmers often returned home with their loads of cotton, their only product of a year's labor, because there was no market for it. The crop lien system helped to worsen the farmer's plight. Under this plan a farmer pledged the crop he had not yet planted in return

[1] U. S. Department of Agriculture. *Yearbook*, 1901, pp. 699, 709, 754.

for his "furnish." When, with his borrowed money, he had bought seed, feed, and groceries at unusually high prices and added as much as thirty percent in interest, the crop sometimes no more than paid his debts. Railroads, free to adjust rates and handling, "took as much from the farmer as possible without taking all." [2] By handing out free passes,[3] railroad companies corrupted so many public officials that farm organizations were powerless against them. So desperate was the rural economy that Mary Elizabeth Lease advised farmers to "raise less corn and more *Hell.*" [4]

Farmers moved to town in search of work. Small businessmen, pressured from the shops by powerful combinations, entered the industrial labor force. Hundreds of thousands of foreign laborers arrived on the labor market. Consequently wages came down without bringing a similar decline in prices of manufactured goods.

Accompanying the growth of large cities came an increase in social ills. New problems brought new institutions. During this period the Woman's Christian Temperance Union was organized (1874) to combat the excessive use of alcohol and the Salvation Army was formed (1879) to help all who gave way to the corrupting forces of industrialization.

Also as a direct result of urbanization with its improved mobility and concentration of people, the churches became less significant in social life, and this, in turn, produced a slackening of interest in the church and a marked increase in the number of the "unchurched."

A spirit of reform swept the country—economic and social. Farmers, laborers, the unemployed, and small businessmen, frustrated in their attempts to rise from mudsill level in the new society by manipulations of powerful industrial leaders, reacted with a myriad of reform movements. The Grange, the Farmers Alliance, and the Populists beckoned farmers to fight for a better share of American prosperity, while labor unions promised a better life for nonagricultural workers. When the railroads operating east of the Mississippi announced wage cuts in 1877, a major struggle ensued and in turn gave rise to an increasing awareness of the significance of the labor force to all society. The American Federation of Labor came to the forefront with a campaign for the eight-hour workday.

The Pulpit Begins to Act

Pulpit response to industrialization and the spirit of reform that swept the country was slow, confused, and almost disastrous. American ministers counseled themselves that economic and social uprisings were not proper

---

[2] *Progressive Farmer*, July 31, 1888; cited in John Hicks, *The Populist Revolt* (Minneapolis: The University of Minnesota Press, 1931), p. 85.
[3] *Ibid.*
[4] Hicks, *The Populist Revolt*, p. 160.

concerns of the church. Under pressure for pulpit sanctions of reform movements on the one hand and for stabilizing the established economic order on the other, ministers generally denied the responsibility of the church in such matters. Affirming that their mission was to spread the gospel, not to be involved in politics, many preachers ignored the social turmoil within their own communities. Published sermons of the period suggest that universals replaced specifics in most Sunday morning services. Church leaders resisted with complacency efforts of a few to make basic readjustments in church teachings to meet the social, economic, and moral changes.

When the waves of protest reached such proportions that they engulfed almost every segment of American life, however, the church could no longer remain aloof. Religious leaders inevitably were forced to play an active role in guiding the response to industrialism; they were forced to consider the collective influence of Christianity on society as a whole. But in its effort to ameliorate growing social and economic evils and to guide the country from the brink of revolution, the church became involved in directing its own internal reform. Clashes between the forces of reform and the established order goaded the church into an internal controversy as to what Christian teachings were most applicable to economic conflict.

The developing reaction tended to become polarized. At one pole were those who experienced a growing conviction that the church ought to be concerned about the problems of the day and involved in the effort to find solutions for them. At the other pole were conservative groups. New denominational entities, such as the Church of God, the Christian and Missionary Alliance, the Church of the Nazarene, the Assemblies of God, the Free Methodists, and the Pentecostal Church emerged as a result of dissatisfaction with both extremes.

Responses to the Issue

Sharp differences among religious leaders of the time revolved around this proposition: that the kingdom of God should be built through social reform. Lines were clearly drawn. Those who urged adaptation and implementation of the proposition were the progressives or liberals, the "social gospelers." Those who resisted and opposed change and defended the time-honored conservative views and methods were the "pietists."

"The church is a social institution," said Shailer Mathews, professor of New Testament History at the University of Chicago in 1894 and champion of the social gospel in the midwest. He continued:

And the present duty of the church? If it would be as significant as its past and its Founder make possible, it can no longer preach merely an individualistic salvation. It must educate the social sympathies of its children; it must have its answer from the countingroom as well as from the pulpit; it must train its members to trust their Christian impulse to aid with whatever cause is true and beautiful and sane; it must teach that, if there can be no regenerate society without regenerate men, neither can there be regenerate men without a regenerate society.[5]

He saw the social gospel, not as a new alternative way of finding individual salvation, but as the natural and inevitable impact on society of regenerate individuals who have simply banded together in mutual esteem and in making common cause to spread the gospel among their fellowmen. Others went further and urged that reformed social institutions were a means of grace, even *the* means of grace.

Probably the majority of ministers in their pulpits did not even mention social and economic problems arising from the industrial revolution.[6] They rationalized that the pulpit was a place from which to proclaim the gospel, not a place for agitating for social and economic reform. The preacher's job was to preach about Jesus, not to direct the nation's economy. God's way, the Reverend William L. Butler told his congregation in Mayfield, Kentucky, in the early 1880's, is the way of the New Testament. "All this application of Christian money outside of the fellowship of the New Testament," he maintained, "is a protest of the wisdom of man against God's way."[7] He advised against the church taking any part in reform efforts. C. H. Winders, in a sermon before the national convention of leaders of the Christian Church, Disciples of Christ, summarized the position of those choosing to ignore social and economic questions:

Men are ever ready to condemn the church because it does not espouse their particular scheme looking toward social, political, moral or religious reform. "Bid my brother divide the inheritance with me," men are everywhere saying. And the church is right when it answers with Jesus, "Who made me a judge or a divider over you? Take heed, and beware of all covetousness, for a man's life consisteth not in the abundance of the things which he possesseth."[8]

Many ministers of the era were so committed to the ideal of personal regeneration that they expressed little concern for the economic or social improvement of society in general. Typical of these men were Charles G. Finney and Dwight L. Moody. Both were aware of the ills of society; yet both saw the remedy, not in terms of social movements and corporate actions, but rather in the natural outcome of the conversion of individuals from lives of sinfulness to lives of holiness. Finney saw the world's greatest need, not in

[5] Shailer Mathews, *The Church and the Changing Order* (New York: The Macmillan Company, 1909), pp. 5-6.
[6] In the writers' estimate, less than five percent of available sermons of the period mention social or economic problems of the era.
[7] F. D. Srygley, *Biographies and Sermons* (Nashville: By the author, 1898), p. 111.
[8] The Christian Church. *Centennial Convention Report* (Cincinnati: Standard Publishing Company, 1909), p. 276.

terms of an improved society in general, but in terms of regenerated individuals as the essence of an improved society.

Moody, a pre-millennialist, was convinced that society was steadily deteriorating and would continue in this way until the bodily return of Christ to earth—an event which he believed to be imminent.[9] He believed that a person's faith was an individual matter and was not more than incidentally influenced by the milieu of the society in which he lived:

"Except a man be born again, he cannot see the kingdom." How are you going to get in? Going to try to educate men? That is what men are trying to do, but it is not God's way. A man is not much better after he is educated if he hasn't got God in his heart. Other men say, "I will work my way up." That is not God's way and the only way is God's way—to be born again.[10]

He thought only in terms of an individual's spiritual experience, rather than of the the impact of Christianity upon society in general.

A large segment of the ministry tried to pacify disgruntled farmers and laborers. Blaming the monetary system for the farmers' plight,[11] conservative ministers felt free to encourage them to accept poverty without trying to alter the economic and social order. "It is said that a dollar a day is not enough for a wife and five or six children," Henry Ward Beecher told one congregation:

No, not if the man smokes and drinks beer. . . . But is not a dollar a day enough to buy bread with? Water costs nothing; and a man who cannot live on bread is not fit to live. What is the use of civilization that simply makes man incompetent to live under the conditions which exist?[12]

On other occasions he was known to have roundly denounced railroad employees for their unwillingness to endure their lot without complaint, though he personally had no need to practice the virtues of austerity which he so vociferously preached.

The Conservative Defense

Church leaders most responsible for changing the image of the church during the reform period were probably those who defended big business against attack by labor and farm groups. Preaching, as they did, that economic growth was a product of spirituality, these religious leaders aroused the sensitivity of the poor and solidified the forces of reform. Labor's protestations that unionism would insure, not destroy, profit seemed only to goad conservative church leaders into proclaiming more vehemently that

[9] E. T. Thompson, *Changing Emphases in American Preaching* (Philadelphia: The Westminster Press, 1943), p. 126.

[10] Dwight L. Moody, a sermon, "On Being Born Again," *New Sermons, Addresses and Prayers by Dwight Lyman Moody* (Cincinnati: Goodspeed, 1877), p. 124.

[11] Hicks, *The Populist Revolt*, p. 87.

[12] *The Christian Union*, August 1, 1877, p. 93.

the rise of unions meant the collapse of capitalism and perhaps the collapse of the church. The Grangers' revolt, the railway strikes, and the Haymarket riot aroused in these leaders what Andrew Carnegie called "a nationwide crusade against anarchism." [13]

The religious press became vocal on the issues of the day, most organs staunchly resisting change and assuming the posture of conservative fundamentalism. *The Watchman* called for troops to put a "pitiless stop" to the strikes of 1894.[14] *The Congregationalist* suggested the Gatling gun as the best way to deal with a mob of workers.[15] *The Christian Advocate* denounced anyone who would speak in defense of the men condemned to hang for their part in the Haymarket affair,[16] and *The Christian Union* urged that pulpit advocates of anarchism be suppressed.[17] Reactionary preachers failed to note that police had shot down strikers unnecessarily or that the Haymarket meeting had been peaceable until police broke it up. So violently opposed were some church leaders to the advancements by reformers that they demanded the actual slaughter of picketing and demonstrating groups. Reformers were branded as ungodly and inhuman, while those who crushed the efforts for reform were called "Soldiers of the Cross."

The bitterness that poured from the conservative pulpit seemed endless. One clergyman told his congregation:

There are times when mercy is a mistake and this is one of them. . . . What a sorry set of ignoramuses they must be who imagine that they are fighting for the rights of labor in coming together to prevent other men from working for low wages because, forsooth, they are discontented with them.[18]

Not only did clergymen propose to meet violence with more ruthless violence, but they also demanded strict legislation to avert future collective protests. One church leader wanted to make it a crime "to starve a poor man, or rob a rich one."[19] Another believed "the whipping post should be revived."[20] An even more bitter minister maintained that no treatment would be too severe for "men who, in a country like the U. S. instigate or aid . . . revolution."[21] Some even wanted legislation to prevent businessmen from conferring with labor leaders. One Christian writer warned, "Extend the rights of the state to compelling of men or corporation to confer with representatives of labor and you have despotism." [22]

[18] Andrew Carnegie, "Wealth," *North American Review*, CXLVIII (June, 1889), 653-54.

[14] *The Watchman*, April 12, 1893, p. 1.

[15] *The Congregationalist*, May 13, 1887, p. 162.

[16] *The Christian Advocate*, October 6, 1887, p. 641.

[17] *The Christian Union*, May 13, 1886, p. 295.

[18] *The Christian Union*, July 25, 1887, p. 62; and August 1, 1887, p. 82.

[19] *The Christian Advocate*, May 2, 1878, p. 280; and June 13, 1878, p. 376.

[20] *The Congregationalist*, February 27, 1878, p. 68.

[21] *The Churchman*, October 28, 1892, p. 496.

[22] *The Christian Advocate*, July 14, 1892, pp. 460-61.

Holders of the sanguine position based their belief on the philosophy that the wealthy become wealthy because they are godly and the poor are poor because they are sinners. *The Congregationalist* characterized the unemployed as "profane, licentious, filthy, vermin-swarming thieves, petty robbers and sometimes murderers, social pests and perambulatory nuisances." [23] Strikes grew out of "corrupt human-nature," according to this point of view,[24] and strikes in turn represented the most "withering and outrageous despotism . . . in the world." [25] A writer for *The Independent* saw all strikers as public enemies, "worse than wild beasts turned loose upon Society." [26] They were, in the eyes of another clergyman, "reckless desperadoes to whom the most fiendish excesses of the days of the Commune of Paris were due." [27]

Some church leaders opposed to the progress of labor tried to "reason" with rather than suppress reformers. These "reasoners," who were less vengeful but just as vehement as their fellow reactionaries, filled churches, classrooms, papers, books, and magazines with their message of discouragement for advocates of change. Noah Porter, president of Yale University, argued that property rights are derived from a higher law than the law of man.[28] Daniel Gregory, author of the most popular textbook on Christian ethics of the day, held a similar belief. God put the power of acquisitiveness in man for a good and noble purpose, wrote Gregory.[29] John D. Rockefeller's explanation to the first graduating class at the University of Chicago that "the good Lord gave me my money," [30] expressed the position echoed in a flood of contemporary books that financial success results from practicing Christian ethics.

Whether through benevolence, faith, or the conviction that their best financial interest would be served, industrialists chose to support the church. The Rockefellers, the Drews, the Carnegies, and others financed the construction of fine, new edifices in urban areas as well as the training and salaries of the ministers in the pulpits who plied their congregations with the gospel of wealth. Students in church-endowed universities were advised that wealth and godliness go hand in hand.

Meanwhile, congregations in the poorer churches heard soothing messages of the wonderful life after death. Some Protestant ministers rejoiced that poverty existed in such abundance that the wealthy could express their

[23] *The Congregationalist*, February 27, 1878, p. 68.
[24] *The Christian Advocate*, July 23, 1885, p. 470.
[25] *The Independent*, February 3, 1887, p. 17.
[26] *Ibid.*
[27] *The Congregationalist*, August 2, 1877, p. 16.
[28] Noah Porter, *Elements of Moral Science* (New York: Charles Scribner's Sons, 1885), p. 368.
[29] Daniel Gregory, *Christian Ethics* (Philadelphia: Eldridge & Brother, 1875), p. 224.
[30] John Flynn, *God's Gold* (New York: Harcourt, Brace & Company, 1932), p. 306.

229

Christianity by giving alms,[31] while some Catholic leaders championed the position that people should "let well enough alone." [32] Leaders from the most conservative clergy ignored protestations of the poor even when church prestige and authority with the working man went into obvious decline. "God has bestowed upon us certain powers and gifts," said James McCosh, president of Princeton, "which no one is at liberty to take from us or to interfere with." [33] But even more patronizing and more frustrating to the hard-pressed producing class were comments from the pulpit such as those made by Bishop William Lawrence that, "Godliness is in league with riches. Material prosperity is helping to make the national character sweeter, more joyous, more unselfish, more Christlike." [34]

Because so many urban Protestant ministers chose to cultivate the middle and upper classes who controlled industrial development rather than support the course of workingmen toward reform, church membership among laborers declined sharply.[35] As a result, once prominent ministers lost prestige not only with the poor but also with their supporters. Preachers were replaced in large numbers on boards of trustees of universities by businessmen and lawyers. From 1860 to 1930, the percentage of clergymen on boards of private universities dropped from thirty-nine to seven. They felt a similar decline in their economic standing.[36] In gaining the support of industrialists the church suffered a general loss of influence. One historian observed, "Never before had the church been materially more powerful or spiritually less effective." [37]

The condescending attitude of some church leaders caused many workers to lower their evaluations of the church. In the Pullman strike, the religious press was generally hostile to the American Railroad Union.[38] The Presbyterian General Assembly called for increased evangelism as a result of the Haymarket riots.[39] Whereas such pulpit proclamations were sincere, workers apparently looked upon them as mockery.

[31] M. A. Selby, "Non-Sectarian Charities," *Watchman Examiner*, December, 1892, pp. 438-39.

[32] *Catholic World*, January, 1888, p. 437.

[33] James McCosh, *Our Moral Nature* (New York: Charles Scribner's Sons, 1892), p. 40.

[34] William Lawrence, "The Relation of Wealth to Morals," *World's Work* I (January, 1901), 286-90.

[35] Samuel Hays, *Response to Industrialism* (Chicago: The University of Chicago Press, 1960), p. 72.

[36] *Ibid.*

[37] Henry Steele Commager, *The American Mind* (New Haven: Yale University Press, 1959), p. 172.

[38] Henry F. May, *Protestant Churches and Industrial America* (New York: Harper & Brothers, 1949 [Octagon Books, 1963]), pp. 108-9.

[39] The Presbyterian General Assembly, *Minutes*, 1886, p. 183.

Growing Sentiment for Reform

Meanwhile, in both Protestant and Catholic churches a small group of reformers worked toward complete Christianization of American society—in government, in commerce, and in private life. Rebel forces began to call from the pulpit for economic and social reform. They meant to plug the gaps in their spheres of influence created by time and industrial revolution. Churchmen who were the first to conclude that a change of attitude was necessary to save the church began with rather timid suggestions of realignment. As early as 1886, growing support of labor could be seen. The strike of 1886 brought less denunciation from the church than did the 1877 labor troubles. In 1886 some blamed the violence on low wages and unscrupulous acts by management.[40] *The Watchman* criticized workers for the acts at the Haymarket, but asked at the same time for an evaluation of the needs of specific industries instead of calling for the Gatling gun.[41] Old certainties had begun to lose strength.

Russell H. Conwell was a spokesman for the transition. While serving as pastor of Grace Baptist Church in Philadelphia he became increasingly concerned about the social implications of the gospel, particularly in terms of education. As a result he founded Temple College, now Temple University, in 1888, a school geared to serving the community rather than denominational leadership needs. He was a man in the tradition of Finney and Moody, but with strong social concerns. He understood the church to be a fellowship of believers, and therefore led in the development of a social program for his congregation that was unknown in his day. He felt that the society of regenerate persons ought to do more than enjoy common faith and fellowship; they ought to contribute to the improvement of their society, especially by the establishment and maintenance of schools, hospitals, and other such means of social betterment. But he did not believe in the church entering the political arena. Of this he said, "Teach men to be good and the government will be right." [42]

Various Adaptive Positions

Slowly there arose a new concern for the sins, not only of individuals, but of society in general. The leaders in this concern were crusaders for a better society: better working conditions for the laborers, improvement of economic standards, greater cultural advantages for all. They wished to regenerate all of society by raising the standard of living.

Ministers who did pick up the cross of the poor did so with visions of re-

[40] May, *Protestant Churches and Industrial America*, p. 99.

[41] *The Watchman*, September 12, 1889, p. 51.

[42] Agnes R. Burr, *Russell H. Conwell and His Work* (Philadelphia: John C. Winston, 1923), p. 34.

forming the system that produced poverty. They interpreted continued labor violence and economic injustice perpetrated upon workers by industry as evidence that the time had come when able-bodied men could no longer make a respectable living wage.[43] They believed businessmen to be captured by a system in which competition had become so keen that to survive required following an ethic of expediency. For instance, Walter Rauschenbusch believed that industrialism had caused great human deterioration:

If some angel with prophetic foresight had witnessed the epoch, would he not have winged his way back to heaven to tell God that human suffering was drawing to its end? Instead of that a long-drawn wail of misery followed wherever the powermachine came. It swept the bread from men's tables and the pride from their hearts.[44]

He argued that the capitalistic system and Christianity were in direct conflict. Competition in commerce, he said, exalted selfishness over dignity of moral principles and appealed to man's most base motives.[45]

Feeling that so many wrongs, so much human suffering resulted from swift industrial growth, a few ministers believed that the pulpit should be the center of a great crusade in the name of God. Consequently, they joined with labor organizations in trying to change sweatshops into well-ventilated, well-ordered places to work and in trying to move children from the production lines into the schools. Washington Gladden, Josiah Strong, Francis Peabody, and others urged aggressive action by those deprived of the fruits of their labor. An ex-Methodist minister, Samuel Fielden, was exhorting the crowd in Haymarket Square when the police stepped in to break up the meeting and touched off the Chicago riot. Methodist minister William H. Carwardine of Pullman, Illinois, preached that increased striking was the only defense of the strikers in the Pullman dispute. The atmosphere in Pullman, he said, was one of suspicion and tyranny. Press stories of company contributions to the poor were mere propaganda;[46] the strike was caused by company tyranny.[47] By forming a Federal Council of Churches, reformers managed to unite their efforts toward social and economic change.

By the turn of the century, reform preachers were convinced that economic and social reform could be achieved. Thus, influential leaders were willing to speak more forthrightly on social and economic injustices. In 1875 few ministers would have branded hard-nosed business procedure as sinful. Yet, early in the new century, Cornelius Woelfkin of the Fifth Avenue Baptist Church in New York City told his congregation, "The hard-hearted,

[43] *Christian Union*, November 26, 1885, pp. 5-6.

[44] Commager, *The American Mind*, p. 175.

[45] Walter Rauschenbusch, *Christianity and the Social Crisis* (New York: The Macmillan Company, 1920), p. 265.

[46] William H. Carwardine, *The Pullman Strike* (4th ed.; Chicago: C. H. Kerr and Company, 1894), p. 25.

[47] *Twentieth Century*, July 12, 1894, pp. 2-3.

tight-fisted businessman, who grinds down employees, and in selfish greed achieves his ambition at the expense of wounded feelings, broken hearts, and discouraged lives" is in sin.[48] By 1915 perhaps a majority of churches with large congregations had disciples of the humanity movement in their pulpits.

Catholics were slower, generally, than Protestants to progress toward championship of individual rights. Churchmen Peter Dietz, John A. Ryan, William Kerby and others fought to develop new attitudes within Catholic congregations toward charity, workers' rights, poverty, and intemperance,[49] while Cardinals Gibbons and Griffon[50] dissuaded Rome from condemning the labor movement.[51] Yet not until 1891 did Pope Leo XIII act officially to justify social insurance and eight-hour-day legislation.[52] The Catholic Church, however, lagged behind in progress toward intellectual liberalization so much that large employers of industrial labor gave considerable monetary support to the Roman Church, allegedly as a means of keeping the great number of foreign-born workers under control.[53] Although some priests persisted in fighting for reform, generally they were overwhelmed by their tradition-minded superiors.[54] Bishop Chatard, for example, turned thumbs down on reform with the admonition that "the law of absolute equality is a figment of the wild brain of the agitator, coquetting with the ignorance of the mass of mankind." [55] Nevertheless those crusading priests, the ones able to persevere in reform efforts, enjoyed greater sanctuary from outside coercion than did Protestant ministers who depended on congregational approval to retain their pulpits.[56]

The concern now became one of Christian leadership for the new reforms. James M. Buckley told his congregation that those who would change established institutions would do so to no avail unless Christian principles were used to change them.[57] Archbishop Ireland of St. Paul urged that the Bible be used as the guide for reform. The Bible, he said, is a "great book of holy social work for men. The miracles of our blessed Lord were primarily exercised for the good of the body, for the temporal felicity of

[48] Cornelius Woelfkin, *Religion: Thirteen Sermons* (New York: Harper & Brothers, 1928), p. 95.

[49] Robert D. Cross, *The Emergence of Liberal Catholicism in America* (New York: Harvard University Press, 1958), p. 111.

[50] *Ibid.*

[51] William Warren Sweet, *The Story of Religion in America* (New York: Harper & Row, 1939 [1950]) p. 508.

[52] Cross, *The Emergence of Liberal Catholicism in America*, p. 109.

[53] *Ibid.*, p. 34.

[54] *Ibid.*, p. 107.

[55] William Chatard, "Catholic Societies," *American Catholic Quarterly Review*, IV (April, 1879), 218.

[56] J. A. Ryan, *Social Doctrine in Action* (New York: Harper & Brothers 1941), p. 114.

[57] Jesse Hurlbut, *Sunday Half Hours with Great Preachers* (Cincinnati: John C. Winston, 1907), p. 572.

man." [58] The Rev. Gerald Smith called upon businessmen to "see the splendid opportunity here for ministry to the thousands in their employ." Men of means, he maintained, should welcome the privilege of providing safeguards for their workers.[59] Washington Gladden wrote,

The church is not in the world to save itself, but to save the world; and when it exhibits no power to regenerate the community in which it stands, it is clear that the salt has lost its savor and is good for nothing but to be cast out and trodden under foot of men. . . . It is impossible, therefore, to segregate the church from the community. The very function of the church is found in its organic relation to the community.[60]

He expressed the aim of the reformers when he criticized the wage system as being "anti-social and anti-Christian." It is necessary, he said, to incorporate " 'Thou shalt love thy neighbor as thyself' into the relationship of employer and employees." [61] He saw the function of Christianity and the church to be the molding of perfect man into a perfect society—he found it impossible to separate individual man from his society and asked the question, "Can it be true that there are churches bearing the name of Jesus Christ which are understood to be churches for the 'lower classes'; churches in which considerations of wealth or rank or culture largely determine membership?" [62]

A new generation of hard-hitting social reformers emerged from the shambles of division within almost all major religious organizations. Peter Dietz, C. M. Sheldon, John Ryan, Walter Rauschenbusch, George Herron, William Kerby, and W. D. P. Bliss led a growing array of liberal-minded ministers dedicated to improvement within the nation and within the church.

Some reformers promoted the belief that the poor are more blessed than the wealthy and the farmer more blessed than the city dweller. They gave hope to the poor for both the afterlife and for the future on earth by identifying blessedness with production. Nathaniel Butler argued that a man should be valued "not by the richness and abundance of what his life contains, but by the value of its output." [63] Output, said John Bates Clark, professor of political economy at Columbia University, is necessary not only for increased gross products but also for the value that both the creativity

[58] James H. Moynihan, *The Life of Archbishop John Ireland* (New York: Harper & Brothers, 1953), p. 36.

[59] Gerald Birney Smith, "The New Heaven and the New Earth," in Theodore Soares (ed.), *University of Chicago Sermons* (Chicago: The University of Chicago Press, 1915), p. 289.

[60] Washington Gladden, *The Christian Pastor and the Working Church* (New York: Charles Scribner's Sons, 1903), pp. 40, 41.

[61] Commager, *The American Mind*, p. 172.

[62] Gladden, *The Christian Pastor and the Working Church*, p. 31.

[63] Smith, "The New Heaven and the New Earth," p. 262.

and material goods have for the workers themselves.[64] The farmer, particularly, was to be envied. "Every man's life is ennobled in the measure in which he lives for the future," explained the Rev. Alexander Maclaren; "a man that gets his wages once in a twelve-month will generally be, in certain respects, a higher type of man than he who gets them once a week." [65] For the most part, however, the preachers of social change lauded the virtues of all workers, urging them to be prudent and wise in commercial affairs, work for reform, and, above all, follow Christ. The Rev. R. E. Thompson, a Presbyterian, put this clerical advice into simple language by admonishing workers in their zeal for reform to "shun radicalism, save, work hard, and avoid liquor and tobacco." [66]

Preachers who sought to improve the lives of the poor by declaring them morally equal or even better than their economic superiors, by condemning wrong perpetrated upon them, and by urging them to work harder to improve the living conditions of their fellow workers, found approval among the wealthy as well as among the poor. These ministers were again leading rather than following. The farmer had good reason to believe that he worked harder, longer, under worse conditions, and for less pay than his fellow producers, and he, no doubt, was pleased to hear that God approved. Factory workers and miners apparently approved preaching that bonded them economically and spiritually with a society that socially rejected them.

Clergymen still differed as to how the church should view the results of industrialism; but by the turn of the century most had had enough firsthand experience with the frustrations of the deprived masses to believe that the church had a responsibility to work for social reform. The church had gained monetarily by fighting farm and labor movements, but it had lost prestige. Now, by admitting that the church erred in this, preachers brought fresh enthusiasm to the American pulpit with a new social gospel.

Clergymen who identified the cause of reform with the cause of Christ waged their crusade with considerable vigor. The pulpit seemed to gain new strength as a result of this identification. Carey E. Morgan explained this new source of power to the international convention of the Disciples of Christ in Toronto, Canada, in 1913. The spur of social consciousness is successful in fighting disease, ignorance, and poverty because Jesus Christ is back of social consciousness, she said, and, since every battle for industrial improvement is supported by social consciousness, the Lord would be in the

[64] John Bates Clark, "The Society of the Future," *The Independent*, LIII (July 18, 1901), 1651.

[65] Alexander Maclaren, *Christ in the Heart* (New York: Funk and Wagnalls, 1905), p. 95.

[66] R. E. Thompson, *Hard Times and What to Learn from Them. A Plain Talk with Working People*, a pamphlet, Philadelphia, 1877. Cited in Henry F. May, *Protestant Churches and Industrial America*, p. 93.

pulpit with every preacher of reform.[67] The Rev. W. A. Williams lauded the results of social gospel preaching. He told his eastern Kentucky congregation that people "are beginning to realize as never before that no man can amass wealth or wisdom without the aid of his fellow man." [68]

As the young century entered its second decade, words of hope and remedies for social ills poured in in increasing volumes from liberal churchmen. College students heard chapel speakers such as Ernest D. Burton at the University of Chicago contrast material wealth and moral wealth, condemning all who block progress toward making life better for everyone. Readers of official church publications read such words of hope as those of the Rev. James Tufts, professor of philosophy at the University of Chicago, who maintained that people were increasing their efforts to make law and government more responsive to men's needs, to give education and physical care as well as to guard life and property.[69] Congregations heard from the pulpit such pronouncements as those of the Rev. Nathaniel Butler that taking an active interest in common welfare, justice, honesty, fellowship, housing reform, industrial education, parks and playgrounds, and general social betterment is the way to perform God's will.[70] Church officials heard their leaders declare what Mrs. Harris Cooley of Cleveland told the Christian Woman's Board of Missions in 1909, that because two million children in America under fifteen years of age were engaged in heavy manual labor and because twenty-five percent of the entire population lived on the border of destitution, the church should become as homelike as the union hall and concern itself vitally with abolition of child labor, a living wage, and all the problems of the toiling, hopeless masses.[71] Members of some small sects heard such blissful prognostications as those of the Rev. Gerald Smith, Baptist professor of theology at the University of Chicago, who envisioned the day "when the nation which preserves a 'jail' will be promptly judged defective in its discernment of righteousness." [72]

Whereas the clergy had stressed charity, it now stressed justice. Whereas it had stressed hope in the afterlife, it now stressed hope for *this* life. "We are beginning to believe that poverty need not exist," said Charles Horne; "we see in the near future an almost indefinite elevation of the standard of living; and we throw the whole authority of Christianity into the scales in favor of the two great modern ideals, that work shall be equitably remun-

---

[67] Carey E. Morgan, *Fellowship with Christ* (St. Louis: Christian Board of Education, 1914), p. 48.

[68] W. A. Williams, "The Star of Bethlehem," unpublished pencil manuscript of a sermon, with place Lexington, Kentucky, about 1903, pp. 8-10. In possession of the Rev. William Williams, Campus Ministry, Murray State College, Murray, Kentucky.

[69] James Tufts, "The Test of Religion," Soares, *University of Chicago Sermons*, p. 101.

[70] Soares, *University of Chicago Sermons*, p. 262.

[71] Mrs. Harris Cooley, *Centennial Convention Report*, Cincinnati, 1909, pp. 58-59.

[72] Soares, *University of Chicago Sermons*, p. 288.

erated and that wealth shall be equitably distributed." [73] Russell Conwell visualized the day when "the cause of Christ will be so administered as to influence the greatest possible number of people, and use all the powers, social and educational, for the purpose." [74]

A large number of religious leaders gave only verbal support and token service to the need for social action. Enough made only superficial gestures toward social reform to prompt one critic to comment that churches confused "doing good" with "saving men from drunkenness, rescuing fallen women, sending flowers to the local hospital, organizing a basketball team for the young folks, maintaining a settlement house in the slums, supporting a missionary in darkest Africa, or holding forums for the discussion of current affairs." [75] This half-hearted effort of some ministers suggests that even those not fully convinced of the righteousness of the social gospel were convinced of its expediency. Rauschenbusch was deeply disturbed by the general lethargy of the church in the direction of revitalizing society and its unwillingness to assume its true role and lamented:

The failure of the church to undertake the work of a Christian reconstruction of social life has not been caused by its close adherence to the spirit of Christ and to the essence of its Christian task, but to the deflecting influence of alien forces penetrating Christianity from without and clogging the revolutionary moral power inherent in it.[76]

The deflecting influence was, as he saw it, being exerted in large part by the fallacious pre-millennialism of many devout and earnest but misguided Christians who viewed the evils of the day as "signs of the times," a necessary precondition to the imminent bodily return of Christ to establish his Kingdom on the earth.

By 1915, however, the social gospel was a major influence in America. Against great and determined opposition, reform preaching had nettled the conscience of Americans and won at least verbal support of most church leaders. Rauschenbusch expressed the faith of the reformers when he said:

To a religious man his contemplation of the larger movements of history brings profound sense of God's presence and overruling power. . . . Christ is imminent in humanity and is slowly disciplining the nations and lifting them to share in his spirit.[77]

Summary

That the Christian social movement became a major influence on American thought by 1915 was a result of labor and farm movements. Economic

[73] Charles Horne, *The Romance of Preaching* (New York: Fleming H. Revell Company, 1914), p. 286.
[74] Hurlbut, *Sunday Half Hours with Great Preachers*, p. 591.
[75] Commager, *The American Mind*, p. 168.
[76] Rauschenbusch, *Christianity and the Social Crisis*, p. 198.
[77] *Ibid.*, p. 209.

deprivation of the majority caused many to leave the established church and develop new sects.[78] Increased wealth of the few caused established churches to become the church of the upper middle class.[79] The resulting loss of membership and prestige to established churches forced a reappraisal of the position of the church on economic and social affairs. The whole concept of what constituted God's law was changed. Gladden explained that what men called natural law was really the unnatural law of greed and strife, whereas natural law, really is the law of brotherhood, sympathy, fellowship, and mutual help and service.[80]

Slowly the attitude supported by the pulpit shifted from strong opposition to any reform efforts to philosophical approval of reform objectives. Although ministers generally remained reticent on public affairs within their communities throughout the 1875–1915 period, rebels in the pulpit and realistic gains by reformers forced a conciliatory attitude on the part of even the most conservative churches.

Reform preachers were determined to help provide the fruits of Christian principles during man's life on earth. They endeavored to meet the challenge of guiding the entire population to better economic and social conditions through employing Christian principles in business and government. They were dedicated to the objective that religion would no longer be merely a sufferance.[81] Because some courageous men of God identified the cause of the poor with the cause of Christ and because reactionary preachers proved ineffective, by 1915 the church had gained new vitality. Membership was growing, enthusiasm increasing, and leadership improving. A new, more powerful voice from the pulpit preached social reform without doubt of propriety and without fear of retribution.

[78] Elmer T. Clark, *The Small Sects in America* (New York and Nashville: Abingdon-Cokesbury Press, 1949), p. 16.
[79] William Sweet, *The Story of Religion in America*, pp. 345-71.
[80] Commager, *The American Mind*, p. 172.
[81] Stowe Persons, "Religion and Modernity, 1865-1914," from James Smith and Leland Jamison, *The Shaping of American Religion* (Princeton: Princeton University Press, 1961), p. 374.

12

PREACHING ON ISSUES OF WAR AND PEACE 1915-1965

Jess Yoder

Wars in twentieth-century America were massive nationwide efforts which cut deeply into the life and spirit of the people. During this century America rose to become the most powerful nation of the world. Technological advances such as telstar communication, supersonic travel, space projects, radar networks, computer systems, and atomic power were incorporated into our military program bringing new dimensions to the issues of ethical morality, religious faith, human justice, and social responsibility. Democratic government in America places the responsibility for the handling of national affairs upon the citizens. Thus responsible citizens must reconcile the acts of war in each new situation with their own consciences and their religious beliefs.

The message of Jesus and the prophets has been summarized in the dual commandment: "Thou shalt love the Lord thy God with all thy heart, and thou shalt love thy neighbor as thyself." The scriptures tell men that they are brothers with one Father. They admonish men to live peaceably, to do justice, to love all mankind, and to return good for evil. Warfare that is established on hatred, enemy relationships, and returning evil for evil naturally conflicts with the love commandments. Preachers, priests, and rabbis therefore have always needed to respond to the basic issues which wars raise. Though the church's response to war has varied, three positions with a long historical tradition have also found expression in the twentieth century: pacifism, the crusade, and the just war.[1] Religious pacifists refuse to participate in any war because their faith precludes it. Proponents of the just war doctrine see war as a means of halting and punishing evil and restoring good, and crusaders fight for an ideal, a holy cause, which they seek to establish upon a recalcitrant world. The crusader participates in war with enthusiasm because he is establishing the right; the proponent of the just

---

[1] Roland H. Bainton, *Christian Attitudes Toward War and Peace* (Nashville: Abingdon Press, 1960), pp. 14-15; see also John C. Bennett, *Christians and the State* (New York: Charles Scribner's Sons, 1958), pp. 166-67.

war participates out of a sense of duty to mete out judgment; and the pacifist, refusing to take arms, chooses to suffer injustice in order to redeem society. The distinction between the just war and the crusade is not always easily drawn because these positions are not mutually exclusive. However, the attitude of the American churches concerning World War I stands in sharp contrast to their attitude concerning World War II; the former attitude approaches that of the crusade, while the latter conforms more to the just war view. Since pacifists refuse to participate in war, their position is readily recognizable. In addition to the Mennonites, Brethren, and Quakers, who are pacifists in doctrine, there are pacifist ministers and laymen in every Protestant denomination as well as among Catholics and Jews in America.

At the turn of the twentieth century the conservative and fundamentalist sectors of Protestantism were fighting the doctrine of evolution and the findings of biblical scholarship while the liberal forces were entering the threshold of the "Christian Century." Progressive reform legislation was passed to curb monopolies, prevent child labor, improve working conditions, guarantee human rights, and equalize wealth. Many enthusiasts of the new idealism expressed in these reforms also supported the advocates of American territorial expansion and increased military power. The American mission to nations and the march of the flag were joined. Optimists envisioned a new era of peace, brotherhood, and prosperity for society. Though churchmen had mixed feelings about the Spanish-American war, the peace movements which followed were welcome reassurances of America's real intention.

One of the avowed purposes in the formation of the Federal Council of the Churches of Christ in America in 1908 was to further the cause of world peace.[2] Ray H. Abrams points out that sermons, denominational journals, and conference proceedings up to about 1911 indicated a lukewarm interest in peace, but that after this date the effect of the influences for peace began to be noticeable and arbitration of international disputes was a popular theme.[3] The establishment of the Hague Peace Palace and Pan-Americanism gave further encouragement to the peace movement. The interest of churches in peace prompted Andrew Carnegie to endow with $2,000,000 a newly created international organization of Catholics, Protestants, and Jews—the Church Peace Union.[4] The efforts of the Church Peace Union and other peace groups were abruptly halted when the first World Peace Congress meeting at Constance, Germany, in August, 1914, was broken up by Germany's declaration of war and her confiscation of

---

[2] Charles S. Macfarland, *Pioneers for Peace Through Religion* (New York: Fleming H. Revell Company, 1946), pp. 34-35.

[3] Ray H. Abrams, *Preachers Present Arms* (New York: Round Table Press, 1933), p. 10. I am heavily indebted to Abrams, professor of sociology, the University of Pennsylvania, for much of the material presented here on World War I preaching.

[4] *Ibid.*, p. 9.

transportation for troop mobilization. In December of 1914, another peace group, the Fellowship of Reconciliation, was organized. It became one of the most influential organizations concerned with issues of war and peace and is still active.

The United States and World War I

In 1914 when war was declared in Europe most American churchmen supported the neutrality leadership of President Wilson. Later, after the sinking of the *Lusitania* in 1915, the response from the pulpits was mixed. Cardinal Gibbons said that the fact that some Americans were foolish enough to travel by endangered ships is no reason for us to declare war and sacrifice thousands of our young men.[5] Frederick Keller of the Evangelical Lutheran Church in Cleveland held that "Germany is absolutely justified in sending to the bottom a boat which carried nearly one-half million dollars worth of munitions of war."[6] In contrast Ferdinand Blanchard of the Euclid Avenue Congregational Church said it was time to put to an end this "crime against civilization. . . . The hour for tolerant neutrality has passed,"[7] and Cortland R. Myers of Tremont Baptist Temple charged that "the German government is in league with hell."[8] As time passed, the sinking of the *Lusitania* received stronger condemnation.

The first step toward American involvement in the war focused on the preparedness issue. In 1915 the Conference Committee on National Preparedness urged ministers to deal with the theme of military preparedness in their Thanksgiving sermons. *The New York Times* reported that as a result of this effort sermons in New York almost universally favored military preparedness.[9] Many ministers echoed the sentiments of Theodore Roosevelt who castigated pacifists as "cravens, cowards, poltroons, and eunuchs" and considered them "probably the most undesirable citizens that this country contains."[10] Bible students of the Second Presbyterian Church in Cleveland were urged to give dimes for a battleship.[11] Charles LeRoy Goodell of St. Paul's Methodist Church in New York opposed Wilson's appointment of Newton D. Baker to Secretary of War because he leaned too heavily toward pacifism.[12] In his book *Is Preparedness for War Unchristian?* Baptist clergyman Leonard G. Broughton of Tennessee said, "I believe that preparedness as at present interpreted in this country is distinctly Christian."[13]

[5] *The New York Times*, May 11, 1915, p. 4.
[6] Abrams, *Preachers Present Arms*, p. 29.
[7] *Ibid.*
[8] *Ibid.*
[9] *The New York Times*, October 18, 1915, p. 4.
[10] *The Advocate of Peace*, LXXVIII, No. 4 (April, 1916), 116.
[11] *Cleveland Leader*, February 21, 1916, p. 4.
[12] *The New York Times*, April 3, 1916, p. 13.
[13] Leonard G. Broughton, *Is Preparedness for War Unchristian?* (New York: Doran, 1916), p. 169.

241

Rabbi Samuel Schulman of New York saw no "contradiction between promoting peace and preparedness." [14] On May 13, 1916 a division of 130 clergymen participated in a preparedness parade in New York.

Not all the clergy supported the preparedness call. The Church Peace Union remained active in its opposition to the war. In contrast to Theodore Roosevelt's militant position, Secretary of State William Jennings Bryan said the United States should not "get down and wallow in this mire of human blood." [15] But during the three-year period from 1914 to 1917 the predominant emphasis of the clergy shifted from advocating neutrality and exploring peace through arbitration to favoring United States participation in the war. On March 11, 1917, the New York Federation of Churches favored the war by a vote of 158 to 52.[16] Cardinal Gibbons changed his position of two years earlier and called upon Catholic young men to take their places in the front ranks.[17] The YMCA became the main agency of Protestants to support the war. "Whatever else the Red Triangle may have symbolized," said Abrams, "its record fits into the picture for what it really was—a big machine organized to promote the business of killing Germans." [18] As soon as war was declared, the Federal Council of the Churches of Christ in America pledged its full support. The Roman Catholic Church organized the National Catholic War Council to coordinate activities within the church, meet the needs of Catholics in the armed services, and to represent the church officially.[19] Jews coordinated their work under the Jewish Welfare Board.

A Holy Crusade

By the time America had entered the war it had become a holy cause, and most churchmen endorsed it wholeheartedly. The Federal Council of Churches in conjunction with the Committee of Public Information sought to present the "moral aims of the war." One of the stated aims was "to win the war against autocracy and to make the world safe for democracy and democracy safe for the world." [20] Over six hundred meetings were held, and 33,334 ministers were reached through this effort.[21] The moral and theological justification for the war was preached throughout the nation. One of the most common themes was that the Germans were enemies of the kingdom of God. Thus to fight the Germans was to promote the cause of the

[14] *The Advocate of Peace*, LXXVIII, No. 5 (May, 1916), 137.
[15] *The New York Times*, February 4, 1917, p. 12.
[16] *The Literary Digest*, LIV, No. 12 (March 24, 1917), 820-21.
[17] *The New York Times*, April 6, 1917, p. 10.
[18] Abrams, *Preachers Present Arms*, p. 172.
[19] For a fuller account, see Michael Williams, *American Catholics in the War* (New York: The Macmillan Company, 1921).
[20] Abrams, *Preachers Present Arms*, p. 146.
[21] *Ibid.*

Kingdom. "The standards and ideals of Christ must prevail in our entire civilization," said Henry Churchill King addressing the Federal Council at Washington, D.C., in 1917. He said that the church "cannot lay down nor be indifferent as to whether its fruits abide, for Christianity is democratic to the core." [22]

Missionary Samuel McCrea Cavert said that regardless of how the war originated, "it is rapidly becoming clearer every day that it is now developed into a conflict between forces that make for the coming of the Kingdom of God and forces that oppose it." [23] A California Baptist minister, James A. Francis, said he looked upon the enlistment of every American soldier as he did on the departure of a missionary for Burma.[24] The Rev. James Vance declared, "We have tried to keep out of this war, but we are in it because we believe that the cause is right, and because we feel that in it we can serve Christ." He said that the great Captain of our salvation is asking us as a nation whether we can drink of the cup that he drank of, or be baptized with the baptism that he was baptized with.[25]

The "kingdom of God" theme which recurred in many sermons of this period came from the theology of the "social gospel." Catholics, who were less influenced by this theological position, endorsed the war because the cause was just.[26] Fundamentalists, who opposed the social gospel emphasis, supported the war because the Bible says government is ordained of God and Christians are to submit to such authority that the will of God might be accomplished. Advocates of the social gospel position commonly viewed war as the means to attain a just cause.[27] The question, "What would Jesus do?" raised in Charles M. Sheldon's popular book *In His Steps*, posed a problem for those stressing Christian discipleship. Would Jesus fight and kill to establish a righteous cause? The Methodist Episcopal minister J. Wesley Johnston said, "Christ was the greatest fighter the world has ever seen." [28] Harold Bell Wright of the Disciples of Christ wrote, "The sword of America is the sword of Jesus." [29] George A. Gordon from his Boston pulpit charged that it is absurd to say Jesus was a pacifist. Some ministers ob-

---

[22] Macfarland, *Pioneers for Peace Through Religion*, p. 43.

[23] *The Biblical World*, I, No. 6 (December, 1917), 351. Cavert was general secretary of The Federal Council of the Churches of Christ in America.

[24] Devere Allen, *The Fight for Peace* (New York: The Macmillan Company, 1930), p. 40.

[25] Macfarland, *Pioneers for Peace Through Religion*, p. 15. Vance was minister of the First Presbyterian Church, Nashville, Tennessee, and executive committee chairman, the Federal Council of Churches.

[26] The Catholic view comes from Augustine's code of war. See Bainton, *Christian Attitudes Toward War and Peace*, pp. 95-100.

[27] Walter Rauschenbusch, the leading exponent of the social gospel movement, remained a pacifist throughout the war; however, most of his followers did not.

[28] *Christian Work*, CIII, No. 26 (December 29, 1917), 807.

[29] Harold Bell Wright, "The Sword of Jesus," *The American Magazine*, LXXXV, No. 2 (February, 1918), 56.

jected to calling Jesus a fighter using the sword. Responding to the Rev. Gordon, Henry Winn Pinkham, a Unitarian minister of Melrose, Massachusetts, said:

Somehow, it does not seem easy to conceive the Savior as the . . . inspirer, helper and friend of the soldier as he rushes to stick his bayonet into the guts of a brother man. . . . Somehow the Christian heart shudders—mine does at any rate, if not Dr. Gordon's—at the thought of Jesus clad in khaki, with a bomb in his hand, or turning the crank of a machine-gun to spatter wounds and death among his fellow men.[30]

Many clergymen supporting the war not only believed that fighting was Christlike, but they considered pacifism to be un-Christlike and immoral as well as un-American. Edward Leigh Pell of Virginia stated: "We fight pacifism not only because it is contrary to the teachings of Christ, but because its whole tendency is to make a yellow streak where you want a man." [31] Harry Emerson Fosdick considered the pacifist position to be immoral on the grounds that pacifists share in other evils but refuse to share in this one. Fosdick argued that personality is the one absolute value in the world and that "bayonets do not reach as far as personality; they reach only physical existence. We must win the war," he said, "for this world has no hope with a triumphant Germany, and if Christianity does not stop the war it will have failed." [32]

In addition to settling the theological issues in favor of the war, clergymen became active in promoting the war effort. They sold liberty bonds, served as army chaplains, and preached patriotism. Church buildings often became recruiting centers.[33] Bishops of the Methodist Episcopal Church pledged that their members would give $80,000,000 for Liberty Loans.[34] A Liberty Anthem was prepared for congregational rallies. Liberty Loan organizations provided ministers with pamphlets, sermon illustrations, prooftexts, and outlines of hate-Germany propaganda. The Liberty Loan Campaign leader was Walter Laidlaw, executive secretary of the New York Federation of Churches. In *Christian Work*, a full-page appeal for people to buy bonds advertised in large bold letters: "Kill the Hun, Kill His Hope." [35]

"If you turn Hell upside down you will find 'Made in Germany' stamped on the bottom," said the popular preacher Billy Sunday.[36] In a *New York*

---

[30] Abrams, *Preachers Present Arms*, quotes from a pamphlet by H. W. Pinkham, *Was Jesus a Pacifist?*

[31] Edward Leigh Pell, *What Did Jesus Really Teach About War?* (New York: Fleming H. Revell Company, 1917), p. 99.

[32] Harry Emerson Fosdick, *The Challenge of the Present Crisis* (New York: Association Press, 1918), p. 39.

[33] Abrams, *Preachers Present Arms*, p. 82.

[34] *The Christian Advocate*, XCIII, No. 14 (April 4, 1918), 423.

[35] *Christian Work*, CV, No. 15 (October 12, 1918), 447.

[36] Abrams, *Preachers Present Arms*, p. 79.

Times article he said the German-American conflict was as Hell against Heaven.[37] "The man who breaks all the rules but at last dies fighting in the trenches is better than you Godforsaken mutts who won't enlist," [38] he said on another occasion. The epitome of the holy crusade was expressed in an *Atlantic Monthly* article written by the rector of the Church of the Savior in Akron, Ohio:

The complete representative of the American church in France is the United States Army Overseas. Yes, an army with its cannons and rifles and machine-guns, and its instruments of destruction. The church militant, sent, morally equipped, strengthened and encouraged, approved and blessed by the church at home. The army today is the church in action, transforming the will of the church into smashing blows. Its worship has its vigil in the trenches, and its fasts and feasts; its prayers are in acts, and its choir is the crash of cannon and the trilling ripple of machine guns.[39]

One of the most unfortunate aspects of preaching during World War I was that a number of clergymen enthusiastically proclaimed the gospel of German hatred. Their claims were often based on rumors, lies, and fantastic atrocity stories. Germans were portrayed as barbaric Huns who would cut off the hands of children, drink from human skulls, and rape enemy women and intentionally infect them with syphilis. The Kaiser was called the Devil and the German people were the inhabitants of Hell. Dr. Dwight Newell Hillis, a Congregational minister and lecturer, was well-known for his sermons, books, and lectures filled with German atrocities.[40] Speaking of the Germans he said, "These brutes must be cast out of society." [41] A Methodist Episcopal bishop in Montana asserted, "The real reason for the war was to vindicate God Almighty against the brutal philosophy of damned men." [42]

Cornelius Woelfkin of the Fifth Avenue Baptist Church in New York and other ministers supported the American Defense Society's proposal that the Hun language should not be taught or spoken by loyal Americans.[43] In addition German songs, operas, and classical music were castigated along with performers of German origin or background, irrespective of their attitude toward Germany. From his Brooklyn pulpit Dr. Hillis falsely accused the celebrated American violinist Fritz Kreisler of sending his income from concerts to Austria. He declared, "Every night that Kreisler is paid $1,000

[37] *The New York Times*, February 19, 1918, p. 11.
[38] *The World Tomorrow*, I, No. 2 (February, 1918), 43.
[39] George Parkin Atwater, "Peter Stood and Warmed Himself," *The Atlantic Monthly*, CXXI (April, 1918), 521.
[40] Dwight Newell Hillis, *German Atrocities* (New York: Fleming H. Revell Company, 1918); Abrams, *Preachers Present Arms*, gives further description of the activities of Hillis, pp. 96 ff.
[41] Dwight Newell Hillis, *The Blot on the Kaiser's Scutcheon* (New York: Fleming H. Revell Company, 1918), p. 57.
[42] *The New York Times*, April 8, 1918, p. 15, quotes Bishop Richard J. Cooke.
[43] *The New York Times*, April 1, 1918. p. 11.

Austria can buy fifty rifles with which Germany can kill our boys." [44] Kreisler had to cancel concerts because of these false allegations. Many clergymen openly condemned Senator La Follette and others who did not take a hard anti-German line.

Pacifists and World War I

As the controversies on the issues of preparedness and the example of Jesus reveal, a number of clergymen took the pacifist position and opposed the war. John Haynes Holmes, a Unitarian minister in New York, held that "war is never justifiable at any time or under any circumstances," it is "an open and utter violation of Christianity." [45] Episcopal Bishop Paul Jones said, "As I love my country, I must protest against her doing what I would not myself do because it is contrary to our Lord's teaching." [46] Norman Thomas, Presbyterian, John Nevin Sayre, Episcopalian, and A. J. Muste, Congregationalist, were all pacifist ministers active in promoting peace through the Fellowship of Reconciliation as well as the pulpit.[47] Rabbi Judah L. Magnes, later chancellor of Hebrew University in Jerusalem, was an influential pacifist among the Jews. Dr. Edwin Dalberg, Baptist, later president of the National Council of Churches, said that in 1917 his seminary graduating class was faced with the moral issue: "Would participation in the war be pleasing to the mind of Christ?" About fifteen of the class "felt that war was a sin against God." Some felt they could do Red Cross work or be army chaplains; others felt they must stay out of it altogether, "even to the point of resisting military conscription and the selective service act." [48]

Ministers of the historic peace churches—Friends, Mennonites, and Brethren—were conscientious objectors. Though their sermons were seldom printed or published, their articles of faith and conference resolutions clearly articulate the doctrine of biblical nonresistance. They participated in relief ministries and government approved service projects for conscientious objectors. The "rhetoric" of these ministries was considered an expression of the Christian faith which could not be separated from doctrinal confession.[49] During the war some ministers and church leaders of the peace churches

[44] *The New York Times*, November 27, 1917, p. 9.

[45] Abrams, *Preachers Present Arms*, p. 199, quotes from a sermon Holmes preached at the Church of the Messiah, April 1, 1917.

[46] *Ibid.*, p. 200.

[47] Nat Hentoff, *Peace Agitator: The Story of A. J. Muste* (New York: The Macmillan Company, 1963).

[48] From a sermon, "The Minister and War," broadcast over WSYR, Syracuse, New York, May 6, 1940.

[49] See Guy F. Hershberger, *War, Peace, and Nonresistance* (Scottdale, Pennsylvania: The Mennonite Publishing House [Herald Press], 1944) and Elton Trueblood, *The People Called Quakers* (New York: Harper & Row, 1966).

were harassed by burning crosses, yellow paint on their church doors, and the like. The treatment of some conscientious objectors in World War I is an embarrassing chapter in American history.[50]

Though the majority of the clergy supported the war effort, the total spectrum ranged from opposing the war categorically to jingoistic crusading. In his thorough analysis of the views of ministers on World War I, Abrams contends that in spite of the church's claim to knowledge of ethical values and depth of spiritual insight, the evidence on wartime hysteria reveals that the ecclesiastical hierachy and church leadership displayed no superior quality of moral judgment as has been assumed. "At least," he says, "their speeches and conduct differed in no wise from the the the mass of the people whom they had undertaken to lead." [51]

When the Clamor Ended

When the war came to a close the nation's political leadership was divided on Wilson's proposals for armistice and the League of Nations. Americans called for a domestic policy that returned to "normalcy" rather than one that was concerned with international affairs. Presumably the satanic forces of evil had been defeated, the war to end war was won, and the righteous were now left to rule the earth. But churchmen were not able to motivate the victors to continue on the path of righteousness and Kingdom-building. Economic upheaval, bootlegging, discriminatory immigration laws and labor practices, political scandals like the Teapot Dome affair, and laxity in morals were disheartening to the Rauschenbusch idealists. It was not the enlightened conscience that ultimately brought the much needed social legislation, but a severe economic depression.

Reflection on World War I had a sobering effect on many Christian leaders and intellectuals. The Nye Committee investigation revealed that munitions makers played an important role in fomenting and prolonging the war.[52] Many wartime atrocity stories were found to be fabrications of propagandists. Laswell's studies on war propaganda were disillusioning to ministers who learned that they had been duped and manipulated.[53] The renunciation of war and the call to repentance came loud and clear in the 1920's. The Chicago Federation of Churches, representing fifteen denomina-

---

[50] Norman Thomas, *The Conscientious Objector in America* (New York: Viking Press, 1923); J. S. Hartzler, *Mennonites in the World War* (Scottdale, Pennsylvania: The Mennonite Publishing House [Herald Press], 1922); Margaret E. Hirsh, *The Quakers in Peace and War* (New York: Doran, 1923).

[51] Abrams, *Preachers Present Arms*, p. 124.

[52] The Senate committee headed by Gerald P. Nye of North Dakota began to examine the role of munition industries in 1934. A popular exposé entitled *Merchants of Death*, by H. C. Engelbrecht and F. C. Hanighen was published the same year.

[53] Harold D. Lasswell, *Propaganda Techniques in the World War* (New York: Knopf, 1927).

tions, was on record stating: "In humble penitence for past mistakes and sincere repentance for our want of faith and devotion to the ideals of the Kingdom of God . . . we declare ourselves as unalterably opposed to war." [54] The World Alliance for Friendship through the Church declared, "The war system and the Gospel of Jesus Christ are diametrically opposed and irreconcilably opposed." [55] At Garrett Biblical Institute, 124 of 125 faculty members and students declared that they would not participate in future wars.[56]

Leading churchmen during the twenties and thirties took the pacifist position. Reinhold Niebuhr asked men to repent and be done with war; Fosdick proposed never to bless war again. Sherwood Eddy, YMCA secretary, became an absolute pacifist. Samuel McCrea Cavert, general secretary of the Federal Council of Churches, after expressing his disillusionment, said, "I have come slowly but clearly to the conclusion that the church in its official capacity should never again give its sanction to war or attempt to make war appear as holy." [57] Rabbi Stephen S. Wise viewed his support of World War I with everlasting regret and pledged himself never to support any war again. Charles C. Morrison, editor of The Christian Century, became a pacifist and called upon the clergy never again "to put Christ in khaki or serve as recruiting officers." [58] The long list of ministers who took the pacifist position in this period between the wars included Ralph W. Sockman, Ernest F. Tittle, Henry H. Crane, George Buttrick, Bernard Iddings Bell, Charles E. Jefferson, Harold A. Bosley, and E. Stanley Jones.

In Europe the postwar crisis shook the foundations of liberal theology. Defeat, destruction, and depression made the utter sinfulness of man more deeply felt. Barth and Brunner reemphasized Reformation theology which taught that man is by nature a sinner incapable of being righteous. The saving hope of man is the sovereignty, judgment, and grace of God, not man's progressive enlightenment.

The theological revival in Europe soon made a profound impact upon American theologians and ministers. Whereas European neo-orthodoxy took the Word as its starting point, American neo-orthodoxy started from an analysis of the nature and predicament of men.[59] That analysis showed man to be self-centered and evil. Studies in psychology also agreed that man is basically egotistical. The problem of man was not his inability to know good from evil, but the fact that he could not eradicate himself from evil. This

[54] Sherwood Eddy and Kirby Page, The Abolition of War (New York: Doran, 1924), p. 193.
[55] Quoted by Abrams, Preachers Present Arms, p. 235.
[56] Ibid., p. 236.
[57] Ibid., p. 235.
[58] The Christian Century, XLI, No. 5 (January 31, 1924), 134.
[59] Reinhold Niebuhr, The Nature and Destiny of Man. 2 vols. (New York: Charles Scribner's Sons, 1941, 1943).

view was considered to be more realistic than the idealism which stressed man's goodness. Niebuhr saw man as a sinner who must live in the tension between what he ought to do and what he does. Because man was sinful he could not attain Kingdom goodness. The gospel, the forgiveness of God as revealed in Christ, enabled man to live in the face of his predicament. The pardon of God did not make man's behavior righteous; rather, it enabled him to live in this tension by faith in God's promise.

Niebuhr said that love has two dimensions: "the vertical dimension of perfection, of sacrifical love; and the horizontal dimension of concern for all people, of concern for social justices and balances by which it is maintained." [60] He charged that pacifists absolutize sacrificial love at the expense of social responsibility. Social justice holds the prior claim, said Niebuhr, and thus an individual ethic could not be held for a collective situation.[61] He contended that the Christian who objected to participating in war was a responsible citiezn ["in the world"] until coercion or violence entered the scene, and then became irresponsible by withdrawing ["not of the world"]. Admitting the difficulty in determining justice in modern warfare, Niebuhr insisted that one dare not abandon the principle because it was difficult to apply. "A war to defend the victims of wanton aggression, where the demands of justice join the demands of order, is today the clearest cause of a just war." [62] However, in the final analysis Niebuhr placed upon the individual the responsibility for judging whether the war was justified. The judgments of the Christian community could help the individual make that decision.[63]

Then Came the Second One

As the clouds of World War II were approaching, the church again was faced with taking positions and making decisions on issues of war. The prevailing theological emphasis which stressed the sinful nature of man was dramatized by the rise of fascism and the approaching war. Thus in contrast to World War I, World War II was not considered holy; it was not ushering in the kingdom of righteousness, but a tragic manifestation of sin.

Many of the sermons from the World War II period stress lessons the church should have learned from her involvement in World War I. In 1939 George Buttrick, president of the Federal Council of Churches, called upon

[60] Angus Dun and Reinhold Niebuhr, "God Wills Both Justice and Peace," *Christianity and Crisis*, XV, No. 10 (June 13, 1955), 75-78.

[61] Reinhold Niebuhr, "The Heresy of Pacifism," *Church Management*, XVII, No. 3 (December, 1940), 147-48.

[62] Dun and Niebuhr, "God Wills Both Justice and Peace," p. 78.

[63] A response to the Dun and Niebuhr article entitled "God Establishes Both Peace and Justice," was published in the booklet *The Christian and War* (1958) by the Historical Peace Churches and the Fellowship of Reconciliation. This booklet also contains the reprint of the article "Peace is the Will of God" that had prompted the Dun and Niebuhr statement.

churchmen to resist propaganda and hatred and to maintain an unbroken worldwide Christian fellowship.[64] The only way to view the human race, preached Reynold Boden, is found in the words, "One is your Father, and all ye are brethren." [65] Ernest Fremont Tittle said that "if Christians in warring countries pray according to the pattern of prayer given by their Lord, they will not be praying against one another." [66] Franklin D. Elmer called upon his congregation to take Paul's advice and "give up all bitterness, rage, and anger." He entreated them not to join those who would destroy and tear apart the sick world but to join those who hold it together.[67] The church in a divided world must not be divided, said Georgia Harkness.[68] The fellowship theme, commonly found in the preaching of World War II and later, was forcefully articulated in the words from a sermon of Winfield Haycock: "When you think of the two pillars of religion, the fatherhood of God and the brotherhood of man, you see that peace is the affirmation of God because it is the demonstration of the oneness of man. War is the denial of God because it is the destruction of human brotherhood." [69]

In contrast to much of the preaching during World War I which portrayed Jesus as a fighter or at least as not opposed to using the sword, sermons of World War II often stressed that the life and teachings of Jesus condemn war. The Methodist Conference of 1939 said that war is a denial of the ideals of Christ.[70] Fosdick called on the church to abide by the ethics of Jesus which is not merely "ordinary humane decency, loving those who love us, but the radical, sometimes incredible demands of Jesus that we love our enemies, that if smitten on the one cheek we turn the other instead, that we do good to those who hate us and pray for those who despitefully use us and persecute us." Satan cannot cast out Satan, he said; it is love that breaks the course of evil.[71] Reverse the teachings of Jesus and you have the world today—hate your enemies, bomb those that curse you, and shell the life out

---

[64] George Buttrick, an NBC address given September 8, 1939; printed in *The Pulpit*, X, No. 11 (November, 1939), 255-56.

[65] Reynold Boden, pastor at the Church of the Messiah in Los Angeles, a sermon, "Youth and War," *The Pulpit*, X, No. 5 (May, 1939), 103-5.

[66] Ernest Fremont Tittle, minister at First Methodist Church, Evanston, Illinois, a sermon, "Christian Fellowship in Time of Crisis," *The Pulpit*, XI, No. 8 (August, 1940), 18.

[67] Franklin D. Elmer, Baptist minister at Lockport, New York, a sermon, "More Important than Victories in War," *The Pulpit*, XI, No. 8 (August, 1940), 173.

[68] Georgia Harkness, professor at Garrett Seminary, a sermon, "The Fiery Furnace," *The Pulpit*, XII, No. 6 (June, 1941), 121-24.

[69] Winfield Haycock, minister at First Methodist Church, Rochester, Minnesota, a sermon, "War and Peace," *The Pulpit Digest*, XLVI, No. 325 (October, 1965), 21-26.

[70] Ernest Fremont Tittle, a sermon, "The Church in a World at War," *The Pulpit*, X, No. 11 (November, 1939), 241.

[71] Harry Emerson Fosdick, minister at Riverside Church, New York City, a sermon, "Jesus' Ethical Message Confronts the World," *The Pulpit*, X, No. 5 (May, 1939), 100.

of those that despitefully use you, preached George Craig Stewart.[72] Living the gospel of love is more important than victories in war,[73] said Frank Elmer; and Henry Hitt Crane emphasized that the power we possess must conform to the gospel we confess.[74] Albert Edward Day said the cross is the Christian's answer to war just as it was Christ's answer to brutal force. The cross does not conquer enemies; it ends enmity.[75]

A third theme of World War II preaching dealt with the evils of war. When the United States was supplying the allied nations with arms, Tittle, recalling the role of munitions sales in the First World War, asked, "Will we Americans want to make money through sales of bombing planes that will be used to rain death and destruction on open towns and cities?"[76] When congressmen were seeking to change the embargo act in order to supply our allies with armaments, Boynton Merrill, Congregationalist minister, warned against the lure of profits.[77] When war begins, truth dies, and moral judgment surrenders to hysteria, said Albert Edward Day. He regretted that in the last war he preached propaganda and hatred.[78] In war we ape the enemies we condemn and hate, said Fosdick.[79] Reynold Boden called modern warfare "organized mass murder, in which babies get killed as well as men." He pointed out that the grim statistics of World War I included 13,000,000 civilians dead, 20,000,000 wounded, 9,000,000 war orphans, 50,000,000 war widows, and 10,000,000 refugees.[80] Technology since the First World War of course magnified the destructive possibilities for World War II.

Even though war was regarded as unholy and sinful, the majority of churchmen believed that Christians should participate in it to avoid a greater evil. Rolland W. Schloerb said:

It is not Christian to kill. But neither is it Christian to allow tyrants to use their power to kill. It is not right to sit back and assume that the refusal to participate in the struggle is Christian. *None of the possibilities with which a person is confronted during these days is absolutely Christian.* They all have something bad about them. Since our sinful acts have caused this kind of world to come to pass, we have no perfectly Christian alternative. To kill men in war or to threaten to

---

[72] George Craig Stewart, Congregational minister at Second Church, Newton, Massachusetts, a sermon, "Four Anchors," *The Pulpit*, X, No. 11 (November, 1939), 247-49.

[73] Elmer, "More Important than Victories in War," pp. 173-75.

[74] Henry Hitt Crane, minister at Central Methodist Church, Detroit, Michigan, in a lecture at Goshen College, Goshen, Indiana, November 28, 1962.

[75] Albert Edward Day, minister at First Methodist Church, Pasadena, California, a sermon, "The Terrible Meek," *The Pulpit* XI, No. 5 (May, 1940), 97-101.

[76] Tittle, "The Church in a World at War," p. 243.

[77] Boynton Merrill, a sermon, "Lest Ye Fight Against God," *The Pulpit*, X, No. 11 (November, 1939), 245-46.

[78] Albert Edward Day, a sermon, "Hitler, America, and God," *The Pulpit*, XI, No. 7 (July, 1940), 149-54.

[79] Fosdick, "Jesus' Ethical Message Confronts the World," p. 101.

[80] Boden, "Youth and War," p. 104.

kill them is not Christian, but it may be the least unchristian of the courses open to us in this kind of world. Resort to war is no good, but it may be less evil than any other possibility confronting us.[81]

In a similar note Nelson Rightmyer in an Armistice Day sermon said in times when the hot blood of the killer is inflamed the Christian must be willing to lay down his own life in order that righteousness may prevail. "When we engage in war, we are being unchristian to that extent, but we can justify our actions only because we hope that a still greater evil may be overcome." [82]

In contrast to these views which called upon Christians to fight that justice might result, many pacifist ministers took a stand similiar to that of Alvin J. Beachy. He said that, although he did not condemn "an earnest Christian who goes to war loathing it but feels there is no alternative except to yield to an even greater evil than war itself," he must give a different answer. He said that the time has come for Christians in all nations who wish to follow Christ to say they will have no part in modern warfare's mass slaughter of innocents, and rather than inflict suffering upon others they should suffer infliction.[83]

A number of sermons emphasized war as the judgment of God upon both sides. As for Jesus, said Clarence Macartney, so for us there is an hour appointed. "It was not that America entered into the war; it was not the wicked plot of Hitler or Japan; not an anti-aircraft shell, a naval gun, a hand grenade, or a bayonet thrust, but the will and the plan of God." [84] War is man's attempt to shape his own destiny, but all men must subject themselves to the sovereignty of God, said Paul E. Scherer.[85] In a sermon dealing with the cold war Richard Niebuhr stressed the illusions of power and blindness to the sovereignty of God. "One purpose the Almighty has in using the enemy as his instrument is to make us good in accordance with our own standards of what is good." Secondly, he said, we overestimate the evil of the enemy and also forget that the power of evil is limited. We must compare the power of the enemy not with our own power but with the

[81] Rolland W. Schloerb, minister at Hyde Park Baptist Church, Chicago, Illinois, a sermon, "An Uneasy Conscience About Killing," *The Pulpit*, XIV, No. 9 (September, 1943), 203.

[82] Nelson Rightmyer, professor at the Divinity School in Philadelphia, Armistice Day sermon, *The Pulpit Digest*, XXVIII, No. 127 (November, 1948), 12.

[83] Alvin J. Beachy, minister at First Congregational Church, Somerville, Massachusetts, *The Pulpit Digest*, XXXVIII, No. 235 (November, 1957), 25-27.

[84] Clarence Edward Noble Macartney, minister at First Presbyterian Church, Pittsburgh, Pennsylvania, a sermon, "Killed in Action," *The Pulpit Digest*, XXII, No. 95 (November, 1945), 16.

[85] Paul E. Scherer, minister at Holy Trinity Lutheran Church, New York City, a sermon preached at the Chicago Sunday Evening Club, "The Day of the Lord is Darkness," *The Pulpit*, XIV, No. 3 (March, 1943), 51-53.

power of the Almighty.[86] Such an emphasis implied that, while one should not hesitate to participate in war, he should realize the outcome is in the hands of God who judges all men and nations according to his purposes.

Ministers affiliated with the National Association of Evangelicals also emphasized the sovereignty of God and the divine appointment of rulers. Evangelist Billy Graham is a well-known minister of the group which took the wars of the Old Testament as its ethical norm and regarded war waged by the state to be in accord with the will of God. The position of the state must be righteous, however, for the Christian to fight. He must use biblical principles to evaluate whether or not the position of the state is good. Carl F. Henry said, "The Bible is still the best text-book on democracy, and Christianity the most effective guardian of our liberties." [87] Christians should fight to defend or establish biblical justice. This view implied that the German Christians who fought for Nazi goals were unchristian and sinful, but the American Christians who killed the Germans in order to destroy Nazism were not committing sin. This attitude to war was a continuation of the holy crusade or righteous war tradition that was more popular in the preaching of the World War I period.

Thus during the Second World War, the holy war, the just war, and pacifism were preached from pulpits across the nation. The prevailing emphasis stressed that war is sinful for the following reasons: it breaks Christian fellowship, it denies the fatherhood of God, it opposes the example and teachings of Jesus, it wastes valuable resources of life and property, and it suppresses moral standards; furthermore, obliteration bombing in modern war kills the innocent and guilty alike. The issues of dishonesty found in deceptive war propaganda, high profit taking by war industries, and settling disagreements by fear and force rather than justice were also raised in sermons preached during World War II.

As in World War I, the historic peace churches officially supported the conscientious objector position. Though other denominations did not stress the conscientious objector position as a body, they did insist that their members who took this stand should have the full support of the church. Approximately 12,000 young men coming from every denomination chose civilian public service in lieu of military service.[88] Pacifists did not view their performing humanitarian service as social irresponsibility. Rather, they

[86] H. Richard Niebuhr, a sermon, "The Illusions of Power," *The Pulpit*, XXXIII, No. 4 (April, 1962), 4-7.

[87] Carl F. Henry, professor at Fuller Theological Seminary and editor of *Christianity Today*, "Christianity and the American Heritage," *Vital Speeches*, XIX, No. 20 (August 1, 1953), 623.

[88] The *Directory of Civilian Public Service* of May, 1941 to March, 1947, lists men who served in Civilian Public Service. By denomination there were: Mennonite, 4,665; Church of the Brethren, 1,353; Society of Friends, 951; Methodist, 673; Jehovah's Witnesses, 409; Congregational Christian, 209; Church of Christ, 199; Presbyterian, 192; Roman Catholic, 149; Christadelphian, 127; Lutheran, 108; Evangelical and Reformed, 101.

often spoke of such service as witnessing, making faith incarnate, and communicating God's will for man. The majority of ministers, while admitting to the sinfulness of war, rejected the pacifist position as unsatisfactory mainly on the grounds of social irresponsibility; it was Christian individualism run amuck. They believed that the Christian commitment called for a realism which pacifism failed to consider. They held that participating in a lesser evil in order to avert a greater evil was the most satisfactory answer.

After the Second One

In contrast to the era following World War I which deemphasized militarism and concentrated on domestic affairs, an arms race between the United States and the Soviet Union developed in the years following World War II. Before the peace treaties were signed the conflict between the communist nations and the western powers was already apparent. America had emerged from the war as the most powerful nation in the world. The atomic bombing of Hiroshima and Nagasaki near the end of the war shocked the world as the realities of the nuclear age became self-evident. Postwar nuclear testing quickly made obsolete the little bomb that wiped out over 100,000 Japanese. But the postwar American nuclear stockpiles for peace were soon rivaled by Russian stockpiles for peace. As the arms race continued, nuclear submarines, radar alert systems, supersonic nuclear bombers, computerized nuclear intercontinental ballistic missiles, and space vehicles were built. Civil defense officials called for nationwide fallout shelter protection. Military experts estimated that a 100-megaton H-bomb would cause a firestorm over an area larger than the state of Vermont.[89] They calculated that a Russian first strike on America might well kill over 30,000,000 Americans before counterforces could be set into action. However, America's retaliatory power could obliterate Russia or any nation from the face of the earth. The offensive strategy of mass retaliation became the keystone of the United States' peace program. Defensive programs as a twenty-billion dollar fallout shelter system or a forty-billion dollar anti-missile missile system were rejected because in addition to high cost they could well be obsolete before completion.

All this technological development and arms buildup naturally was not taking place in a vacuum. At the close of the war Russia had gained immediate control of the nations now known as the Iron Curtain countries in Europe. Communism posed additional threats in Greece, Turkey, Italy, and other nations of Europe. In a few years Germany and Berlin were divided into east and west sectors. After unsuccessful attempts to blockade the

[89] Arthur Waskow, *Civil Defense*, a pamphlet (Philadelphia: American Friends Service Committee, 1961).

western sectors of Berlin, a wall was erected to check the refugee movement and communication with the West. The communist influence extended beyond Europe to the new independent and underdeveloped nations of Africa. In the Far East, China and then Tibet had become communist. Other countries such as Korea, Indonesia, Malaya, Laos, Cambodia, Thailand, and Vietnam were influenced and threatened by communism with varying degrees of success. In 1960 communism invaded the Western hemisphere when Cuba joined the communist ranks.

The cold war era with its complexity of issues presented a challenge to American churchmen. The concerns for social responsibility and justice stressed in wartime preaching, along with the deep awareness of sin, the need for confession and prayer in behalf of one's enemies certainly helped to open up channels for international communication within the church after the war. Churchmen of all nations met not only to discuss doctrines of faith but also the problems of poverty, hunger, nuclear testing, and cold war issues. Many church leaders from behind the Iron Curtain met with the church leadership of western nations in meetings of the World Council of Churches, the International Fellowship of Reconciliation, the Puidoux Conferences, the Ecumenical Council in Rome, and other East-West conferences. Consequently clergymen were not ready to take the hard anticommunist line or endorse measures leaning in that direction. In addition to seeing the fallacy of the "Red or Dead" arguments and realizing the obvious un-godlike nature of a mass retaliation policy, these churchmen refused to accept the emotional stereotypes attributed to communism which their ecumenical experiences repudiated. New York's Union Theological Seminary president, John C. Bennett, called upon Christians to take note of the changes within the communist world and reconsider attitudes shaped by Stalinism immediately after World War II.[90]

One of the most complex issues which ministers encountered in the cold war era was the increasing difficulty of applying the just war theory to the new situation. Many scientists and scholars became nuclear pacifists for survival reasons and, as Arthur Mielke pointed out, have also "taken to their pulpits like the preachers to warn against the potential evil they created." [91] A crisis in Korea, Cuba, or Vietnam could develop into Armageddon as the leaders of nuclear power nations tread the diplomatic brink of the abyss. Moral arguments stressing social responsibility were difficult to defend when a strike would mean from thirty to one-hundred million lives. Methodist Bishop Everett Palmer warned, "American identi-

[90] John C. Bennett, "Changes in the Communist World" (Reprinted from *Concern* for September 1, 1965).
[91] Arthur Mielke, minister at Park Central Presbyterian Church, Syracuse, New York, a sermon, "Hiroshima: Our Guilt and Our Atonement," *The Pulpit*, XXIX, No. 8 (August, 1958), 5.

fication of its will to power with the will of God is quite as monstrous as the Marxist denial of God." [92]

Not all ministers were disturbed by the use of atomic weapons. To some, atheistic communism was to be destroyed regardless of the means or the cost. During the Korean conflict, Daniel A. Poling, editor of *The Christian Herald*, said, "Communism in China, political and military communism must be destroyed. The alternative to that is the communizing of all Asia and of India, with the eclipse of freedom and democracy in the West." [93] Poling supported MacArthur's Far East policy in the Korean crisis. A number of ministers joined the American political right and vigorously preached and crusaded in behalf of anti-communist doctrines. Carl McIntire and the "Twentieth Century Reformation Hour," Billy James Hargis and his Christian Crusade, and Edgar Bundy and the Church League of America are illustrations of the "Christian" anti-communist movement.[94]

The war in Vietnam has created more controversy within America than any prior American war. The strongest opposition has been voiced outside the church in such organizations as SANE, Committee to End the War in Vietnam, The Teach-in Committee, Spring Mobilization Committee, and Student Non-Violent Coordinating Committee. These groups place strong emphasis on the moral issues of the war. They point to the Nuremberg Trials where, by appealing to the conscience of mankind, Nazi officers were condemned for carrying out acts of injustice ordered by superior officers. Soldiers who were, of course, not conscientious objectors have refused to fight in Vietnam and appealed to the Nuremberg principle. While opinion polls have usually indicated a slight majority in favor of the present war policy in Vietnam, the minority voice opposing the war is stronger than during any war of this century.

As in other wars, most denominations do not take a position opposing United States policy. After the Vietnam war began, most of the controversy centered on how the war ought to be conducted, rather than whether it ought to be fought. The American clergy has not responded with any general enthusiasm to the war. Not many sermons for or against the war have been published, especially by ministers who have pulpits. But not all the clergy have been silent. A group of two thousand clergymen concerned about the war in Vietnam did hold a seminar in Washington to study the question. The Fellowship of Reconciliation sent a delegation of clergymen to Vietman to study the question and make proposals. Leaders like Bishop Fulton Sheen, Martin Luther King, Jr., Rabbi Abraham Hershel, Rabbi

[92] Everett Palmer, a sermon, "Lest Patriotism Become Idolatry," *The Pulpit*, XXXI, No. 11 (November, 1960), 19.

[93] Daniel A. Poling, "Don't Talk America into Slavery," *Vital Speeches*, XIX, No. 7 (June 15, 1953), 538.

[94] See the article in this volume by Dale Leathers on "The Thrust of the Radical Right."

Arthur Lelyveld, Bishop James Pike, and Eugene Carson Blake have openly opposed the United States Vietnam policy. Churches have encouraged the president to negotiate or to appeal to the United Nations, but at the time of this writing[95] they seem not to have affected our policy.

The Challenge Now

Where, then, do the world and the church stand now? "War potential in the nuclear age ultimately means ability to wipe out the human habitat. Any society willing to commit such total destruction is in utter revolt against God's purposes in the creation, preservation, and the redemption of mankind," said Howard Schomer.[96] Will the church have a message of hope in a world of wars and rumors of war? Or did that hope disappear when the kingdom of God envisioned at the turn of the century collapsed in the wake of two world wars followed by a nuclear peace? If preaching in America is to be instrumental in bringing peace for mankind, it must take on a role different from that of the past. By and large the preaching on war during this century has echoed United States policies, giving enthusiastic crusading support during World War I and the dutiful support of a penitent sinner during World War II. "The past," said Martin Luther King, "is prophetic in that it asserts loudly that wars are poor chisels for carving out peaceful tomorrows. One day we must come to see that peace is not merely a distant goal that we seek, but a means by which we arrive at that goal. We must pursue peaceful means by which we arrive at that goal. We must pursue peaceful ends through peaceful means. How much longer must we play at deadly war games before we heed the plaintive pleas of the unnumbered dead and maimed of past wars?" [97] Will preaching continue to echo the status quo and proclaim a nuclear salvation for the years that lie ahead?

[95] September, 1967.

[96] Howard Schomer, President, Chicago Theological Seminary, in an address to the Brite Divinity School, Texas Christian University, November 15, 1965. Dr. Schomer was a member of the Fellowship of Reconciliation team visiting Vietnam in July, 1965.

[97] An address by Dr. Martin Luther King, Jr., at The Nation Institute, Los Angeles, February 25, 1967.

13

THE FUNDAMENTALIST-
MODERNIST CONTROVERSY
1918-1930

Allan H. Sager

During the mid-twenties, prohibition enforcement officers were cautioned: "When you see a bulge on a man's hip, do not jump to conclusions; it is as likely to be a Bible as a flask." [1] There was a point behind the jest, for that which has been called "the nation's most spectacular quarrel on religious doctrine," [2] the fundamentalist-modernist controversy, 1918-1930, was in progress.

Fundamentalists, concerned with the consolidation and defense of staunch orthodoxy, and active within almost every major Protestant denomination in the United States, were confronting liberals intent upon refashioning Christianity in the interests of vitality and relevancy. The contending forces made religion, as never before in America, a subject of widespread concern and inquiry.[3]

But the ballyhoo decade of the twenties was generally given to news oddities of an ephemeral nature, and so one may question whether the topics in dispute were vital or superficial. Leading commentators and participants left no doubt how they viewed the controversy. Albert C. Dieffenbach, prominent Unitarian champion of religious liberty, described the fray as "two spiritual worlds, irreconcilable, met in inevitable collision. Nothing

[1] Rollin Lynde Hartt, "Is the Church Dividing?" _The World's Work_, XLVII, No. 2 (December, 1923), 161.

[2] Robert D. Clark, "Harry Emerson Fosdick," A _History and Criticism of American Public Address_, ed. Marie Kathryn Hochmuth, III (3 vols.; New York: Longmans, Green and Company, 1955), 411.

[3] See, for example, O. E. Brown's claim that "as never before, we may safely say, the religious questions are being discussed in all places where men get together, and being discussed as well by men of all types. There is virtually no agency that is meant to contribute to the molding of our more serious public mind that is not devoting time and space to the problem of Modernism." "Modernism: A Calm Survey," _The Methodist Quarterly Review_, LXXIV, No. 3 (July, 1925), 388. News of the controversy was regularly bannered in the great metropolitan dailies and received repeated commentary in popular periodicals of the day such as _The Century Magazine, The World's Work, The Literary Digest, The American Mercury, The New Republic, North American Review_, and _The Forum_.

like it [has] been seen in Christendom in four hundred years." [4] He suggested that the old denominational alignments were giving way to a new cleavage so that "a Fundamentalist Methodist is much closer to a Fundamentalist Episcopalian both spiritually and intellectually than he is to a Methodist Modernist. It is true throughout Protestantism." [5] Harry Emerson Fosdick, noted modernist spokesman, epitomized the momentousness of the basic issues in conflict when he declared that "with multitudes of eager minds in our generation, the decision no longer lies between an old and a new theology, but between new theology and no theology." [6] One of the prominent leaders of the fundamentalists, William Bell Riley, speaking in the tradition of those who repeatedly announced the birth of a "new reformation," heralded the 1919 organization of the World Conference on Christian Fundamentals in Philadelphia as "an event of more historical moment than the nailing up, at Wittenberg, of Martin Luther's ninety-five theses." [7]

Evolution of the Controversy

If the participants, thus envisioning the significance of the conflict, came promptly to the point of open clash, the underlying tensions had long been developing. In the nineteenth century, industrial changes had rapidly transformed post Civil War America from a predominantly rural, pastoral society, in which the Bible as rule book and the church as judge and jury had made a near theocracy of early American life, to a rapidly growing urban, industrial society. The social changes attendant to industrialization were aggravated by new and newly popularized theories in science, especially by the evolutionary hypothesis with its philosophical premise of inevitable progress. Here was cause for conservative religionists to become alarmed. For many of them the logic of the evolutionary hypothesis seemed to demand recognition that man's dignity lay in his rise from brute ancestry, an admission damning to their understanding of the biblical account of creation. While the teaching of the evolutionists raised questions about the factual reliability of the Bible, religious modernists, armed with biblical criticism, a comparative study of religions, and a quickened social conscience, began to call into question entire bodies of teachings and practices which had long been regarded as sacrosanct and unchanging. Thus orthodox Christians felt the attack from two directions.

Conservatives chose to stand their ground and contend for their con-

[4] Albert C. Dieffenbach, *Religious Liberty, the Great American Illusion* (New York: William Morrow and Company, 1927), pp. 63-64.

[5] *Ibid.*, p. 75.

[6] Harry Emerson Fosdick, *Christianity and Progress* (New York: Fleming H. Revell Company, 1922), p. 246.

[7] William Bell Riley, *Inspiration or Evolution* (Cleveland: Union Gospel Press, 1926), p. 185.

victions. Skirmishing, however, was sporadic and ineffectual until it found support in the general post World War I mood of conservatism verging toward reaction. With the postwar world bent on a "return to normalcy," the orthodox found a ready audience among those who resented experiment, innovation, or change of any sort and were ready to denounce those claimants who were glorifying "science" as the new shibboleth of the age. It appeared to many of the orthodox that the scientific spirit, in regarding knowledge as tentative and values as relative, was selling out to a secularism devoid of spiritual foundations. Facing a threat so basic, what was there to do but retire within the impenetrable fortress of an orthodox creed? From this fortress they were to battle both the evolutionist invaders and the modernist subversives. The substance and weaponry of this encounter comprise an informative and rousing chapter in the history of American preaching and public address.

Procedure of Analysis

Granting that effective sermons and speeches on critical issues are vibrant with the immediacy of life—thus being inextricably interwoven with the social fabric of the time—one cannot hope to comprehend, interpret, or evaluate public address and/or preaching apart from a critical examination of the historical setting in which it took place. Reciprocally, the controversy is itself faithfully mirrored in the sermons of the time as Ozora S. Davis has noted: "In spite of the common charge against preaching that it is bound to doctrine and tradition, there is no area of thought and action that is more quickly responsive to the influence of the age than the Christian pulpit. Sermons register trends in popular life with exceeding accuracy and sensitiveness." [8]

Yet it may be questioned whether such religious controversy as occurred in the twenties can ever be properly chronicled. Speaking in the early thirties, Gaius Atkins charged: "The forces are so imponderable, and it has been so largely a drama of faith and doubt confined to what is more hidden

[8] Ozora S. Davis, "American Preaching," *Religious Thought in the Last Quarter-Century*, ed. Gerald Birney Smith (Chicago: The University of Chicago Press, 1927), p. 185. Echoing Davis, Gaius Glenn Atkins declared: "Preaching must, of course, more directly than anything else reflect the changing religious mind. . . . The pulpit of the last forty years has kept on the whole in immediate touch with the restlessness, the quests, the disillusions and the reconstruction of modern society." See *Religion in Our Times* (New York: Round Table Press, 1932), p. 312. In effect, Davis and Atkins were saying that effective preaching during the twenties not only expressed the minds of the speakers, but also gauged the minds of the audience as it implicitly revealed, through the adaptations of the speakers, the current interests, values, belief-systems, prejudices, and caprices shared by the auditors. This chapter is based upon the writer's doctoral dissertation, "The Fundamentalist-Modernist Controversy, 1918-1930, in the History of American Public Address" (Northwestern University, 1963), for which roughly seven hundred and fifty lectures, sermons, addresses, and debates were examined for their pertinency to the study.

than revealed in the life of a generation. How can it all, with its undetermined issues, be made into history now or ever?" [9] Atkins' query is a reminder that religious controversy involves a complexity of human institutions, interests, and ideals; such caution, however, ought not deter us from attempting to unravel some of the tangled involvements. The researcher necessarily looks for the "most essential"—here broadly defined as those features of the age that make more intelligible our understanding of the speakers, their audiences, the specific occasions, and the ideas and propositions in conflict. Because such essentials are wound inextricably around and through less vital supports and, because like ivy on a wall, one cannot separate the growing life from the lifeless support without tearing the former, the following treatment is broadly descriptive rather than highly analytical.

Temper of the Times

The fundamentalist-modernist controversy challenged the attention of a world already occupied by a variety of engrossing interests. The nature and diversity of those interests is indicated by the many labels applied to the twenties. Paul Sann, a sensitive chronicler, used as title for his informal historical excursion, "The Lawless Decade." [10] And lawless it was, as social, civil, criminal, political, and moral laws stood largely ineffectual before a new preoccupation with self-expression. Indeed, the Volstead Act, that law which had the greatest impact on the people, evoked the least obedience.

While "lawless" adequately epitomized the age for many, F. Scott Fitzgerald, official troubadour of the flapper, preferred to christen the decade "the Jazz Age." [11] And without question, it was an age which even in its fun and frolic departed from the conventional score. A whole race was going hedonistic, deciding on pleasure. The flapper and hip flask were fitting symbols, jazz and syncopation its music, and Helen Morgan its typical songstress.

Individualism, though seldom of the Horatio Alger type, ran rampant. At times flamboyant—like Fitzgerald; at times daring—like Lindbergh's conquest of the Atlantic and Trudy Ederle's swim of the English Channel; at times tough—like Hoover's brand of "rugged individualism"; but always symbolizing the "New Freedom" in a "New Era." [12]

The clamor and dissonance of competing individualisms prompted some to think of the period as "the Roaring Twenties." Others hit upon the

[9] Atkins, *Religion in Our Times*, p. 86.

[10] Paul Sann, *The Lawless Decade* (New York: Crown Publishers, 1957).

[11] F. Scott Fitzgerald, "Echoes of the Jazz Age," *These Were Our Years*, ed. Frank Brookhouser (Garden City, N.Y.: Doubleday & Company, 1959).

[12] Labels supplied by Frederick Lewis Allen, one of the period's most popular commentators. Cf. *Only Yesterday* (New York: Harper & Brothers, 1931).

pointedly descriptive title, "the Era of Wonderful Nonsense." And so it was. War-torn nerves craved the anodynes of speed, excitement, and passion—a condition which profit-minded hucksters were quick to exploit. Technological changes added to the turmoil of the age. The automobile and radio, mass produced on the "production line," helped to diminish social isolation.

Far less subtle than the wavelengths of radio were the waves of cynicism and disillusionment which characterized the twenties. This aspect of the psychological climate of the times was pointed up in Harry Emerson Fosdick's sermon on "The Curse of Cynicism": "Theorists are not our chief trouble. Our trouble is a flood tide of moral cynicism. Read our newspapers; go to the theaters and movies; pick up our magazines and novels. You would suspect that most husbands are unclean, most wives unhappy, and all marriages more or less rotten." [13] Fosdick went on to illustrate its effect upon the religious life of the age:

Multitudes of people live habitually in this realm. . . . They eat, drink, and breathe cynicism. They are enfolded by it as by an atmosphere. When, then, they venture into or are dragged into a Christian church and hear, let us say, the beatitudes read, "Blessed are the pure in hearts: for they shall see God. Blessed are they that hunger and thirst after righteousness: for they shall be filled," it is not so much that they theoretically disbelieve the propositions on which such thinking rests as that they cannot understand it. They are like pygmies from the center of Africa listening to Keats' "Ode on a Grecian Urn." [14]

With his usual incisiveness, Walter Lippmann charged: "What most distinguishes the generation who have approached maturity since the debacle of idealism at the end of the War is not their rebellion against the religion and the moral code of their parents, but their disillusionment with their own rebellion." [15] Regarding the dissolution of the ancestral order for the modern man, Lippmann declared: "There is no moral authority to which he must turn now, but there is coercion in opinions, fashions, and fads." [16] The manifest inadequacy of such new "authorities" heightened the disillusionment.[17]

The impact of science and the scientific spirit on the age is illustrated by excerpts from sermons of the period. Unitarian Minot Simons, a minister noted for urging theism as a realistic option in the face of mechanism and humanism, said of the impact of the sciences:

[13] Harry Emerson Fosdick, "The Curse of Cynicism," *If I Had Only One Sermon to Preach,* ed. Charles Stelzle (New York: Harper & Brothers, 1927), p. 120.

[14] *Ibid.,* pp. 122-23.

[15] Walter Lippmann, *A Preface to Morals* (New York: The Macmillan Company, 1929), p. 17.

[16] *Ibid.,* p. 9.

[17] The greatest literary prophet of the disillusionment was Joseph Wood Krutch. Cf. Krutch, *The Modern Temper: A Study and a Confession* (New York: Harcourt, Brace & Company, 1929).

Multitudes of men and women today have come under the influence of the scientific habit of mind. They are no longer willing merely to accept. They desire to know why and what and how. They are subjecting all doctrines and all traditional authorities to a frank scrutiny. Authorities must make good or they are discarded. There is a growing passion for reality in the modern world. It is bringing to pass a new outlook upon the world and a profound desire to discover the truth about it. Ideas are no longer sacred because they are old, but only because they are true.[18]

A second exhibit comes from a sermon by Edward Scribner Ames of the Disciples of Christ, the title of which, cast as query—"What Is Religion For?"—itself suggests the tenor of the times:

We live in a questioning age. Nothing is exempt. All customs, institutions, and especially all idealisms, are under examination. Any refusal to submit to inquiry is regarded as confession of weakness, if not of imposture. Religion cannot take refuge in its sanctity or its mysteries. If it will not answer for itself, then its case is left to critics and on-lookers who may widely miss its inner spirit and intent.[19]

Then with increasing deftness Ames reported how this new spirit specifically affected the function of religion in the twenties:

Every minister now and then is called upon not merely to explain a particular miracle but the miraculous itself; not one article of the creed only, but creeds in general; not this or that ordinance, but the principle of authority back of all ordinances; not merely the meaning of some saying of Jesus, but the significance of the man himself; not one attribute of divinity, but the whole conception of God. Likewise men are insistently asking the ultimate question about religion: What is it for? Why religion? [20]

In summary, the composite effect of the intellectual milieu upon man's purposes, ideals, hopes, and beliefs during the twenties may be sketched:

(1) A method of inquiry and of judgment arose that discredited reliance upon authority and tradition.

(2) Particular beliefs vanished before advancing knowledge of nature, of history, and of mind.

(3) Men acquired increasing voluntary control over conditions and areas that religion traditionally assigned to superhuman powers. At the same time, there arose a sharper awareness that certain phases of life (e.g. "id") were beyond man's conscious control or the seeming guidance of a god.

(4) The whole mental atmosphere changed as ancient fears, attitudes of submission, and reliance upon the dim or the imagined were supplanted by a self-confident realism. If men did not feel more at home in the here and now, at least they were newly disposed to making it a home.

[18] Minot Simons, A Modern Theism (Boston: Beacon Press, 1931), p. 4.
[19] Edward Scribner Ames, "What Is Religion For?" The Christian Century Pulpit, I, No. 5 (February, 1930), 12.
[20] Ibid.

Such was the mood of the age along with the substantive intellectual currents which swept it along.

Pivotal Events

The chronology of the fundamentalist-modernist controversy falls into three sections:[21] the Period of Inception (1918-22) beginning with the postwar heightening of millennial reaction in 1918 and leading up to 1922 when the brewing controversy erupted into open conflict; the Period of Rhetorical Crisis (1922-25) framed by the Fosdick versus Macartney ecclesiastical conflict over modernism, and the Bryan versus Darrow duel over evolution; and the Period of Consummation (1925-30) when the liberals pushed their cause with greater constructive fervency and the fundamentalists grew progressively more dispirited. The milieu of the late twenties simply no longer supported the reactionary orthodoxy which conservatism had become.

The Protest Mounts

As a movement of protest, the first noteworthy conference of fundamentalists was the Philadelphia Prophetic Convention which took place during May of 1918. Five thousand people thronged to its twelve sessions. Fear for the preservation of the historic faith had already been stirred in them by the earlier publication of *The Fundamentals: A Testimony to the Truth.*[22] The war psychology[23] further fanned religious militancy as pockets of protest became consolidated into movement proportions. This budding spirit of militancy for "the old gospel" was both heightened and exploited by the orthodox propagandists. Fundamentalists took the role of defenders of the faith, employing as channels for persuasion Bible and prophetic conferences, fundamentalist schools,[24] special organizations,[25] tractarian propaganda,

[21] This division is suggested by Leland M. Griffin in his article, "The Rhetoric of Historical Movements," *Quarterly Journal of Speech* (April, 1952), pp. 184-88. For another suggested topology useful in the narration of a movement, see C. Wendell King, "Careers of Social Movements," *Social Movements in the United States* (New York: Random House, 1956), pp. 39-57.

[22] Publication of these twelve small volumes, begun in 1909, and distributed widely to some three million religionists in the United States and abroad provided an arsenal of argumentative and illustrative materials which gave unity, respectability, and direction for the orthodox. The significance of these volumes was acclaimed by William Warren Sweet, a responsible church historian, as having actually launched the movement. See Sweet, *The Story of Religion in America* (New York: Harper & Row, 1939), p. 568.

[23] The First World War played an important role in determining the mood and manner of the controversy. The war had spawned militaristic notions of how to deal with threatening forces. On the other hand, victory in war had bred a buoyancy and optimism of spirit which a liberal theology could and did exploit.

[24] Moody Bible Institute in Chicago and its sister institution on the West coast, the Bible Institute of Los Angeles, were most influential during the twenties.

[25] Fundamentalists were instrumental in forming more than a dozen fellowships "beyond the church" of which the World's Christian Fundamentals Association, founded by William Bell Riley in 1919, was most important and longest-lived.

personal correspondence, ecclesiastical and legislative pressures, and polemical preaching and platform speaking. Their apocalyptic and prophetic "Five Points" [26] (regarded as the *sine qua non* of fundamentalism: the infallibility of the Bible, Christ's Virgin Birth, his Substitutionary Atonement, his Resurrection, and his Second Coming) rallied conservative support and provided the textual base for the excoriation of evolutionists, modernists, and other heretics.

Preaching and the Crisis

As the fundamentalist offensive gathered momentum, Harry Emerson Fosdick issued a challenge in a sermon which Robert D. Clark has called "the most sensational and widely-publicized sermon of his generation," [27] "Shall the Fundamentalists Win?" [28] Fosdick stated the differences of conviction dividing the two camps on such matters as the virgin birth of Jesus, the inerrancy of the Scriptures, and the second coming of Christ, and then made his plea that the desirable solution was not a split that would tear the evangelical churches asunder, but a spirit of conciliation that would work out the problem within an inclusive fellowship.

Anything but "a spirit of conciliation" followed as Fosdick himself laments in retrospect: "If ever a sermon failed to achieve its object, mine did. It was a plea for good will, but what came of it was an explosion of ill will, for over two years making headline news of a controversy that went the limit of truculence." [29] Interestingly, Fosdick's congregation at the First Presbyterian Church, New York City, detected nothing inflammatory about the sermon at the time of its delivery. However, the sermon in pamphlet form came to the attention of Ivy Lee, a liberal Presbyterian layman, who was determined, as head of one of the nation's foremost publicity organizations, to supply copies of it to a nationwide audience. Lee divided the sermon into sections, supplied a series of captions, cut out parts of the conciliatory introduction and conclusion, and retitled it, "The New Knowledge and the Christian Faith." [30] The effectiveness for arousal of Lee's version

[26] The fact that fundamentalists could not agree whether five, seven, nine, or more points were "essential" tended to refute their claim to be "united in essentials."

[27] Robert D. Clark, "Harry Emerson Fosdick," *A History and Criticism of American Public Address*, III, 425.

[28] The text of the sermon regarded authoritative by Fosdick is the one based on a stenographic report by Margaret Renton; it is reprinted in *Contemporary Forum, American Speeches on Twentieth-Century Issues*, eds. Ernest J. Wrage and Barnet Baskerville (New York: Harper & Row, 1962), pp. 97-106.

[29] Harry Emerson Fosdick, "The Fundamentalist Controversy," *The Living of These Days: An Autobiography*. (New York: Harper & Row, 1956), p. 145.

[30] Cf. "The New Knowledge and the Christian Faith," reprinted and edited from a sermon preached at the First Presbyterian Church, New York City, May 21, 1922.

of the sermon cannot be disputed, for after its circulation the brewing controversy erupted into open conflict.[31]

The first reply came from Clarence Edward Noble Macartney, a stalwart Presbyterian clergyman of Philadelphia. In a sermon subsequently published under the title "Shall Unbelief Win?" [32] Macartney denounced Fosdick's views as "subversive of the Christian Faith." He enforced the denunciation administratively by insisting that the Philadelphia Presbytery overture the General Assembly of the Presbyterian Church (U.S.A.) that doctrine contrary to the Presbyterian Confession of Faith was being preached from the pulpit of the First Presbyterian Church of New York City. The ensuing action of the Philadelphia Presbytery set off a chain reaction so that by the time the General Assembly met in May of 1923, twelve separate overtures had been filed, ten of which were unfavorable toward Fosdick. The governing powers of the church were thus set to work on the case. The intricate involvements of this action have been traced in careful detail elsewhere.[33] To make the broad outline of the narrative complete, however, it should be noted that after two years of General Assembly debate (in which William Jennings Bryan figured prominently), Judicial Commission rulings, minority reports, political maneuverings, drafting and redrafting of statements, and Presbytery and Session inquiries, Fosdick was asked to "regularize" his position by becoming a Presbyterian minister[34] "subject to the jurisdiction and authority of the Church," or "not to continue to occupy a Presbyterian pulpit." Fosdick declined the invitational ultimatum to become a Presbyterian minister, feeling such action would represent a "retrograde sectarian movement," a "return to the principle of a denominationally 'closed shop'"—a principle completely unpalatable to him as a convinced interdenominationalist.[35] His resignation followed. He preached his farewell sermon to the First Presbyterian Church of New York City on Sunday, March 1, 1925.[36] The sermon, published complete in

---

[31] There were certainly other instances of the sermon's publication (e. g., *The Baptist*, June 10, 1922), but Lee's version was indisputably the most influential.

[32] Speaking of Fosdick's sermon, "Shall the Fundamentalists Win?' Macartney says in his autobiography, *The Making of a Minister*, p. 184: "This extraordinary sermon I answered with one entitled, 'Shall Unbelief Win?' This sermon, too, was printed in pamphlet form and widely circulated."

[33] Cf. *The First Presbyterian Church of New York and Dr. Fosdick* (pamphlet giving no publication details); *Fosdick Case*, Complaint of Walter D. Buchanan and Others to the 136th General Assembly of the Presbyterian Church in the U.S.A. Against the Presbytery of New York in its Answer to the Mandate of the 135th General Assembly of the Presbyterian Church in the U.S.A. (Grand Rapids, 1924); and Fosdick, "The Fundamentalist Controversy." *The Living of These Days*, pp. 144-76.

[34] Fosdick, called as the associate preaching minister of the First Presbyterian Church of New York City in 1918, had been ordained as a Baptist in 1903.

[35] Fosdick, *The Living of These Days*, p. 174.

[36] *The Farewell Sermon of Dr. Harry Emerson Fosdick to the First Presbyterian Church of New York, Sunday, March 1, 1929* (pamphlet giving no publication details).

266

pamphlet form, is noteworthy not only for its rhetorical excellence but as marking an important milestone in the general controversy.

Bryan Speaks for Fundamentalism

Although reaction to Fosdick's sermon of 1922 provided the greatest excitement at the Indianapolis General Assembly of 1923, William Jennings Bryan was able to turn the delegates' attention for a brief time to evolution, his major concern. Increasingly thereafter, evolution was to rival the issue of modernism for central billing in fundamentalist gatherings, climaxing in the Scopes trial of 1925, when it was made to appear that evolution was the only issue at stake.

Bryan's exodus from politics in 1915 was the signal for his giving increasing time to the expression of his religious convictions. On college campuses, before legislative assemblies, in large metropolitan auditoriums, at fundamentalist assemblies, at Bible conferences, and on extended speaking tours, Bryan popularized the cause of fundamentalism, often in strikingly aphoristic terms. It has been estimated that "Bryan delivered as many speeches between 1915 and 1925 as he did in any other decade of his life," and that "practically all of what he said, regardless of the audience or occasion, was colored by his deep religious convictions, in which a firm adherence to fundamentalism [was] dominant." [37] So we may not wholly dismiss as jest Bryan's comment on his heavy speaking schedule during these years: "Men who haven't heard me are so few and far between that in a few years they will be able to draw salaries in a museum;" and again, "On several occasions I have refused invitations to talk, just to show I could go a whole day without making a speech." [38]

The anti-evolution sentiments expressed by Bryan in 1925 as counsel for the prosecution at the Scopes trial represented the crystallization of a lifetime of thinking on the subject of religious fundamentalism. As early as the turn of the century, Bryan had recognized that a force was working to undermine his cherished faith. Unlike those proponents of The Fundamentals who saw the threat to orthodoxy as lying in modernism, Bryan rather laid the blame on evolution. Actually the foremost fundamentalist warrior on both fronts, Bryan chose to concentrate on evolution because he saw it as the more inclusive issue—primarily because it questioned the literal interpretation of the Bible, the very foundation of his faith.

Bryan began his crusade against evolution formally in 1921 with the publication of his pamphlet, "The Menace of Darwinism," and a speech before the Florida Baptist Association in which, with ridicule and invective,

[37] Jack Mills, "The Speaking of William Jennings Bryan in Florida, 1915-1925," *Southern Speech Journal* (January, 1949), p. 168.
[38] *Ibid.*, pp. 168-69. Quotations taken from the Miami *Daily Metropolis*, February 14, 1918, and the Miami *Daily News and Metropolis*, April 23, 1924, respectively.

he charged that Darwin's "guesses" were not fit substitutes for the Word of God.[39]

By 1922 he had carried the fight into what he considered the enemy's stronghold, the colleges and universities of the land. He was then ready to articulate his objections to Darwinism in lectures[40] and publish them for national consumption.[41] His specific objections ("it is an hypothesis, and an hypothesis is nothing more than a guess"; "it has not one syllable in the Bible to support it"; "there is not the slightest shred of scientific evidence to support it"; "it resorts to absurd explanations which tax human credulity"; and "it destroys faith in religion, the only basis of morals") led him to that conclusion for which he fought legislatively: We do not ask that teachers paid by taxation shall teach the Christian religion to students, but we do insist that they shall not teach under the guise of either science or philosophy, anything that undermines faith in God, impairs belief in the Bible, or discredits Christ." [42] Insistence upon this credo led Bryan to the small Tennessee town of Dayton, where, in the summer 1925, he took the witness stand in its defense, answering to the harsh, skeptical reasoning and merciless cross-examination of Clarence Darrow. There in the famed "Monkey Trial," humiliated by Darrow and denied a chance for self-vindication by not being allowed to deliver his speech of summation, Bryan and the cause that he championed were publically disgraced. His death only days after the trial not only spared Bryan from tasting the full bitterness of the disgrace, but also deprived fundamentalism of its most dedicated and articulate advocate. Bereft of that charismatic leader who had supplied for their crusade many of the arguments, most of the aphoristic slogans, and certainly the inspirational dynamic, fundamentalists were unable to sustain a unified offensive and progressively lost ground over the ensuing years.[43]

[39] *Ibid.*, pp. 148-49.

[40] William Jennings Bryan, *In His Image* (New York: Fleming H. Revell Company, 1922); first delivered as the James Sprunt Lectures at Union Theological Seminary, Richmond, Virginia. Bryan claimed that the lectures "provided the opportunity for the presentation of an argument I had had in mind for years—an argument to the heart and mind of the average men, especially to the young" (p. 7). Regarding the title and argumentative framework for the book, he added: "I have chosen 'In His Image' as the title of this series of lectures, because, in my judgment, all depends upon our conception of our place in God's plan. The Bible tells us that God made us in His image . . ." (p. 8).

[41] William Jennings Bryan, "God and Evolution," *The New York Times*, February 26, 1922, Sec. VII, p. 1.

[42] Mills, "The Speaking of William Jennings Bryan," *Southern Speech Journal* (January, 1949), p. 151.

[43] It may, of course, be challenged that it was less Bryan's death than the devastating ridicule to which his beliefs had been publicly subjected that disheartened his followers and reduced them to relative silence. Everett L. Perry's estimate that "the early demise of such an illustrious proponent as William Jennings Bryan seemed to have little effect on the movement," does, however, seem exaggerated. See the dissertation, "The Role of Socio-Economic Factors in the Rise and Development of American Fundamentalism" (University of Chicago, 1959), p. 185.

Between these pivotal events of Fosdick versus Macartney and Bryan versus Darrow, there was a vast array of lesser skirmishings, including the much-publicized New York fundamentalist debates between John Roach Straton, argumentative Baptist minister, and Charles Francis Potter, Unitarian clergyman.[44]

Following the summer of 1925, the climate of the controversy changed. Responsibility for the change was not confined to the faltering influence of the fundamentalists, for a new spirit and strategy among the modernists was evident as well, as Fosdick indicated:

The sum of the whole matter is this: modernism up to date has been largely a movement of protest and criticism. It has originated in reaction against obscurantist assaults on Christian intelligence and against the continuance of meaningless denominational divisions. It inevitably has the faults of its qualities, but it is high time it recovered from them. If it is to serve any abiding purpose it must pass through protest to production, through criticism to creation. Whenever it does that, it wins. The most effective Christian churches that I know today are manned by liberals. Multiply such and the day is won.[45]

Even more pointed than Fosdick's own challenge to the modernists was that of William Pierson Merrill, his liberal New York City Presbyterian colleague, when he charged: "We must learn how to be popular, positive, impassioned, rather than critical, highbrow, and academic. There has been too much water and too little fire about our liberal Christianity." [46]

The Conflict Wanes

By mid-year of 1926, *The Christian Century* carried an article on "Vanishing Fundamentalism" in which was predicted: "It has not yet fully run its fortuitous course. But it is henceforth to be a disappearing quantity in American religious life, while our churches go on to larger issues, finding their controversies in realities that are pregnant and significant for human welfare rather than in hollow and sterile dogmas which are irrelevant even if true." [47]

There were, to be sure, still notable instances of sporadic conflict. Prominent among them was the fight led by John Gresham Machen against a plan for the reorganization of Princeton Seminary which threatened its position as a conservative Presbyterian stronghold. After three years of wrangling over the issue, Machen and his forces suffered defeat in the

[44] Cf. *The Famous New York Fundamentalist-Modernist Debates* (New York: Doran, 1924).

[45] Harry Emerson Fosdick, *Adventurous Religion* (New York: Harper & Brothers, 1926), pp. 273-74.

[46] William Pierson Merrill, *Liberal Christianity* (New York: The Macmillan Company, 1925), p. 166.

[47] "Vanishing Fundamentalism," *The Christian Century*, XLIII, No. 24 (June 17, 1926), 799.

General Assembly of 1929. Promptly, he and his colleague supporters resigned their teaching posts at Princeton Seminary and organized an independent and rival Westminster Theological Seminary in a fundamentalist stronghold, Philadelphia.

The fact that it was the fundamentalists rather than the liberals who were finding it necessary to leave seminaries and churches in the late twenties and early thirties indicated that ecclesiastical power had shifted from the fundamentalists to the modernists. On the other hand, it may hardly be said that the modernists had won a decisive victory, for the fundamentalists were more dispirited than routed. Depicted analogously, the situation was much the same as that described by a scientist, who, when asked who killed off the dinosaurs, replied, "Nobody, the climate changed and they died." Fundamentalists were not defeated; the climate changed and they found themselves no longer a viable force on the American theological scene. By 1930, a whole new slate of issues had been drawn to the fore. Just as fundamentalists early in the twenties were creating wide stir over the "Menace of Modernism," modernists by the turn of the decade were winning the headlines with alarm over such things as the "Menace of the Movies." Sabbath observance, prohibition, divorce, crime, world peace, and other issues—more socio-religious than theological—were capturing central attention. In short, it was time to begin viewing the fundamentalist-modernist controversy as history.[48]

Points of Issue

A study of the rhetoric of the controversy reveals that the three topics most ventilated through the oral medium were the doctrines of Biblical Inspiration, the Virgin Birth, and the Second Coming. A survey of each of these three provides an overview of the clashing homiletic content.

The reason that the authority of the Bible was at issue is suggested by Charles A. Blanchard, president of Wheaton College: "If the Bible is not the very Word of God, we are all at sea on every other article of Faith. . . . I therefore call the doctrine that the Bible is the Word of God, the fundamental of fundamentals."[49] In defense of their doctrine of an inspired Bible, fundamentalists characteristically pointed to three witnesses: the witness of the Bible to its own inspiration, the witness of church history, and the internal witness of the Holy Spirit authenticating its validity as "inspired" to the heart of the believers.

Modernists, on the other hand, claimed that fundamentalists' insistence

---

[48] Stewart Grant Cole produced his dissertation on "The Psychology of the Fundamentalist Movement" in 1929 and published his book *The History of Fundamentalism* in 1931.

[49] Charles A. Blanchard, "The Fundamental of Fundamentals," *The King's Business,* XIV, No. 5 (May, 1923), 459.

upon a rigid scriptural inerrancy (a deduction from the doctrine that the Bible was the inspired Word of a God who cannot err) reflected human insecurity, and that it represented not so much a high view of Scripture as a rigid and over-limited one. Modernists did not consider that errors in the Bible affected its purpose at all—that the reality of a historical event did not depend upon an inerrant account of the event—indeed, that errors were the inevitable accompaniments of the process of a progressive revelation, constituting primitive and temporary forms through which the essential biblical message was passing to maturity.

Many fundamentalists, holding the Bible to be inerrantly factual in every detail, insisted that the biology, zoology, and geology of the Bible was as authoritative as its theology—that it was as much a textbook in science and history as it was a handbook of religion. Most modernists held that all biblical narratives were certainly not literal and exact records of sober, historical fact and that all the scientific references and conceptions contained in the Bible did not agree with the well-established conclusions of modern knowledge. But the Bible's value to them was not diminished by such contentions. Rather, they insisted upon recognition that the Bible's authority was strictly religious and that it was no belittling limitation to say of the Bible that it was an authority *only on God.*

In essence then, fundamentalists argued that the Bible came into existence through a process of divine, supernatural inspiration and that it was to be used as a final, absolute, and infallible authority; modernists, in contrast, denying biblical infallibility and fearlessly discarding whatever affronted their reason or their conscience, chose to interpret the Bible as they interpreted other great literature, preferring an appreciative over an authoritative view of the Bible's religious insights.

Next to the problem of how the Bible was to be regarded, the doctrine most widely debated concerned the Virgin Birth of Jesus. "All the foundations of our faith go when that falls!" charged one fundamentalist clergyman.[50] Fundamentalists argued first that the doctrine of the Virgin Birth was directly and plainly stated as a fact in the gospel narrative. The unbroken testimony of the church to the Virgin Birth, especially as embodied in the Apostles' Creed, comprised a second argument. A third argument for the Virgin Birth was that the uniqueness of Christ's sinless life is best understood when his birth is regarded as supernatural. A fourth reason, hardly an argument, may best be labeled "sentiment." Men and women believed in the doctrine simply because they did not want to give it up. Often, the manner in which these arguments were presented betrayed the fundamentalists' anxiety that with denial of the Virgin Birth was apt to go denial of the virgin life, and so attack upon the Virgin Birth was regarded as a flank attack

[50] John G. Reid, "Is It Fundamental?" *The King's Business,* XV, No. 5 (May, 1924), 277.

upon the whole supernatural estimate of Christ—his life, his claims, his sinlessness, his miracles, and, finally, his resurrection from the dead.

Modernists, of course, countered with their own arguments, such as: (1) the Virgin Birth is scientifically improbable; (2) it is historically questionable; and (3) it is religiously unessential.[51]

To summarize debate on the topic, while some few modernists professed belief in the Virgin Birth and others, for various reasons, did not, all of them agreed that it was not a central affirmation of the Christian faith as fundamentalists insisted. In short, the question at issue was whether or not the doctrine of the Virgin Birth should be an issue.

While some focused upon the doctrine of Biblical Inspiration or the doctrine of the Virgin Birth, others settled upon the doctrine of the Second Coming of Christ as the central dogma of the movement. As J. Frank Norris, colorful leader of Southern fundamentalists, put it: "When a man tells me he believes in the literal, personal, bodily, visible, imminent return of the Lord to this earth as King, I know what he believes on every other question. I know that he believes the Bible literally, I know what he believes concerning the Godhead, I know what he believes concerning the Virgin Birth, . . . I know that he is not a Modernist." [52]

The doctrine of the Second Coming had decided social repercussions. Many fundamentalists declared that indeed a glorious future was sure to come, but that it would come through the arbitrary stroke of God, not through the struggles of men to realize illusive social ideals. They shared the belief that the world was essentially wicked and evil and that not only would it remain so but would grow more so until God himself finally destroyed it. Indeed, the logic of this position pushed to the conclusion that the worse the world got, the more reason there was for hope in the imminent Second Coming.[53] For a sizable number of fundamentalists, the mission of the church was envisioned, not as representing a catalyst for the betterment of society, but as constituting an ark which, as in the days of the flood, spirited an elect coterie of souls out of impending social disaster. Society—if at all it could be saved—was to be saved soul-by-soul.

Modernists had no patience for a save-your-own-soul-and-get-out-of-this-devil's-world-as-quickly-as-possible view, and registered their objections with labels such as "intellectually unbelievable," "psychologically catastrophic," and "ethically reprehensible."

[51] See, for example, Joseph Lewis, *The Bible Unmasked* (New York: The Freethought Press Association, 1926), p. 197; and Harry Emerson Fosdick, "Shall the Fundamentalists Win?" *Contemporary Forum*, p. 105.

[52] William Henry Smith, *Modernism, Fundamentalism, and Catholicism* (Milwaukee: Morehouse Publishing Company, 1926), pp. 41-42.

[53] See the report on a sermon by John Roach Straton who was called the "archbishop of fundamentalism." "Dr. Straton Thinks Return of Christ at Hand," *The Christian Century*, XLI, No. 52 (December 25, 1924), 1672.

The issue then, in summary, was this: Fundamentalists held that the ultimate hope of the world lay in the Second Coming of Christ which would bring to a consummation his redeeming work in the complete salvation of all his people and the final destruction of all sin; modernists, in contrast, proclaimed the gradual evolution of the human race and the betterment of world conditions as men increasingly realized the necessity of putting into practice, in all phases of life, the teachings of Jesus.

Homiletic Distinctions

The clash between modernists and fundamentalists was as evident in homiletic technique as it was in homiletic content. Generally, oratory during the controversy ran the gamut from the fiery, impassioned exhibition of unrestrained fanaticism to the cool, reflective cadences of reasoned discourse. There was heterogeneity in oratorical styles and rhetorical purposes. The language of the disputation tended to be rich in connotative meanings, heavy with antitheses, exaggerated, and generally heightened. The acrimony of the dispute betrayed many participants into vituperative speech with such frequency that it became a dominant characteristic of the controversy.[54] In composition, fundamentalists tended to be direct and concrete; with few notable exceptions, modernists tended toward abstractions and the theoretical. Fundamentalist orators generally exhibited their passion to "defend the faith." Modernist speaking was characteristically less heated and less urgent. For the fundamentalist, controversy seemed to be a vocation (to "be Christian" was to defend Christianity); for the modernist, participation in the controversy was more often an avocation. Fundamentalists, by and large, accepted the role of propagandists and manipulators of opinion. Few, if any, gained prominence as originators of ideas. Such "newness" as was evident among them expressed itself largely in novel strategies and aphorisms for defense. Modernists, given to creative thought and the spirit of experimentation, lauded and practiced innovation. Their inventiveness aggravated fundamentalist defensiveness.

Fundamentalists, often more adept in stirring the listeners when in face-to-face debates with modernists before live audiences, brought considerable knowledge, skill, and confidence to bear upon the effective presentation of their authoritarian-based propositions. Implicit if not explicit in their public address was the contention: thus saith the Bible, the church, holy tradition,

[54] The oratory of this controversy furnishes a rich deposit of vituperative speech and bold exhibits of the strategy of ridicule to which students of these special rhetorical phenomena might turn with special profit. In the history of American public address, perhaps no other decade lent so hospitable a climate for these phenomena as did the twenties. What the ethos of the age supported, the spokesmen exploited.

inherited faith, or hallowed habit. Modernists, on the other hand, revealed in their sermons that they handled their subjects more as a quest than as a pronouncement based upon some authority. Sermons tended to be less an exposition of some historical or textual particular than a trail of inquiry through some forest of perplexity. Often the marks of thinking-aloud are evident: vague generalization, more negation than affirmation, and lack of precise definition leading to no specific conclusion. Yet, certain modernist spokesmen won a sympathetic and understanding following by revealing their abilities for intellectual subtlety, paradox, meaningful symbolic retranslation of abiding verities, and their general concern for a validated, contemporaneous relevancy.

Fundamentalist spokesmen characteristically made appeal to such specific wants as security, self-respect and pride, loyalty, and competition and rivalry. Modernist spokesmen appealed rather to man's desires for freedom, honor and duty, love and friendship, and adventure. The supports used to buttress these appeals were generally consistent with the speakers' theological and philosophical undergirdings. Fundamentalist spokesmen characteristically used traditional authority, relying most heavily upon biblical and historical source materials used in the forms of definition, illustration, testimony, and repetition or restatement. Modernists were more likely to employ scientific, literary, and experiential sources which they typically used in the forms of specific instances, factual information, illustrations, and comparison or contrast.

Much used representative phrases of fundamentalism such as "Jesus saves," "the Bible is the Word of God," "the Blood which cleanseth from all sin," and "born-again Christians" were central symbols about which sermons and prayers tended to cluster. Recurring phrases in modernist rhetoric were oriented more toward method than content, including "it is a fact no longer to be questioned," "we have at length learned," "we no longer think of," "scholars generally agree," and "the consensus of learned opinion is."

Fundamentalists, though conservative in thought, were, with minor exception, anything but restrained in physical behavior on the platform. Instead of using pulpits, a number of them paced the platform to emphasize a forceful method of address. Modernists seemed generally to prefer and practice more restraint in delivery, though one cannot charge that they were typically deficient in physical vitality and expressiveness.

Among all the speakers in the controversy, William Jennings Bryan had no peer in vocal effects. His pure, bell-like tones had the power and carrying quality that made it possible for 15,000 people, seated in the open air, to hear him without the aid of loudspeaker systems. The press, biographers of his time, friends and foes alike agreed that his voice was phenomenal.

274

Summary

The fundamentalist-modernist controversy was noteworthy in the history of American theological disputes for being primarily a "pulpit controversy." [55] In contrast, for example, with the struggle against modernism within the Roman Catholic Church, which was largely a documentary exchange among the hierarchy,[56] the fundamentalist-modernist dispute among Protestants excited and involved the laity. Fundamentalist and modernist leadership knew they had to carry their ideological skirmishing to the "grass roots" of the church if they wished a decisive victory, and they knew equally well that there was no better way to reach the laity than through the medium of public address.

The controversy drew into its services many of the ablest religious leaders and spokesmen of the day. Fosdick, Macartney, Bryan, Darrow, and possibly Riley would surely be listed in any Who's Who of rhetorical greats of the twenties. William Jennings Bryan became the unchallenged leader of the lay forces of fundamentalism. No man in America knew so well as he the formidable strength of the country's religious conservatism or possessed the strength of belief and oratorical genius to rally that conservatism into militant action. In contrast, Harry Emerson Fosdick, "modernism's Moses," disclaimed polemical intent and simply championed the cause of "an intellectually hospitable, tolerant, liberty-loving church." In the struggle for that cause, Fosdick was distinguished neither as an administrator nor as an ecclesiastical potentate, achieving leadership position rather largely through the clarity and persuasiveness of his oral and written works.

The multiple, variegated, and complex skirmishes during the controversy were of three types, illustrated by the following samples: (a) conflicts between religious groups and secular groups—e.g., the Scopes trial; (b) conflicts between different religious groups or denominations—e.g., the Straton-Potter debates; and (c) conflicts within a single religious group or denomination—e.g., the Fosdick case in the Presbyterian Church.

Cultural currents played a large part in aggravating the conflict. Indeed, modernism's ascendancy, though creditable in part to the leadership of such men as Harry Emerson Fosdick, William P. Merrill, Shailer Mathews, Ernest Fremont Tittle, and Percy Stickney Grant, must be largely attributed to its alignment with four forces prominent in the contemporary culture: (a) the basic assumption of science that reason is the sole trustworthy guide in a

[55] Used in a broadly inclusive sense to refer to all forms of public address in the ecclesiastical context.

[56] See Alec R. Vidler, *The Modernist Movement in the Roman Church* (Cambridge: The University Press, 1934). The term "modernist" as an ecclesiastical designation of a theological position had its origin in the encyclical *Pascendi Dominici Gregis* in 1907. For the broad outline modernism traced within the Roman Catholic Church, see the dissertation, "The Fundamentalist-Modernist Controversy, 1918-1930, in the History of American Public Address," pp. 167-71.

world that is rational and law-bound; (b) the democratic ideal of an authority residing in the breasts of free and intelligent men who refuse to be coerced by legislative, ecclesiastical, or supernatural restrictions that run counter to reasoned convictions of right and duty; (c) the genius of Protestantism itself, popularly interpreted as allowing for marked individualism in religion; and (d) that individualistic *Zeitgeist* of the twenties which sanctioned libidinal self-expression and debunked obeisance to traditional norms and conventions.

Points at issue were ostensibly theological. They are best recast in summary so as to point up the defensive posture of the fundamentalists: (a) against the inroads of higher criticism, fundamentalists proclaimed and defended the doctrine of an inspired, infallible Word, factually authoritative throughout and generally to be literally interpreted; (b) against the optimistic romanticism of a liberal, socially oriented Christianity, fundamentalists proclaimed man's total enslavement to sin, a depravity which, they claimed, led to social upheaval and despair unless touched by the redemptive power of him whose Second Coming would at once vindicate the righteous and destroy both the corrupt and the evil social order they inhabited; and (c) against the intrusion of evolution, science, and naturalism into theology, fundamentalists offered a heightened supernaturalism encompassing the doctrines of the Virgin Birth (Jesus' supernatural origin) and the special, fiat creation of man (man's supernatural origin).

Fundamentalist and modernist spokesmen rallied significantly contrasting audiences. Fundamentalists, despite declared evangelistic and proselytizing intent and marked success in adapting their oratory to their various "believing" audiences, were yet not appreciably successful in capturing the ecclesiastically noncommitted. The single most adequate explanation would seem to be that fundamentalist spokesmen were, for the most part, speaking more to themselves than to the age. Their rhetoric was cast more as a celebration of the obvious for the "committed" than as an appeal to the "sideliner" to join their cause. Championing ideas that they felt were—or should be—of paramount concern to the masses, they appealed chiefly to common men of partisan, parochial interests. While the fundamentalists characteristically addressed themselves to the *Volksgeist* of an elderly, rural population, modernists sought to abet the *Zeitgeist* of a growing, progressive liberalism. Modernist spokesmen seemed to be speaking more to an age than to a particular composite of people.[57] Significantly, intellectuals and cosmopolites, when at all they could be drawn into the controversy, tended to support those modernist spokesmen who stressed both the complexity of issues and man's native ability to surmount his problems.

The most successful spokesmen of both camps as judged by noncomba-

[57] It might be argued that modernists were speaking less to the "age" than to fellow modernists whom they regarded as leaders in the "new age."

tants were those who shunned conventionalized and formulistic utterances, choosing rather to speak with simplicity, clarity, directness, and concreteness. In an age when foundations are shaken, men look for facts and truths naked and unadorned. Truth itself seems so necessary and hunger for it becomes so poignant that any marked artistry in its presentation seems like an impertinence. Men of the twenties, tutored by science that the "best" and "most important" truth seldom if ever wears the rich garments of eloquence, were generally suspicious of trombone tones and the bunting-draped platform.

Finally, "victory" was decisive for neither party to the controversy. Fundamentalists underestimated the strength and far-flung pervasiveness of the modern culture they resisted and defied, and in turn, overestimated their tactics in persuasion to turn the cultural tide. Modernists underestimated the deep-seated resistance to innovations and somewhat overestimated their powers to transmute a budding *Zeitgeist* into a modified *Volksgeist*. Nonetheless, the skirmish ranks as a historic conflict on the American theological scene, providing strikingly contrasting elements both of homiletic content and technique—elements which, to this day, push themselves, however temporarily, into public consciousness whenever an articulate spokesman, a cogent expression, a supportive climate, and a voluntary and motivated listening audience unite in the arena of public address.

14

NEO-ORTHODOXY AND THE AMERICAN PULPIT

_____Harold Brack_____

In his autobiography Harry Emerson Fosdick warns against identifying neo-orthodoxy with fundamentalism. He emphasizes the reality of wide variations and changing emphases within neo-orthodoxy. Then he hazards a generalization, "There is one common quality which characterizes the neo-orthodox movement as a whole: its discontent with the liberal theology current in the late nineteenth and early twentieth centries." [1] Fosdick cites neo-orthodoxy's opposition to liberalism's emphasis on the immanence of God, its reliance on reason, and its easygoing tolerance. He suggests, nevertheless, that it was liberalism that laid the ground for neo-orthodoxy. Dr. Fosdick preached during the period of neo-orthodoxy's emergence in this country.

We have to keep in mind that as a major theological movement neo-orthodoxy has both intercontinental and interdenominational dimensions. Roman Catholics have been prompted to a rediscovery of the extensive work of Thomas Aquinas with the aid of Étienne Gilson and Jacques Maritain. Some Anglicans have given particular attention to Berdyaev's philosophic and theological contributions, while Protestants on both sides of the ocean have turned anew to Luther, Calvin, Wesley, and read avidly the works of Barth, Brunner, Niebuhr.

Neo-Orthodoxy Defined

Neo-orthodoxy emphasized the historical character of Christianity. It pointed to the biblical record of the mighty acts of God and lifted up the ministry, death, and resurrection of Jesus of Nazareth. Such an emphasis led to a revival of the doctrine of the Word of God. This revived doctrine of the Word of God declared that the Bible is an authoritative witness to the Divine self-disclosure. Hence preaching, i.e. proclamation, rests on God's Word.[2]

[1] Harry Emerson Fosdick, *The Living of These Days* (New York: Harper & Row, 1956), p. 249.

[2] Hugh Ross Mackintosh, *Types of Modern Theology* (London: Nisbet and Company, 1949), p. 288.

278

Dwight E. Stevenson caught the spirit of this revival when he declared, "Our motivation is urgent, for until the Bible again becomes a living book, Christianity cannot become a living faith." [3]

Neo-orthodoxy also insisted on a more realistic view of man with full recognition that man is a sinner. Man's denial of God's lordship was declared to be the basic issue. In his work dealing with the thought of Reinhold Niebuhr, church historian Gordon Harland observes, "Niebuhr's rich and profound analysis of man's sin is quite generally regarded as his most valuable contribution to contemporary theology." [4] Frequently overlooked is Niebuhr's parallel emphasis on God's grace and the particular attention which he gave to forgiveness and redemption.

Americans tend to identify neo-orthodoxy with the names of Karl Barth, Emil Brunner, and Reinhold Niebuhr. Niebuhr is the theologian primarily responsible for transmitting Barthianism to America. There were, too, forerunners like Edwin Lewis who in one of his Fondren Lectures entitled "An Appeal to the Preacher" asserted:

You are to declare what God in Christ has revealed himself to be, and this will set you squarely against the numerous bizarre theisms which are the fashion of our time. You are to declare God's unchanging hatred of sin both because of what it is in itself and because of what it does for human life, but you are also to declare what that great Deed is—call it incarnation.[5]

Generally neo-orthodoxy is thought of as a critical response to a liberal theology which was less historically and more subjectively and psychologically inclined.[6] Neo-orthodoxy opposed preoccupation with altering the social order without wisdom and power from above and the notion of inevitable social evolution and progress. Particularly did it take issue with liberalism's inadequate emphasis on grace. A sample of this opposition appears in Reinhold Niebuhr's objection to the preaching of Norman Vincent Peale.

The Christian religion is one of repentance and faith, sin and grace. Christianity stresses the idea that man tends to think more of himself than he should and there can be no real meeting with God, except through repentance and the confession of sin.

The basic sin of this new cult is its egocentricity. It puts self instead of the cross at the center of the picture. Christianity insists that you cannot have faith without repentance, and since the very ideas of sin and repentance are negative,

---

[3] Dwight E. Stevenson, *Preaching on the Books of the New Testament* (New York: Harper & Row, 1956), p. 6.

[4] Gordon Harland, *The Thought of Reinhold Niebuhr* (New York: Oxford University Press, 1960), p. 76.

[5] Edwin Lewis, *The Faith We Declare* (Nashville: Cokesbury Press, 1939), pp. 218-19.

[6] Charles Clayton Morrison, *What Is Christianity?* (New York: Willet, Clark and Company, 1940), pp. 76-77.

the positive thinkers simply leave them out, or at best, gloss them over. The result is a partial picture of Christianity, a sort of half-truth.[7]

Another example of this criticism as it pertained to social programs advocated by liberal Christiaity is voiced by Elmer G. Homrighausen:

Now the goal of my faith, socially, is the Kingdom of God. This kingdom is in the world, operating wherever men realistically evaluate themselves in the face of true revelation. But this kingdom cannot be identified with any social program.
I am not so foolish as to believe that this kingdom will come by sheer human effort. Nor do I think that this kingdom will come by an "inherent necessity" in the nature of the universe automatically to produce a perfect world.[8]

Neo-orthodoxy, then, is to be understood as a movement which had substantial impact in Roman Catholic, Anglican, and Protestant communions on both sides of the Atlantic with its emphasis on the historical character of Christianity and its return to the Word of God as the theological ground of Christian faith. In the United States the spokesmen for neo-orthodoxy engaged in a sharp critique of a liberal Christianity with its emphasis on the altering of social structures and its reliance on psychological and sociological approaches. Barthians reaffirmed that we must first see man as a sinner who stands in need of redemption. The fundamental ground of the social problem, they declared, is man's rejection of God's sovereignty. Commenting on the impact of Barth and Niebuhr, in his review of the Lyman Beecher lecture series, Edgar DeWitt Jones remarked, "It has revived the doctrine of the 'exceeding sinfulness of sin,' and that is a revival long overdue."[9]

Positive Responses to the Movement

American preachers responded to this movement in a variety of ways. A number joined it while others opposed it—some because they confused it with the old orthodoxy. Many entered into dialogue with it, and still others naïvely affirmed it. There were even those who ignored it.

Elmer G. Homrighausen is one of those preachers who became an American exponent of the general Barthian point of view. A recipient of the doctor of theology degree from Dubuque University, he assisted in the translation of two volumes of Karl Barth's sermons. He served as minister of the First English Reformed Church of Freeport, Illinois, and later as

[7] Allan R. Broadhurst, *He Speaks the Word of God* (Englewood Cliffs, New Jersey: Prentice-Hall, 1963), p. 56.
[8] Charles S. Braden, *Varieties of American Religion* (New York: Willet, Clark and Company, 1936), p. 102.
[9] Edgar DeWitt Jones, *The Royalty of the Pulpit* (New York: Harper & Brothers, 1951), p. 113.

minister of the Carrollton Avenue (Evangelical and Reformed) Church in Indianapolis. Having served on the faculty of the theological school at Princeton for many years, he became its dean in 1955.

He has expressed the neo-orthodox position clearly and succinctly:

> The real cause of our social and personal disease can be plainly seen today. The remedy lies alone in a life of obedience to God, whose we are by sheer grace, in spite of our sins, and in whom we all cohere as brothers of a common, self-revealing Father.[10]

Paul E. Scherer has also preached in the neo-orthodox vein. Pastor of Holy Trinity Church in New York City for fifteen years, he became a member of the faculty at Union Theological Seminary in 1945. He is well known for his radio preaching on Sunday vespers and through his books of sermons.

In one of his sermons preached on the text of I Peter 2:9, we have an indication of his support of the neo-orthodox stance:

> We have to recover something instead of commemorating it.
> For one thing, the immediacy of that encounter, as Dr. Brunner calls it, in which a man, fully to be a man, finds himself before the face of the living God, with nothing between.[11]

The conclusion of the sermon indicates how Scherer has developed this insight of Brunner's until it points emphatically to the ultimate sovereignty of God.

> What we mean to do about all this is decisive beyond any thought we have had. You cannot deplete human existence morally and spiritually as the last four centuries have depleted it, to the point not of high tragedy but of dismal triviality and farce, and then expect to transform it with a United Nations. You cannot transform it with anything less than a faith that has a Cross in the middle, and the kind of people gathered round that God Himself will underwrite.[12]

Reinhold Niebuhr was known for his preaching as well as his lecturing and surely deserves to be included with those preachers who propounded the neo-orthodox view. During his early ministry he served a church in Detroit, Michigan, where many came to hear him preach. It was not until 1928 that he began teaching at Union Theological Seminary. He delivered the Lyman Beecher Lectures in 1945, and his preaching met with enthusiastic response at such universities as Harvard, Yale, and Princeton. Edgar DeWitt Jones has aptly described the uniqueness of Niebuhr's preaching:

[10] Braden, *Varieties of American Religion*, pp. 106-7.
[11] Andrew W. Blackwood, *The Protestant Pulpit* (Nashville: Abingdon Press, 1947), p. 273.
[12] *Ibid.*, pp. 275-76.

It is as different from the typical great and good sermon which soothes and comforts the hearer, as the patter of gentle raindrops on the roof differs from a storm, with the wind tearing at the cornices and the trees bending and breaking under the violent assault of all nature. On the one hand the hearer feels himself to be the object of God's goodness, and, on the other, he is not at all sure he has any claim on the love or goodness of God. Rather, he is moved to think of himself as a poor and miserable sinner.[13]

This appraisal takes on added significance when we set it alongside Niebuhr's own comments about "moralistic preaching."

This is why all moralistic preaching which does not reveal the religious heights which stand over every specific moral ideal of justice is also so incapable of coming to terms with the political realities of our existence. It always substitutes ideals of love for the political necessities of justice. It wants people of changed heart to grant their fellow men love so that their fellow men will not have to demand justice. It always suggests that the brutal realities of politics are necessary only because people haven't heard and been charmed by the ideal of love. It does not realize that if all men professed Christ and even if they understood his gospel so well that they felt under the tension of the commandment, "Thou shalt love thy neighbor as thyself," the fact of sin would still make political and economic coercion for the establishment of justice necessary. Moralistic preaching which makes love a substitute for justice merely increases the moral confusion of our day.[14]

Analytical Responses to Neo-Orthodoxy

Another response of the American pulpit was to enter into dialogue with neo-orthodoxy. Preachers sought to engage in serious conversation with the revived orthodoxy. Harold A. Bosley in the introduction of his book *Sermons on Genesis* rejoices in the renewal of concern about the Bible. Moreover, he takes pains to point out how he nurtured this renewed concern for the Bible in the First Methodist Church, Evanston, Illinois, where he was then a minister. So far he is in accord with the emphasis on the Bible and biblical preaching. However, he enters into dialogue with neo-orthodoxy when he raises the difficult question of how we find validation for biblical insights:

This is to make the hard point that, if insights of the Bible are not validated within our own experience, there is no reason either in the traditions of our faith or anywhere for us to accept them as normative. The insight brought to us by tradition must be tested in our experience—and we must judge of its adequacy.
I am concerned over the way this approach throws the door open to all sorts of individualistic temptations from which the movement called biblical theology,

[13] Jones, *The Royalty of the Pulpit*, pp. 143-44.
[14] Reinhold Niebuhr, "Moralistic Preaching," *The Christian Century*, July 15, 1936, p. 986.

on the one hand, and the resurgence of the authority of the church, on the other, are trying to save us. But I would be less than candid if I did not admit that I am now as afraid of guards as of the culprits.[15]

Bosley goes on to illustrate that while it is an unquestioned fact that there are a number of clearly delineated theological points of view in the Bible, we are occasionally urged to accept one definite biblical theology as normative. He responds to this appeal, "Biblical theologies, yes, but a biblical theology, no." [16]

In the same volume Bosley laments, with his concluding sermon "You Must Not Go Back," the preference of his generation for almost any form of religious authoritarianism to any kind of liberalism. Describing the liberal as one who sees merit in other religions and believes that Christianity can learn from them, and who believes that we are still pursuing and seeking to discover truth in an unfinished task, Bosley observes that authoritarianism, whatever its stripe, denies these views. He goes on to plead for the liberalism in religion which, Fosdick tells us, neo-orthodoxy has attacked.

The Lyman Beecher Lectures of professor of homiletics Halford E. Luccock also question neo-orthodox positions. While acknowledging the significance of neo-orthodox contributions, he expresses a grave concern about their weaknesses. First, he observes that too frequently neo-orthodox preaching simply takes for granted things which large numbers of people are seriously questioning. Thinking persons, for example, are asking, not "what is the Christian message?" but "why should anyone even pay any attention to it?"

Luccock further analyzes the weakness of neo-orthodox preaching on such themes as the transcendence of God, a recovered sense of sin, dependence on God, and what he regards to be a "minimizing of the priority of Jesus."

The strong affirmation of God in Barth and many others has been a needed message. . . . But in the correction of that there is often too much discontinuity. The gap between God and his creation is made too great for man's need, and for the biblical conception of God, the creator.[17]

His comment on neo-orthodox preaching on sin follows a similar pattern.

Again, the recovered sense of sin comes through in much preaching as a devaluation of man. Salvation begins by the operation of grace, but it is wholly unwarranted to distort that truth to deny any good in natural man, or to say, as some said, that all social effort for betterment is futile.[18]

[15] Harold A. Bosley, *Sermon on Genesis* (Apex ed.; Nashville: Abingdon Press, 1958), p. xv.
[16] *Ibid.*
[17] Halford E. Luccock, *Communicating the Gospel* (New York: Harper & Brothers, 1954), p. 59.
[18] *Ibid.*, pp. 59-60.

Likewise he points to the danger of a serious omission in neo-orthodox preaching in its heavy emphasis upon dependence on God. "The needed preaching of dependence on God may be so extreme that it overlooks the other end of the bridge between God and man, man's responsiveness." [19]

Walter Russell Bowie, whose career includes service as rector of St. Paul's in Richmond, Virginia, and Grace Church in New York City, Lyman Beecher lecturer, and professor of homiletics in the Protestant Episcopal Theological Seminary in Virginia, voiced a similar warning about the preaching issuing from a neo-orthodox orientation.

That is why there is mortal danger in the subtle defeatism which can be created by the very orthodoxy which dwells—but may dwell one-sidedly—upon its message of the sovereignty and judgment of God. God *is* sovereign, but his decisive sovereignty may want to exercise itself through human individuals alert enough and brave enough to be his instruments. A world in crisis cannot be saved by a pessimistic and paralyzing theology which disintegrates belief in what men can do. We need instead the kind of preaching which will be a flame of faith— faith that Christian men and women, in their churches and as citizens, under God can make a better world.[20]

With these criticisms in mind it is interesting to discover Bishop Gerald Kennedy turning to Reinhold Niebuhr for support in a sermon titled "Who Speaks for Hope!" [21] This sermon was preached at the First Methodist Church in Pasadena, California. Describing Niebuhr as "one of our greatest contemporary theologians," Bishop Kennedy quotes the following passage from Niebuhr's *The Irony of American History.*

Nothing that is worth doing can be achieved in our lifetime; therefore we must be saved by hope. Nothing which is true or beautiful or good makes complete sense in any immediate context of history; therefore we must be saved by faith. Nothing we do, however virtuous, can be accomplished alone; therefore we are saved by love. No virtuous act is quite as virtuous from the standpoint of our friend or foe as it is from our standpoint. Therefore we must be saved by the final form of love which is forgiveness.[22]

Harry Emerson Fosdick entered into dialogue with neo-orthodox leaders and also preached some of their major themes. Those who think of him as a liberal recalling his sermon "Shall the Fundamentalists Win?" (May 21, 1922) will be interested in one of Loral W. Pancake's conclusions in his Master's thesis, "Theological Liberalism in the Life and Ministry of Harry Emerson Fosdick."

[19] *Ibid.,* p. 61.
[20] Walter Russell Bowie, *Preaching* (Nashville: Abingdon Press, 1954), p. 161.
[21] Gerald Kennedy, *Who Speaks for God?* (Nashville: Abingdon Press, 1954), p. 129.
[22] Reinhold Niebuhr, *The Irony of American History* (New York: Charles Scribner's Sons, 1952), p. 63.

Dr. Fosdick's modernism has never been of the extreme kind. The fungus growth at which Doctors Walter M. Horton and Reinhold Niebuhr shake their fists so fiercely is what Dr. Fosdick would call a caricature of modernism. . . . Dr. Fosdick has stood with the evangelical tradition and preached the great doctrines of God and Christ and grace and regeneration with a consistency and power. . . .[23]

If we read Fosdick's concluding paragraph from his Christmas sermon Christ Himself Is Christianity," we can observe an emphasis on Jesus Christ that would be compatible with neo-orthodoxy's thrust; yet at the same time we can see traces of Fosdick's personalism.

Christmas means this at least: a personality has come into the world concerning whom millions believe that he is the answer. Even Paul never said, I know what I have believed. The mystery of life so deep, the confusion of the world so great, he sometimes did not know what he believed. What Paul said went deeper: "I know him whom I have believed." That is Christianity! I wish I could persuade someone here who never has accepted it, to accept it now. I am not inviting you to sign a theological creed on the dotted line. I am not inviting you to join a sectarian denomination, and subscribe to its peculiarities. I am inviting you to see Christ, his revelation of God, his basic principles, his way of life, his spirit and quality, and so seeing him, to say, He is the answer! [24]

A look at his sermon, "The Church Must Go Beyond Modernism," could lead one to ask if Fosdick, in some areas, might even be classified as a proponent of neo-orthodoxy. Surely his discussion of "sin" seems to sound the neo-orthodox theme.

Underline this: *Sin is real.* Personal and social sin is as terribly real as our forefathers said it was, no matter how we change their way of saying so. And it leads men and nations to damnation as they said it did, no matter how we change their way of picturing it. For these are times, real times, of the kind out of which man's great exploits have commonly been won, in which, if a man is to have a real faith he must gain it from the very teeth of dismay; if he is to have real hope, it must shine, like a Rembrandt portrait, from the dark background of fearful apprehension; if he is to have real character, he must achieve it against the terrific down-drag of an antagonistic world; and if he is to have a real church, it must stand out from the world and challenge it, not be harmonized with it.[25]

One would also expect that those of neo-orthodox persuasion would applaud Fosdick's sermon titled "The Modern World's Rediscovery of Sin." Indeed, the title alone ought to draw a round of applause from them.

[23] Loral W. Pancake, "Theological Liberalism in the Life and Ministry of Harry Emerson Fosdick" (unpublished Master's thesis, Drew University, 1946), pp. 119-20.

[24] Harry Emerson Fosdick, *On Being Fit to Live With* (New York: Harper & Brothers, 1946), p. 193.

[25] Harry Emerson Fosdick, *Successful Christian Living* (New York: Harper & Brothers, 1937), p. 159.

What we are saying is that no man understands himself until he has faced the presence in himself of some such share in what our fathers called "original sin." In this regard we often deceive ourselves because sin can take such a high polish. Sometimes sin is gross and terrible. It staggers down the street; it blasphemes with oaths that can be heard; it wallows in vice unmentionable by modest lips. Then prosperity visits sin. It moves to a fine residence; it seeks the suburbs or gets itself domiciled on a college campus. It changes all its clothes. It is no longer indecent and obscene; its speech is mild, its civility is irreproachable. But at heart it is the same old sin, self-indulgent, callous, envious, cruel, unclean. As anybody may easily observe, sin takes on a very high polish.[26]

Surely, I would be remiss if I did not add that Fosdick's concern for biblical preaching was dramatized by his Lyman Beecher Lectures in which he devoted the entire series of lectures to the Bible exclusively. Edgar DeWitt Jones in his commentary on Fosdick and these lectures asserts, "The peoples of other countries think of Dr. Fosdick as first among American preachers, just as they think of Dr. Niebuhr as first among our theologians." [27]

Yet it was also Dr. Fosdick who, in his January, 1929, *Atlantic Monthly* article "What Is the Matter with Preaching?" gave impetus to "life situation" preaching. Neo-orthodoxy took strong exception to this kind of preaching because it feared that such led to an inadvertent acceptance of cultural norms.

A sermon preached by Edward D. Gates in the First Presbyterian Church of Peoria, Illinois, on September 17, 1950, and entitled "Time Is Running Out" is an excellent example of what neo-orthodoxy feared. The sermon rehearses the mighty acts of the United States rather than the mighty acts of God. Its eloquence in praising the nation is attested to by its receipt of an honor medal and a sum of $1500 from Freedoms Foundation Awards presented by General Omar Bradley at Valley Forge, Pennsylvania.[28]

Dr. Fosdick in turn had some reservations about neo-orthodoxy's effect on preaching.

In a few cases especially, I never had heard at Union such homiletical arrogance, such take-it-or-leave-it assumption of theological finality, such cancellation of the life and words of the historic Jesus by the substitution of a dogmatic Christ. My first contacts with neo-orthodoxy's effect upon the preacher were very disillusioning.[29]

Responses of Opposition

In addition to those who supported the neo-orthodox position and those who sought to enter into meaningful dialogue with it, there were those who

[26] Harry Emerson Fosdick, *Living Under Tension* (New York: Harper & Brothers, 1941), p. 118.

[27] Jones, *The Royalty of the Pulpit*, pp. 101-2.

[28] Harold F. Harding, *The Age of Danger* (New York: Random House, 1952), pp. 472-80.

[29] Fosdick, *The Living of These Days*, p. 247.

opposed neo-orthodoxy. Indeed Harvey H. Potthoff, professor of theology at Iliff School of Theology, describes that school's resistance to the movement. "During the heyday of neoorthodoxy, when many were rejecting all forms of philosophical theology and affirming the 'wholly other' God, Iliff held steady with a natural theology, laying the foundations for a deepened neo-liberalism." [30]

Edward Scribner Ames who served as pastor of the University Church of The Disciples of Christ, Chicago, Illinois, clearly stated some of this opposition.

Theologians have exalted God so much and debased man so far that it has become almost impossible for them to believe that men are truly the children of God, sons of God. No wonder it seems to them that only a miracle of conversion and of mysterious rebirth could bring men into this relation. We have become familiar with the idea that God is to be identified with the "personality-evolving activities of the cosmos." This conception is more acceptable, for it includes those activities of self-criticism and imagination within man himself by which he strives for the realization of ideals. We are workers together with God in the process of redemption. In very real ways we must work out our own salvation.[31]

So far we have considered some of the major emphases of neo-orthodoxy (the Bible as Word of God, Sin and Alienation, Grace, the Centrality of Christ) and have noted a variety of responses to this movement by the American pulpit. We must take a few moments to suggest the range of its impact on those concerned with influencing and educating preachers.

Homiletics and Neo-Orthodoxy

David MacLennan, senior minister at Brick Presbyterian Church, Rochester, New York, and contributor to *Church Management*, makes reference in his *Resources for Sermon Preparation* to Barth's study of Romans, to Brunner's interpretation of salvation as something which has happened, is happening, and will happen, and to the neo-orthodox emphasis on God as "the wholly other." He goes on to show how this emphasis saves us from easy sentimentalism or becoming "pally" with the Lord.[32]

Joseph Sittler in *The Anguish of Preaching*, the publication of his Zimmerman Lectures designated to deal with some aspect of effective preaching, turns to Barth and his understanding of church dogmatics. He describes

[30] Harvey H. Potthoff, "The Seminary and the New Day," *Christian Advocate*, December 1, 1966, p. 10.

[31] Braden, *Varieties of American Religion*, p. 73.

[32] David MacLennan, *Resources for Sermon Preparation* (Philadelphia: The Westminster Press, 1957), p. 69.

Christianity as a historical religion and speaks of becoming a "community by the word of God." [33]

The Preaching Ministry Today, written by Rolland W. Schloerb, minister of Hyde Park Baptist Church in Chicago, and published two decades earlier than Sittler's work, emphasizes the debt we owe Karl Barth for directing our attention to the historical givenness of the Christian revelation.[34]

Baptist Faris D. Whitesell in his *Power in Expository Preaching* refers to "the neo-orthodox pattern which claims that preaching should re-enact the redemptive deeds of God in Christ so that the hearer is confronted with the living Christ in judgment and redemption." [35]

Methodist Ronald E. Sleeth makes reference to Barth's view that preaching and sacrament are two modes of proclamation, and refers us to *Church Dogmatics* I/1 in his book *Proclaiming the Word*.[36]

Congregationalist Carl S. Patton takes issue with Niebuhr's observation that "moral" preaching leaves people cold, and with the indictment of contemporary preaching for saying too little about sin.[37] Under the heading "Giving the Primacy to God," Presbyterian Andrew W. Blackwood cites Brunner's warning that progressively the church is losing its awareness of what it is and what it is for.[38]

The writing of these authors, mostly teachers of preaching, suggests the richness and variety with which neo-orthodoxy has permeated the instruction in preaching in American theological schools. Especially is this true if we think of the numerous lectures and textbooks already cited in this essay which indicated the way in which American preaching responded to neo-orthodox doctrine. Since neo-orthodoxy was such a prominent matter of concern we are moved to ask one more major question: What have been the contributions of neo-orthodoxy to homiletical theory?

Impact on Homiletical Theory

Let us begin our answer by turning to Barth himself who describes both the biblical and the theological character of preaching.

[33] Joseph Sittler, *The Anguish of Preaching* (Philadelphia: Fortress Press, 1966), p. 63.

[34] Rolland W. Schloerb, *The Preaching Ministry Today* (New York: Harper & Brothers, 1946), p. 35.

[35] Faris D. Whitesell, *Power in Expository Preaching* (New York: Fleming H. Revell Company, 1963), p. xiii.

[36] Ronald E. Sleeth, *Proclaiming the Word* (Nashville: Abingdon Press, 1964), pp. 22-23.

[37] Carl S. Patton, *The Preparation and Delivery of Sermons* (New York: Willet, Clark and Company, 1938), pp. 28, 132-34.

[38] Andrew W. Blackwood, *Biographical Preaching for Today* (Nashville: Abingdon Press, 1954), p. 184.

Preaching follows from the command given to the Church to serve the Word of God by means of a man called to this task. It is this man's duty to proclaim to his fellow men what God himself has to say to them, by explaining, in his own words, a passage from Scripture which concerns them personally. . . . There is no basis in human experience for the concept of preaching. It is a purely theological concept resting on faith alone. As has been said, it is directed to one end only: to point to divine truth.[39]

In these paragraphs Barth contributes a definition of preaching to the general body of homiletical theory, a definition which, if rigorously applied, would probably necessitate reclassifying a number of the addresses which are discussed in this volume on the assumption that they are sermons. Let us take a second look at the criteria which Barth suggests.

1. Preaching is a response to God's command to serve the Word of God.
2. Preaching is an explanation of a passage of scripture which concerns the congregation.
3. Preaching is a purely theological concept resting on faith alone.
4. The sole end of preaching is to point to divine truth.

Contemporary works in homiletics emphasize both the biblical and theological nature of preaching with a concern similar to Barth's. For example, Presbyterian James D. Smart, in an introduction to his book of sermons *The Recovery of Humanity*, holds that expository preaching is indispensable because we are called to a ministry of the Word of God. He further declares that the preacher must put himself wholly at the service of that other Word. Smart warns: "What is at stake here is the Biblical and Reformed conception of the ministry." [40]

Truman B. Douglass, Congregationalist, in his Lyman Beecher Lectures relied on the neo-orthodox position when he declared: "Preaching is essentially a telling of the mighty acts of God." [41] He did give something of an extra-biblical interpretation when he also suggested that the present ecumenical reformation could be regarded as a contemporary sign of "new and mighty acts" and in this sense be preached.

Donald G. Miller of Virginia's Union Theological Seminary describes the central concern of preaching as such a rehearsing of "the story of God's redeeming action in Christ that it becomes a living reality in the act of

[39] Karl Barth, *The Preaching of the Gospel*, trans. B. E. Hooke (Philadelphia: The Westminster Press, 1963), pp. 9, 11.

[40] James D. Smart, *The Recovery of Humanity* (Philadelphia: The Westminster Press, 1953), p. 14.

[41] Truman B. Douglass, *Preaching and the New Reformation* (New York: Harper & Brothers, 1956), p. 116.

preaching." [42] He declares unequivocally, "Only preaching which sets forth the Bible story can do this. And that which fails to do it is something other than preaching." [43]

President Frederick W. Schroeder of Eden Theological Seminary describes the preacher as a witnessing ambassador and concurs with Barth that authority in preaching comes from the Word itself. He adds, "Authority in the pulpit can scarcely be conveyed unless there is evidence that the minister himself has come under the authority of the divine Word." [44]

While the preceding comments all are intended to suggest a definition of preaching, they also have strong implications for other areas of homiletical theory such as the aim or purpose of preaching, the content of preaching, and the motivation for preaching.

Conclusion

So it can be fairly said that neo-orthodoxy not only had an impact on the kind of preaching which was done in American pulpits, but it also caused teachers of preaching to reconsider basic questions about the nature and purpose of preaching.

Some observers, however, feel that the main influence of neo-orthodoxy on American preaching was primarily limited to the environment of theological schools and their immediate geographical surroundings and that it did not actually raise the theological level of preaching to any marked degree. At least this seemed to be the essence of Robert J. McCracken's comment in one of his Stone Lectures delivered at Princeton Theological Seminary:

> Even allowing for the revived interest in theology and the influence of neo-orthodoxy, here is where American preaching is weakest. The impression is prevalent among us that a doctrinal sermon in the nature of the case can hardly be other than ponderous, if not dull, and that to our practical-minded people it is bound to seem abstruse and academic. [45]

In response to McCracken we note that neo-orthodox preaching is not necessarily doctrinal, and point out that his generalization about doctrinal preaching is called into question by such strong proponents as Ernest Fremont Tittle whose final book was entitled *The Gospel According to Luke*

[42] Donald G. Miller, *The Way to Biblical Preaching* (Nashville: Abingdon Press, 1957), p. 14.

[43] *Ibid.*, p. 15.

[44] Frederick W. Schroeder, *Preaching the Word with Authority* (Philadelphia: The Westminster Press, 1954), p. 119.

[45] Robert J. McCracken, *The Making of the Sermon* (New York: Harper & Brothers, 1956), p. 45.

—*Exposition and Application.* Especially striking is Halford Luccock's foreword which emphasizes the fundamentally biblical and theological character of Tittle's preaching and at the same time lifts up Tittle's "passionate devotion to Christian social action, which made him a dependable leader and fighter against the great social evils of our time." [46]

[46] Ernest Fremont Tittle, *The Gospel According to Luke* (New York: Harper & Brothers, 1951), p. vii.

15

THE ECUMENICAL MOVEMENT

———————John W. Carlton———————

A distinguished church historian has observed that "two drives have consistently marked church history—the movement toward expansion, the other toward integration." [1] The nineteenth century provides a striking illustration of expansion, and the twentieth century is characterized by the quest for an integrative unity. For all those who have viewed with embarrassment and concern the "fissiparous tendency" of American Protestantism the ecumenical movement is perhaps the most enheartening occurrence in modern Christian history. Hardly any denominational body within Christendom has remained untouched by the aspirations for Christian unity that have marked our time. The all-embracing goal of a community of Christians united in the confession of a common faith, bound together by ties of Christian charity, nurtured by Word and Sacrament, and manifesting to the world a fellowship that transcends human barriers, has wrought a revolution in the temper and spirit of our times. William Temple, the late archbishop of Canterbury, once hailed this movement to overcome the persistent self-righteous fragmentation of the people of God as the great new fact of our time.

The goal of ecumenical unity involves far more than the prudential reunion of unreconciled churches or the quest for mere oneness in order to tidy up a world of bewildering variety. Charles Clayton Morrison, former editor of *The Christian Century*, describes the objective of the ecumenical movement as "the restoration of visible and functional unity to the body of Christ which is the community of Christian believers throughout the world." [2] The movement is an attempt to find and manifest the oneness of Christ's church in the whole world.

Both historical and pragmatic developments have contributed to the bold

[1] John T. McNeill, *Modern Christian Movements* (Philadelphia: The Westminster Press, 1954), p. 130.
[2] Henry Smith Leiper, "Reunion and the Ecumenical Movement," *Protestant Thought in the Twentieth Century*, ed. Arnold Nash (New York: The Macmillan Company, 1951), p. 268.

ecumenical thrust of our century. For one thing, despite the proliferation of sects in our country, it should be noted that the religious scene in America has never been quite as diversified as the official records would suggest. A critical examination of the statistics of church membership will reveal that in the middle of the twentieth century two-thirds of all church members belonged to three religious groups: Roman Catholic, Baptist, and Methodist. Over nine-tenths were attached to the ten leading denominations. Moreover, as the distinguished historian Henry Steele Commager has suggested, "religious allegiance was not unlike political allegiance: inherited rather than assumed, dictated, often, by geography or by interest rather than by intellectual conviction, it was embraced without solemnity, changed without spiritual travail, abandoned without pain." [3] We all recognize that frequently church membership is dictated by such matters as accessibility, convenience, social programs, and ministerial leadership rather than by dogmatic distinctions. Indeed, there is a pronounced impatience with the defensive militancy of reactionaries who are eager to assert old dogmatisms. We are seeing afresh the obvious futility of old sectarian alignments in coping with contemporary issues of life and thought. Yet with the loosening of denominational ties today we must not lose sight of the fact that twentieth-century Christianity in America has witnessed some violent conflicts between those who wished to modernize Christianity's expression of its faith and those who wanted to take up the cudgels for literalism and traditional expressions of orthodoxy. Forty years ago Harry Emerson Fosdick, embroiled in the fundamentalist-modernist controversy, lamented:

A great deal of our contemporary Christianity constitutes one of the most embittering influences in our society. It does not weave men into a brotherhood; it does not mollify asperities, prejudices and hatreds; it rather baptizes them so that men indulge freely in their antipathies as a sacred duty. [4]

Years later, as minister of the Riverside Church in New York, Dr. Fosdick declared in a sermon:

Nothing more challenging confronts us Christians today than the fact that this impression made by Christ of size, of universality of outlook and spirit, is distinctly not the impression made by our sectarian churches. I speak from inside the church, loving it, after a lifetime of ministry believing in it and loyal to it, but I am deeply concerned about its trivialities, its sectarian littleness. To have a Master and Lord who impresses even unbelievers with his universal range and sweep, and then to have churches, supposed to represent him, which impress even believers as much too petty and small-minded to meet the world's need— that is a tragedy. [5]

[3] Henry Steele Commager, *The American Mind* (New Haven: Yale University Press, 1950), p. 188.
[4] Harry Emerson Fosdick, *Adventurous Religion* (New York: Harper & Brothers, 1926), pp. 280-81.
[5] Harry Emerson Fosdick, *What Is Vital in Religion* (New York: Harper & Brothers, 1955), p. 24.

While we have not arrived at any era of theological unanimity, it is gratifying to live in a time when the embittering atmosphere of sectarian controversy, majoring on trivial discriminations of belief and practice, has given place increasingly to more rational conversation and to an emphasis upon an inclusive Christianity dedicated to the creation of personal character and social righteousness.

Healing Forces

The practical exigencies of the missionary enterprise have helped to shape an ecumenical spirit. Bishop Charles Henry Brent (1862-1929), first missionary bishop of the Philippine Islands and an ardent leader in the ecumenical movement, argued that the fragmentation of Christendom frustrated missionary advance. He viewed sectarianism as "the cult of the incomplete," an evident loss of wholeness and thus a diseased condition. The churches of South India, representing a small and beleaguered minority surrounded by non-Christian populations, discovered that they could ill afford the luxury of their divisions. The World Missionary Conference in Edinburgh in 1910 took seriously the problem of denominational divisions imposed from the West which were so obviously irrelevant to the situation of recent converts who had come from the great non-Christian religions.

Surely the realities of a world sundered by the conflicting claims of secular humanism, existentialism, and communism demand from the church a more united front. For all its high-minded and sensitive concern for humane values, humanistic faith has cut itself loose from the claims of any historic religious faith. Within much existentialist thought there is a philosophy of cosmic resignation which runs counter to the Christian faith. Communism rejects supernaturalism and identifies evil with the economic system of its adversaries, a stance which stifles self-criticism and makes naïve self-righteousness inevitable. These philosophies, with their failures as guides to human life, have contributed to the cosmic hallowe'en of dark witchery and fear that enfolds us all.

Beyond these forces and facts we must reckon with the rediscovery within the past fifty years of some essential dimensions of the gospel. We have come to appreciate afresh the theological reality of the church—that to be in Christ is to be in the church. This added theological depth has provided a needed corrective of the pragmatic temper of American Christianity. It has helped to foster the church's heightened sense of mission to the world and its diminishing concern with institutional prestige and self-preservation. The lively theological dialogue among churchmen today, with its open confession of the partial and relative nature of truth which each historic group of Christians possesses, has contributed to the richness of our Christian heritage.

Disquieting Forces

Given these historical and pragmatic developments which have strengthened the ecumenical spirit of our time, perhaps it would be instructive to look at some of the underlying causes of the initial fragmentation of American Christianity. A significant factor was the transplanting to American soil of representatives of practically all the religious groups of Europe, both right- and left-wing. By the middle of the nineteenth century America had become the repository of these transplanted offshoots. These religious groups learned to get on peacefully together in the new world. Indeed, they luxuriated under the vivifying sun of religious freedom and found stimulation for life and expansion in the almost unlimited social and geographical space.

To be noted also is the "sectarian" tendency of the American denominations, a development aptly summarized by Sidney E. Mead, former president of the American Society of Church History:

The constellation of ideas prevailing during the Revolutionary epoch in which the denominations began to take shape were: the idea of pure and normative beginnings to which return was possible; the idea that the intervening history was largely that of aberrations and corruptions which was better ignored; and the idea of building anew in the American wilderness on the true and ancient foundations.[*]

Accenting the primacy of the beliefs and practices of primitive Christianity, many of the left-wing sects sought to justify their peculiar interpretations and practices by insisting that their own views and policies conformed to this standard more than those of their rivals.

We note further that the individualism of the frontier, combined with revivalism, found intellectual and emotional expression in the various denominations. Internal quarrels erupted in the older denominations as they fought the battle of revivalist techniques versus the catechetical methods of the fathers. Churches were divided into "revivalist" and "anti-revivalist" factions such as the "New Sides" and "Old Sides" among the Presbyterians, and the "New Lights" and "Old Lights" among the Congregationalists. The preaching of such men as Theodore J. Frelinghuysen, Gilbert Tennent, Jonathan Edwards, and Devereux Jarratt helped to shape the early revivalist tradition in America. Revivalism directed its appeal to radical conversion, and "preachableness" in revivals became a normative criterion for doctrines. Under such an impetus the conception of the church gradually lost the sacramental dimension, and the institutional ministry became less formal and more charismatic and instrumental. Preachers feared a "dull uniformity" more than "enthusiasm." A few had the wisdom to urge a middle course in preaching between "the contortions of an epileptic zeal" and "the numbness

[*] Sidney E. Mead, *The Lively Experiment* (New York: Harper & Row, 1963), p. 111.

of a paralytic one." Anecdotal preaching, with total neglect or strange twists of exegesis and dubious application, characterized much proclamation.

Sectional and racial schisms produced rancor and division, especially in the traumatic era of the Civil War. The language of many clergy before, during, and after the war often accentuated hatred. Southern churches sought to espouse the myth of the lost cause, and northern churches identified them-selves with national expansion and aggrandizement. Religion ran the gamut from "private piety" to "manifest destiny."

Denominational competition was an inevitable development given the free church idea under church-state separation. The free churches were con-fronted with a western migration, and this "virgin territory for evangelization" fostered rivalry among them in the vast market of souls. The competition re-leased tremendous energies, and in the ensuing battles for souls there was little concern for ethics. Baptist-Methodist rivalry was sometimes forgotten as the two groups combined against Presbyterians and Episcopalians. The latter served as an ever-present and welcome whipping boy for those eager to attack "forms" and liturgical niceties. Of course, the competition was between Christian groups holding divergent forms of the same faith, with shifting patterns of antagonism and challenge and, consequently, of alignments and cooperation. Roman Catholic immigration from Ireland, Germany, and southern Europe produced Catholic-Protestant tensions. A Roman Catholic threat could effectually unite all the other groups. Traditional alignments in the competitive pattern occasionally broke down as "Evangelicals" and "Unevangelicals"—of whatever brand—hurled their weapons at each other.

Ecumenical Spokesmen

The past half century has brought monumental advances in the attempt to reverse this long drift into division. At the turn of this century relatively little concern for Christian unity appeared except in the trenchant writings of such stalwarts as Josiah Strong, Philip Schaff, and William Reed Hunting-ton, but the earlier years were not without ecumenical pathfinders who helped to open the road to Christian unity.

John Eliot (1604-90), a pioneer Protestant missionary among the Indians, envisioned a union of the Presbyterian and Congregational "parties" and, in the practical urgencies of his missionary task, developed a combined Presby-terian-Congregational polity. It is significant that much later these two de-nominations joined together in the "Plan of Union" (1801-52) which served to unite them in the tasks of evangelism in their western mission work. Pro-vision was made for "union congregations" where desired and for the settle-ment of Presbyterian ministers in Congregational churches and vice versa. Despite its rejection in 1837 by old-school Presbyterians and in 1852 by the

Congregationalists, this Plan of Union partially united the national evangelistic forces of two major denominations.

Thomas Campbell (1763-1854) published in 1809 his *Declaration and Address*, an apologia for Christian unity and the fundamental document of the Disciples movement, which issued an appeal to transcend sectarian divisions through a restoration of the church to its "primitive unity, purity, and prosperity." Creeds were regarded as human opinions only, the "tangled underbrush" that obscures the church's goal of pristine purity. Campbell proposed a union of all Christians based upon "the pure spring of Bible truth" without added tests of creed or ritual. Thomas Campbell's son, Alexander (1786-1866), became a pronounced advocate of his father's views in his plea for Christian union, *Christianity Restored* (1835). He reiterated the idea that the "formal principle" of the new reformation was the restoration of primitive Christianity. The Campbells proposed no ecclesiastical carpentry by which a new church could be built out of the coordinated denominational machinery of merging churches. They placed the problem of church union on an individual, personal plane, forcing those who felt as they did to forsake their old denominations. In the early twentieth century such Disciples leaders as Peter Ainslie called the denomination to move beyond polemics to a new sense of ecumenical mission. In his Reinicker Lectures at the Episcopal Theological Seminary in Virginia, Dr. Ainslie declared:

An infidel world is the price we are paying for a divided church. The time is at hand when the honor of Christ and the salvation of a world must rise above our pride of party and contentment of divisions in obedience to the will of God on earth. Sectarianism must be abolished. Henceforth let no man glory in his denomination; that is sectarianism: but let all men glory in Christ and practice brotherhood with men; that is Christianity.[7]

Among the prominent churchmen who articulated with prophetic force the longing for a wider unity among Protestants we must mention Professor Samuel Simon Schmucker (1799-1873), a distinguished Lutheran. His *Fraternal Appeal to the American Churches: with a Plan for Catholic Union, on Apostolic Principles*, published in 1838, called for the formation of the "Apostolic Protestant Church," whose doctrinal *sine qua non* and the uniting basis of the constituent denominations was to be a united confession based upon the "fundamental" doctrines of Protestantism expressed in and common to all Protestant creeds. He proposed open communion and a free interchange of ministry.

A significant contribution to the quest for Christian unity was made by a distinguished Episcopalian, William Reed Huntington (1838-1918). In *The Church Idea: An Essay Toward Unity* (1870) he outlined a platform of essentials of Anglicanism on which churches could unite. He considered

---

[7] Peter Ainslie, *If Not a United Church—What?* (New York: Fleming H. Revell Company, 1920), p. 103.

Reformation confessions too long and involved—"old battleships"—whereas for him the times called for a "modern ironclad with heavy guns and few," with the latter amply provided by the Apostles' and Nicene creeds. Huntington named four "essentials" of Anglicanism as the basis for reunion discussion: (1) the Holy Scriptures as the rule and ultimate standard of faith; (2) the primitive creeds as a sufficient statement of faith; (3) the two sacraments ordained by Christ; and (4) the historic episcopate as the keystone of governmental unity. These "essentials," with slight modifications, were approved by the American Episcopal House of Bishops and the Anglican Lambeth Conference and became the "Chicago-Lambeth Quadrilateral" which boldly thrust to the fore crucial matters of faith and order that had to be faced in unity discussions.

Among the true ecumenical statesmen was the American Episcopal missionary bishop Charles Henry Brent, to whom reference has been made. The spirit of the World Missionary Conference at Edinburgh in 1910 profoundly moved Bishop Brent. He wrote after that meeting: "I was converted. I learned that something was working that was not of man in that conference, that the spirit of God was preparing a new era in the history of Christianity." [8] As senior chaplain with the American expeditionary forces in Europe in World War I, Bishop Brent pointed to the fellowship of thirteen hundred chaplains, representing every phase of conviction and yet interpreting "the lesser in terms of the greater, the church in terms of the Kingdom of God," as a living reality that could be perpetuated in civil life. In a famous sermon on "The Call to Unity" he observed that the apostle Paul "strikes sectarianism of all ages between the eyes by calling divisions 'carnal.'" Acknowledging that most of us are "devotees of the cult of the incomplete—sectarianism," he added:

God has used, beyond anything we had a right to expect, our divided Christendom. But now that we know the sin and disaster of sectarianism we cannot hope that he will use it much longer. . . . Let us keep the purpose of unity firm in our hearts and look on all Christians of whatever name, as brothers beloved. It is thus that, by practicing unity, we shall gain unity. [9]

The cause of ecumenicity was ably championed also by one of Bishop Brent's fellow Episcopalians, Bishop C. P. Anderson of Chicago, in the Hale Memorial Sermon preached in St. Paul's Church in Chicago on the Sunday before Advent in 1917. Noting that "sectarianism is necessarily incapable of thinking nationally or acting internationally or moulding the world conscience," Bishop Anderson went on to ask:

[8] Alexander C. Zabriskie, *Bishop Brent*, Crusader for Christian Unity (Philadelphia: The Westminster Press, 1948), p. 145.

[9] Charles Henry Brent, "The Call to Unity," *A Treasury of Great Sermons*, ed. Daniel A. Poling (New York: Greenberg, 1944), pp. 146-51.

Can the churches remain static while the whole fabric of society is undergoing structural changes? Can a fossilized traditionalism supply the spiritual dynamic to the new age? Dare the churches go on preaching a disintegrated Christ to this newborn era which is hailing internationalism and the progressive solidarity of brotherhood as its new saviours? Must not the churches expect to undergo something as revolutionary as what is going on around them?[10]

Bishop Anderson described the ecumenical venture as "the recovery of a lost conscience on the unity of the body of Christ" and a liberation from "the tyranny of inherited pride, prejudice, and ignorance." [11] He acknowledged the conspicuous role of Anglicanism in the advocacy of church unity, but the bishop went on to chide that communion for timidity in practice and for shrinking from the consequences of its own corporate actions. The sermon was a clarion call for Anglicanism to abandon self-consciousness in a "self-forgetful adventure for the visible unity of the people of God."

Organizational Beginnings

The ecumenical consciousness of men such as Bishops Brent and Anderson helped to mobilize the forces for unity which brought about the World Conference on Faith and Order at Lausanne in 1927, when over four hundred delegates representing over one hundred churches convened, explored their ecclesiastical divisions, and issued a unanimous statement on "The Church's Message to the World." A Continuation Committee carried the deliberations further, summoning the next conference for Edinburgh in 1937.

A major area of ecumenical development concerned with Christian service and common ethical action, eventually called "Life and Work," first achieved organizational expression in the Evangelical Alliance, organized in London in 1846. As a champion of religious liberty the Alliance achieved much, but it bore no official relationship to the communions. Josiah Strong (1847-1916) was the last conspicuous secretary of the American branch of the Alliance. In 1898 he resigned to assume an active role in the organization of the Federal Council of the Churches of Christ in America. The Federal Council was founded in 1908, with a membership comprised of about thirty American denominations, including many of the major bodies. Among its professed goals was that of securing "a larger combined influence for the Churches of Christ in all matters affecting the moral and social condition of the people, so as to promote the application of the law of Christ in every relation of human life." [12] In a sermon delivered in Washington, D.C., in 1933, on the twenty-fifth anniversary of the Federal Council, Albert W. Beaven, a distinguished Baptist who was then president of the Council, observed:

[10] C. P. Anderson, *The Work of the Church on Behalf of Unity* (Milwaukee: The Young Churchman Company, 1917), p. 21.

[11] *Ibid.*, p. 26.

[12] Williston Walker, *A History of the Christian Church* (New York: Charles Scribner's Sons, 1959), p. 540.

Twenty-five years ago there was no central agency through which Protestant-ism as a unity could come into relation with the other two major religious groups in America—the Roman Catholic and the Jewish. Today the Council maintains relations of friendly understanding, which, while calling for no com-promise of conviction, make it possible for the three bodies to join from time to time in cooperative undertakings in behalf of social betterment and human welfare.

Twenty-five years ago there was no way of expressing the collective Christian conscience on social problems. Today the new statement of "Social Ideals," as revised and expanded last year, constitutes the most widely recognized platform of Christian social effort, and the Council is recognized as one of the powerful forces working for social justice, fair treatment for labor and international peace.

Before the formation of the Council there was no agency for rallying church influence against racial prejudice and friction, or in behalf of mutual under-standing. Today the Federal Council is engaged in a persistent educational cam-paign against lynching, a campaign which recent events show to be terrifyingly necessary. It opposes unjust discrimination against Negroes in our economic and civic life. In its own structure and life the Federal Council is a great inter-racial movement, uniting the four leading Negro denominations with the white bodies in a common fellowship and a joint approach to common tasks. This is one of the most noteworthy instances of inter-racial collaboration anywhere in the world.[13]

In 1950 the Federal Council merged with a number of interdenominational agencies in the United States engaged in enterprises of home and foreign missions, stewardship, religious education, and women's work to form the National Council of the Churches of Christ in the U.S.A. Meanwhile, forces were at work on the world scene to bring churches together in common ethical action notwithstanding their doctrinal cleavages. Through the vision and energy of a Swedish Lutheran, Nathan Söderblom, the first Universal Christian Life Conference on Life and Work met at Stockholm in 1925. A Continuation Committee furthered the aims of the movement. The Commit-tee became the Universal Christian Council for Life and Work in 1930, and it issued the call for a second world gathering, the Conference on Church, Com-munity, and State at Oxford in 1937.

The World Council Evolves

For more than twenty-five years the three movements calling for cooperation in the missionary task of the church, life and work, and faith and order pursued their independent ways, a separation which could not continue, given those within each movement who envisioned a broader goal. In Amsterdam on August 22, 1948, representatives from one hundred forty-six churches and

[13] Albert W. Beaven, *The Lift of a Far View* (Philadelphia: The Judson Press, 1936), pp. 113, 115.

forty-four countries convened and completed the organization of the World Council of Churches. The World Council adopted as its basis a very simple doctrinal formula: "a fellowship of churches which accepts our Lord Jesus Christ as God and Savior," and it was made clear that the Council would have no constitutional authority over the member churches. Thus it disavowed any role as a "super-church." Indeed, it is not even a church at all, but, as Albert C. Outler, professor of theology at Southern Methodist University, suggests, it is

a rallying point for the ecumenical movement as a whole—a facility created and supported by its member churches to help them find the ways and means for effective ecumenical study, negotiation, and action. . . . Its chief significance is as an earnest of the Christian will-to-unity, a pledge of obedience to our Lord's command, a mode of reception of God's gift of unity. The World Council is the token between the churches that they have convenanted together to seek Christian unity according to God's will and by whatever pattern he may lead us to seek and to accept.[14]

The meeting of the World Missionary Conference at Edinburgh in 1910 had symbolized the missionary thrust of the church as a global fellowship. A Continuation Committee of that Conference was established which, by 1921, had become the International Missionary Council. An American Methodist layman, John R. Mott (1865-1955), became its first chairman. This Council, with the longest experience of any of the agencies in international work and with a strong organizational structure, maintained its separate existence for a time; but after the World Council of Churches came into formal existence in 1948, the two bodies defined themselves as "in association" with each other, a relationship that proved so vital that a plan for full integration was drafted eight years later.

Church Union

One of the areas of ecumenical achievement is that of organic church union. The United States has provided conspicuous examples of intra-confessional unions, notably among the Lutherans and the Methodists. In other lands trans-confessional unions across denominational lines have produced further consolidation. The United Church of Canada, comprised of Methodists, Congregationalists, and a majority of the Presbyterians, came into being in 1925. By far the most significant movement for church union was the coming together of episcopal and nonepiscopal churches in South India. After long years of immense labor on theological thought, and after securing

[14] Albert C. Outler, *The Christian Tradition and the Unity We Seek* (New York: Oxford University Press, 1957), p. 5.

unbelievably complicated official decisions required from the constituent bodies in India, with their ties in other lands, the Church of South India was inaugurated in 1947, bringing to final reality union negotiations among the Presbyterians, Congregationalists, Episcopalians, Methodists, and Anglicans.

On the American scene an audacious proposal for church union was made in a sermon preached in Grace Cathedral, San Francisco, by Eugene Carson Blake, then stated clerk of the General Assembly of the United Presbyterian Church in the U.S.A., on December 4, 1960.[15] Speaking not in an official capacity but as a minister of the Presbyterian Church "privileged and required to preach the Word," Dr. Blake proposed to his host congregation that the Protestant Episcopal Church join with his own denomination in inviting the Methodist Church and the United Church of Christ "to form with us a plan of church union, both catholic and reformed." Deploring the popular image of the church as "social groups pulling and hauling, propagandizing and pressuring for their own organizational advantage," Dr. Blake urged that "with the whole church we hold ourselves alert for the surprises with which the Lord of history can alter the tempo of our renewal and for the new forms with which the eternally recreating God can startle us while he secures his church."

In the sermon he cited the principles of reunion that are obviously important in the catholic tradition: (1) We must honor the "visible and historical continuity with the church of all ages before and after the Reformation," including a ministry with proper orders and ordination. He proposed that, without adopting any particular theory of historic succession, the reunited church "shall provide for the consecration of all its bishops by bishops and presbyters both in the apostolic succession and out of it from all over the world from all Christian churches which would authorize them to take part." (2) Persons in the catholic tradition would deem important the confession of the historic trinitarian faith "received from the apostles and set forth in the Apostles' and Nicene Creeds." (3) Significant to all is the administration of the two sacraments, which are to be recognized as "a true means of grace and not merely a symbolic memorial."

Dr. Blake then enumerated bases of reunion that would be important to persons in the Reformation tradition: (1) They would stress the principle of continuing reformation under the Word of God, with the Bible serving as "God's instrument to speak His Saving Word to Christians and to the Church." They would keep Word and Sacrament "equally and intimately united in understanding and appreciation." (2) Recognizing the monarchical

[15] For a full text of the sermon and perceptive reactions to the proposal consult *The Challenge to Reunion*, ed. Robert McAfee Brown and David H. Scott (New York: McGraw-Hill, 1963).

and authoritarian dangers inherent in the episcopacy and the bureaucratic perils native to nonepiscopal churches, Dr. Blake appealed for a truly democratic government rooted in the recognition that, while some are separated and ordained to the ministry of Word and Sacrament, all Christians are to be ministers of Christ. Historically Protestants have sought to make decisions through "ordered groups of men under the guidance of the Holy Spirit," hence the importance of respecting "the responsible freedom of congregations," including the election of their pastors. (3) The reunited church will of necessity include within its catholicity diverse forms of theological formulation and varied approaches to worship and liturgy. Bishop James A. Pike, who was present when Dr. Blake's sermon was delivered, characterized it as "the most sound and inspiring proposal for the unity of the church in this country which has ever been made in our history." Other comments were not so effusive. Father George H. Tavard, a leading Catholic ecumenist writing in the *Catholic Register* (January 20, 1961), questioned whether the proposal was either "catholic" or "reformed." Truman B. Douglass expressed fear that an "ecumenical battle fatigue" might ensue which would deplete the vigor needed to carry through the proposal. Yet it is significant to note that, as Dr. Robert T. Handy observes, the four churches named in the Blake proposal were not four but actually eleven sizable bodies at the beginning of the twentieth century. The sermon has evoked much appreciative comment and searching criticism. All four of the denominations mentioned in Dr. Blake's proposal have subsequently given official approval to joint discussions of its implementation. On April 9-10, 1962, forty representatives from the various churches met in Washington, D.C., to engage in "preliminary and exploratory sessions." They formed a body called "The Consultation on Church Union" and elected President James I. McCord of Princeton Theological Seminary as chairman.

Rome Acts

Even a cursory treatment of the ecumenical movement would be incomplete without reference to the far-ranging and imaginative sweep of Roman Catholic reform. The attitude of Rome toward the great Protestant ecumenical gatherings at Lausanne, Edinburgh, and Oxford was quite rigid, with only a modicum of personal and unofficial cooperation. There is today, however, a gratifying manifestation of a new mood, with exciting ecumenical conversation going on among Roman Catholic, Orthodox, and Protestant bodies. The monumental significance of the pontificate of John XXIII, permanently turning the tide and marking perhaps the terminus of the counter-Reformation, needs little reiteration in our time. We are abandoning old stereotypes of Catholicism as a closed, complacent, sectarian body. Influential and perceptive literature on the ecumenical movement is being produced by Roman Catholic scholars.[16] One of the vital forces in Roman Catholic renewal is the prodigious amount of biblical and theological work within that tradition in recent years. Biblical commentaries have been produced by a galaxy of Roman Catholic scholars, and a new vigor has gripped their theological seminaries. Indeed, a distinguished Protestant churchman has suggested that

it may be true that just at the moment we Protestants are abandoning kerygmatic theology and moving into a theological no-man's land, characterized by the erosion of faith and the loss of all biblical authority, Roman Cathlicism is moving into a fresh recovery of the *kerygma* and will become in our time the champion of biblical faith.[17]

Augustin Cardinal Bea, a major draftsman in the unfolding designs of Catholic ecumenicity, in delivering the Charles Chauncey Stillman Lectures at Harvard University, hailed the "authentic Christian openness" that marks present dialogue and called for bold definition and clear statement of differences. He added:

It stands to reason that overcoming the differences is not a search for compromises. Faith must not be confused with politics. Charity without truth will flicker but briefly. Love for the truth, the absolutely unbroken love for the truth is for all of us simply fidelity to Christ and to his Church. The Church is not the controller, the master of the truth, but its minister, its servant. She preaches the truth she has received from Christ, explains it, keeps it undefiled.[18]

He appealed for an intelligent restatement of traditional doctrinal formulas, reiterating the Pope's explicit statement that "the *substance* of the ancient teaching of the deposit of faith is one thing, the *manner* in which it is expressed is another." The cardinal emphasized that "irrevocably fixed" points of doctrine by no means exhaust "the treasure-trove of divine revelation." He called for continuing dialogue on matters not yet proclaimed as binding upon all: problems regarding the membership of non-Catholic Christians in the church, problems of the union of all Christians with Christ, questions re-

---

[16] Consult, e.g., Edward Duff, S.J., *The Social Thought of the World Council of Churches* (New York: Association Press, 1956); John Courtney Murray, S.J., *We Hold These Truths* (New York: Sheed and Ward, 1960); George H. Tavard, *The Catholic Approach to Protestantism* (New York: Harper & Brothers, 1955); and Gustave Weigel, S.J., *A Catholic Primer on the Ecumenical Movement* (Westminster, Maryland: Newman Press, 1967) and *Catholic Theology in Dialogue* (New York: Harper & Row, 1961).

[17] James I. McCord, "The Ecumenical Imperative," *The Drew Gateway*, XXXV, No. 3, 126.

[18] Samuel H. Miller and G. Ernest Wright, eds., *Ecumenical Dialogue at Harvard: the Roman Catholic-Protestant Colloquium* (Cambridge: Harvard University Press, 1964), p. 33.

lating to the constitution of the church, practical matters pertaining to the relief of the suffering and oppressed, and concerns of public worship, particularly its language and rites. Catholics and Protestants alike need an enduring and patient hope as we follow the slow rhythm that marks this ecumenical advance.

The Resistance

To be reckoned with also are large denominational groups who are indifferent to or critical of the ecumenical movement as a whole. Southern Baptists, with their heavy stress upon the autonomy of the local congregation and the fear of any centralized authority, have, as a denominational body, consistently remained aloof. Indeed, this denomination was once dubbed "the problem child of American Protestantism" in this respect. The fact that Baptists around the world present no uniform pattern of relationship to the ecumenical movement is often bewildering to members of other religious bodies. There are significant groups of Baptists within the World Council: the British Baptists and, within the United States, the American Baptist Convention and the National Baptist Convention. It is obvious that these bodies, with a strong congregational ecclesiology, have arrived at a *modus operandi* which enables them to cooperate with the World Council without peril to either doctrine or polity. Yet outside the World Council are large national bodies of Baptists in Latin America, Europe, Canada, and Australia. Southern Baptists have consistently declined membership. Why this ambivalent situation among the Baptists? Professor William R. Estep writes in answer:

The dynamic of Baptist life is part of the explanation. Vigorous growth in areas of relative freedom has produced a heady wine that has torn asunder the Old World wine skins. Proliferation and even fragmentation of the Baptist witness has been one of the results. Baptists rival the Holiness movement in the variety of their denominational structures. Baptist individualism, congregational polity, differing doctrinal emphases, strong personalities, geographical and cultural isolation, limited educational attainments, and strong conservative tendencies with some interesting liberal sidelights contribute their share in creating a rather confused picture.[19]

Among Southern Baptists in particular the great accent upon the autonomy of the local congregation has served to further an anti-ecumenical posture. The denomination's "official" response to the invitation to join the World Council included this statement:

[19] William R. Estep, *Baptists and Christian Unity* (Nashville: Broadman Press, 1966), p. 127.

Our convention has no ecclesiastical authority. It is in no sense the Southern Baptist Church. The thousands of churches to which our Convention looks for support of its missionary, benevolent, and educational program cherish their independence and would disapprove of any attempted exercise of ecclesiastical authority over them.[20]

This same view, reiterated through the years, is weakened by the fact that this body's membership in the Baptist World Alliance was achieved through a decision made by the Convention, not by the congregations. Moreover, in the Convention's annual meetings, programs and goals are presented and promoted by the denomination's professional staff, operating through boards, functioning as the equivalent of other denominational headquarters. Some of the factors that have contributed to Southern Baptist rigidity concerning the ecumenical movement are still active, but there is a growing ecumenical spirit among them. This is evident in Southern Baptists' very active participation in local councils of churches and in the increasingly restless and vocal minority, particularly among the younger ministers, who are openly critical of the denomination's rigidity on the issue of ecumenicity. In a sermon to his congregation a leading young Southern Baptist clergyman said:

To think that we possess all of the fullness of Christianity in our tradition is spiritual blindness indeed. The particular meanings that have come to us through our own unique experience are matched by the particular meanings that have come to other parts of the Body. And God would have us all share in this multi-splendored reality by sharing with one another. Yet this will never come to pass if we cut ourselves off from every other group and say, "We do not need you." [21]

An increasing number of Southern Baptists would share the viewpoint of Professor Theron D. Price of Furman University that we are "in much greater danger, at present, of failing to make our witness to the whole Church by isolation than of losing the distinctiveness of that witness by association." [22]

Any consideration of "non-cooperating Protestants" and the ecumenical movement must include the Lutheran Church, Missouri Synod. While this group is not unconcerned with the unity of the church, they have insisted that agreement in statement of doctrine is prerequisite to cooperation or union. Also outside the ecumenical movement at present are certain Christian groups that cooperate with one another but not under the aegis of the World Council. They have designated themselves "Evangelicals," and, accenting doctrinal orthodoxy as they see it, have spurned association with the

[20] *Annual of the Southern Baptist Convention,* 1940, p. 99.

[21] John R. Claypool, a sermon, "Our Oneness and Our Differences," delivered at the Crescent Hill Baptist Church, Louisville, Kentucky, February 7, 1965.

[22] Theron D. Price, "A Southern Baptist Views Church Unity," *Christian Unity in North America,* ed. J. Robert Nelson (St. Louis: Bethany Press, 1958), p. 88.

World Council because of their fear of centralization, a super-Church, and anxieties over the Council's "minimizing of theology" in what to Evangelicals is an insufficient creedal statement. This refrain may be heard in a sermon by Carl F. H. Henry, editor of *Christianity Today*, addressed to ecumenists from a "conservative evangelical perspective":

Across the years ecumenical leadership and affiliation have reflected humanist, liberal, neo-orthodox, and neoliberal as well as evangelical points of view. It is not difficult to list prominent ecumenical theologians who deny such basic Christian doctrines as the virgin birth of Jesus, his messianic self-consciousness, his substitutionary and propitiatory atonement, his bodily resurrection, or his personal and visible return. In Faith and Order conferences the loss of the Bible as an authoritative canon of sacred writings is obvious. Present-day ecumenism distills its theological consensus from the diverse promulgations of contemporary Christendom; the great ecumenical creeds of the past, on the other hand, arose through a determination to champion the scripturally revealed doctrines over against heretical deviations. . . .

It is no accident of twentieth-century Christianity, therefore, that the ecumenical movement as an ecclesiastical phenomenon has been paralleled by serious theological turbulence. For the third time in our century, Continental Protestantism has tumbled into a morass of doctrinal uncertainty. Sad to say, this theological confusion has been sheltered and even promoted by an ecumenical Christianity which prizes tolerance above truth and union above unction.[23]

The "Evangelical's" criticism often stems from his assumption that the pervasive interest of the World Council of Churches is the external unification of all Protestant bodies into one vast organization. Some Pentecostal groups, emphasizing the direct and present activity of the Holy Spirit and the emotional heightening of religious experience, have maintained a highly critical attitude toward prevailing institutional forms of church life.

Many individuals within all these groups assume quite sincerely that they will better serve as custodians and teachers of truth by remaining apart and "particular"—that aloofness indicates seriousness, whereas ecumenical en-

---

[23] Carl F. H. Henry, "Christ and His Embattled Legions," *Sermons to Men of Other Faiths and Traditions*, ed. Gerald H. Anderson (Nashville: Abingdon Press, 1966), pp. 147-48. The following sermons represent a different point of view and an affirmative assessment of the goals and achievements of the ecumenical movement: Roland H. Bainton, "Our Protestant Witness," *The Pulpit* (December, 1948); Eugene Carson Blake, "When Conviction Tests Cooperation," *The Pulpit* (November, 1957); Robert S. Bilheimer, "The Christian Hope," *Pulpit Digest* (August, 1954); Archibald C. Craig, "In One All Things," *Pulpit Digest* (March, 1959); Henry Smith Leiper, "Toward Worldwide Community," *Pulpit Digest* (September, 1958); Johannes Lilje, "Moving Toward a World-wide Unity," *Pulpit Digest* (July, 1958); J. Robert Nelson, "One in Christ," *Pulpit Digest* (November, 1959); Ronald E. Osborn, "Scandal of an Ecumenical Church," *The Pulpit* (January, 1954); Liston Pope, "That All May Be One," *Best Sermons, 1962*, ed. G. Paul Butler (Princeton: D. Van Nostrand, 1962), pp. 143-48; Edward Hughes Pruden, "United Nations and Divided Churches," *Best Sermons, 1949-50*, ed. G. Paul Butler (New York: Harper & Brothers, 1949), pp. 76-83.

PREACHING IN AMERICAN HISTORY

counter implies indifferentism in the search for truth. Devoted partisans of
the ecumenical movement question such an assumption and are often tempted
to dismiss conservative critics as obscurantists and obstructionists. It *is* a
striking fact that fundamentalists and "neo-evangelicals," sometimes motivated
by merely "anti-ecumenicalism," seek in their conclaves a unity among
intransigents. However, we shall do well to avoid invidious stereotype in our
appraisal of these groups. The fact is that, if the ecumenical movement is to
express the *wholeness* of the church, we must take proper account of the type
of churchmanship they represent.

Conclusion

Now far past the invigorating days when it was "the great new fact of
our time," the ecumenical movement is at a more critical stage in its career.
The intervening years have brought a more realistic view of the residual
problems it faces. While there has been no diminishing of vitality among
devoted advocates, many recognize the need to "broaden the base of ecumenical participation." Now, as never before, the movement needs the vigor
and vision of lay and clerical church leadership.

In a factually divided Christendom we are committed to yearn, work, and
pray for the realization of the undivided community of the faithful. Robert
E. Cushman, dean of the Divinity School of Duke University, states our
mission:

The ecumenical challenge today, then, includes and fosters the consciousness of
a new and larger divine vocation that is quite trans-denominational. It engenders
a larger loyalty that is at odds with particularistic loyalties and self-defensive denominational self-consciousness. It is productive of a new spirit, a spirit of openness, a spirit more sensitive of God's power to transcend differences than of man's
capacity to sharpen them through pride.[24]

In this venture hopeful signs increase that the cause is supremely worthful.
The Christian community has lived through a long night of isolation. Harsh
realities must yet be faced and overcome. In this time of faithful working
and waiting for the ecumenical movement to come to the fruition of its aims,
perhaps it will be salutary to recall some words of Horace Bushnell (1802-
76). In an era of abrasive theological conflict, he yearned and worked for a
catholic and comprehensive unity that would "soften asperities and
prejudices." With typical realism he wrote:

If any one asks, when shall these things be?, we may well enough refer him to
the geologists for an answer. For if God required long ages of heaving and fiery
commotion to settle the world's layers into peace and habitable order, we ought

[24] Robert E. Cushman, "The Ecumenical Challenge to Methodism," *The Drew
Gateway*, XXXV, No. 3, 138.

308

not utterly to despair if the geologic era of the church covers a somewhat longer space of time than we ourselves might prescribe.[25]

Although we move "with painful gait and slow" on the long uncharted road, perhaps, under God, we are on the way to that fullness and fulfillment of the Body of Christ that will bring a new day in universal church history.

[25] H. Shelton Smith, ed., *Horace Bushnell* (New York: Oxford University Press, 1965), pp. 125-26.

16

THE THRUST OF THE RADICAL RIGHT

Dale Leathers

"*God calls us through the Holy Spirit to serve him in the need of our neighbors*" is the current rallying cry of liberal Christianity in America.[1] Centralized religion and government both operate from the premise suggested by the caption—a society must help the individual solve problems for which society is responsible. This position outrages an increasingly verbal and affluent portion of America's clergymen. The outrage comes because clergymen of this persuasion have a deep distrust of man and the society he shapes.

The Right in Religion Defined

"Freedom-loving Christian Americans need to stay on their guard to avoid being deceived or confused by those who would weaken their Christian faith under a false concept of brotherhood," warns Billy James Hargis.[2] Hargis is a reactionary. Like his fellow reactionaries he is bitterly opposed to all forms of collectivism. His denunciation of the ecumenical movement is no less bitter than his condemnation of the welfare state. In an age of societal commitment to civil and personal rights the reactionary pulpit strives to remove social conscience from our daily lives.

For this reason ministers of Hargis' persuasion have such epithets as extremist, hatemonger, fright peddler, bigot, anti-intellectual, fascist, and rightist applied to them. The actual characterization of the reactionaries' ideological position is often equally inflammatory. Rabbi Solomon S. Bernards, writing for the Anti-Defamation League, asserts that the reactionaries "find great satisfaction in building philosophies and ideologies of everyday living based

[1] Margaret Williamson, ed., *Concern and Response* (New York: Friendship Press, 1962), p. 186. This book is the official report of the Second National Conference on the Churches and Social Welfare.

[2] Billy James Hargis, *The Facts About Communism and Our Churches* (Tulsa, Oklahoma: Christian Crusade Publications, 1962), p. 145.

on fear, intolerance, and blindness. These movements endanger the very core of a free society." [3]

Among the reactionary responses to current issues we find: the civil rights revolution depicted as a Red plot to "mongrelize America"; the United Nations condemned as a "hot-bed of international Communist intrigue"; foreign aid attacked as a "campaign to bankrupt the nation"; medicare denounced as "creeping socialism"; mental health programs assailed as drives to "brainwash" America; and the United States Supreme Court decisions on school prayers, desegregation, and the right to dissent cited as evidence of communism in high places and the "treason" of Chief Justice Earl Warren.[4] Critics dismiss the reactionaries' view of political and social reality as ridiculous.

To many Americans the motivation of the reactionary pulpit is as suspect as its anti-humanitarian stance on social issues. Reactionary ministers are characterized as "prophets of the 60's come to the cure of our Communist-fed minds with bibles [sic] in their hands and their pockets ajingle with gold. . . . What they have discovered is the Red Menace which is everywhere, and to fight it much bread must be cast upon the waters. And the bread for the best of them will run over a million dollars a year." [5] Such epithetic responses neither objectively define nor describe the reactionary preacher of this decade, however.

Technically, the preachers under study here are not just reactionary; they are revolutionary reactionaries. Such reactionaries are revolutionary because they want to destroy America's political institutions; they are reactionary because they look to a much earlier America for strength. This definition is based on the reactionaries' response to traditions, institutions, and values. With this orientation in mind Clinton Rossiter defines seven political types— revolutionary radicals, radicals, liberals, conservatives, standpatters, reactionaries, and revolutionary reactionaries.[6] Rossiter suggests that revolutionary radicals and revolutionary reactionaries are the "closest of neighbors" in a definitional sense. Both groups agree that present institutions, traditions, and values are oppressive, diseased, and untrustworthy. They differ in that radicals have a messianic commitment to the future while the reactionary is equally committed to the past. Both are revolutionary without qualification. They would not substitute; they would destroy the present institution, tradition, and value complex of the United States without replacement.[7]

Reactionary persuasion in America has both a secular and a sacred branch,

[3] Solomon S. Bernards, *The Radical Right and Religion* (New York: The Anti-Defamation League of B'nai B'rith, 1965), p. 2.

[4] *Countering Extremism: A Primer for Americans* (New York: American Jewish Committee, Institute of Human Relations, May, 1966).

[5] New York *Post Daily Magazine*, March 31, 1964, p. 1.

[6] Clinton Rossiter, *Conservatism in America: The Thankless Persuasion* (New York: Vintage Books, 1962), pp. 12-14.

[7] *Ibid.*, p. 11.

though the basic value system for the two branches is nearly indistinguishable. Robert Welch with his John Birch Society is the most prominent American reactionary who is not a preacher. Besides Welch, the most prominent secular reactionaries are Dr. Fred Schwarz who heads the Christian Anti-Communism Crusade, Clarence Manion who reaches upward of two hundred and fifty radio stations on his Manion Forum, Kent and Phoebe Courtney who cover fifteen southeastern states with their radio version of their newspaper *The Independent American*, and Dan Smoot with the Dan Smoot Report which reaches seventy radio stations and forty television stations weekly.

Since the National Council of Churches has become a central target of reactionary broadcasters, the NCC's Bureau of Research and Survey keeps records of what it calls "Radical Right Broadcasters." The Bureau reports that "nine of the leading Radical Right broadcasters account for over seven thousand programs a week over radio and television stations.[8] These broadcasters are identified as Howard Kershner, Clarence Manion, Dan Smoot, R. K. Scott with America's Future, Kent and Phoebe Courtney, Edgar Bundy with the Church League of America, H. L. Hunt with Life Line, Carl McIntire with the Twentieth Century Reformation Hour, and Billy James Hargis with the Christian Crusade.

Despite the publicity given to many of the secular reactionaries, the religious arm of American reaction is most significant today for at least two reasons. American reaction, of whatever form, is a religious manifestation and not political in terms of its generative values; increasingly, the strength of American reaction is found in the pulpit. Billy James Hargis puts the matter most directly when he asks, "What in the world do you think all these little Birch Committees, or McIntire or Hargis or Smoot or Manion committees are? They are nothing but God's people who have been fed liberal pap all these years wanting a chance to associate with people of like religious faith. The John Birch Society itself is nothing but a religious expression." [9]

The two strongest voices for American reaction among clergymen are those of Carl McIntire and Billy James Hargis. While countless preachers across the nation, particularly in the Bible Belt, advocate their brand of Americanism, McIntire and Hargis stand alone in their ability to attract and expand a nationwide audience. This is even more impressive since they are resisting the mainstream of ideological expression in America at present. As the New York *Post* puts it, "There is, then, a Darwinian force at work in the midst of the great Fundamentalist stream, and in the end the only ones who have come up . . . in fighting condition are the Rev. Dr. Carl McIntire of Collings-

[8] *Information Service*, Saturday, October 10, 1964. *Information Service* is a biweekly publication of the Bureau of Research and Survey of the National Council of the Churches of Christ in the United States of America.

[9] Interview with Dr. Billy James Hargis, founder-director of the Christian Crusade, at Crusade Headquarters, Tulsa, Oklahoma, March 11, 1965.

wood, N. J., and the Rev. Dr. Billy James Hargis of Tulsa, Oklahoma." [10] Fletcher Coates, executive information director for the National Council of Churches of the U.S.A., says unequivocally that "McIntire and Hargis are the most influential preachers on the far right." [11]

Carl McIntire warns "the beloved" that "we must fight now. We must work now. We must sacrifice now. Some of you may go to your savings; some of you may be able to sell some land and other things; but a million dollars will do marvels right now. Let these men know that there is a God in Israel in whom we delight. The doors may be closed before long." [12] "The beloved," of course, are the devout followers of the Rev. Carl McIntire. While Robert Welch possesses the strongest *secular* voice of the American right today, Carl McIntire's is clearly the strongest *sacred* voice. McIntire presently achieves national exposure with radio, but he labored for a long period of time in obscurity. "From 1935 to 1960, despite intensive efforts, he [McIntire] made little progress in his campaign. But in the early sixties his newspaper, the *Christian Beacon*, set up a subsidiary called the 20th Century Reformation Hour to broadcast McIntire's dissident views, which until then had been heard only over a small radio station in Chester, Pennsylvania. He now broadcasts over some 600 radio stations and reaches millions of people daily." [13] From 1960 to 1967 McIntire's radio coverage doubled, tripled, and quadrupled. Since late 1965, his goal has been to broadcast his thirty-minute radio program over a thousand radio stations; he currently is heard in all but three states of the Union. He boasts a larger sustained audience than any other reactionary persuader. [14]

The purpose of McIntire's radio preaching is twofold. He wants "to bring before the Christian public in the United States the facts about Communist infiltration of religion" and to point out "the inroads being made by liberal theologians who deny the basic creeds of Christian belief." [15]

Hargis is less concerned about purely religious issues than McIntire. He is determined to preserve the Constitution and Christianity with considerable emphasis on the Constitution. Thus, Hargis warns his followers that "this is a time for God's people to pray for the continuation of freedom of speech and to actively engage in this fight to preserve Constitutional concepts and orthodox Christianity." [16]

Hargis has organized his Christian Crusade for two reasons. He wants a

[10] New York *Post Daily Magazine*, March 31, 1964, p. 1.
[11] Telephone interview with Fletcher Coates, executive information director for the National Council of Churches, New York, April 28, 1967.
[12] Official letter of Dr. Carl McIntire to his followers, Twentieth Century Reformation Hour, Collingswood, New Jersey, n. d.
[13] Bernards, *The Radical Right and Religion*, p. 11.
[14] Official letter of Dr. Carl McIntire (see n. 12).
[15] Carl McIntire, biographical brochure, *Testimony to Christ and a Witness for Freedom* (Collingswood, New Jersey: Twentieth Century Reformation Hour, 1965), n. p.
[16] Billy James Hargis, *Christian Crusade*, April, 1965, p. 34.

Constitutional America; he wants a Christian America. Since Hargis stresses the "un-American" and "un-Christian" nature of communism, the communists would appear to be his chief concern. But they are not. Hargis is equally concerned about the "un-American" and "un-Christian" activities of liberals. His central objective is to expose both the communists and the liberals. As Hargis puts it, he "not only will attempt to expose the Communist conspiracy internally, but will also focus a spotlight of truth upon those organizations and men who have aided and abetted the cause of Communism by word or deed, whether intentionally or unintentionally." [17]

The success of preachers like McIntire and Hargis since 1960 is suggestive of a definite trend among clergymen fighting collectivism and communism. In the West, the Voice of Americanism, Dr. W. S. McBirnie, typifies the increasingly secular interests of this portion of the American pulpit. When the suave, articulate McBirnie arrived in Glendale, California, he found a Baptist congregation without crusading tendencies. Within a matter of a few years he (1) converted the Baptist congregation into the United Community Church of Glendale with the implied purpose of fighting communism and liberalism; (2) built a new split-level building to house the Voice of Americanism, a fifteen-minute radio program which expanded from a handful of regional outlets in the early 1960's to over ninety outlets across the nation at present; (3) built a new "Center for American Research and Education." Despite the fact that two of McBirnie's major enterprises, the Voice of Americanism and the Center for American Research and Education, are avowedly secular in purpose, McBirnie began an interview with this writer by asserting that "as a minister I do not believe that the church has any business mixing in politics." [18]

Theology of the Right

Ideologically, America's reactionary pulpit is identifiable and quite homogeneous in position. The dichotomization of theology into "mirror Christianity" and "apostate Christianity," the polarization of issues into "Americanist" and "socialist," and the compartmentalization of man's motivation

---

[17] Billy James Hargis, *The Real Extremists: The Far Left* (Tulsa, Oklahoma: Christian Crusade Publications, 1964), p. 7.

[18] Interview with Dr. W. S. McBirnie in his recording studio at Voice of Americanism Headquarters in Glendale, California, May 5, 1967. Throughout the hour and one-half interview McBirnie repeatedly stressed his hope that he would not be classified as an extremist. In his *Lexicon for Americans* he classifies "political and ideological social movements" from Extreme Left to Extreme Right: Communism-Socialism, Menshevism, Nazism, Marxian-Socialism, Socialism, Fabianism, Liberalism, Monarchism, Constitutional Conservatism, Capitalism, and Anarchism. He lists both Capitalism and Anarchy on the Extreme Right as opposed to the Right. Significantly, he stressed in the interview that his is the philosophy of Capitalism.

as either "man-centered" or "God-centered" is representative of the reactionary voice in contemporary preaching.

The reactionaries' theology is circumscribed by a political and moral dimension. Irving E. Howard isolates the theological creed of today's reactionary preacher by writing in *The Christian Alternative to Socialism* that "present day Americans are committing idolatry by seeking security and equality through government action. They have put the State in the place of God and, consequently, have set in motion a process which will eventually destroy the fabric of society." [19] The touchstone of reactionary theology is an inversion, if not an outright contradiction, of the justifying premise for the social gospel: man must not be a keeper of his own brother, because each man best promotes the general interest by promoting his own.[20] Reactionary theology asserts that (1) materialistic and social inequities are sanctioned by God, (2) attempts to equalize opportunity and assure minimum standards of living constitute "thievery" in contravention of "God's law," and (3) complete governmental disregard for individual needs is true humanitarianism—to cater to the needs of the underprivileged is to glorify man at the expense of God. Thus society's "have nots" should "accept the inequalities of life as part of God's plan for them." [21] To seek aid is sinful, for the "citizen in the small cottage, if he had this faith, did not envy the man in the big house, because the man in the small cottage accepted economic inequality as a part of God's will for him until, with God's help, he could improve his situation." [22] Likewise measures to equalize opportunity are apostatic for "both socialism and welfare statism defy the moral laws of God. Both practice legalized thievery." [23] Self-interest becomes a noble motive in the reactionary pulpit for "the competitive profit-seeking businessman, if he believes in God, is the true humanitarian, while the agnostic welfare stater denies the dignity of man because, in all his pseudo-charity, he acts upon the assumption that man 'lives by bread alone.' " [24]

The political nuances of reactionary theology were captured by the Rev. W. S. McBirnie. The central issue, claims McBirnie, is whether "society is

[19] Irving E. Howard, *The Christian Alternative to Socialism* (Arlington, Virginia: Better Books, 1966), p. 28. Howard's new book represents an authentic and fair treatment of reactionary theology. The book has been prominently advertised in Hargis' monthly magazine, *Christian Crusade*, as the definitive treatment of reactionary theology. Prominent reactionary broadcaster Howard E. Kershner has written the introduction to Howard's book, and in it he asserts that "few men understand the relationship of scriptures to freedom, free government, and economic well-being better than Mr. Howard." Howard started out as a minister, but from 1954 to the present time he has been assistant editor of *Christian Economics*.

[20] *Ibid.*, p. 61.
[21] *Ibid.*, p. 9.
[22] *Ibid.*
[23] *Ibid.*, p. 22.
[24] *Ibid.*, p. 9.

responsible for man or man for society." [25] McBirnie was quick to polarize the issue by claiming that the world is divided between two issues. Liberal theology "says if you can improve society you can improve man. This is the philosophy that says slums cause crime." [26] In direct opposition is reactionary theology, for this "is the theology of capitalism and Christianity in its simple, New Testament sense. If you want to start to improve things, start with man himself. Improve man and he will improve society." [27]

The moral dimension in reactionary theology is inextricably related to the political. Reactionaries argue that it is morally wrong to invest the government, or any secular institution, with the power to protect or assure a man's civil rights. No matter how noble the motivation, "the sinful bent of human nature will corrupt those [governmental] decisions," [28] and, more importantly, such acts may result in the "fracturing of a personal right to property," the original and most sacred right.[29]

The reactionary preacher is highly vexed by a liberal theology which converts belief in the social gospel into action through the National Council of Churches. To people like Hargis, McIntire, Bundy, the Robert Joneses, and McBirnie the theological thesis is: save man, and society will take care of itself. To the same reactionary preachers theological antithesis is: save society, and man becomes worthy of salvation. The Rev. David Noebel, a colleague of Hargis and a reactionary preacher of note in his own right, sums up the reactionary's disdain for religion with a social conscience. At reactionary rallies throughout the country Noebel bitterly attacks the National Council of Churches as the institutional voice of the social gospel. In a recently released pamphlet entitled "Religion Is Red," Noebel begins his polemic agains the NCC by asking, "Does the National Council of Churches Speak for You?" His contempt for liberal theology, as represented by the NCC, becomes manifest in the secondary questions he raises to determine whether the NCC speaks for "you":

(Does the National Council of Churches Speak for "You?")
1) When it accepts a Socialist-Communist Economic Creed?
2) When it substitutes the "Social Gospel" for the Gospel of Jesus Christ?
3) When it sponsors the World Council of Churches which has communists on its central committee?
4) When it urges the weakening of the Walter-McCarran Immigration Act hence opening the flood gates to Marxist-oriented peoples?
5) When it employs identified communist-fronters to translate, revise and publish the Revised Standard Version of the Bible?

[25] Interview with W. S. McBirnie.
[26] Ibid.
[27] Ibid.
[28] Howard, The Christian Alternative to Socialism, p. 18.
[29] Interview with W. S. McBirnie.

316

6) When it sponsors study material that follows the current line of Soviet policy? [30]

The dispute between the reactionary pulpit and the liberal pulpit is neither superficial nor academic. The two pulpits stand diametrically opposed as to the message of Christianity, its interpretation, and its implementation. The voice of liberal Christianity speaks more and more to man's physical, emotional, cultural, and social needs. To the reactionary preacher this is apostasy.

The declared enemies of the reactionary pulpit are liberal theology and institutionalized liberal religion. Liberal theology is most succinctly translated as the social gospel, and the acting organ of that theology is the National Council of Churches. The past president of the National Council of Churches, J. Irwin Miller, has captured the rationale for a theology which reactionary preachers find so blasphemous. In a speech appropriately titled "The Theological Basis for Social Action," he argues for an action-oriented religion, for "Jesus in his own life offered us the example of the prophetic concept of religion. When he came upon suffering, he stopped to relieve it. When he came upon injustice, he moved to correct it. When he encountered wickedness, he spoke out to condemn it." [31]

Reactionaries preach that the true believer serves God best by serving his own self-interest, while they disregard the nonspiritual needs of their fellowman and denounce collective attempts to meet those needs. The liberals, like Miller, preach that the " 'weightier matters' of the law are justice, and mercy, and faith—qualities which cannot be expressed except in right responses, and right actions in difficult and challenging social situations." [32] To the dismay of the reactionary preacher, the liberal church has never been so actively involved in programs of social action. [33]

In summary, the nakedly conflicting thrust of reactionary and liberal theologies is captured in the creed of the social gospel: in the lifetime of this world, we will be judged by those generations to whom we hand on our society, according to whether it is better or worse than the one we received;

[30] Fernando Penabaz, *Crusading Preacher from the West* (Tulsa, Oklahoma: Christian Crusade Publications, 1965), pp. 175-77.

[31] J. Irwin Miller, address, "The Theological Basis for Social Action" (New York: Office of Public Interpretation, National Council of the Churches of Christ in the U.S.A.). Delivered at the Convention of Christian Churches, St. Louis, Missouri, October 19, 1958. Fletcher Coates of the information department at the National Council of Churches claims that this speech remains the best justification for the liberal church's active attack on social problems.

[32] *Ibid.*

[33] Williamson, ed., *Concern and Response*, p. 16. A recent survey conducted under the auspices of the National Council of Churches indicates that homes for the aged, hospitals, neighborhood houses, and settlements, and institutions for the care of children were the most important of the churches' welfare agencies. However, other welfare measures included child placement and adoption, day nursery, clinic or dispensary, convalescent care, temporary shelter, family welfare social education and action and chaplaincy in prisons and hospitals.

317

and, at the last time, we will thus be judged by the only wise Judge.[34] Even in theory this social gospel is apostasy to the reactionary preacher; in practice it is heresy.

The Right as a Response

The reactionary pulpit has been stunned and embittered by the rapid and inexorable movement of American society. The reactionaries sought institutional simplicity in politics and government; they got complexity. They sought to increase local autonomy; they got increased regulation from federal agencies. They sought to dissociate themselves from societal concerns—and society dissociated itself from the reactionaries. At first, the reactionary pulpit assumed that the societal drift to collectivism was a fad. Developments of the last three decades have convinced them that the trend toward highly centralized government and religion is irreversible without some dramatic means of alarming the American public.

The problems which excite reactionary preachers and give reactionary rhetoric its strident quality are clearly identifiable. Reactionary preaching is increasingly a protest to collectivism in its two forms—the ecumenical movement and the welfare state. The unprecedented growth of political and religious collectivism in the United States has amounted to a direct repudiation of the reactionary pulpit. Specifically, since the advent of the New Deal, reactionary preachers have been faced with the following problems: (1) the social gospel is no longer a fanciful theory but an institutional reality in the United States; (2) the welfare state has not collapsed of its own inertia but grows at an accelerating rate; (3) the vast majority of Americans participating in religious and political life continue to approve both forms of collectivism; and (4) the reactionary cause from 1933-60 was highly unsalable.

The combined weight of these historical factors has disillusioned the reactionary preacher, but it has done more. Reactionaries are now convinced that society is basically sick. Society needs more than modification of its institutions. Society needs an ideological revolution which will destroy the present institutional framework of the United States and reject those groups which are responsible for the proliferation of governmental and religious institutions.[35]

[34] Miller "The Theological Basis for Social Action."

[35] For the most illuminating look at the reactionaries' stand on political issues and their rejection of present societal institutions, see Kent Courtney, *Tax Fax* No. 26. Number 26 is one of the more revealing issues in an extensive pamphlet series on major political issues sponsored by *The Independent American*, New Orleans, Louisiana. These pamphlets illustrate quite graphically that the reactionaries want to abolish the Supreme Court, as we know it, the graduated income tax, social security, civil rights legislation, the National Council of Churches, the United Nations, and NATO.

The Right Organizes

The reactionary pulpit of this decade is gaining strength as an organ of protest to two political developments—the New Deal and communism. Reactionary preachers have found a popular cause and, hence, a loyal following through their distinctively vitriolic protest to these two political developments. Men like Carl McIntire and Robert Jones became religious outcasts, at least to the religious establishment, by rejecting the alleged alliance between liberal religion and the New Deal. The new breed of reactionary preachers, like Hargis, McBirnie, and Noebel, became religious malcontents by rejecting the alleged alliance between "New Frontier socialism" and communism. To illustrate, at twenty-three Carl McIntire entered Princeton Theological Seminary to study under the prominent fundamentalist scholar John Gresham Machen. Machen was devoted to a form of biblical individualism which brooked no interference by the state to help those who cannot help themselves. He felt that the social gospel emphasis at Princeton Theological Seminary was beginning to compromise his principles. Machen soon left Princeton to set up his own Westminster Seminary in Chestnut Hill, Pennsylvania, in 1931, and McIntire followed. Machen and McIntire identified strongly with each other in denouncing the heretical acts of the United Presbyterian Church of America. They saw the Presbyterian Church endorsing the welfare measures of Franklin Roosevelt's New Deal. Subscribing to the social gospel was bad enough, but translating it into relief programs run by the federal government was outright heresy. Machen and his pupil McIntire repudiated the regular Presbyterian mission board and set up the Independent Board of Presbyterian Foreign Missions.[36]

Both men became increasingly defiant in their struggle against the centralized authority of the United Presbyterian Church of America. In 1936, McIntire and Machen went on trial for causing "dissension and strife" before the General Assembly of the Presbyterian Church. At this trial, "McIntire was found guilty on three counts; and the General Assembly of the Church, upholding the prior decision of the Synod, voted his dismissal from the ministry of the United Presbyterian Church." [37]

The act of expulsion helps explain much of the bitterness which is so endemic to McIntire's radio speaking and his public speeches in general. Since then, many of McIntire's actions have had at least the appearance of retaliatory efforts in response to the expulsion. He not only has bitterly opposed the ecumenical movement, but he has set up organizations for the expressed purpose of frustrating the ecumenical leaders. In 1941, Carl McIntire founded the American Council of Christian Churches, and in 1947 he

[36] Harry and Bonaro Overstreet, *The Strange Tactics of Extremism* (New York: W. W. Norton, 1964), p. 150.
[37] *Ibid.*

began work to form the International Council of Christian Churches.[38] An apparent major objective of both organizations is to frustrate the ecumenical ambitions of both the National Council of Churches and the World Council of Churches.

Reactionary preachers of McIntire's generation were reacting in part to the welfare measures of the New Deal. Nonetheless, in the late 1930's and 1940's they were primarily concerned with the impact of collectivized government on theology and religious institutions; their concern was still primarily with sacred matters, not secular, The next generation of reactionaries, Hargis, Noebel, McBirnie, and others, was concerned with secular matters from the start. McIntire's generation of reactionary preachers drew inspiration from rejecting the apostatic alliance between collectivized religion and government in the forms of the ecumenical movement and the New Deal. In contrast Hargis' generation of preachers find inspiration in attacking the alliance between collectivized government "under God" and collectivized government without God. The former type of collectivism is seen as represented by the New Deal, Fair Deal, New Frontier, and the Great Society; the latter type is seen as "atheistic" communism. Hargis is perhaps the best case in point.

Unlike McIntire, who has delivered weekly sermons from his own pulpit for the last three decades, Hargis preached to his own congregation for only seven years, from 1943 to 1950. Since then, communists, not Christian sinners, have been his chief concern. In 1943, Hargis completed his study for the ministry in a year and one half at Ozark Bible College in Bentonville, Arkansas, and was ordained into the ministry at the age of eighteen. Following his May 30, 1943, ordination he became pastor of the First Christian Church at Sallisaw, Oklahoma. When twenty, he left Sallisaw to accept the pastorate at the First Christian Church in Granby, Missouri.[39]

A pivotal point in Hargis' career seemed to come in Sapulpa, Oklahoma. He was visiting a minister there and expressed his concern that communist influences might be taking control of Christianity in this country. The fellow pastor's indifferent response—so what?—was an affront which shocked young Hargis to the core of his fundamentalist philosophy. In fact, he was enraged. *His* response was rapid and purposeful. "He persuaded his church to pay for a 'religious' radio broadcast, and the response from listeners was a revelation of the numbers he could reach through this means. . . . In 1950, he resigned to launch the campaign to save America from Communists and Liberals." [40] Within a year Hargis incorporated as a religious, nonprofit-making body called the Christian Echoes Ministry, Inc., now popularly known as Christian

[38] McIntire, *Testimony to Christ and a Witness for Freedom.*

[39] Mary Lou Betts, "Billy James Hargis: Orator in the Anti-Communist Movement" (unpublished Master's thesis, Department of Speech, California State College, Long Beach, California, 1963), p. 23.

[40] Arnold Forster and Benjamin R. Epstein, *Danger on the Right* (New York: Random House, 1964), p. 72.

Crusade. By 1952, he had radio outlets scattered throughout America's heartland and collected over $70,000. His attack on the liberal-communist alliance did not have the same sting with republican Dwight Eisenhower in office as it began to have in 1960 with liberal democrat John F. Kennedy as president. Hargis' basic theme then was the same as it is now, for he warns that "the anti-God philosophy of communism has influenced the entire liberal camp. It is Adam defying God all over again. The underlying reason for the liberals' defiance of the historic American way and orthodox New Testament Christianity, is their disbelief in God and the Bible." [41]

Values of the Right

The rhetoric of the reactionary pulpit constitutes a distinctive body of discourse. This reactionary discourse can best be understood by isolating the value system which moves the reactionary preacher and by analyzing the burdens that value system creates when it is superimposed upon the value system of liberal America.

Ralph T. Eubanks and Virgil L. Baker write that "behind the proposals and theses of public utterance are value propositions. In a sense, human values are fundamental in rhetoric," [42] and the reactionary pulpit is most easily understood by isolating reactionary value orientations. Such value orientations suggest both how the rhetoric operates and why it operates the way it does. Conceptually, the reactionary preacher expends more energy describing the nature of God, man, and country than on all other concerns. The reactionary's value orientations spring directly from his vigorous response to evil men attacking his God and his country.

The reactionary preacher's view of God is that of the fundamentalist. This God is not only empirically unknowable but fearfully omnipotent and an avenger. This God demands complete subservience. The fundamentalist's God demands abject conformity to a set of spiritual mandates, not to make fellow man's lot better on earth, but to avoid his vengeance after death. John Gresham Machen pictures a God who elicits nonrational commitment to the afterlife from his followers. He writes that "one attribute is absolutely necessary in order to render intelligible all the rest. That is the awful transcendence of God." [43]

---

[41] *Christian Crusade (A Progress Report 1963-1964).* Special edition of monthly magazine for Christian Crusade members, p. 1.

[42] Ralph T. Eubanks and Virgil L. Baker, "Toward an Axiology of Rhetoric," *Quarterly Journal of Speech,* XLVIII (April, 1962), 158. See Stanley F. Paulson, "Social Values and Experimental Research in Speech," *Western Speech,* XXVI (Summer, 1962), 136; and Edward D. Steele and Charles W. Redding, "The American Value System," *Western Speech,* XXVI (Spring, 1962), 83-91, for a defense and application of value analysis in rhetorical criticism.

[43] John Gresham Machen, *Christianity and Liberalism* (New York: The Macmillan Company, 1923), p. 62.

God's fearful omnipotence serves to reinforce a sense of subservience among reactionaries. Such subservience inevitably leads to a fear reaction and need for certainty. By his nature, then, the fundamentalist God is God of the frightened believer who feels a need for absolute certainty—a certainty so uncharacteristic of this world.

Reactionary rhetoric mirrors and reinforces this image of a transcendent and vengeful God. In a speech suggestively entitled "Christ—the Great Destroyer," Billy James Hargis warns his followers to "love your enemies; indeed, pray for your enemies, that they may be saved and not perish—but do not be deceived by them; do not go along with them in their deceit. Their lot is damnation; why make damnation your lot by taking heed to THEM?" [44]

The reactionary's view of the nature of man is as central to his value orientation as his view of the nature of God. Man is an abject sinner under the just condemnation of God. Man is basically suspect; man is untrustworthy; man is evil. Billy James Hargis is convinced not only that man is evil to the core of his being but that the degree of man's wickedness is increasing. Thus, Hargis is forced to the alarming conclusion that "Satan is the God of this world. . . . Evil forces are at work in countless ways and through manifest channels." [45] Carl McIntire is given to describing man as "desperately wicked" in his exhortatory radio sermons. McIntire is convinced that man is inherently evil and that man will never turn from his wicked ways without the intervention of God. Characteristically, in his radio prayers he implores God to lead man from his evil ways: "And Thou hast told us that fear of the Lord is the beginning of wisdom and to depart from evil—that is understanding. And wilt Thou give us an understanding of evil, that we may not follow it?" [46] The reactionary pulpit is highly sensitive to the pervasive nature of man's sinning. Each preacher is convinced of the inevitability of God's punishment for the unrepentant; each preacher stresses the consciousness of sin through the consciousness of hell.

The third reactionary value orientation, which is essential in fully disclosing how reactionary rhetoric works, involves the reactionary's view of his country. Just as reactionary preachers agree as to the nature of God and man, unanimity of opinion characterizes their view of America. Billy James Hargis spoke as the voice of American reaction when he said,

The only thing I will assume is, one, that America is right and, second, that God is right. And those are the only two things that I assume. I assume that you agree that America is the greatest country in the world and that you agree that Jesus Christ is everything he said he was and from there I will go. We've got to

[44] Billy James Hargis, address, "Christ the Great Destroyer" (Berne, Indiana: Economy Printing Concern, 1960), p. 162.
[45] *Christian Crusade*, May, 1965, p. 12.
[46] McIntire radio broadcast of January 29, 1965.

build some base. Now I'm not going to argue about America; I'm not going to argue about Christ."[47]

In summary, reactionaries subscribe to a set of values which minimize, indeed deny, the possibility that man may be the master of his destiny on earth. They emphasize the unknowable nature of an omnipotent God; at the same time they emphasize the unknowing nature of impotent man. Men are born evil and untrustworthy. All groups are conspiratorial because they inevitably are formed by evil men—all men are innately bad men. These values of course clearly identify the fundamentalist creed. In fact it is quite clear that American fundamentalism has been a major factor in shaping American reaction. Richard Hofstadter, among students of the far right, early recognized the relationship between American fundamentalism and American reaction.[48]

Social Institutions Rejected

The reactionaries have discovered a respectable way to cultivate the value of patriotism through the anti-communist issue. At the beginning of this decade, McIntire and Hargis began to stress the internal threat of communism in the United States. At the same time, the Twentieth Century Reformation Hour and the Christian Crusade gained national prominence. Reactionary value orientations now cluster around the alleged threat of communism. As the reactionaries see it, their vengeful God is enraged because his guileless country, America, is under attack by the guileful forces of communism.

Until 1960, reactionary preachers struggled with three major problems, the increasing popularity of the ecumenical movement, the increasing dominance of liberal government, and the increasing unpopularity of their own theology of self-interest. In short, reactionary preachers had a vested interest in somehow talking these problems into nonexistence. With the political change of 1960, the communist issue allowed more exploitation, and these preachers had an effective way of attacking all three problems. They could simply deny the reality of appearances, because of deception from within by the communists.

[47] Interview with Billy James Hargis.

[48] Richard Hofstadter, "Pseudo-Conservatism Revisited: A Postscript," *The Radical Right*, ed. Daniel Bell (Garden City, N.Y.: Doubleday & Company, 1963), p. 103. Hofstadter waited until 1964 to write that "if this essay were to be rewritten today, there is one force in American life, hardly more than hinted at in my original formulation [reference is to the *New American Right* (New York: Criterion Books, 1955)] that would now loom very large indeed and that is fundamentalism. The little that we know from the press about the John Birch Society, the Christian Crusade of Dr. Fred Schwarz, and the activities of the Rev. Billy James Hargis has served to remind us how much alive fundamentalism still is in the United States, and how firmly it has now fixed its attention on the fight against Communism as it once concentrated on the fight against evolution."

323

Reactionaries assert the impossibility of acquiring knowledge empirically because the empirical world is untrustworthy. This means that the reactionary persuader is forced to use nonempirical means to acquire knowledge. Reactionaries are convinced that citizens of the United States cannot gain knowledge empirically because the communists control every major type of institutionalized communication in the United States today. They assert that honest communication would merely subvert the purposes and undermine the actions of the communist conspirators. In short, for the communists to prosper they must deceive. Reactionary preachers charge that the communists are perpetrating an evil plan upon the American people. The communists have gained virtual control of three sources of institutionalized communication in America—the press, the liberal politician, and the liberal clergyman. The communist's potential to deceive, therefore, is beyond comprehension.

Billy James Hargis makes the typical reactionary charge against the liberal press by exclaiming that "infiltration of the free press in free nations is a necessary tactic of Communism, and is being accomplished easily in America, and in other free nations as well." [49] McIntire makes the same charge, but in biblical prose. He attacks *Life* and *Look* magazines for deceiving the American people. He dismisses the two mass circulation periodicals as representative of a deceitful liberal press.[50]

Hargis concentrates on the allegedly deceitful nature of the liberal politician by lamenting that "you would have to lead an Anti-Communist movement to know what the liberals are capable of—the hatred, incriminations, intimidations and coercions they constantly throw at the leaders of the Anti-Communist cause. . . . It is this lawless spirit that is preached by the Communists, and practiced by far too many liberals that we oppose." [51] Hargis' biographer Fernando Penabaz is less restrained in his blanket indictment of the communists and liberal politicians. "The smears, the lies, the half-truths, the innuendos, the false images, the guilt by association techniques . . . all whittle down the influence exercised by Hargis among his supporters," Penabaz complains, and merely confirms the deceitful nature of the liberal politician and the world.[52]

[49] Billy James Hargis, an address, *A Free Press—Leading America Leftward* (Tulsa, Oklahoma: Christian Crusade). Delivered periodically at anti-Communist rallies throughout the United States since 1960.

[50] Carl McIntire, Twentieth Century Reformation Hour radio broadcast, January 22, 1965.

[51] Billy James Hargis, *The Real Extremists: The Far Left* (Tulsa, Oklahoma: Christian Crusade Publications, 1964), p. 143.

[52] Penabaz, *Crusading Preacher from the West*, p. 236. Fernando Penabaz, who wrote this official biography of Hargis, is Hargis' top news analyst and an exiled lawyer from Castro's Cuba. Penabaz is convinced that the communists have virtual control of the country. During an interview with the author in Tulsa, Oklahoma, in March, 1965, Penabaz charged that "the Russian torpedo boats are cruising within the three mile limit in front of Ft. Lauderdale." In the last year Billy James Hargis has moved Penabaz from Christian Crusade headquarters in Tulsa, to Miami, Florida—presumably to

McIntire is just as quick to charge the liberal politician with duplicity. He refers his listeners to "this full page ad that was put in the New York *Times* questioning the mental health and condition of Barry Goldwater." [53] Deception was clearly the object when liberal politicians cast doubt on the mental health of, first, General Edwin Walker and, then, Barry Goldwater. McIntire claims that the denials of Walker and Goldwater were inevitable since "they don't want to be railroaded off to some mental institution." [54] The insinuation of mental instability was unfair because it put both men on the defensive in McIntire's view. McIntire concludes that "General Walker and Barry Goldwater are men who have been under terrific attack by the liberal element," for purposes of misleading the public.[55]

The cruelest blow to the reactionary is the alleged deception of the American clergy. Hargis complains bitterly that these same "busy churchmen who are engaged in this destructive work have convinced far too many people in our churches that anti-Communists engaged in exposing the suicidal error of their fallacious reasoning are really the ones doing the deceiving." [56] W. S. McBirnie amplifies the same theme by asserting, with a knowing nod of the head, that he can name any number of communist preachers in Los Angeles,[57] Among laymen, Myers G. Lowman has perhaps gained most notice with his persisting charge of duplicity in the liberal clergy.[58] But the reactionary pulpit mounts the most consistent and unified attack on the liberal pulpit. Without apparent misgivings, reactionary ministers turn on their liberal counterparts and charge that "we have barely scratched the surface of the voluminous record of participation in communist front activity by clergymen. No one knows the exact number of clergymen and front affiliations but thousands have participated. Many of these participating have been persons in leadership capacity within the National Council of Churches or its predecessor, the Federal Council of Churches." [59]

Reactionaries agree that, because of the pervasive influence of communism on American life, knowledge cannot be acquired by empirical means. This assumption grows directly from the value system of the reactionary pulpit.

---

bring the anti-communist message to the unusually appreciative ever-expanding audience of Cuban exiles in Miami.

[53] Carl McIntire, Twentieth Century Reformation Hour, radio broadcast, KQRS, Golden Valley, Minnesota, January 23, 1965, 6:00-6:30 A.M.

[54] *Ibid.*

[55] *Ibid.*

[56] Hargis, *The Facts About Communism and Our Churches*, p. 115.

[57] Interview with W. S. McBirnie.

[58] Myers G. Lowman, *A Compilation of Public Records of 658 Clergymen and Laymen Connected with The National Council of Churches* (Cincinnati, Ohio: Circuit Riders, 1962), p. 40. Lowman charges that "contrary to the assertions of top executives of the National Council of Churches, the Communist-front apparatus still receives the support of a large number of clergymen. In 1960, Communist fronts had the support of more than 1,200 Protestant clergymen."

[59] Hargis, *The Facts about Communism and Our Churches*, p. 52.

The most bizarre elaboration of the assumption comes, however, from the secular arm of American reaction and Robert Welch. Welch is convinced that the average citizen cannot possibly know on the basis of what he observes, because of what he calls the "Principle of Reversal." Through the application of this principle, warns Welch, the communists make the lie seem to be a fact and the fact a lie. What the communists would have you believe are the greatest strengths of America, they have made into America's most disturbing weaknesses, through the insidious process of infiltration. Welch illustrates the virtual impossibility of gaining the truth from experience, today, with the example of the Protestant clergy. He asserts that the clergy comprise "the very group where the ordinary American would least suspect, or expect to find, Communists or Communist sympathizers, and undoubtedly has the largest percentage of Consymps of any group of similar size in America." [60] To Welch this alleged duplicity of the clergy is striking confirmation for his conviction that the empirical world is untrustworthy. On the basis of the facts at hand, how could most Americans possibly know of communism in the clergy, asks Welch. They could not, for "the Protestant ministry in America should have been, and by all natural logic would be expected to be, in the very forefront of militant opposition to the Communists; a source of great danger to their schemes and a magnifier of their weaknesses." [61]

Immaculate Perception

The rhetoric of the reactionary pulpit has, then, coalesced around the startling contention that virtually all institutionalized voices in America are to be mistrusted and opposed—such respected institutional bulwarks as the labor movement, the ecumenical movement, and the mass media are to be denounced and suspected of duplicity. This epistemological bias, that experience is untrustworthy, circumscribes reactionary rhetoric. This bias dictates that reactionary values be nonexperiential. Abraham Kaplan, though not writing about reactionaries, reinforces this point when he asserts that "allowing *a* role to values is not what makes for bias; what makes for bias, rather, is allowing them only a role that insulates them from the test of experience; they are prejudicial when they are prejudged." [62]

Such bias is, of course, not confined to reactionary rhetoric. Bias is of overriding importance in reactionary rhetoric, however, because one belief is based on another belief rather than on facts. Since the reactionary views all forms

[60] Robert Welch, address, *Through All the Days to Be* (Belmont, Massachusetts; John Birch Society). First delivered in the Shrine Auditorium in Los Angeles, California, April 11, 1961.
[61] *Ibid.*
[62] Abraham Kaplan, *The Conduct of Inquiry* (San Francisco: Chandler Publishing Company, 1964), p. 386.

of contemporary communication as untrustworthy, he must deny any factual basis for his beliefs.[63] For this reason the reactionary is unwilling to embrace even the theologically respectable position that one should explain as much as possible by fact before relying on belief.[64]

The reactionary claims that belief provides its own warrant or justification. But those Americans who trust appearances contend that "belief cannot establish its own legitimacy." [65] From this perspective "belief is secondary. Before belief, therefore, come seeing and knowing. These take precedence over belief. Any serious examination of human modes of thinking and speaking will bear this out." [66]

This is heady stuff for the reactionary audience, because a new respectability comes with the charge that we can no longer trust appearances. The somewhat unpalatable burden of recent history is removed—maybe the apparent popularity of the welfare state is an illusion, possibly the ecumenical movement is a formidable opponent only on paper, and, better yet, the apparent unpopularity of the reactionary position from 1930-60 may be attributed to the oppressive control of the popular press by communists. Indeed, the epistemological bias, which gives rise to such hopes, serves to strengthen the very values which made the bias acceptable. Initially, this bias eliminates the possibility that a reactionary may alter his values on the basis of what he sees or experiences. This bias makes for the inflexibility of values popularly associated with the reactionary. Reactionary values are self-perpetuating since there is no way to verify or disprove the propositions which spring from these values. Finally, this bias removes the need to defend one's values by the traditional methods of applying evidence, for the "assent of belief is, as it were by nature, unqualified and without reservations." [67] The result of this epistemological bias, then, is a feedback of continuous reinforcement for the reactionary speaker and the values which give him sustenance.

The reactionary rhetoric which has such an obvious ability to compel the in-group is destined to repel the out-group for the same reasons. The reactionary preacher has been faced with a dilemma in this decade. He has been faced with two alternatives which are both highly undesirable: (1) he can maintain, as he does, that appearances are so uniformly deceiving that anti-communists cannot gather the necessary facts on which to base wise decisions; unfortunately for the reactionary, the vast majority of Americans do believe in the reliability of appearances and constitute the "deceived," "un-

---

[63] Kaplan has referred to this epistomological bias as the "dogma of the immaculate perception."

[64] See John Herman Randall, *The Role of Knowledge in Western Religion* (Boston: Beacon Press, 1958); or Paul Tillich, *Biblical Religion and the Search for Ultimate Reality* (Chicago: The University of Chicago Press, 1955) in support of this point.

[65] Josef Pieper, *Belief and Faith* (New York: Pantheon Books, 1963), p. 34.

[66] *Ibid.*

[67] *Ibid.*

committed" audience that the reactionary wants to reach; or (2) he can maintain that appearances are uniformly reliable to attract the larger "uncommitted" audience, but if he does so he must disown the very value orientations from which his persuasion springs.

In choosing the first alternative, the reactionary preacher dissipates his potential to adapt to the out-group. Forced to spin out an elaborate deductive structure to indicate what he is, the reactionary alienates more and more people as the web of apparent rationalization grows. In terms of values he not only defies popular consensus but, epistemologically, he uses belief rather than fact to defend those values.

The irony of it all may be that the reactionary sees the dispute as one of fact, not value. Regrettably for him, he is forced to deny the authenticity of what most Americans consider to be facts. For "the beloved," the committed crusaders, and the reactionary audience in general, the reactionary persuader thereby creates a rhetoric which is functional beyond dispute. Unfortunately for the reactionary preacher, as he placates the in-group, he alienates the out-group. His rhetoric of protest has become anathema to many Americans.

Education as a Tool of the Right

The opponents of reactionary preaching do not consider the reactionaries to be straw men or mere nuisances. Officials of the AFL-CIO, National Federation of Teachers, the Anti-Defamation League, the American Civil Liberties Union, the National Council of Churches, and many other liberal organizations are convinced that American reactionaries are a serious threat to some of America's most basic values.[68] Since the National Council of Churches is the favorite target for reactionary preachers, the response of the NCC is perhaps the best case in point. Reactionary attempts to infiltrate liberal churches have been so alarming, claims Fletcher Coates, executive information director for the NCC, that the council has developed a special information service for combating reactionary propaganda. A recent NCC release on available literature reveals reactionary preaching as the subject of fully one third of the sources—sample titles include "The Far Right and the Churches," "The Radical Right," and "The Radical Right and Religion." The NCC has been forced to mobilize its resources to combat the reactionary charge of communism in the high command. Publicity releases frequently

---

[68] Correspondence between officials of each of these organizations and the author confirms the fact that many liberal organizations are not only disturbed by the reactionary pulpit, but that they are mounting major informational programs to meet the reactionary threat.

cite a speech by FBI assistant director William C. Sullivan, which denies communist influence in the NCC.

Liberal clergymen as well as laymen are indeed upset by the reactionary pulpit. They have established comprehensive information programs to offset the impact of reactionary charges of apostasy, heresy, and communist control. Churches, labor unions, teachers' associations, and civil rights groups now issue special prefabricated information packets to members for meeting reactionary attacks. These church and civic groups are making a concerted effort to reach their confused or uncertain members with information and instructions on how to use the information.

Harry and Bonaro Overstreet note that these national groups have become obsessed with the "highly practical question of how local groups can best handle attacks from the Radical Right." [69] The targets of the reactionary pulpit are responding with carefully planned attempts to disseminate factual information. Whether it is the American Jewish Committee or the National Mental Health Association, the response to the contemporary reactionary is very similar. Such organizations have built up a comprehensive collection of research materials which facilitate their direct and telling response to predicable charges by reactionary preachers.

The response of the reactionary audience has also been to seek information, but not from the traditional sources—they cannot be trusted. Reactionary preachers seek to inform, if not indoctrinate, in at least two ways. First, reactionaries are going, increasingly, to their own training centers with anti-communist summer schools, centers for the study of "Americanism," anti-communist leadership conferences, and "Americanist" seminaries as the most popular educational vehicles. Reactionary preachers claim that the need for in-group education, free from the communist influence of public schools, is compelling. For men like Hargis the reactionary promise of salvation by education is no longer a dream but a reality:

In announcing our plans to build a Christian Crusade Headquarters in January, this was the dream that inspired it . . . a Center for Christian Conservatives . . . [where] supporters and helpers of all anti-Communist groups . . . can meet together month after month to fellowship, co-ordinate, create, and seek the guidance of God. Let's face it . . . all the odds are against us, as far as wealth, prestige, power, press etc. are concerned. But the greatest fact of all is the sole possession of Christian conservatives.[70]

Carl McIntire and Billy James Hargis were the first reactionary preachers to establish anti-communist summer schools to help combat the communist

[69] Overstreet, *The Strange Tactics of Extremism*, p. 24.
[70] *Christian Crusade*, March, 1965, p. 23.

menace through education. In these summer schools the reactionary message is transmitted by way of seminars. Anti-communist students are instructed by such teachers as General Edwin Walker, Robert Welch, Dan Smoot, Major Pedro Diaz Lanz, Kent Courtney, Dr. Bob Jones, Sr., Dr. Bob Jones, Jr., and Tom Andrews.[71] In 1965, Billy James Hargis advertised six summer sessions at his Christian Crusade Anti-Communist Youth University, Manitou Springs, Colorado, with the reminder that "on June 6th of this year, the Summit will open its 3rd year of summer seminars, designed to teach the Christian conservative youth of America the unvarnished truth regarding communism, socialism and their traceable offspring in the fields of religion, economics, politics, education and culture." [72] Here students may, to use Hargis' own advertisement, "Study the Dialectical Materialism at the Summit as well as Fabianism, the United Nations, Communist Tactics, Disarmament, and the Marxist N.C.C." [73]

While geographically distant, Carl McIntire's anti-communist summer school is very similar. The Twentieth Century Reformation Hour now owns the Christian Admiral, a hotel, at Cape May, New Jersey. Here, much like Hargis, McIntire holds summer school. McIntire introduces the Christian Admiral as a new addition to the Twentieth Century Reformation Movement. Such summer schools are perhaps the most graphic result of the reactionary preacher's attempt to isolate his followers from an untrustworthy world of vindictively bad men. McIntire enunciates the reactionary rationale for such education when he says that the Christian Admiral "had been founded to meet the great need of bringing Christians and patriots together that they might be informed, inspired, comforted, and challenged to face the issues which confront free men today—the Communist conspiracy and its drive upon the West, creeping Socialism as promoted by a false Kingdom of God ideology, the apostasy from belief in the infallible Scriptures which abounds on every hand." [74]

Secondly, the reactionaries seek to inform the in-group with an unrelenting and apparently limitless supply of reactionary literature. A visit to the headquarters of Billy James Hargis and W. S. McBirnie revealed one striking similarity. Both men have their headquarters literally stacked with pamphlets and brochures of every type, and they keep a full staff of secretaries busy mailing their releases to the reactionary brethren. The reactionaries' published literature has at least two identifying characteristics. It is voluminous; it covers virtually every conceivable topic. For variety of release, Hargis' Christian Crusade is undoubtedly champion. For example, Hargis advertises an infinite variety of pamphlets. Representative titles include "Current Com-

---

[71] *Christian Crusade*, May, 1965, p. 6.
[72] *Ibid.*
[73] *Ibid.*
[74] McIntire, *Testimony to Christ and Witness to Freedom*, n. p.

munist Party Lines Promoted by the National Council of Churches," "Radicalism of the Left . . . Americans for Democratic Action," "The Snake in Our Schoolroom . . . UNESCO We Put It There," and "Unmasking Martin Luther King Jr., the Deceiver." [75] To fit every need Hargis has other reactionary pamphlets at 25 for $1, 12 for $1, 5 for $1, and 3 for $1. Twenty-six of Hargis' 12½ minute anti-communist speeches on 16mm. black and white sound films may be purchased for $65 each or rented for $15. All this is in addition to Hargis' weekly and monthly newspapers, the *Weekly Crusader* and *Christian Crusade*, billed as The National Christian American Monthly. Among the better-selling books which Hargis has authored are *The Facts About Communism and Our Churches, Communist America . . . Must It Be,* and *The Real Extremists: The Far Left.*

A carefully contrived system of in-group education is the most characteristic response of the reactionary in the struggle with collectivism. The fact that Hargis, McIntire, McBirnie, and others are rapidly expanding this type of education suggests that the reactionary audience finds it the most suitable way to respond to the threat of a deceiving society which is deceitful because its institutional thrust is in contravention of God's law, and its apostatic leaders are out to confuse and mislead the people.

There can be little doubt that vast sums of money are being poured into the reactionaries' attempt at education by isolation. Forster and Epstein estimate that well over $14,000,000 is spent on reactionary propaganda each year. Recently, 70 or more foundations, 113 business firms and corporations, 25 public utilities, and 250 individuals were identified as having contributed at least $500. Foundations of considerable substance are heavy contributors such as O'Donnell Foundations of Dallas, Alfred P. Sloan Foundation of New York, William Vokers Foundation, Ada Hearne Foundation, Harnischfeger Corporation, Glenmede Trust Company of Philadelphia, and others. Significant corporations like Technicolor Inc., Schick Safety Razor Company, Flick-Reddy Corporation, Allen-Bradley Corporation, Henry Regnery Company, and, of course, Dr. Ross Dog and Cat Food Company have either made substantial contributions directly to the reactionary persuaders or have sponsored their programs.[76]

In summary, the reactionaries aim to isolate their followers from an evil world with an exclusive education system. The liberal establishment is well aware of this strident and affluent voice in the American pulpit and is girding for a long fight. A recent release from the National Council of Churches warned:

[75] *Do Something . . . Help Billy James Hargis Fight Communism.* A pamphlet, current listing of items available from the Christian Crusade headquarters, Tulsa, Oklahoma.
[76] Forster and Epstein, *Danger on the Right,* Appendix.

With varying emphasis the hundreds of organizations on the radical right agree that one target of theirs is the great majority of churches and churchmen who believe that the gospel has both individual and social relevance. . . . It is, however, well for churchmen to be acutely aware that the churches are only one and, for most right wingers, a secondary target. The primary challenge is to the basic philosophy of democracy and to government itself as we have it.[77]

[77] *Information Service*, Saturday, October 10, 1964.

POPULAR VS. EXPERIMENTAL RELIGION

Leroy Davis

During the past twenty years a polarity has been established between popular and experimentalist forms of preaching. The terms of this polarity may be deceptive due to the fact that no agreed-upon terminology has been accepted into general use to describe the phenomenon. Admittedly the terms "popular" and "experimental" are artificial and even hyperbolic. Their viability is based upon the degree to which they describe the practice which results from the words used by persons at either end of the polarity, characterized as fundamentally theological in nature; highly dichotomous at the popular extremity and unitary at the other.

Definitions

Popular religion is the usually observed activities, programs, ideas, bureaucracies, and orientations of the church at large. The emphases of popular religion are stability, conservatism, traditionalism, and a lack of involvement in concerns outside the institutional church. Experimentalism stresses social involvement, non-dogmatic theology, new and different ministries such as the industrial missions, and a disinterest with the minutiae of parochial life. The designations of the polarity are thus behavioral in nature. They correspond more to practice than to statements. There is, however, a characteristic pattern to the preaching which corresponds to the activities of the polarity, but it is more subtle than a behavioral description. Some facets of the definition of the polarity cannot be encapsulated in a formal definition. Generally speaking, the polarity under consideration has been described as liberal-conservative, Christian-pharisaic, communist-Christian, true-false, and false-true—depending upon the viewpoint of those making the description. The essential reason for this choice of terminology is that popular religion tends to be normative or popular in the customary usage of the term. In relation to the normative practice of religion, any deviation from it can be described as an experiment or a trial of something new. Even if experimentation with ideas or activities reflect biblical patterns, in relation to the status quo of normative or popular religion these practices would be new. Therefore, from the perspective of contemporary church life, popular religion denotes the generally accepted patterns. Experimentalism denotes change from the established pattern of church life.

The definition of the polarity is additionally complicated because persons tend to be humanly inconsistent in their resistance to categorizations. For example one person might maintain an experimentalist position with regard to civil rights, but a popular view in relation to birth control. Thus it is necessary to examine the specific issues involved in the polarity for effective discussion. A number of these emphases are the subjects of individual essays in this collection.

The popular-experimental polarity of American church life is well known to persons aware of what is happening in the church. An examination of church literature shows it in sharp relief. On the one hand is the approach taken by the Ecumenical Institute of Chicago whose *Bulletin* contains a lead article entitled "Cybernetics: Meta-images of the Twentieth Century." [1] Included in that issue are numerous reports of social undertakings in the Chicago area. This is, for purposes of definition, an example of an experimentalist approach. The *Christian Century* typically carries articles indicative of this end of the polarity. Representing the other end of the polarity are the editorial views expressed in the November 11, 1966 issue of *Christianity Today*. In discussing the report of the British Council of Churches, *Sex and Morality*, the editors express themselves quite clearly:

Although the report rightly opposed the *Playboy* version of deified eros and recommends increased instruction on sexual matters by schools and churches, it shares the shortcomings of *the theological pap dispensed by members of the new theology*. It assumes that man in his existential situation is able to determine truth and wisdom better than Bible and may jettison biblical teaching when the occasion calls for it.

On the subject of alcoholism, the same editors take a clear stand. "The epidemic of alcoholism is a national scandal. The real solution is not to try to avoid excessive drinking. It is not to drink at all." [2]

The speech delivered by Billy Graham at the Berlin Congress of 1966 indicates another aspect of the polarity. Quoting the statement of a person with whom he was to take issue, Mr. Graham said:

The redemption of the world is not dependent upon the souls we win for Christ. . . . There cannot be individual salvation. . . . Salvation has more to do with the whole society than with the individual soul. . . . We must not be satis-

[1] "Cybernetics: Meta-images of the Twentieth Century," *Bulletin of the Ecumenical Institute of Chicago*, III, No. 2.

[2] *Christianity Today*, XI, No. 34 (November 11, 1966).

fied to win people one by one. . . . Contemporary evangelism is moving away from winning souls one by one to the evangelization of the structures of society.

Mr. Graham then stated his own position: "We cannot accept this interpretation of evangelism. Evangelism has social implications, but its primary thrust is the winning of men to a personal relationship to Jesus Christ." Again for the purpose of definition, the approach taken by Mr. Graham would be placed in the popular end of the polarity, while the views with which he disagreed would be found in the experimentalist camp.

The Dichotomous Nature of Popular Preaching

Popular preaching is religious preaching. It begins with the assumption that contained within the Bible or the tradition of the church are capsulated truths that can be communicated by statement and illustration. Popular preaching is religious preaching because it explicates the text through the use of other religious insights and homely examples. Popular preaching seldom moves outside the sphere of church and home because these are the focuses of popular religion.

Undergirding the popular approach to preaching is a tacit theology. The theology of popular preaching is characterized by its lack of systematization, thus making generalization difficult. It is certain, however, that such theology is characterized by an anti-intellectual approach. There is little room for questioning in it. This is very clearly indicated by the monologic approach of popular preaching. If questions do arise, they are treated as obstacles to the digestion of the true faith, rather than as opportunities for growth. When the problem of doubt is raised in popular preaching it comes forth as an evil to be beaten down by the passage of time or through a massive dose of prayer. These two approaches are characterized by, "When I was young like you I had difficulty believing," and "Pray earnestly to your heavenly Father that the sin which blinds your eyes from the truth may be removed."

One of the interesting contrasts in popular preaching is that, while being anti-intellectual, it is highly cerebral. The cerebral nature of this preaching stems from its separation from most of the aspects of life. Because it is so removed, emotional content, save for pulpit sentimentality, is lost. Herein also lies the great difficulty which many preachers evidence in relating their biblical "truths" to existence.

A second characteristic of the theology undergirding popular preaching is its interesting combination of historical and nonhistorical approaches. Quite often the popular sermon begins with some kind of scriptural reference that forms the basis for the "truth" to be communicated. This reference is treated as being historical in nature, but without its appropriate context. Without that context the event or saying is thereby removed from the historical plane and elevated to the realms of nonhistory. It is thus not subject to interpretation by historical, i.e., human standards.

A typical use of biblical material can be seen through a brief analysis of a sermon preached on the text, "Behold, I make all things new," taken from Revelation 21:5. Following a few brief references to biblical passages that apparently indicate that Christians are to be happy about new things, this sermon is divided into three sections headed by the appropriate propositions: newness comes through sleep, conversion, and death. From a theological point of view, it would be difficult to take issue with the resurrection motif around which the sermon revolves. However, the text is only tangentially related to the main point of the sermon. This is customary practice. No reference is made to the context of the text, nor to the fruits of an exegesis of the passage.[3]

The more serious outcome of this approach is that the transfer of biblical events from a former world to a different one creates an almost insurmountable gulf between biblical content and human beings. The resurrection event, for example, through its treatment as an event belonging to a world different from the one now in existence prevents it from being associated with the vitally significant resurrection experiences of life. The term resurrection is not used to describe the growth of persons into fuller life through trial and testing because the Christian event is removed from the level of human experience. The classic example of the nonhistorical dichotomy of popular theology as expressed in preaching has to do with the picture of Jesus presented. Jesus is often received as the sweet young man who loved children and conversed in dulcet tones, probably in Elizabethan prose. The church has, of course, been debating the picture of Jesus for centuries, and it may be that no honest and complete depiction can be made of him. But one certainty remains—if he was historical, he was a man.

An interesting example of the typical treatment of the young man Jesus is to be found in a sermon by Methodist Richard C. Raines, entitled, *And Jesus Grew*. Speculating upon the home life of the boy Jesus, Mr. Raines stated:

And so Mary and Joseph insisted upon not being a drifting home, accommodating itself to the social pressures, but being the kind of home where the atmosphere encouraged their children to grow up into their full measure of the stature of Christ [?] . . . Strong against the tyranny of empire and the turbulence of resentment in their people's hearts and against the lax and easy ways, and the race prejudice [defined as the prejudice of the Jews toward others] and nationalism, Joseph and Mary created an environment where *this ineffably sensitive little boy* [Jesus] could grow up and appropriate all of his best of the tradition, history

[3] D. Reginald Thomas, a sermon, "Newness, a Miracle of God's Grace," *Things That Are to Be* (Philadelphia: The Evangelical Foundation, 1965).

336

and environment, and seemingly be *immune from the corruption and the strain of the worst.*[4]

This idealized picture of the atmosphere in which Jesus grew up and of the kind of child Jesus was is directly related to the nonhistorical base of popular preaching. Without sound exegesis which takes into account historical settings, viewpoints such as that quoted above can appear to be as viable history. The impact of these speculative views on theology and the church is enormous in that they tend to define the nature of Christian life. Such an idealized and therefore removed picture of Jesus tends to place all Christian insight into the same intellectually idealized and removed sphere.

The contrasting views of J. Ernest Somerville, pastor of the First Presbyterian Church of Philadelphia, Pennsylvania, are interesting in this connection:

It is difficult to see how such an approach to the Christian gospel can be reconciled with the life and ministry of the young man of Nazareth. If we can somehow read of him with fresh eye, unclouded by the weak, effeminate, too often woebegone and totally imaginary portraits that have been painted of him, we shall surely find instead the story of a man who loved life and who loved the people and who brought always with him a sense of vitality and color and joy. To the adherents of the straight and narrow, he must be, of course, as one English cleric described him, some years ago, Jesus the heretic. He came, after all, offering life. Life, he said, to the full; more abundant, bubbling up, running over.[5]

The lack of historical orientation leads directly to the literalist approach of popular theology in preaching. Because of the literal approach dogmas of the past are not called into question, even when they have nothing to do with the biblical account. This opens popular theology to the possibilities of including almost any notion that fits in with its general approach.

Theological literalism implies far more than the "literal" truth of biblical events. Its effect is to deny opportunity to question the premises upon which the structure is based. One of the more notable premises to be challenged recently is that concerning sex. While the popular pulpit extolls the singular virtue of connubial bliss, a revolution is taking place. In general, the position of popular preaching about sex can be effectively summarized as "no." Sex in the pulpit, so to speak, is still a dirty word according to popular theology. This attitude has great implication for the debate over the Virgin Birth with which James Pike is notably involved. His contention, echoing many theologians, is simply that there is meaning in this symbol which can be extracted and perhaps symbolized more meaningfully for our time. The opposition to this proposal quite likely stems from the popular notion that since sex is only for weak humanity, it has no place in its theology. The

---

[4] Richard C. Raines, a sermon, "And Jesus Grew," p. 3. (Mimeographed.)
[5] J. Ernest Somerville, a sermon, "The Straight and Narrow," *The Protestant Hour* (New York: United Presbyterian Church, 1966).

premises regarding sex are the faulty link in the arguments regarding the Virgin Birth.

The premises of popular religion and preaching are being called into question by the experimentalists. Popular theology is a hermetic whole, all parts of which are necessary for its continued existence. Theological literalism is not primarily related to the historical nature of biblical events. It is a total approach that is useful in defending a structure if one accepts the premise that that which is real is tangible, and that religious reality existed in time past sufficiently unlike the present so that it cannot be weighed now. Literalism means that the faith is described in terms of physically observable realities which have been elevated so that they cannot be examined as history. The literalist is enabled, thus, to have his cake and eat it too.

Popular preaching is dichotomous in nature. It contains a schism between Bible and man, thought and emotion, idea and application, the eternal and the now. This dichotomous approach results in the artificial polarities of sacred and secular, clergy and laity, belief and action, church and state. On its lowest level the dichotomy results in such things as the notion that church work is done in the church, that Monday through Saturday are intrinsically different from Sunday. In terms of preaching, the minister talks and the congregation listens.

Popular preaching is based upon the separation of speaker and hearer. The signification of separation is the institutional sanction given the preacher. He is set apart from others; or more properly, set into a different context. He becomes a part of that world about which he speaks and into which he attempts to guide others through preaching and church activity. The common attitudes about clergymen such as their separation into a more holy environment reveal a great deal about the theology which is tacitly, if not openly, preached. They all point to an underlying dichotomy. It is worthy of note that a dichotomy is a division of an essential whole into two parts.

The Unitary Nature of the Experimentalist Position

At some point after the Second World War the experimentalist reaction to popular preaching began in earnest. This development has led to ministries, such as the industrial missions, in which small-group discussion has replaced the sermon as the prime means of communication. Teaching, counseling, and other nonparochial ministries have mushroomed in the Protestant scene during recent years. These all involve means of communication that displace the sermon from its primacy. The churches, in addition, have given much attention to other types of communication, including periodicals, books, and pamphlets. In part, these developments represent a search for more effective means of communication than sermons.

There are two factors which impinge upon the development of the experimentalist position that are significant in this context. The first of these is the widespread importation of techniques of biblical study from Europe. The second is the attitude of life's relativity that grew from the involvement of persons in the Second World War. It is possible that the polarity under consideration would have been less obvious had not the postwar period been characterized in the churches by an attempted rampant return to the normalcy of innocence. During the fifties, churches tended to try to reestablish the patterns they maintained prior to worldwide conflict and despite the newer awarenesses of many persons. It was probably this effort which cast the experimental position in sharp relief as many preachers attempted to wrestle with the newer issues confronting them. Thus the experimentalist position can be seen both as an effort to deal realistically with the thoughts and events following the Second World War, and as a reaction against the general response of the churches in the postwar period.

The technique of biblical study known in what used to be called liberal seminaries, for many years prior to 1945, became available to many more persons through seminaries and through publications. It is important in this context that many members of the laity began reading and being stirred by viewpoints which opened new dimensions to their faith at the same time that their future preachers were being educated in these insights. A core of reasonably open-minded and informed hearers was created for the message of the experimentalist clergy. As these biblical studies developed, an attitude began to emerge that was strikingly at variance with the literalist position. The newer approach stressed a historical foundation which has culminated in such well-known treatments as Anglican bishop John A. T. Robinson's *Honest to God*. Such an undertaking as this makes a direct attack upon the dichotomy of popular religion through its historical approach. This constitutes a sundering of the literalist position by depriving it of its ability to elevate its premises above human speculation and criticism. The attempt of the experimentalists was, and continues to be, the discovery of the essentials of the faith.

This quest has been played out on the American scene in the person of Episcopal bishop James A. Pike. He has become a symbol of the experimentalist position, and it is often difficult for persons outside professional theological study to disengage the movement from his person. His writings are voluminous, and a rather good presentation of his odyssey was presented in the November 11, 1966 issue of *Time* magazine. The relationship of the two positions, popular and experimental, is shown with the greatest of clarity in the controversy surrounding Pike.

The second factor significant in the development of the experimentalist approach was the deep sense of relativity in life and in values that entered the mainstream of American life after 1945. This has been the cornerstone of the existentialist approach in literature and the arts. Sartre, Green, Albee,

Joyce, Camus, Kafka, Silone, and Faulkner, among others, are illustrative of the emotional content in the experimental approach. Therein resides a wrestling with many issues of life, probably most significantly with the issue of human evil and degradation. The innocence of popular theology is at striking variance with the existential-experimental approach. Anger, despair, loneliness, relativity, and meaninglessness are foreign to the popular approach but are woven throughout the experimental understandings. Although seldom stated philosophically, the issues to which many experimentalists address themselves in sermons have to do with these problems, either in the individual sense or in their cultural ramifications.

In the mature experimentalist expression, the human situation is treated with compassion and sensitivity. For example, Gordon M. Torgerson, while recognizing that life is harsh, denying, depriving, and often engulfed in darkness, affirms a resolution in terms of a radical association with Jesus through other persons.

In that week in Jerusalem, in so many ways, I had gone down to the level of Jesus. I had done it physically. In a greater sense I knew we had to do it spiritually—to get down through the clutter of the centuries . . . to get through this overlay of spiritual rubble on which we have built. Every man must do his own excavating . . . to get down deep to the original condition of faith. To get down to the level of Jesus, in a world of hate, we must still be able to express love. In a world of blindness to hold out hope of sight; in a world of intolerable burdens to help one another bear them; in a world of allurement, detachment, rationalization, to know that real Christianity is inescapable. When we get to that level we hear a voice saying, "Take up your cross and follow Me." [*]

The depth of insight into humanity, the emphasis upon common humanity, and the lack of concern with inherited minutiae indicates that the mature experimentalist approach is far more substantial than the label might indicate.

The civil rights issue has become something of a useful dividing line between experimentalist and popular clergymen. The issue at stake is not legal rights and prerogatives of minority groups, but rather a definition of what constitutes human beings. Popular religion is committed to a position of the ins and outs, whereby those outside are viewed as being less than fully human. The experimentalist view is that the means by which that division is determined reflects the sickness of a culture trapped in its own despair and seeking alleviation through an attempt to cut off the sickness by isolating a portion of the culture.

Experimentalists have been concerned to preach in many areas that bring the popular pole into opposition. The clearest example of this occurred in the 1964 national elections wherein the popularists had a clearly defined presi-

[*] Gordon M. Torgerson, a sermon, "On Getting Down to the Level of Jesus," pp. 5-6. (Mimeographed.)

dential candidate, as did the experimentalists. The issue soon degenerated into a dispute as to whether the clergymen held the prerogative of discoursing upon "political" matters. The experimentalists maintained that God's concern for persons is worked out by persons in the events of life. Thus there is no limit to the involvement of clergymen in any phase of life, since it all belongs to God anyway. The popularists tended to maintain that religious concerns transcend political affairs and the two should not be related. The establishment of a relationship between them would only be to the detriment of the removed nature of religious understanding. The argument was based, of course, upon the theological assumptions of popular religion. On the theological level, the experimental position tends to reduce to something approaching the radical Barthian position of God and man as the two basic realities. Many experimentalists do not, of course, think of themselves as being in the Barthian school of thought, but the underlying unitary approach is best characterized by that theologian. Whereas the popular position unites God, the Bible, the clergy, theology, Christ Jesus, and the church in one aspect of its dichotomy in opposition to the Devil, contemporary literature, the laity, practical thinking, mankind, and the secular world; the experimentalists tend to group all but God and Jesus, to some extent, into one category encompassing human experience.

The outstanding characteristic of the experimentalist viewpoint is its fluidity. To some this appears as indecision or even iconoclasm, but to others it represents a time of transition in which the certainties to come are not as yet formulated. The best sermonic indicator of this tendency is the reluctance of experimentalists to base their presentations upon theological truths, preferring rather to extract a theological insight from human experience and to use other than religious frameworks for their presentation.[7]

The experimentalist position is tied to the processes of change which are seen to be relevant to the unsettled changes of the contemporary period. In opposition to the popular approach, which is to attempt to maintain a steady position in the time of change, the experimentalists have tended to become involved in that change. If done wholeheartedly, this means that little if anything is exempt from questioning and criticism.

The Ethical Polarity

Thus far we have attempted to discuss some of the underlying understandings and insights involved in the polarity between popular and experimentalist preaching. While a general polarity exists, it is seen best in the specific issues and activities to which preachers address themselves. These issues include ecumenism, war and peace, civil rights, world affairs, and na-

[7] Lloyd Averill, a sermon, "The Context of Decision." (Mimeographed.)

tional politics, among others. Other essays in this volume having to do with these issues constitute additional data upon which a general description of the polarity can be made.

The issues of the polarity existing between popularists and experimentalists, being involved with activity as well as words, are probably most effectively considered under the general category of ethics. While something of an ethical revolution has taken place with which the experimentalists are intimately associated, popular pulpit ethics have remained virtually unchanged. The tendency of the popular approach is to view ethics within the framework of popular theology where the matters of concern are personal morals and the behavior appropriate to the church. The experimentalists, on the other hand, tend to view the structures of life, including its many institutions, as being of ethical concern.

Preaching seems to have its greatest effect when dealing with ethical concerns. This is especially the case with popular preaching. Two factors make ethical preaching on the popular level effective. The first of these is the veiled or blatant use of anxiety and guilt-provoking consequences of unethical behavior. Secondly, popular ethics is customarily concerned with matters such as attendance at church, giving of money, and generalities describing the value of work, the evils of sex, leisure, and alcohol. The concerns of popular ethics tend to be either very limited or shrouded in generalities large enough that contact with life situations of real ethical concern is minimized. Thus preaching on ethical matters of this nature can be said to have a rather significant impact, relative to its context. It is possible to infer some of the aspects of the impact of popular religious preaching simply from the meaning of the word "religious." Regardless of the several meanings this word has had in the past, it has now come to be restricted largely to the fulfillment of quasi-legal minutiae. When something, usually of little consequence, is performed in fulfillment of an expectation, whether having to do with the church or staying on a diet, it is said to be done religiously. The opposite, of course, is to undertake something scientifically. In our culture this means to do it with intelligence, understanding, and thoroughness. The contrast involved in these two words is that of significant, meaningful activity versus vacant repetitiveness. The definition of religious is directly related to the character of religious preaching. It presents itself as being concerned with the little things of life, the niceties of biblical words and personal relationships. Good taste dictates that real issues are seldom broached. From this approach to preaching stem the religious activities of the church—activities repeated endlessly as an end within themselves. The two are intimately related, the one reinforcing the other. The perceived content of preaching is seen reflected in the activities undertaken in and by a church, individually and collectively.

The premise of popular ethical preaching is that there are certain well-defined standards against which behavior can be measured. Experimentalist ethical preaching does not tend to accept as normative the literalist and often incorrect interpretations of biblical and other standards. The experimentalists tend to include in their ethical purview the institutions of men as well as individuals. It is the nature of institutions to be compromised in some manner or another, and the ethical norms applied to institutions must take account of the ambiguities of human groups, whether they be business, community, social, or church groups.

The impact of experimental ethical preaching is probably more diffuse than that of the popular. It is unfortunate that publications such as *Playboy*, have taken some of the experimentalist views and constructed hedonistic viewpoints which appear to have the sanction of experimentalist ethical theology. Such undertakings as those of *Playboy* tend to identify experimentalist ethics with libertine hedonism. Such an identification is, of course, patently reductionistic.

Preaching based upon popular ethics has three major emphases: legalism, pietism, and moralism. These emphases devolve from the dichotomy of popular theological understanding. Due to the elevation of theological understanding from life, a gap between ethical insight and human activity is generated. Roman Catholic ethical thought bridges this gap through the principles of natural law derived from reason, while Protestantism, on the other hand, has no effective casuistry save that subjectively apprehended through personal revelation. In either case, the end products are the three emphases given above which serve the purpose of expressing on the human level that which is felt to be true on the divine.

Legalism is the attempt to make the biblical and theological proscriptions applicable to human existence within a literalist context. Thus maxims such as the "Golden Rule" and the "Ten Commandments" are applied to personal situations as specific guidelines for behavior, without regard for the human historical context of those statements. Without a historical sense, they are envisioned as divine regulations to be applied without modification to human life. Moreover, there is no latitude possible in responding to these regulations because they are encompassed about the mores and folkways of the portion of culture which is involved in popular religion. As was mentioned earlier, due to the uncritical acceptance engendered by the literal approach, concerns similar to those already held easily become a part of the structure. The content of legalistic ethics includes, therefore, a host of cultural understandings which interpret and determine proper ethical conduct. The attitudes expressed by preachers relative to divorce, for example, reflect particular cultural norms that have tenuous relationship to biblical injunction.

Pietism is the individualization and subjectivization of legalistic maxims. It is based upon the framework in which the church operates, namely in terms of individual persons as those persons relate to the church. Pietism is the opposite of community commitment. From the pietistic emphasis comes the concern with doing "spiritual" things that "elevate" the individual. Involved also is a tendency to equate rightness with that which makes one feel subjectively good. The pietistic viewpoint stresses an individually concerned ethic which is guided by subjective feelings of goodness. This is, of course, tantamount to feeling good because one has lived up to certain expectations.

Moralism is the reduction of legalistic maxims to levels readily attainable by persons. Because the foundation of the ethic is made absolute and hence removed from life, it is impossible for persons to maintain perfect obedience to it. Instead of utilizing the approach of forgiveness to mediate the discrepancies between desire and fact, moralism reduces the demands to simple, repetitive rules. The connection between moralism and the contemporary meaning of "religious" is at once apparent. The contribution of moralism is to make absolute the cultural concomitants of popular ethics, such as those concerning alcohol, smoking, attending church every Sunday, giving money to the church, and so forth. It is possible, therefore, to fulfill the ethical imperative through obedience to readily observable regulations. This is, obviously, what Jesus called Phariseeism.

Popular pulpit ethics, even when sophisticated through the use of the more lax folkways of some aspects of society, remain legalistic in orientation. There is no essential difference between the injunction to drink in moderation and that of abstinence. Both are regulations, regardless of their content. Popular ethics has almost nothing to say about work, recreation, politics, mental health, cybernetics, labor unions, war, economics, law, education, or any of the other realities of life. This has to do partially with its pietistic individualism and with its separation of existence from its ethical foundations. The best examples of popular ethics are the various codes of conduct adopted by organizations. When examined closely they reveal themselves to be little more than a statement of current practice, which is the moralistic heart of popular ethics.

In radical distinction to the legalistic ethic of popularism is the situational or contextual approach of the experimentalists. Situational ethics attacks the legalistic approach through its emphasis upon the context of decision. This emphasis is derived from the experimentalists' concern to draw the fundamental distinction between God and man rather than between church and world. In so doing, the artifically elevated biblical maxims become a part of human experience in all its ambiguity. In that context they are no longer absolutes, but partake rather of the quest of persons to discover the meaning of ethical conduct in their lives and institutions. The experimental approach is neither existential nor antinomian. It is an attempt to confront the *meaning* of behavior within living situations.

344

The experimentalist approach to ethics concerns itself basically with decision-making prior to an action. That is, it does not accept absolutely binding rules for determining *ex post facto* whether that which has been undertaken is right or wrong. Since it operates in the gray area of prior decision, it is not concerned to judge after the fact. It is, thus, much more open and tolerant than popular ethics. Popularists view this approach, of course, as not being ethics at all. Experimentalism bases its ethics upon a universal law of love, with love treated as a verb rather than as a noun. It has, therefore, little systematic content, being a methodology rather than a substantive ethics. In place of rules, this approach utilizes questions about what is necessary, the means to obtain it, the motivations governing the potential event, and the foreseeable consequences. This is not very much different from the approach of John Dewey.

The experimentalist approach is based ultimately upon a commitment to the person of Christ Jesus and devolves from the character of that relationship. It is, thus, personal and relational in nature. This is in distinction to the popular approach through the regulation derivitive from personal relations with that person. Popular ethical preaching is based upon unexamined regulations, taken as being absolute in nature, while the experimentalist approach is that of ascertaining the better response in given contexts. Experimental preaching is, therefore, built upon a dual foundation of various substantive ethics, whether Christian or not, and upon living situations. Through asking questions, rather than applying rules, decisions of conduct are reached. This involves repeated wrestling with the fundamentals of human relationships as they relate to the basic relationships of man and God.

One of the dilemmas involved in assessing the ethical preaching polarity is that the proponents of the respective positions often either have not made their positions clear, or else not been understood in the spirit in which they have spoken and written. For example, Dr. David B. Watermulder in preaching upon the second commandment had the following to say about situational ethics:

This ancient commandment also strikes at another of modern idolatries—the religion of easy tolerance which becomes almost totally permissive. We find it suggested in the new books on what is called "contextual ethics" or "situational ethics," . . . Indeed, the so-called new ethic is not new at all. From time immemorial men have erected their images and idols in the name of the living God. These words may easily be misunderstood. Anyone who has heard me, year in and year out, knows that I am not appealing to a rigid, brittle legalism which cancels out the mercy, acceptance and forgiveness of a loving Heavenly Father. . . . Truly tolerance, on the other hand, does not come from an obey-the-impulse, do-as-you-please philosophy. Our ethical decisions—sexual and social, private and public— do not come out of isolation from the past—its laws, traditions, experience and revelation. *Nor can we make them without thinking of the future—the consequences of our attitudes.*[8]

Due to the fact that Dr. Watermulder appeals to the same propositions as do contextual theologians, one is tempted to conclude the polarity is founded more upon misunderstanding than upon a difference of opinion. There is, of course, some truth in that allegation, for men of sensitivity and learning would tend to base their ethical understandings upon a dual consideration for the value of tradition and the importance of ascertaining the consequences of behavior within contemporary contexts.

Not all religious leaders are able to balance the past and the present, and so the polarity does tend to represent a striking difference of opinion. The popular ethical position was succinctly stated by at least one clergyman in a controversy over the music of Duke Ellington, a performance of which had been scheduled by an ecumenical church group.

The Rev. John D. Bussey of the Bethesda Baptist Church, said yesterday he drew up the resolution opposing the performance because the orchestra leader's life is "opposed to what the church stands for." Mr. Bussey cited Ellington's "nightclub playing and the fact the music is just considered worldly." He said that when persons become Christians "they stop their worldly ways." [9]

It is sometimes not recognized that the popular views of the Baptist minister quoted above are essentially the same as those of persons from different social groups. A survey of attitudes of Episcopal church women was undertaken by the diocese of California, and it was discovered that most of them discounted ritual observance, doctrinal orthodoxy, and familiarity with the Bible as "very important" indicators of religiousness. By contrast ninety percent said how much a person helps his fellowman is very important in determining his religiousness. Despite the conviction that true religiousness is closely allied with ethical behavior, the women preferred to see the institutional church devote itself to ritual and personal matters.

The most important functions of the church were felt to be providing the sacrament (ninety-three percent) and educating children in traditional Christian beliefs (ninety-two percent). Due to the differing socio-economic levels of the Baptist and Episcopal churches, the popular approach takes differing forms but in essence is the same. Lower socio-economic populism tends to base its withdrawal from the world upon an appeal to the folkways of the "nice" people of the lower middle class. The Episcopalians tend to base their withdrawal from the world on the fact that the church should not be soiled by coming into contact with the sordidness of social inferiors. There is no

[8] David B. Watermulder, a sermon, "Our Images and Idols" (Bryn Mawr, Pennsylvania: The Sermon Distribution Fund, n. d.).

[9] *Washington Post,* December 1, 1966, p. B-7.

essential difference between these views. Both rationalize the withdrawal of the church from life.[10]

The fundamental differences between the groups of the polarity arises from the differing view of Scripture they hold. The popular view comes from its general literalist base and is typified by D. Reginald Thomas' sermon, "Standards by Which We Are Judged." Although the message culminates in assertions regarding the importance of ethical deeds as well as words, its basis is literalist. In seeking the ex post facto standards by which persons are to be judged, Mr. Thomas concludes that "we have from Jesus himself the standard of judgment in the verse concerning the judgment and separation of the worthy from the unworthy." The verses which were from Jesus himself were Matt. 25:31-36, 41-43.[11]

In distinction to the literalist approach to ethics is the situational, as typified by Letty M. Russell:

If we are willing to put our trust in God's love, then in each situation in life we will seek the way to treat other persons justly, with mercy and faithfulness. Then we find certain aids given to us to carry out such relationships with other people. . . . One, the Bible gives us the knowledge of the way God acts and wants us to act, and the example of Christ's life. This knowledge is not given to us as a set of rules, but as a guide for living, to help us and give us advice in trying to make dicisions.[12]

In the experimentalist view, there is room for ambiguity and uncertainty.

There are few things that are absolutely black and white. Under some circumstances, the Protestant Church says that divorce can be justified. To those who say all divorce is sin, we can respond that it's possible to have greater sin (unwholesomeness—damage to life) with two people maintaining a home.[13]

The same preacher, in dealing with alcoholic beverages, ultimately based his argument upon contextual understandings.

My concluding statement would be that each of us has to face the subject on a personal basis. We all have to ask whether drinking will hurt us as individuals, whether it creates any concern for our family or associates, . . . and whether it is good for society. We need to ask whether our drinking is encouraging someone else who may be destroyed by alcohol. This is not a matter that can be settled by laying down hard fact and fast rules. Such rules have not worked in the past and they will not work now. This is a matter for individual decision on the part of every Christian man and woman.[14]

[10] *Washington Post*, December 31, 1966, p. A-11.

[11] D. Reginald Thomas, a sermon, "Standards by Which We Are Judged," *Judgment and Christmas Messages* (Philadelphia: The Evangelical Foundation, 1966), pp. 7-8.

[12] Letty M. Russell, a sermon, "Right and Wrong," p. 3, March 1, 1964. (Mimeographed.)

[13] Gordon M. Torgerson, a sermon, "The Really Great Divorce," p. 1. (Mimeographed.)

[14] Gordon M. Torgerson, a sermon, "The Problem of Modern Drinking," p. 6. (Mimeographed.)

The polarity between the popularists and experimentalists does not tend to arise in the public view unless representatives of the experimentalist position make statements or undertake activities that result in a reaction by the popularists. It is most unusual for the differences to emerge clearly and in writing. One of the clearest examples of the polarity occurred in the Episcopal diocese of Washington in the summer of 1966.

The polarity came into public view when the *Washington Post* of July 10, 1966, carried an article based upon a vestry resolution by All Souls Church, made available to the press. That article stated:

> One of Washington's major Episcopal Churches has halved its annual contribution for the mission program of the Diocese of Washington because it says the money is used to finance public demonstrations and to influence legislation. The parish's officials apparently meant to register their objection, among other things, to the involvement in social activities of the dioceses suffragan bishop, the Right Rev. Paul Moore, Jr.

The resolution passed by that vestry in June 1966 and sent to a number of Episcopal parishes in the diocese justified its action as follows: "On February 22, 1966," the resolution stated, "we heard our own Suffragan Bishop approve the application of economic pressures by minorities against business to gain their ends, so we are sure the Church will approve the reduction in our giving." The resolution went on to state:

> Whereas our laymen believe in the separation of Church and State, we do not want our contributions to the Lord's work used to propagandize controversial state subjects such as so-called "Fair-employment," sale or rental of private property, termination of nuclear defense experiments, . . . nor do we approve the use of church funds or personnel to foster public demonstrations or marches that tend to breed disrespect for law and order and the property rights of others.

The vestry preferred that the church restrict its activities to the "Fundamental spiritual concerns that effect [sic] the destinies of the souls of its members and nonbelievers."

The response of the bishops of the diocese, mailed to the clergymen of the diocese, started in part:

> We do not need to belabor the reason for the Church's involvement in social matters. Ever since Moses demanded better labor relations for the Israelites in Egypt, the people of God have known that justice was a concern of the Almighty and, therefore, our concern. The prophets, Jesus, himself, in his confrontation with the powers-that-be in Jerusalem, the apostles, and the Church down through the ages, have shown that one cannot carry out the demand to love one's neighbor without struggling to better the conditions in which he lives.

Involvement in the ethical concerns of the world beyond the church is probably one of the more significant dividing lines between popular and experimental ethics. The experimentalist view has been succinctly stated by Letty M. Russell:

Christ is the Lord of the whole world and he is at work guiding men and helping them to gain freedom from poverty, prejudice, ignorance and disease. Where other groups of people, be they revolutionaries, politicians, freedom riders, school teachers, are doing the job of helping men to have a share of God's creation, they seem more and more to be the hands and feet of Christ and not the church which meets on Sunday to pray, and forgets the world in which it lives.[15]

In addressing himself to the Vietnam conflict, Norman DePuy effectively summarized the growing experimentalist position in regard to the role and function of the ministry in ethical matters:

You feel, by now, that I overlook the complexities of power and the necessity for the President to get elected and to satisfy the warmonger in our society. Not at all, I am not President. I can afford to look at the thing first as a Christian, then as a Republican, or whatever. And further, the compromises the President will rightly make will be strongly determined by the mentality of the populace. Altering that mentality is my profession as a preacher, and yours as a Christian.[16]

The experimentalist view of ethics is broad and diffuse. Norman DePuy, editor of *Missions*, grouped together some of the experimentalist concerns in his column:

I'll never be able to tell you how a man can all himself be a Christian and yet be a segregationist. I'll never be able to tell you how the mainstream churches can be blithely ignorant of the very pointed things Jesus said about pacifism, to say nothing of the pacifism of the Cross. I'll never be able to explain, if I live to be a thousand and four, how so many Christians can treat mission as if it were an option. I'll forever be stunned by people who feel that they have grasped the wonderful, profound grace of God merely because they do not say bad words. I am awed by Christians who worry more about someone who drinks wine with his dinner than they do over a child who dies in Asia for the want of a cup of rice.[17]

Involvement in the concerns and needs of the world casts a distinctive character upon the experimentalist movement. In addition to the experimentalists' disenchantment with mere words, there is a certain zeal for a return to the simplicity of biblical thought and action. Mr. Lloyd Averill in *Holy Partisans and Godly Troublemakers* has indicated both the experimentalist emphasis upon activity and the biblical simplicity of approach:

And perhaps in this movement for civil rights God is also driving us Christians out of our sanctuaries and into the streets, out of our isolation from the world

[15] Letty M. Russell, a sermon, "These Men . . . Who Have Turned the World Upside Down," p. 1. (Mimeographed.)

[16] Norman DePuy, *Current*, VI, No. 28 (September 15, 1965), 3. (Bulletin of the First Baptist Church, Moorestown, New Jersey.)

[17] Norman DePuy, "Oh, for a Nice Warm Category," *Missions*, CLXIV (November, 1966), 10.

and into involvement with the world, as he himself became involved with the world in Jesus Christ. Perhaps this is his way of teaching us that prayer and professions of love are not enough; to labor is to pray, and work is love made visible. Perhaps he is seeking to draw us out of our old irrelevance and to give us fresh pertinence.

Those of you who make no pretense at being Christians will have to settle these things with your own conscience in your own way. For the moment I am not particularly interested in what you do or don't do, or in what you think or don't think. But the time has come for those of us who call ourselves Christians either to give up our unholy tolerance and our misplaced devotion to social harmony or to give up calling ourselves Christians. Indeed, it may be time for some of us, at least, to confess, by the grace of God that what we try to pass off as tolerance is really moral indifference, and what we try to peddle as devotion to social concord is really cowardice. Because the truth is that we have not cared enough to share the Bible's prejudice, and we have not dared enough to become godly troublemakers.[18]

The ethical polarity between popular and experimental positions can be characterized as the difference between a church-related ethic and a world-related ethic. Since the experimentalists tend not to recognize as great a difference between church and world as do the popularists, the ethical approach of the experimentalists tends to be more unitary than the dichotomous popular position. One of the great difficulties involved in treating these ethical positions is the fact that ethical understanding is in such a state of flux that generalizations about it can be tentative at best.

Conclusion

The polarity between popular and experimental preaching has been seen to be characterized by a fundamentally different theological approach. Popular preaching is based upon a dichotomous theological outlook that influences the preaching and activities based upon it. Experimentalist preaching, on the other hand, tends to be based upon a more unitary approach with much emphasis given to human situations and institutions. This polarity has arisen from the attempt of the experimentalists to deal meaningfully with the issues which have arisen in American culture following the Second World War. Popular preaching, conversely, has tended to disregard these issues in an attempt to maintain its prewar approach. Had popular religion been able to incorporate some of the changes resultant from the period following the Second World War, the experimentalists would constitute merely an advance fringe of the church rather than an extremity of polarity.

This polarity has tended to be seen most graphically in the respective actions undertaken by representatives of each group. There has been little

[18] Lloyd Averill, a sermon, "Holy Partisans and Godly Troublemakers," pp. 4 and 8. (Mimeographed.)

discussion of the fundamental differences dividing these groups. As time passes, however, it will become increasingly necessary for the groups to define their respective positions. This hopefully will result in a fruitful theological debate that will bring to the surface the issues of the time. The development of an appropriate and stable theological outlook, influencing the whole operation of the church, may be the most significant result of this polarity.[19]

[19] The sermonic extracts presented in this essay have been kindly provided by the authors. The extracts were chosen because of their representativeness and because of the stature of the preachers. We do not intend any classification of individual preachers into the artificial and hyperbolic categories used in the essay. This is an essay about ideas, not personalities.

18

SEPARATION OF CHURCH AND STATE

_____Charles Stewart_____

When the religious issue flared up during the 1960 presidential campaign, it was but a continuation of a long-standing controversy. Most American colonies were settled according to religious beliefs: Puritans in Massachusetts, Quakers in Pennsylvania, Catholics in Maryland, Anglicans in Virginia. The majority sect frequently became the established church, and the state enforced its beliefs and practices.[1] Cruel intolerance was not uncommon in some colonies. In spite of campaigns for religious freedom and the separation of church and state by men like Roger Williams, William Penn, and Lord Baltimore, only four colonies had no established churches on the eve of the American Revolution. Rhode Island alone had complete separation of church and state and no laws unfavorable to Catholics and non-Christians.[2]

The intermingling of religions during the Revolutionary War, together with a wave of religious indifference and skepticism, created a more tolerant atmosphere and lessened the influence of established churches. A movement toward religious liberty resulted.[3] In December, 1785, an act of the Virginia Assembly guaranteed religious freedom and a policy of no established church in Virginia. Other states followed the example and prepared the way for national action when the Constitutional Convention convened in 1787.[4]

James Madison, Thomas Jefferson, and Patrick Henry—all from Virginia—argued for constitutional guarantees.[5] The final draft of the Constitution,

---

[1] Anson Phelps Stokes, _Church and State in the United States_, I (3 vols.; New York: Harper & Brothers, 1950), 152-63. Loren P. Beth, _The American Theory of Church and State_ (Gainesville, Florida: The University of Florida Press, 1958), pp. 33-39.

[2] Beth, _The American Theory of Church and State_, p. 59.

[3] Anson Phelps Stokes and Leo Pfeffer, _Church and State in the United States_ (New York: Harper & Row, 1964), pp. 33-39.

[4] Beth, _The American Theory of Church and State_, pp. 62-65; and Stokes, _Church and State in the United States_, I, 366-97.

[5] Stokes and Pfeffer, _Church and State in the United States_, pp. 39-40, list the following as major spokesmen for religious freedom: Benjamin Franklin, John Witherspoon, George Mason, Isaac Backus, George Washington, Patrick Henry, Samuel Livermore, Thomas Paine, John Carroll, Thomas Jefferson, James Madison, and John Leland.

however, contained only a single clause directly concerning religion; it read, "No religious Test shall ever be required as a Qualification to any office or public Trust under the United States." [6] Madison, Henry, and others were dissatisfied. The single clause said nothing about establishment of a state church or religious freedom. Soon after Washington's inauguration, Madison submitted several amendments to the new Constitution. The first clause of the First Amendment, passed by Congress in 1789 and ratified by the states in 1791, read: "Congress shall make no law respecting an establishment of religion, or prohibiting the free exercise thereof." [7] These constitutional guarantees far exceeded those of other eighteenth-century nations.

Thomas Jefferson wrote optimistically in 1802 that the Constitution had erected "a wall of separation between church and state." [8] Nearly constant assaults and defenses, however, have made the "wall of separation" resemble a sieve. Congregationalism remained the state-favored church in Massachusetts until 1833; only Protestants could serve in the New Hampshire legislature until 1852; and persons holding public offices in New Jersey were limited to Protestants until 1874.[9] Succeeding generations of clergy debated such state limitations as well as tax exemption of churches, governmental aid to parochial schools, and religious observances in public schools. Indeed, the proper degree of separation between church and state remained questionable. Sixty years after Jefferson's declaration, for instance, the Rev. Henry W. Bellows of New York, one of the most prominent clergymen in America, declared "Nothing can be less real than the imaginary separation between Church and State in this country." [10]

Controversies over Church and State

By the 1830's, Protestants were viewing with alarm the ever-growing Roman Catholic minority. Papal claims to complete control over its members and pronouncements against separation of church and state convinced Protestant spokesmen that the "wall of separation" was in grave danger.[11] Groups like the American or Know-Nothing Party tried to prevent Catholics from gaining

[6] Thomas James Norton, *The Constitution of the United States: Its Sources and Its Application* (New York: America's Future, 1943), p. 279.

[7] *Ibid.*

[8] Thomas Jefferson, *Writings*, ed. H. A. Washington, VII (9 vols.; New York: John O. Riker, 1853-54), 113. Jefferson made this statement in a letter to the Danbury Baptist Association of Connecticut, January 1, 1802. Photograph of the letter is in Stokes, *Church and State in the United States*, Vol. I.

[9] Stokes and Pfeffer, *Church and State in the United States*, pp. 76-82.

[10] Henry W. Bellows, *The State and the Nation—Sacred to Christian Citizens* (New York: J. Miller, 1861), p. 4.

[11] Pope Pius IX's encyclical "Syllabus of Errors," issued in 1864, contained the following declarations: "The State has not the right to leave every man free to profess and embrace whatever religion he shall deem true. . . . It has not the right to separate itself from the Church. . . . It has not the right to exclude the pontiff or clergy from all dominion over temporal affairs."

any local, state, or national political office. Above all, Protestants feared either a Catholic or pro-Catholic candidate winning the presidency. The so-called religious issue, usually the assertion that the Catholic church was controlling one of the presidential candidates, entered into the elections of 1856, 1876, 1884, and 1896.[12]

The twentieth century has witnessed continued furor over the separation of church and state. Most old issues have remained unresolved, and new controversies have arisen over birth control, federal aid for parochial schools, bus transportation for students in parochial schools, and prayer in the public schools. Theodore Roosevelt, Taft, and Wilson all faced charges of being pro-Catholic.[13] The most heated battle took place in 1928 when Alfred E. Smith, a practicing Catholic, won the Democratic nomination for president. The religious issue played a major role in a bitter campaign; Smith was soundly defeated. Following World War II, the United States Supreme Court more and more was placed in the position of determining violations of the constitutional provisions separating church and state.

The decade of the 1960's may well prove to be the peak of controversy over this question. Its first year saw the nomination and election of the first Roman Catholic president; its second has been called the "most important single year in the legal history of American church and state relations" [14] because of the volume of court cases on the issue; and succeeding years have witnessed a continuing series of momentous Supreme Court decisions concerning governmental sponsorship of religious activities. The pulpit has been actively involved in all these controversies, particularly concerning itself with the 1960 campaign of John F. Kennedy and the Supreme Court decisions on prayer and Bible reading in the public schools.

A Roman Catholic for President, 1960

After Alfred E. Smith's presidential defeat in 1928, the religious issue lay dormant in the political world for nearly thirty-two years. Political tacticians felt that a Catholic's religion alone would send him to certain defeat; thus,

---

[12] Stokes, *Church and State in the United States*, II, 392-421; and David Ellis Walker, Jr., "Invention in Selected Sermons of Ministers Opposing the Election of a Roman Catholic Presidential Candidate: 1960" (unpublished Master's thesis, The University of Florida, 1961), pp. 13-22, contain discussions of the religious issue in presidential campaigns.

[13] Walker, "Invention in Selected Sermons," pp. 17-19. Roosevelt was suspect because of his previous efforts to persuade the pope to appoint Archbishop John Ireland a cardinal. Taft was criticized for having paid Catholic friars for their land in the Philippines while he was governor of those islands. Wilson was suspected by some of being a Catholic or at least pro-Catholic.

[14] George R. LaNoue, *A Review of Church-State Legal Developments 1961-62* (Background Reports, National Conference of Christians and Jews, September, 1962), p. 17.

no political party wanted to nominate a Catholic for either the presidency or the vice-presidency.[15]

John Fitzgerald Kennedy, a young, popular, and ambitious senator from Massachusetts, a Roman Catholic, disagreed with the party professionals. He wanted to be president of the United States, and he thought he could win. Kennedy started preparing for the presidential nomination soon after losing a bid for the vice-presidential nomination in 1956. By late fall 1959, his religious affiliation and potential candidacy were being aired in the religious and secular presses, but his impressive showings in the Wisconsin and West Virginia primaries really brought his religion into full national view.[16] His nomination at the Democratic national convention in July assured the "religious issue" a prominent role in the campaign.[17]

Undoubtedly some clergymen opposed Kennedy and his Catholic faith through sheer prejudice. However, it seems likely that most clerical opposition occurred because of sincere convictions that a Catholic in the White House could mean an end of religious liberty and the separation of church and state in America. For clergymen with this conviction, the threat was increased by two known facts: (1) anti-Catholic feeling had declined since the 1928 campaign of Alfred E. Smith, and (2) the percentage of Catholics in the population of the United States had increased sharply since the twenties.[18] Kennedy stood a good chance of winning the presidency. Anti-Kennedy sermons emanated from pulpits even before the Democratic convention; they continued to do so until election eve. Clerics did not hesitate to express their fears:

We call upon all Americans, let us preserve our Christian heritage for our wonderful children and their children! We must not turn our families over to Catholicism by electing a Roman Catholic as President or Vice-President. NOW IS THE TIME TO STOP ROME'S MARCH INTO THE WHITE HOUSE. SPEAK UP . . . SPREAD THE TRUTH . . . SAVE AMERICA . . . VOTE AGAINST A ROMAN CATHOLIC FOR PRESIDENT.[19]

[15] Theodore H. White, *The Making of the President 1960* (New York: Atheneum Publications, 1961), p. 55.

[16] *Ibid.*, pp. 78-114. A good discussion of the growth of the religious issue during the 1960 presidential campaign.

[17] Thirteen anti-Kennedy sermons were studied. They ranged in time from February to November, 1960, and included Church of Christ, Baptist, Methodist, United Church of Christ, and fundamentalist clergy. Sermons against the religious issue were very difficult to locate. Five sermons were studied in detail. They ranged in time from September to November, 1960, and included Baptist, Methodist, Jewish, and Roman Catholic clergymen. In addition, the writer reviewed written communications of clergymen concerning the religious issue.

[18] White, *The Making of the President 1960*, pp. 238-42; and Walker, "Invention in Selected Sermons," pp. 21-22.

[19] Bob Grube, "A Roman Catholic President? NO!" *Western Voice* (Englewood, Colorado), June 23, 1960, p. 4. The sermon was delivered in May.

Preaching Enters National Politics, 1960

Sermons contained references to the "Roman Church," to "Roman Hierarchy," and to "Rome" rather than to "Roman Catholic," "Catholic," or "Vatican." Purely partisan appeals crept into some sermons. The Rev. Harvey W. Springer, pastor of the First Baptist Church of Englewood, Colorado, exclaimed, "Our liberties have cost rivers of sacrificial Protestant blood," and, "This country must be run by Protestant Americans." [20]

On the opposite pole were clergymen who contended that religion should never be a political issue. This conviction led a great many ministers to refuse even to mention the election from their pulpits. Reinhold Niebuhr wrote later, "I have never preached an election sermon taking a party side and I regard such sermons as very nauseous." [21] Other clerics seemed to feel that any preaching on Kennedy's religion would be an admission that religion was a legitimate campaign issue. As the campaign progressed, however, some clergymen felt compelled to answer the mounting charges against Kennedy and Catholicism. They did so with reservations. For instance, the Rev. James William Morgan of the University Methodist Church, Austin, Texas, stated, "As the weeks have gone by, I have sadly realized that I cannot possibly speak on this Reformation Sunday and ignore this issue. . . . But, oh, how painful to thread your way through these issues and be utterly fair!" [22] Morgan and others were afraid that, if the anti-Kennedy, anti-Catholic sermons remained unchallenged, a rise of religious intolerance and dissension would result. Rabbi Robert I. Kahn of the Congregation Emanu El in Houston, Texas, declared that anti-Catholic preaching was a "breach of the wall of separation," and warned that the religious issue "has aroused a religious war . . . a conflict which is tearing this nation apart." [23] Defenders of John Kennedy and Catholicism tended to devote their sermons to answering the basic arguments developed in the opposition's preaching.

Catholicism, Church and State

Although anti-Kennedy sermons varied in degree of emotionalism and in particulars, the basic theme was the same: The Roman Catholic Church, in theory and in practice, opposes the American tradition of religious freedom and the separation of church and state. Clergymen supported the *theory* part of their thesis by quoting passage after passage from "official" Catholic sources, often with little or no personal commentary. The amount of evidence

[20] Harvey W. Springer, a pamphlet, *Catholicism in America*, pp. 9 and 11. Delivered several times throughout the country in the fall of 1960.

[21] Letter from Reinhold Niebuhr to David Ellis Walker, Jr., November 18, 1960

[22] James William Morgan, "Reformation Day and the Election," p. 1. (Typed manuscript.) Delivered on October 30, 1960.

[23] Robert I. Kahn, "The Religious Issues in the Presidential Campaign," p. 6. (Typed manuscript.) Delivered on October 7, 1960.

was remarkable. However, "official" remained undefined. Statements like "absolute authority rests in Rome," [24] and "Remember, now, in the Roman Catholic Church there is but one voice and source of authority in faith and morals, namely the Pope" [25] appeared to define "official" as papal pronouncements under the power of infallibility. Analysis of evidence used, however, revealed these characteristics of "official" sources: (1) any statement ever made by any Pope,[26] (2) statements by the Catholic hierarchy, (3) statements in Catholic newspapers and periodicals, and, importantly, (4) any book containing the imprimatur of a bishop.[27] Sermons contained a variety of both old and very recent materials, many of which were documented to the extent of citing page numbers and naming the bishops under whose imprimaturs the sources were published. The *Catholic Encyclopedia*, Catholic textbooks, Pope Pius IX's "Syllabus of Errors," and an April, 1948, issue of *Civiltà Cattolica* appeared repeatedly in anti-Kennedy sermons. All these sources claimed that the Roman Catholic Church, the one true church, should have state support, and they even questioned the right of existence of other religious sects.

Churchmen pointed out that these views were advocated in the United States as well as in foreign, Catholic-dominated countries. "But do any Catholics in America believe such things? Definitely!" The Rev. Robert Lovell of the Temple Baptist Church, Champaign, Illinois, declared, "Fathers Ryan and Boland in their *Catholic Principles of Politics* (issued under Cardinal Spellman's imprimatur), plainly assert that the Roman Catholic religion is the one true religion, that the Roman Catholic Church must establish itself as the State Church in the United States, and that the state should recognize and support it." [28]

Catholics for Separation

Anti-Catholic preaching tended either to ignore the existence of Catholic pronouncements *for* the separation of church and state or to dismiss them

[24] Batsell B. Baxter, a pamphlet, *A Dangerous Doctrine*, p. 16. Delivered on October 9, 1960, Hillsboro Church of Christ, Nashville, Tennessee.

[25] Harold A. Bosley, "Why I Cannot Now Vote for a Roman Catholic for President." Contained in previously cited thesis of David Ellis Walker, Jr., p. 158. Delivered on February 28, 1960, First Methodist Church, Evanston, Illinois.

[26] James A. Pike, *A Roman Catholic in the White House* (Garden City, N.Y.: Doubleday & Company, 1960), pp. 70-79, contains a good discussion of the confusion and controversy over papal infallibility and how infallibility might affect the actions of a Roman Catholic president.

[27] Albert J. Nevins, ed., *The Maryknoll Catholic Dictionary* (New York: Grosset and Dunlap, 1965), p. 288. Imprimatur is defined as "Permission from a competent ecclesiastical authority to publish a book that may be safely read without damage to faith or morals." This, of course, does not make a book an "official" statement of the Roman Catholic Church.

[28] Robert Lovell, "The Religious Issue," p. 4. (Mimeographed.) Delivered on October 23, 1960.

as "unofficial." The second practice inevitably produced inconsistencies. For example, the Rev. Batsell B. Baxter of Nashville, Tennessee, refuted a sermon given by the Rev. Gustave Weigel, a theologian from Woodstock College in Maryland, in the following manner:

Professor Gustave Weigel . . . stepped forward to express his views only recently, not as an official spokesman for the Roman Catholic Church, but as a distinguished Jesuit theologian. . . . We appreciate Professor Weigel's statement of his own views; we wish they were the official statements of his church. . . . Finally, until such time as the Pope himself declares this to be the doctrine of the Church, the rest of us will simply take such statements as Professor Weigel's for what he openly declares it to be—an expression of his own personal views and not the official position of the church.[29]

Earlier in his sermon Baxter had stated, "I shall quote only from those sources that the Catholics themselves have given authority by the placing of the bishop's imprimatur upon the flyleaf of the book." [30] Interestingly enough, Weigel's sermon met this criterion. Helicon Press of Baltimore published the sermon in October, 1960, under the imprimatur of Francis P. Keough, Archbishop of Baltimore. Thus, Baxter dismissed as "unofficial," and therefore unacceptable, statements of a "distinguished Jesuit theologian" while in the same sermon he quoted as official Church doctrine eight passages from common Catholic textbooks.

Defenders of Roman Catholicism could not deny the staggering amount of evidence presented in anti-Kennedy sermons to prove that the Church was opposed in theory to the "wall of separation between church and state." Nevertheless, the charge had to be answered. Of the sermons studied, only Gustave Weigel's attempted to show that there was no "official" Catholic position. "For the last thirty years within Catholic theology there has been much thinking and writing on the Catholic doctrine of Church and State," Weigel said. "Theological investigation is going on and clarification is being reached by an academic debate in Catholic circles." [31] He concluded, "The full investigation has not yet been ended and it will go on for some time to come." Weigel and other clergymen who openly opposed the religious issue admitted the existence of extreme pronouncements by Catholic hierarchy and writers, but they quoted statements of American and Vatican hierarchy, ranging in time from 1787 to 1960, that supported a strict separation of church and state. Kennedy's antagonists, they concluded, were guilty of selecting only those sources that supported their fears. Referring to the so-called "unofficial" American Catholic pronouncements, James William Mor-

[29] Baxter, A Dangerous Doctrine, pp. 18-20.
[30] Ibid., p. 3.
[31] Gustave Weigel, S.J., a pamphlet, Church-State Relations: A Theological Considera-tion, p. 10. Delivered on September 27, 1960, Shrine of the Most Blessed Sacrament, Chevy Chase Circle, District of Columbia.

gan of Austin, Texas, exclaimed that the "significant thing is that Rome has not silenced these opinions and this silence speaks volumes." [32]

Churchmen also argued that Protestants were guilty of the charges they were leveling at Catholicism. One minister declared that "while we complain, we must also look at some of our pronouncements about Rome. Both of us must recognize that our words and persecutions of each other both stand condemned by God." [33] Rabbi Kahn of Houston, Texas, accused anti-Catholic clergymen of wrenching Catholic sources "out of context so as to mean the opposite of what they were intended to say" and of "every kind of distortion, every kind of prejudice-arousing trick." [34] Although evidence of such practices was available, Rabbi Kahn offered none.[35] The basic arguments in defense of Catholicism seemed excellent, but they lacked both development and substantial proofs. Perhaps the hesitancy of clergymen to become involved in an issue they opposed so strongly, and the danger of being accused of partisan preaching, led them to generalize.

Catholicism Against Separation

The Catholic Church's opposition to religious liberty and the separation of church and state was not theory alone, Kennedy's opposition contended, but was practiced throughout the world "wherever the Roman Catholic Church is in control." [36] Was not Vatican City a sovereign nation? And did not the Catholic Church control its diplomatic corps, police force, stamps, currency, passports, and government? No better proof was needed that the Church believed in union of church and state. Some clergymen reasoned that the Vatican City, admittedly a tiny nation with little temporal power, could be ignored if it was the only instance of Catholic interference in matters of "state." They, of course, were quick to show it was not. Spain, Colombia, or both, served as illustrations of Roman Catholic intolerance

[32] Morgan, "Reformation Day and the Election," p. 4.

[33] *Ibid.*

[34] Kahn, "The Religious Issue in the Presidential Campaign," p. 7.

[35] The following instance of questionable editing appeared in a sermon that was quoting John A. Ryan and Francis J. Boland, *Catholic Principles of Politics* (New York: The Macmillan Company, 1952), p. 320. The parts in italics were deleted when the passage appeared in the sermon: "Suppose that the Constitutional obstacles to persecution [proscription was the correct word] of non-Catholics have been legitimately removed *and they themselves have become numerically insignificant:* what then would be the proper course of action for a Catholic State? *Apparently* the latter state could logically tolerate only such religious activities as were confined to the members of the dissenting group. *It could not permit them to carry on general propaganda* nor accord *their organization* certain privileges *that had* formerly *been* extended to all religious corporations, for example, exemption from taxation. *While all this is very true in logic and in theory, the event of its practical realization in any state or country is so remote in time and in probability that no practical man will let it disturb his equanimity or affect his attitude toward those who differ from him in religious faith.*

[36] Baxter, *A Dangerous Doctrine*, p. 7.

and suppression in all but one of the sermons studied. Clerics presented detailed and lengthy descriptions of persecutions in Spain, especially persecutions of Protestant congregations and ministers. Statistics on Colombian suppression varied in *sermons studied,* ranging from 89 to 116 Protestant leaders murdered, 34 to 200 Protestant churches confiscated, and 49 to 66 Protestant churches destroyed. Paraguay, Argentina, and Mexico were mentioned occasionally as nations having laws unfavorable toward non-Catholics. This bleak picture of Roman Catholic intolerance led the Rev. Frederick H. Haag, pastor of the Congregational church in Walla Walla, Washington, to warn that "a disquisition now may forestall an Inquisition to some future date." [37]

Catholic intolerance and interference in matters of state were not just foreign problems, churchmen pointed out, but they were serious threats to the United States as well. The church's size and increasing influence in America frightened non-Catholic clergymen. "I do not believe that Communism is the greatest threat to the United States of America," Harvey W. Springer declared in the First Baptist Church of Englewood, Colorado. "Roman Catholic power in America is persuasive and substantial, outnumbering Communist power in official membership by about 490 to 1." [38] Speakers claimed that 2,055 Catholic nuns, brothers, and priests were already teaching in the public schools of twenty-one states, that nineteen states had free bus transportation for parochial school students, that seventy percent of the teachers in Chicago and ninety percent of the teachers in New Orleans were Catholic, and that only Catholics could be elected mayor in Chicago, Buffalo, and other cities. Robert Lovell of Champaign, Illinois, summarized the kinds of Catholic interference that bothered Protestant clergymen:

Attempts to force non-Catholic hospitals and doctors to conform to Catholic ideas of medical ethics; Catholic pressure to remove welfare agencies that have birth control clinics from local community chests; Catholic attempts to secure public money to support its parochial schools; these arouse our Protestant resentment and fears.[39]

More than anything else, churchmen feared Catholic control of the immense presidential powers. Harvey W. Springer referred to millions in governmental funds that Congressman John W. McCormack of Massachusetts had allegedly obtained for Catholic programs, and asked, "If a mere Congressman can do that, what could a Catholic President do?" [40] "Remember," the Rev. Onesimus J. Rundus of Des Moines, Iowa, warned, "if you have a Roman Catholic President—he'll be backed by nearly one hundred Roman

[37] Frederick H. Haag, "Dare We Elect a *Roman* Catholic for President?" p. 5. (Mimeographed.) Delivered in the summer of 1960.
[38] Springer, *Catholicism in America,* pp. 7-8.
[39] Lovell, "The Religious Issue," p. 3.
[40] Springer, *Catholicism in America,* p. 16.

Catholic members of the House and a good number of Romans in the Senate."[41]

Defenders of Catholicism did not attempt to deny, nor could they have under the circumstances, the examples of Catholic intolerance and interference in foreign countries. Instead they employed the same tactics as they had in refuting the alleged theoretical position of the church on separation of church and state. First of all, clergymen accused Kennedy's opponents of selecting only those Catholic countries, Spain and Colombia in particular, that would support their arguments. "The Catholic can only answer: Look about you!" the Rev. Gustave Weigel of Woodstock College exclaimed. "The heads of state in West Germany and France are Catholics. This is also true in Ireland. Catholics will soon be a majority in Holland. . . . Do non-Catholics in those lands feel any oppression or do they even show any fear of such an event?" he asked.[42] James Morgan of Austin, Texas, discussed France and Ireland and concluded, "Not all Roman Catholic countries are like Spain."[43] Secondly, churchmen claimed that Protestants were guilty of the very practices for which they were condemning the Catholic church. "It is true that Catholicism is established by law in some countries," Weigel said, "it is equally true that such establishment is found in lands called Protestant."[44] He listed England as his prime example. "Until recently," Rabbi Kahn remarked, "a Jesuit priest could not even set foot in Protestant Sweden."[45]

What about a Catholic President; would Catholics bring strong pressure upon him? "Of course they would," the Rev. Blake Smith of the University Baptist Church in Austin, Texas, pointed out. "A President is always under pressure. Did we not bring strong pressure on the President to prevent the appointment of an Ambassador to the Vatican?"[46] Rabbi Kahn argued that the wall of separation between church and state is equally breached when Catholics want state funds for their schools or Protestants want a released time program for religious instruction in public schools, when Catholics want birth control prohibited and Protestants want to prohibit the liquor traffic, when Catholics want to ban books and movies and Protestants want to enforce blue laws on Sunday, and when clergymen tell their congregations how to vote in political elections.[47]

[41] Onesimus J. Rundus, "Are American Liberties at Stake?" *Western Voice* (August 25, 1960), p. 4, col. 3. Delivered in May, 1960, in the First Federated Church.

[42] Weigel, *Church-State Relations*, p. 13.

[43] Morgan, "Reformation Day and the Election," p. 5.

[44] Weigel, *Church-State Relations*, pp. 13-14.

[45] Kahn, "The Religious Issue in the Presidential Campaign," p. 2.

[46] Blake Smith, "Religion and the Presidency," p. 7. (Mimeographed.) Delivered on September 11, 1960.

[47] Kahn, "The Religious Issue in the Presidential Campaign," pp. 5-6.

Kennedy in Preaching

The presidential candidate himself received scant attention in most sermons. Churchmen generally belittled Kennedy's past record on church and state, his statements for lay independence from the Roman Catholic hierarchy, and his dramatic speech before the Greater Houston Ministerial Association. A 1950 incident served as "undeniable proof" in nearly every sermon studied that Kennedy had been and would continue to be a "part of the docile flock of the Church." The Rev. William A. Criswell, pastor of the First Baptist Church in Dallas, Texas, related the incident as follows:

During the second World War, the American Ship, Dorchester, was sunk by enemy fire. The four chaplains on the ship, two of whom were Protestants, one Jewish, and one Catholic, all gave their life preservers to four sailors and went down with the ship. . . . After the war, the father of one of the Protestant chaplains, Dr. Daniel A. Poling, conceived the idea of building an inter-church chapel in Philadelphia, Pennsylvania, in memory of the four chaplains. In the fall of 1950, he proposed to celebrate the occasion and to dedicate the chapel with a banquet. . . . The honorable Charles P. Taft, Mayor of Cincinnati, Ohio, was invited to speak for the Protestants. Senator Herbert H. Lehman was invited to speak for the Jewish faith, and John Kennedy . . . was invited—and accepted —to speak for the Catholic faith. Dr. Poling relates how Mr. Kennedy notified him at the last minute that . . . he would have to cancel his appearance due to the fact that his Eminence Denis Cardinal Dougherty had requested him not to speak at the banquet and not to appear . . . and I quote John Kennedy, "As a loyal son of the church, I have no other alternative but not to come." [48]

The emotional impact of this story must have been great with many Protestant congregations, but it was often heightened by concluding questions like, "Is my President of the United States to be a man who could not come into one of my services lest he be contaminated by walking into the precincts of a Protestant church?" [49] Kennedy's attempted explanations of the Dorchester incident were all but ignored from the pulpit.[50] When the Catholic press criticized the candidate's independence from the hierarchy, it supplied opposition clergymen with an additional windfall of evidence. Typical was the Rev. Harry R. Butman's reaction from his pulpit in the Congregational Church of the Messiah in Los Angeles:

What Senator Kennedy has done is adopt for himself the Protestant principle of the right of private judgment. The serious view which the Roman Church takes of Senator Kennedy's declaration of a layman's independence is to be seen in the instant and critical reaction of the Catholic press to his statements.

[48] William A. Criswell, a pamphlet, *Religious Freedom, the Church, the State, and Senator Kennedy*, pp. 5-6. Exact date unknown.

[49] *Ibid.*, p. 6.

[50] Pike, *A Roman Catholic in the White House*, pp. 126-29, discusses the incident and Kennedy's explanations of it on December 8, 1959, and January 15, 1960.

He has been assaulted by Catholic diocesan papers and by the influential *Commonweal*. But chiefly he came under censure by the official Roman newspaper.[51]

After quoting an article from the "official Roman newspaper," *L'Osservatore Romano*, he concluded, "In short, this article says that Roman Catholic magistrates do not make the rules, they obey them; magistrates are subject in all matters to the church." Thus, a Catholic president would be under complete control of the Church. Not only were Kennedy's pronouncements disproved by the Dorchester incident and criticized by the Catholic press, clergy argued, but, at best, his statements were "unofficial." "Much as we might like to believe Al Smith or John Kennedy or anyone else when they proclaim the position advanced by American Catholic leaders," the Rev. Harold A. Bosley told his congregation at the First Methodist Church of Evanston, Illinois, *"we cannot forget that it is unofficial, that it contradicts the official position."* [52]

From the pulpit of the Third Baptist Church in St. Louis, the Rev. Sterling Price alluded to alleged Catholic persecutions and interference in governmental affairs and declared, "Your church's record in church and state matters makes so much noise the American voters have difficulty hearing what you say." [53]

Clerical opposition to religion as a campaign issue said little in defense of John F. Kennedy. Rabbi Kahn of Houston stated that "no one who heard" Kennedy speak in Houston "could possibly doubt where he stands on the separation of church-state." [54] Few of Kennedy's opponents would have disagreed with this statement, for their point was not the sincerity of Kennedy's personal beliefs but his ability to carry them out under pressure from his church. Defenders of Kennedy and Catholicism did not mention the all-important Dorchester incident. Indeed, such clergymen seemed to fear the accusation that they were supporting candidate Kennedy rather than speaking against the religious issue. For instance, immediately after his reference to Kennedy's Houston speech, Rabbi Kahn remarked, "Again, let me assure you, I do not solicit your vote for any candidate in this election." [55]

Results of the Campaign

The debate over the religious issue continued until November 8, election day. The outcome of the election is history; John Fitzgerald Kennedy became the first Roman Catholic President of the United States. The margin of

[51] Harry R. Butman, "Church, State, and the Magistrate," p. 3. (Mimeographed.) Delivered on September 25, 1960.

[52] Bosley, "Why I Cannot Now Vote," p. 161.

[53] Sterling L. Price, a pamphlet, *The Catholic-Protestant Dilemma*, p. 3. Delivered on September 11, 1960.

[54] Kahn, "The Religious Issue in the Presidential Campaign," pp. 7-8.

[55] *Ibid.*, p. 8.

victory, only one-tenth of one percent of the popular vote, was the closest presidential election of the twentieth century. Had Kennedy's religion been an asset or a liability in his narrow victory? Some observers felt that the anti-Catholic and pro-Catholic votes had canceled out each other.[56] But Louis H. Bean, a noted political analyst, argued that the religious issue had actually helped Kennedy. He reasoned that people vote *for* a candidate out of pride and *against* him out of prejudice. "And many more, I believe, voted from pride than from prejudice," [57] Bean concluded. On the other hand, the results of a study by the Survey Research Center of the University of Michigan showed that Kennedy's religion had been a definite hindrance.[58] Researchers found a clear correlation between frequency of church attendance and percentage of Protestants voting for Richard M. Nixon. The Michigan researchers cautioned, "We need not assume . . . that each defection pictured here represents a sermon from the pulpit and an obedient member of the congregation" voting against a Catholic candidate.[59] Those attending church regularly or often, however, were more likely to have heard one or more carefully organized and supported anti-Kennedy sermons. Perhaps the decision by most clergymen who opposed the religious issue to remain silent was ill-conceived, for persons who read or heard anti-Catholic arguments were seldom exposed to counterarguments. The Michigan researchers said that the religious issue probably cost Kennedy a net loss of 2.2 percent of the national vote. "There is every reason to believe," they concluded, "that these preliminary estimates underestimate the importance of religion in the 1960 vote, and, in particular, underestimate the magnitude of the anti-Catholic vote." [60]

Following the election, many of Kennedy's staunchest opponents united behind him as the new president. Dr. Ramsey Pollard, president of the Southern Baptist Convention and a vocal opponent of Kennedy during the campaign, stated, "Kennedy's election should help religious coexistence. But everything depends on what he does—that is, if he keeps his promises about the separation of church and state." [61] The three years of Kennedy's administration saw the wall of separation protected if not strengthened, and the pressure of the Catholic hierarchy proved to be no obstacle. The question remained, however, whether the religious issue would raise its head if another Catholic candidate tried for the presidency or vice-presidency. The answer

[56] White, *The Making of the President 1960*, pp. 355-58.

[57] Louis H. Bean, "Why Kennedy Won," *The Nation*, November 26, 1960, pp. 408-10. *The New York Times*, November 20, 1960, p. E 5, said that a "narrow consensus" of observers felt that Kennedy had gained more than he had lost because of his religion.

[58] Philip E. Converse *et al.*, "Stability and Change in 1960: A Reinstating Election," *American Political Science Review*, June, 1961, pp. 276-77.

[59] *Ibid.*, p. 276.

[60] *Ibid.*, p. 278.

[61] *Newsweek*, November 28, 1960, p. 82.

was not long in coming. In 1964, William E. Miller, a Roman Catholic congressman from New York, was nominated for the vice-presidency by the Republican Party. Miller's religion was rarely mentioned during the ensuing campaign, and Catholics voted heavily for the Democratic ticket. Perhaps one threat to the "wall of separation," if it ever existed, has ended.

Prayer and Bible Reading in the Public Schools

Except for minor rumblings over federal aid to parochial schools, the early part of John F. Kennedy's administration witnessed little conflict over the wall of separation between church and state. This was due in part to Kennedy's firm position in favor of separation.

During this period of relative calm, the case of *Engel* v. *Vitale* was wending its way through the lower courts to the Supreme Court of the United States. Five parents of school children in New Hyde Park, New York, brought suit in 1958 against a New York Board of Regents' prayer recited as a morning ritual in the New York public schools.[62] The prayer read, "Almighty God, we acknowledge our dependence upon Thee, and we beg Thy blessings upon us, our parents, our teachers and our country." On the final day of its 1961 term, June 25, 1962, the Supreme Court decided six to one that the Board of Regents' prayer violated the First Amendment's guarantees of religious freedom and the separation of church and state.[63] No governmental agency, the Court decided, could compose or require prayers for the public schools.

Pulpit Response

Reaction to the Supreme Court's decision was immediate and furious. Francis Cardinal Spellman of New York exclaimed that "the decision strikes at the very heart of the Godly tradition in which America's children have for so long been raised." [64] "God pity our country when we can no longer appeal to God for help," [65] declared the Rev. Billy Graham. In Congress Representative George Andrews of Alabama remarked that the Court had "put the Negroes in the schools and now they've driven God out." [66]

The pulpit assailed and defended the Regents' Prayer decision and predicted further Supreme Court actions on religious activities in the public schools. Nearly a year later, on June 17, 1963, the Supreme Court closed its 1962 term by declaring in *Abington* v. *Schempp* that required Bible reading

[62] Philip B. Kurland, "The School Prayer Cases," *The Wall Between Church and State*, ed. Dallin H. Oaks (Chicago: The University of Chicago Press, 1963), pp. 142-44 and 147-50.

[63] Two justices did not vote. One was ill and the other was appointed after the case had been debated before the Court.

[64] *The New York Times*, June 26, 1962, p. 17, col. 3.

[65] *Indianapolis Star*, June 26, 1962, p. 1, col. 7.

[66] *The New York Times*, June 26, 1962, p. 16, col. 8.

and the recitation of the Lord's Prayer as specified in statutes of Pennsylvania and Maryland were also violations of the First Amendment to the Constitution. Reaction was again immediate, but less vituperative than in 1962, perhaps because that reaction had actually never ended. The pattern of opposition was the same: most Catholic and fundamentalist Protestant clergy, on opposite sides during the 1960 presidential election, tended to oppose the decision, while liberal Protestant and most Jewish churchmen accepted and even praised the decision.[67]

Clerical defenders of the decisions accused their opponents of reacting emotionally without bothering to read the Court's opinions. The Rev. Charles C. Hoskinson of the First Congregational Church in Glen Ellyn, Illinois, cited several "emotional and almost violent" reactions against the decisions and concluded, "As I have read comments such as these, I have wondered whether the people who made them had read the court's decision." [68] Analyses of sermons against the Court indicate that speculations like Hoskinson's were probably accurate.[69] Only one sermon studied for this essay quoted from the Court's majority opinions, and these passages did not include the *reasons* for the decisions. Only one clergyman attempted to refute arguments favoring the decisions. None tried to show that the prayers and readings actually made students more religious or moral. In fact, two clergymen admitted that such practices had little religious value. "When they read from the Bible, without comment, a brief passage or two, perhaps their devotional life was not being greatly enriched," the Rev. Marion L. Matics of Brooklyn said, "but at least they were being taught respect for the fundamental religious tradition which has made this nation great." [70]

Pulpit Opposition

A major strategy of anti-Court clerics appeared to be an attempt to discredit the 1962 and 1963 decisions without dealing directly with either the Court's majority opinions or explanations offered after the fact. Thus some speakers attacked those people who were responsible for taking the cases to the Supreme Court. "Persons who carried this [*Abington* v. *Schempp*] to the highest court were a Unitarian couple in Abington, Pa., and an atheist in Baltimore, Md.," the Rev. Charles E. Fair, pastor of the Alsace Lutheran

---

[67] Kurland, "The School Prayer Cases," pp. 145-46.

[68] Charles C. Hoskinson, "Prayer Prescribed and Proscribed," pp. 4-5. (Typed manuscript.) Delivered on November 11, 1962.

[69] Eight sermons and numerous statements of Catholic and Protestant clergymen opposed to the decisions were studied in detail for this essay. The sermons ranged in time from July, 1962, to spring, 1966, and included Episcopalian, Methodist, United Church of Christ, Lutheran, and fundamentalist clergy. Roman Catholic opinion was found mainly in statements made immediately following each Court decision.

[70] Marion L. Matics, "Obituary for Children's Prayers," p. 3. (Mimeographed.) Delivered on June 23, 1963, in Christ Church Bay Ridge (Episcopalian).

Church in Reading, Pennsylvania, stated. "This case was not brought forth by a Roman Catholic, Protestant, or Jewish family!" [71] The word atheist was repeated often in sermons opposing the school prayer decisions; clergymen obviously realized its emotional value. The Rev. Fair asked later in his sermon, "Incidentally, what do you know about the atheist woman from Baltimore who carried this case to the Supreme Court? A divorcee with two sons, she has been quoted in a nationwide magazine." After citing a particularly damaging passage from the magazine article, he concluded, "It is both shocking and insulting to learn of her attitude and yet she has won her case and upset this religious tradition that has existed in thousands of schools for years." [72]

Perhaps it was inevitable, with many vocal groups like the John Birch Society and the Christian Anti-Communist Crusade warning of widespread Communist conspiracies, that both the Supreme Court and its decisions would be associated with communism. "I do not know if there are any Communists on the Supreme Court," the Rev. Ronald A. Brunger told his congregation in the Methodist Church of Marysville, Michigan, "it really seems impossible that this could be true, but obviously the Supreme Court has made a decision to please the Communists." [73] Clergymen felt that the Court had outlawed the basic differences between religious America and atheistic Russia. James Francis Cardinal McIntyre of Los Angeles declared that the decisions could "only mean that our American heritage of philosophy, of religion and of freedom are being abandoned in imitation of Soviet philosophy, of Soviet materialism and of Soviet-regimented liberty." [74]

In addition to attempts to discredit the Court's decisions, sermons proposed four main reasons why the decisions were wrong. First of all, churchmen argued, the Supreme Court had made an excessively narrow interpretation of the First Amendment to the Constitution. The Rev. Paul T. Stoudt of Quakertown, Pennsylvania, for instance, contended that "church and state must be forever separate in the U.S.A., but religion and the state must be forever united." [75] Clergymen like Stoudt tried to distinguish between "religion" and "church," but lack of development often allowed their argument to become an attack on the "wall of separation" itself. "Atheists and free-thinkers," a Methodist clergyman declared, have been attacking religious customs in public schools as "a violation of their shibboleth, 'Separation of Church and State.'" [76] The Rev. Harry R. Butman of Los Angeles, a vocal

[71] Charles E. Fair, "Bible-Prayer-Public Schools," p. 2. (Mimeographed.) Delivered on June 23 and 30, 1963.
[72] *Ibid.*, p. 8.
[73] Ronald A. Brunger, "Which Way—America?" p. 6. (Mimeographed.) Delivered on July 1, 1962.
[74] *The New York Times*, June 19, 1963, p. 18, col. 1.
[75] Paul T. Stoudt, "The Church and the State," p. 11. (Handwritten manuscript.) Delivered in spring of 1966, First United Church of Christ.
[76] Brunger, "Which Way—America?" p. 6.

opponent of Kennedy in 1960 because of Roman Catholic views on church and state, commented in 1964 that "the legal separation of Church and State in America is rapidly become a dangerous spiritual divorce." [77]

The decisions were wrong also, clerics contended, because they were contrary to American history and tradition. "It is obvious that little by little it [Supreme Court] is discarding religious traditions hallowed by a century and half of American practice," the Most Rev. Patrick A. O'Boyle of Washington, D.C., said.[78] Franklin, Jefferson, Lincoln, Theodore Roosevelt, and Wilson had offered prayers, clerics recalled; could all these have been wrong? To many speakers, the prayers and readings had to be constitutional simply because they had never before been declared unconstitutional. One minister argued:

Think, my friends—if it was constitutional and American to have religion in the schools in 1790; if it was constitutional and American to have religion in the schools in 1840 (when people were living who had participated in the Revolution); if it was constitutional and American to have religion in the schools in 1895; it is constitutional and American to have religion (but not sectarian religion) in our schools in 1962! [79]

According to the clergymen, the Supreme Court was wrong, in the third place, because such decisions were part of "a continuing series of actions to remove God entirely, and every mention of Him from all public and governmental life." [80] The Rev. Marion Matics of Brooklyn summed up this concern when he termed the ban of prayers and Bible readings as "another straw in the rising wind of secularism." [81] Preachers like Matics saw the two Court decisions as only a continuation of a movement against all religious activities connected with the state: chaplains in the armed services and in Congress, mentions of God in the national anthem, the Pledge of Allegiance, and "America," inscriptions on coins, tax exemption of churches, draft exemptions for clergymen, baccalaureate services in public high schools and colleges, and even the prayer said at the beginning of each session of the Supreme Court. Extreme predictions were frequent. For instance, the Rev. Onesimus J. Rundus of Des Moines, Iowa, asked his congregation, "Will our children sing, 'Our Father's God to Thee,' or will they wonder who or what was our God and not know to whom to sing? . . . Or worse yet," he concluded, "will we leave behind laws that will make it illegal for them to sing

[77] Harry R. Butman, "A Nation Under God," p. 1. (Mimeographed.) Delivered on July 5, 1964, in the Congregational Church of the Messiah.
[78] *The New York Times*, June 18, 1963, p. 29, col. 6.
[79] Brunger, "Which Way—America?" p. 6.
[80] Kenneth L. Whitney, "Supreme Court on Prayer," p. 2. (Typed manuscript.) Delivered on July 7, 1963, St. Andrew's-by-the-Sea Protestant Episcopal Church, Nags Head, North Carolina.
[81] Matics, "Obituary for Children's Prayers," p. 1.

about God?" [82] This secularization was taking place, clerics warned, "just when Divorce, Crime and Immorality is [sic] soaring completely out of bounds." [83] "Meanwhile, the moral fabric continues to deteriorate, and our children and young people are quick to sense the trend," [84] one minister commented. He cited several reports of juvenile crime and vandalism and concluded sarcastically, "By all means, keep our children protected from the Lord's Prayer and from Bible readings in the schools. They might learn to believe in God. They might learn decency and self-respect. Wouldn't it be terrible if they learned the Ten Commandments?" [85] All this immorality and banning of religion in the public schools added up to one thing according to opposition clerics, a turning away from God, "from the rock of faith on which America was founded." [86] Ministers warned of imminent punishment from God, and cited passages from the Old Testament, Deuteronomy in particular, that related how God had punished Israel when its people became evil and turned to false gods. "God cannot close His eyes to the immorality, the irreligiousness, the Godlessness of our land," Onesimus Rundus told his congregation. "It is quite likely that He may choose to use Russia or some other atheistic nation to punish us just as He used Assyria and Babylon to punish Israel and Judah." [87] Anti-Court clergymen obviously viewed the decisions on prayer and Bible reading as a religious tragedy.

The Court was wrong, fourthly, said the clergymen, because it was allowing minorities to usurp the rights of the majority. "Important as minority rights are, the majority has rights too," [88] the Rev. Kenneth L. Whitney of Nags Head, North Carolina, remarked. He continued by asking the question posed by Dean Griswold of Harvard: "In a country which has a great tradition of tolerance is it not important that the minorities, who have benefited so greatly from that tolerance, should be tolerant too?" [89] Ministers pointed out that the states had provisions for excusing any child who objected to the religious rituals. "Isn't it strange that when non-believers in the Lord Jesus Christ were granted the privilege of being excused from Bible reading and the Lord's Prayer, they were not content with this courtesy," Charles E. Fair of Reading, Pennsylvania, declared, "they insisted that every pupil in every classroom in every school in every school district in every state of the union be subject to their wishes and rights." [90]

Only one solution seemed both feasible and acceptable—an amendment

[82] Onesimus J. Rundus, "Whither America," p. 8. (Mimeographed.) Delivered on December 27, 1964, in the First Federated Church, Des Moines, Iowa.
[83] Ibid., p. 5.
[84] Matics, "Obituary for Children's Prayers," p. 4.
[85] Ibid.
[86] Brunger, "Which Way—America?" p. 7.
[87] Rundus, "Whither America," p. 3.
[88] Whitney, "Supreme Court on Prayer," p. 2.
[89] Ibid.
[90] Fair, "Bible-Prayer-Public Schools," pp. 10-11.

to the Constitution allowing nonsectarian religious practices in the public schools. More than a hundred bills were introduced into Congress, all with the purpose of overruling the Supreme Court's decisions. Hope rested mainly on proposed amendments in the House of Representatives by Frank Becker of New York and in the Senate by Everett Dirksen of Illinois. Ministers called upon their congregations to write their congressmen in support of these amendments.

Court Defenders

Although the Supreme Court came under attack from many directions, adequate defenders generally appeared in the ranks of liberal Protestant and Jewish clergymen.[91] They applauded the decisions on prayer and Bible reading and attempted to refute opposing arguments. The main strategy of such clerics seemed to be to strike at the weakest aspect of anti-Court preaching: the lack of consideration, knowledge, or both, of what the Court had actually decided. The Court's proponents frequently began by reviewing the reactions against the 1962 and 1963 decisions. They quoted statements from the pulpit and Congressional opposition and tried to reveal these as sheer emotionalism. "All in all it sounded as though the Court had dealt the forces of religion a mortal blow," commented the Rev. John D. King, pastor of the United Presbyterian Church in Westminster, Colorado.[92] These emotional reactions were prevalent, a Baptist minister declared, because "most people know what they think of this decision; but an amazingly large percentage apparently do not know what the Court decided." [93]

The Court's clerical defenders apparently felt that their congregations would support the decisions once the facts were known. Their sermons related the history of *Engle v. Vitale* and *Abington v. Schempp*, the reasons for the suits, the lower courts' decisions and, above all, the crucial question that faced the Supreme Court. "Remember," the Rev. J. Ray Robinson, pastor of the Citadel Square Baptist Church of Charleston, South Carolina, stated, "the question asked of the Supreme Court was—can any group representing our federal, state, county, or city government tell me the prayer that I or my children must pray in the public schools? *This is the question, the only question, that they were asked.*" [94]

The next step was twofold: first, isolate the actual Court decisions and,

[91] Seventeen pro-Supreme Court sermons were studied for this essay. They ranged in time from July, 1962, to February, 1965, and included Presbyterian, Methodist, Universalist, Congregational, Jewish, Baptist, and Episcopalian clergymen.

[92] John D. King, "On Prayer and Public Piety," p. 1. (Typed manuscript.) Delivered on August 5, 1962.

[93] Jack H. Manley, "The Supreme Court Decision," p. 3. (Mimeographed.) Delivered on July 8, 1962, in Fairfax Baptist Church, city and state unknown.

[94] J. Ray Robinson, a pamphlet, *Right or Wrong: The Supreme Court Decision in the New York School Prayer Case*, p. 2. Date unknown.

second, cite the reasons for them. Speakers turned directly to the majority opinions to find the decisions handed down. After quoting at length from these opinions, clergymen invariably drew the same conclusion: "The Supreme Court did not ban prayer," but declared "unconstitutional the composing of official prayers by the government." [95] In other words, a Congregational clergyman concluded, "the State can neither enhance nor deter religion." [96] Liberal clerics cited several reasons why the unpopular Court decisions were the best and only ones possible. First, any movement, however slight, of government into the realm of religion violates the First Amendment's provision on establishment of religion. Second, governmentally prescribed religious rituals violate the wall of separation between church and state. "This has become a deeply cherished American principle," Rabbi Robert I. Kahn of Houston, Texas, stated. "And it ought not to become an empty shibboleth." [97] Kahn and others reviewed the history of church-state relationships from Roman times through the American colonial period and elaborated upon the inherent evils of union of church and state. Our founding fathers would have praised the Court's decisions, clergymen agreed. The third reason the Court decisions were right was given as America's increasingly pluralistic nature. No religious exercise, clergymen contended, could satisfy all elements in the public schools. "Is our society Christian?" the Rev. Donald L. Rogan of Morgantown, West Virginia, asked. "If so, what sort of citizens are Jews, Unitarians, Mormons, 7th Day Adventists, Christian Scientists, etc.?" [98]

What practices, then, did the Supreme Court rule unconstitutional, clerics asked, and of what value were they? Some preachers objected to the New York Board of Regents' prayer because it was "largely self-centered and heavily nationalistic" and "counter to the counsels and examples of Christ as to the appropriate use and phrasing of prayer." [99] Churchmen also objected to the use of prayers and Bible reading as classroom rituals. After all, they contended, Christ himself declared in his Sermon on the Mount that "Alms should be given in secret—prayer should be private—and fasting should go unnoticed." [100] Not only were the content and uses of prayer and scripture questionable, but the alleged worth of such practices was challenged.

[95] Kenneth V. Kettlewell, "Freedom of Religion in Our Land," p. 1. (Mimeographed.) Delivered on February 17, 1963, Oak Hill United Presbyterian Church, Akron, Ohio.

[96] Philip E. Kunz, "Christian Education," *Montclair Times* (Montclair, New Jersey), date unknown, delivered in the Union Congregational Church, Upper Montclair, New Jersey.

[97] Robert I. Kahn, "Vote Against Prayer and for God. Shall We Amend the First Amendment?" p. 6. (Mimeographed.) Delivered on April 10, 1964, Congregation Emanu El.

[98] Donald L. Rogan, "Sermon on the Supreme Court Decision on School Prayers," p. 1. (Typed manuscript.) Delivered on July 1, 1962, Trinity Church (Episcopalian).

[99] Donald W. Morgan, a pamphlet, *The Supreme Court Decisions: Their Meaning for Us*, p. 2. Delivered on September 8, 1963, Congregational Church, Rutland, Vermont.

[100] King, "On Prayer and Public Piety," p. 1.

The Rev. Earl M. Brooks of Muncy, Pennsylvania, recalled a common objection to the Court's actions, "Why take Bible reading and prayer out of the school—after all, what harm does it do?" This "is precisely the point," he added, "Bible reading and prayer as we know it today in our schools is quite a nice harmless little routine—would one dare to say, 'a meaningless ritual?' " [101] Brooks had revealed earlier in his sermon that the attorney for Baltimore in *Abington v. Schempp* had "maintained that one purpose of the practice [reciting prayers at the start of school]—according to many teachers —was to *calm* the students before classes began." [102] Speakers concluded that the highest Court had actually ruled against worthless and questionable religious practices in the public schools. Sermons also attacked such "religious" practices for unfairness to children who might oppose them. Provisions for excusing children existed in most communities, clergymen admitted, but they presented examples of teachers either failing to make the provisions known or punishing children who refused to take part in the rituals.

Having shown what the Supreme Court had ruled against and why, churchmen tried to show what the Court had *not* done. For one thing, the "Court did not even outlaw prayer in the public schools," only prescribed prayer.[103] For a second, it did not ban God from the schools. "People who believe that God can be taken in and out of the schools by court action on devotions certainly must have a strange concept of God," remarked the Rev. Donald H. Fado, pastor of the Methodist church in Hanford, California.[104] Moreover, clerics pointed out, the justices had said nothing against the Pledge of Allegiance, the national anthem, "America," inscriptions on coins, prayers in Congress, and a host of other national recognitions of God. One minister commented, "What has been lost . . . is nothing more than the government's right to give its token support to religion-in-general." [105]

Pro-Court clergymen concluded that the decisions were in the best interests of *all* Americans, and that the Court deserved praise, not uninformed, emotional criticism. Consider the dangers reverse decisions would have created, clerics asked their congregations. "Would we actually want the state to have the power to write prayers for our children to recite?" [106] Ministers warned their congregations that the state, or any majority, could then impose its own prayers on public school students. They reminded hearers that areas of the United States were heavily Catholic, Jewish, and even Buddhist. "Would

[101] Earl M. Brooks, "Bible Reading, Prayer and the Public School," p. 4. (Mimeographed.) Delivered on September 29, 1963, Muncy Presbyterian Church.
[102] *Ibid.*, p. 3.
[103] Manley, "The Supreme Court Decision," p. 3.
[104] Donald H. Fado, "A Time to Refrain from Embracing," p. 3. (Mimeographed.) Delivered on June 24 and 28, 1964.
[105] King, "On Prayer and Public Piety," p. 2.
[106] Fado, "A Time to Refrain from Embracing," p. 2.

you, as a Protestant, want your child to participate in the Rosary each morning before classroom instruction began in the public schools?" asked the Rev. Leroy C. Hodapp, pastor of the First Methodist Church in Bloomington, Indiana. Hodapp declared that "If we persist in arrogant self-righteous attempts to use any arm of the state to propagate the Christian faith, we shall be helping to dig the grave of our own religious freedom." [107] Other clerics saw increased friction among religions as the end result of governmentally prescribed prayers. "There is enough religious conflict now," Rabbi Robert I. Kahn of Houston stated, "Shall we add to it at the level of young children?" [108]

The Court's defenders examined two solutions to the dilemma of religion in the public schools. One was to make prayer legal by adopting an amendment to the Constitution. Speakers reviewed a number of proposed amendments, and they concluded that, at its worst, an amendment could leave Americans with "no safeguard whatever against a government-sponsored, government-controlled, pressure-group-oriented, majority-imposed religion." [109] At its best, an amendment would create endless questions: which version of the Bible, which version of the Lord's Prayer, and even which God? Clergymen predicted that administrators would try to reduce frictions by choosing so-called nonsectarian passages of the Bible. "In other words," the Rev. Donald Fado of Hanford, California, said, "we would read sections which really don't have much to say." [110] The second solution was offered in most pro-Court sermons as the one most in line with American traditions of religious liberty and the separation of church and state:

Let him who is so upset at the possibility of prayers going out of the schools dedicate himself to praying in his home and in his church the more fervently. The strength of our country does not depend upon *where* the prayers are offered but upon *whether* the prayers are offered. The strength of our country does not depend upon our schools opening with prayer each morning. Stronger we would be as a nation, if all our homes opened with prayer each morning. [111]

Lack of parental responsibility and religion in the home caused juvenile delinquency, clergymen contended, not the Supreme Court's ban on religious ritualism in the public schools.

[107] Leroy C. Hodapp, "The Great American Dilemma," p. 3. (Mimeographed.) Delivered on December 2, 1962.

[108] Kahn, "Vote Against Prayer and for God," p. 4.

[109] Arthur W. Mielke, "The Six Most Important Religious Events of 1964," p. 3. (Mimeographed.) Delivered on January 10, 1965, in the First Presbyterian Church, Buffalo, New York.

[110] Fado, "A Time to Refrain from Embracing," p. 2.

[111] Kettlewell, "Freedom of Religion in Our Land," p. 3.

Developments

In the years since the *Engel* v. *Vitale* and *Abington* v. *Schempp* decisions, public and pulpit furor have gradually lessened, and the tide of public opinion seems to have turned against an amendment that would make school prayer and Bible reading constitutional. Representative Frank Becker of New York maneuvered the House Judiciary Committee into holding open hearings on his proposed amendment during the spring of 1964. The hearings revealed much dissatisfaction with the Court's decisions, but they also revealed strong support of the Court by various Catholic, Jewish, and Protestant groups.[112] Through the summer and fall of 1964, Becker tried unsuccessfully to obtain the required number of congressional signatures to force his bill out of committee. The Becker Amendment appears to have gradually faded away. The Senate, at the instigation of Everett M. Dirksen of Illinois, conducted open hearings on possible school prayer amendments during August, 1966. The majority of witnesses, Catholic, Protestant, and Jewish, opposed moves to reverse the Court's decisions.[113] A few weeks later the Senate voted against Dirksen's proposed amendment. The controversy continues, however, and Senator Dirksen has vowed to continue his "crusade" until the Supreme Court's decisions are overruled.

There are several reasons why Congressional proposals have not received the necessary support of congressmen, the general public, or clergymen. First, the consequences prophesied by the Supreme Court's antagonists have not materialized. Second, the justices have refused to hear suits against the "under God" phrase in the Pledge of Allegiance and "In God We Trust" on coins. These actions indicated that the Court was not trying to eliminate all mention of God from American life as some clergymen had charged. And, third, many able and vocal clerics have defended the Court's decisions and have refuted its opposition. The emotional messages of anti-Court clergymen, many of whom seemed either unaware of what the Court has said or willing to ignore it, were probably adapted to and effective with many congregations —especially those that would not be exposed to counterarguments. But these audiences have not been enough to bring about Congressional action. The Court's opponents had to marshal a large portion of the public and clergymen against the Court if they were to reverse the 1962 and 1963 decisions. They have failed thus far to do so.

[112] U. S. House of Representatives. *School Prayers.* Hearings Before the Committee on the Judiciary, House of Representatives, 88th Congress, 2d Session, on Proposed Amendments to the Constitution Relating to School Prayers and Bible Reading in the Public Schools, 1964. See also Joseph P. Zima, "A Study of Major Issues, Contentions, and Arguments at the 1964 House Judiciary Committee Hearings on School Prayers" (unpublished Master's thesis, School of Speech, Kent State University, 1965).

[113] U. S. Senate. *School Prayer.* Hearings Before the Subcommittee on Constitutional Amendments of the Senate Committee on the Judiciary, 89th Congress, 2d Session, on Senate Joint Resolution 148, relating to Prayer in the Public Schools, 1966.

19

THE PULPIT AND RACE RELATIONS
1954-1966

William Pinson[1]

On May 17, 1954, America's racial revolution burst into the open. In a momentous decision the Supreme Court of the United States declared that segregation in public schools was unconstitutional. With staggering rapidity other court decisions coupled with legislative action began to topple the walls of segregation.

Historical Background

Segregation had been the pattern of relationship between black and white in America for decades. Obviously a practice of such wide acceptance and long standing would not be rooted out easily. Thus the Supreme Court's "Black Monday" decision—as the segregationists referred to it—ignited into full flame a revolution which had been smoldering for years.

A number of factors had contributed to the unrest over segregation. World War II had witnessed thousands of Negro soldiers fighting to defend a nation which they came to believe granted them only second-class citizenship. Following the war, a worldwide scrutiny of democracy threw a searching spotlight on the United States. Obvious to all was the inconsistency of pledging "liberty and justice for all" while denying both liberty and justice to a huge Negro minority. Many citizens began to feel strongly that the deeds of Americans should match their creed.

In the postwar period the United States vied with the Soviet Union for world support of its ideology. Since the majority of the world's people were colored, segregation placed the United States at a serious propaganda disadvantage. Many government officials were eager to see this disadvantage removed.

Changes in the Negro community paved the way for the civil rights revolution. The 1950's saw the Negro population more numerous, educated, af-

[1] Mr. James Heath acted as research assistant and aided greatly in gathering material for this essay.

fluent, skilled, and mobile than ever before. Having tasted of the better life, they now wanted to eat fully of the fare America offered. And Negro leadership had developed to lead the masses to the promised land.

Much of this leadership centered in civil rights organizations. Prior to the 1954 decision, the NAACP had been the most active group battering at segregation. After 1954, a number of other organizations came into being—or grew in strength. CORE, SNCC, and the Southern Christian Leadership Conference were the best known. Whereas the NAACP had majored on legal strategy in the courts, the other groups fostered sit-ins, marches, speeches, and demonstrations to advance the Negro cause.

The move toward desegregation did not go unchallenged. The 1954 decree stiffened and institutionalized the segregationists' resistance to change. The Ku Klux Klan, the Citizens' Councils, and the American Nazi Party gained strength. Segregationists used smear tactics, violence, and threat of violence to intimidate advocates of desegregation. Millions of other Americans were less zealous but nonetheless dedicated to the idea of segregation.

The role the churches played in the racial revolution is difficult to describe. For the most part they did not play a leading part in the struggle. Neither did they merely sit on the sideline and watch; they could not. They were faced with decisions forced on them by the revolution: whether to speak or to be silent; whether to desegregate facilities and institutions or not; whether to support the pro- or anti-segregationists; whether to back the radicals or the moderates. Much of the role of the churches is indicated in policy statements and denominational action, but important also was the preaching.

Preaching in favor of civil rights was by no means unheard of prior to 1954. Evidence indicates, however, that outside of a few groups, especially the Unitarians, such sermons were rare. After 1954, many congregations heard an increasing number of sermons on race relations and civil rights.

Preachers and Issues

The clergymen of America divided into three rather distinct groups over the issue of race. The largest group by far at the outset was composed of ministers dedicated to silence. For various reasons these persons chose to remain quiet and to ignore the revolution. After 1954, this group began to diminish.

As race relations became a popular cause, more and more men foresook silence and began to speak out for civil rights. As a result, a second group, made up of those who called for the end of segregation and discrimination, increased in size. The group was by no means homogeneous. Some members were merely mildly critical of social injustice and pleaded for more love in human relations. Others marched in civil rights demonstrations and participated in sit-ins—acts which drew the criticism of their milder colleagues. Yet, in spite of differences, these pro-civil rights preachers were dedicated to the eradication of segregation, discrimination, and racial prejudice.

A third group of preachers proclaimed the virtues of segregation and declared that any effort to abolish the practice was against the will of God. Many segregationist pastors were convinced that the Negro was an inferior being and that it was necessary to keep him separated from the white community.[2]

Members of each of these groups were found in all parts of the nation and within almost every denomination.[3] Both blacks and whites were numbered in all three categories.[4]

The conflict between pro- and anti-segregationists disturbed the tranquillity of many denominations. Southern Baptists, for example, had in their ranks outspoken segregationists as well as severe critics of segregation. Negro Baptists had such diverse types as J. H. Jackson, who pleaded for obedience to the law even if the law upheld segregation, and Martin Luther King, Jr., who led out in civil disobedience.

Many of the ministers who opposed segregation were younger, had more formal education, and professed more concern for social action in general than those who were its defenders. Segregationists were usually more conservative in theology—and in economics, politics, and other areas—than their opponents. The pro-civil rights advocates tended to come from denominations where religious concern was directed toward social involvement and action.

Several factors encouraged the increase of the civil rights advocates in the years following 1954. The racial revolution continued to gain momentum. Many were swept into support of the civil rights movement by its sheer popularity. Others for the first time became aware of the Negroes' needs and were moved to speak in their behalf. Many denominations made pronouncements supporting civil rights and tended to encourage local pastors to speak to the issue. Seminary students graduated better prepared to deal with the issues of race than were students of earlier generations. Religious leaders, such as Billy Graham, Eugene Carson Blake, Norman Vincent Peale, Rein-

---

[2] Segregationist sermons became less numerous in the late 1950's and early 1960's. This was true for at least two reasons: (1) the segregationists had set forth their basic arguments and had little more to add; (2) civil rights gained popularity and the segregationists had to buck public opinion.

[3] To determine the precise number or percentage of preachers from each denomination who were in each of the three categories is not possible. Neither is it feasible to calculate how many sermons were related to race. Estimates and generalizations in this chapter are based on observations by leaders in the main religious groups in America.

[4] The Black Muslims are difficult to classify. Their spokesmen, in a sense, were preachers. In their addresses they advocated black supremacy and often urged a form of segregation to keep the black from contamination by the white. Yet, they also favored certain aspects of the civil rights movement.

hold Niebuhr, and Carl F. H. Henry, spoke out in behalf of the Negro and thus encouraged others to do likewise. An increasing amount of pro-civil rights printed material furnished information for sermons.

By the mid-1960's, some preachers who had been vocal in the movement began retreating to the silent middle; others expressed doubts. This was due in part to the slowdown of the total movement. It had bounded forward without pause for over a decade, and many began to realize that problems compounded by centuries of neglect were not to be solved by a decade of concern. Also a so-called "white backlash" developed and made preaching on race relations less popular than it had been in the early 1960's. New causes engaged the attention of the minister—war in Vietnam, poverty in America, and renewal in the church. Thus, civil rights preaching, though still relevant, was not fresh and lost much of its urgency.

Authority, Appeals, and Arguments

Both the segregationists and the civil rights advocates based their messages on many sources. Each claimed the authority of God and the Bible. They also based the rightness of their stand on the nature of man, on law and reason, on the lessons of history, the data of science, and the teachings and writings of prominent individuals.

Most ministers who spoke to the race issue were skilled in the art of persuasion. They appealed to reason and to the emotions—especially pride, patriotism, love, fear, anger, pity, and the sense of duty. The numerous arguments used in the sermons of the time fall into categories largely determined by the nature of the appeal.[5]

Opponents of civil rights contended that reason clearly dictated segregation. Segregationists insisted that the white man was superior to the black man. They reasoned, therefore, that the white race must be kept from black contamination and that segregation was obviously the best way to maintain this racial purity. They warned that the civil rights movement would lead to the destruction of the white man's civilization because it would result in intermarriage and the end of racial purity.

Segregationists declared that the Negro was better off in America than anywhere else in the world. To them it was obvious that their system worked for the progress of the black as well as for the protection of the white.

Opponents of integration further reasoned that God would not have made different racial types if he had not intended for them to remain distinct; thus, segregation was considered natural. It had the further advantage of

---

[5] In a limited essay, an extensive listing of pro- and anti-segregation arguments used in sermons is impossible. The arguments presented in this chapter are, therefore, merely representative. They were all widely used, however. Because of wide use, only actual quotations will be footnoted. As far as possible, quotations are from sermons in published books.

378

easing tension between the two races since it clearly defined the Negro's place and encouraged him to stay in it.

When the civil rights movement occurred, there was widespread fear of communism. The segregationists capitalized on this fear by labeling the movement as communist inspired and directed. In an address before the Synod of Mississippi of the Presbyterian Church in the United States, G. T. Gillespie of Belhaven College said, "It is not without significance, however, that a very considerable part of the violent agitation against segregation stems from sources outside the negro [sic] race, and outside of America, and coincides with the world-wide movement for racial amalgamation which has its fountainhead in Moscow." [6]

Knowing the desire of most people to stand with the majority, the opponents of civil rights insisted that most Americans—black and white—preferred a segregated society. Outside agitators caused the trouble, the segregationists insisted. In his Mississippi Synod address, Gillespie insisted, "The Southern negro . . . is happier and better adjusted, than can be said of any comparable number of his race at any time in their history or in any part of the world today." [7] And a Baptist preacher speaking to the Joint Assembly of the state of South Carolina declared:

It's some of those two-by scantling, good-for-nothing fellows who are trying to upset all of the things that we love as good old Southern people. . . . They don't know us, and I'm glad. Let them stay where they are, wherever they are, but leave us alone. We get along fine. We are not having any trouble. [8]

Civil rights advocates, not to be outdone, had ample arguments to support their cause. They were adept at pointing out the inconsistencies of the segregationist position. They asked, for example, why, if segregation existed to prevent interbreeding of the races, there were millions of mulattoes in the South, the most thoroughly segregated section of America. Preachers favoring civil rights insisted that segregation harmed everyone involved, diminished the prestige of the United States in the world, and caused a decline in the effectiveness of evangelism and missions.

While the anti-segregationists sometimes displayed prejudice toward the prejudiced and hate toward the hatemongers, they usually sounded a note of love, concern, justice, and sympathy. A favorite technique was to describe

[6] G. T. Gillespie, "A Christian View on Segregation," an address presented before the Synod of Mississippi of the Presbyterian Church in the United States, November 4, 1954, p. 3. Printed pamphlet available from Citizens' Councils, Greenwood, Mississippi.

[7] Ibid., p. 7.

[8] W. A. Criswell, "Christianity and Segregation," an address presented to the Joint Assembly of South Carolina. Printed booklet, n. d., n. p. Mr. Criswell is pastor of the First Baptist Church, Dallas, Texas. In 1968, however, Mr. Criswell came out strongly against segregation in churches and pleaded for an open-door policy in regard to churches and race.

vividly the plight of the Negro and then appeal for Christians to act in love to help the downtrodden. Using this technique, a Negro preacher declared:

The Negro, once principally a small farmer, under the impact of contracting agriculture has become a displaced, unskilled, unhoused semi-migrant herded into the ghettos of the cities, themselves unprepared to absorb him. In these conditions of chaotic change his fragile family life has been shattered, his labor wasted or exploited, and thick walls of discrimination crush his hopes and opportunity. The Negro did not do this himself—it was done for him.[9]

In vivid fashion, white preachers described the injustice, cruelty, violence, and suffering inflicted on the Negro. David G. Colwell, at the time pastor of the First Congregational United Church of Christ in Washington, D. C., spoke of "injuries of vital sensitive parts of the human anatomy inflicted by the cruel and abusive use of cattle prods." [10]

Sermons which applied the requirements of Christian love to modern racial problems were common among the ranks of the pro-civil rights preachers. The appeal of the nonviolent revolution, headed effectively by Martin Luther King, Jr., was largely to love. King preached that love ultimately would triumph over hate and prejudice. In his hands, love became a tool to batter down the doors which prejudice had closed to the Negro. By nonviolence and love or goodwill in action the Negro and his white sympathizers would overcome their opponents. King declared:

To our most bitter opponents we say: "We shall match your capacity to inflict suffering by our capacity to endure suffering. We shall meet your physical force with soul force. . . . We cannot in all good conscience obey your unjust laws, because non-cooperation with evil is as much a moral obligation as is cooperation with good. Throw us in jail and we shall love you. Bomb our homes and be assured that we will wear you down by our capacity to suffer. One day we shall win freedom, but not only for ourselves. We shall so appeal to your heart and conscience that we shall win *you* in the process, and our victory will be a double victory." [11]

Both pro- and anti-civil rights preachers insisted that the sciences bolstered their position. They often cited material from anthropology and sociology.

Both sides also appealed to the prestige of authority figures. Segregationists quoted with zeal statements by Thomas Jefferson, Abraham Lincoln, and even David Livingstone declaring the black man to be inferior to white. Various scientists were cited to prove white supremacy. On the other hand,

[9] Martin Luther King, Jr., "Beyond Discovery, Love," an unpublished sermon presented to the International Convention of Christian Churches in Dallas, Texas, September 25, 1966, n. p. (Mimeographed.)

[10] David G. Colwell, "As if in a Foreign Country," *The Pulpit Speaks on Race*, ed. Alfred T. Davies (Nashville: Abingdon Press, 1965), p. 136.

[11] G. Paul Butler, ed., *Best Sermons*, IX (New York: D. Van Nostrand, 1964), 277.

those opposing segregation also displayed scientific studies and statements by famous men to defend their position.

Both camps strongly appealed to the senses of duty and social responsibility. White suprematists argued that it was the duty of the white man to protect his civilization. They insisted—as long as segregation laws were on the books—that citizens should obey the law. Civil rights advocates meanwhile declared that democracy cannot exist apart from social justice, and that justice called for the elimination of segregation. They also called on citizens to obey the law of the land—the laws abolishing segregation.

Biblical and Theological Arguments

That which distinguished the sermons on race relations from the thousands of other speeches on the subject was a heavy emphasis on the Bible and theology.

The segregationists produced many texts to prove their cases; they claimed that the Bible from Genesis to Revelation supported segregation. Speaking of the first chapter of Genesis, Carey Daniel, author of the sermon *God the Original Segregationist*, insisted that "God made all His different creatures to be separated and segregated according to their different kinds and different species, and man is no exception to the rule." [12]

Perhaps the favorite text used against the Negro was Genesis 9, the so-called "Curse of Ham." According to the segregationists' interpretation of this passage, God cursed all the descendents of Ham to servitude and turned their skin black. Joshua 9 and Jeremiah 13:23 were used to support the contention that the Bible taught black skin was a symbol of the Negro's evil nature and that he was to be a "hewer of wood and drawer of water" forever. To further insure segregation, God confounded the languages of the people in the Tower of Babel experience. One minister discussed the Genesis 11 passage:

Let me say that the human race was fully integrated at the Tower of Babel. . . . This was the darkest day thus far in human history subsequent to Adam's fall. Satan was nearer to a complete victory in that day than he ever has been since. . . . God, Himself, had to come down and deal directly with the situation. Segregation was born at Babel and our God was the creator of it. [13]

The whole Old Testament was interpreted by the white supremists as an appeal for racial purity. They pointed out that God severely punished the Israelites for intermarriage with other people; thus he must be vitally concerned about the preservation of the purity of racial stock.

[12] Carey Daniel, *God the Original Segregationist and Seven Other Segregation Sermons* (Dallas, Texas: By the author, n. d.), p. 15.
[13] Byron M. Wilkinson, "Fusion of the Races," printed sermon available from Hatcher Memorial Baptist Church, Richmond, Virginia, p. 6.

The New Testament also served as a support for the segregationists' position. According to their view, every leading figure in the New Testament, including Jesus, was a segregationist. They insisted that Jesus never called for amalgamation; rather, he emphasized racial differences. As one preacher put it: "The incarnation of God in Christ did not change His views on racial segregation." [14] An often quoted passage in the New Testament was Acts 17:26 which was said to prove that God had established the division of the races. And, thundered the segregationists, what God has put asunder, let not man join together!

Many preachers who opposed integration recognized the need to evangelize and treat Negroes with kindness. But they insisted that this could be done apart from race mixing. They declared that the Bible calls men to concern for the souls of all men and to spiritual unity but that spiritual unity did not require social unity. In fact, integration was declared to be anti-Christian. T. Robert Ingram, an Episcopal priest, declared:

I believe that integration is un-Christian! Further, I believe that integration is anti-Christian! . . . I believe that the integration movement is one very important facet of a world-wide, highly-organized, centuries-old assault on mankind's greatest treasure—our faith in Jesus Christ. . . .
Every person who believes . . . in what we today call "integration," is also declaring that he believes Christ spoke falsely, and that Christ is not ruler and sovereign over all things in Heaven and in earth. . . .
Integration is important . . . because if we accept it, it will snatch us who accept it away from the throne of grace! [15]

Defenders of the Negroes' rights also used the Bible to support their stand. Their approach utilized fewer proof texts and more appeals to general biblical truth.

Yet, the anti-segregationists did have favorite texts. Among them were Matthew 22:34-40 (love for God, neighbor, and self), Acts 17:26 (God made of one blood all nations), and I Peter 1:17 (God is not a respecter of persons). It should be noted that while the segregationists leaned heavily on the Old Testament, their opponents depended more specifically upon the New Testament.

Rather than pluck verses here and there to build their case, civil rights proponents usually talked more about the biblical view of God, man, salvation, and the church in relation to race. They had much to say about God. He created all men. He is just and is no respecter of persons. He showers his love on all people regardless of color. And Christians are to be like God, insisted the preachers. "God demands justice for all of us, and we must de-

[14] Daniel, *God the Original Segregationist*, p. 11.
[15] T. Robert Ingram, "Why Integration Is Un-Christian!" sermon reprinted from *The Citizen*, the Citizens' Council, Plaza Building, Jackson, Mississippi, n. d., n. p.

mand it for one another." [16] "As God makes no distinctions in His relationship to man, so He would have us make no distinctions in our relationships."[17]

The will of God for man, declared the opponents of discrimination, rules out segregation. Joseph W. Ellwanger, pastor of St. Paul Lutheran Church in Birmingham, Alabama, preached, "It is important for us as followers of the Christ to see clearly that God is not neutral toward segregation—nor can we be neutral—because, as Paul wrote several times in his letter to the Ephesians, it is God's plan to unite all things in Christ." [18] The fact that those in the New Testament who carried out the will of God did so without discrimination was given as further evidence that God abhors prejudice. Often cited were the experiences of Peter and Cornelius, Philip and the Ethiopian eunuch, Philemon and Onesimus.

The Christian preachers insisted that the most complete understanding of what God is like is to be gained in Jesus Christ. Thus, the example of Jesus in human relations became the ideal for all to follow. Civil rights sermons pointed out that Jesus broke down the barriers of segregation which existed in his day. Francis Gerald Ensley, bishop of the Methodist Church, declared:

He lived in a segregated society. "Jews have no dealings with Samaritans." Yet, he could make a Samaritan the hero of a parable. He lived at a time when Rome and all her lackeys were hated as were the Nazis by the Europe they subdued a quarter century ago. Yet, he healed a centurion's servant and called a publican—a Roman henchman—down out of a tree to eat with him.[19]

For many the incarnation was the reason for their involvement in the race problem. They argued that since in the incarnation God became involved with humanity to help man, they must become involved with the oppressed in order to help them. Many also saw in the cross an indication that redemption comes only through suffering. They were, therefore, willing to suffer for the cause of civil rights. The promoters of brotherhood further declared that because Jesus had ministered to them without discrimination, they must minister to others in like fashion.

Almost as important as the emphasis on the nature of God was that on the nature of man. Sermons favoring the cause of racial justice insisted on the unity of the human race. They declared that all men were created in the image of God and were, therefore, worthy of dignity and respect. Gerald Kennedy declared:

[16] Gerald Kennedy, "Dedicated to a Proposition," *The Pulpit Speaks on Race*, ed. Alfred T. Davies, p. 75.

[17] Lloyd L. Ramseyer, *The More Excellent Way* (Newton, Kansas: Faith and Life Press, 1965), p. 85.

[18] Joseph W. Ellwanger, "God's Plan: To Unite All Things in Christ," *The Pulpit Speaks on Race*, ed. Alfred T. Davies, p. 41.

[19] Francis Gerald Ensley, "On Loving One's Neighbor as Oneself," *The Pulpit Speaks on Race*, ed. Alfred T. Davies, p. 54.

The Christian church comes into our world with an idea about man and his ultimate nature. It proclaims the worth of every human creature and the universal brotherhood of all of us. There is no biblical support for prejudice or for the artificial distinctions of color and class.[20]

A strong appeal was also made to look upon men as individuals, not as members of racial groups. James Armstrong, pastor of the Broadway Methodist Church in Indianapolis, Indiana, stated, "Prejudice does not see the *individual* as a growing, dreaming, yearning, laughing, crying, aching child of God. And that's exactly what he is, no matter who he is or where he's from." [21] And these individuals were to be treated as equals, regardless of their status in life. As one minister said, "The fact that a brother is weaker than we are, that he is indeed our inferior, is all the more reason that we should accept him as our brother." [22]

The nature of the church was also used to argue against segregation. Preachers pointed out that the church belonged to God, not man. It was God who determined the makeup of the church, not man. Segregated churches, therefore, were declared to be an affront to the God who loved all men and called all men to him through his Son. Eleven o'clock on Sunday morning was lamented as the most segregated hour of the week.

Approaches in Preaching

Race relations sermons were both direct and indirect, general and specific. The most rabid segregationists often dealt directly with race. Their sermons were topical in nature and dealt exclusively with this one issue. The titles of some indicate their forthrightness: "God the Original Segregationist," "A Mongrel America Tomorrow," "Why Integration Is Un-Christian!" and "A Christian View on Segregation." These messages could not be misunderstood. They did not skirt the issue. The preacher stated the point and declared with no quibbling that segregation was the will of God and that any Christian worth his salt would staunchly defend the system.

The most outspoken of the civil rights advocates also dealt directly with race in their sermons. This was especially true of the leaders of the movement such as Martin Luther King, Jr. Other ministers—both black and white —spoke directly on the race issue too. The number of immediately available printed sermons directly advocating support of the civil rights movement far outnumber sermons directly damning the movement.

Other sermons dealt with the racial problem indirectly. Various techniques were employed to approach the subject obliquely. One way was to preach on

[20] Kennedy, "Dedicated to a Proposition," p. 71.
[21] James Armstrong, "Long Minutes," *The Pulpit Speaks on Race*, ed. Alfred T. Davies, p. 17.
[22] Warren Tyree Carr, "On Reviving a Doctrine," *The Pulpit Speaks on Race*, ed. Alfred T. Davies, p. 175.

a general theme, such as love or the will of God, and make one of the applications to race. Another was to preach from a text and to relate the teaching to current issues, one of which obviously was race. Segregationists often inserted comments on the race issue into sermons on other topics.

In areas where the racial issue was especially explosive the proponents of civil rights often used the indirect approach. One pastor explained why:

In a situation such as this I believe that a pastor must speak prophetically but also wisely. When the matter of race relations is brought up on a larger context of man's total response to the gospel and not as a specific, isolated subject, the defenses are often penetrated more effectively. As a result my preaching on this subject is usually a part of the application of a Scripture lesson to many facets of life.[23]

Sermons on race were also both general and specific. On both sides of the issue the majority of messages called for response and action of generality. The consensus of many evaluating the preaching supporting civil rights was that it was very general. Ian McCrae of the Department of Christian Action and Community Service of the Disciples of Christ maintained:

Such sermons are generally couched in such vague terms as to enable the congregation to agree in principles since no specific suggestions are being made. There are not too many people in congregations now that are going to vote against the brotherhood of man as long as this does not call for any particular action which disrupts their present mode of living.[24]

Malcolm P. Calhoun of the Division of Church and Society of the Presbyterian Church in the United States said, "Generally, preaching has not been specific enough to arouse much response in the congregation." [25]

In the main the pro-civil rights sermons called for love, brotherhood, better human relations, and other general responses. Often the insistence was that the only hope for better race relations was for men to learn to love their fellowman, and this could happen only when they were "right with God." Thus much of the preaching was directed to the individual—his attitudes and actions—rather than to social, legal, and economic action.

Some sermons were specific, however. Messages supported or condemned efforts to desegregate public schools. Significant civil rights steps evoked definite censure or praise—the 1954 decision of the Supreme Court of the United States, the civil rights act of 1957, 1960, 1964, and 1965, demonstrations, marches, and sit-ins. Other messages were designed to elicit a specific response from the congregation, such as a decision to accept or to refuse Negroes who came for worship or membership.

[23]Letter from Melvin D. Hugen, pastor of the Eastern Avenue Christian Reformed Church, Grand Rapids, Michigan, December 7, 1966.
[24] Letter from Ian McCrae, Department of Christian Action and Community Service of the Disciples of Christ, October 13, 1966.
[25] Letter from Malcolm P. Calhoun, October 13, 1966.

An example of a sermon which set forth rather specific suggestions is "Law and Order and Christian Duty" by Eugene Carson Blake, stated Clerk of the United Presbyterian Church in the U.S.A. In it he recommended: (1) to encourage Congress to pass stronger civil rights legislation; (2) to join some civil rights organization; (3) to encourage fair treatment of Negroes with regard to training and employment; (4) to pray for the Negro community and those who lead out in civil rights activities; (5) to lead out in making it possible for anyone who has the financial resources to buy and rent in your community; and (6) to protest when you hear people slamming the civil rights movement.[26]

Other Sermon Characteristics

To read through the sermons preached on race in the 1950's and 1960's is to be struck by a number of characteristics common to most of the messages: ridicule directed to the opposition; refutation of contrary arguments; firmness of conviction; urgency; highly emotional and oratorical statements. Some of these characteristics are illustrated in the following passages from a sermon by Thomas Kilgore, Jr, of the Second Baptist Church, Los Angeles:

The spirit of a developing and growing America has never been a spirit of gradualism. We have never been satisfied in this great country with snail's pace progress. When Great Britain attempted to strangle our initiative and keep us in a subservient position we declared ourselves independent and engaged in a powerful arms struggle in the late eighteenth century to certify our rights to move on unhampered.

We were not gradualists in embracing the tools of the Industrial Revolution. We moved with almost lightning-like speed from an agrarian economy to the most powerful industrial complex in the world. In scientific research we have startled the world with our discoveries and inventions, and in transportation we have few peers. *Gradualism! Status quo! Wait! The time is not ripe!* These are not American expressions. We have always been ready to move ahead. Why, then, the cry for gradualism as the American Negro emerges in his fight for first-class citizenship? Why ask him to be gradual? Why ask him to wait? Crispus Attucks did not wait at the Boston Common. He rushed forth with courage and with love of country to be the first to spill blood in the American Revolution. The thousands of Negro soldiers who fought in the Civil War did not wait. . . . In subsequent years they have done the same at San Juan Hill, at Okinawa, on Normandy Beach, and at Heart Break Ridge.[27]

One of the greatest criticisms of the civil rights movement was that racial problems cannot be solved by law. Martin Luther King's refutation of this argument is characteristic of pro-civil rights preaching:

[26] Eugene Carson Blake, "Law and Order and Christian Duty," *The Pulpit Speaks on Race,* ed. Alfred T. Davies, pp. 115-17.

[27] Thomas Kilgore, Jr., "Segregation, Discrimination, and the Christian Church," *The Pulpit Speaks on Race,* ed. Alfred T. Davies, pp. 147-48.

Let us never succumb to the temptation of believing that legislation and judicial decrees play only minor roles in solving this problem. Morality cannot be legislated but behavior can be regulated. Judicial decrees may not change the heart, but they can restrain the heartless. The law cannot make a man love me, but it can keep him from lynching me. . . . The habits, if not the hearts of people, have been and are being altered everyday by legislative acts, judicial decisions, and executive orders. Let us not be misled by those who argue that segregation cannot be ended by the force of law.[28]

Sermons on race, especially by segregationists, sometimes ridiculed the opposition mercilessly. Carey Daniel, pastor of the First Baptist Church of West Dallas, Texas, was one of the hardest hitting of the anti-civil rights preachers. He thundered:

All "American" integrationists should be given a one-way ticket across the Rio Grande River. There in Mexico, Central and South America they would find the Finished Product of the Race-Mixer's Art—white, black, and yellow people all intermarried, blended into a duke's mixture and stirred into a slow brown gravy. They would soon sicken of that comparative heathenism and yearn to return to the White Man's civilization which once they had scorned.[29]

In a sermon entitled "After His Kind" Daniel further declared:

When some Communist comes along with his anti-God and anti-Christ philosophy, teaching that the races should be mongrelized and that the White race should be Africanized, if necessary at the point of a bayonet, there are literally millions of Americans who will accept that teaching as law and gospel. . . . There are multitudes of dupes who will swallow that demoniacal doctrine hook, line and sinker.[30]

Certain features were more characteristic of pro-civil rights sermons than addresses by segregationists. Among these were self-rebuke, confession of the church's sin, and calls for repentance. For example, William O. Byrd, minister of the First Methodist Church in New Orleans, Louisiana, declared, "Too often the Church (or rather the caricature we make of His Holy Body on earth) became molded and shaped by pious prattle, mouthing its love of the Supreme Law Giver and Lover of All Life while dragging behind the Supreme Court in human relations." [31] Frederick West, in a sermon entitled "The Word Is Near You," declared, "God is calling to us Christians and our segregated, but priceless, churches to repent and to live as new creatures in Christ Jesus in the church and in the rest of society's public institutions." [32] And E. J. Kearney, a Southern Baptist, in 1957 preached:

[28] King, "Beyond Discovery, Love," n. p.
[29] Daniel, *God the Original Segregationist*, pp. 38-39.
[30] *Ibid.*, p. 17.
[31] G. Paul Butler, ed., *Best Sermons*, VIII (New York: D. Van Nostrand, 1962), 271.
[32] R. Frederick West, "The Word Is Near You," *Preaching on Race* (St. Louis, Missouri: The Bethany Press, 1962), p. 88.

I am ashamed that the highest court of our land has to enjoin upon us by decree of law the Bible doctrine that all men are made equal in the sight of God. I am ashamed that the church has kept her tongue in cheek ere these years and failed to cry out against the injustices of our day—both social and racial. . . . But the pulpit has been embarrassingly quiet on the subject of race relations—lest it cost us our pulpits.[33]

Reactions

From 1954 to the mid-1960's, a barrage of words about race was loosed by preachers. Did these sermons have any effect on the racial pattern as a whole in the United States? Such a question can be answered only by informed speculation. A number of denominational spokesmen expressed pessimism over the effect of sermons designed to better race relations. In 1966, Ian McCrae wrote, "My reaction is that the pulpit has had very minimal effect on the climate of civil rights and race relations in our denomination or in the nation." [34] At the same time Grover Bagby of the General Board of Christian Social Concerns of the Methodist Church wrote: "I would say that both in the North and in the South, the church is still largely irrelevant to the crucial, cutting edges of the civil rights question." [35] But the accuracy of such statements is not really determinable. As Rabbi Roland B. Gittelsohn stated, "As to what precise, practical effect my preaching has had in their lives, I wish I knew some device which would enable preachers to measure this not only on the subject of race but quite generally." [36]

It seems fair to assume that pro-civil rights preaching had some positive effect. It helped create a climate of open discussion about race. It encouraged those actively engaged in the civil rights movement. It put into circulation a mass of material about race from a religious point of view. It informed lawmakers that many in the church were in favor of civil rights legislation. It stimulated a number of ministers and churchmen to campaign actively for social and legal action to reduce discrimination. Quite possibly such preaching was partially responsible for a number of active churchmen in high government posts taking a leading role in civil rights legislation.

The effect of anti-segregation preaching within churches and denominations was by no means uniform. In certain areas and within some religious groups these sermons contributed to the elimination of segregation as an official policy in thousands of churches and church-related institutions. Many preachers directly attacked segregation in the church. Of course, not all the shake-up in racial policies of churches during the 1950's and 1960's can be

---

[33] E. J. Kearney, "The Church's Responsibility in Race Relations," mimeographed sermon in files of author, p. 2.

[34] Letter from Ian McCrae, October 13, 1966.

[35] Letter from Grover Bagby, October 12, 1966.

[36] Letter from Roland B. Gittelsohn, Rabbi of Temple Sinai, Long Island, New York, November 14, 1966.

traced directly to sermons, but sermons certainly contributed to building a climate of opinion which made such changes possible.

On the other hand, the effect of segregation sermons was small. Such sermons apparently served to deepen the convictions of segregationists, but they were of little effect in changing opinion or policy. Of course, anti-civil rights messages defended the status quo. Their purpose for the most part was not to stimulate but rather to prevent change. In churches and communities where segregation was held to tenaciously, one may guess with some basis that sermons contributed to the effectiveness of the holding action.

While the effects of sermons in regard to social change are difficult to determine, the responses to sermons on race are more obvious. Pro-civil rights sermons were met with far more pronounced reaction than messages expressing the opposite view. In some instances the minister advocating the end to segregation and racial discrimination was praised by both black and white members of the community. Sometimes his hearers entered in active support of the Negroes' cause, and his church experienced an increase in attendance and contribution. More often, however, the response was negative, even violent.

The degree of adverse reaction was in proportion to the people's commitment to segregation and fear of change. Where prejudice was deep, belief in segregation strong, and fear of changed circumstances great, reaction to pro-civil rights sermons was often violent. Suggestive of this sort of response are these: Church members withheld financial support or withdrew from the church; church officials and members demanded that the minister stop speaking on race and confine himself to "preaching the gospel";[37] hostile letters, threatening phone calls, and public ridicule harassed the preacher and his family. Other more violent responses were less common but received more publicity. A number of ministers were forced to leave the church where they had preached on race. Several were attacked and beaten by mobs. Loss of property was often experienced: churches and the homes of many pro-civil rights preachers were bombed and/or burned. Some ministers were killed for their stand on race. Shot and beaten to death, they became the martyrs of the cause. In most cases the severest violence came because the ministers were not content to confine their efforts to sermons. Rather, they became active participants in civil rights demonstrations and programs.

In contrast to the fate of pro-civil rights preachers, the segregationist ministers fared rather well. They experienced practically no loss of job or physical abuse. Their churches, composed of persons who agreed in the main

---

[37] The following were the most common charges leveled against civil rights preaching: (1) such preaching mixed religion and politics; (2) it was a social gospel approach to the Christian faith; (3) it detracted preachers from speaking to save souls; (4) preaching on controversial subjects would hurt the church; (5) the civil rights movement was in error and did not deserve the support of the clergy.

with segregationist views, seldom opposed such preaching. A very few opponents of civil rights were the butt of scorn, ridicule, and social ostracism. However, as public sentiment grew, the strong segregationist waned in influence and by the mid-1960's many churches would not accept as pastor a rabid segregationist.

Conclusion

Preaching was a significant aspect of the civil rights revolution of the 1950's and 1960's. Martin Luther King, Jr., one of the leaders of the revolution and himself a Baptist minister, made of preaching a weapon to batter down the walls of segregation. Many other black and white preachers used sermons to urge support of the civil rights movement. Preachers also sermonized against civil rights and for segregation. Most racist sermons were heard in white churches, but the Black Muslims often set forth a similar line.

While no precise accounting is possible, likely more sermons were preached on race than any other social issue during this period. Yet, great hosts of ministers in most denominations said little or nothing. Few preached on the issue to the extent that they became known as "race preachers." But numbers of men bucked public opinion, risked their jobs—and even their lives—to take a stand, to relate their view of religion to life. This they did as they spoke from pulpits about race.

20

THE CHALLENGE
OF THE SECULAR

_____Leroy Davis_____

During the past two decades the church has been called upon once again to define its relationship to the world. The need for redefinition has come about because of changes which have taken place in the secular world. There have been two basic responses to the call of the secular. The first, the expressive, was reflected in the attempted return to normalcy following World War II. The second response, the instrumental,[1] stressed the need for greater involvement in worldly affairs. The first response tended to incorporate a tacit definition of the church as a holy, spiritual, otherworldly institution. The second response tended to develop a definition of the church which stressed its similarities to other institutions in nature and task.

Definition of the Polarity

The expressive polar position views the church as an institution set apart from the world. The instrumental polar position sees the church as a part of the world. Since representatives of both polar positions appeal to the same sources, i.e., the Bible, history, contemporary events, and theology, it is not possible to claim that one position is necessarily more "true" than the other or that one position is necessarily predicated upon firmer foundations. The real difference between the polar positions is to be found, not in methods of exegesis or in analysis of events, but in the assumptions maintained. It is quite possible to find sources to which appeal can be made to justify either position, but these are secondary to the assumptions basic to each position. The expressive group tends to assume that the church ought to be separated from the world in some sense, while the instrumental group tends to assume that the church ought to be a part of the world.

Extreme models of either position appear. For example, the preaching of

---

[1] The words "instrumental" and "expressive" have been taken from Talcott Parsons and E. A. Shils, eds., _Toward a General Theory of Action_ (Cambridge: Harvard University Press, 1951).

Carl McIntire, Billy James Hargis, and ministers of the American Council of Christian Churches would be classed in the expressive polar position, but the bulk of expressive preaching is probably not too closely related to the views of that group. Conversely, Bishop James Pike, the Rev. Malcolm Boyd, Fr. James Groppi, and Dr. James Kavanaugh would be placed in the instrumental category, but they would be no more representative of the membership of this category than Carl McIntire is of the other.

The polarity can perhaps be best defined through reference to two recent books both authored by preachers. In the first, Paul Ramsey[2] made the following statement:

My thesis is that, if such an examination is undertaken, we will no longer be able to speak and act as if there is a closer identification between Christian social ethics and the policy making of the Secular City than was asserted even in the Middle Ages. In the *contents* of ecumenical ethics there needs to be some way to tell some difference between the spiritual and temporal power. Yet I fear that to propound this thesis even in an age that is assertedly post-Christian will only brand the author as one who believes the church to be a spiritual cult with no pertinent social outlook.[3]

Continuing, Ramsey examined the assumption of the "new" Christian ethics:

The *ad hoc* theology that today gives seeming warrant to this almost complete identification of Christian social ethics with social policy making is the view that the relevant contemporary knowledge of God and his claims upon us and the judgment and grace he enacts over humankind comes from "what God is doing in the world."[4]

Ramsey then termed this approach "a fig leaf to cover the unseemly parts of a disintegrated Christian understanding . . . an evident secularization of the church."[5]

In politics the church is only a *theoretician*. The religious communities as such should be concerned with *perspectives* upon politics, with political doctrine, with the direction and structures of the common life, not with specific directives.[6]

Ramsey also contended that the religious communities "need to stand in awe before people called political 'decision makers,' or rather before the majesty of topmost political agency." Ramsey's theological justification for this view is that:

Political decision and action is an image of the majesty of God, who also rules by particular decrees. God says, "Let there be . . ."; and his word becomes deed

---

[2] Paul Ramsey, *Who Speaks for the Church?* (Nashville: Abingdon Press, 1967).
[3] *Ibid.*, p. 20.
[4] *Ibid.*
[5] *Ibid.*, p. 21.
[6] *Ibid.*, p. 152.

and actuality. So also earthly magistrates have the high and lonely responsibility of declaring what shall actually be done.[7]

He concluded with these words, "Let the church be the church and let the magistrate be the magistrate. Let both keep their distances. May there be less confusion of these roles."[8]

In contrast to Ramsey's views are those of Harvey Cox[9]:

No doubt it is hard for us to concede that God works through secularization, the revolution against the remnants of religious world views. But he does.[10] . . . It is crucial to recall that God is working his reconciliation *in the world*. It is the world's renewal in which the church is privileged to participate. The church is not the only community of renewal, but it participates gladly and thankfully in the totality of that renewal.[11] . . . We have suggested that in Jesus of Nazareth we encounter a God who discloses himself through activities that threaten the status quo, through something like what we now call revolution.[12] . . . We have been emphasizing all along that in a secular age the mission of the church must assume a secular style.[13]

It is obvious that there are considerable differences between the viewpoints of Ramsey and Cox. For purposes of definition, Ramsey's views would be labeled expressive; those of Cox, instrumental. It is notable that neither position contains an argument for noninvolvement of the church in the world. Aside from their theological orientations, that which distinguishes them is the *means* by which they feel the church should be involved in "secular" affairs. The expressive position presents the view that it is the business of the church to deal with generic understandings from which individuals derive their own concrete actions, and with the development of persons who will act rightly in the world. The instrumental view tends to maintain that it is the business of the church to change not only individuals, but also the structures and the context of human life through direct involvement of the church in "secular" affairs. Neither position maintains that the church should not be involved; separation does not mean non-involvement. The bulk of sermonic debate over involvement in the "secular" tends to take place on the level of the *means* of involvement, not on the level of whether there should or should not be involvement.

Some would assert that the expressivists really don't want to see the church involved in the world, and that their statements about means are but a cover-up for their real views. If such a contention were to be made, the converse would also have to be made, namely, that the instrumentalists want to do

[7] *Ibid.*, p. 153.
[8] *Ibid.*, p. 157.
[9] Harvey Cox, *God's Revolution and Man's Responsibility* (Valley Forge, Pennsylvania: Judson Press, 1965).
[10] *Ibid.*, p. 33.
[11] *Ibid.*, p. 69.
[12] *Ibid.*, p. 103.
[13] *Ibid.*, p. 104.

away with anything called church. Such reductionism would result in the expressivists calling the others communists, and the instrumentalists calling their opposites sacred cows or pious isolationists. Without being too reckless then, the positions of polarity under consideration are distinguished primarily by the respective approaches taken to involvement of the church in the world or the secular. The expressive position tends to represent the view that it is the business of the church to set forth general principles relative to secular affairs and to develop persons who are able to be constructively involved in the world. The instrumental position tends to be that of involvement of the institutional church in changing the context of personal life, as well as individuals, through direct involvement in specific programs or activities. Zealots on both ends of the continuum would be reluctant to accept such moderate definitions.

Development of the Polarity

This polarity has always been present, only its current form is different from those which have preceded it. The question then arises: Of what larger development is the current polarity a part?

An early emphasis is apparent from the biblical tendency toward two differing orientations to the world. The world was created by God, and when God looked upon it he found it to be good, but the Hebrew people were called upon to separate themselves from their more "worldly" neighbors.

Further, the New Testament seems to contain two differing views about the world. One is that the world is an evil place from which escape should be sought (cf. James 1:27 and I John 2:15-16). The other is that the world is loved by God and that it is good that persons live in it (cf. John 3:16). While it is not difficult to reconcile these views through word studies or theological gymnastics, it does appear that these views of the world represent differing outlooks on life and religion. The expressivists do tend to look upon the world as having a contaminating effect upon the church, so that it must remain somewhat aloof if it is to carry out its purpose of redeeming the world. The instrumentalists tend to view the world as where God is, and so involvement in it is a good thing.

Another view of the current polarity has to do with an understanding of whether the church *is* or whether the church *does*. A church which *is* is established either theologically or politically and exists as a part of the culture which surrounds it. It performs certain well-defined tasks which contribute to the maintenance of the culture. Using a sales motif, it represents God through the sanctification of certain cultural phenomena which are defined as helpful to cultural existence. The church which *is* gives its blessing to the family, the country, worship, traditions, the Boy Scouts, the P.T.A., the flag, motherhood, capitalism (sometimes to modified socialism), hard work, holy

394

war (defined as any war undertaken by the society), "safety in the streets," and so on. The church which *is* is concerned to maintain certain cultural phenomena because they are considered to be "right." In return, the church which *is* is protected by the culture so long as it sanctifies the right things and does not intrude into that which it sanctifies. The church which *is* is separated of necessity so that it can maintain the moral fiber and strength of the culture without contamination by the difficult and compromising nature of secular affairs. Its function is to bless and sanctify.

The church which *does* is quite different. Here the conception is that something called the gospel is a revolutionary program which takes precedence over any cultural institutions. It is not concerned to maintain, but to tear down the old and build up something new. It is dissatisfied with cultural institutions and is eager to get about the task of doing something to effect a change in a direction that will be more "right." Thus, the church which *does* is concerned for the brotherhood of man, the fatherhood of God, open housing, equal rights for everybody, an end to war (it does not recognize a holy war), food for starving children, and is against police brutality, tyranny, and middle-class America. These things, according to the definition of the church which *does*, are more "right" than the things which the church which *is* considers to be "right." This is why we maintained earlier that the real differences in the polar structure have to be sought on the level of assumptions.

Throughout history there have been church groups which maintained and others which sought change. If Niebuhr is correct,[14] most religious institutions began as revolutionary undertakings and gradually became maintaining groups in the culture, thus giving rise to more revolutionary groups. Certain conditions have prevailed at times when new religious expressions have arisen. The most important of these is the coming to awareness by a group that it does not need to accept disenfranchisement. When persons move toward a refusal of that which has been their lot, whether social, religious, or political, they create "problems."

The creation of "problems" forces those not immediately causing the "problems" to decide upon the degree to which they desire to become involved. Involvement, within this developmental scheme, means involvement in "problems." The "problems" and the consequent solutions can be identified, of course, in any number of ways. For example, when a riot breaks out in an American Negro ghetto, the problem tends to be identified as either a form of insurrection against the established order or as a justifiable redress for grievances. The solution to insurrection is repression by force; the solution for a justifiable redress of grievances is to give the revolutionaries what they want. The maintaining church which *is* will tend to identify the problem as

[14] H. Richard Niebuhr, *Social Sources of Denominationalism.* (New York: Meridian Books, 1957).

insurrection, while the revolutionary church which *does* will tend to identify the problem as a justifiable expression of grievances. Both kinds of churches will be involved in the problem, but in very different ways. Since the church which *is* is established, it tends to be involved on the level of dispensation of spiritual or material blessings commonly known as paternalism. It will give to the "less fortunate" as long as they do not constitute a threat to the established order, in other words, when they accept their "place." When they, in this case ghetto Negroes, no longer desire to be so accepting of their lot, the church which *is* becomes concerned with that great euphemism for Negro revolution, "crime in the streets." The church which *does* tends to be involved on the level of "living with" those who have the potential for revolution. It, thus, tends to be identified with them and there is little transition in its views, except for the liberals who savor a kind of total immersion in "problems" until the talking stops and the action begins. We have used the example of Negro rights or rebellion, depending on how one looks at it, but there have been many more revolutions taking place which have contributed to the creation of "problems" which the title of this essay calls the challenge of the secular.

Bearing in mind that cultural developments take place which give rise to "problems" requiring involvement decisions by the church, it is possible to set forth a few of the "problem" areas or revolutions that currently challenge the church. These contribute to the development of the polarity since by their very existence they induce the church to respond.

One of the greatest revolutions which is taking place is basically philosophical in nature. Growing out of the findings of behavioral sciences it has come to emphasize the qualities of human relationships and psychological health as being of religious concern. In place of discipline and obedience, it holds out the ultimate goods of growth and freedom, both cultural and personal. Such a view has a profound effect on the operation of a church, on clergy-laity relations, on programming, and on every other facet, including worship. The church which *is* has tended to react to this revolution by ignoring the revolution, since this is the first stage in reaction to a revolution, but there are signs in sermonic material that pseudo-psychological approaches to personal problems are growing.

Recently two sermons in different churches were preached on the same text, Matt. 13:24-30. In one case, the preacher took the more or less traditional approach to the passage by placing emphasis upon the judgment to come in the last days when the good and the bad will be separated. Significantly, however, this preacher did perceive the nonjudgmental aspect of the parable. He did not develop the thought, but coming out of a quite rigid expressive background and context, it was most unusual. In the second case the preacher placed his whole emphasis upon the proposition that symbolic weeds are an important aspect of life and that persons should learn more about accepting them than getting rid of them. Both preachers made attempts to bring the gospel into relation with the everyday experiences of persons. The former attempted to do it through an "application" of biblical truth to human situations. The latter began with a psychological proposition and used the biblical materials in a typological framework to develop his theme. Random listening to and reading of sermons tend to indicate that personal problems are receiving an increasing amount of sermonic attention, despite the differences in homiletic approaches and conclusions. The full impact of the revolution is being felt in churches which *do* when they begin to lay aside "religious" terminology and begin programming for growth.

Another aspect of the development of the polarity is the worldwide movement toward nationalism. Aside from upsetting some cherished notions about the world in general, this movement challenges the missionary activities of the churches which *are*. During the late 1940's, a new concept in missionary activity began to emerge into popular awareness. In place of the paternalistic exportation of American culture in the guise of mission, some persons were saying that missionary activity needed to respect the culture indigenous to the missionary area. There grew an awareness of the need for reciprocal missionary work which is rather popular at this time. In a time of emerging nationalism, churches involved in missionary activity cannot help becoming involved on the level of *doing*.

One of the more significant revolutions which has contributed to the development of the polarity has been the rise of pragmatic, materialistic, and technological philosophies. These approaches to life and religious interpretation have tended to emphasize the importance of a sensorially based epistemology in contrast to that derived from the philosophical idealism of the past. The "newer" approaches have tended to reject the notion that thoughts about God or formulations of divinity have any independent existence. These approaches emphasize the point that talk about that which cannot be sensed and measured is just noise. In extreme forms, this view culminates in the proposition that God is dead, since God himself cannot be smelled or measured on a spectrograph. Action is seen as more meaningful than talk. What is involved are competing philosophical orientations. Christian idealism—with its emphasis on an external world of religious ideas—is being increasingly challenged by a view which maintains that ideas have no reality. The thinking of right thoughts is set in conflict with the doing of right actions. The question, "Does it work?" conflicts with the query, "Is that the right way to state that?" The philosophical revolution on the popular level—where many tend to be unaware that philosophical considerations are deeply involved in their attitudes—has had a serious impact on the development of the polarity. Once ideas lose their independent existence, religious talk becomes mere speculation and the whole enterprise descends rapidly to the level of thoughtless and somewhat frenetic activity.

The catalog of revolutions contributing to the development of the polarity would fill a good-sized text. Among them are changes in biblical studies, existential philosophy, new theologies, industrialization, technology, cybernetics, communication, advertising and marketing practices, music, the Negro ghettos, ecumenism, the megalopolis, the labor movement, in short, all the revolutionary changes which have taken place in the past few decades, including new concepts of armament and warfare. Just which factors are more important than others is probably a matter of subjective judgment. The key principle, however, is that revolutions are taking place which require decisions about involvement in them. It is almost impossible to avoid awareness of them due to the hydra-like character of the communications industry. In response to these changes, which take place almost entirely outside parochial existence but in which our culture is deeply enmeshed, the church which *is* tends to try to maintain, while the church which *does* tends to try to revolutionize and relate itself directly to the changes.

In reaction to these developments, the church which *is* tends to maintain a certain kind of preaching which emphasizes individual faith as a response to change. It is expressive preaching because it places a premium on loving and approving that which it seeks to maintain. Expressive preaching esteems that which is established. The church which *does* tends to develop a certain kind of preaching which emphasizes the need for change in the structure of society. It is instrumental preaching because it places a premium on getting things done.

The Context of Preaching

Since preaching does not take place *in vacuo*, it is important to examine briefly the contexts of expressive and instrumental preaching. These contexts tend to differ in many ways, but the chief among them is probably dependent upon financial and social considerations. As a general rule, it is probably true that the expressive position tends to be representative of socially and economically established church groups, while the instrumental position tends to be representative of nonestablished church groups. In this connection I maintained in an earlier essay in this volume that popular preaching (the equivalent of expressive) was dichotomous in nature. That is, it reflected the orientation that religious life and experiences were distinct from secular life and experiences. I also maintained that experimental (could be likened to instrumental) preaching reflected a unitary approach. These distinctions are useful because expressive preaching tends to reflect the idea that institutional involvement in "secular" concerns is inappropriate. While it would be difficult to establish a causal relationship, it is probably fair to state that the greater the degree of social and economic status possessed by a group, the less inclination there is toward institutional involvement with those less well off.

A dichotomous position prevents "secular" problems from arising into "religious" awareness. Where basic needs for housing and education and food exist, it is not too surprising that these concerns should find their way into the "religious" views of the instrumentalists on the level of institutional involvement.

Of some importance in this regard is the incongruous lack of religious institutional involvement by American Jewish religious bodies. While there is no lack of clerical involvement or money for "secular causes," or talk about involvement, the Jewish institutions tend to remain as aloof as do some Roman or Protestant ones.

Intrinsic to the expressive position, which is the second contextual observation to be made, is an emphasis upon clerical pastoral counseling as a major concern and activity. The instrumentalists, on the other hand, tend toward more of an emphasis upon what is sometimes called social work. The reason for this contrast is not difficult to discover. If one adopts the position that the secular world sometimes hurts persons, then one can conclude that it is the task of the church to help heal those individuals who have been hurt *out there.* If, however, one feels that the harmful effects of secular life have been caused by an absence of ethical conviction, then one may conclude that the structure of secular life should be changed so as to prevent persons getting hurt. In these contrasting views lie the characteristic attitudes of the respective institutions. There can be no doubt that expressionist groups assist those in need, but their involvement tends to come from outside the situation and after the fact. The instrumentalist groups tend to emphasize immediate institutional involvement to deal with issues before the fact and from the inside.

A third contextual aspect of the polar positions is to be seen in the different emphases placed upon program and activities. The expressionist context tends to favor the development of internally oriented activities, while the instrumental context tends to seek externally directed activities. Typical expressive programming includes the normal run of groups: church school, women's groups, men's groups, youth groups; all of which tend to be involved either in study (usually biblical) or in service to the church. "Outreach" or "mission" groups tend to be basically concerned with increasing revenues or membership. Instrumental programming, to the contrary, tends to be oriented to the world; even when some traditional forms are maintained. For example, an instrumentally oriented institution can make use of church school and other educational forms for involvement purposes by utilizing materials that thrust the learner into the concerns of the world. The distinguishing mark, however, of the instrumental institutions is their programming for redress of social evils. Such programming is seen as integral to the life of the church rather than peripheral to it.

Finally, the immediate context of both kinds of preaching—the pattern of

399

public worship—tends to be different. Where it is possible, the instrumentalists tend toward greater flexibility and simplicity of worship patterns, together
with a freer and more relaxed atmosphere which can border on sloppiness
denoting a lack of concern with the liturgical exercise. The expressivists, conversely, tend more toward a certain rigidity of worship experience.

There are, undoubtedly, more aspects to the context of preaching, but
these have been discussed to open this dimension at least a little.

Sermonic Representation of the Polarity

In this section we will endeavor to present a number of illustrations of
the polarity, which are taken mostly from sermonic material. Quotations
from sermons do not imply a firm categorization of the preachers. This essay
is concerned with ideas and not personalities. For a general overview of the
polarity two nonsermonic sources will be used. The expressive point of view
can probably be typified by the following editorial comment taken from
Christianity Today:

The social-action hierarchy is attempting to defuse Paul Ramsey's ecumenical
bombshell—*Who Speaks for the Church?*—by verbal magic. "Good medicine
for those who are too heedless in making pronouncements on specific matters
of policy," writes John Bennett in *Christianity and Crisis*. He then goes on to
defend ecclesiastical endorsements of legislation and to carry forward his theology
of an anti-American, pro-Communist God. . . . The tragedy of ecumenical
Christianity—in the midst of its social-action fanaticism—is more than method-
ological miscarriage; it is the ideological loss of the truth of revelation.

[Roger] Shinn notes that the secularists, for whom whatever happens in history is God's activity, cannot distinguish authentic from false revolutions (or,
as we would prefer to say, legitimate from illegitimate alternatives). But the
secular theologians are not alone in their chaos. Writes Shinn: "Nobody knows
what justice is. . . ." One would think that, given this major premise, churchmen
would either forego pontificating in the public arena or else return to the revealed will of God. Unless they do so, they may be speaking the vocabulary of
redemption while fueling the fires of godless revolution.[15]

In contradistinction, the Ecumenical Institute in Chicago suggested:

From the earliest, man has struggled to envision a world composed of those
structures by which he could realize a fully human life. In the 20th Century, an
explosion of possibilities has occurred, radically altering man's ability to plan
and create the social constructs in and by which he lives. . . . [The new man]
is engaged in the total social process in his every concrete action in order to
pioneer in the formulation of social structures which minister to all people
everywhere. . . . Both the symbolic and reflective dimensions of the new church
undergird the pioneering activity of these missional people. The new church
does not have a mission—it is a mission in history. As mission it is constantly

[15] *Christianity Today*, XII (November 24, 1967), 27.

expending itself on behalf of all that is, and all that shall be. It loves the world by bearing the liberating Word and creating the structures of justice which make human life human.[16]

It is fortunate for the purposes of this essay that the Rev. Norman R DePuy responded to an article in *Reader's Digest* entitled "Should the Church 'Meddle' in Civil Affairs?" by J. Howard Pew, president of Sun Oil Company. Mr. Pew stated in part that the "mainstream" churches are failing their members "(1) by succumbing to a creeping tendency to downgrade the Bible as the infallible Word of God and, (2) by efforts to shift the church's main thrust from the spiritual to the secular." [17] The Rev. Mr. DePuy retorted in a sermon:

Mr. Pew argues that a man has no concern with Caesar because he renders his utmost to God; that if a man is hungry we have no responsibility to help him feed himself (get a job); that if a man is in jail, we have no responsibility for justice. . . . Is there any part of the world which is not God's? Is there some animal that God told Adam he should not name (control) because it was outside the province of the sacred, that is, of God and His will? According to Pew, if we are making war, God does not care; international peace is not the province of religion, in spite, evidently, of Jesus' very clear teaching. Did Jesus mean peace between individuals in the church pews; and not for the youngster killed in his fox hole because foolish old men are too proud to talk around the table (U.N.)? Of course, the root of brother Pew's error is in thinking that people are individuals and not social beings. You are a person only when you are in relationship; that is Jesus' greatest commandment. Relationship is simply another term for society. When you say individuals must be changed, you are saying that society must be changed, or you can put it in the opposite way: when society is changed, individuals will be changed. Individuals and society are synonymous! Every last one of the men Pew accused of loving society more than "souls," on the contrary, is vitally interested in the hearts of men. But they believe, as do I that to tell a hungry, disillusioned, frightened man that God loves him, while not giving him anything to eat, to hang on to, is like challenging a man with his leg in a cast to break the record for the hundred yard dash. Nonsense! [18]

One of the characteristic aspects of the polarity under consideration is that persons arguing from both positions ground their views in biblical understanding. The difference between the use of biblical understandings is well illustrated by the following quotations:

Where did all this get started, anyway? Where did the notion come from that the seriousness of my Christian commitment is to be measured by the number of tread marks on my chest where I have allowed myself to be run over rather than cause a fuss? Where did we get the idea that faith is the absence of con-

[16] *The Declaration of the Spirit Movement of the People of God Century Twenty* (Chicago: Journal of the Ecumenical Institute, 1967), p. 12.

[17] J. Howard Pew, "Should the Church 'Meddle' in Civil Affairs?" *Reader's Digest*, LXXXVIII (May, 1966), 49-54.

[18] Norman R. DePuy, First Baptist Church, Moorestown, New Jersey, May 25, 1966, unpublished sermon.

viction and love is the refusal to take sides? Well, I'll tell you one thing: we
didn't get it from the Bible! Some one once described the Bible as "the most
thoroughly prejudiced set of books ever penned." Of course the Bible is prejudiced! When it comes to the problem of social injustice, there is not an open
mind to be found anywhere in the Scriptures. When it comes to the problem
of human exploitation, there is not an agnostic in sight. When it comes to the
problem of personal or political tyranny, there is no equal time for the tyrant on
the biblical agenda.[19]

and:

Jesus did not come to upset the status quo. He came to transform it by supernatural power. Jesus builds his kingdom by unique and godly means exclusively,
"not by might nor by power but by my spirit," sayeth the Lord. It is the conviction of this preacher that one of the saddest spectacles in the history of the
Christian church is the fact that the church so often today is reduced to implementing what they think of as Christ's program in history by human, worldly,
secular means. Trying to impose godly goals in worldly ways. It does not work,
it will not work, it cannot work. You do not bring in the kingdom of Jesus Christ
by legislation or education or demonstration. "My kingdom is not of this world,
else would my servants fight, that I should not be delivered to the Jews." There
remained one grand fundamental task before his earthly mission was fulfilled,
one fundamental prerequisite to his reign in history and beyond history, one
condition which must be met if the kingdom of our Lord and Savior Jesus
Christ is to be extended and effectuated. He must be delivered, delivered for
our transgression. Jesus Christ had to die on the cross, there was no short-cut to
his kingly reign.[20]

The same preacher took issue with a certain dramatic presentation held at
a church in New York:

Another news item . . . reported that the Judson Memorial Baptist Church in
New York's Greenwich Village had a dance program which included a number
in which a man and a woman, both naked, moved across the stage in face to face
embrace! "Knowing the judgment of God that they which commit such things
are worthy of death, they not only do the same but have pleasure in them that
do them." There is no mystery about the popularity of modern pornography and
obscenity. Pleasure in such things is the inevitable end of secular culture.[21]

The views of the pastor of Judson Memorial Baptist Church are particularly
illuminative of the issues included in the polarity.

We have seen develop here [Judson Memorial Baptist Church] a human, com-
munal sanctuary—not meaning a holy and special place where holy and special

[19] Lloyd J. Averill, "Holy Partisans and Godly Troublemakers," Kalamazoo College
Chapel, Kalamazoo, Michigan, p. 1.
[20] Richard C. Halverson, "Art Thou a King?" Fourth Presbyterian Church, Washington, D. C., April 3, 1966, p. 3.
[21] Richard C. Halverson, "Righteousness Exalteth a Nation," Fourth Presbyterian
Church, Washington, D.C., p. 6, n. d. (most of the sermons used in this essay are
undated since they are not published formally).

things are said and expected, but a commune where all things may be said. . . . In a world where painful exactions and unbearable stereotypes are made of persons, it is altogether fitting and a joy to find a place, a community of persons, where the expectations are only that we be tolerant of each other's search for our identity and meaning in this life—where the only blasphemy is any hurried or frenetic pressure that people embrace some abstract gospel or liberal ideology or vocational commitment. The only heresy is the failure to share with another (when it is desired) where we are in the pilgrimage, and what we are able to believe and in some measure act upon. . . . The church is not just a religious sector carved out of the world, it is a "happening" in the world and wherever it occurs in authenticity it is a miracle and a surprise to believers and non-believers alike. . . . My friends, when is this platform upon which I am standing an altar, when a stage, when a sculpture upon which our children play? How many times is the theatre an unexpected ritual of joy and delight while the worship service is a dull, repetitious play? So many of our distinctions are unwarranted when the walls that separate and divide us are broken down and all our life together are the vessels of revelation and miracles of human relationships.[22]

In connection with the expressive-instrumental polarity, some basic doctrinal questions have arisen. The Rev. Frederic M. Hudson analyzed the problems involved in the following fashion:

Radical theology is suggesting that both the Bible and the Church at large interpret God in quite another way, as Being-in-Himself, and this disparity between professional theologians and the Church at large, over the reality of God is the major crisis in Christianity today. Sophisticated theologians who march off to Selma or organize Viet Nam protests because they believe "God is acting" (symbolically, of course, as a configuration of faith-history, not arguable as ordinary history) live in a different theological world from the majority of Churchmen, and alas, from the majority of Biblical attestations to God. This is at the crux of the failure of the ecumenical and renewal efforts of this century, which have as their cornerstone a neo-orthodox reconstruction of the doctrine of God. While professional theologians have been trying to reconstruct a doctrine of God in terms of historical categories, the Church at large has proceeded with the assumption that God has a religious meaning, i.e., a holy Being who inspires cosmic piety through awe, reverence, holiness, and obedience. . . . So here is the central issue for debate. It is a problem of exegesis or Biblical interpretation. If God is demythologized, then how are we to interpret the traditional functions of God in a secular fashion without making man himself into a god? How do judging, forgiveness, repentance, and obedience take place in ordinary history? Is it theologically responsible to speak of faith as a manner of handling the experiences of life rather than as belief in something or someone? These, I think, are the crucial questions.[23]

Dr. Herschel H. Hobbs made an analysis of the same problem, but concluded with an assertion of the expressive viewpoint:

[22] Howard Moody, "My Ten Years in a Quandry: Some Immodest and Irreverent Reflections on a Decade at Judson Church," Judson Memorial Baptist Church, New York, New York, pp. 1-2. n. d.

[23] Frederic M. Hudson, "Musings on the Death of God," Colby College Chapel, Waterville, Maine, pp. 2-3, 5, n. d.

There is a type of modern religion called Humanism. It places religion on the basis of man and his relation to other men. It is designed to change a man's environment, but it is powerless to change the man. It fills his stomach, but leaves him with an empty soul. Thus it leaves too much to be desired. Now, do not misunderstand me. True religion does have a social aspect. But it does not begin there. It begins with a right relationship with God, and from that relationship expresses itself in a right relationship toward men. Anything short of that leaves you with a void in your heart.[24]

Representative of expressivist preaching is the quotation below which could be heard thousands of times on Sunday mornings in slightly differing forms, indicating the expressivist attitude toward the certainties of doctrinal faith:

We don't need to be resentful of every new excursion into theology, as though some word from a bright young man who aches to break into print is about to fell us. We can even welcome any ideas which challenge our basic grasp of Christianity, for they should serve to clarify and strengthen what we really do believe. Said Theodore Beza, the reformer, "The church is an anvil which has worn out many hammers." The hammers are hitting, and sometimes we may be led to think the anvil is about to be shattered, but it has happened before and will happen again.[25]

It is toward incarnational theology that many instrumentalists are turning, as is illustrated in the quotation below:

If you want it said in doctrinal terms this is a truly Incarnational theology, that is, it is what the coming of Jesus was about. It is what his life was about. It is what the church is about; holy worldliness rather than otherworldliness. "The Word was made flesh and dwelt among us." The Word, a spiritual concept, entered the flesh, a material concept, and in so doing wiped out all the false distinctions between temporal and eternal, secular and holy, heavenly and worldly. Henry Scott Holland used to say, "the more you are interested in the Incarnation, the more you must be concerned about drains." Yes, drains and slums and disease and hunger and poverty; not in some condescending pity that would offer a touch of soothing ointment for the symptoms of a deep-rooted disease, but rather because God so loved the world. . . . We are in the world and we must live in the world.[26]

The expressivists have sometimes been challenged for their seeming complacency in the face of serious problems. "The Christian message directs the Church not unto itself where it manicures its souls on foam rubber cushions

---

[24] Herschel H. Hobbs, "More than Religion," *The Ten Commandments* (Fort Worth, Texas: Southern Baptist Convention, 1961), p. 3.

[25] David B. Watermulder, "The Reality of God," Bryn Mawr Presbyterian Church, Bryn Mawr, Pennsylvania, 1966.

[26] J. Ernest Somerville, "The Law of the Second Wind," *The Protestant Hour* (New York: United Presbyterian Church, U.S.A., 1966), p. 73.

but into a world where it may dirty and even infect its hands in servitude to human need." [27] Expressivists have, of course, responded:

We are not unmindful of the criticism that evangelical Christiaity has no social consciousness, no social awareness; that evangelical Christians are interested only in the individual and his eternal salvation; that evangelical Christians are indifferent to social evils. This simply is not true. Historically, evangelical Christianity has been acutely aware of human need in the social dimension. The preaching of the Gospel of Jesus Christ has inspired and implemented the greatest social movements for renewal and rehabilitation in history. To be sure, there are glaring exceptions as in everything, but the rule is, that men and women, hearts sensitized by new life in Christ have been crusaders, individually and corporately against all manner of social exploitation and inhumanity . . . of course we must not neglect the temporal need of the poor—to do so is sub-Christian; but we are not fulfilling our Lord's mission in history if we fail to preach the Gospel to them. Without the elevating power of the Gospel we condemn them to their perennial dilemma however much else we may do for them. In the war on poverty, the only adequate weapon is the Gospel of Jesus Christ.[28]

Although the expressivist position takes cognizance of social problems, as has just been indicated, their primary emphasis is placed upon the "spiritual" needs of mankind:

Looking again at the world a more serious situation exists. Turn wherever you will, and spiritual need abounds over physical need. The world is a seething cauldron because downtrodden peoples are seeking a better life. Their basic need is spiritual—not economic. Indeed, for the most part their spiritual dearth has produced their material condition. But dwelling in spiritual darkness they see the better life only in terms of material blessings. And atheistic Communism is thriving upon both needs.[29]

The expressive position appears to be that if persons in difficulty have the gospel preached to them, and if they accept it, they will set about the task of getting their own material blessings, as did out nineteenth-century midwestern forefathers. In obvious contrast to this approach is the following:

He [God] is where the bigotry and immaturity of some is met by the passion for justice of others; he's in the struggle of a man and a woman to find the fulfillment of their lives in marriage; he's where men attempt to be whole and human in their dealings with one another; he's in the protests men erect against the structures of society which warp lives and distort personalities; he's where men gather themselves in communities and seek the meaning of brotherhood, even fraternities and sororities. I make bold to suggest it's not God's way to be

[27] David O. Woodyard, "The Student and the Church," Denison University Chapel, Granville, Ohio, p. 4, n. d.

[28] Richard C. Halverson, "War on Poverty," Fourth Presbyterian Church, Washington, D. C., March 2, 1966, pp. 1, 6.

[29] Herschel H. Hobbs, "The First Question Man Asked," Best of "The Baptist Hour" (Fort Worth, Texas: Southern Baptist Convention, 1961), p. 20.

present in religious calisthenics where men pride themselves on their piety. God is where the action is, where things are happening. And as you participate in what he's doing, you'll begin to know who he is. When you lay hold of life, its source lays hold of you. . . . I've wrestled for years with how I grow in that and share its meaning with others. More times than not frustration has been afoot of frustration. The brutal fact is that none of us can deliver Christ to another.[30]

As we indicated earlier, the basic estrangement between the polar positions has more to do with "secular" issues than with "religious" ones. In November of 1967, Dr. Cotesworth P. Lewis of Williamsburg, Virginia, preached a sermon when the president of the United States was in attendance. The text of the sermon was, "The people that walked in darkness have seen a great light: they that dwell in the land of the shadow of death, upon them hath the light shined" (Isaiah 9:2). The passage in the sermon which occasioned indirect remarks by the president, debate in the press, and an apology to the president from the vestry of Bruton parish is as follows:

The overshadowing problem before us is in the international realm. The political complexities of our involvement in an undeclared war in Vietnam are so baffling that I feel presumptuous even in asking questions. But since there is a rather general consensus that something is wrong in Vietnam (a conviction voiced by leaders of nations traditionally our friends—leading military experts—and the rank and file of American citizens)—we wonder if some logical, straightforward explanation might be given without endangering whatever military or political advantage we hold. Relatively few of us plan even the mildest form of disloyal action against constituted authority. "United we stand, divided we fall." We know the necessity of supporting our leader. But we cannot close our Christian consciences to consideration of the rightness of actions as they are reported to us —perhaps erroneously, perhaps for good cause (of which we have not been apprised). We are appalled that apparently this is the only war in our history which has had three times as many civilian as military casualties. It is particularly regrettable that to so many nations the struggle's purpose appears as neo-colonialism. We are mystified by news accounts suggesting that our brave fighting units are inhibited by directives and inadequate equipment from using their capacities to terminate the conflict successfully. While pledging our loyalty— we ask humbly, WHY?

The sermon concluded with the words:

The years ahead will be painful. We may be compelled to think new thoughts and walk in new paths. Emerging young men and women who will gradually take over must have more understanding than we have had. The future looks terrible; but . . . (as in every strategic juncture of history) he [God] will infuse the essential factor into the equation—something we could never suspect as a possibility—to make the future glorious.[31]

[30] David O. Woodyard, "The Name Will Come Later," Denison University Chapel, Granville, Ohio, pp. 3-4, n. d.

[31] Cotesworth P. Lewis, Bruton Parish Church, Williamsburg, Virginia, November 12, 1967, pp. 1-2.

Subsequent to press reaction and numerous inquiries, the full text of the sermon was made available, together with a covering letter, part of which is quoted below.

Perhaps someday it will be understood that my remarks in Bruton Parish Church, November 12, were neither derogatory to nor critical of the President—as many of those attending in a spirit of worship agree. Deplorable misconstructions have been drawn from the occasion by lifting portions out of context, by impugning motives, and by imagining ideas which were never stated or inferred. My outline and intent was simple, kindly, and religious: (1) when things seem hopeless (2) and man does his righteous best, (3) God gives reason for hope. Since I was incapable of making specific recommendations, I sought by examples from Scripture and history to give encouragement.[32]

This sermon could hardly be called an example of revolutionary instrumentalism. As a sermon, it stands clearly in the expressive tradition. Dr. Lewis wrote to us that "the Vietnam section [of the sermon] is not a purely secular intrusion into a Christian Service of Worship. I feel so strongly that in line with our ordination vows to teach nothing contrary to the Scriptures, we must base all our presentations in and out of the pulpit, on Christian motivation clearly observable and provable by Scripture." In essence, this sermon follows the general view of Paul Ramsey which we quoted earlier. It is a sermon that asks questions and seeks to provide a basis for hope. However, the reaction to even the raising of questions by a preacher belonging to one of the oldest and most prestigious families in Virginia which must certainly be termed established, is indicative of the highly charged atmosphere of the polarity.

The climate of the polarity is rather well revealed by the following editorial opinion:

We would like to think this evident collapse (of the image of the clergy) has occurred because great, prophetic voices among the clergy are calling the people to righteousness. Frankly, we see and hear little evidence to this effect. Perhaps the collapse has occurred because the public is weary of clergymen who, having no spiritual message, seek to identify some pet political nostrum with the will of God. Since clergymen have never demonstrated any particular acumen in the field, the political sorties are not apt to be edifying. . . . Here, again, we see the logical consequences of clericalism. When the church and clergy eschew their historic role, exchanging it for a mess of political pottage, we are apt to see what we see now. It is time for a quick change.[33]

As for the future, it is possible that the polar positions may become more and more hyperbolic until some additional factor enters which alters their relationship. We submit these final two quotations as a summary and as indicators for the future:

[32] Cotesworth P. Lewis, Bruton Parish Church, Williamsburg, Virginia.
[33] *Church and State*, XX (March, 1967), 4.

There are so many places that we could be putting our lives on the line in behalf of other men. Who will be the advocates before the power structures of our society, for people victimized by unjust laws? There is an endless number of ways the church can act, use its power and respectability to influence in behalf of other men's needs, to feed hungry people, to succor and console the victims of injustice, to protest the duplicity of a policy that guarantees territorial integrity to a people against Communist zealots, but not against racial fanatics.[34]

and,

What do these times require of us as men and women who bear the name of Christ? Well, it seems to me that you don't have to weigh the matter long before concluding in the first place that these times require us to return to the Bible.[35]

Conclusions

The expressive-instrumental polarity in contemporary American preaching has been defined in terms of the nature or kind of involvement favored by preachers relative to the problems that have arisen through numerous revolutions in the secular world. The expressive polar position maintains that the church should provide generic guidance to the culture and seek to inculcate gospel virtues in persons. The instrumental view holds that it is the business of the church to seek change in the structure of our culture and that persons discover the gospel through their involvement in specific secular problems. We have set this polarity within the context of the history of revolution by the disenfranchised. These persons, when unwilling to accept their given roles create problems which force the church to decide how it will respond. The problems are seldom "religious" in their entirety and tend to be relative to social and economic and personal needs. While one cannot discount the "religious" factor in providing impetus to a specific revolution, the religious views associated with the respective positions appear to have more to do with providing a rationale for them. Both polar positions can ground their views in biblical understanding with little difficulty, leading to the obvious conclusion that both are in some part true, but that neither has a full grasp of biblical exegesis.

We have presented a few sermonic extracts to illustrate the polarity; they were chosen because of their representative character. We have made no attempt to classify particular preachers, both because individual preachers could be reclassified if different categories and definitions were used, and

---

[34] Howard Moody, "The Signs of the Silent Church," Judson Memorial Baptist Church, New York, N. Y., June 11, 1967, pp. 3-4.

[35] D. Reginald Thomas, "The Christian's Duty Today," A Nation Under God (Philadelphia: The Evangelical Foundation, 1965), p. 32.

because many preachers maintain inconsistent (for our purposes) views on specific problems involved in the polar situation.

One final observation remains to be made. If our analysis of the polarity and its development is correct, then we have tacitly defined the nature of the church as a responsive, rather than innovative, institution. If the church is responsive, there is little point, on the one hand, of berating the institution because it does not carry the torch of revolution prior to social upheaval, and, on the other hand, to decry the involvement of the church in changes which take place in the world. The responsive church will follow the culture and it will respond to it. As long as the church is an institution, it is a part of the culture. It would be facile to assume that there is one and only one expression of the church for all times and places. Ultimately, the criteria by which the church will be judged are not ours to make, nor do we have much of a grasp upon them. Our need is to talk and work together so as to discover, as best we can, what our role at this time should be.

BIBLIOGRAPHY

(The numbers in parentheses following each bibliographic entry refer to the chapters to which the works are most relevant)

Abrams, Ray H. *Preachers Present Arms*. New York: Round Table Press, 1933. (12)

Addison, Daniel D. *The Clergy in American Life and Letters*. London: Macmillan & Company, 1900. (7)

Allen, Devere. *The Fight for Peace*. New York: The Macmillan Company 1930. (12)

Allen, Frederick Lewis. *Only Yesterday*. New York: Harper & Brothers, 1931. (13)

Allen, Leslie H., ed. *Bryan and Darrow at Dayton: The Record and Documents of the Bible-Evolution Trial*. New York: A. Lee, 1925. (13)

Ames, William. *Workes*. London, 1643. (2)

Andrews, Charles M. *The Colonial Period of American History: The Settlements*. New Haven: Yale University Press, 1964. (3)

Armstrong, George D. *The Christian Doctrine of Slavery*. New York: Charles Scribner, 1857. (8)

Atkins, Gaius Glenn. *Preaching and the Mind of Today*. New York: Round Table Press, 1934. (13)

Atkins, Gaius Glenn. *Religion in Our Times*. New York: Round Table Press, 1932. (13)

Auer, J. Jeffrey, ed. *Antislavery and Disunion, 1858-1861: Studies in the Rhetoric of Compromise and Conflict*. New York: Harper & Row, 1963. (8)

Ayer, Alfred J. *The Foundations of Empirical Knowledge*. London: Macmillan & Company, 1947. (16)

Bacon, Leonard W. *A History of American Christianity*. New York: Charles Scribner's Sons, 1901. (8)

Bailyn, Bernard. *The New England Merchants in the Seventeenth Century*. Cambridge, Massachusetts: Harvard University Press, 1955. (2)

Bainton, Roland H. *Christian Attitudes Toward War and Peace*. Nashville: Abingdon Press, 1960. (12)

Baldwin, Mary. *The New England Clergy and the American Revolution*. Durham, North Carolina: Duke University Press, 1928. (1)

Baptist Fundamentals, Addresses Delivered at the Pre-Convention Conference at Buffalo, June 21-22, 1920. Philadelphia: Judson Press, 1920. (13)

411

Barnes, Albert. *The Church and Slavery*. Philadelphia: Parry and McMillan, 1857. (8)

Barnes, Gilbert H. *The Antislavery Impulse, 1830-1844*. New York: Appleton-Century, 1933. (8)

Barnes, Gilbert H., and Dumond, Dwight L., eds. *The Letters of Theodore Dwight Weld and Angelina Grimke Weld and Sarah Grimke, 1822-1844*. 2 vols. New York: Appleton-Century, 1934. (8)

Barnes, William W. *The Southern Baptist Convention, 1845-1953*. Nashville, Broadman Press, 1954. (8)

Barth, Karl. *The Preaching of the Gospel*. Trans. B. E. Hooke. Philadelphia: The Westminster Press, 1963. (14)

Baskerville, Barnet. "The Cross and the Flag: Evangelists of the Far Right," *Western Speech*, XXVII (Fall, 1963), 197-207. (16)

Beardsley, F. G. *Charles G. Finney: A Study in Evangelism*. New York: American Tract Society, 1937. (11)

Becker, Carl L. *The Declaration of Independence: A Study in the History of Political Ideas*. New York: Random House, 1942. (8)

Beecher, Henry Ward. *Evolution and Religion*. New York: Fords, Howard Shilbert, 1885. (10)

Beecher, Lyman. *Beecher's Works*. Cleveland: John P. Jewett and Company, 1851. (6)

Beecher, William C., and Scoville, Samuel. *A Biography of Rev. Henry Ward Beecher*. London: S. Low, Marston, Searle and Rivingtons, 1888. (8)

Behrends, A. J. F. *Socialism and Christianity*. New York: Baker and Taylor, 1886. (11)

Bell, Daniel. *The New American Right*. New York: Criterion Books, 1955. (16)

Bell, Daniel. *The Radical Right*. Garden City, N.Y.: Doubleday & Company, 1963. (16)

Bennett, John C. "Christian Ethics and the National Conscience," Bell Lecture Number Six. Boston: Boston University Press, 1965. (17)

Bennett, John C. *Christians and the State*. New York: Charles Scribner's Sons, 1958. (12)

Beth, Loren P. *The American Theory of Church and State*. Gainesville, Florida: The University of Florida Press, 1958. (18)

Betts, George Herbert. *The Beliefs of 700 Ministers and Their Meaning for Religious Education*. New York: The Abingdon Press, 1929. (13)

Blanshard, Paul. *God and Man in Washington*. Boston: Beacon Press, 1960. (18)

The Blue Book of the John Birch Society. Belmont, Massachusetts: Printing particulars not released, 1961. (16)

Bosley, Harold A. *Preaching on Controversial Issues*. New York: Harper & Brothers, 1953. (1, 19)

Bradford, William. *History of Plimoth Plantation*. Commonwealth edition. Boston: Wright and Potter Printing Company, 1901. (3)

Brady, Tom. *Black Monday*. Winona, Mississippi: Association of Citizens' Councils, 1955. (19)

Brady, Tom. "Segregation and the South." Greenwood, Mississippi: Citizens' Councils, Educational Fund, 1957. (19)

Brookhouser, Frank, ed. *These Were Our Years*. Garden City, N.Y.: Doubleday & Company, 1959. (13)

Broughton, Leonard G. *Is Preparedness for War Unchristian?* New York: Doran, 1916. (12)

Brown, Robert McAfee, and Scott, David H., eds. *The Challenge to Reunion.* New York: McGraw-Hill, 1963. (15)

Broyles, A. J. "John Birch Society; a Movement of Social Protest of the Radical Right," *Journal of Social Issues,* XXIX (April, 1963), 51-62. (16)

Bryan, William Jennings. *Bryan's Last Speech.* Oklahoma City: Sunlight Publishing Society, 1925. (10)

Bryan, William Jennings. *Bryan's Last Word on Evolution.* Chicago: The Bible Institute, Colportage Association, 1925. (13)

Bryan, William Jennings. *In His Image.* New York: Fleming H. Revell Company, 1922. (13)

Bryan, William Jennings. *Orthodox Christianity Versus Modernism.* Chicago: Fleming H. Revell Company, 1924. (13)

Bryan, William Jennings. *Seven Questions in Dispute.* New York: Fleming H. Revell Company, 1924. (13)

Bryan, William Jennings, and Bryan, Mary B. *The Memoirs of William Jennings Bryan.* Chicago: John C. Winston, 1925. (13)

Bulkeley, Peter. *The Gospel Covenant . . . Preached in Concord in New England.* London, 1651. (2)

Bultmann, Rudolf. *Theology of the New Testament.* Trans. Kendrick Grobel. New York: Charles Scribner's Sons, 1951. (1)

Burggraaff, Winfield. *The Rise and Development of Liberal Theology in America.* New York: Board of Publication and Bible-School Work, 1928. (13)

Burr, A. R. *Russell H. Conwell: The Work and the Man.* Philadelphia: John C. Winston, 1905. (11)

Burr, Agnes R. *Russell H. Conwell and His Work.* Philadelphia: John C. Winston, 1923. (11)

Bushnell, Horace. *Building Eras in Religion.* New York: Charles Scribner's Sons, 1881. (7)

Bushnell, Horace. *Christian Nurture.* New Haven: Yale University Press, 1947. (7)

Bushnell, Horace. *Nature and the Supernatural, as Together Constituting the One System of God.* 2d ed. New York: Charles Scribner, 1858. (7)

Bushnell, Horace. *Sermons on Living Subjects.* New York: Charles Scribner's Sons, 1876. (10)

Buswell, J. Oliver, III. *Slavery, Segregation, and Scripture.* Grand Rapids, Michigan: William B. Eerdmans, 1964. (19)

Campbell, E. Q., and Pettigrew, T. F. *Christians in Racial Crisis: A Study of Little Rock's Ministry.* Washington: Public Affairs Press, 1959. (19)

Carnegie, Andrew. "Wealth," *North American Review,* CXLVIII (June, 1889), 653-54. (11)

Carwardine, William H. *The Pullman Strike.* 4th ed. Chicago: C. H. Kerr and Company, 1894. (11)

Cassara, Ernest. *Hosea Ballou.* Boston: Beacon Press, 1961. (5)

Cavert, Samuel McCrea. *On the Road to Christian Unity.* New York: Harper & Brothers, 1961. (15)

Chapman, J. W. *The Life and Works of Dwight L. Moody.* Chicago: W. E. Scull, 1900. (11)

Chapman, Stuart W. "The Protestant Campaign for the Union." Unpublished Ph.D. dissertation, Department of History, Yale University, 1939. (9)

Chatard, William. "Catholic Societies," *American Catholic Quarterly Review*, IV, (April, 1879). (11)

Chauncy, Charles. *Seasonable Thoughts on the State of Religion in New England, a Treatise in Five Parts.* Boston, 1743. (4)

Cheever, George B. *God Against Slavery: and the Freedom and Duty of the Prophet to Rebuke It, as a Sin Against God.* Cincinnati: American and Reform Tract and Book Society, 1857. (8)

Cheney, Mary Bushnell. *Life and Letters of Horace Bushnell.* New York: Charles Scribner's Sons, 1905. (7)

Cherry, Conrad. *The Theology of Jonathan Edwards.* Garden City, N.Y.: Doubleday & Company, 1966. (2)

Chesler, Mark, and Schmuck, Richard. "Participant Observation in a Super-Patriot Discussion Group," *Journal of Social Issues*, XIX (April, 1963), 18-30. (16)

Clark, Elmer T. *The Small Sects in America.* Nashville: Abingdon Press, 1949. (11)

Clark, John Bates. "The Society of the Future," *The Independent*, LIII (July 18, 1901). (11)

Clark, Robert E. D. *Darwin: Before and After.* London: The Paternoster Press, 1958. (10)

Clebsch, William A. "Baptism of Blood: A Study of Christian Contributions to the Interpretation of the Civil War in American History." Unpublished Ph.D. dissertation, Union Theological Seminary, 1957. (9)

Cole, Charles C., Jr. *The Social Ideas of the Northern Evangelists, 1826-1860.* New York: Columbia University Press, 1954. (7, 8)

Cole, Stewart G. *The History of Fundamentalism.* New York: Richard R. Smith, 1931. (13)

Commager, Henry Steele. *The American Mind.* New Haven: Yale University Press, 1950. (11)

Commager, Henry Steele. *Theodore Parker: Yankee Crusader.* Boston: Little, Brown and Company, 1936. (8)

Conwell, Russell. *Acres of Diamonds.* New York, 1890. (11)

Cox, Harvey. *God's Revolution and Man's Responsibility.* Valley Forge, Pennsylvania: Judson Press, 1965. (20)

Cross, Barbara. *Horace Bushnell: Minister to a Changing America.* Chicago: The University of Chicago Press, 1958. (7)

Cross, Barbara, ed. *The Autobiography of Lyman Beecher.* Cambridge, Massachusetts: The Belknap Press of Harvard University, 1961. (6)

Curti, Merle. *The Growth of American Thought.* New York: Harper & Row, 1943. (6)

Cuyler, Cornelius C. *The Signs of the Times: A Series of Discourses Delivered in the Second Presbyterian Church, Philadelphia.* Philadelphia: William S. Martien, 1839. (7)

Dandeneau, Richard J. "The Rhetorical Invention of Conservatism: An Analysis of the Assumptions of Contemporary Conservative Thought." Unpublished Ph.D. dissertation, Southern Illinois University, 1962. (16)

Darrow, Clarence. *The Story of My Life.* New York: Charles Scribner's Sons, 1932. (13)

Davies, Alfred T., ed. *The Pulpit Speaks on Race.* Nashville: Abingdon Press, 1965. (19)

Dexter, Henry M. *As to Roger Williams and His Banishment from the Massachusetts Plantation.* Boston: Congregational Publishing Society, 1876. (3)

Dieffenbach, Albert C. *Religious Liberty, the Great American Illusion.* New York: William Morrow and Company, 1927. (13)

Douglass, Truman B. *Preaching and the New Reformation.* New York: Harper & Brothers, 1956. (14)

Drake, Thomas E. *Quakers and Slavery in America.* New Haven: Yale University Press, 1950. (8)

Dumond, Dwight Lowell. *Antislavery Origins of the Civil War in the United States.* Ann Arbor, Michigan: The University of Michigan Press, 1959. (8)

Dumond, Dwight Lowell. *A Bibliography of Antislavery in America.* Ann Arbor, Michigan: The University of Michigan Press, 1961. (8)

Dunham. Chester Forrester. "The Attitude of the Northern Clergy Toward the South, 1860-1865." Unpublished Ph.D. dissertation, Department of History, The University of Chicago, 1939. (9)

Eddy, Sherwood, and Page, Kirby. *The Abolition of War.* New York: Doran, 1924. (12)

Edwards, Jonathan. *The Distinguishing Marks of a Work of the Spirit of God, Applied to That Uncommon Operation That Has Lately Appeared on the Minds of Many of the People in New England.* New York: 1832. (4)

Edwards, Jonathan. *A Faithful Narrative of the Surprising Work of God in the Conversion of Many Hundred Souls in Northampton, Massachusetts, A.D. 1735.* London: Printed for John Oswald, 1735. (4)

Edwards, Jonathan. *Freedom of the Will.* Ed. Paul Ramsey. New Haven: Yale University Press, 1957. (4)

Edwards, Jonathan. *Selected Sermons of Jonathan Edwards.* Ed. H. Norman Gardiner. New York: The Macmillan Company, 1904. (4)

Edwards, Jonathan. *Thoughts on the Revival of Religion in New England, and the Way in Which It Ought to Be Acknowledged and Promoted.* New York: Dunning and Spalding, 1832. (4)

Edwards, Jonathan. *A Treatise Concerning Religious Affections.* Ed. John E. Smith. New Haven: Yale University Press, 1959. (4)

Edwards, Jonathan. *The Works of President Edwards in Four Volumes.* New York, [Robert Carter and Brothers, 1881] 1843. (4)

Edwards, Jonathan. *The Works of President Edwards, In Ten Volumes.* New York: S. Converse, 1829. (4)

Engstrom, Theodore W. *Master Preachers of All Ages.* Grand Rapids, Michigan: Zondervan, 1951. (6)

Eubanks, Ralph T., and Baker, Virgil L. "Toward an Axiology of Rhetoric," *Quarterly Journal of Speech,* XLVIII (April, 1962), 158. (16)

Fast Day Sermons: or, The Pulpit on the State of the Country. New York: Rudd and Carleton, 1861. (8)

Finney, Charles G. *Lectures on Revivals of Religion.* Oberlin, Ohio: E. J. Goodrich, 1868. (11)

Finney, Charles G. *Memoirs of Rev. Charles G. Finney Written by Himself.* New York: Fleming H. Revell Company, 1876 [also, New York: A. S. Barnes, 1876]. (6, 7, 11)

Finney, Charles G. *Sermons on Gospel Themes.* Oberlin, Ohio: E. J. Goodrich, 1876. (7)

Finney, Charles G. *Sermons on Important Subjects.* 3rd ed. New York: John S. Taylor, 1836. (7)

Finney, Charles G. *Sermons on the Way of Salvation*. Oberlin, E. J. Goodrich, 1891. (7)

Fish, Henry C. *Pulpit Eloquence of the Nineteenth Century*. New York: Dodd, Mead & Company, 1871. (6)

Fletcher, Joseph. *Situation Ethics*. Philadelphia: The Westminster Press, 1966. (17)

Forster, Arnold, and Epstein, Benjamin R. *Danger on the Right*. New York: Random House, 1964. (16)

Forsyth, Peter Taylor. *Positive Preaching and the Modern Mind*. London: The Independent Press, 1949. (1)

Fosdick, Harry Emerson. *Adventurous Religion*. New York: Harper & Brothers, 1926. (13)

Fosdick, Harry Emerson. *As I See Religion*. New York: Harper & Brothers, 1932. (13)

Fosdick, Harry Emerson. *The Challenge of the Present Crisis*. New York: Association Press, 1918. (12)

Fosdick, Harry Emerson. *Christianity and Progress*. New York: Fleming H. Revell Company, 1922. (13)

Fosdick, Harry Emerson. *The Farewell Sermon of Dr. Harry Emerson Fosdick to the First Presbyterian Church of New York, Sunday, March 1, 1925*. New York: Privately printed, 1925. (13)

Fosdick, Harry Emerson. *The First Presbyterian Church of New York and Dr. Fosdick*. New York: Privately printed, 1924. (13)

Fosdick, Harry Emerson. *The Living of These Days: An Autobiography*. New York: Harper & Row, 1956. (13, 14)

Fosdick, Harry Emerson. *Living Under Tension*. New York: Harper & Brothers, 1941. (14)

Fosdick, Harry Emerson. *On Being Fit to Live With*. New York: Harper & Brothers, 1946. (14)

Fosdick, Harry Emerson. *Shall the Fundamentalists Win?* A sermon preached at the First Presbyterian Church of New York, May 21, 1922, as stenographically reported by Margaret Renton. New York: Privately printed, 1922. (13)

Fosdick, Harry Emerson. *Successful Christian Living*. New York: Harper & Brothers, 1937. (14)

Foster, Frank Hugh, *A Genetic History of the New England Theology*. Chicago: The University of Chicago Press, 1907. (7)

The Fundamentals: A Testimony to the Truth. 12 vols. Chicago: Testimony Publishing Company, 1909-12. (13)

Furniss, Norman F. *The Fundamentalist Controversy, 1918-1931*. New Haven: Yale University Press, 1954. (13)

Gabriel, Ralph Henry. *The Course of American Democratic Thought*. New York: The Ronald Press, 1956. (9)

Gabriel, Ralph Henry. "Evangelical Religion and Popular Romanticism in Early Nineteenth Century America," *Church History*, XIX (March, 1950). (6)

Gardiner, Clinton. *Biblical Faith and Social Ethics*. New York: Harper & Brothers, 1960. (17)

Giboney, Ezra P., and Potter, Agnes M. *The Life of Mark A. Matthews*. Grand Rapids, Michigan: William B. Eerdmans, 1948. (13)

Gingerich, Melvin. *Service for Peace*. Scottdale, Pennsylvania: Herald Press, 1949. (12)

Gladden, Washington. *The Christian Pastor and the Working Church.* New York: Charles Scribner's Sons, 1903. (11)

Gleason, Robert. "Situational Morality," *Thought,* XXXII (1957) 533-58. (17)

God Hath Spoken. Twenty-five Addresses Delivered at the World Conference on Christian Fundamentals, May 25 to June 1, 1919. Philadelphia: Privately printed by the Bible Conference Committee, 1919. (13)

Gray, Asa. "The Origin of Species by Means of Natural Selection." Vol. II of *Major Crises in American History.* Ed. Merrill D. Peterson and Leonard W. Levy. New York: Harcourt, Brace & World, 1962. (10)

Griffin, Edward D. *A Series of Lectures, Delivered in Park Street Church, Boston.* 3d ed. Boston: Crocker and Brewster, 1829. (7)

Griffin, Leland M. "The Rhetorical Structure of the 'New Left' Movement: Part I," *Quarterly Journal of Speech,* L (April, 1964), 113-35. (16)

Gustafson, James. "Context Versus Principles: A Misplaced Debate in Christian Ethics," *Harvard Theological Review,* LVIII (1965) 171-202. (17)

Hackner, Willibold, "Disturbances of the Social Equilibrium," *Catholic World,* November, 1887. (11)

Harding, Vincent. *Must Walls Divide?* New York: Friendship Press, 1965. (19)

Hargis, Billy James. *The Facts About Communism and Our Churches.* Tulsa, Oklahoma: Christian Crusade Publications, 1962. (16)

Hargis, Billy James. *The Real Extremists: The Far Left.* Tulsa, Oklahoma: Christian Crusade Publications, 1964. (16)

Hargis, Billy James. "The United Nations Hoax," an address recorded for commercial sale with cover endorsement by Matt Overtic, former FBI counterspy. Los Angeles, California: Key Records. (16)

Hargis, Billy James. "What's Wrong with America?" an address delivered on the Berlin Crisis during the summer of 1961. Tulsa, Oklahoma: Christian Crusade Publications. (16)

Harland, Gordon. *The Thought of Reinhold Niebuhr.* New York: Oxford University Press, 1960. (14)

Hartzler, J. S. *Mennonites in the World War.* Scottdale, Pennsylvania: The Mennonite Publishing House (Herald Press), 1922. (12)

Heckman, Oliver Saxon. "Northern Church Penetration of the South, 1860-1880." Unpublished Ph.D. dissertation, Department of History, Duke University, 1939. (9)

Henretta, James A. "Economic Development and Social Structure in Colonial Boston," *The William and Mary Quarterly,* XXII (January, 1965), 75-92. (2)

Henry, J. Clyde, ed. *The Making of a Minister: Autobiography of Clarence Edward Macartney.* Great Neck: Channel Press, 1961. (13)

Hentoff, Nat. *Peace Agitator: The Story of A. J. Muste.* New York: The Macmillan Company, 1963. (12)

Hershberger, Guy F. *War, Peace, and Nonresistance.* Scottdale, Pennsylvania: The Mennonite Publishing House (Herald Press), 1944. (12)

Hieronymus, Frank L. "For Now and Forever: The Chaplains of the Confederate States Army." Unpublished Ph.D. dissertation, The University of California at Los Angeles, 1964. (9)

Hillis, Dwight Newell. *The Blot on the Kaiser's Scutcheon.* New York: Fleming H. Revell Company, 1918. (12)

Hillis, Dwight Newell. *German Atrocities.* New York: Fleming H. Revell Company, 1918. (12)

417

Hirsh, Margaret E. *The Quakers in Peace and War.* New York: Doran, 1923. (12)

Hodge, Charles. *Essays and Reviews.* New York: Robert Carter and Brothers, 1857. (7)

Hodge, Charles. *What Is Darwinism?* New York: Scribner, Armstrong and Company, 1874. (10)

Hofstadter, Richard. *The American Political Tradition and the Men Who Made It.* New York: Vintage Books, 1958. (8)

Hooker, Thomas. *The Application of Redemption.* London, 1656. (2)

Hooker, Thomas. *The Covenant of Grace Opened.* London, 1649. (2)

Hooker, Thomas. *The Faithful Covenanter.* London, 1644. (2)

Hooker, Thomas. *The Saints Guide.* London, 1645. (2)

Hooker, Thomas. *The Soules Exaltation.* London, 1638. (2)

Hooker, Thomas. *The Soules Humiliation.* London, 1637. (2)

Hooker, Thomas. *The Soules Ingrafting into Christ.* London, 1637. (2)

Hooker, Thomas. *The Soules Preparation.* London, 1632. (2)

Hooker, Thomas. *A Survey of the Summe of Church Discipline.* London, 1648 (2)

Hooker, Thomas. *The Unbelievers Preparing for Christ.* London: 1638. (2)

Howard, Irving E. *The Christian Alternative to Socialism.* Arlington, Virginia: Better Books, 1966. (16)

Hubbard William. *A General History of New England, from the Discovery to 1680.* Cambridge: Hillard and Metcalf, as reprinted entire. Boston: Charles C. Little and James Brown, 1848. (3)

Hudson, Winthrop S. *Religion in America.* New York: Charles Scribner's Sons, 1965. (6)

Huxley, T. H. "Mr. Darwin's Critics," *Darwiniana.* New York: D. Appleton and Company, 1898. (10)

"The Immutability of Species," *Catholic World,* X (November, 1869). (10)

James, William. *Varieties of Religious Experience.* New York: Modern Library, 1929. (10)

Janson, Donald, and Eismann, Bernard. *The Far Right.* New York: McGraw-Hill, 1963. (16)

Jenkins, William Sumner *Pro-Slavery Thought in the Old South.* Chapel Hill, North Carolina: The University of North Carolina Press, 1935. (8)

Johnson, Charles. *The Frontier Camp Meeting.* Dallas, Texas: Southern Methodist University Press, 1955. (6)

Johnson, James W. *Fundamentalism Versus Modernism: A Layman's Viewpoint.* New York: The Century Company, 1925. (13)

Johnson, William A. *Nature and the Supernatural in the Theology of Horace Bushnell.* Lund: CWK Gleerup, 1963. (7)

Kelsey, George D. *Racism and the Christian Understanding of Man.* New York: Charles Scribner's Sons, 1965. (19)

Kennedy, Gail. *Evolution and Religion: Problems in American Civilization.* Boston: D. C. Heath, 1957. (10)

Kennedy, Gerald. *Who Speaks for God?* Nashville: Abingdon Press, 1954. (14)

Kerr, Harry P. "The Rhetoric of Political Protest," *Quarterly Journal of Speech,* XLV (February, 1959), 146-52. (16)

King, C. Wendell. *Social Movements in the United States.* New York: Random House, 1956. (13)

King, Martin Luther, Jr. *The Measure of a Man*. Philadelphia: Christian Education Press, 1959. (19)

King, Martin Luther, Jr. *Strength to Love*. New York: Harper & Row, 1963. (19)

Krutch, Joseph Wood. *The Modern Temper: A Study and a Confession*. New York: Harcourt, Brace & Company, 1929. (13)

Kuhns, Frederick Irving. *The American Home Missionary Society in Relation to the Antislavery Controversy in the Old Northwest*. Billings, Montana: Privately printed, 1959. (8)

Kurland, Philip B. *Religion and the Law of Church and State and the Supreme Court*. Chicago: The University of Chicago Press, 1962. (18)

Lasswell, Harold D. *Propaganda Techniques in the World War*. New York: Knopf, 1927. (12)

Lawrence, William, "The Relation of Wealth to Morals," *World's Work*, I January, 1901. (11)

Lee, Robert. *The Social Sources of Church Unity*. Nashville: Abingdon Press, 1960. (15)

Lehmann, Paul. *Ethics in a Christian Context*. New York: Harper & Row, 1963. (17)

Lepley, Ray, ed. *The Language of Value*. New York: Columbia, 1957. (16)

Lewis, Edwin. *The Faith We Declare*. Nashville: Cokesbury Press, 1939. (14)

Lewis, Joseph. *The Bible Unmasked*. New York: The Free-thought Press Association, 1926. (13)

Lippmann, Walter. *American Inquisitors, a Commentary on Dayton and Chicago*. New York: The Macmillan Company, 1928. (13)

Lippmann, Walter. *A Preface to Morals*. New York: The Macmillan Company, 1929. (13)

Loewenberg, Bert J. "The Controversy Over Evolution in New England," *New England Quarterly*, VIII, No. 2 (June, 1935). (10)

Luccock, Halford E. *Communicating the Gospel*. New York: Harper & Brothers, 1954. (14)

Lymen, Jesse. *Sunday Half Hours with Great Preachers*. Cincinnati: 1907. (11)

Macartney, Clarence Edward. *Christianity and Common Sense*. Chicago: John C. Winston Company, 1927. (13)

Macartney, Clarence Edward. *Things Most Surely Believed, a Series of Sermons on the Apostles' Creed*. Nashville: Cokesbury Press, 1930. (13)

Macfarland, Charles S. *Pioneers for Peace Through Religion*. New York: Fleming H. Revell Company, 1946. (12)

Machen, John Gresham. *The Attack Upon Princeton Seminary: A Plea for Fair Play*. Princeton: Privately printed, 1927. (13)

Machen, John Gresham. *Christianity and Liberalism*. New York: The Macmillan Company, 1923. (13)

Machen, John Gresham. *The Separateness of the Church*. A sermon preached in the chapel of the Presbyterian Theological Seminary, Princeton, New Jersey, on Sunday, March 8, 1925. Calcutta, India: The Evangelical Literature Trust, 1925. (13)

Machen, John Gresham. *The Virgin Birth of Christ*. New York: Harper & Brothers, 1930. (13)

Machen, John Gresham. *What is Faith?* New York: The Macmillan Company, 1925. (13)

Mackintosh, Hugh Ross. *Types of Modern Theology*. London: Nisbet and Company [1937], 1949. (14)

Maclaren, Alexander. *Christ in the Heart.* New York: Funk and Wagnalls, 1905. (11)

Manion, Clarence. Radio broadcasts of the *Manion Forum* for the months of January-June, 1965, Elkhart, Indiana. (16)

Marryat, Captain Frederick. *A Diary in America,* ed. S. W. Jackman. New York: Alfred A. Knopf, 1962. (6)

Martin, John Bartlow. *The Deep South Says "Never."* New York: The Macmillan Company, 1959. (19)

Mascall, E. L. *Words and Images: A Study in Theological Discourse.* New York: The Ronald Press, 1951. (16)

Maston, T. B. *The Bible and Race.* Nashville: Broadman Press, 1959. (19)

Maston, T. B. *Segregation and Desegregation.* New York: The Macmillan Company, 1959. (19)

Mather, Increase. "The First Principles of New England, Concerning the Subject of Baptisme and Communion of Churches." Cambridge, Massachusetts, 1675. (2)

Mathews, Donald G. *Slavery and Methodism: A Chapter in American Morality, 1780-1845.* Princeton: Princeton University Press, 1965. (8)

Mathews, Shailer. *The Church and the Changing Order.* New York: The Macmillan Company, 1909. (11)

Mathews, Shailer. *The Faith of Modernism.* New York: The Macmillan Company, 1924. (13)

Mathews, Shailer. *The Growth of the Idea of God.* New York: The Macmillan Company, 1931. (13)

Mathews, Shailer, *et al. Contributions of Science to Religion.* New York: D. Appleton and Company, 1924. (13)

Matthews, Mark Allison. *In the Beginning, God—and Other Talks.* Chicago: Bible Institute Colportage Association, 1924. (13)

May, Henry F. *Protestant Churches and Industrial America.* New York: Harper & Brothers, 1949 (Octagon Books, 1963). (11)

McCosh, James. *Our Moral Nature.* New York: Charles Scribner's Sons, 1892. (11)

McCosh, James. *The Religious Aspect of Evolution.* New York: Charles Scribner's Sons, 1890. (10)

McCracken, Robert J. *The Making of the Sermon.* New York: Harper & Brothers, 1956. (14)

McIntire, Carl. "Biblical Christian Unity," a pamphlet. Collingswood, New Jersey: Twentieth Century Reformation Hour, 1965. (16)

McIntire, Carl, "Communist Victory in the World Council of Churches," a pamphlet. Collingswood, New Jersey: Twentieth Century Reformation Hour, 1965. (16)

McIntire, Carl. "Men in a Hurry—Building the One World Church," a pamphlet. Collingswood, New Jersey: Twentieth Century Reformation Hour, 1965. (16)

McIntire, Carl. "The Social Creed of the Church," a pamphlet. Collingswood, New Jersey: Twentieth Century Reformation Hour, 1965. (16)

McKee, Elmore McNeill, ed. *Preaching in the New Era.* Garden City, N.Y.: Doubleday, Doran, and Company, 1929. (13)

McKee, Elmore McNeill, *et al. What Can Students Believe?* New York: R. R. Smith, 1931. (13)

McLoughlin, William Gerald. *Modern Revivalism*. New York: The Ronald Press, 1959. (6)

McNeill, John T., ed. *Calvin: Institutes of the Christian Religion*. 2 vols. Trans. Ford Lewis Battles. Philadelphia: The Westminster Press, 1960. (2)

Merrill, William Pierson. *The Freedom of the Preacher*. New York: The Macmillan Company, 1922. (13)

Merrill, William Pierson. *Liberal Christianity*. New York: The Macmillan Company, 1925. (13)

Miller, Donald G. *The Way to Biblical Preaching*. Nashville: Abingdon Press, 1957. (14)

Miller, Perry. *Errand into the Wilderness*. Cambridge, Massachusetts: Harvard University Press, 1964. (2)

Miller, Perry. *Jonathan Edwards*. New York: W. Sloane Associates, 1949. (4)

Miller, Perry. *The New England Mind: From Colony to Province*. Cambridge, Massachusetts: Harvard University Press, 1953. (2)

Miller, Robert Moats. *American Protestantism and Social Issues, 1919-1939*. Chapel Hill, North Carolina: The University of North Carolina Press, 1958. (13)

Miller, Samuel H., and Wright, G. Ernest, eds. *Ecumenical Dialogue at Harvard: The Roman Catholic-Protestant Colloquium*. Cambridge, Massachusetts: Harvard University Press, 1964. (15)

Morgan, Edmund S. *Visible Saints*. New York: New York University Press, 1963. (2)

Morrison, Charles Clayton. *What Is Christianity?* New York: Willet, Clark and Company, 1940. (14)

Morrison, Charles Clayton, ed. *The American Pulpit*. New York: The Macmillan Company, 1925. (13)

Morton, Nathaniel. *New England's Memoriall*. Cambridge: Printed by S. G. and M. F., 1669. (3)

Munger, Theodore T. *Horace Bushnell: Preacher and Theologian*. Boston: Houghton Mifflin Company, 1899. (7)

Nash, Arnold S., ed. *Protestant Thought in the Twentieth Century*. New York: The Macmillan Company, 1951. (13)

Neill, Stephen, ed. *Twentieth Century Christianity*. Garden City, N.Y.: Doubleday & Company, 1961. (15)

Nelson, J. Robert, ed. *Christian Unity in North America*. St. Louis, Missouri: Bethany Press, 1958. (15)

Newton, Joseph Fort. *If I Had Only One Sermon to Prepare*. New York: Harper & Brothers, 1932. (13)

Newton, Joseph Fort, ed. *Best Sermons 1924*. New York: Harcourt, Brace, 1924. (13)

Newton, Joseph Fort, ed. *Best Sermons 1925*. New York: Harcourt, Brace, 1925. (13)

Newton, Joseph Fort, ed. *Best Sermons 1926*. New York: Harcourt, Brace, 1926. (13)

Newton, Joseph Fort, ed. *Best Sermons 1927*. New York: Harcourt, Brace, 1927. (13)

Nichols, James H. *History of Christianity, 1650-1950*. New York: The Ronald Press, 1956. (4)

Niebuhr, H. Richard. *Christ and Culture*. New York: Harper & Brothers, 1951. (13)

Niebuhr, H. Richard. *Social Sources of Denominationalism.* New York: Meridian Books, 1957. (20)

Niebuhr, H. Richard, and Williams, Daniel D., eds. *The Ministry in Historical Perspective.* New York: Harper & Row, 1956. (6)

Niebuhr, Reinhold. *The Irony of American History.* New York: Charles Scribner's Sons, 1952. (14)

Niebuhr, Reinhold. *Leaves from the Notebook of a Tamed Cynic.* Chicago: Willett, 1929. (12)

Niebuhr, Reinhold. *Moral Man and Immoral Society.* New York: Charles Scribner's Sons, 1932. (17)

Niebuhr, Reinhold, "Moralistic Preaching," *The Christian Century,* July 15, 1936. (14)

Niebuhr, Reinhold. *The Nature and Destiny of man.* 2 vols. New York: Charles Scribner's Sons, 1941, 1943. (12)

Oaks, Dallin H. *The Wall Between Church and State.* Chicago: The University of Chicago Press, 1963. (18)

Olbricht, Thomas H. "Christian Connexion and Unitarian Relations, 1800-1844," *Restoration Quarterly,* 9:3, 1966. (5)

Oliver, Robert T. *History of Public Speaking in America.* Boston: Allyn & Bacon, 1965. (6)

Olmstead, Clifton E. *History of Religion in the United States.* Englewood Cliffs, New Jersey: Prentice-Hall, 1960. (6)

Outler, Albert C. *The Christian Tradition and the Unity We Seek.* New York: Oxford University Press, 1957. (15)

Overstreet, Harry, and Overstreet, Bonaro. *The Strange Tactics of Extremism.* New York: W. W. Norton, 1964. (16)

Pancake, Loral W. "Theological Liberalism in the Life and Ministry of Harry Emerson Fosdick." Unpublished Master's thesis, Drew University, 1946. (14)

Parker, Theodore. *Additional Speeches, Addresses and Occasional Sermons.* 2 vols. Boston: Little, 1855. (8)

Parker, Theodore. *The Collected Works of Theodore Parker.* Ed. Frances Power Cobbe. 14 vols. London: Trubner and Company, 1863. (8)

Parker, Theodore. *Speeches, Addresses and Occasional Sermons.* 2 vols. Boston: Crosby and Nichols, 1852. (8)

Pate, Lloyd. *Reactionary.* New York: Harper & Brothers, 1956. (16)

Pearson, Roy. *The Ministry of Preaching.* New York: Harper & Brothers, 1954. (19)

Pell, Edward Leigh. *What Did Jesus Really Teach About War?* New York: Fleming H. Revell Company, 1917. (12)

Penabaz, Fernando. *Crusading Preacher from the West.* Tulsa, Oklahoma: Christian Crusade Publications, 1965. (16)

Persons, Stowe. "Evolution and Theology in America," *Evolutionary Thought in America,* ed. Stowe Persons. New Haven: Yale University Press, 1950. (10)

Pike, James A. *Doing the Truth.* New York: The Macmillan Company, 1965. (17)

Pike, James A. *A Roman Catholic in the White House.* Garden City, N.Y.: Doubleday & Company, 1960. (18)

Poling, Daniel A. *Huts in Hell.* Boston: Christian Endeavor World, 1918. (12)

Pope, Liston. *Kingdom Beyond Caste.* New York: Friendship Press, 1957. (19)

Posey, Walter B. *The Presbyterian Church in the Southwest, 1778-1838.* Richmond: John Knox Press, 1952. (8)

Potthoff, Harvey H. "The Seminary and the New Day," *Christian Advocate*, December 1, 1966. (14)

Preston, John. *The New Covenant*. London, 1629. (2)

Preston, John. *Riches of Mercy to Men in Misery*. London, 1658. (2)

Quimby, Rollins W. "Recurrent Themes and Purposes in the Sermons of the Union Army Chaplains," *Speech Monographs*, November, 1964. (9)

Ramsey, Paul. *Basic Christian Ethics*. New York: Charles Scribner's Sons, 1950. (17)

Ramsey, Paul. *Who Speaks for the Church?* Nashville: Abingdon Press, 1967. (20)

Ramseyer, Lloyd L. *The More Excellent Way*. Newton, Kansas: Faith and Life Press, 1965. (19)

Randall, John Herman. *The Making of the Modern Mind*. Rev. ed. Boston: Houghton Mifflin Company, 1940. (13)

Rauschenbusch, Walter. *Christianity and the Social Crisis*. New York: The Macmillan Company, 1920. (11)

"Religion and the Radical Right," *Christian Century*, LXXIX (April 11, 1962), 446-48. (16)

Rice, Madeline Hook. *American Catholic Opinion in the Slavery Controversy*. New York: Columbia University Press, 1949. (8)

Riley, William Bell. *Addresses Delivered by W. B. Riley in the Debates Between Maynard Shipley and W. B. Riley*. Chicago: Privately printed, 1925. (13)

Riley, William Bell. "The Challenge of Orthodoxy," an address delivered at the World Conference on Christian Fundamentals, Chicago, June 13, 1920. (13)

Riley, William Bell. *Inspiration or Evolution*. Cleveland: Union Gospel Press, 1926. (13)

Riley, William Bell. *The Menace of Modernism*. New York: Christian Alliance Publishing Company, 1917. (13)

Rossiter, Clinton. *Conservatism in America: The Thankless Persuasion*. New York: Vintage Books, 1962. (16)

Rossiter, Clinton. *The First American Revolution*. New York: Harcourt, Brace & World, 1956. (2)

Rossiter, Clinton. *The Political Thought of the American Revolution*. New York: Harcourt, Brace & World, 1963. (8)

Rossiter, Clinton. *Seedtime of the Republic*. New York: Harcourt, Brace & World, 1953. (3)

Rouse, Ruth, and Neill, Stephen C., eds. *A History of the Ecumenical Movement: 1517-1948*. Philadelphia: The Westminster Press, 1954. (15)

Roy, Ralph Lord. *Apostles of Discord*. Boston: Beacon Press, 1953. (16)

Ryan, John A. *Social Doctrine in Action*. New York: Harper & Brothers, 1941. (11)

Sandys, Sir Miles. *Prudence the First of the Foure Cardinall Virtues*. n. p., 1635. (2)

Sann, Paul. *The Lawless Decade*. New York: Crown Publishers, 1957. (13)

Schloerb, Rolland W. *The Preaching Ministry Today*. New York: Harper & Brothers, 1946. (14)

Schroeder, Frederick W. *Preaching the Word with Authority*. Philadelphia: The Westminster Press, 1954. (14)

Schwarz, Fred. *You Can Trust the Communists*. Englewood Cliffs, New Jersey; Prentice-Hall, 1960. (16)

423

Sellers, James. *The South and Christian Ethics.* New York: Association Press, 1962. (19)

Shenks, Caroline L. "The Biblical Anti-Slavery Argument of the Decade 1830-1840," *Journal of Negro History,* XVI (April, 1931), 132-57. (16)

Sherman, Billy Don. "The Ideology of American Segregationism." Unpublished Th.D. dissertation, Department of Christian Ethics, Southwestern Baptist Theological Seminary, 1966. (19)

Sherwin, Mark. *The Extremists.* New York: St. Martin's Press, 1963. (16)

Shriver, Donald W., Jr., ed. *The Unsilent South.* Richmond, Virginia: John Knox Press, 1965. (19)

Shurtleff, Nathaniel. *Records of the Governor and Company of the Massachusetts Bay in New England.* 5 vols. Boston: William White, 1853-54. (2)

Silver, James W. "The Confederate Preacher Goes to War," *North Carolina Historical Review,* XXXIII (1956). (9)

Simons, Minot. *A Modern Theism.* Boston: Beacon Press, 1931. (13)

Sittler, Joseph. *The Anguish of Preaching.* Philadelphia: Fortress Press, 1966. (14)

Sittler, Joseph. *The Structure of Christian Ethics.* Baton Rouge: Louisiana State University Press, 1958. (17)

Sleeth, Ronald E. *Proclaiming the Word.* Nashville: Abingdon Press, 1964. (14)

Smart, James D. *The Recovery of Humanity.* Philadelphia: The Westminister Press, 1953. (14)

Smeltzer, Wallace Guy. *Methodism on the Headwaters of the Ohio.* Nashville: The Parthenon Press, 1951. (1)

Smith, Gerald Birney, ed. *Religious Thought in the Last Quarter-Century.* Chicago: The University of Chicago Press, 1927. (13)

Smith, H. Shelton, Handy, Robert T., and Loetscher, Lefferts A. *American Christianity: An Historical Interpretation with Representative Documents.* 2 vols. New York: Charles Scribner's Sons [1960], 1963. (4, 7, 8, 11)

Smith, James, and Jamison, Leland. *The Shaping of American Religion.* Princeton: Princeton University Press, 1961. (11)

Smith, Timothy L. *Revivalism and Social Reform.* Nashville: Abingdon Press, 1957. (6)

Smith, William Henry. *Modernism, Fundamentalism, and Catholicism.* Milwaukee, Wisconsin: Morehouse Publishing Company, 1926. (13)

Smith, Wilson. *Professors and Public Ethics: Studies of Northern Moral Philosophers Before the Civil War.* Ithaca, New York: Cornell University Press, 1956. (8)

Soares, Theodore, ed. *University of Chicago Sermons.* Chicago: The University of Chicago Press, 1915. (11)

Speech Association of America. *A History and Criticism of American Public Address.* 3 vols. New York: Russell and Russell, 1960. (8, 13)

Staudenraus, P. J. *The African Colonization Movement, 1816–1865.* New York: Columbia University Press, 1961. (8)

Steele, Edward D. "Social Values in Public Address," *Western Speech,* XII (Winter, 1958), 39. (16)

Stevenson, Dwight E. *Preaching on the Books of the New Testament.* New York: Harper & Row, 1956. (14)

Stoddard, Solomon. *The Efficiency of the Fear of Hell to Restrain Men from Sin.* Boston, 1713. (2)

Stoddard, Solomon. *The Falseness of the Hopes of Many Professors*. Boston, 1708. (2)

Stoddard, Solomon. *The Safety of Appearing at the Day of Judgment*. Boston, 1687 (2nd ed., 1729). (2)

Stoddard, Solomon. *Three Sermons Lately Preach'd at Boston*. Boston, 1717. (2)

Stoddard, Solomon. *A Treatise Concerning Conversion*. Boston, 1719. (2)

Stoddard, Solomon. *The Way for a People to Live Long in the Land That God Hath Given Them*. Boston, 1703. (2)

Stokes, Anson Phelps, and Pfeffer, Leo. *Church and State in the United States*. 3 vols. New York: Harper & Row, 1964. (18)

Stonehouse, Ned B. *J. Gresham Machen, a Biographical Memoir*. Grand Rapids, Michigan: William B. Eerdmans, 1955. (13)

Straton, John Roach. *The Famous New York Fundamentalist-Modernist Debates, the Orthodox Side*. New York: George H. Doran, 1924, 1925. (13)

Straton, John Roach. *The Old Gospel at the Heart of the Metropolis*. New York: George H. Doran, 1925. (13)

Sweet, William Warren. *The American Churches*. Nashville: Abingdon-Cokesbury, 1948. (1)

Sweet, William Warren. *Religion in Colonial America*. New York: Charles Scribner's Sons, 1942. (1)

Sweet, William Warren. *Religion in the Development of American Culture 1765-1840*. New York: Charles Scribner's Sons, 1952. (6)

Sweet, William Warren. *The Story of Religion in America*. New York: Harper & Row [1939], 1950. (6, 11, 13)

Tavard, George H. *The Catholic Approach to Protestantism*. New York: Harper & Brothers, 1955. (15)

Taylor, Hubert V. "Slavery and the Deliberations of the Presbyterian General Assembly, 1833-1838." Unpublished Ph.D. dissertation, Northwestern University, 1964. (8)

Thomas, Norman. *The Conscientious Objector in America*. New York: Viking Press, 1923. (12)

Thompson, E. T. *Changing Emphases in American Preaching*. Philadelphia: The Westminster Press, 1943. (11)

Thornwell, James H. *The Collected Writings of James Henley Thornwell*. Ed. John B. Adger and John L. Giradeau. 4 vols. Richmond: Presbyterian Committee of Publication, 1873. (8)

Tillich, Paul. *Morality and Beyond*. New York: Harper & Row, 1963. (17)

Tilson, Everett. *Segregation and the Bible*. Nashville: Abingdon Press, 1958. (19)

Tittle, Ernest Fremont. "Does It Make Any Difference What a Man Believes?" Sermon preached in the First Methodist Episcopal Church, Evanston, Illinois, October 9, 1921. (13)

Tittle, Ernest Fremont. *The Gospel According to Luke*. New York: Harper & Brothers, 1951. (14)

Tittle, Ernest Fremont. *A Mighty Fortress*. New York: Harper & Brothers, 1950. (14)

Tittle, Ernest Fremont. *The Religion of the Spirit*. New York: Abingdon Press, 1928. (13)

Tittle, Ernest Fremont, *et al. What Religion Means to Me*. Garden City, N.Y.: Doubleday & Company, 1929. (13)

Torrey, Reuben Archer. *The Fundamental Doctrines of the Christian Faith*. New York: Fleming H. Revell Company, 1918. (13)

Torrey, Reuben Archer. *How to Be Saved and How to Be Lost: The Way of Salvation and the Way of Condemnation Made as Plain as Day*. New York: Fleming H. Revell Company, 1923. (13)

Tracey, Joseph. *The Great Awakening*. Boston: Charles Tappan, 1845. (4)

Trueblood, Elton. *The People Called Quakers*. New York: Harper & Row, 1966. (12)

Trumbull, Benjamin. *A Complete History of Connecticut*. New Haven, 1818. (4)

Turner, Arlin, ed. *The Negro Question. A Selection of Writings on Civil Rights in the South*. Garden City, N.Y.: Doubleday & Company, 1958. (19)

Turner, Frederick Jackson. *The Frontier in American History*. New York: Henry Holt & Company, 1921. (6)

Tyler, Alice Felt. *Freedom's Ferment: Phases of American Social History to 1860*. Minneapolis: The University of Minnesota Press, 1944. (6, 7)

Tyler, Bennet. *Memoir of the Life and Character of Rev. Asahel Nettleton*. Hartford, Connecticut: Robins and Smith, 1845. (7)

Vanderlaan, Eldred C., ed. *Fundamentalism Versus Modernism*. New York: H. W. Wilson, 1925. (13)

Van Dusen, Henry P. *World Christianity*. Nashville: Abingdon Press, 1947. (15)

Vidler, Alec R. *The Modernist Movement in the Roman Church*. Cambridge, Massachusetts: The University Press, 1934. (13)

Wadsworth, Charles. "A Sermon Preached in the Arch Street Presbyterian Church, April 11, 1858." Philadelphia, 1858. (7)

Walker, Brooks R. *The Christian Fright Peddlers*. Garden City, N.Y.: Doubleday & Company, 1964. (16)

Walker, David Ellis, Jr. "Invention in Selected Sermons of Ministers Opposing the Election of a Roman Catholic Presidential Candidate: 1960." Unpublished Master's thesis, The University of Florida, 1961. (18)

Ware, Henry, Jr. "Jesus the Mediator," *The Works of Henry Ware, Jr*. Boston: James Munroe and Company, 1847. (5)

Weigel, Gustave, S.J. *A Catholic Primer on the Ecumenical Movement*. Westminster, Maryland: Newman Press, 1967. (15)

Weisberger, Bernard A. *They Gathered at the River*. Boston: Little, Brown & Company, 1958. (6)

Welch, Robert. *The Politician*. Belmont, Massachusetts: Printing particulars not released, 1961. (16)

West, R. Frederick. *Preaching on Race*. St. Louis, Missouri: The Bethany Press, 1962. (19)

White, Eugene E. "Cotton Mather's *Manuductio ad Ministerium*," *The Quarterly Journal of Speech* XLIX (October, 1963), 308-19. (2)

White, Eugene E. "Master Holdsworth and 'A Knowledge Very Useful and Necessary,'" *The Quarterly Journal of Speech*, LII (February, 1967), 1-16. (2)

Wilberforce, Samuel. "The Origin of Species," *Quarterly Review*, CVIII (July, 1860). (10)

Wilbur, Earl Morse. *A History of Unitarianism in Transylvania, England, and America*. Cambridge: Harvard University Press, 1952. (8)

Wiley, Bill I. "Holy Joes of the Sixties: A Study of Civil War Chaplains," *Huntington Library Quarterly*, XVI (1953). (9)

Williams, Michael. *American Catholics in the War*. New York: The Macmillan Company, 1921. (12)

Williams, Roger. *The Bloudy Tenent of Persecution* (London, 1644) as reprinted entire and in facsimile, ed. S. L. Caldwell, Providence, Narragansett Club Publications, Providence Press, 1867. (3)

Williams, Roger. *The Bloudy Tenent Yet More Bloudy*. (London, 1652) as reprinted entire and in facsimile, ed. S. L. Caldwell, Providence, Narragansett Club Publications, Providence Press, 1870. (3)

Williams, Roger. *Letters of Roger Williams*, ed. John R. Bartlett. Providence, Narragansett Club Publications, Providence Press, 1874. (3)

Williams, Roger. *Mr. Cotton's Letter Lately Printed, Examined and Answered* (London, 1644) reprinted entire and ed. R. A. Guild, Providence, Narragansett Club Publications, Providence Press, 1867. (3)

Winslow, Ola Elizabeth. *Master Roger Williams, a Biography*. New York: The Macmillan Company, 1957. (3)

Winslow, Ola Elizabeth. *Meetinghouse Hill: 1630–1783*. New York: The Macmillan Company, 1952. (1)

Winthrop, John. *History of New England*. Ed. James Kendall Hosmer. New York: Charles Scribner's Sons, 1908. (3)

Winthrop Papers, ed. The Massachusetts Historical Society. Boston: Plimpton Press, 1931. (3)

Woelfkin, Cornelius. *Religion: Thirteen Sermons*. New York: Harper & Brothers, 1928. (11)

Wrage, Ernest J., and Baskerville, Barnet, eds. *Contemporary Forum, American Speeches on Twentieth-Century Issues*. New York: Harper & Row, 1962. (13)

Wright, Conrad. *The Beginnings of Unitarianism in America*. Boston: Beacon Press, 1966. (5)

Wright, Conrad. *Three Prophets of Religious Liberalism: Channing, Emerson, and Parker*. Boston: Beacon Press, 1961. (5)

Ziff, Larzer. *The Career of John Cotton: Puritanism and the American Experience*. Princeton: Princeton University Press, 1962. (2)

INDEX

/